EAST ASIAN LABOR AND EMPLOYMENT LAW

This book discusses international labor and employment law in the East Asia Region (EA), particularly with regard to China, South Korea, and Japan. It explores and explains the effects of globalization and discusses the role played by international labor law as it affects lawyers, business, labor, labor unions, and human resource management and the labor issues that can arise in dealing in EA trade and investment.

The text and the readings (from area experts) are organized and written to provide the reader with a broad understanding and insight into first the global dimensions of the fast-emerging area of labor and employment issues (e.g., global legal standards and their interplay with domestic and foreign laws) and second how these laws and approaches play out in specific EA countries (comparing global approaches with the specific laws of each country on four common agenda items: regulatory administration, workers' rights, trade unions, and dispute resolution). The book should be of interest not only to lawyers, students, human resource personnel, and government officials, but also to business investors, managers, and members of the public interested in the growing phenomenon of changing labor laws and societies in China, South Korea, and Japan.

Ronald C. Brown is a Professor of Law at the University of Hawaii, where he has served as Associate Dean and as Director of the University's Center for Chinese Studies. He has worked in China under the USIA's Professional-in-Residence Program, served as a consultant with the World Bank, served as a Distinguished Fulbright Scholar who taught at Peking and Tsinghua University Law Schools, and lectured throughout Asia on comparative labor law topics.

Professor Brown currently serves as an active labor arbitrator. His teaching specialties include labor and employment law, employment discrimination law, arbitration, Chinese law, Asian international and comparative labor and employment law, and U.S.–China labor and employment law. He has authored numerous articles and two books: *Understanding Labor and Employment Law in China* (Cambridge University Press, 2010) and *Understanding Chinese Courts and Legal Process: Law with Chinese Characteristics* (1997).

East Asian Labor and Employment Law

INTERNATIONAL AND COMPARATIVE CONTEXT

RONALD C. BROWN
University of Hawaii Law School

CAMBRIDGE
UNIVERSITY PRESS

CAMBRIDGE UNIVERSITY PRESS
Cambridge, New York, Melbourne, Madrid, Cape Town,
Singapore, São Paulo, Delhi, Mexico City

Cambridge University Press
32 Avenue of the Americas, New York, NY 10013-2473, USA

www.cambridge.org
Information on this title: www.cambridge.org/9781107018334

First published 2012

Printed in the United States of America

A catalog record for this publication is available from the British Library.

Library of Congress Cataloging in Publication data

Brown, Ronald C.
East Asian labor and employment law : international and comparative context / Ronald C. Brown.
p. cm.
Includes bibliographical references and index.
ISBN 978-1-107-01833-4 (hardback)
1. Labor laws and legislation – Asia. I. Title.
KNC403.B76 2012
344.501–dc23 2011040844

ISBN 978-1-107-01833-4 Hardback

Contents

Preface

EAST ASIAN LABOR AND EMPLOYMENT LAW: INTERNATIONAL AND COMPARATIVE CONTEXT

Introduction

A mid-sized U.S. employer in Toledo, Ohio, contemplated investing somewhere in China, South Korea, or Japan. Its goal was to reduce its costs in manufacturing and supplying certain products. It currently has a collective-bargaining agreement with its employees and needs to decide whether to close its U.S. plant, subcontract with a foreign company, or set up operations overseas; but where and how can profits be maximized and competitive advantages enhanced? Must seniority be followed in selecting which key employees can be offered relocation to the foreign facility? Whose laws apply? Do those countries have labor and employment laws? Are they enforced? Certainly many business decisions will need to be made, but how significant are the labor issues that must be considered and how costly if mistakes are made?

Within the developing world, the populous Asia and Pacific region dominates, accounting for more than fifty-seven percent of all employment. The two giants, China and India, have 26.0 percent and 14.8 percent of world employment, respectively.[1]

This book discusses international labor and employment law in the East Asia Region (EA), particularly with regard to Japan, South Korea, and China. Part I introduces globalization – economic integration, cross-border business involving capital, labor, and global production and assembly lines. Also discussed are the effects of globalization on labor, labor unions, business, human resource management, law, and lawyers. From this globalization and its effects come the need for international lawyers, business personnel, and human resource directors who are knowledgeable

[1] CHANGING PATTERNS IN THE WORLD OF WORK 19, *citing*, ILO: Global Employment Trends Model database (Geneva, 2006). See www.ilo.org/public/english/employment/strat/wrest.htm.

and culturally sensitive and who understand the issues that can arise in dealing in EA trade and investment. Not all issues are legal, but they still have clear implications for a company's wellness (e.g., cheap labor may be viewed by some as exploitive labor), as Sears, NIKE, and Liz Claiborne learned in earlier years. Practitioners soon discover that in today's global economy they need at least a basic awareness of not only U.S. or home-country labor and employment laws, but also of international and foreign legal issues that often are implicated.

Part II of the book deals with global legal standards and their interplay with domestic and foreign labor and employment laws. Understanding labor and employment law in its international context reveals that law itself is becoming globalized, as is an increasing percentage of the labor force. The book addresses how these changing demographics also change the dynamics of regulation; and, as the Eastern and Western cultures mix, new perspectives are raised concerning whether *labor rights* and practices may cross over into *human rights*. Some thoughtful analysis may be required to set aside one's own biases and understand another culture's approach to legal rights, as for example protecting the safety of a pregnant woman in the workplace involving issues of gender discrimination. The laws in EA derive from legal heritages and legal systems that embrace different pieces of Western traditions. Knowing how a civil law system or one blended with common law or socialist law characteristics operates facilitates successful lawyering involving foreign trade and investment. Whether there has been an "*Asianization*" of law in EA is debatable, but the impact in EA of globalization causing a convergence of global labor standards and local labor and employment laws is real.

Confronting the international labor and employment lawyer are three levels of law: domestic, international, and foreign. For example, a U.S. company needs to consider and coordinate gender issues in the workplace under Title VII of the Civil Rights Law, International Labor Organization (ILO) standards, and the particular EA country's laws. Also in play may be industry or company codes of conduct, extraterritorial application of U.S. laws, or the Alien Tort Claims Act. Wal-Mart has been embroiled in litigation in California touching on some of these issues.

Part III, for comparative purposes, examines global approaches to four "agenda items": a) regulatory sources, structures, and administration; b) workers' labor rights and benefits; c) labor unions, national and international; and d) dispute resolution of labor rights and interests.

Part IV examines the EA legal regimes of Japan, South Korea, and China (including reference to Hong Kong and Taiwan) as they regulate their labor and employment. Also considered are global institutions' measurements of these countries' compliance with international global standards.

Lastly, Part V provides a number of illustrative issues or themes common within the EA countries and raises questions about the various approaches that would be taken by the labor and employment laws of each. These approaches are then compared to each other through questions to see where the "best practice" or comparative advantage might lie or identify an area needing reform. The issues examined include: a) hiring and discrimination; b) labor contracts, individual and collective; c) working conditions and benefits; and d) employer discipline, termination, and alternative dispute resolution (ADR).

Although this book is useful as a textbook or source book, it is also written for those interested in gaining *competitive* advantages in the Asian markets by better understanding the *comparative* advantages of the various labor law regimes in China, Japan, and South Korea. The readings and text are organized and written to provide the reader with a broad understanding and insight into first the global dimensions of the fast-emerging area of labor and employment issues and second how in specific Asian countries these laws and approaches play out. In this regard, the book should be of interest not only to lawyers, students, human resource personnel, and government officials, but also to business investors, managers, and members of the public interested in the growing phenomenon of changing labor laws and societies in Japan, South Korea, and China.

International Labor and Employment Law: From Periphery to Core[2]

Marley S. Weiss

If we were to rank areas of labor and employment law by the level of change in the past twenty-five years, international labor and employment law would surely be near the top. It is no exaggeration to say that this field has been transformed during the past two and a half decades. As an area of specialty practice, international labor and employment law has fully emerged. This time period witnessed the information and telecommunication revolution, paralleled by quantum leaps forward in the global trade order and regional integration regimes. Internationalization of markets for and supply chains in goods and services has profoundly affected the practice of domestic labor and employment law, the balance of power between capital and labor, and the content of the employment relationship. The globalization of markets in goods, services, capital, and labor has led to the embedding of comparative labor and employment law within the practice of domestic labor and employment law. The globalization of labor markets also has resulted in the incorporation of elements of immigration law into the heart of employment law practice.

Changes in international trade law, as well as technology-driven changes in the economics of trade and investment, have stimulated new approaches to the substantive, procedural, and remedial aspects of international labor law. The content of law school curricula and continuing legal education programs increasingly responds to these new bodies of law and legal practice. Cumulatively, these dramatic changes in law, economics, and society have brought American labor and employment law practice to the

[2] Marley S. Weiss, International Labor and Employment Law: From Periphery to Core, 25 *ABA J of Labor & Employment Law* 487–88 (2010). [Footnotes omitted.] The author, Professor of Law at the University of Maryland School of Law, has served as the academic/employee co-chair of the International Labor and Employment Law Committee of the ABA Section of Labor and Employment Law.

cusp of an immense transformation in how employment and labor law is practiced in connection with transnational activities.

. . . .

IV. The Next Step: Strategic Thinking in the Practice of Labor and Employment Law

Finally, the coming of age of international labor law is increasingly reflected in practitioners' resort to the type of strategic and comparative thinking more familiar in U.S. domestic law. Strategic planning to minimize labor/employment obligations, economic burdens, and liability exposure, heretofore used by businesses in site selection and plant relocation decisions about moving from one U.S. state to another, now plays a role in decisions of multinationals about whether to outsource work from the United States to a Brazilian subcontractor. Even smaller businesses engage in comparative analysis of national law, industrial relations systems, and international obligations in making decisions about mergers, acquisitions, joint ventures, offshoring or outsourcing business activities, brand licensing, and other transnational transactions.

Transnational trade union confederations and global workers' rights networks are deploying countervailing corporate campaigns, consumer boycott appeals, and legal strategies on the international plane. As in a domestic labor dispute or corporate campaign, unions and workers' rights advocates strategically analyze potential sources of economic pressure, such as consumer boycotts, withholding of investment by sovereign wealth funds with corporate social responsibility mandates, and publicity campaigns. They utilize both domestic and international legal proceedings for the legal remedies they may supply and for the additional publicity and veracity a legal ruling can provide to fuel public political, economic, and social pressure campaigns. Legal submissions utilizing the frameworks available at the ILO, UN Global Compact, U.S. free trade agreement-based labor rights, international corporate codes of conduct, and other international arrangements provide an international framework within which labor organizations and multinational corporations strategize and navigate.

Although few of these international instruments afford relief to victimized workers and trade unions, or deterrent sanctions against employers or even nation-states, they do play an important role in mobilizing political pressure to change policy in noncompliant nation-states and induce corporate compliance with core international labor rights, even in the absence of strong national- or local-level enforcement. U.S. domestic statutes such as the Alien Tort Claims Act provide a stronger deterrent effect against both companies and governments by affording potentially massive tort remedial awards for the worst violations of workers' rights.

Management lawyers analyze choice of law, choice of forum, election or combination of procedures and remedies, comparative labor costs, industrial relations systems, and labor and employment law regimes as they advise regarding site selection decisions, capital redeployment decisions, and trade union development of countervailing transnational affiliations, mobilization, and economic and political pressure campaigns.

With an ever-shrinking globe, and an ever-intensifying international integration of markets and work, one must anticipate that these trends will continue and intensify in the coming years.

Acknowledgments

The content of this book derives from working experiences in Asia and countless visits over the past decades to East Asia, including China, Japan, South Korea, Hong Kong, and Taiwan, and meetings, consulting, teaching, providing seminars and training, and working on joint projects on law and labor and employment-related projects with legal practitioners, academics, business personnel, and government officials. The format and organization of the book evolved from my law school course on Asian International and Comparative Labor and Employment Law, which I have taught at the University of Hawaii Law School and in Asian law schools for the past two decades and which appears to have been successful in introducing the legal environment of East Asia and educating law students during that time.

During this period of continually discovering and discussing with countless numbers of legal practitioners, academics, students, business personnel, and government officials the development and importance of international labor and employment law, I have come to understand that this area of the law is very significant as a discrete and concrete subject area that involves citizens, workers, businesses, unions, and governments. The economics and politics of labor and employment laws and labor relations can be volatile and affect economic development, social stability, labor unrest, and the success or failure of business operations, as well as the welfare and safety of the employees performing the work under varying workplace environments. I am grateful for the permissions granted by the authors for some of the materials used in this book, as they and their expertise have expressed it in the voice of firsthand knowledge and perspective.

The time for specialized emphasis and knowledge of the approaches and requirements of labor and employment laws and practices in this region of the world is now. The tide of trade and business investment, and even adventure for many, has moved from trans-Atlantic to trans-Pacific. This book seeks to address the legal background of the region, provide an introduction to the reader of the many sophisticated regional and global developments presently occurring in East Asia, and place them in an international and comparative context; yet leave the many factors and variables raised, but not fully analyzed, for subsequent discussions and decisions by lawyers, students, business and human resource personnel, and those interested in the combined localization and globalization of the workplace environments now taking place in East Asia. The law in each country changes rapidly, and the EA country materials are not necessarily intended to be specific and current but rather to provide sufficient basis to understand the legal parameters and spur on further inquiry.

I also want to acknowledge the support of the University of Hawaii Law School and the significant technical assistance provided to me on this project by my research assistants at the Law School, Aeri Yum and Sara Lee. Aeri Yum, already a health specialist, transformed into a wonderfully capable foreign legal researcher, using her meticulous medical skills to collect and analyze the many laws and articles of possible relevance to my teaching a course on Asian labor law as well as for use in this book. She also successfully organized and obtained the required copyright permissions. Sara Lee, a second-year law student, more recently has assisted greatly in adding to Aeri's work and putting this book in proper form and formatting. Lastly, I wish to acknowledge my wife, Mangmang, who has assisted and supported me over the years in the many projects in Asia relevant to this book. Her keen mind, legal background, inherent understanding of "Chinese and Asian characteristics," and her time and support are always an asset to me as I move forward.

I

Perspective

Globalism and Its Impacts

"Globalization" is a phenomenon that has moved domestic and foreign businesses, as well as developed and developing countries, ever closer. It is sometimes described as economic integration. Often the business motivation is to take advantage of cheaper labor and lax law enforcement, but there are many reasons why U.S. and European Union (EU) businesses trade and invest in and with Asia, including market expansion. While some of the practices by hosting countries may appear unfair and exploitive and fuel the "race to the bottom," this trade and investment also bring jobs and technology to those countries and lower-priced products for consumers in the European Union and the United States.[1] Cross-border and foreign business revolve around corporate activity performed by labor (and sometimes involving labor unions) and serviced by lawyers. With increases in foreign direct investment (FDI) in East Asia, the use of outsourcing, global production systems, and offshore production has also grown. With this growth, new challenges abound for lawyers and human resource managers to comply with the myriad laws that arise in domestic, foreign, and international forums.

In all cases, significant labor and employment issues will be raised because human resources are the fuel of this economic activity. In understanding the impacts of globalism on international and comparative labor and employment issues in Asia, some perspective on the global economic and production systems affecting employment is provided because these systems often are the underpinnings of the evolving changes in workplace regulation. Globalization can be described as the "hub" of a wheel, with

[1] Jim Dator et al., Fairness, Globalization, and Public Institutions: East Asia and Beyond (2006). *See also* Labour Law in an Era of Globalization (Joanne Conaghan et al. eds., 2004). This collection of "[e]ssays consider[s] the consequences of such developments as accelerating international economic integration and wage competition, a decline in the capacity of the nation-state to steer economic progress, the proliferation of contingent employment relationships, and the significantly increased participation of women in paid work." Book Notes, 29 Law & Soc. Inquiry 299, 304 (2004).

its emanating spokes transmitting impacts on labor, labor unions, human resource management policies, law, and law practice, in ways described next.

A. ECONOMIC INTEGRATION: BUSINESS FLOWS AND EXPANDING LEGAL ISSUES

1. *Cross-Border Business*

a. Economic Integration

Economic integration within communities, regions, nations, and internationally has occurred in some form for thousands of years, but never at today's pace. The reality is that, whereas global merchandise exports in 1913 were eight percent of the world's gross domestic product (GDP), today they are more than twenty percent;[2] capital exports, historically coming from industrialized countries, today also come from emerging market nations.[3] An interesting phenomenon has occurred in recent decades wherein many corporations are geographically fragmented, with portions of their business operations diversified; and further, some forty percent of U.S. merchandise trade is being done *intrafirm*, which combines with increasing numbers of firms being involved in *global supply chains*.[4]

Author Thomas L. Friedman has made the case that the "world is flat."[5] Not all accept that globalization has flattened the world outside the business community,[6] but, within the business realm, Federal Reserve Chairman Ben Bernanke explains this aspect of globalization as "global economic integration,"[7] which is at the epicenter of the hub of globalization.

Global Economic Integration: What's New and What's Not?[8]

Ben S. Bernanke, Chairman, Federal Reserve

When geographers study the earth and its features, distance is one of the basic measures they use to describe the patterns they observe. Distance is an elastic concept, however. The physical distance along a great circle from Wausau, Wisconsin, to Wuhan, China, is fixed at 7,020 miles. But to an economist, the distance from Wausau to Wuhan can

[2] Chairman Ben S. Bernanke, Speech at the Federal Reserve Bank of Kansas City's Thirtieth Annual Economic Symposium: Global Economic Integration: What's New and What's Not? (August 25, 2006), *available at* http://www.federalreserve.gov/newsevents/speech/bernanke20060825a.htm (last visited Oct. 3, 2010).

[3] *Id.*

[4] *Id.*

[5] Thomas L. Friedman, The World is Flat (2005).

[6] Joseph E. Stiglitz, Making Globalization Work (2006).

[7] Bernanke, *supra* note 2.

[8] *Id.*

also be expressed in other metrics, such as the cost of shipping goods between the two cities, the time it takes for a message to travel those 7,020 miles, and the cost of sending and receiving the message. Economically relevant distances between Wausau and Wuhan may also depend on what trade economists refer to as the "width of the border," which reflects the extra costs of economic exchange imposed by factors such as tariff and nontariff barriers, as well as costs arising from differences in language, culture, legal traditions, and political systems.

One of the defining characteristics of the world in which we now live is that, by most economically relevant measures, distances are shrinking rapidly. The shrinking globe has been a major source of the powerful wave of worldwide economic integration and increased economic interdependence that we are currently experiencing. The causes and implications of declining economic distances and increased economic integration are, of course, the subject of this conference. The pace of global economic change in recent decades has been breathtaking indeed, and the full implications of these developments for all aspects of our lives will not be known for many years. History may provide some guidance, however. The process of global economic integration has been going on for thousands of years, and the sources and consequences of this integration have often borne at least a qualitative resemblance to those associated with the current episode. In my remarks today I will briefly review some past episodes of global economic integration, identify some common themes, and then put forward some ways in which I see the current episode as similar to and different from the past. In doing so, I hope to provide some background and context for the important discussions that we will be having over the next few days.

A Short History of Global Economic Integration

As I just noted, the economic integration of widely separated regions is hardly a new phenomenon. Two thousand years ago, the Romans unified their far-flung empire through an extensive transportation network and a common language, legal system, and currency. One historian recently observed that "a citizen of the empire traveling from Britain to the Euphrates in the mid-second century CE would have found in virtually every town along the journey foods, goods, landscapes, buildings, institutions, laws, entertainment, and sacred elements not dissimilar to those in his own community." . . . This unification promoted trade and economic development.

A millennium and a half later, at the end of the fifteenth century, the voyages of Columbus, Vasco da Gama, and other explorers initiated a period of trade over even vaster distances.

. . . .

Global economic integration took another major leap forward during the period between the end of the Napoleonic Wars in 1815 and the beginning of World War I. International trade again expanded significantly as did cross-border flows of financial capital and labor. Once again, new technologies played an important role in facilitating integration: Transport costs plunged as steam power replaced the sail and railroads replaced the wagon or the barge, and an ambitious public works project, the opening of the Suez Canal, significantly reduced travel times between Europe and Asia. Communication costs likewise fell as the telegraph came into common use.

. . . .

The structure of trade during the post-Napoleonic period followed a "core-periphery" pattern. Capital-rich Western European countries, particularly Britain, were the center, or core, of the trading system and the international monetary system. Countries in which natural resources and land were relatively abundant formed the periphery. Manufactured goods, financial capital, and labor tended to flow from the core to the periphery, with natural resources and agricultural products flowing from the periphery to the core. The composition of the core and the periphery remained fairly stable, with one important exception being the United States, which, over the course of the nineteenth century, made the transition from the periphery to the core. The share of manufactured goods in U.S. exports rose from less than 30 percent in 1840 to 60 percent in 1913, and the United States became a net exporter of financial capital beginning in the late 1890s.

For the most part, government policies during this era fostered openness to trade, capital mobility, and migration. . . . A growing appreciation for the principle of comparative advantage, as forcefully articulated by Adam Smith and David Ricardo, may have made governments more receptive to the view that international trade is not a zero-sum game but can be beneficial to all participants.

. . . .

Unfortunately, the international economic integration achieved during the nineteenth century was largely unraveled in the twentieth by two world wars and the Great Depression. After World War II, the major powers undertook the difficult tasks of rebuilding both the physical infrastructure and the international trade and monetary systems. The industrial core – now including an emergent Japan as well as the United States and Western Europe – ultimately succeeded in restoring a substantial degree of economic integration, though decades passed before trade as a share of global output reached pre-World War I levels.

. . . .

Postwar economic re-integration was supported by several factors, both technological and political. Technological advances further reduced the costs of transportation and communication, as the air freight fleet was converted from propeller to jet and intermodal shipping techniques (including containerization) became common. Telephone communication expanded, and digital electronic computing came into use. Taken together, these advances allowed an ever-broadening set of products to be traded internationally. In the policy sphere, tariff barriers – which had been dramatically increased during the Great Depression – were lowered, with many of these reductions negotiated within the multilateral framework provided by the General Agreement on Tariffs and Trade. Globalization was, to some extent, also supported by geopolitical considerations, as economic integration among the Western market economies became viewed as part of the strategy for waging the Cold War. However, although trade expanded significantly in the early post-World War II period, many countries – recalling the exchange-rate and financial crises of the 1930s – adopted regulations aimed at limiting the mobility of financial capital across national borders.

Several conclusions emerge from this brief historical review. Perhaps the clearest conclusion is that new technologies that reduce the costs of transportation and communication have been a major factor supporting global economic integration.

. . . .

A second conclusion from history is that national policy choices may be critical determinants of the extent of international economic integration. Britain's embrace of free trade and free capital flows helped to catalyze international integration in the nineteenth century.

. . . .

A third observation is that social dislocation, and consequently often social resistance, may result when economies become more open. An important source of dislocation is that – as the principle of comparative advantage suggests – the expansion of trade opportunities tends to change the mix of goods that each country produces and the relative returns to capital and labor. The resulting shifts in the structure of production impose costs on workers and business owners in some industries and thus create a constituency that opposes the process of economic integration. More broadly, increased economic interdependence may also engender opposition by stimulating social or cultural change, or by being perceived as benefiting some groups much more than others.

The Current Episode of Global Economic Integration

How does the current wave of global economic integration compare with previous episodes? In a number of ways, the remarkable economic changes that we observe today are being driven by the same basic forces and are having similar effects as in the past. Perhaps most important, technological advances continue to play an important role in facilitating global integration. For example, dramatic improvements in supply-chain management, made possible by advances in communication and computer technologies, have significantly reduced the costs of coordinating production among globally distributed suppliers.

Another common feature of the contemporary economic landscape and the experience of the past is the continued broadening of the range of products that are viewed as tradable. In part, this broadening simply reflects the wider range of goods available today – high-tech consumer goods, for example – as well as ongoing declines in transportation costs. Particularly striking, however, is the extent to which information and communication technologies now facilitate active international trade in a wide range of services, from call center operations to sophisticated financial, legal, medical, and engineering services.

The critical role of government policy in supporting, or at least permitting, global economic integration, is a third similarity between the past and the present. Progress in trade liberalization has continued in recent decades – though not always at a steady pace, as the recent Doha Round negotiations demonstrate. Moreover, the institutional framework supporting global trade, most importantly the World Trade Organization, has expanded and strengthened over time. Regional frameworks and agreements, such as the North American Free Trade Agreement and the European Union's "single market," have also promoted trade. Government restrictions on international capital flows have generally declined, and the "soft infrastructure" supporting those flows – for example, legal frameworks and accounting rules – has improved, in part through international cooperation.

In yet another parallel with the past, however, social and political opposition to rapid economic integration has also emerged. As in the past, much of this opposition is driven by the distributional impact of changes in the pattern of production, but other concerns have been expressed as well – for example, about the effects of global economic integration on the environment or on the poorest countries.

What, then, is new about the current episode? Each observer will have his or her own perspective, but, to me, four differences between the current wave of global economic integration and past episodes seem most important. First, the scale and pace of the current episode is unprecedented. For example, in recent years, global merchandise exports have been above 20 percent of world gross domestic product, compared with about 8 percent in 1913 and less than 15 percent as recently as 1990; and international financial flows have expanded even more quickly. But these data understate the magnitude of the change that we are now experiencing. The emergence of China, India, and the former communist-bloc countries implies that the greater part of the earth's population is now engaged, at least potentially, in the global economy. There are no historical antecedents for this development. Columbus's voyage to the New World ultimately led to enormous economic change, of course, but the full integration of the New and the Old Worlds took centuries. In contrast, the economic opening of China, which began in earnest less than three decades ago, is proceeding rapidly and, if anything, seems to be accelerating.

Second, the traditional distinction between the core and the periphery is becoming increasingly less relevant, as the mature industrial economies and the emerging-market economies become more integrated and interdependent. Notably, the nineteenth-century pattern, in which the core exported manufactures to the periphery in exchange for commodities, no longer holds, as an increasing share of world manufacturing capacity is now found in emerging markets. An even more striking aspect of the breakdown of the core-periphery paradigm is the direction of capital flows: In the nineteenth century, the country at the center of the world's economy, Great Britain, ran current-account surpluses and exported financial capital to the periphery. Today, the world's largest economy, that of the United States, runs a current-account deficit, financed to a substantial extent by capital exports from emerging-market nations.

Third, production processes are becoming geographically fragmented to an unprecedented degree. Rather than producing goods in a single process in a single location, firms are increasingly breaking the production process into discrete steps and performing each step in whatever location allows them to minimize costs. For example, the U.S. chip producer AMD locates most of its research and development in California; produces in Texas, Germany, and Japan; does final processing and testing in Thailand, Singapore, Malaysia, and China; and then sells to markets around the globe. To be sure, international production chains are not entirely new: In 1911, Henry Ford opened his company's first overseas factory in Manchester, England, to be closer to a growing source of demand. The factory produced bodies for the Model A automobile, but imported the chassis and mechanical parts from the United States for assembly in Manchester. Although examples like this one illustrate the historical continuity of the process of economic integration, today the geographical extension of production processes is far more advanced and pervasive than ever before. As an aside, some interesting economic questions are raised by the fact that in some cases international production chains are managed almost entirely within a single multinational corporation (roughly 40 percent of U.S. merchandise trade is classified as intra-firm) and in others they are built through arm's-length transactions among unrelated firms. But the empirical evidence in both cases suggests that substantial productivity gains can often be achieved through the development of global supply chains.

The final item on my list of what is new about the current episode is that international capital markets have become substantially more mature. Although the net capital flows of a century ago, measured relative to global output, are comparable to those of the present, gross flows today are much larger. Moreover, capital flows now take many more forms than in the past: In the nineteenth century, international portfolio investments were concentrated in the finance of infrastructure projects (such as the American railroads) and in the purchase of government debt. Today, international investors hold an array of debt instruments, equities, and derivatives, including claims on a broad range of sectors. Flows of foreign direct investment are also much larger relative to output than they were fifty or a hundred years ago. As I noted earlier, the increase in capital flows owes much to capital-market liberalization and factors such as the greater standardization of accounting practices as well as to technological advances.

Conclusion

By almost any economically relevant metric, distances have shrunk considerably in recent decades. As a consequence, economically speaking, Wausau and Wuhan are today closer and more interdependent than ever before. Economic and technological changes are likely to shrink effective distances still further in coming years, creating the potential for continued improvements in productivity and living standards and for a reduction in global poverty.

Further progress in global economic integration should not be taken for granted, however. Geopolitical concerns, including international tensions and the risks of terrorism, already constrain the pace of worldwide economic integration and may do so even more in the future. And, as in the past, the social and political opposition to openness can be strong. Although this opposition has many sources, I have suggested that much of it arises because changes in the patterns of production are likely to threaten the livelihoods of some workers and the profits of some firms, even when these changes lead to greater productivity and output overall. The natural reaction of those so affected is to resist change, for example, by seeking the passage of protectionist measures. The challenge for policy makers is to ensure that the benefits of global economic integration are sufficiently widely shared – for example, by helping displaced workers get the necessary training to take advantage of new opportunities – that a consensus for welfare-enhancing change can be obtained. Building such a consensus may be far from easy, at both the national and the global levels. However, the effort is well worth making, as the potential benefits of increased global economic integration are large indeed.

---

b. Foreign Direct Investment

In the global economy, foreign direct investment (FDI) is an ever-growing ingredient that requires appropriate legal services.[9] It is distinguishable from foreign portfolio

[9] FDI has been explained as follows: "Foreign direct investment, in its classic definition, is defined as a company from one country making a physical investment into building a factory in another country. The direct investment in buildings, machinery, and equipment is in contrast with making a portfolio investment, which is considered an indirect investment. In recent years, given rapid growth and change in global investment patterns, the definition has been broadened to include

investment and different from foreign trade. Host countries, especially in developing countries, welcome FDI as a source of technology transfer, expertise, and sometimes foreign currency (in China's case). They are also mindful of the risks of a foreign takeover of sensitive industries (e.g., communications, banks). FDI may be used in several ways, such as establishing a new business or investing in or joining, merging, or acquiring an existing business. FDI is expanding as businesses seek to gain a competitive advantage through increased market share, reduced costs coming from cheaper labor, lower shipping costs, or lax law enforcement. For example, in the recent merger and acquisition (M&A) in China of Anheuser-Busch and Harbin Brewery Group Ltd., the transaction resulted in increased market share, an exchange of valuable expertise, connections, and for better or worse, a Chinese labor force with a bundle of labor-law issues.

Unlike foreign trade, there is an absence of international regulation of FDI, leaving it to bilateral or multilateral arrangements. The challenge to international lawyers is to understand the foreign laws or enough of them so that they can diligently engage and monitor foreign lawyers. These arrangements can take place through agency (or correspondent) offices, foreign offices, or international legal networks, as described later in the article by Robert Pritchard. He has noted that in the future, lawyers specializing in FDI and other forms of international business will also need to demonstrate a high level of cross-cultural understanding if they are to realize their full potential as facilitators of FDI, as well as protectors of their client's interests.[10]

the acquisition of a lasting management interest in a company or enterprise outside the investing firm's home country. As such, it may take many forms, such as a direct acquisition of a foreign firm, construction of a facility, or investment in a joint venture or strategic alliance with a local firm with attendant input of technology, licensing of intellectual property. In the past decade, FDI has come to play a major role in the internationalization of business. Reacting to changes in technology, growing liberalization of the national regulatory framework governing investment in enterprises, and changes in capital markets profound changes have occurred in the size, scope, and methods of FDI. New information technology systems, decline in global communication costs have made management of foreign investments far easier than in the past. The sea change in trade and investment policies and the regulatory environment globally in the past decade, including trade policy and tariff liberalization, easing of restrictions on foreign investment and acquisition in many nations, and the deregulation and privatization of many industries, has probably been the most significant catalyst for FDI's expanded role. The most profound effect has been seen in developing countries, where yearly foreign direct investment flows have increased from an average of less than $10 billion in the 1970s to a yearly average of less than $20 billion in the 1980s, to explode in the 1990s from $26.7 billion in 1990 to $179 billion in 1998 and $208 billion in 1999 and now comprise a large portion of global FDI. Driven by mergers and acquisitions and internationalization of production in a range of industries, FDI into developed countries last year rose to $636 billion, from $481 billion in 1998. (Source: UNCTAD)" Jeffrey P. Graham & R. Barry Spaulding, *Understanding Foreign Direct Investment*, http://www.going-global.com/articles/understanding_foreign_direct_investment.htm (last updated June 18, 2005). *See also* DONALD M. DEPAMPHILIS, MERGERS, ACQUISITIONS, AND OTHER RESTRUCTURING ACTIVITIES 150 (2005).

10 Robert L. Pritchard, *The Lawyer's Role in Foreign Direct Investment and the Global Economy*, 18 INT'L BUS. LAW 358 (1990) [Footnotes omitted]. Mr. Pritchard served as Chairman of the International Legal Practice Committee of the Law Council of Australia. Although these comments were circulated some years ago, the principles discussed remain insightful. *See, e.g.*, John O. Haley, *Law and Culture in China and Japan: A Framework for Analysis*, 27 MICH. J. INT'L L. 895 (2006); Teemu Ruskola, *Legal Orientalism*, 101 MICH. L. REV. 179, 181–88 (2002).

The number of international labor and employment lawyers, as a special area of this practice, has mushroomed, as described subsequently.

The Lawyer's Role in Foreign Direct Investment and the Global Economy[11]

Robert L. Pritchard

The world is going through an era when foreign direct investment (FDI) is increasing rapidly. It is therefore opportune to review the place of FDI in the global economy and the lawyer's role in facilitating FDI. . . . [The 1980's] witnessed a dramatic increase in Japanese FDI, mainly for the purpose of securing market access and shifting production facilities abroad. In the past, much of Japanese FDI was made for the purpose of securing raw material supplies from resource-rich countries. In the future, FDI will continue to increase as more and more . . . firms join US and European multinationals and others in expanding their businesses into a truly global marketplace.

What Is FDI?

There are two basic categories of foreign investment: one is FDI and the other is foreign portfolio investment (which includes corporate debt). Worldwide, FDI represents between 15 and 20 percent of total foreign investment and this percentage is rising. . . . [12] FDI may be defined as the capital invested in an enterprise or a real asset by a nonresident which gives the investor a significant influence, either potential or actual, over

[11] Pritchard, *supra* note 10.

[12] The impact of cross-border investments on the world economy has risen dramatically over the past decades. Between 1973 and 2000 worldwide annual FDI flows increased fiftyfold from $25 billion to $1.271 billion. The contribution of FDI to world welfare (the cumulative GDP of all countries) rose to seventeen percent compared with a mere six percent in 1980. Hans Christiansen & Mehmet Ogutcu, *Foreign Direct Investment for Development: Maximising Benefits, Minimising Costs*, GLOBAL FORUM ON INTERNATIONAL INVESTMENT (DEC. 5–6, 2002), *available at* http://www.oecd.org/dataoecd/54/33/2764465.pdf. It is reported that

> [g]lobal foreign direct investment (FDI) inflows remained stagnant in 2010 at an estimated $1,122 billion, comparing to $1,114 billion in the previous year, representing a 0.7 percent growth, announced United Nations Conference on Trade and Development (UNCTAD) here on Monday. "We have seen the global economic recovery, we have seen that trade and industrial output fully recovered to pre-crisis level," however, "FDI remains stagnated, and still at its lowest level," said Zhan Xiaoning, Director of UNCTAD Investment and Enterprise Division, referring to the fact that global FDI in 2010 was twenty-five percent below the pre-crisis average between 2005 and 2007. The results came out of an UNCTAD annual survey titled "Global and Regional FDI Trends in 2010," which had registered divergent performances between developed economies and developing economies. Mired in financial crisis, FDI in developed economies has not yet moved out of the declining trend. UNCTAD estimation indicates FDI in this group of economies to have fallen by seven percent in the past year, down to $526.6 billion. . . . On the other hand, FDI to developing economies and economies in transition, for the first time in history, exceeded the investment flows to developed economies, taking up fifty-three percent of the total global FDI in 2010. (*UN body says global foreign direct investment inflows remain stagnant in 2010*, GLOBAL TIMES, Jan. 18, 2010, http://business.globaltimes.cn/world/2011-01/613560.html)

the key policies of the enterprise or over the use of the asset. The threshold level which gives a 'significant influence' is rather arbitrary. For statistical purposes, most countries use a threshold of 10 per cent or more of the ordinary shares or voting stock. FDI may involve: (i) the acquisition of an existing enterprise; (ii) the establishment of a new enterprise; (iii) the reinvestment of earnings, or (iv) the purchase of land, buildings, and other assets. Joint ventures, whether incorporated or unincorporated, are one form of FDI. The other category of foreign investment is foreign portfolio investment. Portfolio investment involves the purchase of debt or equity in an enterprise by a non-resident, but does not involve any transfer of control over the use of assets.

What Causes Global FDI?

The overall level of global FDI and its flow to individual countries is a function of three concurrent factors:

- global savings imbalances, which determine the total flows of foreign investment;
- the comparative advantages of countries in particular industries, which explain why investment (but not necessarily foreign investment) is likely to occur; and
- inter-firm organisational factors, which explain why a firm's corporate strategy will cause it to undertake FDI. The implications of inter-firm organisational factors are discussed further below.

Regulation of Global FDI

Whereas world trade is regulated by the GATT [and now, the WTO], there is no corresponding multilateral body governing FDI. The United Nations has been unsuccessfully attempting for many years to institutionalize its Code of Conduct for Transnational Corporations. The World Bank's International Centre for the Settlement of Investment Disputes (ICSID) has received wider acceptance but is limited to the role of resolving disputes rather than preventing them. Under the OECD Declaration on International Investment and Multinational Enterprises, OECD member countries recommend to multinational enterprises operating in their territories the observance of the (OECD) Guidelines.

The OECD guidelines lay down standards for the activities of multinational firms. In relation to taxation, for example, firms are expected to refrain from modifying the tax base on which they are assessed by any practices which do not conform to an arm's length standard. The OECD Guidelines are not aimed at introducing differences of treatment between foreign and domestic firms; wherever relevant, they reflect good practice for all. Observance of the OECD Guidelines is, however, voluntary and is not legally enforceable.

In the absence of any multilateral framework, FDI continues to be regulated by host country legislation and by bilateral treaties. For example, in the case of Australia and Japan, the relevant bilateral treaty is the Australia–Japan Treaty of Friendship and Cooperation (the Treaty of Nara), signed in 1976. The treaty provides for most favoured nation status in investment for both countries.

In the 1960s, the United States dominated FDI. Today there is a much wider spread of investor countries including the US, Western Europe, and North Asia (especially Japan [and now China]). Also, most industrial countries have become both home and host countries at the same time. There is therefore wide recognition of the benefits of FDI and less pressure to introduce de facto anti-US measures than there has been in the past.

Why Should Host Countries Allow FDI?

Any country which wishes to invest more than it saves must be financed by foreign savings. The recipient country has an initial choice between official borrowing by the government to finance public investment and non-official flows to finance private investment. The remaining choice for the recipient country is between foreign portfolio investment (which includes corporate debt) and FDI. The latter has the following advantages over portfolio investment:

- FDI is normally accompanied by the transfer of technology and operating know-how;
- FDI is likely to provide superior market knowledge;
- FDI is likely to promote improved management performance;
- FDI reduces vulnerability to downturns in world economic conditions by tying foreign repayments to ability to pay;
- FDI helps to reduce volatility in financial markets.

Why Should Host Countries Restrict FDI?

From the point of view of the host country's national interest, FDI carries the potential risk that decisions of national importance to the host country may be made abroad in disregard of the national interest of the host country or may even be influenced by the national interest of the foreign investor's home country. This potential risk is not particularly grave; it needs to be weighed up in the context of the fact that the host country retains the unfettered right to set the rules governing business activities within its borders and to impose taxes and other imposts on such activities.

In their national interest, host countries may wish to restrict FDI in sensitive areas (for example, in defence industries, banking, the media and rural real estate). However, any such restriction imposes economic costs by dampening down the overall level of economic activity and reducing the inflow of foreign technology and operating know-how.

Why Do Firms Undertake FDI?

In discussions of FDI, the emphasis is usually on the question of why a firm invests in *a given country*. It is useful to change the emphasis and ask instead why a firm chooses to *invest* in a given country as its preferred method of doing business there.

A foreign firm may have an advantage in product development, process technology, or market knowledge. To exploit this advantage, it may adopt a globalisation strategy, but it need not necessarily choose FDI as being the best strategic route to implement that strategy.

We need to ask, in the case of a horizontal investment, why should not the foreign firm simply license its production technology to a local firm? After all, local firms should have superior knowledge about operating in their own country. Or, in the case of a backward vertical integration into a raw material or parts supplier, why should not the foreign firm choose instead a long-term procurement contract?

One common misconception is that firms undertake FDI solely to exploit some relative locational advantage in the host country, such as low political risk, low wages, low real estate costs, attractive investment incentives, high skill levels, the presence of raw materials or energy, or to get around a tariff barrier. These factors can explain why a country has a comparative advantage in a particular industry. They can therefore explain why domestic or foreign investment is likely to occur, but they cannot explain which one will occur, i.e. the particular attraction for a foreign investor as opposed to a domestic investor.

If FDI cannot be explained primarily by locational factors, to what is it due? FDI can best be explained by inter-firm *organisational factors*, in particular, transaction costs. By 'transaction costs' are meant the costs of communication, administration, and marketing which accompany an economic exchange. Whether they be firms or individuals, both parties in an economic exchange incur costs of negotiating, drawing up, monitoring, supervising performance of, and perhaps even enforcing, formal or informal contracts.

Lawyers have a special part to play in the process of economic exchange. Transaction costs therefore usually involve legal expenses, especially if the transaction needs to be documented in a formal contract. A formal contract between arm's length parties needs to specify in detail issues of quantity, quality, price, and delivery, as well as the consequences of all perceived future circumstances which may affect either or both parties. Alternatively, if the parties prefer to base their relationship on trust, there are heavy non-legal costs involved in the efforts and length of time needed to establish and maintain a higher degree of rapport between the parties.

Another cause of transaction costs is that even formal contracts often carry an element of uncertainty because of changing circumstances. Take the case of a manufacturing firm which has a strategic concern to secure the long-term supply or to stabilise the price and quality of its raw material needs. Such a firm must weigh up the transaction costs of establishing the necessary degree of rapport with arm's length suppliers against the confidence it would have in the behaviour of a foreign branch or affiliate. It does not invest in a country simply because the raw material is cheap or abundant there. The decision by a firm to undertake FDI is almost invariably a trade-off between, on the one hand, the costs of carrying out international transactions with another, separate firm and, on the other hand, the costs of internalising the transactions and operating a foreign branch or affiliate in an unfamiliar, perhaps quite uncertain, environment.

Whichever strategic route is chosen by a foreign firm, its lawyer will usually be called upon to contribute to its successful implementation. Quite often, a lawyer's advice will be essential to making an informed decision on which business route to take.

Global FDI is Likely to Increase

There is always a risk that a host country firm may be unresponsive to requests for greater cooperation and instead behave opportunistically. This will increase the risk to the foreign firm that the contract will need to be enforced. In any case, complex and unforeseen situations can arise in which contracts may be unenforceable. These risks have always provided an inducement for firms to undertake FDI.

. . . .

Why Do Firms Undertake Joint Ventures?

Joint ventures in a foreign country offer an intermediate choice between an arm's length relationship and a wholly-owned investment. By comparison with an arm's length relationship, the foreign firm expects that, once the joint venture is established, future transaction costs will be lower. It is therefore willing to incur the transaction costs inherent in forming the joint venture.

By comparison with a wholly-owned investment, the foreign firm expects that, although control has to be shared, the transaction costs of the joint venture will be justified by the additional confidence which the foreign firm can derive from the involvement and local knowledge of the host country partner.

Differences in National Legal Systems

The most obvious and fundamental legal constraint in the expansion of global FDI is that national legal systems differ from one to another, in many cases radically. This poses the risk for foreign investors that they may misunderstand the law of a particular country unless they develop an awareness of its unique cultural, social and political context. This danger is compounded as between Western and . . . [Eastern] legal systems. Western lawyers and businessmen inevitably interpret their own laws based on Western assumptions – assumptions as to the political, economic, cultural, and social circumstances prevailing in their own countries – assumptions which may themselves be part of Western culture.

By contrast . . . [Eastern] law tends to reflect Confucian social values. There is almost always an undercurrent notion that the individual should demonstrate his moral superiority and preserve social harmony by adjusting his moral 'rights' to the forces of nature and to the needs of others. A contract is therefore seen in [Eastern] cultures as an expression of a long-term cooperative relationship between the parties, rather than as a determinant of that relationship, as it is seen under English common law.

In addition, internationally, there remains a virtual legal vacuum in the field of business regulation. Despite the treaty-making efforts of governments and the more wide-sweeping initiatives of bodies such as the United Nations and the International Chamber of Commerce, a vast amount remains to be done to create a regime which will provide the level of legal stability needed by firms involved in the international marketplace.

All of this emphasizes the merit of mutual trust and understanding as the foundation of all long-term business relationships. But it is not enough by itself - carefully designed legal structures and smooth international legal processes are necessary as well. The role of the lawyer is crucial in all of this.

Foreign Merger and Acquisition (M&A) Activity

Because of the absence of international rules, the process of FDI is usually very slow. The pressure of current economic conditions is nevertheless very intense. For many firms, therefore, there is insufficient time (i) to study carefully product-market opportunities in the traditional way; (ii) to design and construct off-shore production facilities in the most ideal strategic location; (iii) to establish efficient distribution systems where none existed before; (iv) to put reliable management in place; and (v) wait for profits.

Many more businessmen are now studying M&A opportunities in foreign countries in order to adjust their businesses to the global economy at a more adequate rate. Sometimes a takeover can accelerate dramatically the rate of adjustment – an entire corporation, with its know-how, its people, its facilities, its investments, and its flow of existing profits, can be quickly acquired (or even disposed of) by a relatively straightforward transaction through a stock exchange. M&A activity is, of course, subject to strict domestic legal regulation in most countries. This is intended to guarantee that all shareholders are afforded fair and equal treatment. Here, the skilled lawyer plays a pivotal role in ensuring that the spirit and requirements of the legislation are observed.

. . . .

The ILO has studied the flow of FDI and its effects on economies and employment; some of its findings are discussed next.

Changing Patterns in the World of Work[13]

ILO

. . . .

Impact of Increased Investment by Multinational Enterprises on Jobs

39. Foreign direct investment (FDI) has grown faster than trade in most years since 1990. Changes in trade patterns described above mirror trends in FDI. Most FDI continues to go into the large markets of developed countries, but since the 1990s there has been a marked rise in FDI flows to the group of developing countries that has successfully focused on exports. This followed measures by a number of countries to attract FDI, such as the easing of controls on inward flows and repatriation of profits, as well as the establishment of export processing zones. Mergers and acquisitions (M&A) of existing assets also grew much faster than investment in new assets (Greenfield FDI), especially in countries that carried out extensive privatization of their public enterprises.

40. Annual flows of FDI vary with the business cycle but over the past 15 years, about two-thirds of all inflows on average went to developed countries – mostly from other developed countries. Developing countries account for about one-third of all inflows but only around 10 per cent of outflows. These shares were up to 36 per cent and 13 per cent, respectively, in 2004. Increasingly, China has come to dominate inflows of FDI to developing countries, while the United States remains the main source of outward investment. One of the most striking features of world FDI is the concentration on a relatively small number of home and host countries. In the 2002–04 period, 15 of the top 20 countries for FDI outflows were also in the top 20 for inflows [these included China, Japan, and South Korea]. The top five developing economy recipients – China, Hong Kong (China), Brazil, Mexico, and Singapore – accounted for over 60 per cent of total flows to developing countries.

[13] Juan Somavia, *Changing Patterns in the World of Work*, Int'l Labour Conference 9th Session 2006, *available at* http://www.ilo.org/public/english/standards/relm/ilc/ilc95/pdf/rep-i-c.pdf (last visited Sept. 23, 2010). Published by the International Labour Organization (2006).

41. By 2004, the 690,000 foreign affiliates of at least 70,000 multinational enterprises (MNEs) accounted for 10 per cent of world output, one-third of world exports, and around 10 per cent of investment (gross capital formation (GCF)). The growth of the sales of foreign affiliates of MNEs outpaced world exports markedly over the period between 1982 and 2004. The ILO estimated that direct employment by MNEs was approaching 100 million in 2000 – an increase from about 40 million in the mid-1970s. At approximately 3.4 per cent, this represents a relatively modest contribution to total world employment.

. . . .

42. The job-creating potential of FDI is one of the main reasons cited by governments for policy changes to attract MNEs. This has led to concern that countries may weaken labour protections as an incentive to inward investors. An OECD study on policy competition for FDI suggests that the danger of increasing downward pressure on labour standards always exists. Nonetheless, it concludes that there is "no robust evidence that low-standard countries provide a haven for foreign firms". This finding is confirmed by a detailed ILO analysis of the possible links between FDI flows and stronger freedom of association, collective bargaining rights and democracy. Despite some evidence that these rights are associated with higher labour costs even after accounting for productivity gains, it would seem that the economic and social stability that freedom of association as a basic building block of democracy engenders is attractive to foreign investors.

43. As described above, the job-creating potential of FDI can be overstated. Empirical research in developing countries does not show strong employment and labour market effects. A rising share of FDI in total investment tends to reduce the overall employment elasticity while shifting the pattern of labour demand in favour of high-skilled labour. Rising wage inequality is a consequence. On the positive side, a rising share of FDI in total investment leads to an improvement in the average quality of employment for both high-skilled and low-skilled labour.

. . . .

QUESTIONS

1. What are the forces driving companies to engage in Foreign Direct Investment?
2. Enumerate the alternative legal forms of entering the foreign market and their relative advantages and disadvantages.
3. What are the competitive advantages to the host country to accept and encourage FDI?
4. What is the meaning of "getting the China price"?
5. What regulations govern the process of FDI?
6. What would you anticipate are the labor standards in a country that encourages FDI?

c. Global Production Systems, Outsourcing, Offshoring, and Employment

Globalization has brought real changes in production systems, which, in turn, have directly affected employment arrangements. Diffused production and network-centric control by companies such as NIKE with its 900-plus suppliers and nearly

700,000 workers throughout 50 countries have changed the nature of governance and legal advising. Global governance rules are primarily facilitative and protective of property rights, but lacking in enforceable standards in labor, such as the International Labor Organization's (ILO) core labor standards. The impact of these production systems on wages and working conditions varies, with many of these industries having oligopolies on top and supplier competition on the bottom, creating pressure to keep costs (wages) low. Real and sham "social responsibility" provisions and codes of conduct have been introduced in an attempt to self-regulate, often amid allegations that they are to appease offended customers who may otherwise boycott products made in substandard conditions.[14]

Another related phenomenon affecting the new realities of global employment are the changes brought by cross-national systems of production, with their large amount of *outsourcing* and *offshoring* and their impact on employment, as discussed in the below excerpts.[15] Added to this is the evolution of many business organizations from vertical (such as General Motors) to horizontal operations (such as NIKE).

Cross-National Systems of Production

Global Production and Local Jobs: New Perspectives on Enterprise Networks, Employment, and Local Development Policy[16]

Sandra Polaski

Global Production, Local Jobs

Through the processes of globalization, economic activities performed in a variety of regions and countries are becoming increasingly integrated into cross-national systems of production. In industries such as automobiles, electronics, and garments, the chain of value-adding activities leading to a final product is organized in *global networks* creating new interdependencies between firms, industries, and labour markets. Although these networks are transnational in scope, they comprise specialized clusters of activities that remain strongly embedded in local industries and communities. Local embeddedness is particularly pronounced with regards to labour resources, which are much less mobile than capital, products, and information within the global economy.

The interactions between the global dynamics of production networks and the local operation of labour markets and labour market institutions... generate new growth opportunities, as local firms can access new markets and resources by connecting to

[14] Discussed in Section II.B.1.

[15] Reprinted by permission of the publisher from "*Global Production Systems and Employment: New Reality, New Policy Challenges*," Sandra Polaski (Washington, DC; Carnegie Endowment for International Peace, 2004), http://www.carnegieendowment.org [hereinafter Roundtable Discussion]. Gary Gereffi, Int'l Labor Org. 7th Nobel Peace Prize Social Policy Lectures: The New Offshoring of Jobs and Global Development: An Overview of the Contemporary Global Labor Market (2005), *available at* http://library.fes.de/pdf-files/gurn/00062.pdf (last visited Sept. 21, 2010).

[16] Roundtable Discussion, *supra* note 15.

global networks. Global linkages also provide a means to acquire new skills and capabilities, enhancing the value content of local activities and their potential for sustainable growth. Both the quantity and quality of local jobs can *potentially* be increased in that process. At the same time, global connections might provide an unstable basis for growth and development. Locational advantage and the competitiveness of local firms have to be constantly realigned to the restructuring of global production networks. Moreover, becoming integrated into global networks can divide and fragment local industries and societies, marginalizing those economic actors that fail to develop strong global linkages.

. . . .

Structure and Dynamics of Enterprise Networks

To examine the implications of global production networks for local jobs in industrial clusters . . . a number of approaches [are] developed at two levels of analysis: the global and the local. At the global level, the *global commodity chain (GCC)* framework offers key insights on the structure and dynamics of international production networks. A global commodity chain can be broadly defined as a set of networks clustered around one final product or service and linking firms, industries and communities to one another across the world economy. Adopting such a framework involves three important shifts in our conceptualization of production: (1) from industries as homogeneous groups of activities to value chains cutting across and within industries; (2) from firms as self-contained units to networks spanning across organizations; and (3) from national frames of reference to complex interactions between local and global perspectives.

Industries are traditionally defined with reference to a homogeneous group of products, with the assumption that firms involved in the production of such products perform fairly similar activities. By contrast, a *value chain* is formed by a set of *complementary activities* that may belong to different industries – for example, the apparel chain involves textile producers, apparel manufacturers, and retailers – or be differentiated within one industry – apparel firms might be specialized in product design or product manufacturing. Adopting such a chain perspective helps to understand the new forms and logic of competition. In today's fast-changing competitive environment, firms are placing greater emphasis on integrating complementary activities within a flexible and responsive network aimed at reducing cycle times, improving quality and cost control, and facilitating the diffusion of innovation within the network.

These networks increasingly cut across firms' boundaries. As shown by evidence from a number of industries such as automobiles, garments, and electronics, their emergence is being driven by the strategies of large *lead firms* that are reacting to intensified competitive pressures by developing new relationships based on a mix of cooperation and market links with a variety of satellite firms across the globe. Such relationships can be seen as forming *strategic networks*, in which lead firms are constantly engaged in attracting and selecting members, in sustaining network relationships by managing conflicts and learning, and in building the structure and culture of the network.

. . . .

Local Learning, Industrial Upgrading, and Employment

. . . .

Learning dynamics in global production networks have important implications for employment. Upgrading strategies at the local level are likely to involve the adoption of new work systems and human resource management practices based on employee skills development, employee involvement, and the retention of skilled workers through higher wages and improved working conditions. However, as some firms improve their network position, others might take over lower value-added activities, which are more vulnerable to competitive pressures and less conducive to innovative employment practices. The quality of employment might thus become increasingly differentiated according to firms' positions within production networks. In this context, some analysts point to a growing polarization between a shrinking core and an expanding periphery. These new patterns of segmentation might develop within or between locations, depending on the specific characteristics of local industries and labour markets, and on their place and role in global networks.

Innovative Policies at the Local Level

The development of global production networks is placing new demands on policy makers, who need to redefine their role in relation to changes in the forms and logic of competition. . . . Labour market institutions in particular are seen as capable of playing an important role in developing workers' skills, raising standards, and contributing to build up intangible assets. Because skills and capabilities are essential sources of competitive advantage, industrial and labour policies appear as increasingly interlinked, reinforcing the need for a systemic approach to policy.

An equally important shift concerns the relationships between the actors involved in policy making. As emphasized by the growing literature on economic governance, neither the state nor the market can satisfactorily do it alone. Just as enterprises are transforming their modes of operation in order to build sustainable competitive advantage, state and non-state institutions – including employers' and workers' organizations – are striving to find new, flexible ways of interacting between themselves, and with businesses, in order to support industrial competitiveness and foster social cohesion. In particular, the promotion of effective integration of local firms within global production networks seems to rely increasingly on networking strategies between local institutions, supporting agencies, and enterprises. In this regard, firms are seen less as pure recipients of support and more as potential partners. Enterprises themselves are exploring new possibilities to team up with other actors for social action, for instance as they react to mounting global and local pressures for ethical sourcing and more socially responsible behaviour. Such innovative policy initiatives, "policy networks" and "tactical alliances" are particularly evident at the local level, in specialized industrial clusters where globalization pays more, or hits harder, and where consensus about collective interests is easier to achieve.[17]

. . . .

[17] No longer does a single firm control all of a company's activities (e.g., General Motors in the 1960s), but rather the system operates from a network-centric perspective and a firm is disconnected from the customers it serves – for instance, NIKE now has 900 suppliers and 650,000 workers spread over 50 countries. Although there has been a diffusion of production, the control has solidified on the retail side as a result of consolidation among top-tier firms and a proliferation among potential suppliers. *Id.*

OUTSOURCING AND OFFSHORING. Global outsourcing has been increasing, particularly since the 1980s, and combines two distinct business activities: "outsourcing" and "offshoring." Outsourcing is merely a business decision to make or buy goods or services. Offshoring refers to the decision to move the supply of goods and services from domestic to overseas locations.

Globalization, Employment, and Economic Development: A Briefing Paper[18]

Gary Gereffi and Timothy J. Sturgeon

The Great Global Job Shift

A cover story in the February 3, 2003, issue of *Business Week* highlighted the impact of global outsourcing over the past several decades on the quality and quantity of jobs in both developed and developing countries (Engardio, Bernstein, and Kripalani, 2003). The first wave of global outsourcing began in the 1960s and 1970s with the exodus of production jobs in shoes, clothing, cheap electronics, and toys. After that, routine service work, like credit-card receipt processing, airline reservations, and the writing of basic software code began to move offshore. Today, the computerization of work, the Internet, and high-speed private data networks have allowed a wide range of "knowledge work" to become more footloose.

Global outsourcing reveals many of the key features of contemporary globalization: it deals with international competitiveness in a way that underscores the growing interdependence of developed and developing countries; a huge part of the debate centers around jobs, wages, and skills in different parts of the world, and there is a useful focus on how the chain of activities is organized across firms and country boundaries, and where in the chain value and employment is created. There are enormous political as well as economic stakes in how global outsourcing plays itself out in the coming years, particularly as well-endowed and strategically positioned economies increase their participation in global value chains. Countries like India, China, the Philippines, Mexico, Russia, parts of Eastern Europe, and South Africa are loaded with college graduates who speak Western languages and can handle outsourced information-technology work. India is particularly well positioned in this regard.

The extent of global outsourcing is impressive. In 2001, about 90% of all consumer electronics sold in the United States were produced offshore, as were 80-85% of footwear, toys, luggage and handbags, watches, clocks, games, and television sets, 70% of bicycles, 60% of computers, and 57% of apparel (USITC, 2002). The vast majority of these imports came from developing countries, which accounted for 55–60% of the knitted fabrics and undergarments exported in the world, nearly 50% of transistors and semiconductors, and 36% of computers (UNCTAD, 2002: 57). Most of these figures have risen sharply in the past decade.

[18] Gary Gereffi & Timothy J. Sturgeon, *Globalization, Employment, and Economic Development: A Briefing Paper*, *in* INDUSTRIAL PERFORMANCE CENTER WORKING PAPER SERIES, *available at* http://web.mit.edu/ipc/publications/pdf/04-007.pdf (last visited Sept. 21, 2010).

The rise of global outsourcing has triggered waves of consternation in advanced economies about job loss and the degradation of capabilities that could spell the disappearance of entire national industries. Many have dismissed these concerns, arguing instead that global outsourcing should be embraced as a mechanism for economies to shift out of low-value activities and old industries, freeing up capital and human resources for higher-value activities and the development of newer industries and cutting-edge products (*The Economist*, 2004a; 2004b). But clearly such assurances are of little comfort to those whose economic survival has been placed in jeopardy by direct competition with firms and workers with low wages and increasingly high skills.

Global outsourcing has also triggered a debate about the benefits and costs of globalization for developing countries. Some claim that it has been extremely beneficial, but others argue that global outsourcing has led only to "immiserizing"[19] growth and a "race to the bottom," as developing countries compete with one another to offer transnational companies the lowest operating costs (Kaplinsky, 2000; 2001). The emergence of China and, to a lesser extent, India, as important nodes of activity – or hubs – in global value chains has expanded the global labor force so significantly that globalization is likely to bid down the living standards not only for unskilled work and primary products, but increasingly for skilled work and industrial products as well.

Despite popular notions to the contrary, global outsourcing has not meant a wholesale transfer of economic activity out of developed economies and into developing ones. A large and important set of activities have remained rooted, at least so far, in advanced economies, even as they have become tightly linked to activities located elsewhere. The cumulative effect is that cross-border linkages between economies and firms have grown more elaborate. Firms are less likely to simply make products and export them; they increasingly participate in highly complex cross-border arrangements that involve a dizzying array of partners, customers, and suppliers. Global outsourcing has given rise to a new and important set of economic structures in the world economy that we refer to as "global value chains."

The spread of global value chains has created a new level of fluidity in the international economy that appears to be having a profound impact on the quantity and quality of jobs generated throughout the world. The acceleration of outsourcing in the 1990s signaled the "deverticalization"[20] of the modern corporation, as defined in the 1970s by Alfred Chandler. Instead of continually growing in size and scope, the trend was for greater specialization and focus on "core competencies." This process created new interdependencies between lead firms and suppliers as each value chain actor learned

[19] This is defined as economic growth that makes the country worse off. Bhagwati (1958) coined this term for growth that expands exports and worsens the terms of trade sufficiently that real income falls. Johnson (1955) had shown that a market distorted by a tariff could lose from growth and had also, independently, worked out conditions for Bhagwati's result. *See* Alan V. Deardorff, DEARDORFFS' GLOSSARY OF INTERNATIONAL ECONOMICS, http://www-personal.umich.edu/~alandear/glossary/i.html (last visited May 31, 2011).

[20] This term has been defined as when "vertical organizations own more of their supply chains and therefore focus less on core competencies. So vertical food conglomerates own farms, processing plants, manufacturing facilities, and warehouses. Companies 'deverticalize' by selling and outsourcing major supply chain segments while retaining control of their core business. Deverticalization can eliminate weak links in the supply chain and allow core divisions to grow." *On the Buzzword Watch*, LOGISTICSMGMT.COM, http://www.logisticsmgmt.com/article/CA145620.html (last visited Apr. 10, 2010) (on file with author).

how to quickly and effectively combine distinct and complementary sets of capabilities with other actors in the chain.

In the increasingly globalized economy of the late twentieth century, it became logical to complement outsourcing with offshoring – that is, the practice of moving discrete value chain activities to places with lower operating costs, specialized capabilities, large markets, or all three. For advanced industrial economies like those in North America and Europe, offshore manufacturing platforms offered low-cost and increasingly high-quality alternatives to making goods at home. While offshore assembly was initially done by the subsidiaries of multinational firms, growing capabilities in the supply base led to the emergence of both an independent set of developing country suppliers in places like Taiwan and a cadre of huge "global suppliers" headquartered in developed countries with extensive worldwide operations.

The difficulty is that the bounds of global outsourcing are unknown – what began as simple assembly work in the 1960s and 1970s has rapidly spread up and down the value chain into a wide range of goods and services. Virtually all consumer products sold by developed country retailers today are made entirely or to a significant extent in offshore factories located in developing countries. Even products that require precision manufacturing, like hard disk drives and many kinds of semiconductors, are becoming "high-tech commodities" made in capital-intensive facilities in Southeast Asia and elsewhere. Certain kinds of software programming and hardware design can now be done more cheaply in places like India, Taiwan, South Korea, and the Philippines than in the United States, Europe, or Japan, and a growing array of knowledge-intensive business services, such as engineering, design, accounting, legal and medical advice, financial analysis, and business consulting, are now beginning to move offshore as well. The implications of these shifts for the future of white-collar and skilled factory work have become an explosive political issue in developed economies, even as developing country governments pin their hopes on global outsourcing as a key driver for economic development.

. . . .

Starting Point: Outsourcing, Offshoring, and Global Outsourcing

Global outsourcing has been gathering pace since the 1980s. This process combines two quite distinct phenomena: outsourcing and offshoring. "Outsourcing" is a standard aspect of all businesses, which frequently and continually need to make the decision to "make or buy" specific inputs and services (Williamson, 1975, 1985). While companies regularly decide whether they wish to produce goods and services "in house" or buy them from outside vendors, the trend in recent years has shifted in the direction of "buy." Major manufacturers such as the "Big Two" American automakers, General Motors and Ford, have spun off their huge internal parts divisions as independent suppliers., and many businesses have outsourced a wide range of services, such as accounts receivable, insurance, and logistics, to specialized firms in industries like electronics., manufacturing itself has become a service.

"Offshoring" refers to the decision to move the supply of goods and services from domestic to overseas locations. These activities may be carried out in facilities owned in whole or in part by the parent firm, by transnational suppliers, or by local suppliers. The geographic shift of industries is certainly not a new phenomenon. In the early twentieth century in the United States, many industries that were established in

New England, such as textiles, apparel, footwear and furniture, began to move to the U.S. South in search of abundant natural resources and cheaper labor, frequently in "right to work" states that made it difficult to establish labor unions. The same forces behind the impetus to shift production to low-cost regions within the United States eventually led U.S. manufacturers to cross national borders to places like Mexico, Japan, and Singapore, and eventually to most of East Asia. Another major driver of industry re-location have been trade rules, which either tilted the balance for market access in favor of local production or reduced tariffs in outward processing trade (or production sharing) to the point where manufacturing offshore for the home market became highly attractive.

The search for capabilities also weighs heavily in the location decisions of firms. As the capabilities of both global and local suppliers matured in the 1980s and 1990s, lead firms in the United States, Europe, and to a lesser extent Japan, began to move more extensively toward an international contracting model that utilized the capabilities of suppliers, contractors, and intermediaries to implement their offshoring strategies. This trend leads us to the term "offshore outsourcing," or perhaps better, "global outsourcing."

The Expansion of the Global Supply Base in Asia

Today China has established a critical mass of infrastructure and factory capacity that makes it the world's most important global outsourcing platform for manufacturing. It has an unparalleled mix of economies of scale, industrial diversification, and domestically funded infrastructure, buttressed by the world's largest inflows of foreign direct investment (FDI). Together these make China's export-oriented factories a critical link in global value chains. But China is not alone. There are low-cost, high-quality offshore manufacturing platforms in many parts of Asia, as well as Mexico, South America, and Eastern and Central Europe. These far-flung locations are coming to be better integrated and more connected with one another on a daily basis, which is critical to the emergence of a global supply base.

. . . .

China's economic growth, averaging 8% a year since 1978, has not only made it into a global Goliath, but it has also become the major engine for intraregional trade in developing Asia. According to the Asian Development Bank (2004), "(China) is the world's biggest consumer of copper, tin, zinc, platinum, steel, and iron ore; second biggest of aluminum and lead; third largest of nickel; and fourth largest of gold. It is now the world's second-largest oil consumer [after the United States], and accounted for 35% of the global rise in oil demand in 2003." China's large trade surplus with the United States is closely linked to its widening trade deficit with East and Southeast Asia. China has become the single largest export market for Japan and the East Asian newly industrializing economies, and it accounted for nearly 80% of Japan's increase in exports in 2003. China's demand for intermediate components from its East and Southeast Asian regional trading partners, which supplied China with over half of its total imports in 2003, has grown sharply, thereby fueling the precipitous rise of China's exports of final goods to non-Asian industrial economies.

Participants in Asia's regional production chain have pushed each other to move from low value-added sectors to high value-added sectors in the past decade by "vertical specialization" in global value chains. China has established a strong comparative advantage in the downstream stages of production, largely as a result of massive inflows of FDI and its abundant supplies of low-cost labor. Meanwhile, Japan and the newly industrializing economies of Hong Kong, South Korea, Taiwan, and Singapore supply China with high technology and relatively high value-added inputs and finished products, and Southeast Asian economies (Indonesia, Malaysia, Philippines, and Thailand) export significant quantities of primary products to China (Asian Development Bank, 2004).

. . . .

Without FDI, and in particular the capital equipment and skills brought to China by foreign firms, China's development over the past ten years would have looked very different. At the same time, the strategies of many of the world's largest and most important companies now appear to be inextricably integrated with the capabilities that exist on the ground in China.

Global outsourcing is also emerging up and down the value chain in the once-sacrosanct services sector. The offshore provision of services began with low-value-added activities, such as back office transactions and call centers, and it now includes activities more closely associated with knowledge work, such as software programming, engineering, design, accounting, legal and medical advice, and a broad array of other professional services.

. . . .

Global Buyers and Global Suppliers: The Employment Implications of the New Global Supply Base

A powerful trend in the most recent phase of global outsourcing, in both manufacturing and in services, is the shift of activities to an increasingly competent set of suppliers, contract manufacturers, and intermediaries – in other words, a deepening of the "outsourcing" facet of globalization. When work is "handed off" to independent suppliers, several things happen.

First, the supplier can gain economies of scale and scope by pooling its resources across a broad customer base. Second, the existence of highly competent independent suppliers lowers the barriers to globalization for firms, including small and medium-sized firms, which have not yet shifted any activities offshore. Third, the separation of routine and labor-intensive functions from non-routine, skill-intensive functions, and the passing of the former to independent firms, eases the introduction of two-tier wage and benefit structures.

The emergence of a global supply base lowers the costs of and barriers to globalization, and so encourages more firms to adopt global outsourcing strategies. When smaller, less competent firms move in this direction, markets are created for a broader array of functions to be outsourced, and this drives suppliers to bundle additional functions and increase their range of competence. This bundling and packaging of functions by suppliers lowers barriers further, and a cycle of supplier upgrading and increased outsourcing is set in motion. Sturgeon and Lee (2004) have referred to this process as "industry co-evolution." Clearly, the role of lead firms in driving this process forward has been critical, especially when we consider the increased involvement of huge retailers like Wal-Mart and Costco in pushing their suppliers to lower costs and increase quality by consolidating production in low-wage locations such as China. Taking the role of buyers seriously places the development of East Asia and Mexico in a new light, and leads us to notions such as "supplier-oriented industrial upgrading" that supports "demand-driven development" in response to the needs of increasingly powerful "global buyers."

In terms of employment effects, these points provide few answers, but usefully identify the process of global outsourcing as a historical one that may accelerate rapidly after long periods of experimentation and supply-base upgrading by pioneering firms. Once an offshore supply base comes into being and then reaches a critical level of competence and scale, barriers to entry fall (for buyers and other lead firms, but not for suppliers) and global outsourcing can really take off. We have seen such surges in global outsourcing in manufacturing industries, sometimes referred to as an "outsourcing tear," and the feeling among many observers seems to be that we are on the brink of such an event in the realm of services.

The measurement of globalization's impact on service sector employment, as in manufacturing, is clearly a vexing issue. As Dossani and Kenney put it, "How significant service offshoring will be for developed country employment patterns is difficult to calculate." Like manufacturing, the globalization of services started with multinational firms in fields like accounting and consulting setting up offices in offshore locations to access new markets, followed by the movement of centralized labor-intensive functions, often referred to in services as "back-office" work (such as call centers and bill processing) to places with pools of educated, low-cost labor.

. . . .

Clearly global-scale integration and coordination is needed in the labor movement to match the same trends in the global economy, but it is also clear that devising and implementing strategies to address labor issues in specific industries requires understanding who the actors in global value chains are and what governs the relationships between them.

. . . .

For developing countries, the implications of the new global supply base are a hotly debated topic. One view is that the functional and geographic fragmentation of value chains can serve to lock developing countries into low-value activities because these activities can remain physically distant from higher-value activities in the chain. Another view is that it is not so easy to distinguish high- from low-value activities, and that there has been a great deal of upgrading in all kinds of value chain functions, not least because of the requirements for tight coordination, high quality, and extremely disciplined and technology-intensive supply-chain management methods that make global value chains tick. Furthermore, the immense concentration of "low-value" activities that have been pooled to gain economies of scale has given a great deal of leverage to these huge new global factories and global back offices, and the countries that contain them. The real worry, in this view, is for the places that continue to be entirely excluded from participation in global value chains.

. . . .

QUESTIONS

1. Provide examples of a "global commodity chain" and a "value chain."
2. Consider the *competitive* advantages vis-à-vis employment by the business choices of the employer in doing cross-border business.

3. What are the implications of the OECD statement, "[w]hile offshoring has no real impact on the overall numbers of workers in employment, it can reduce demand for low-skill workers [in the sending country], probably because businesses tend to move the most routine production stages overseas." Do you agree or disagree, and why?
4. There are also practical risks associated with outsourcing work. Some of those are listed next in the insightful comments of an international lawyer. Are any more likely to occur in East Asia than elsewhere?

Emerging Market/China Outsourcing Issues: A Speech[21]

Dan Harris

. . . .

In choosing whether or not to outsource, U.S. companies typically weigh the perceived benefits of outsourcing versus the perceived risks.

The perceived benefits typically are one or more of the following:

- Reduced costs
- Having an outside company handle the non-core aspects of the business
- Better quality/operational performance
- Around the clock work force

All of these benefits can be realized by outsourcing to an emerging market country, particularly the lower costs and the 24/7 work force.

But of course, there are risks to outsourcing as well, including the following:

- Your vendor will do a bad job
- Your vendor will do a bad job, yet still expect full payment
- Your vendor will steal your data
- Your vendor will steal your Intellectual Property
- Your vendor will steal your trade secrets
- Your vendor will sell your data or IP or trade secrets to one of your competitors
- Your vendor will use your data or IP or trade secrets to compete with you
- Your vendor will cost more than expected in the short term due to transition costs
- Your vendor will cost more than expected in the long term
- Your company will lose its innovation edge because someone else is doing its key work
- Your vendor's personnel tomorrow will be different from your vendor's personnel today
- Your company's morale will be negatively impacted by your outsourcing
- Suing and collecting meaningful damages from your vendor may be difficult
- Politics will impair the project
- The price will change due to currency fluctuation

[21] Dan Harris, *Emerging Market/China Outsourcing Issues: A Speech*, China Law Blog (November 21, 2010), http://www.chinalawblog.com/2010/11/emerging_market_china_too_outsourcing_issues_a_speech.html.

- An inability to secure visas will impair the project
- Crime will impair the project
- You might face export control issues
- You might face Foreign Corrupt Practices Act issues (FCPA)
- You might get snared in your vendor's labor/employment law issues
- You might get snared in your vendor's bankruptcy

Nearly all of the above risks are present even when you outsource domestically, but nearly all of these risks will be greater when you outsource overseas and nearly all of these risks will be even greater still when you outsource to an emerging market country.

. . . .

QUESTIONS

1. Explain the differences, *comparative* consequences, and the possible advantages for employment of outsourcing, offshoring, and global outsourcing.
2. Explain and compare global commodity chains and value chains.
3. Distinguish global outsourcing from offshoring. Why choose one over the other?
4. Is the use of foreign labor in your home country a viable alternative to outsourcing and offshoring; how do they differ?

2. *Global Impacts*

The effects of globalism on employment are often direct and diverse. Globalism may affect the employment relationship and working conditions, labor unions, business practices, and human resource management (HRM) policies. The promise of globalism is to raise the economic tide and provide increased jobs, wealth, and benefits for all. Of course, all don't benefit; and for those who do, the benefits may fall sporadically and unevenly.

Labor unionism has declined in recent decades; has it declined because of the impacts of globalism that arm many employers with less expensive options? Globalism also motivates labor unions to unite across national borders, as is discussed later. Business decisions relating to labor and employment have become ever more significant as employers seek to maximize their competitive advantages. This has caused some interesting phenomena, such as a unionized Wal-Mart in China versus its having no unionized companies in the United States. One of the challenges is how best to coordinate HRM policies and practices between domestic and foreign locations – harmonize or diversify?

Labor union supporters measure job creation as against job losses caused by employment displaced through outsourcing, offshoring, or relocation. Employers may measure new employment relationships through job flexibility and low costs often achieved by increased use of "contingent" (or irregular) workers. These workers, such as part-time, casual, or leased employees, often fall outside labor regulations; and it is for that reason they are employed in the contingent status. Employers may feel compelled to conduct business in this manner in order to stay competitive, even though it is argued such an approach is a "race to the bottom" on labor standards because they are competing with overseas employers with low-paid workers and fewer enforced labor standards. In attempts to keep costs low, workers' wages and working conditions are sometimes compromised. In overseas locations there are periodic reports of worker abuse. Many of these reported cases involve local subcontractors of foreign employers. In that case, although not directly involved in legal issues, the foreign employer may be caught up in public relations issues.

Another aspect of globalization is the global workforce, with a component being about 175 million migrant workers from poorer countries migrating to wealthier countries for employment on foreign soil. This "insourcing" brings in foreign nationals as workers rather than using foreign workers in their home location, which raises additional labor and employment law issues.

---

a. Labor and Employment

GLOBAL TRENDS IN LABOR MARKETS

Labour Market Trends and Globalization's Impact on Them[22]

Unemployment and the loss of jobs in developed countries are quite commonly associated with globalization. That globalization has a negative impact on labor is described below as emanating from changing business conditions:

- Multinationals have exported jobs from developed countries to developing countries through foreign investments and outward production in special economic zones.
- Through trade liberalization, governments have encouraged the replacement of domestically produced goods with goods produced abroad.
- The increased application of technology, especially in globally operating companies, can reduce the use of and dependence on labour.

. . . .

---

[22] Labour Market Trends and Globalization's Impact on Them, *available at* http://actrav.itcilo.org/actrav-english/telearn/global/ilo/seura/mains.htm (last visited Sept. 21, 2010). Copyright © International Labour Organization [hereinafter Labour Market Trends]. *See also* Kevin Kolben, *Labor and Employment Law*, 61 IND. & LAB. REL. REV. 580, 580 (2008) (reviewing GLOBALIZATION AND THE FUTURE OF LABOUR LAW (John D. R. Craig & S. Michael Lynk eds., 2006)). This collection provides an "understanding [of] how traditional modes of workplace and labor regulation are affected by globalization[ ]" and discusses "what should be the policy and regulatory responses to this phenomenon, particularly at the supranational and international levels." *Id.*

An opposing view, set forth, for example, by the IMF and the OECD, is that globalization (e.g., through foreign investment, trade, new technology, and liberalization) contributes to growth, which is the key to employment. Unemployment, on the other hand, is mainly due to governments' failure to adopt sound macroeconomic and labour market policies. However, the OECD, in particular, has also recognized that globalization makes workers increasingly vulnerable, as discussed below.

OECD Employment Outlook Summary – 2007 Edition[23]

. . . .

Globalisation – the freeing up of worldwide trade – has raised people's incomes in the OECD area. For example, OECD countries that see a 10 percentage point increase in trade openness enjoy about a 4% rise in per capita income.

Despite these gains, there is considerable public ambivalence about globalisation. While globalisation has helped raise the incomes of many workers, some – particularly the low skilled – have fared less well and there is now genuine public concern that globalisation is squeezing salaries and damaging workers' conditions in OECD countries. How justified are these fears?

There is some evidence that deepening trade over the past few decades has increased both earnings inequality and insecurity for OECD workers. But some important caveats need to be kept in mind. Firstly, it is difficult to separate the impact of globalisation from that of technological change or structural reform and, secondly, the impact is not as great as is popularly understood.

The impact of globalisation on workers varies, and is determined in part by their skill levels. While offshoring has no real impact on the overall numbers of workers in employment, it can reduce demand for low-skill workers, probably because businesses tend to move the most routine production stages overseas.

More profoundly, globalisation is one of a number of factors – including domestic policy reform and technological change – contributing to greater flexibility in both salaries and labour demand, which have both become much more responsive to economic shocks.

As an indicator of this change, the wage elasticity of labour demand increased from 0.2 to 0.5 (in absolute value) between 1980 and 2002. This translates to a more dynamic labour market which places a premium on being mobile and having the right skills. Indeed, increased foreign competition leads to increased job switching.

[23] OECD Employment Outlook: OECD Multilingual Summaries (2007 ed.), *available at* http://www.oecd.org/dataoecd/28/32/38798341.pdf (last visited Sept. 20, 2010). More open markets, global trade, and investment don't inevitably lead to greater prosperity and more jobs. Thus, workers and trade unions pointing to adverse effects of globalization, in particular the loss of jobs, stagnating wages and increasing inequality, have good reasons to do so. *OECD: Impact of globalisation makes workers increasingly vulnerable*, TUAC News (July 2007), http://old.tuac.org/News/default.htm (last visited Sept. 20, 2010); *see also* Michel Camdessus, Managing Director of the Int'l Monetary Fund, Address at the Sixteenth World Congress of the Int'l Confederation of Free Trade Unions: The Impact of Globalization on Workers and Their Trade Unions (June 26, 1996), *available at* http://www.imf.org/external/np/sec/mds/1996/MDS9613.HTM (last visited Oct. 3, 2010).

On income inequality, the share of national income accounted for by workers' wages has fallen, quite sharply in some countries. There is also a growing gap in earnings, but it is largely accounted for by sharp increases in earnings among the top 10% of earners, rather than by falls at the bottom end of the earning range. The extent to which globalisation is contributing to these changes is unclear. However the changes in earnings distribution at least suggest that globalisation is allowing small elites of workers and investors to pull away from everyone else.

. . . .

———

CHANGING EMPLOYMENT RELATIONSHIPS. The clear trend in employment relationships is for the employer to establish an arrangement that maximizes flexibility and lowers costs while maintaining productivity. This drive for competitive advantage and profitability results in an increased number of "contingent" (irregular) employees. These include part-time, casual, and leased employees who typically have lower labor costs and are free from much of the labor regulations provided to regular employees.

———

A New Labor Law for a New World of Work: The Case for a Comparative-Transnational Approach[24]

Katherine V. W. Stone

. . . .

II. Pressures Shaping the Employment Relationship Today

A. *Flexibilization*

. . . .

In recent years, employers in many countries have dismantled their internal labor market job structures and abandoned the implicit promises that went along with them. In their place, employers have created new types of employment relationships that give them flexibility to cross-utilize employees and to make quick adjustments in production methods as they confront increasingly competitive product markets.

. . . .

Firms are creating a new employment relationship in which regular, full-time work has become contingent in the sense that the attachment between the firm and the worker has been weakened. The "recasualization of work" has reportedly become a fact of life all along the employment spectrum from blue collar workers to high-end professionals and managers.

[24] Reprinted with permission by Katherine V. W. Stone, *A New Labor Law for a New World of Work: The Case for a Comparative-Transnational Approach*, 28 COMP. LAB. & POL'Y J. 565 (2007). Copyright © Katherine V. W. Stone.

The changing employment patterns are evident in a series of new work practices that employers have instituted over the past decade. The new work practices include innovations such as broadbanding that are designed to give employers flexibility to cross utilize employees across job titles and departmental lines. They also include compensation practices such as pay-for-performance and bench-marking that attempt to match employees' pay to their individual contribution and to their value in the external labor market. Other features of the new employment relationship are a flattening of hierarchy and an increase in discretion to ever lower ranks of employees. The latter is an effort to capture employee knowledge, skills, and imagination for firm goals. To cultivate and capture employee knowledge, skills, and imagination, firms have designed various types of workforce empowerment programs to give bounded discretion to relatively low level employees.

The new employment relationship also involves a change in the implicit contract between the employee and the firm. Instead of giving employees an implicit promise of employment security, today's employers implicitly promise employability security – the ability to acquire skills that will enhance their opportunities in the labor market. Employers also no longer promise their employees orderly promotional opportunities but rather promise opportunities for employees to network and gain skills that will prepare them for other jobs outside the firm. In the new "boundaryless" employment relationship, employees are expected to manage their own careers, rather than to expect long-term employment from a single firm.

. . . .

The mismatch between today's flexible work relations and conventional union practices has led companies to resist unions more fiercely than ever. Indeed, unions have had a difficult time gaining a foothold in companies such as TRW and Hewlett Packard that have been at the vanguard of the new human resource revolution. Some companies, such as General Electric, engaged in aggressive deunionization first in order to restructure their labor relations. The move to flexible employment practices has thus been one of the factors feeding management's assault on unions.

2. Globalization

Globalization is the cross-border interpenetration of economic life. It is the result of many well-known factors, including new telecommunications and computer technologies that enable firms to produce, distribute, and market all over the world; new trading regimes that reduce trade barriers and foreign exchange restrictions; and the rise of multi-national corporations and production networks whose long supply chains span continents. As a result of globalization, national borders are becoming permeable to products and capital flows from all around the globe.

Trade unionists and progressive policy makers have long feared that globalization will mean the demise of hard-won labor standards and workplace rights in the Western world. Many economists have found that companies are moving low-skilled jobs to low-wage, low union density countries, thereby leaving depressed wages and increased unemployment in their wake.

Globalization not only undermines domestic labor standards directly, it also undermines the strength of domestic labor organizations. As capital mobility increases, businesses have an incentive as well as an ability to relocate to countries with lower labor standards. The result is that unions have less power at the bargaining table in their home countries because they are always bargaining against the threat of relocation. In practice, this means that companies are less likely to yield to union demands. Unions, in turn, scale back their demands out of fear of triggering business flight.

Globalization also diminishes the level of domestic labor-protective regulations. Companies prefer to produce in legal environments that offer the least protections for labor and, when feasible, they shift production to capture the resultant lower labor costs. As a result, nations compete for business using lower labor standards to attract businesses, a dynamic known as "regulatory competition." Regulatory competition leads non-labor groups to oppose labor regulation on the grounds that business flight hurts them. Thus, regulatory competition can trigger a downward spiral in which nations compete with each other for lower labor standards while labor, having lost its historic allies at the domestic level, is thus rendered powerless to resist.

Globalization could be an impetus toward international labor solidarity and cooperation, but without meaningful international labor standards, it can pit labor organizations in one country against those in another. For example, unions in developed countries have advocated supra-national legislation that would equalize labor standards and hence decrease the likelihood of capital flight, but unions in less developed countries have resisted these measures and attacked them as protectionist. Some unions have attempted to organize workers across national and regional borders and bargain for parity. However, while such a strategy has a lot of potential, it is also problematic. Countries have markedly different labor laws and collective bargaining systems, so that it is difficult for unions in one country to collaborate with unions in other countries in a way that jointly harnesses their economic weapons and furthers their common bargaining goals.

Finally, globalization can lead to the deterioration of labor's political power. National labor movements operate in the context of a particular regulatory environment. Labor's political power is undermined when the locus of labor regulation moves from a national to an international arena.

3. Privatization

A third trend that is reshaping labor relations is privatization. The term "privatization" usually refers to policies that shift responsibilities and resources from the public to the private sector. However, in current parlance, the term also refers to the neo-liberal ideology that underlies the shift from the public to the private realm. In the United States, the neo-liberal assault on New Deal social policies has had two goals. First, it attempts to shift responsibility for social welfare out of the public domain and into the arena of private contract. And second, it attempts to move the locus of social legislation away from the federal government and back to the states. Both of these intellectual and political attacks on the New Deal have been garnering strength over the past twenty years, and have contributed to the weakening of labor protection.

. . . .

The shift in the site of regulation has been accompanied by a shift of responsibilities and resources from the public sphere to the private sector. One area where this shift has occurred is in the adjudication of labor rights violations. Increasingly, employers are requiring employees to waive their rights to a public forum and agree instead to bring any claims of labor rights violations to a private forum that is crafted and often controlled by the employer. The Supreme Court has upheld the use of mandatory private arbitration tribunals for adjudicating claims under the discrimination laws, and lower courts have upheld them for many other types of employment claims. Employment law is thus becoming a body of law that is interpreted by private arbitrators outside of the public eye. As employers move more and more disputes about labor rights out of public fora, the resolution of employment disputes become invisible and the decision makers become unaccountable. There also fails to develop a body of publicly-known jurisprudence that can provide a normative basis for the assertion of labor rights by others.

. . . .

Each of the three dynamics described above contributes to union decline and a diminishment of labor rights. Flexibilization increases employers' incentive to avoid unions because they perceive unions as promoting rigidity, uniformity, job protections, and narrow job definitions. Globalization increases employers' desire to avoid unions and labor regulations in their quest for lower labor costs. In addition, global production chains, enhanced transportation and communication, and lower trade barriers give employers considerable leverage to avoid unions altogether, or limit their effectiveness where they exist. Privatization fosters policies that have diminished legal protection for labor rights and collective bargaining and have contributed to rapidly growing income inequality.

. . . .

I suggest that we need to change the focus, or at least the locus, of our research. We need to become at the same time, comparative, transnational, and intensely local. The threat of flexibilization requires us to be comparative – to understand how flexible work practices are undermining established collective labor relations and to explore efforts in different places to adapt organizational forms to the new work practices. The threat of globalization requires us to be transnational – to imagine the possibilities of cross border unionism and of transnational labor regulation. And the threat of privatization requires us to be intensely local – to understand how the public and private spheres are joined in our specific national context, and to formulate strategies in the localized context for the reinvention of the social safety net.

. . . .

While these approaches benefit the employer, there are ill effects on employees who have fewer labor protections. They also provide an economic incentive to employers to "race to the bottom" on labor standards. Additionally, there can be an even darker side brought by the changing global production systems and their effect on workers. If foreign labor and employment laws do not adequately regulate and protect workers, then the risk of unscrupulous employers (often local subcontractors of foreign employers) taking advantage of workers and exploiting them is a real concern. There are many advocate groups who point out specific cases of the ill effects of the dark side of globalized businesses.[25] The victims are often young women, as illustrated below in the garment industry.[26]

[25] China Labour Bulletin, http://www.china-labour.org.hk/en/ (last visited Sept. 20, 2010).

[26] Ruth Domoney, *Briefing on the Chinese Garment Industry*, (Feb. 2007), *available at* http://www.labourbehindthelabel.org/images/pdf/chinabriefing.pdf (last visited Sept. 20, 2010); Alison A.

Lastly, the economic factors in globalism also fuel the ever-increasing number of migrant workers who leave their country in search of jobs and opportunities in industrialized countries. In this case, it is not the FDI going to the foreign location, but rather the foreign worker going to a foreign location.

As the ILO reports below, global labor trends and changing patterns of work provide the setting within which globalism impacts employment relationships.

Changing Patterns in the World of Work[27]

. . . .

6. This Report is an effort by the International Labour Office, the secretariat of the Organization, to understand better the strength and direction of the global trends that are shaping working lives. It is by no means definitive, as much because of the complexities of the world of work as the lack of information and data. By setting out in summary form the scale and pace of the global transformation under way, it aims to provide a context for debates about the policies and institutions needed to grasp opportunities for creating decent work for all and to lessen the uncertainties that rapid change provokes.

. . . .

B. Trends in the global labour market

. . . .

56. In 2005, of the 4.6 billion people of working age in the world, over 3 billion, around two-thirds, were either working or looking for work. Of these, 84 percent live in the developing countries of Asia and the Pacific, Africa, Latin America, and the Caribbean, as well as the transition countries of the Confederation of Independent States (CIS) and South Eastern Europe. The remaining 16 per cent live in the EU and other Western European countries, North America, Japan, Australia and New Zealand.

57. Within the developing world, the populous Asia and Pacific region dominates, accounting for more than 57 per cent of all employment. The two giants, China and India, have 26.0 per cent and 14.8 per cent of world employment, respectively. . . .

58. From 1995 to 2005, the number of unemployed – those wanting to work but who could not find regular employment – rose from 157.3 million to 191.8 million, an increase of 21.9 percent. This pushed up the unemployment rate from 6 to 6.3 per cent. The East Asian and Latin American crises, the ensuing recessions, as well as the Central and Eastern European and CIS countries in transition are the major factors contributing to this rise in global unemployment. Despite relatively brisk growth of the global economy between 2002 and 2005, the global unemployment rate only declined from 6.6 to 6.3 per cent. Although the unemployment rate is widely used as an indicator of labour market tightness and vulnerability, the poor have no choice but to work in many developing countries with high poverty and an absence of safety nets. Their work is often of an

Gormley, *The Underground Exposed: The United States Corporation's Use of Sweatshops Abroad, and the Abuse of Women*, 25 SUFFOLK TRANSNAT'L L. REV. 109 (2001) [Footnotes omitted].

27 Juan Somavia, *Changing Patterns in the World of Work*, Int'l Labour Conference Ninth Session 2006, *available at* http://www.ilo.org/public/english/standards/relm/ilc/ilc95/pdf/rep-i-c.pdf (last visited Sept. 23, 2010). Published by the International Labour Organization (2006).

irregular nature, unproductive, and poorly rewarded, but does not fall within a strict definition of unemployment.

. . . .

The number of unemployed stood at 205 million in 2010, essentially unchanged from the year earlier and 27.6 million higher than in 2007, with little hope for this figure to revert to pre-crisis levels in the near term. The global unemployment rate stood at 6.2 per cent in 2010, versus 6.3 per cent in 2009, but still well above the rate of 5.6 per cent in 2007. . . . [28]

In contrast to many regions around the world, the labour market in East Asia has recovered relatively quickly. . . . In 2011, economic growth is projected to slow to 8.6 percent, while the unemployment rate is expected to show little change at 4.0 percent. . . . [29]

. . . .

Global workforce implications manifest themselves in many ways, including the ways in which businesses respond to these changes. Next are observations and advice given to management to survive and find advantage in the changing demographics and configurations of the modern globalizing workforces.

Getting Beyond Trends: Recognizing Today's Global Workforce Implications[30]

Steven Landberg

The recent announcement by three of the U.S.'s largest companies – Ford, Dell, and Walmart to begin massive workforce expansions in China and India is just the latest evidence of the transformation of once regionalized workforces into a unified global reality. The growing recognition of the realities of this unified global workforce has awakened U.S. enterprises with both positive and negative reactions. There is growing fear among workers of multinationals of job losses as enterprises take more aggressive steps to leverage skilled lower cost workers to respond to competitive challenges from global competitors and as leaders take advantage of hard-to-find global workforce capabilities for their organizations. It is critical for every organization seeking to maintain its own workforce driven advantage to reflect upon their global workforce model in light of these global workforce developments to best understand the implications for its marketplace, customers, competitors, and internal capabilities and develop a strategic approach for addressing this rapidly evolving situation.

Key Global Workforce Trends

Major global workforce trends are accelerating and impacting almost all organizations and individuals in the USA as the world's largest and most developed economy. Whether

[28] ILO, Global Employment Trends ix (2011), *available at* http://www.ilo.org/wcmsp5/groups/public/–dgreports/–dcomm/–publ/documents/publication/wcms_150440.pdf.

[29] *Id.* at 41.

[30] Steven Landberg, Claymore Partners Perspectives: Getting Beyond Trends: Recognizing Today's Global Workforce Implications, *available at* http://www.claymorepartners.com/dwnld/global_workforce_planning.pdf (last visited Sept. 30, 2010).

an organization is developing its own globalized worker ranks or simply competing with a competitor's, it must actively determine whether to tap into this unified resource. These trends should be identified and leveraged to provide a basis for developing a global workforce approach with implications for each industry and organization. How an organization responds in addressing the challenges will clearly impact their future success. Few will be spared the rapidly evolving realities of a global workforce. While each organization needs to identify the major global workforce trends that are impacting their business, a summary of key global workforce trends includes:

- Expansion of global economic trade for both manufacturing and service sectors with lower barriers and greater knowledge and availability;
- Rapid emergence of 40% of the world's population becoming a vibrant part of the global economy and workforce with China and India's economic development growing at over double that of the developed economies (>7% vs. 3%)
- Growing use of global workforce for outsourcing and offshoring service oriented jobs as well as manufacturing jobs;
- Rise in level of education and skills of the global workforce, especially in India and China (India is producing about 400,000 engineering graduates annually versus only about 30,000 in the USA);
- Advanced and low cost telecommunications and internet connectivity have enabled service and knowledge worker displacement globally to lower cost environments (online collaboration tools will further enhance global connectivity in the near future as well)
- Continued pressure on productivity gains and lower labor costs to remain competitive in a global economy with increasing reachable large lower cost labor pools.

. . . .

Major Workforce Model Implications

Going Global is finally affecting us at home. As a result of the global and USA workforce trends, there is expected to be continual pressures and shifts with significant implications for organizations, which drive both near term and long-term workforce decisions. By and large, future organizations – regardless of the boundaries of their customer markets – will be forced to reconsider workforce models and make key decisions regarding what the future state of their workforce. Firms will examine new options born of these emerging implications and determine whether global options like contingent workers, outsourcing or offshore staff augmentation will be leveraged – and if these global workforce options are tapped – what model for managing and developing that workforce will be utilized. While the workforce model implications are not always as clear as the workforce trends, organizations nonetheless need to incorporate their views on the implications into their business strategies and human resource planning efforts.

While no single list could capture the entire major workforce model implications of these global workforce trends, U.S.-based businesses should consider this short list of implications:

- Shift more standardized service and knowledge work to lower cost environments that are capable of delivering quality output

- Develop operating business models that integrate global workforces to better take advantage of cost and service levels benefits via strong business processes and collaboration tools
- Invest in the education of your workforce to further enhance the value added and productivity of your core talent base
- Obtain/develop global executives to lead and effectively manage global workforces
- Continue to employ baby boomers via alternative work solutions including contract employment, remote work, part time work
- Increase the role of HR as a strategic asset focused on addressing global workforce trends/implications vs. utilizing primarily as a transaction support function
- Develop global workforce management, talent acquisition and retention approaches:
  - Employ a global talent mindset, which extends beyond the current "diversity" mentality/approach;
  - Utilize comprehensive workforce planning approaches integrating permanent, contract/temporary, outsourcers, offshorers, and consultant workforce resources with a global perspective
  - Deploy global workforce strategic planning processes as a critical business planning process.

A Strategic Approach for Addressing the Global Workforce Crisis/Opportunity

. . . .

While critical, these efforts are only ultimately anchored by the company's mindset about workforce. Adoption of a global mindset is the first step for an organization to establish a basis for a strategic global workforce planning approach. That needs to start at the top of an organization with an increase in global executive talent, training, and experience. Organizations need to shift from viewing businesses as international vs. domestic to global businesses and further imbed a global mentality into their overall business perspectives inclusive of workforce planning and implementation efforts. There are few organizations that can avoid the implications of a global workforce today. It is time to embrace that change and determine how to leverage the opportunities and embrace being global.

. . . .

A "darker" implication of global competiveness, often reported as a by-product of globalism, is the existence of "sweatshops" and workplaces that are abusive and violate labor laws, though to be sure they have existed for a long time. They exist in most countries and may reflect no more than greedy lawbreakers. However, they also do exist in East Asia, most often reported in China, sometimes involving U.S. investors, and this implication raises additional labor and employment law concerns.

The Underground Exposed: The United States Corporations' Use of Sweatshops Abroad and the Abuse of Women[31]

Alice A. Gormley

. . . .

II. Women and Sweatshops

Sweatshops exist in nearly every part of the world, and have a colorful history. Sweatshops date back to the late eighteen hundreds when employers would sweat as much profit out of each worker as possible. Sweatshops and forced labor substitute the notion of the usual course of business, thereby excusing sweatshop labor practices. This accepted practice has the greatest impact upon young women, whom these sweatshops hide from the public behind locked doors, denying them their basic human rights. For American corporations though, it is a "race to the bottom" in which "there is always someplace, somewhere, where clothing can be made still more cheaply." Corporations, however, afford little concern for the human beings this practice affects.

. . . .

Multinational corporations (MNCs) employ two strategies that allow United States corporations to maintain sweatshops abroad with little interference. The MNCs' first strategy to blur the lines between a retailer and manufacturer is to contract and outsource production. MNCs shift responsibility so that consumers do not fully know, nor can they easily ascertain, where garment production occurs. The second strategy MNCs employ is their ability to relocate production anywhere in the world, forcing developing nations to accommodate and comply with MNCs' standards. For example, if workers demand higher pay, less hours, or better working conditions, the MNCs simply relocate to an area where workers are willing to meet the MNCs' demands. Threats to relocate, and subsequent location shopping, deplete women's economic bargaining power, which ultimately decreases their ability to combat MNCs' inhumane and undignified conditions.

MNCs implement monitoring systems within their factories to meet United States and United Nations policies; these devices have little effect since outside forces do not examine them. Without outside threats or government scrutiny, these monitoring systems are inadequate because often times the MNCs only implement the system, without ever enforcing better working standards, or altering existing working conditions. In addition, there is little redress for MNCs' violations because the sweatshop women, although the backbone of the garment industry, lack the strength to fight against the power of international capitalization. Lack of efficient force on MNCs perpetuates sweatshop women's exploitation and inhumane treatment.[32]

. . . .

---

[31] Alison A. Gormley, *The Underground Exposed: The United States Corporation's Use of Sweatshops Abroad, and the Abuse of Women*, 25 SUFFOLK TRANSNAT'L L. REV. 109 (2001) [Footnotes omitted].

[32] Migrant workers, of whom women now represent nearly half, constitute a growing share of the world's workforce. In 2000 there were more than eighty-six million migrant workers throughout the world, with thirty-four million of these in developing regions. Taking into account those not economically active, about 175 million people were residing outside their country of birth or citizenship, accounting for about three percent of the world's population. Increasing international labor migration in Somavia, *supra* note 27.

GLOBAL WORKFORCE. Another aspect of the interrelationship of globalism and labor, in addition to cross-border hiring of workers or contractors, involves the migration of a "global workforce," moving generally from poor to rich countries to perform work. The push-pull phenomenon draws on workforce needs and competitive advantage, as discussed next. It raises issues as to what the implications are of this migration on foreign, international, and domestic labor and employment laws.

Globalisation and Migration: Some Reflections on the Connection between Two Inter-Related Global Phenomena[33]

Antonios K. Papantoniou, Doris Peschke, and Torsten Moritz

Globalisation and migration represent two of the most dynamic global socio-political trends of our present time. While both have their own driving dynamic, they are highly interrelated. Globalisation has an ambivalent and somehow contradictory influence on the current migratory flows. On the one hand, it creates situations and conditions which increase the pressure and intensify the desire to migrate. Growing economic inequalities, extreme poverty, breaking down of national economies, declining of traditional industry, environmental degradation, revival of tribal, ethnic, and religious fundamentalism, conflicts and wars, to name only a few of the direct or indirect results of globalisation, contribute towards migration understood as a "survival strategy." A considerable number of the estimated 150 million people working outside their countries of origin have been forced into migration by the economic consequences of the globalised economy.

The revolution in communication; the easiness and low cost of information flow and geographical movement of persons; the daily projection of prosperity and affluence pictures at a global scale; the cultivation through the mass media of the illusion of an increased familiarity with the North and accessibility of the Western way and quality of life to everyone living in the Western countries intensify the desire of participation – particularly among those who, for political or economic reasons, lived up to now isolated and deprived – and constitute a great temptation and an urge towards taking over the risk to migrate.

The functioning of a national economy increasingly depends on the fast availability of a (small) number of high-skilled migrants and a higher number of migrants belonging to the pool of low-paid workers (often undocumented workers constituting cheap and flexible but also vulnerable labour force). The capacity to manage and steer migration

[33] Antonios K. Papantoniou et al., "Globalisation and Migration: Some Reflections on the Connection between Two Interrelated Global Phenomenon," Council of Europe, Apr. 2002 (on file with author), *available at* http://docs.google.com/fileview?id=0B5vm9beLyq1sNGM4NTRhYmQtYzJkZC00NGYwLTk0ZDAtZGQxY2VkYWY1ZGM3&hl=en (last visited Sept. 21, 2010). For an opposing view, which is there are not enough data to document the link between migration and globalization, see Labor Market Trends, *supra* note 22. It is suggested that "[S]uch countries can also increase exports by making dynamic use of the comparative advantage of their low-cost labor. Trade tends to reduce migration through the creation of additional employment and accelerated economic growth in exporting countries. The increased tradability of skill- and knowledge-intensive services opens up new opportunities for high-wage jobs in the migrant-sending countries, and can be expected to induce skilled workers to stay in their home country" *Id.*

movements towards a country has thus become an important element of the global competitiveness for a global economy.

In addition, the demographic developments in most Northern industrialised countries will pose enormous challenges to the societies. A far greater percentage of the population will be part of the older generation with more demands on the social and health services. At the same time, most of these societies will decrease in numbers dramatically over the next years. While most of the related problems require structural responses, they will also require active migration policies. A number of countries, among them major European states, have already started active recruiting policies.

On the other hand, globalisation constitutes a restraining force, counteracting migration. Globalisation prioritises [sic] the importance of capital and downgrades significantly the role and relative power of the labour in the globalised economy. Particularly in the developed economies of the North since the early 70's the value of the unskilled labour force has dramatically decreased, resulting in the official stop of immigration. The EU countries decided to apply – even though unsuccessfully – a policy of zero migration, imposing continuously new and additional controls, restrictions, and barriers to the entry of migrants originating from the so called "third countries."

The downgrading of the significance of the factor of labour partially explains also the fact that powerful governments, TNCs [transnational corporations], and the globalising IGOs like WTO and IMF, while undertaking intensive efforts to achieve freedom of movement of goods and capital, show a limited interest to promote the free movement of persons, if so it is often restricted to the global elite.

In parallel, TNCs transferring their economic activities where labour is cheap, flexible and unregulated, environmental protection minimal, and taxes very low, contribute indirectly in counteracting migration. However, as recent surveys show this trend is far less important than originally anticipated.

Global exchange at present is dominated by a few countries, and even more so corporations, which have the freedom, and resources, to travel and to decide where they want to stay, produce, or sell. This domination extends to the migratory movements. One of the most significant repercussions of globalisation on migration is the transfer of the economic policies of privatisation and deregulation on the formation of migratory movements. While until the decade of the 60's, migratory movements were organised and took place with the participation and the collaboration of states and enterprises, the actual migrations constitute a purely private enterprise and are linked to many entepreunerial risks. In the context of the globalising markets, the global, fast and flexible movement of labour (a small percentage of highly skilled workers as well as a big number of cheap, often undocumented workers) becomes an important key element of successful economic development. Labour migrants could thus be key players in the process towards a globalising economy – both as those largely profiting from and setting the agenda of globalisation as well as potential objects and victims of globalisation processes.

....

The transfer of money by migrants constitutes an important economic contribution to the national economy for a lot of countries of the South. For many countries, the money sent home by migrants is one of the most important sources of foreign currency earnings. In many cases, these transfers help to create an unofficial social security system: families of migrants manage to survive despite their own financial difficulties – thanks to the transfers by relatives, who migrated. The World Bank estimates that remittances by migrant workers amount to 65 billion USD per year. The national economy of Turkey for example annually receives around 3 billion USD from remittances of migrant workers, compared to 1.5 billion in official development assistance.

These few examples show the interrelated nature of globalisation and migration. A long-term economic development strategy, which is aiming at rebalancing globalisation will not create any sustainable results without taking into consideration the phenomena of migration. Monitoring and analysing migration trends as well as trying to monitor and to influence migration policies thus needs to become an integral part of any development strategy in the times of globalisation. On the other hand, any efforts to influence migration policy will remain patchwork if not complemented by an analysis of the trends of globalisation and the promotion of sustainable models of economic globalisation.

. . . .

QUESTIONS

1. How does globalization impact profits of the corporations versus wages of the workers?
2. What is the risk to a country that has a high Gini coefficient and an ever-growing wage gap between the rich and poor?
3. How and why is East Asia significant in labor and employment issues in a globalizing economy?
4. How are the configurations of the employment relationship changing?
5. Why might an employer want to hire foreign or domestic migrant workers?
6. What impact does the migrant labor workforce have on the employment of labor and the benefits of social security provisions? Does this contribute to the "race to the bottom"? Does this contribute to a "brain drain"?

b. Labor Unions

The transnational unions and confederations of domestic and international unions that work on global issues have existed for some time and are discussed in Part III.C of this book.[34] Impacts of globalization on domestic labor unions cause responses varying from little concern to vocal opposition by those unions claiming it displaces domestic jobs and puts competitive pressures on U.S. employers to lower labor costs.

There has been some movement by U.S. domestic unions to directly bridge the international divide by undertaking joint efforts to coordinate and cooperate not only with international confederations, but also with specific foreign unions in an effort

[34] Alan Hyde & Mona Ressaissi, *Unions Without Borders: Recent Developments in the Theory, Practice, and Law of Transnational Unionism*, 14 CAN. LAB. & EMP. L.J., 47 (2009), *available at* http://papers.ssrn.com/sol3/papers.cfm?abstract_id=1323807 (last visited Sept. 21, 2010); *see also ICFTU Trade Union Guide to Globalisation*, *available at* http://www.icftu.org/pubs/globalisation/globguide.html (last visited Sept. 21, 2010).

to pressure employers for job protections and benefits. Toward that end, in one case coordinated activities involved the attempt by the International Longshoremen's Association (ILA) to link with Japanese labor unions to apply economic pressures in Japan to further the ILA's labor dispute in the United States.[35] American unions also have begun to coordinate programs in China to further joint union interests.

As expected, there are different points of view on how globalization affects labor unions and what responses are most appropriate.

UNION PERSPECTIVES AND INTERNATIONAL ACTIVITIES

Labor Unions and Globalization[36]

. . . .

Webster's defines a labor union as "an organization of workers formed for the purpose of advancing its members' interests in respect to wages, benefits, and working conditions." Explaining the relationship between globalization and labor unions necessarily involves asking a series of polemical questions about the effect of increased capital flows on wages, regulations, and worker bargaining power. The explanation of this relationship often depends on the political position of the person writing or speaking on the subject. The articles selected [below] will explore the diametrically opposed views of 'anti-establishmentarians' and 'establishmentarians' with regards to globalization and labor unions.

Last April 2001, AFL-CIO President John Sweeney addressed the 17th World Congress of the International Confederation of Trade Unions (ICTFU) in Durban, South Africa, on the topic of globalization. The 50-year old ICTFU represents 125 million working people in 213 national trade unions from 145 countries. In discussing the topic of globalization, Sweeney expressed concerns shared by most labor union supporters throughout the world when he asserted that "[g]lobal capital and corporations have enlisted state power to free them from civilizing rules." Sweeney continued his critical appraisal of economic globalization by stating that "[t]he global economy that corporations have forged can only be tamed by the international solidarity of working families everywhere . . . [w]e must commit to pressuring our governments to champion the cause of building enforceable workers' rights into the rules of the global market." Because of this critique and other similar critiques made by international labor organizations, unions are usually portrayed

[35] Int'l Longshoremen's Ass'n v. NLRB, 56 F.3d 205 (D.C. Cir. 2005). The National Labor Relations Board examined this activity and held it was an unlawful secondary boycott in violation of U.S. labor law, but the decision was reversed and remanded by the U.S. Court of Appeals for the District of Columbia. The issue was whether the National Labor Relations Board reasonably concluded that an American labor union violated the secondary boycott provisions of the National Labor Relations Act through its communications with Japanese unions that threatened to refuse to unload in Japan cargo that had been loaded in the United States by nonunion labor.

[36] Reprinted with permission from the University of Iowa Center for International Finance & Development, http://ebook.law.uiowa.edu/ebook/. Univ. of Iowa Ctr. Int'l Fin. & Dev., *Labor Unions & Globalization*, http://blogs.law.uiowa.edu/ebook/issues/globalization/reading-table/labor-unions (last visited June 21, 2011). *See also* Christian Lévesque & Gregor Murray, *Local versus Global: Activating Local Union Power in the Global Economy*, 27 LAB. STUDIES J. 39 (2002).

as being part of the 'anti-globalization' movement. In all major demonstrations from Barcelona and Sidney to Seattle and Quebec City, labor unions have been a very visible part of the 'anti-globalization' or 'global economic justice' movement. Labor unions argue that globalization, as it is currently constituted, favors the interests of multinational corporations and global capital to the detriment of working people around the world.

Briefly, the argument made by labor unions is that countries are forced to compete among themselves to attract the attention and the investment capital of companies. In competing with each other, countries invariably drive down wages, reduce tax rates, and eliminate legislation protecting workers and the environment, among other things. By creating favorable conditions for corporations in terms of lower costs, fewer taxes, permissive laws, and higher taxes through competition, the argument is that this causes a 'race to the bottom' in living standards for workers. Accordingly, the bargaining position of workers and labor unions is severely weakened as corporations play countries against each other to make the lowest bid. In summarizing the consequences of the 'race to the bottom effect', consequences that allegedly do more than simply harm workers, Economist Robin Hahnel explains that

> The 'race to the bottom effect' is real. Liberalization of trade and international investment does put downward pressure on . . . wages [and] labor standards . . . Third World peasants and workers do not enjoy the beneficial effect one might otherwise expect from increased international investment and specialization in labor intensive manufacturing in their countries. By strengthening the bargaining power of global capital versus any and all with whom it negotiates, liberalization of trade and investment leads to downward pressure on wages, labor standards, and environmental standards in First World and Third World countries.

However, establishmentarian supporters of globalization affirm that the 'race to the bottom effect' is largely an illusion and that economic globalization "improves the living standards of the vast majority of people," workers included. Pro-globalizers John Micklethwait and Adrian Wooldridge argue that the 'race to the bottom' critics are mistaken on at least four grounds: first, critics believe that employers are only concerned about the price of labor, when they are really concerned about the value of labor. As Micklethwait and Wooldridge explain, "what employers want is not cheap workers but productive ones . . . [a]nd the most productive workers are usually those with the best education, access to the best machinery, and a support system that includes things like good infrastructure."

Second, Micklethwait and Wooldridge claim that critics are mistaken about the ease and willingness of corporations, allegedly unmoored from their nations of origin, to simply relocate to more business-friendly countries around the globe. To support this claim, the authors state that "[d]uring the Justice Department's investigation of Microsoft, Bill Gates could not have threatened to move his operation to the Bahamas, even though Microsoft has relatively few fixed assets. Microsoft depends not just on a supply of educated workers . . . but also on its close relationship with American universities."

Third, the authors argue that critics exaggerate the 'hostility' of corporations toward labor unions and labor standards. They do agree with critics that all corporations at all times tend to react unfavorably to labor unions because "they [labor unions] want to shackle their [corporations'] freedom of maneuver with inflexible rules about, say, hiring and firing." However, globalization allegedly does not worsen this fundamental antipathy between corporations and unions. Regarding labor standards, Micklethwait and Wooldridge assert that corporations, especially multinational corporations, tend to improve working standards in pursuing the goal of increasing productivity.

Finally, the authors state that critics wrongly entertain the idea that "globalization is a zero-sum game: that if the rich are getting richer as a result of globalization, then the poor must be getting poorer." Instead of a zero-sum game, where a fixed amount of wealth is inequitably distributed among the global rich and poor, Micklethwait and Wooldridge argue that globalization creates more wealth, increases efficiency, and improves "the lot of everybody."

. . . .

Which of the above positions most accurately explains the relationship between globalization and labor unions? The summaries of articles below were selected not to provide an answer to this question, but rather to encourage the reader to continue researching the topic.

Union Leaders Seek Globalization[37]

In this article, Sheila Cherry accuses America's largest organized labor organization, the AFL-CIO, of using globalization to advance its political agenda. Together with the International Confederation of Free Trade Unions (ICFTU), the AFL-CIO has been actively campaigning to internationalize its union drive. However, Cherry claims that the AFL-CIO is deaf to criticism of its policies swelling among the rank and file membership. She states that the AFL-CIO has unnecessarily allied itself to the Democratic Party in opposition to the Republican Party, and that this alliance has resulted in more concern of the union leadership for supporting Democrats favoring free-trade initiatives than protecting the interests of American workers. Cherry claims that American workers are much more concerned with the competitive job loss caused by globalization. Accordingly, she argues that the international organizing efforts of the AFL-CIO are not for the purpose of improving the lives of working people in the U.S. and around the world, but for increasing union membership to build political strength to elect union-supported Democrats to office.

Yes to Globalization, But Protect the Poor[38]

Bill Jordan, the General Secretary of the International Confederation of Free Trade Unions, claims that globalization has the potential to create prosperity for everyone on the planet, but that globalization is currently only serving the interests of the wealthy. He claims that the objective of the international labor movement with regards to globalization is to ensure that the benefits of increased economic output are shared by all. He argues that the policy for achieving this objective is to be found in the implementation of international core labor standards and in the growth of global trade unionism.

[37] Univ. of Iowa Ctr. Int'l Fin. & Dev., *Id.* For full article, see Sheila R. Cherry, *Union Leaders Seek Globalization*, BNET.com, July 23, 2001, http://findarticles.com/p/articles/mi_m1571/is_27_17/ai_76844630/ (last visited Oct. 3, 2010).

[38] Univ. of Iowa Ctr. Int'l Fin. & Dev., *Id.* For full article, see Bill Jordan, *Yes to Globalization, But Protect the Poor*, N.Y. TIMES, Dec. 21, 2000, http://www.nytimes.com/2000/12/21/opinion/21iht-edjordan.t.html (last visited July 29, 2010).

He maintains that core labor standards would protect workers in developing market countries from inhumane treatment and workers in developed countries from sweatshop competition abroad. He also asserts that global trade unionism will guarantee a more equitable distribution of the economic benefits of globalization between companies and workers.

....

GLOBAL EXCHANGES AND COOPERATION OF U.S. LABOR UNIONS. Another illustration of the effects of globalism on labor unions is where it brings coordination and cooperation between domestic labor unions and foreign labor unions on a wider and continuing scope. An example involves the recent exchanges between American unions led by the Service Employees International Union (SEIU), and the cooperation agreement between the SEIU and China's Council and China's Shanghai Municipal Trade Union Council, affiliated with the All China Federation of Trade Unions (AFCTU) and the Los Angeles County Federation of Labor. This is the first time a U.S.-central labor council has established "sister-city" relations with a central labor council in China. Descriptions of the visits follow, first the American account, followed by the Chinese account.

L.A. Labor Builds Solidarity in Shanghai[39]

Kent Wong participated in a historic delegation of the Los Angeles County Federation of Labor to establish formal relations with the Shanghai Municipal Trade Union Council. In July 2007, the delegation led by María Elena Durazo met with union leaders in Shanghai and Beijing, visited four different worksites, and met with labor representatives at the national, provincial, municipal, and local levels. This is the first time a U.S.-central labor council has established sister-city relations with a central labor council in China. In the last year, unions in China have successfully organized seventy Wal-Mart stores and four hundred McDonald's and KFC restaurants. China adopted new labor laws strengthening worker rights the week before the L.A. County Federation of Labor arrived in China. There are about 134 million union members in China. In Shanghai alone, there are more than 6 million union members. The L.A. County Federation of

[39] UCLA Ctr. Lab. Research&Educ., *L.A. Labor Builds Solidarity in Shanghai*, LAB. EDUC. NEWS (2007), *available at* http://www.labor.ucla.edu/publications/newsletters/pdf/07sumfall.pdf (last visited Sept. 21, 2010). A more detailed description of the visit, from the Chinese point of view, is reported in, Wang Jiao Ping, *Change to Win Delegation Visits China*, THE WORKERS' DAILY, May 22, 2007, http://www.ihlo.org/LRC/ACFTU/250907.html (last visited Sept. 21, 2010). *See also* NEW CHINA NEWS, *U.S. Trade Union Leaders: U.S. and China Trade Unions make their first move to deepen cooperations* (She Li-Na ed., May 23, 2007), *available at* http://www.clntranslations.org/file_download/13/CLNT_CtoWin_deeper_ cooperation.pdf (last visited Sept. 21, 2010) (trans. from Chinese version, *available at* http://www.shaanxi.cn/admin/pub_newsshow.asp?id=1056371&chid=100009 (last visited May 26, 2007)) [hereinafter NEW CHINA NEWS]. For a report on the return visit by the Chinese, see SEIU Local 721, President's Report to the Executive Board (Feb. 18, 2009), *available at* http://localsdev.seiu.org/about/President's%20Report%202009-02.pdf (last visited Sept. 21, 2010).

Labor met with the Shanghai Teachers Union president and discussed a new proposal to establish an exchange program for high school teachers and students between the two cities that would begin in 2008. During the visit to the Port of Shanghai, the third largest port in the world, representatives of the ILWU and the Shanghai Maritime Union discussed the dock workers' working conditions and health and safety issues, and pledged to strengthen relations between the unions.

. . . .

The American unions' mission to gain cooperation with China's All Federation of Trade Union (ACFTU) began in the early 2000s. SEIU's President Andy Stern stated he visited China as early as 2002 because "our employers are all in China. So, the largest security and food service companies in the world are moving to China. Wal-Mart is in China. They are not directly our union's employers, but obviously we have a lot of interest there, and we're very helpful on working with the Chinese on organizing. We go there because our employers have gone there, and what we learned in the U.S. is that as employers get larger, we're less able to affect their behavior. As they grow globally, we begin to think more globally as well. China is the mother lode for American corporations." He added, "[D]espite the fact there are geographical borders, our employers are global and we don't have the strength when we are just in our country. When we represent a small number of employees in a large corporation, we can't influence [its] behavior. We're on the verge of having global unions. Capital and trade and companies have gone global – how come unions shouldn't be global? It doesn't make sense for the workers."[40]

Change to Win Delegation Visits China[41]

Wang Jiao Ping

. . . .

The delegation leader, Change to Win President Anna Burger, told reporters that reforms in China and Chinese trade unions give the impressions that establishing a close and friendly relationship with the All-China Federation of Trade Unions (ACFTU) is the only course.

On 18 May, the 21-member delegation of Change to Win, headed by Anna Burger, began their 9-day visit in China. This was the first official visit from Change to Win since its establishment in 2005, and marked the establishment of a friendly bilateral Sino-American relationship at the national trade union level.

. . . .

"Despite being here just a very short time, we have gained a lot because we share many common issues." Anna Burger said that, "Chinese unions face difficulties in promoting

[40] Renuka Rayasam, *SEIU's Andy Stern: Going Global*, U.S. News & World Rep., June 5, 2007, http://www.usnews.com/usnews/biztech/articles/070605/5stern.htm (last visited Sept. 21, 2010).

[41] Wang Jiao Ping, *Change to Win Delegation Visits China*, *supra* note 39. For an American publication's portrayal of the visit, see Mei Fong & Kris Maher, *U.S. Labor Leader Aided China's Wal-Mart Coup*, WSJ, June 22, 2007, *available at* http://walmartwatch.org/blog/archives/wsj-u-s-labor-leader-aided-chinas-wal-mart-coup/ (last visited June 7, 2011).

collective bargaining such as union organizers' specialized knowledge, improvement of negotiating skills, difficulties in honoring contracts etc...., but these are all issues that we also face. Problem solving brings us closer together. We are very willing to let Chinese unions share and learn from Change to Win's collective bargaining skills. At the same time Chinese unions participated in the drafting of labor law legislation in a positive way, and this is a worthwhile experience to draw from."

....

The Service Employee International Union (SEIU) president Andy Stern is called by American media as a "progressive and practical labor leader." As early as 2002, the SEIU president led delegations to China, opening a new phase in Chinese American union contacts. In 2005, after the SEIU president and seven national trade unions established the Change to Win federation, he remained steadfast in trying to enhance understanding and dialogue between Chinese and American unions.

....

Andy Stern told reporters, "Each country's trade union organizations should enhance dialogue and cooperation. By protecting the interests of workers, this allows them to enjoy the benefits of economic growth. Globalization is the backdrop that each country's union organizations are faced with and which we struggle against together." Chinese union leaders equally have a deep understanding of these matters, which made Stern extremely delighted.

....

The next case describes an attempted coordination of mutual self-help activities between American and Japanese labor unions to further the labor demands of the American union. The case falls under U.S. domestic labor law, which in this instance was found not to have been violated.

International Longshoremen's Association, AFL-CIO, v. National Labor Relations Board, Respondent, Canaveral Port Authority, et al.[42]

EDWARDS, *Chief Judge:* This case requires us to decide whether a domestic labor union commits an unfair labor practice under the National Labor Relations Act ("NLRA" or "Act"), 29 U.S.C. § 151 *et seq.* (1988), by seeking the support of Japanese unions in connection with labor disputes involving nonunion employers in the United States. Petitioner International Longshoremen's Association ("ILA") seeks review of a decision of the National Labor Relations Board ("NLRB" or "Board") holding that the ILA violated section 8(b)(4) of the Act, 29 U.S.C. § 158(b)(4), by establishing a secondary boycott through the actions of its putative agents, the Japanese unions. Because we hold that the Board erred in attributing the actions of the Japanese unions to the ILA, we grant the petition for review and remand the case to the Board.

In 1947, Congress amended the NLRA with the enactment of the Labor Management Relations Act, ch. 120, 61 Stat. 136 (1947) ("LMRA"). A principal provision of the

[42] Int'l Longshoremen's Ass'n v. NLRB, 56 F.3d 205 (D.C. Cir. 2005).

LMRA was the section 8(b)(4) proscription of "secondary boycotts . . . *See International Longshoremen's Ass'n v. Allied Int'l, Inc.*, 456 U.S. 212, 225 (1982) (stating that Congress drafted section 8(b)(4) "to protect neutral parties, the helpless victims of quarrels that do not concern them at all") (internal quotations omitted). However, in drafting section 8(b)(4), Congress did not create a "sweeping prohibition" on all forms of secondary boycotts. *Local 1976, United Bhd. of Carpenters v. NLRB*, 357 U.S. 93, 98 (1958). Rather, the provision "describes and condemns specific union conduct directed to specific objectives." *Id.* Thus, section 8(b)(4)(i) specifically targets union actions to engage in, or induce or encourage others employed in commerce to engage in, a strike or refusal to work on goods, *see* 29 U.S.C. § 158(b)(4)(i), and section 8(b)(4)(ii) prohibits union actions to threaten or coerce persons engaged in commerce, *see id.* § 158(b)(4)(ii), where in either case the object of such action is to force a person to cease using or otherwise dealing in the products of another, *see id.* § 158(b)(4)(B). In this case, the ILA did neither.

The undisputed facts reveal that the ILA merely requested assistance from Japanese labor unions in its dispute with two nonunion stevedoring companies engaged in Florida's citrus fruit export trade. In response, the Japanese unions gave notice that their members would refuse to unload any fruit in Japan that had been loaded in Florida by nonunion workers. As a consequence of this threat, all Florida–Japan citrus shipments were redirected to new ports of embarkment during the 1990–1991 export season. The parties adversely affected by these actions – the two stevedoring companies and one neutral party – filed unfair labor practice charges against the ILA.

Upon reviewing the unfair labor practice charges, the Board held that the ILA had violated the prohibition against secondary boycotts. In reaching this conclusion, however, the Board could not rely on section 8(b)(4)(i), for, although the ILA arguably induced or encouraged other employees to refuse to handle goods, the employees to whom the ILA's entreaties were addressed were Japanese longshoremen, who are not employed by a person "engaged in commerce" as the Act requires. 29 U.S.C. § 158(b)(4)(i). Nor could the Board find that the ILA's actions, standing alone, fell within the scope of section 8(b)(4)(ii), because the Japanese unions, not the ILA, issued the alleged threats that created the boycott. Nevertheless, the Board held that the ILA's actions fell within the scope of section 8(b)(4)(ii) pursuant to a theory of agency law. Under this theory, the Board held that the Japanese unions acted as the agents of the ILA merely because the ILA requested the Japanese unions' actions and benefited from the results of those actions.

In its petition for review, the ILA claims that the Board's agency theory is untenable. We agree. Not only is the Board's theory completely without support in nearly 50 years of NLRB and judicial precedent interpreting the secondary boycott provision of the NLRA, but it flies in the face of the common law agency principles that Congress sought to incorporate into the Act. Put simply, the ILA and the Japanese unions were completely independent entities; neither exercised any control over the other. If they were bound together at all, it was by a spirit of labor solidarity, but such a spiritual link is too frail to render one union the agent of another. Thus, we reject the Board's theory and remand the case for further consideration.

. . . .

QUESTIONS

1. What is the impact, if any, and to whom, on the "race to the bottom"?
2. Is global cooperation among labor unions a good idea? If so, why; if not, why not?
3. What is the legal risk to a U.S. labor union, if any, of cross-border union coordination of conduct by a foreign union?

c. Business: Wal-Mart Illustration

Many of the impacts of globalism on business are discussed throughout other sections; however, it is instructive to observe how the world's largest retailer deals with its labor and employment law issues overseas in Asia. Wal-Mart has long engaged in global operations and it now has its supply center located in China. In a recent study it was found that it, like other multinational corporations (MNCs), generally adapts to host-country institutional, political, and regulatory environments.[43] It also concluded that rather than seeking to dominate the host-country's labor laws, it adapted to local and national-level labor regulation and industrial relations systems and possibly even functioned in certain contexts as a labor rights catalyst in both its host and home countries.

Wal-Mart is Coming, but it's Not All Bad: Wal-Mart and Labor Rights in its International Subsidiaries[44]

Kevin Kolben

. . . .

As countries have liberalized their FDI regulations, foreign MNCs have been rapidly increasing their investment and operations, particularly in emerging markets, such as China and India. But what is the impact of these large MNCs on domestic labor law regimes, and what is the impact of these regimes on the conduct of foreign corporations? Should the legal response to the regulation of MNCs and international capital take place at the transnational or the local level? Are domestic labor regulatory regimes increasingly irrelevant in the regulation of global capital, or is sovereignty challenged and regulatory capacity weakened through competition for FDI? Do MNCs conduct themselves differently in their foreign operations than they do their home operations?

This article contributes to this discussion by examining how Wal-Mart, the largest corporation in the world, conducts itself in its foreign retail operations with respect

[43] Kevin Kolben, *Wal-Mart is Coming, but it's Not All Bad: Wal-Mart and Labor Rights in its International Subsidiaries*, 12 UCLA J. INT'L L. & FOR. AFF. 275 (2007).

[44] *Id.* However, adaptation to legal issues alone does not guarantee successful business operations in Asia. In South Korea it was reported that Wal-Mart failed to adapt to local customer demands and was forced to sell out and leave Korea. It was suggested that Wal-Mart had not done adequate cultural due diligence on the customs of South Korean customers. Choe Sang-Hun, *Wal-Mart Selling Stores and Leaving South Korea*, N.Y. TIMES, May 23, 2006, http://www.nytimes.com/2006/05/23/business/worldbusiness/23shop.html (last visited Sept. 21, 2010).

to industrial relations practices and respect for labor rights – specifically the rights to freedom of association and collective bargaining.

. . . .

Therefore, there might be natural cause for concern that when Wal-Mart enters a foreign market, it will bring its home-country practices with it. . . . [A]s Part II shows, while Wal-Mart is fiercely anti-union in its home operations, its subsidiaries do not necessarily act the same way abroad. Rather than simply exporting its rather distinct animus towards unions and collective bargaining, Wal-Mart is surprisingly sensitive and responsive to domestic institutional, political, and regulatory environments. This means that Wal-Mart, with degrees of nuance and variation, peacefully co-exists with unions and engages in collective bargaining in most countries outside of North America.

. . . .

Wal-Mart could paradoxically serve as a catalyst that can lead to improved labor conditions and regulatory regimes in host countries, and possibly in home countries as well.

. . . .

E. China: Corporatism with Chinese Characteristics

. . . .

1. *Chinese Labor Law and the ACFTU*

. . . .

After increasing pressure from the ACFTU and the Chinese government, in November 2004, Wal-Mart announced that "[s]hould associates request formation of a union, Wal-Mart China would respect their wishes and honor its obligation under China's trade union law." At the same time, Wal-Mart suggested that there were no unions because workers had "not requested that one be formed," but that "employees can take voluntary action if they so desire."

. . . .

Pressure from the Chinese government increased in the form of threats of more stringent application of health and safety and sanitation regulations. There was also discussion of a proposed legal amendment to the labor law, clearly aimed at Wal-Mart, that would force foreign companies to unionize.

. . . .

Finally, without Wal-Mart's knowledge, a group of workers formed a union in a store in the southeastern city of Quanzhou on July 29, 2006.

. . . .

Soon thereafter, unions were formed at stores in Shenzhen (Wal-Mart's first store in China) and Nanjing. Wal-Mart, according to Chan, went into anti-union mode, holding meetings and even threatening to terminate the contracts of workers who joined the union. But within one to two weeks of the initial union formation, something caused Wal-Mart to change tactics and reach out to the ACFTU with an olive branch. Wal-Mart officials met with ACFTU officials to discuss the entry of unions in all Wal-Mart stores, and began to make statements that were unprecedented from Wal-Mart. Joe Hatfield,

Wal-Mart's China CEO and an old time Wal-Mart executive, announced in a written statement that "I fully anticipate working collaboratively with leadership from ACFTU and Union organizations at all levels to create a model working relationship," and that the company's "mutual aim is to establish grassroots unions within each Wal-Mart store throughout China." Organizing spread to other Wal-Mart stores, and soon unions formed in all of them.

The ACFTU used the successes at Wal-Mart to organize unions in other foreign firms, such as Eastman Kodak, Dell, and a Taiwanese company manufacturing Apple iPod parts called Foxcomm. The local ACFTU branch in Guangdong aimed to set up unions in the 300 companies that were part of the Fortune 500, although the head of the union assured foreign investors that the union does not "protect rights for the sake of protecting rights, but rather mobilize[s] the initiative of workers to promote the development of enterprises." By the beginning of 2007, the ACFTU reported that there were branches at 60% of foreign owned enterprises. Even McDonald's and KFC were reported to be explicitly allowing unions in their branches. The ACFTU's success drew criticism from the bastion of union-free workplace advocacy, the *Wall Street Journal* editorial page, which was concerned that the creation of ACFTU unions in Wal-Mart might lead to a transfer of U.S.-style collective bargaining and employer–union conflict into the Chinese industrial relations system.

. . . .

F. Japan: Industrial Cooperation

Wal-Mart entered the Japanese market in March 2002 through the acquisition of a 6.1% stake in the Japanese supermarket Seiyu. In late 2005, it increased its share to a majority 53% stake in the company and installed a Wal-Mart executive as CEO. There are, as of this writing, 392 stores in Japan, and all of these stores are unionized with the Seiyu Workers' Union, which is an affiliate of the JSD union. Once Wal-Mart took over Seiyu, a major objective was to take the ailing chain into profitability by extending some of Wal-Mart's practices into the Japanese retailer, such as methods to increase labor productivity. However, this transfer of practices did not seem to extend to union relations. Labor relations have been described as "normal" by UNI, and in 2004, there was an agreement between the union and Seiyu (as well as two other companies) to allow part-time employees to join the union, purportedly to ensure high quality personnel. This meant that 14,000 more Seiyu workers would become union members and be covered by the CBA.

. . . .

Thus, Wal-Mart bought a unionized company with pre-existing, cooperative union relations, and entered into an industrial relations context where unions and employers try to work collaboratively for the good of the company. It has not intervened or tried to change that dynamic.

III. Making Sense of Wal-Mart

As the country narratives above illustrate, Wal-Mart's relationships with unions and collective bargaining structures in its foreign operations are, if not seamless, much less conflict-ridden than they are in the United States. Wal-Mart, one of the fiercest opponents of unions and unionization in America, generally complies with host country regulations and norms concerning freedom of association and collective bargaining, and fits into the broad norms of the retail sectors in which it operates. Where it has deviated from this path, it has often been forced to conform to prevailing standards.

Thus, as a broadly applicable conclusion, with some small variations, Wal-Mart adapts to the practices of the country and the retail sector in which it operates and does not export, at least in any directly comparable way, its home-country approach to unions to the host country. It tends to comply with the domestic laws and industrial relations systems, as well as with the norms of the society and the organized retail sector in the country in which it operates. . . .

. . . .

As can be seen, the implications of the effects of globalization on businesses involve numbers of issues, many of which interact with domestic labor law regulatory schemes.

QUESTIONS

1. How important to the foreign employer are the nonlegal, cultural factors in operating businesses in East Asia? Give an example.
2. Why, in your opinion, did Wal-Mart change its approach to labor unions and permit them to be established in China?

d. HRM

Issues in human resource management (HRM) abound and are immersed in the global complexities of foreign and domestic labor and employment law requirements regarding hiring, benefits, working conditions, industrial relations, discipline and termination, dispute resolution, and post-employment issues.

Employees working for companies operating on foreign soil may include executives sent to manage the operations, some technical employees to oversee operations, and local employees to staff and operate the company. A common pattern is to eventually "localize" management. Certain documentation may be required for the U.S. workers, including visas and work permits. Most companies will have special benefits and an orientation regarding the new social and business cultural environment.

As businesses cross borders, legal questions arise as to whose laws apply, which laws, and to whom? Likewise, in drafting HRM policies, these legal answers provide business managers the basis under which the provisions are issued and to whom. For example, will U.S. sexual harassment law be applied in East Asia; if so, to whom? Does severance pay need to be paid to all Chinese employees or does it depend on the nature of the employment relationship; and, what about the American employees?

Global Human Resource Strategy[45]

Roger Herod

Introduction

. . . .

[T]he rapid pace of business globalization has blurred the distinctions between domestic and international human resources to such an extent that large numbers of human resource professionals without any prior international experience have found themselves confronted with unexpected challenges, such as establishing and supporting "offshore" manufacturing operations and call centers. Understanding the critical and unique issues involved in managing the human resource issues of global operations is becoming an essential requirement for the career development of all ambitious human resource professionals.

Critical Strategic Global Human Resources Challenges

This chapter will focus on a number of the most critical and often "immediate" challenges faced by human resource professionals involved in supporting international operations:

1. Gaining acceptance as a business partner
2. Establishing new operations
3. Involvement in mergers and acquisitions
4. Recruiting for key positions
5. Developing compensation and benefits strategies
6. Establishing and maintaining global ethical standards

Gaining Acceptance as a Business Partner

. . . .

The challenge is not an easy one. Business development executives frequently prefer to appoint their own candidates to manage international projects and operations. Human resource managers are often excluded from international merger and acquisitions until the deal has been concluded and then left to try to resolve a myriad of cultural, organizational, and policy issues after the event. However, once human resource managers have been able to prove that their contribution to the international business development process is equally valuable to those of finance and marketing executives, their "place at the table" is generally assured.

45 Reprinted with permission from *International HR Journal* (Winter 2007), derived from the introductory chapter of *International Human Resources Guide*, © 2007 Thomson Reuters.

Establishing New Operations

Even relatively small companies are now looking globally, whether to source raw materials, market their products, or find cheaper methods of manufacturing. Human resource managers are finding themselves being asked to help establish new operations . . . [and] [e]stablishing a comprehensive staffing plan for the new operation is the critical first step:

1. What is the timeline for establishing the new operation?
2. What are the short and long term staffing requirements and the timeframe?
3. What level of expertise and skills are required?
4. Which positions will need to be filled immediately?
5. What is the availability of suitable local candidates?
6. Which positions will require expatriates and short term assignees either for management control purposes or to provide the necessary technical and professional support?

. . . .

If no specific policy dealing with business ethics exists, it is crucial to develop one and to make sure it is widely communicated across the organization, including any international operations. These are the types of issues that the policy needs to address:

- The need for employees to comply with all applicable laws [including the Federal Corrupt Practices Act] and regulations, specifying who to contact internally in the event of any question
- Prohibition on payments to public officials
- Prohibition on political contributions
- Guidelines regarding "facilitating payments"
- Authorization procedures for transactions and disposition of assets
- Approval procedures for payments
- Maintenance and retention of records

Summary

The rapid and complex pace of globalization has created immense challenges for human resource managers involved in developing and managing international businesses. Gaining acceptance as a business partner is critical for human resource managers want to make an effective contribution to the success of their company's global business initiatives. In fact, human resource managers have to take a leadership role in many of these initiatives. Establishing new offshore operations and call centers, taking a proactive role in evaluating the human resource aspects of potential mergers and acquisitions, and developing staffing strategies to secure the critical resources needed for new international ventures are all examples of the type of leadership needed to be an effective human resource executive in this challenging new environment.

Workers Without Borders: The Age of the Global Employee[46]

Stephen J. Hirschfeld

. . . .

III. Key Issues When Managing a Multinational Workforce

. . . .

B. Employee Handbooks

Employee handbooks are critical personnel tools for managing employees in many jurisdictions. . . . We note, however, that local laws may require differing levels of employee consent to change work rule provisions to the employee's detriment.

When numerous jurisdictions are involved, some employers choose to develop different handbooks for each jurisdiction. While this is one option, other national or international employers prefer to address the contingencies associated with multi-jurisdictional operations and regulations simply by stating their general policies in the handbooks, noting that variations will occur whenever necessary to comply with applicable laws.

. . . .

C. Document Retention

Up-to-date and effective document retention policies and practices are critical for the multinational employer. In the wake of the Enron and Arthur Andersen debacles, people everywhere are becoming more cynical about corporations and the actions they will take to keep from airing their dirty laundry. There are also significant legal ramifications to "losing" documents. For these reasons, a sound document retention policy is essential. Each jurisdiction has laws that require employers, in varying degrees, to maintain various employment records and failure to comply with these laws can result in fines and other penalties. Given the multitude of regulations and substantial penalties that they impose, most companies would prefer to have a single policy for all employees and operations.

. . . .

D. Equal Employment Opportunity Law Policies

In the United States, Title VII of the Civil Rights Act of 1964 prohibits employment discrimination. . . . Although more and more countries are banning sexual harassment, they do not address this problem uniformly. Thus, although U.S. citizens working abroad [may be] covered by American equal employment opportunity laws, foreign citizens working in foreign countries are not covered by these statutes.

Multinational organizations with employees who are either American and doing work overseas or are foreign doing work in the U.S. face a difficult task. On the one hand,

[46] Stephen J. Hirschfeld, Panelist, Inter-Pacific Bar Association Eighteenth Annual Conference: Workers Without Borders: The Age of the Global Employee (April 2008), *available at*, http://www.ipba2008.com/panels/panel14.html (last visited Sept. 22, 2010) (on file with author).

they must diligently apply American equal employment opportunity laws. On the other hand, depending on the requirements of the foreign country, they must also navigate and apply the foreign employment laws.

. . . .

E. Compensation Issues

"Compensation," "Pay," or "Wage and Hour" issues are extremely rule-ridden and complex. Certain jurisdictions have more rules and greater employee protections than others. Many jurisdictions have overlapping laws within them – such as in the individual states in the U.S., where the employer must master two sets of laws: the individual state law and federal law.

. . . .

F. Medical Leave Policies, Including Workers' Compensation Compliance Issues

For anyone doing business or intending to do business in more than one jurisdiction, it is essential to realize that there can be great disparities in the laws regulating employee leaves. There can also be overlapping laws within a single jurisdiction, making the task of managing a multi-jurisdictional workforce particularly daunting. Is the company a covered employer under a particular leave statute? Is the employee an eligible employee for purposes of obtaining a leave? Is there any notice requirement that triggers the leave? Does the employee have a right to time off and for how long? To what salary and/or benefits is the employee entitled? Is there job protection and for what duration? At what point in time can an employee be terminated? These are all questions that an employer should be asking any time an employee is absent or requests some kind of extended leave. The employer must also determine within each jurisdiction that it is doing business: (1) what rules and laws apply to the company; (2) what rules and laws apply to the employee; and (3) what rules and laws apply to the employee's specific issue. Understanding that there are significant differences in both the substantive requirements of leave laws, as well as the sources for such leaves, is a critical first step in being able to develop and implement appropriate leave policies. Only by having an understanding of the subtleties in this area can an employer expect to successfully adapt its policies to each state or country's legal requirements.

. . . .

G. Labor Activism

In recent years, a number of multinational employers have experienced increased pressure from not only their own workforce regarding various aspects of the company's employment practices, but also from local activists and labor groups. These groups are injecting themselves into what used to be a strictly employer–employee dialogue by claiming that they are now being asked to intervene in labor and employment law areas of global concern. These groups bring to public attention alleged violations of labor rights issues through the use of corporate campaigns, special internet websites and organized protests. Through heightened exposure, they call for multinational employers to be transparent with respect to their companies' labor practices.

. . . .

H. Handling Business Competition, Non-Compete and Trade Secret Issues

For any employer, the need to achieve a competitive advantage by protecting the creation and maintenance of its proprietary trade secret information is of critical importance. The age of employee mobility makes it more important than ever for multi-jurisdictional employers to have written trade secret policies in place, as well as agreements with each employee memorializing their understanding of the company's rights to the information, and the obligations to protect the integrity of that data.

. . . .

I. Post-employment Issues

The reality of the current working world is that innumerable employees across the world are released from their jobs on a daily basis. Virtually every termination – regardless of whether it is voluntary resignation or a for-cause discharge – carries with it the possibility of subsequent litigation. Moreover, termination of employment is an area where both the substantive and procedural laws of each jurisdiction vary greatly. That is, there can be great variations in the laws of different jurisdictions concerning such issues as: (1) grounds for termination, (2) procedures for termination, (3) notice requirements, (4) levels of compensation, (5) methods of enforcing employee rights; (6) payment and type of compensation due, if any; (7) severance requirements, if any, and (8) whether there is any judicial or administrative oversight of the termination process.

. . . .

IV. The Essential Reasons for Employment Law Training

Another key issue that a global employer needs to consider is whether and to what extent training should be provided to managers and employees in the above-mentioned substantive areas. Is training a good place to invest limited resources? If so, who should be trained? What subjects should be covered? Who should do the training? To what extent should the company use outside resources? What about the logistical issues in training employees at different sites? How do you train supervisors on various policies when the supervisors manage a workforce that extends across several jurisdictions? Should diversity training be given? How do you measure the qualifications of an outside trainer? How will the success of the training efforts be determined? Answering these and other questions is an important step to embarking on any effective training program.

. . . .

In planning an effective training program, the global employer should consider whether to include cultural diversity training for its multinational workforce. Cultural diversity programs can be beneficial for improving working relationships, which ultimately leads to greater productivity and greater sensitivity to customer's needs. By educating managers on how to recognize and understand various cultural assumptions, a company can provide an environment that fosters effective cross-cultural communication skills, avoids misunderstandings, and promotes an atmosphere of trust and mutual support that transcends cultural boundaries.

. . . .

QUESTIONS

1. Employment relationships have been changing in recent decades with increased use of contingent employees. How much of this is attributable to globalism?
2. Discuss the effects of globalism on employment relationships.
3. What will influence a business decision whether to relocate from a country whose labor laws are being newly enforced (e.g., China), or bend to the local reality and adapt, as in the Wal-Mart illustration?
4. What is the effect on "competitive advantage" of a country's meeting ILO core labor standards?
5. How do HRM issues correlate with legal issues and the rendering of legal advice?
6. What are the top three issues for employers to consider in HRM regarding globalization?

3. *International Labor Law Practice*

With the onset of globalism, the role and practice of international labor and employment lawyers have mushroomed in recent years and as long as businesses require employees to staff and operate them, it will be a growth area. With China's economy as the world's second largest economy, growing by double digits and recently overtaking Japan, there has been a steady flow there of American and European investment, growing numbers of workers employed by them, and the corresponding need for lawyers to service them. Likewise, trade unions that have gone global and reach across international borders for mutual assistance and cooperation have growing needs for international labor and employment lawyers to represent them.

Many practical questions must be understood. Outside the United States, it is common to bar foreign lawyers from taking the qualifying bar examination necessary to practice law inside the country. If so, how does one use the American lawyer in the United States or operating from offices located in the foreign country and coordinate with licensed lawyers inside these countries? Are the legal training, ethical requirements, licensing to practice, and functions of lawyers in China, Japan, and South Korea similar to those in the United States? If not, what are the differences and are there potential risks that need to be guarded against?

The Practice of International Labor and Employment Law: Escort Your Labor/Employment Clients into the Global Millennium[47]

Donald C. Dowling

I. Introduction

International labor and employment law, as a practice area, is still just a tiny corner of labor and employment law practice, but its importance in the new millennium is exploding.

. . . .

The demand chiefly comes from multinationals scrambling to become (and claiming to be) global. *Going global* – as opposed to remaining a mere multinational – is a hot business trend, akin to what *total quality* was years ago. Of course, the globalization trend has a profound effect on labor unions and many individual employees.

. . . .

II. What International Labor and Employment Law Practice Is Not

Appreciating that international labor and employment law practice is at last coming into its own means nothing until one understands what international labor and employment practice actually is. Because international issues have not traditionally been on labor and employment lawyers' radar screens, many labor/employment specialists do not understand the international field, and they make wrong assumptions about what it must be.

Indeed, plenty of labor/employment practitioners out there still insist that international labor and employment practice does not even exist. These practitioners point out that every country has its own discrete employment law system and that any lawyer who advises on foreign labor/employment law is merely practicing overseas law without a license. Alas, while this analysis perhaps used to make sense, in the new global millennium it is no longer quite so simple.

This article demonstrates why international labor and employment law practice is an increasingly viable – indeed, vital – concentration within labor and employment law practice. Because international labor/employment law practice is so poorly understood, I have to start by clearing up the misconceptions. I begin by discussing what the practice of international labor and employment law is not.

[47] Donald C. Dowling, Jr., Partner, International Employment, White & Case LLP, *The Practice of International Labor and Employment Law: Escort Your Labor/Employment Client into the Global Millennium*, 17 Lab. L. 1 (2001). *See also* Donald C. Dowling, *What Is International Employment Law Practice* (2007), http://www.whitecase.com/publications_10052007/. Mr. Dowling, now a partner at White & Case, New York City, responds to the question of what is the future of the international employment law practice: "A. Corporations' focus on compliance, together with the globalization trend, push multinationals to take a global approach to many (if not all) aspects of human resources and employment law compliance. Multinationals in the global information age increasingly wrestle with cross-border talent problems and increasingly demand counselors even more fluent in international employment law concepts as they are themselves. This demand will spur growth in the practice of international employment law in coming years." *Id.* at 6.

A. *Single Foreign-Country Employment-Law Practice*

A scenario that happens all the time is as follows: A U.S. labor/employment lawyer sitting in an office in Cleveland or Sacramento or wherever receives a call from a frantic client, a U.S.-based multinational. Breathlessly the client announces, "We need to fire a guy in our Paris office immediately," or "We've just announced we're shutting down our Sao Paulo factory and we don't know what we need to do," or "Our Tokyo people just made a job offer to a sales manager who is demanding a written employment contract," or "Our plant manager in Sydney says we might be getting a union. What can we do?" These are all urgent and important questions, but none involves international labor or employment law: Each involves merely a single country's foreign employment laws. When any one single country is the site of employment, the residence of the employees in question, and the place of controlling law, there is no cross-border or international issue – even if the employer's parent company is a multinational based elsewhere (for example, in the United States).

. . . .

International employment-law practitioners have to be intimately familiar with the wildly different issues that arise under foreign (local) employment laws because international employment practice constantly involves questions of multiple countries' foreign laws simultaneously. Multiple foreign-country law problems are, by definition, cross-border and hence international. Cross-border projects that simultaneously raise issues under a cluster of foreign countries' domestic employment laws require the oversight of a single international employment expert collecting answers or opinions from local practitioners in each country involved and molding them together into a global solution for the client.

. . . .

B. *Public International (Diplomatic) Employment-Law Practice*

Because international employment-law practice does not involve single-country foreign practice, many labor/employment lawyers assume it must involve public-international or diplomatic employment law (such as treaty-drafting for the ILO, government dispute resolution under NAFTA's North American Agreement on Labor Cooperation [NAALC], and international employment-standards projects for the UN and the WTO).

. . . .

However, public international employment law kicks up plenty of issues that land in private practitioners' laps. A good example is the diplomatic focus on labor standards in international trade treaties, which leads to lots of international employment-law work, drafting multinationals' codes of conduct. Another example is the dispute-resolution body of the NAFTA labor side agreement, the NAALC. Although open only to nations as parties, most NAALC disputes implicate individual companies' employment practices (NAALC cases, though, are rare).

C. *Inbound-Employer Law Practice*

Often American employment lawyers who represent foreign-based multinationals in matters involving U.S. operations think of these matters as involving international employment law, but really they do not. Local employment-law practice representing an overseas-based client is more likely to raise cross-cultural problems than cross-border legal ones.

. . . .

D. *Immigration Law Practice*

Immigration is relevant to international labor and employment law practice chiefly to dismiss it: The practice of immigration law is a discrete area unto itself. Immigration is not a branch of international employment law. Why? First, immigration law is not strictly international law because it involves whether an alien is entitled to a visa under local domestic laws of a host country: An immigrant may have crossed borders, but the legal issues have not.

. . . .

III. Practice for Multinational Companies[48]

Having disposed of what international employment law practice is not, now I can drill down to what the practice actually is. The best way to understand international employment as a law-practice field is to look at the contexts in which international employment lawyers actually work. Labor and employment lawyers define their practice contexts according to *who their clients are*: employers, labor unions, or individual employees. These three groupings define *international employment-law practice*. I begin with the biggest of these three practice contexts: practice for multinational-company clients.

. . . .

A. *Global Legal-Compliance Audits*

A multinational that globalizes its talent operations quickly realizes how little headquarters knows about the human resources policies and practices the company offers around the world – and whether its own overseas human resources programs comply with local laws. So multinationals embarking on talent-globalization projects often start with a worldwide employment-law compliance audit. International employment law practitioners (in liaison with local employment experts, of course) are the ideal candidates to quarterback these projects.

B. *Global Policies and Handbooks*

When multinationals think about globalizing human resources procedures, the common knee-jerk reaction is to try to propagate a single set of employment policies, a single global handbook, or a single form employment contract (countries from Mexico to Chile to China to all of the European Union [EU] require employers to give each employee a written employment contract or statement). Unfortunately, the radically

[48] For discussion of the types of American-style employment practices a multinational company may seek to retain in a foreign host country, see Donald C. Dowling, Jr., *U.S.-Based Multinational Employers and the Social Contract Outside the United States*, 26 LAB. & EMPLOYMENT L. J. 77 (2010).

different employment laws of the world make these projects, in many respects, impossible. But it is possible – and desirable – for a globalizing multinational to articulate overall employment philosophies and objectives and implement them locally. International employment lawyers often help lead these projects, translating global talent aspirations into collections of local employment policies that mesh with one another.

. . . .

C. Global Labor Relations

Related to globalizing employment policies is the issue of globalizing labor relations. Plenty of U.S.-based employers actually forget about unions, because only nine percent of the U.S. non-government workforce is unionized. Abroad, though, unions are statistically far more likely to represent a company's workers.

Actual union representations and collective bargaining will always be inherently local. . . .

D. Human Rights, Civil Rights, and Codes of Conduct

The highly charged politics after the 1999 WTO riots in Seattle catapulted onto international employment-law agendas a range of issues involving multinationals' human rights, civil rights, codes of conduct, and minimum employment guarantees around the world. Just ask McDonald's or Nike.

. . . .

Codes of conduct are corporate pledges of minimum employment standards ensured around the world – not only in a multinational's own employment operations, but, often, even in suppliers' workplaces.

. . . .

E. Global Employee Benefits, Compensation, and Stock Options

. . . .

The lesson is that globalizing benefits is a key piece to globalizing a company. Right now, most multinationals are taking huge steps toward globalizing compensation and benefits, starting by articulating a global rewards philosophy and implementing it through global rewards programs – although huge differences among the world's health care, social security, and mandatory benefit-law systems make full uniformity impossible.

. . . .

F. Data Privacy and Global Human Resources Information Systems

Another big problem is starting to send multinationals scrambling to international employment law practitioners: data privacy. Multinationals employing people worldwide need to ensure foreign data privacy laws accommodate their global personnel information systems – systems like human resources information systems (HRISs), global performance management, and global benefits/stock options.

. . . .

The philosophy underlying these data laws is tough for Americans to grasp. The First Amendment affirmatively grants the right to traffic information about others.

. . . .

A multinational's overseas employees think very differently. Workers abroad can be surprisingly circumspect to HR data about themselves that their employer – especially if it is a faceless American giant – inputs into its computers and transmits to God knows where. Data privacy laws are designed to quell concerns like these. The problem is that in globalizing a personnel system in this era of e-HR, HRISs, and PeopleSoft, the data laws' effect can be downright Luddite-like. American multinationals aiming to globalize HRISs hit a wall when some lawyer explains that they cannot use their own databases for otherwise legitimate business purposes.

Unfortunately, U.S.-based multinationals face even bigger data-privacy problems than their locally based competitors abroad because data-protection countries erect huge barriers to transmitting personal data offshore. (The countries fear that scofflaws will send personal data about local citizens abroad to do what would be – in the data's country of origin – illegal.) These barriers frustrate U.S. multinationals whenever headquarters decide to roll out global performance management, stock options, or HRISs.

. . . .

G. Global Mergers and Acquisitions

. . . .

What this all means to international employment lawyers should be obvious: U.S. companies are not accustomed to ceding employment issues more than a sliver of their M&A radar screens, but neglecting to include an employment expert on a team doing a global deal invites disaster. Besides piloting global human-resources due diligence before a closing, international employment practitioners need to guide the back end of any global deal in post-merger integration, ensuring the transaction succeeds and brings the intended synergies.

A more mundane but equally important employment law aspect to international M&A (and to international business law practice generally) is accounting for the employment ramifications of corporate form. Abroad, how a company is structured can determine many of its employment obligations. In Europe, for example, certain labor law obligations (ranging from the duty to recognize local country and European works councils to the need to appoint labor representatives on a company's board) can turn on what corporate form a business chooses. In Mexico and other Latin countries, computations under employee profit-sharing laws turn on whether a business employs its workers directly or through a separately incorporated services company subsidiary. Lawyers who structure corporations abroad simply must account for labor law in a merger-and-acquisition deal.

H. Global Layoffs and Plant Shutdowns (Collective Redundancies)

Talking about the synergies in a global merger-and-acquisition deal sounds good, but in real life, synergies often mean overlap; thus, synergies often lead to laying off unneeded workers whose jobs duplicate positions in the acquiring company. Even outside the

M&A context, market pressures and global restructuring projects push multinationals to have global layoffs and shut down factories.

U.S. multinationals, unfortunately, tend to be bad at global layoffs. American businesses are steeped in their unique and peculiar employment-at-will doctrine, which even other Anglo-system countries like England, Canada, and Australia rejected years ago. U.S. employment lawyers say that America's employment at will has eroded away, but theirs is a historical, not an international, perspective. By comparison to other countries, employment at will is alive and well in the U.S. and explains why America's employers are the world's most trigger-happy when it comes to layoffs, downsizing, and plant shutdowns.

. . . .

IV. Practice for Labor Unions

Having run through the areas that international employment practitioners cover when they represent multinationals, I now turn to union-side international practice. The range of issues here is every bit as broad.

A. *International Employment and Local Organizing/Collective Bargaining*

A basic role for union-side international practitioners is supplying international information for local organizing campaigns and collective bargaining. Union-side practitioners who are familiar with foreign laws and collective bargaining agreements feed union organizers data on overseas work practices (especially data about a target multinational's superior offerings abroad). For years, U.S. unions have exploited, as an organizing tool, the fact that foreign employers offer better worker protections and broader benefits.

. . . .

B. *Cross-Border Union Initiatives against Multinational Employers*

Union-side international lawyers do a lot more than summarize foreign laws and collective agreements. They also structure initiatives among the unions in different countries that represent a single multinational's workers. Cross-border union alliances compare notes in collective bargaining and apply cross-border pressure (such as through global boycotts) to win concessions.

. . . .

C. *International Politics and Public Relations*

Union-side international lawyers also play a key role in politics and public relations. One piece of this is advising on international boycotts and initiatives regarding international work issues.

. . . .

Union international lawyers also petition governments to enforce labor treaties like NAFTA's NAALC labor-side agreement.

. . . .

A big piece of international union lawyers' political and public relations work goes into lobbying to ratify ILO conventions and to inject labor standards into international trade treaties.

. . . .

V. Practice for Individual Employees and Executives

Law practice representing individual employees – including executives – differs substantially from union-side practice, even though both pit talent against employers. Most employment lawyers who represent individuals have largely domestic practices and do not concentrate internationally. But as more and more employees work as immigrants and expatriates, cross-border employment issues increasingly pop up, such as when executives' lawyers are asked to negotiate expatriate agreements and to resolve disputes after expatriate postings sour. The legal issues here, not for novices, include such arcana as international taxation; offshore pension accruals; cross-border social security equalization; and friendship, commerce, and navigation treaties.

The threshold issue, often dispositive, in representing individual employees internationally – be it contract drafting or dispute resolution – is the question of whose law applies.

. . . .

The answer to this choice-of-law question is both.

. . . .

VI. Conclusion

. . . .

As soon as lawyers' clients realize how many huge problems can be solved – and how much money can be saved – by retaining an international labor and employment lawyer, international labor and employment law will thrive as a critical sub-concentration within labor and employment law practice

. . . .

A further more practical summary encapsulating the above description was recently presented by the same author.

What Is International Employment Law Practice?[49]

Donald C. Dowling

. . . .

Q. *Then what kinds of client matters do international employment lawyers work on?*
A. Globalization means certain human resources issues that a decade ago would have been relegated to overseas control, now get driven from U.S. headquarters.

[49] Dowling, *What is International Employment Law Practice?*, *supra* note 47.

As such, corporate headquarters now tend to seek international employment law advice on 15 types of matters:

1. Global employee contract documents, handbooks, codes of conduct, ethics codes, discrimination/harassment/diversity policies, other global human resources policies, affinity groups – and global training
2. Global whistleblower hotlines (compliance with Sarbanes-Oxley §301 and foreign data privacy and labor laws)
3. Global reductions-in-force and workforce restructurings
4. Global compensation, benefits, commission, bonus, equity and severance pay plans
5. Global human resources information systems (compliance with foreign data privacy laws)
6. Global employee communications (compliance with labor and language laws)
7. Human resources in international mergers and acquisitions (due diligence and contract drafting through post-merger integration)
8. Cross-border labor representation strategy (union/works council alignment; foreign negotiations over headquarters global mandates; response to global "corporate campaigns" and secondary boycotts)
9. "Sweatshop" (supplier) codes of conduct and monitoring (compliance with local laws and corporate policies on human rights)
10. Human resources issues in "offshoring" and international outsourcing
11. Overseas independent contractors (avoiding *de facto* employee liability)
12. Global applicant background checks/screening, and global employee surveillance (video, computer)
13. Headquarters-driven global oversight of local employment law compliance
14. Duty of care/managing exposure to employee personal injury claims arising abroad (terrorism, pandemics, dangerous assignments, employee security)
15. Expatriates (secondment arrangements, benefits, terminations, repatriation)

Q. *Since international employment lawyers are not licensed in foreign jurisdictions, their chief role on these projects would seem to be collecting and packaging advice from foreign lawyers. Right?*

A. No. When international employment lawyers get together and "talk shop," their biggest frustration is the misunderstanding that their practice means shuttling back and forth as intermediaries between U.S. clients and foreign counsel. Like other types of international lawyers (international business lawyers, international arbitration lawyers, international tax lawyers), international employment practitioners advise clients on cross-border legal strategies and principles that apply across jurisdictions. Gathering advice on specific foreign local rules, like all legal research, can be critical. But local advice-gathering is not necessarily the main "value-add" of an international law practice, and in fact – like domestic legal research – is often efficiently delegated to junior lawyers.

American employment-at-will is unique in the world. The other side of that coin is that the labor/employment law principles arising outside the US are radically different from our doctrines stateside. To advise US-based clients on outside-US human resources strategies, an international employment lawyer needs to understand foreign employment law principles well enough to discuss them in a cold phone call from a client or prospective client. This means being ready to distinguish, for example:

- unfair dismissal damages vs. wrongful dismissal damages vs. statutory severance pay vs. payment in lieu of notice
- collective redundancies for an ETO (economic, technical, or organizational) reason vs. unjustified redundancies
- vested rights vs. acquired rights in the transfer of undertakings context individual consultation vs. collective information and consultation vs. worker participation
- works councils in member states of the European Union vs. European Works Councils vs. Asian worker committees
- white unions vs. enterprise unions vs. independent trade unions vs. trade union confederations vs. trade union political parties
- sectoral collective bargaining agreements vs. enterprise-level agreements
- transposition of social directives vs. direct effect
- model contractual clauses vs. binding corporate rules vs. safe harbor
- statutory termination procedures vs. mandated employer-issued DDPs (dismissal and disciplinary procedures)
- mandatory profit sharing vs. *agüinaldo*
- employment services companies vs. foreign operating subsidiaries
- dual employer liability vs. PE (permanent establishment) liability
- positive action vs. victimization
- bullying and mobbing vs. moral and psychosocial harassment
- end-of-service gratuities vs. superannuation

Expect in-house employment lawyers and human resources professionals at multinational clients already to understand the terms on this list. Sophisticated clients seek outside international employment law advisors who have mastered these concepts well enough to offer creative strategies – not go-betweens who need to call foreign lawyers to clarify terms. Beyond addressing these foreign law principles, international employment lawyers also advise U.S.-based clients on why and how, overseas, they need to replace, or radically restructure, many American-made human resources tools tailored for the unique U.S. employment-at-will environment, such as:

- employment-at-will clauses and handbook disclaimers
- detailed employee handbooks
- mandatory applicant and employee consents/acknowledgements
- union avoidance strategies
- applicant drug testing and credit checks
- diversity plans/metrics, race/ethnicity tracking, affirmative action plans and affinity groups
- fraternization/nepotism policies and employee dating restrictions
- expressly anonymous, mandatory whistleblower hotlines
- adverse impact analysis
- health care benefits, and other benefits restricted to regular full-time employees
- vacation and retirement benefits that increase with job tenure

. . . .

The Lawyer's Role in Foreign Direct Investment and the Global Economy[50]

Robert L. Pritchard

Need for international legal Links

. . . .

(a) Agency or Correspondent Relationships

This is still the most common method by which lawyers handle international business. Typically, a client still consults his domestic lawyer in his home country office. The domestic lawyer then retains a foreign lawyer as his agent or correspondent in the host country to carry out the foreign components of the task.

. . . .

As the rate of FDI has increased, direct consultation of lawyers in the host country has become more frequent. Rather than operate indirectly, through his domestic lawyer, the client retains the host country lawyer directly.

(b) Foreign Offices

. . . .

A foreign office not only channels business into the home base of the law firm, it also provides overseas services to domestic clients of the law firm who have ventured abroad. Many firms find, however, that foreign offices are a great drain on their financial and human resources.

There are three other difficulties for lawyers in operating a foreign office.

- Location – for most lawyers there is no established pattern in the flow of foreign legal work to justify the operation of a foreign office in a particular location.
- Range of services – clients typically expect a law office to provide a full range of services. This is difficult for a small office with a limited number of personnel.
- Accreditation problems: in the case of Japan, for example, all practicing Japanese lawyers must be members of the Japan Federation of Bar Associations (Nichibenren). There are only about 15,000, an extremely small figure for an economically advanced country with a population of 120 million. About half of these practise individually. Most of the remainder practise in groups of two or three. There is a shortage of skilled international lawyers. In recognition of this, Japan now offers limited accreditation for foreign lawyers. This is a most welcome development and further liberalisation of the accreditation rules will no doubt be considered. It would certainly be welcomed by foreign lawyers.

(c) International Legal Networks

This is the most recent trend in the evolution of international relationships between lawyers. To cater for what they see as a common global challenge, law firms from

[50] Robert L. Pritchard, *The Lawyer's Role in Foreign Direct Investment and the Global Economy*, 18 INT'L BUS. LAW. 358 (1990). Mr. Pritchard served as Chairman of the International Legal Practice Committee of the Law Council of Australia.

different countries are increasingly forming international legal networks. These networks adopt cooperative approaches towards addressing the international problems which firms encounter as they undertake international business.

Some Conclusions

It is clear that lawyers will have an increasingly crucial role in the globalisation of the world economy, particularly as FDI continues to increase. . . .

Lawyers have always been adept at advising clients not only on local laws but also on the political and social context in which such laws are administered. In future, lawyers specialising in FDI and other forms of international business will also need to demonstrate a high level of cross-cultural understanding if they are to realise their full potential as facilitators of FDI as well as protectors of their clients' interests.

. . . .

Lawyers in different countries have different training and often play different roles than expected by an American lawyer first venturing into the foreign deal. An anecdotal perspective of one experienced lawyer follows.

Working with Korean and Chinese Attorneys[51]

Dan Harris

Asian attorneys have different expectations and perceptions of their roles than American attorneys. Since no two legal systems in Asia are exactly alike, I will focus on China and Korea.

Working with Lawyers in Korea

In Korea as in Japan, the overwhelming majority of people who go to law school never pass the bar. This scarcity of lawyers gives Korean lawyers a very high social status (think U.S. medical doctors in the 1950s), and this, in turn, can pose many problems for foreign lawyers and clients needing legal help in Korea. The fact that Korea does not allow foreign law firms compounds the problem. The four most common problems I see in retaining Korean lawyers are:

1. *Non-responsiveness is the norm.* American lawyers generally see their role as helping clients achieve their goals and keeping their clients informed. Korean lawyers operate far more independently. They consider themselves the legal experts and can get offended when questioned. According to their perspective, a client should trust them, not ask questions, and not expect updates.

[51] Dan Harris, *Working with Korean and Chinese Attorneys*, The Complete Lawyer (December 9, 2008), http://www.thecompletelawyer.com/international-business/asia/working-with-korean-and-chinese-attorneys-394.html (last visited Oct. 3, 2010). Of course, everyone's experience may differ.

This obviously does not work well for American clients. Two excellent Korean law firms have admitted to me they "always get fired" when they work directly with American companies or with American lawyers inexperienced with Korea. If a Korean lawyer has a hearing scheduled in a case, I email him the day before to urge him to provide me with a full report by the next day, at the latest. I usually send another email reminder after the hearing concludes and if I do not have a timely report, I call.

2. *Your matter is not important.* Most Korean lawyers have plenty of work and any one matter from an overseas client is not likely to be of paramount importance to them. This may mean your Korean lawyer will not fight hard on a particular motion where the chances of winning are low; he or she would rather stay in the good graces of a judge or fellow lawyer than challenge the status quo. I try to get around it by hiring "outsider" lawyers if my case is going to be particularly difficult or contentious, or by attending the hearing if it is particularly important. I also always make clear, upfront, that a good result for this client will lead to more work from my other clients.

3. *The Korean lawyer's role is different.* Korean lawyers tend to view themselves as "above it all." I learned this when, trying to settle a case, we offered $900,000 and the Korean company on the other side offered to pay us $700,000. I asked the Korean lawyer to go back at $850,000 and I could feel his reluctance. I say "feel" because while he was telling me he would go back at $850,000, he was also asking me questions to let me know he did not think he should go back at $850,000. Weeks then passed with no updates and vague responses to my emails. Then, out of the blue, a US-educated paralegal from the firm called me to say the $850,000 offer had never been passed on because the Korean lawyer considered it beneath him to negotiate "as though at a flea market." I do not know if that paralegal was put up to the call by the attorney or if he did it on his own, but I have since learned to control negotiations myself. It is not just in negotiations that the Korean lawyer sees himself as above the fray. If you do not put pressure on your Korean lawyer, you can pretty much assume that numerous time extensions will delay your case for years.

4. *Confidentiality? What's that?* Korean lawyers simply do not respect the attorney–client privilege as American lawyers do. I try to handle confidentiality problems by using the same few lawyers in Korea for all of my firm's clients. Because I provide so much work to these attorneys, I have a personal relationship with them, which makes it less likely that they will hurt me by hurting my client. It also decreases the incentive for the Korean lawyer to hurt my client because doing so will cut off a regular stream of work.

Working with Lawyers in China

There are many lawyers in China scrambling for work, but most of them have neither the experience nor the language skills to handle international clients. The problem is that most either do not know this or will not admit it. The four most common problems I see in retaining Chinese lawyers are:

1. *Chinese law firms often aren't "firms" as we understand the term.* There are very few really good Chinese international law firms in China and many of them are not really firms at all; they are a collection of solo practitioners. Many American companies think they are using the best lawyer in a firm for a particular matter

when in fact that lawyer has the case not because of his skill set but because he or she is the one who brought the case in.

2. *Chinese lawyers are rarely power brokers.* The importance of connections isn't as strong as it once was, though it is still a factor in certain industries and certain parts of the country. Chinese lawyers are usually not well connected (even if they are reluctant to admit it) so hiring a lawyer as a power play is rarely recommended. China's good lawyers are very smart and very well educated, but if they were truly well connected, they would most likely have a top position in the government or with a big company, and they would never have attended law school in the first place.
3. *The Chinese lawyer's role is different.* Chinese lawyers far too often see their role as doing what the client tells them to do rather than telling the client what should be done. If a client calls me and says she wants to do A, my knee-jerk response is to ask why. The typical Chinese lawyer's response is to say yes.
4. *Chinese lawyers do things the Chinese way.* Chinese companies can get away with all sorts of things in China that American-owned companies cannot. Chinese lawyers tend not to account for this. Chinese lawyers also almost never know the various US law strictures under which American companies must operate. The Foreign Corrupt Practices Act is a classic example. There are also many things American companies can do legally in China that would be a public relations disaster back home. This is particularly true regarding labor relations and environmental stewardship.

There are a whole slew of excellent American law firms with lawyers in China and the safest way to handle your Chinese legal matter is usually to retain an American lawyer who both speaks and reads Chinese.

Interestingly, it is noted that many of these American law firms increasingly are becoming "localized" through the hiring of local lawyers, many of whom have been educated in the United States. And, in some cases, leading non-Chinese lawyers have left their firms to join the local Chinese law firms.[52]

QUESTIONS

1. How useful is it in the U.S. attorney's law practice to understand the legal environment of its Japanese "inbound" clients? Why?
2. When a unionized employee of an American air carrier wants to transfer to China under seniority rights it has under a collective-bargaining contract, but China refuses to issue a visa, is this a question of U.S. law or foreign law? Is this international labor law? Why?

[52] Anthony Lin, *The New China Hands*, 32 AM. LAW. 66 (2010), http://www.law.com/jsp/cc/PubArticleCC.jsp?id=1202446056176 (last visited Sept. 23, 2010).

3. Explain the different law training and functions of an East Asian lawyer versus a U.S.-trained lawyer.
4. How can an American attorney utilizing the legal services of a foreign lawyer hope to adequately monitor the legal advice given and meet ethical requirements? Does it make a difference whether the American lawyer is an "in-house" lawyer?
5. Who is liable for malpractice if the foreign lawyer provides "bad legal advice" to the American lawyer who passes it on as his or her own advice to the client? How can this be best dealt with?

B. INTERNATIONAL AND COMPARATIVE LABOR AND EMPLOYMENT LAW

1. *Evolving Area of International Labor and Employment Law; Employee Rights as Human Rights; Comparative Biases*

a. Globalization of the Law of Labor and Employment

The law itself in this area is in constant development as the pressures of changing trends reshape the employment relationship and raise new challenges for regulation. Questions arise as to what is "international labor and employment law" and what underlies the changing trends? The primary dynamics of change have been categorized as "flexibilization," "globalization," and "privatization."[53] Workplace trends associated with globalization bring a reshaping of the employment relationship, including the increased use of contingent workers, women workers, and migrant workers, and the general decline of the role of labor unions, each of which also is causing pressure to reshape the legal contours of the regulation of the employment relationship.[54]

Questions are also raised about whether the new labor and employment laws will utilize "best practices," be significantly influenced by external standards, or be pressured by the market to "race to the bottom." Even as the HRM practices and the labor and employment laws are changing, so also is the practice of law in this area; and lawyers are finding they must adapt to this new globalization of labor and employment law. How the effects of globalization have been forming and reshaping "international labor law" is discussed next.[55]

---

[53] Reprinted with permission by Katherine V. W. Stone, *A New Labor Law for a New World of Work: The Case for a Comparative-Transnational Approach*, 28 *Comp. Lab. & Pol'y J.* 565 (2007). Copyright © Katherine V. W. Stone.

[54] Roger Blanpain et al., THE GLOBAL WORKPLACE 8–17 (Cambridge Univ. Press 2007).

[55] The subject of international and comparative labor and employment law is increasingly being offered in law school curricula. *See* Michael J. Zimmer, *Two Halves of a Whole: Teaching International and*

Reinventing Labor Law for the Global Economy: The Benjamin Aaron Lecture[56]

Harry Arthurs

. . . .

V. What Kind of New Labor Law System is Developing in the Context of the Global Economy?

. . . [d]espite the inability of many lawyers to detect it, a new labor law is actually emerging in the global economy. This new labor law has not yet begun to affect U.S. domestic labor law, but it is gradually beginning to shape relations between transnational employers and their workers, and to influence the industrial relations and labor law systems of many of America's trading partners and competitors. In the long run, therefore, it may leach back into the United States, just as it did under the New Deal and during the postwar period. This emerging global labor law has at least five components.

The first is international treaties and conventions. Obviously, these have a direct juridical effect only on the countries that sign them – which, in most cases, the United States has not. However, the United States has been arguing for some time that those countries that do not adhere to "core labor standards" should be denied membership in the WTO, in which the United States is very much a dominant player. Ironically, since "core labor standards" are, in fact, taken directly from the ILO's large catalogue of Conventions – many of which the United States has not ratified – if the United States succeeds in making compliance a condition of WTO membership, it will have extended the reach of the ILO not only to cover other countries, but possibly itself as well. Indeed, at least one scholarly study has argued that these standards have already become part of customary international law, adherence to which is already required by the WTO statute.

Moreover, the United States obviously is a member of NAFTA and has signed the so-called "labor side accord," the NAALC. This agreement commits each NAFTA partner to adhere to its own labor laws, establishes a dispute resolution process to ensure compliance, and allows this process to be accessed not only by the other governments, but by their aggrieved citizens. As a result, over the past five or six years, American workers, unions, and social movements have filed twenty or thirty complaints with the NAALC National Administrative Office in Washington against the failure of the Mexican government to extend protection to its own workers, especially in cases involving foreign subsidiaries doing business in the maquiladoras. A number of these complaints have given rise to hearings, and the resulting findings and publicity have embarrassed the

Comparative Employment Law, 25 Int'l J. Comp. Lab. L. & Indus. Rel., 23 (2009), *available at* http://papers.ssrn.com/sol3/papers.cfm?abstract_id=1422701 (last visited Oct. 3, 2010). Professor Zimmer states that the ". . . earlier divide between international law and comparative law in a good number of these areas has narrowed because aspects of both international law and national law are closely related to each other. Understanding either requires understanding both. . . . Labour and employment law is an area where a full understanding involves looking both at international law and at the laws of many different nation states." *Id.*

[56] Harry Arthurs, *Reinventing Labor Law for the Global Economy: The Benjamin Aaron Lecture*, 22 Berkeley J. Emp. & Lab. L. 271 (2001). © 2001 by the Regents of the University of California. Reprinted from Berkeley Journal of Employment and Labor Law. Vol. 22, No. 1, by permission of the Regents of the University of California. [Footnotes omitted].

employers involved, the official Mexican trade unions, and the Mexican government. As a result, some improvements have taken place in the administration of Mexican labor law. More to the point, the complaints process has helped to launch a new independent trade union movement in Mexico, has been the catalyst for much greater cooperation amongst Mexican, Canadian, and American unions, and has also legitimated and reinforced the activities of churches, women's groups, and other social activists on behalf of Mexican workers.

. . . .

The dissemination of "best practices" is the second major component of developing global labor law. This is essentially the optimistic obverse of a process I mentioned earlier, in which the law of the shop is degraded by globalization. The optimistic version begins with the proposition that best practices are indispensable for success in technology-based economies, where human capital is a strategic asset.

. . . .

Third, management is constructing a kind of global labor law in the form of corporate voluntary codes of conduct. These codes, which have been appearing at a great rate over the past decade, have been adopted by individual corporations and sectoral organizations voluntarily, under pressure from labor unions, consumer organizations, and human rights groups and in response to the urgings of national governments the OECD, the ILO, and other international organizations. These codes are "voluntary" in the sense that they are not imposed by law and do not appear to give rise to enforceable third party claims. However, in another sense they are not voluntary. Many were adopted under pressure by reluctant corporations in order to ward off adverse publicity, strikes, boycotts, embargoes, or political and legal sanctions. This pressure may become more intense.

. . . .

Fourth, corporations are not the only actors shaping global labor law. Unions are making a modest contribution too, whether through national unions and labor congresses, international labor bodies such as the so-called "trade secretariats," or ad hoc union alliances built around specific disputes and for limited purposes. Needless to say, union efforts to build solidarity across national boundaries have not been hugely successful, for reasons mentioned earlier. But in a few celebrated cases, unions have been able to win at least battles, if not actual wars. Employers have been forced to abandon plant closings or compensate dismissed workers, improve wages and working conditions, recognize unions, and respect local health and safety standards. In other words, unions have been able to do on a small scale globally what they aspire to do on a large scale nationally.

Fifth, the new actors in the formation of global economy are social movements – women, consumers, university students, religious communities, environmentalists, aboriginal peoples, anti-poverty and anti-child labor activists, and human rights groups. These social movements, often working with unions in both the advanced and developing economies, have been able to arouse public indignation against abusive labor practices which, in turn, has forced retailers, investors, and ultimately governments to bring pressure to bear on offending employers.

It is difficult to imagine that governments, unions, corporations, and social movements might create and administer a system of global labor law by pasting together a collage of treaties and conventions, best practices, corporate codes, ad hoc settlements, and vestigial remnants of national legislation. But this, after all, is pretty much how we originally constructed our "old" system of labor law. Lest we forget, there was collective bargaining before the Wagner Act, employer- and union-sponsored welfare funds before Social Security, and grievance arbitration before the War Labor Board. Thus, I want to conclude by arguing that it is just possible that in these scattered, episodic episodes of rule-making and dispute resolution, we may spy the shape of the future.

. . . .

Extraterritoriality by Other Means: How Labor Law Sneaks Across Borders, Conquers Minds, and Controls Workplaces Abroad[57]

Harry Arthurs

[This article] suggests that transnational flows of technology and capital, goods and services, and ideas and information have brought in their wake changes in political economy and social relations that have transformed regimes of public and workplace governance in all countries. It proposes that the extraterritoriality doctrine operates, if at all, only in the formal sense of not allowing one state to overtly project its law into the territory of another. But extraterritoriality does little to prevent the rules governing employment relations in one country from taking root elsewhere, from shaping foreign labor market norms, institutions, and practices, and from being reproduced, in their original or mutant forms, in foreign systems of labor law. The result is the extraterritorial projection "by other means" of labor law and policy – a form of extraterritoriality that has the potential to enhance as well as undermine labor standards in global enterprises.

. . . .

A New Labor Law for a New World of Work: The Case for a Comparative-Transnational Approach[58]

Katherine V. W. Stone

There are many reasons to study comparative labor law. One is that comparative labor law can reveal the way in which different legal systems approach similar issues differently. That is, a study of comparative labor law can assemble and reveal unfamiliar doctrines and approaches, much as a museum collects and displays unfamiliar artifacts. Alternatively, comparative labor law can serve not only intellectual curiosity, but also instrumental goals. Understanding comparative law and alternative institutional arrangements can

57 Harry Arthurs, *Extraterritoriality by Other Means: How Labor Law Sneaks Across Borders, Conquers Minds, and Controls Workplaces Abroad*, 21 Stan. L. & Pol'y Rev. 527 (2010), *available at* http://papers.ssrn.com/sol3/papers.cfm?abstract_id=1645248 (last visited Sept. 23, 2010).

58 Reprinted with permission by Katherine V. W. Stone, *A New Labor Law for a New World of Work: The Case for a Comparative-Transnational Approach*, 28 Comp. Lab. & Pol'y J. 565 (2007). Copyright © Katherine V. W. Stone.

be useful to fill in gaps in national legal systems of regulation – to provide a source of inspiration and information about alternative regimes when one's domestic regime is deemed to be incomplete or unsatisfactory. The gap-filling use of comparative labor law, like the museum use, emphasizes differences between the domestic regime and the comparative "other." A third, more anthropological approach to comparative labor law seeks to identify and to understand legal differences as one instance of other structural differences that both reflect and constitute the observed differences between nations in their histories and their practices.

Each of the three approaches described involve approaching comparative law as a study in differences. An alternative approach is to study comparative labor law in order to understand not differences but similarities. In this vein, some hope that by identifying similar patterns and homologous legal institutions, they might be able to identify a universal approach to labor regulation and develop a meta-theory of labor regulation.

There is also an intensely practical reason to study comparative labor law. In our increasingly globalized world, cross-border knowledge is increasingly necessary for labor lawyers, corporate lawyers, and others who deal with employment issues in more than one country. It is becoming important for international lawyers to have some knowledge of comparative labor law in order to practice across national borders.

. . . .

QUESTIONS

1. Discuss whether there is "international labor and employment law." Explain why or why not?
2. How, if at all, does the "race to the bottom" affect the internationalization of labor and employment law?
3. Do you agree with Professor Arthurs that extraterritorial effects of foreign labor law have an effect on the local labor laws and practice? Why or why not?

---

b. Global "Common Law"?

As labor and employment law is becoming globalized, there also is an argument that global "common law" is developing. It is suggested that it arises from "precedents" under applications, interpretations, and adjudications of international protocols and rules of global institutions such as WBO, WHO, etc., and that may be viewed as "guiding" or "binding." Perhaps this can be roughly analogized to "customary" law?

These nongovernmental institutional decisions, if not acting as international "precedent" among nations, at least on a domestic level may be binding on a national level and thereby on a local level. For example, a state in the United States may be precluded from acting inconsistently with an obligation found to exist under

WTO adjudications at the national level. This global "common law," to the extent it may exist, can be observed most readily in certain sectors (e.g., health and trade). A question remains whether this may also occur in the area of labor and employment.

Globalization and the Law: Emerging "Global Common Law"[59]

Ronald C. Brown

Global Challenges to Public Institutions and Emerging Local Legal Responses

. . . .

This chapter examines the legal aspects of the individual and multiple impacts of globalization and the responses of national and global institutions, which often come in the form of legal regulations and consequent legal interpretations. Also discussed is how at times global influences bring legal changes, as if there were a "global common law" – both creating legal obligations and, at other times, restricting these local legal changes.

Though international trade, investment, travel, and cultural exchanges have been ongoing for centuries, in recent times, cross-border contacts, dependency, and impacts increasingly occur without choice and with greater intensity. While globalization itself is a neutral term, it quickly acquires connotations in the areas of health, safety, welfare, economics, and politics. The impacts and ripple effects of such phenomena as failing financial markets, SARS, anti-terrorism, music, or the Internet reverberate across the globe, regardless of borders, and local public institutions must grapple with finding appropriate responses.

. . . .

International organizations like the WHO and WTO have widespread effects on creating comparable and compatible responses by governments on agenda items of global concern with local impacts. A clear illustration occurred in 2003 with SARS in East Asia and how governments dealt with it and with the WHO, illustrating the power of global influences on local public institutions, at least regarding certain issues. China was initially prepared to "go it alone," protect its national interests, and deal with SARS in its own way." It quickly became apparent that global cooperation and some integration with "outside" bodies were required to meaningfully deal with the health threat. Public institutions were rapidly transformed and plugged into WHO standards and personnel. China's penchant for nondisclosure was replaced by transparency of its public institutions and practices in dealing with SARS. Government policies and new legislation were quickly put into place to curb the threat.

Joining the WTO is another example illustrating the generation of domestic reforms pursuant to global influences – a case in point, Chinese laws, public institutions, and past practices were all locally reformed in order to meet the mandatory standards of the global organization. Interestingly, by joining the WTO, members submit to a "mini supreme

[59] Ronald C. Brown, *Globalization and the Law: Emerging "Global Common Law,"* in FAIRNESS, GLOBALIZATION, AND PUBLIC INSTITUTIONS: EAST ASIA AND BEYOND ch. 12, at 145 (Jim Dator et al. eds., [hereinafter Brown].

court" to resolve international trade disputes. Such resolutions have required states to change protective laws to keep the nation in compliance with WTO requirements. Thus global responses are made to be compatible with global requirements.

. . . .

Another method of global influence alluded to earlier, is the carrot-and stick approach of certain funding entities, such as the World Bank or IMF that require agreement to bring about reforms in order to receive financial assistance in those projects. While it certainly is a joint project, with domestic needs being met, one can hardly miss the global influence and the local response.

. . . .

What they have in common is that by consent or by economic or social reality (as described below), sovereign decisions are affected or transcended by a "beyond-national-decision interpretation" of an obligation. This results in "global common law" – for example, under the WTO, which may either create or restrict local legal decision-making authority, not only for the nation member under the global institution's dispute-resolving mechanism, but also for the other members who will be guided by that outcome in ordering their own affairs. That is because they know that they, too, could have their decisions brought in that venue.

. . . .

In a long line of decisions in the United States, federal courts have protected the integrity of the federal government in managing the nation's foreign relations vis-à-vis states' attempts to affect it by striking down state legislation that placed risks to the United States' performance of its international obligations. A recent illustration of this was found in 2000 in *National Trade Council v. Natsios*, where the U.S. Supreme Court struck down a Massachusetts law restricting state purchases from companies doing business in Burma (Myanmar). The law had provoked protests from other countries that subsequently challenged the measure under the WTO as being inconsistent with the U.S. government's international obligations under the WTO Agreement on Government Procurement. Thus one can see the interplay among state, national, and global law wherein the national law preempted the state law, due to the national law's requirement to follow the global law. This type of "precedent" is thereafter used as a type of global common law not only by the United States, but also by other countries.

. . . .

The WTO does not invalidate national legislation. Instead, after a series of procedures permitting member retaliation, it provides that follow-up legal issues of how to deal with the offending national legislation be left for the sovereign judgment of the violating nation.

Another field falling under global common law is human rights. An interesting case developed in Tasmania where, due to international pressures from an international organization – the UN Human Rights Commission (UNHRC), under the International Covenant on Civil and Political Rights (ICCPR) – the Tasmanian state government repealed laws that outlawed homosexual acts between consenting adults. In that case, an NGO filed before the UNHRC claiming that Tasmanian law violated Australia's obligations under the ICCPR to respect privacy and equality rights. . . .

Interesting corollary legal issues involve the potential precedential value of global common-law decisions by global legal institutions. Common-law countries with a common-law legal tradition, such as the United Kingdom and the United States, are experienced with the practice of *stare decisis*, whereby once a decision is rendered it is a binding precedent in future similar situations. By contrast, a larger number of countries fall under the civil law legal tradition that historically does not follow that practice of *stare decisis*. Therefore, the "legal reflexes" of countries may vary on how to deal with certain of the global common-law decisions.

Global common law, while certainly very significant in its influence and impact on local decision making by public institutions, is still only piecemeal and limited to certain areas, such as commercial and human rights. While these areas may develop the common-law patterns of decisions toward universal standards of global law (or "customs" of international law), other large areas of a nation's political and cultural identity may or may not succumb to global pressures. Diversity and legal pluralism will continue within nations and any growth toward universality will come not just from the legal compulsion and influence of global common law, but also from social, economic, and cultural global influences or by consent to global norms, based on self-interest. Global common law may well be the beacon that lays out a practical pathway on which to proceed.

Whether global common law will manifest itself in the field of global labor and employment law remains to be seen. Certainly, ILO standards or UN Covenants or interpretations under them could become a common-law "precedent" or "customary" international law, but at this point it is largely a moral obligation without precedential or legal enforcement until ratification or national implementation.

. . . .

---

c. East Asian Harmonization: Regionalization or "Asianization"?

Harmonization of labor and employment laws at a political and regional level is perhaps best illustrated by legal developments in the European Union (EU) where national labor laws aim to harmonize with EU Directives.[60] Regional labor rights

[60] *See* Stephen Hardy & Mark Butler, "European Employment Laws: a Comparative Guide," (2007); European Commission, *EU strategy to promote core labor standards* (July 18, 2001), http://www.eu-un.europa.eu/articles/en/article_33_en.htm (last visited Sept. 23, 2010). For the EU's evolution in developing its labor standards, see Pharis J. Harvey et al., *Developing Effective Mechanisms for Implementing Labor Rights in the Global Economy* (May 10, 2000), *available at* http://www.laborrights.org/files/developing_mechanisms.pdf (last visited Oct. 3, 2010) [hereinafter Harvey]. The *Community Charter of Basic Social Rights for Workers* covers these subjects: the right to freedom of movement; employment and remuneration; the improvement of living and working conditions; the right to social protection; the right to freedom of association and collective bargaining; the right to vocational training; the right of men and women to equal treatment; the right to information, consultation and participation; the right to health and safety in the workplace; the protection of children and adolescents in employment; the protection of elderly persons; protection; of persons with disabilities. In the EU system, "Directives" proposed by the European Commission and adopted by the Council of Ministers require member countries to conform their laws to a European standard. On labor rights, the EU has adopted several Directives on such matters as health and safety, equal treatment of men and women, and consultation with workers. A recent Works Council Directive requires European

regimes are starting to fashion a stronger link between labor rights and trade. The European Union (EU) and the North American Free Trade Agreement (NAFTA) have created institutions and mechanisms to treat issues of workers' rights in connection with economic integration. Regionalization, begun by economic integration, can also be initiated by organizations of communities, for example under APEC or free-trade agreements, like NAFTA, with the development of common legal rules and practices within that community.[61] Can this type of regionalization occur within East Asia and result in the "*Asianization*" of its national labor laws?[62] If so, will it come by government direction or by the global influences bringing a convergence of labor standards? Although most think such an "Asianization" is not likely, there have been some identifiable activities relating to labor issues in the Asia Pacific Economic Cooperation (APEC) meetings, and a suggestion for using South Korea as a hub, as discussed later.

Historical perspectives are useful in understanding common contemporary legal developments in East Asia. Although political integration is not likely, it is useful to analyze the factors and the impacts of globalization of the law in East Asia and to pay some attention to whether the similarities or dissimilarities of legal developments predominate. Is there increasing confluence and uniformity or will existing diversity and legal pluralism continue; and what is the implication, if any, for the possible "Asianization" of labor laws in this region? If it does occur, what is the implication, if any, in the resulting laws and their administration; will it have a discernable "East Asian twist"?

In addition to the influences of global laws and standards acceded to by the EA countries (and additional bilateral and multilateral treaties), there are other aspects of law and legal culture that can be described to address the issue of the extent to which there may be a harmonization of the legal systems.[63] Although Japan, China,

companies – defined as firms with 1,000 or more employees in two or more countries – to consult annually with worker representatives on future employment plans. *Id.*

61 Trade agreements linking labor standards are discussed under II. A. 2. *See* Greg J. Bamber, *How is the Asia-Pacific Economic Cooperation (APEC) Forum Developing? Comparative Comments on APEC and Employment Relations*, 26 COMP. LAB. L. & POL'Y J 423 (2005) [hereinafter Bamber]. "Unlike the EU and the North American Free Trade Agreement (NAFTA), APEC is not a trade bloc, but it includes other trade blocs including: 1. the Association of South East Asian Nations +3 (ASEAN's ten members plus China, Japan, and South Korea); 2. NAFTA (Canada, Mexico, and the United States); 3. Australia and New Zealand, which have a long-standing Closer Economic Relations (CER) Free Trade Agreement (FTA). APEC is a loosely coupled economic community, but it is the largest of its type in the world." *Id.*

62 *See generally* Yoichi Funabashi, *The Asianization of Asia*, FOREIGN AFF., Nov.–Dec. 1993, at 75. For an argument that even ILO labor standards imposed in a free-trade agreement do not create or impose harmonized labor standards on the countries, see Lewis Karesh, *U.S. Free Trade Agreements and Labor Rights* (Feb. 2006), *available at* http://www.crnm.org/index.php?option=com_docman&task=doc_download&Itemid=113&gid=445 (last visited Sept. 23, 2010).

63 Ronald C. Brown, *Harmonizing Domestic Labor Law Reforms with Global Labor Law Standards*, *in* INTERNATIONAL ECONOMIC LAW AND CHINA IN ITS ECONOMIC TRANSITION, ch. 10, at 61 (Huiping Chen, ed., 2007).

and South Korea are in different economic positions, they share a common legal culture of being in the "Western legal family," utilizing civil law traditions brought in from Europe and adapted to local use. From that base flows a somewhat common historic use of codes and the roles of lawyers, judges, and prosecutors that now constitute the contemporary legal systems of each, although to be sure, each with its own national characteristics.

Likewise, there is a common bed of reference to Confucian doctrines, creating a certain expectation of order, morality, and law in society and within legal regimes, underpinning or explaining current legal approaches. Also, there are "sociological explanations" of *group interests* over individual interests and *conflict-avoidance* methods being preferred over confrontational means that can be identified and seen to be reflected in laws and legal processes in each East Asian country. However, even those generalizations prove to be more useful as historic insights, as for example in China, the use of mediation is being surpassed by litigation, although mediation remains a part of litigation. While legal education in East Asia had been somewhat similar, in the fall of 2003, Japan began transforming its legal education system to look more like that of the United States. Lastly, with common historic ties, there is also ample evidence of East Asian scholars paying attention to each other's jurisprudence and scholarship.[64]

These common legal threads, when put to the test of practical application, also reflect on the issue of whether there is "Asianization" of law. For some time, there has been an ongoing debate on whether *rule of law* and *human rights* issues should be based and analyzed on *Asian values* rather than Western or American values.[65] That debate continues with no clear consensus. One could also compare substantive areas of law to look for similarities; for example, labor laws. History reveals Japan has a General MacArthur-issued American-style labor law, placed on Japan after World War II, which of course operates totally differently than its U.S. counterpart. China's labor and employment laws, while permitting collective negotiations, have a much different approach than either Japan or South Korea on the role of labor unions in that process. Likewise, since the 1980s, South Korea has been experiencing ongoing changes and reforms in its labor and employment laws, along with the changing political environment.

Therefore, while one can describe commonalities, confluence, and similar approaches under the law, there remains no clear uniform regional path being followed by China, Japan, and South Korea that is separate from global paths. Absent this bed of common regional law or legal approach to nontrade issues, it can be concluded that law would not be the factor to lead toward "unification" or "Asianization." Given the gulf of differences among the East Asian states in terms of economies,

64 Chongko Choi, EAST ASIAN JURISPRUDENCE (2009)

65 William Theodore De Bary, ASIAN VALUES AND HUMAN RIGHTS: A CONFUCIAN COMMUNITARIAN PERSPECTIVE (1998).

culture, and politics, the more accurate observation of the future direction of global laws in East Asia is that they likely will be developing under global law or global common law[66] as opposed to regional or East Asia-specific, "harmonized" law.

Therefore, the ultimate mosaic of global law has patches of global diversity with increasing patches of global, not East Asian, uniformity. So the ultimate face of labor law in East Asia likely will not be an Asian face, but rather a world composite, arising from international obligations and standards.

There is continuing interest in East Asia in coordinating intraregional trade, with its special preferences and benefits, and with its concomitant effects on labor laws and HRM practices. Such interest is illustrated by the activities of the Asia Pacific Economic Cooperation (APEC), discussed below. With APEC including so many countries, what about the Asianization of the discrete area of human resources in East Asia? Can harmonization of trade and labor laws occur at a significant level in this regional area through economic integration or regional cooperation?

APEC[67]

Workers in the Global Economy[68]

Pharis J. Harvey, Terry Collingsworth, and Bama Athreya

Concrete steps have been taken to discuss integration of the economies of Asia through a loose association called Asia Pacific Economic Cooperation (APEC). Despite the lack of any binding agreements on integration and the early stage of the discussions, trade unions and NGOs have used the APEC forums to gather to express solidarity, and to make clear at a very early stage of the discussions that any economic integration must include

66 Brown, *supra*, note 59.

67 Asia-Pacific Economic Cooperation (APEC), *About APEC*, http://www.apec.org/en/About-Us/About-APEC.aspx (last visited May 31, 2011). APEC was established in 1989 to further enhance economic growth and prosperity for the region and to strengthen the Asia-Pacific community. Asia-Pacific Economic Cooperation, or APEC, is the premier forum for facilitating economic growth, cooperation, trade, and investment in the Asia-Pacific region. APEC is the only intergovernmental grouping in the world operating on the basis of nonbinding commitments, open dialogue, and equal respect for the views of all participants. Unlike the WTO or other multilateral trade bodies, APEC has no treaty obligations required of its participants. Decisions made within APEC are reached by consensus and commitments are undertaken on a voluntary basis. APEC has twenty-one members – referred to as "Member Economies" – which account for approximately 40.5% of the world's population, approximately 54.2% of world GDP, and about 43.7% of world trade. APEC's twenty-one Member Economies are Australia; Brunei Darussalam; Canada; Chile; People's Republic of China; Hong Kong, China; Indonesia; Japan; Republic of Korea; Malaysia; Mexico; New Zealand; Papua New Guinea; Peru; The Republic of the Philippines; The Russian Federation; Singapore; Chinese Taipei; Thailand; United States of America; Viet Nam. For discussion of strengths and obstacles to harmonization of the NEA countries, see Tsuneo Akaha, *Asia-Pacific Regionalism and Northeast Asia Subregionalism*, 27 GLOBAL ECON. REV. 20 (1998).

68 Pharis J. Harvey et al., *Developing Effective Mechanisms for Implementing Labor Rights in the Global Economy* (May 10, 2000), *available at* http://www.laborrights.org/files/developing_mechanisms.pdf (last visited Oct. 3, 2010).

provisions to protect workers and the environment. Following the Manila People's Forum in November, 1996, those assembled issued a Plan of Action that included a demand to the governments of APEC countries to honor their existing international commitments, including ILO Conventions ratified, and to "respect, enforce and improve national laws protecting human and labor rights, and where these laws do not meet international standards, to amend them and bring them into compliance." Addressing a particular concern in Asia, the Plan requires that "informal sector workers, migrants, farm workers and free trade zone workers must be included within labor laws and governments must inform migrant workers of their legal rights." The challenges of integrating the extremely diverse economies and cultures of the Pacific basin are enormous. The APEC process must also be viewed as a crucial challenge for advocates for social justice to use the lever of trade to improve labor rights enforcement in countries of Asia that represent some of the most repressive regimes in the global economy.

. . . .

How is the Asia-Pacific Economic Cooperation (APEC) Forum Developing? Comparative Comments on APEC and Employment Relations[69]

Greg J. Bamber

. . . .

VII. Conclusions

The discussion has not focused narrowly on labor law and HR, but has touched on wider political and economic factors. APEC was launched in the period of international realignment after "the cold war." To an extent this echoes the predecessors to the EU having been launched in the period of reconstruction after World War II as a "common market." The EU has developed from such beginnings to influence labor markets, not least by including a "social chapter." Could APEC develop to become a form of an Asia-Pacific Union, with some parallels with the EU? This is conceivable; however, there are at least four hurdles to such a development.

First, APEC covers a much larger terrain and includes more diversity than the EU, for instance, in terms of geography, culture, religions, races, income levels, industry structure, systems of political economy, and stages of economic development. This article mentioned that APEC includes at least four distinct clusters of economies that are at different stages of economic development in terms of their contrasting levels of GDP per capita, for example. It also mentioned four different categories in terms of their development strategies and political economy.

Second, despite the increasing role of China, which has a Communist government, there is usually a greater propensity for there to be right-of-center governments in many of the other Asia-Pacific economies than in Europe. Social-Democratic/Labor politicians and unions have driven the EU's social chapter. As a generalization, moreover, unions

[69] Greg J. Bamber, *How is the Asia-Pacific Economic Cooperation (APEC) Forum Developing? Comparative Comments on APEC and Employment Relations*, 26 Comp. Lab. L. & Pol'y J 423 (2005) [Footnotes omitted].

are weaker and more fragmented in APEC than they are in the EU. For example, in two of APEC's most highly populated members, neither the All China Federation of Trade Unions (ACFTU), nor the Indonesian Trade Union Congress (ITUC) is affiliated to the ICFTU. Although the ICFTU invites such confederations to participate in some APLN activities, unions in APEC economies are not well positioned to press for the inclusion of an EU-style social chapter in APEC. Concerted union action is constrained by a legacy of cold war divisions between union confederations in the Asia-Pacific region, especially between the ICFTU and the ACFTU. Also, there is great variation in the strength of unions in the various APEC economies.

Third, employers' interests have strong influences on most governments of APEC members and such interests generally do not agree that APEC or other international, intergovernmental groups should focus on the contested terrain of employment relations. Employers' interests usually prefer that such matters should be covered by managerial prerogatives if practicable. Employers' interests oppose any notion that APEC might follow the EU's lead in fostering a social chapter. Therefore, an EU-style Asia-Pacific Union would confront even greater obstacles than the EU social chapter. Hence the notion of Asia-Pacific community remains more of an aspiration than a reality. Nonetheless, it seems likely that APEC will continue to develop more influences in labor markets, although such influences will be constrained by prevailing attitudes, ideologies, and political-economy realities.

Fourth, before APEC can make decisions it has to reach unanimity, which is very difficult to achieve among such a diverse group of economies. In the EU there is less diversity and there is scope for making some decisions by majority voting.

In spite of the different forms of attempt by the APLN and ABAC pressure groups to persuade APEC to play a larger role in promoting social or trade agendas, for the foreseeable future APEC will continue to play a much more modest role than the EU. There are no signs that APEC itself is inducing any convergence in terms of patterns of employment relations.

. . . .

Human Resources Development Working Group (HRDWG)[70]

APEC's Labor and Social Protection Network

In 1990, APEC established the Human Resources Development Working Group (HRDWG) to coordinate and implement programs in education, labour, and capacity-building. The HRDWG is focused on narrowing the skills gap and preparing individuals for the knowledge-based economy. It identified eight medium-term priorities in the areas of basic education; labour market; training for executives and SMEs; lifelong

[70] Maria Teresa Garcia & Emmanuel C. Lallana, *Asia-Pacific Economic Cooperation*, *in* Digital Review of Asia Pacific 2009–2010 (Shahid Akhtar & Patricia Arinto eds., 2010), *available at* http://www.idrc.ca/openebooks/456-7/ (last visited May 31, 2011); APEC, *Telecommunications and Information*, http://www.apec.org/en/Groups/SOM-Steering-Committee-on-Economic-and-Technical-Cooperation/Working-Groups/Telecommunications-and-Information.aspx (last visited on May 31, 2001); *Human Resources Development Working Group*, http://hrd.apec.org/index.php/Human_Resources_Development_Working_Group_%28HRDWG%29 (last visited on May 31, 2011).

learning, skills and development; mobility; labour force and workplace; human resource development for trade; and investment liberalization and facilitation.

The HRDWG undertakes various programs through its three networks: the Education Network (1992), Labour and Social Protection Network (2000), and Capacity Building Network.... The Labour and Social Protection Network (LSPN), which first met in Brunei in May 2000, aims to foster strong and flexible labour markets and strengthen social protection, including safety nets through evidence-based interventions, collaboration, technical cooperation, and the provision of labour market social protection information and analysis to address sustainable human resource development across APEC member economies.[71]

The Labour and Social Protection Network (LSPN) is part of the APEC Human Resources Development Working Group (HRDWG).[72] The objectives of LSPN are as follows:

The purpose of the Labour and Social Protection Network is to foster strong and flexible labour markets and strengthen social protection including social safety nets through evidence-based interventions, collaboration, technical co-operation and the provision of labour market and social protection information and analysis to address sustainable human resource development across APEC member economies.

Specifically LSPN will focus on issues and support activities in the following areas:

- Fostering economic development to enhance growth and employment creation and alleviate poverty through effective labour market policies, including such measures as enhancing productivity, labour force participation, and skills development;
- Maximizing the opportunities afforded by globalisation through the development of improved workplace conditions and practices through the adoption of new technologies, effective labour-management relations, improved workplace health and safety practices and labour market adjustment measures to assist workers affected by globalisation; and
- Building capacity to strengthen social protection in APEC member economies through an appropriate combination of active and passive labour market measures, empowering individuals and mitigating dependence through the dissemination and information exchange of effective practices for better social safety net delivery.

[71] *Human Resources Development Working Group*, *id.*

[72] Reprinted with permission by APEC. Labour and Social Protection Network (LSPN), APEC Human Resources Development Working Group, http://hrd.apec.org/index.php/Labour_and_Social_Protection_Network_%28LSPN%29 (last visited Apr. 30, 2011). Potential insight into possible agendas by APEC is suggested in a February 2010 joint meeting with HRDWG, the Economic Committee Chair suggested five potential questions, which could be explored from the HRDWG's viewpoint:

- What are the effects of individual incentives on job/skill improvement?
- With good safety nets, what are the needs for secure employment?
- What is the best way to regulate heavily subsidized sectors?
- How should governments intervene in unregulated sectors (e.g., Japanese preparatory schools); and,
- What are the best ways to minimize excessive precautionary savings?

Summary Report, Human Resources Development Working Group: Human Resources Development Ministerial Meeting Planning Session (Feb. 24–28, 2010), *available at* http://aimp.apec.org/Documents/2010/HRDWG/HRDWG1/10_hrdwg1_summary.doc (last visited May 31, 2011).

Innovative Strategies for Sustainable Human Resource and Economic Development

To meet the demands of the new global economy and promote sustainable growth, APEC economies are developing a variety of innovative human resource development strategies and are incorporating these strategies into broader economic development schemes.

Other approaches to economic development that APEC economies are exploring include innovative strategies for supporting entrepreneurial development and building collaborative public-private partnerships, both of which promote job creation, economic growth, and sustainable economic prosperity.

. . . .

Labour Issues in APEC[73]

Tim Harcourt

1. Introduction – What Are the Key Issues?

1.1 The APEC Process: One of the main challenges facing governments, businesses, and the community in the 1990s has been the integration of the fast-growing economies of the Asia Pacific region. This has been highlighted formally by the recent summits of the national political leaders of the region under the Asia Pacific Economic Cooperation (APEC) banner. Whilst the APEC summits have been considered important (and indeed prestigious) diplomatic events in recent international affairs, the analysis of the economic and social effects of APEC is still in its infancy. All groups in society that have an interest in the APEC process are attempting to understand the implications of economic integration and what APEC can or should do for national economies.

Whilst APEC summits have concentrated on trade liberalisation (including the implementation of the Bogor Declaration) and investment issues, there has been to date no discussion of labour issues or income distribution questions. Labour movements around the region have not been widely involved (and in most cases not invited) to the APEC Leaders' Summits, Ministerial Meetings, Senior Officials Meetings, Economic Committee, Committee on Trade and Investment, Working Groups etc. To date non-government organisations (NGOs) and community groups also have had little involvement. However, it is clear that the APEC leaders are keen to have business input through the APEC Business Advisory Council (ABAC), which continues the work of the APEC Pacific Business Forum (PBF).

The International Confederation of Free Trade Unions (ICFTU) – the international trade union confederation to which the ACTU is affiliated – has taken steps to have a labour-type forum initiated along the same lines as business groups at APEC.[74] A labour

[73] Tim Harcourt, *Labour Issues in APEC*, Australian APEC Study Centre Issues Paper 9, *available at* http://www.apec.org.au/docs/iss9.htm (last visited Sept. 23, 2010).

[74] "In a meeting today [September 3, 2010] with a delegation of the ITUC Asia Pacific Labour Network (APLN), Japanese Prime Minister Naoto Kan stated that he would make his best efforts to achieve agreement on establishing a Labor Forum to enable trade union representation in the Asia Pacific Economic Cooperation (APEC) forum. The Japanese Prime Minister said that in his capacity as host of the

delegation from APEC countries, for example, met the Japanese Prime Minister at the 1995 Leaders' meeting and the Philippines President at the 1996 meeting. However, whilst the host leaders met the delegations on each occasion, there was no plan to issue formal invitations to labour or community groups to future APEC Leaders' meetings. Labour and NGO groups were more like "gate-crashers" than formal invitees at the Osaka and Subic Bay summits.

1.2 What Will APEC Do? Whilst there has been some debate about what form APEC may take (i.e., whether it be an Organisation for Economic Co-operation and Development (OECD) for the Asia Pacific region, or a trade liberalisation -type organisation like the World Trade Organisation (WTO) for the region), there has been little analysis of the economic and social impact of APEC. Some of the views from all quarters – business, union, government, communities – have been positive and upbeat, whilst others have been negative and suspicious of APEC (in the same vein as the scepticism generated about the GATT, WTO, UN, and other international organisations).

The positive views of APEC include several a priori assumptions that:

- the integration of the world's most influential economies must be a positive thing in terms of economic growth, employment, wealth and living standards for the citizens of APEC economies;
- the APEC process will assist the already considerable economic dynamism of the region;
- integration of trade and investment in APEC will assist economic development and enable APEC economies to provide a more equitable distribution of income, particularly in the poorer APEC economies.

On the other hand, there have also been some negative views of the APEC agenda. These consist of the following assumptions:

- that economic integration will lead to a 'race to the bottom' in terms of environmental standards in all APEC economies;
- that economic integration will lead to a 'race to the bottom' in terms of social policies, labour standards and human rights in all APEC economies;
- that APEC will do nothing to improve income distribution and associated social and political stability in APEC economies, particularly in the poorer countries;
- that APEC gives capital major advantages, but gives labour and the community no advantages or any means of defending its hard won gains.

APEC Leaders' Meeting in Yokohama, Japan, on November 13–14, he would approach other governments to achieve their support for a Labor Forum, and would work to ensure decent work was promoted throughout the APEC region." ITUC, *Japanese Prime Minister Backs Call for APEC Labour Forum* (Sept. 7, 2010), http://www.goiam.org/index.php/headquarters/departments/trade-and-globalization/ituc-online/7797-ituc-online-september-3-2010. *See Beating the crisis involving working people and realising decent work Statement of the ITUC ASIA Pacific Labour Network (Nov. 13–14, 2010), available at* http://www.ituc-csi.org/IMG/pdf/Microsoft_Word_-_Final_APLN_statement_2010-20100903124545.pdf (last visited Sept. 23, 2010).

It is important, however, that certain aspects of the APEC process be analysed rigorously rather than relying on a priori views that are either positive or negative.

1.3 Labour's Role in APEC. In terms of labour's role in APEC, the Asia Pacific labour movement has several issues to focus on.

First, it is important to understand APEC and how it will affect workers' employment opportunities, job security, wages, incomes, labour standards, health and safety, etc. Analysis of trade and wages has played an important role in economic literature (see section 3). But APEC is not just about trade, it is also about investment flows, customs procedures, standards and conformance, government procurements, rules of origin, intellectual property, etc. These issues also have potential labour implications.

Secondly, it is important to make a decision about labour's role in the APEC process. For example, do international union bodies become involved in the process formally or do national union centres simply lobby their own national Governments in the lead up to APEC summits? Do individual unions involve their resources in the formulation of individual action plans (IAPs), for example? Do unions negotiate with employers on industry lines based on product market considerations or do they negotiate on a cross-industry collective basis?

There is also a question of how best to use the union movements' scarce resources (relative to those of business and government) by focusing on key parts of the APEC process. For example, the Human Resource Development Working Group would be an appropriate part of the APEC process for union contributions. How APEC economies can improve productivity through investment in human capital by education and training is a key issue in economic development and growth. Unions typically have a good grasp of skills and training issues and could make an important contribution to skill and human resource development.

Thirdly, there is the much more complicated question of social integration in APEC to accompany economic integration. What is the best means of improving living standards in APEC economies? What are the mechanisms by which freer trade and investment lead to improved real wages and living standards for workers and their families? There is also the related question of how global economies have become. If business considers the economy to be 'global' and capital mobile then surely labour issues will take on a more 'global' perspective too. How do we integrate different national labour systems at the same time as capital becomes more mobile and integrated and competition policy becomes international? If we really are serious about having integrated economies, our approaches to workplace issues must also be included in the discussion. Integration should be harnessed to improved living standards and social considerations as well as improving business opportunities and economic expansion.

Fourthly, the labour movement should be aware of the human development/social development aspect of the APEC agenda. The "APEC Economic Leaders' Declaration from Vision to Action" (The Subic Declaration) developed at the 1996 summit in the Philippines recognised that liberalised trade should contribute "... to sustainable growth and equitable development and to a reduction in economic disparities" (Leaders' declaration, point 15). The declaration also recognised that the principles for economic and technical co-operation should be "giving a human face to development" (point 16). The social agenda of APEC includes labour-related issues such as human resource development as well as questions of income distribution and community development. The question is how the labour movement can position itself on the social agenda of the APEC process.

. . . .

Whether and how APEC deals with economic integration or coordination issues could provide the basis upon which labor relations may or may not move toward integration or harmonization.

How these developments of regionalization in East Asia may affect particular labor issues and employment relations from a Korean perspective is discussed next.[75]

Northeast Asia and the Trends of the 21st Century: An Essay on the Northeast Asian Economic Community[76]

Jung-Dong Park

In corresponding to present trends, it is necessary to organize an EU-like community in Asia, especially in the Northeast Asia. The Northeast Asian countries, including Korea, China, Japan, Taiwan, and so on, have similar history, culture, and ethnic background, and therefore, it is easy to carry out cooperative work. With a well- developed transportation and production capacity like what we have right now, not only would each country's territory seem too narrow but an economic integration which is suitable for a broader territory would be accomplished. Further, it will lead to the cultural integration of races within the consolidated area and, eventually, enable a development toward political integration.

. . . .

V. In Place of Conclusion: The Northeast Asian Economic Community and Win-Win Game

In the 21st century, a formation of a national union that is larger than a nation but smaller than the world will be accelerated. The EU, which has undergone the infancy period and is now in adolescence, currently, exists and such trend will continue to speed up with the development of transportation and communication technology. At the same time, the UN will be reorganized, according to unions such as EU and AU (Asian Union), rather than each country as a separate unit.

. . . .

---

75 Bamber, *supra* note 69, at 442–44.

76 Jung-Dong Park, *Northeast Asia and the Trends of the 21st Century: An Essay on the Northeast Asian Economic Community*, *available at* http://www.esri.go.jp/jp/workshop/021118/021118paper2.pdf (last visited Oct. 3, 2010).

Hub of Northeast Asia[77]

Kim Mi-hui

International economic reports today are peppered with acronyms such as EU, NAFTA, MERCOSUR, and ASEAN. This is because these regional blocs standing for the European Union, North America Free Trade Agreement, Mercado Comun del Cono Sur (Southern Cone Common Market), and Association of Southeast Asian Nations, respectively, are the powers in international business, responsible for 43 percent of total global trade volume.

By contrast, Northeastern Asian countries – Korea, China, and Japan – have no such relationship, resulting in a lower global and intraregional trade volume. According to the Korea Institute for International Economic Policy (KIEP), for example, the share of intraregional trade among the three markets was 18.7 percent in 1997, far lower than the EU's 59.7 percent, NAFTA's 43.5 percent, and APEC's 71.1 percent.

But it is time that the three countries consider collaborating strategically to defend themselves against such economic giants, experts around the world say. These critics particularly suggest that the three nations pursue an industrial collaboration plan where they divide labor according to each market's special characteristics and strengths as a way of boosting national and regional competitiveness.

"Each of the three markets has distinctive business characteristics and if they collaborate in such a way that makes the most of the individual strengths, this could boost their trade, restructure their industries in a more competitive way, and position them as the newest regional economic power," Cheong In-kyo, senior research fellow at KIEP, writes in his book on free trade agreements (FTAs).

. . . .

QUESTIONS

1. It has been said that "NEA [East Asia] is a geographic referent rather than a political, much less a cultural community." Does that exclude an "economic" community? Can Asia develop as did the EU into an entity with harmonized labor and employment laws? Explain differences and similarities.
2. If East Asian labor and employment laws were harmonized, what would be the effect on an individual country's competitive and comparative advantages?
3. Whether or not there is Asianization or confluence of labor laws in the region, how might the agenda for HRM set by APEC affect the region?
4. If harmonization occurred, how would the industrial relations system in the APEC countries be affected (e.g., for collective bargaining)? Would it converge to a common model or diversify according to national standards?
5. What would Japan and China think about having South Korea as the "hub"?

[77] Kim Mi-hui, *Hub of Northeast Asia*, Korea Now, Dec. 28, 2002, at 20–21.

d. Are Labor Rights Human Rights?

In looking at UN Covenants, one can see apparent overlaps in some areas between human rights and labor rights, with much having been written on the subject.[78] Ongoing debate continues and the parties contesting it often reflect their countries' stage of economic development.[79] What the significance may be of being either is presented next with discussions often centering on whether rights in the workplace are economic or human rights. Questions persist whether labor laws do or should address human rights and whether worker rights in the workplace should be different from citizen rights in society.

Labor's Human Rights: A Review of the Nature and Status of Core Labor Rights as Human Rights[80]

Roy J. Adams

Introduction

As discussed by Donnelly and Howard (1987), human rights are "rights held by each (and every) person simply as a human being." They are, "by their nature, universal."

Although they may be suppressed or neglected, they may not be legitimately granted nor taken away by states or by nonstate actors. They are rights that, in the words of the International Court of Justice are, "obligatio erga omnes" – that is, they are owed by all to all (Paust 2002:2).

As a class of rights, labor rights have two generally understood meanings. In the broader meaning, labor rights encompass a range of worker rights covered in the International Bill of Rights, which includes the United Nations' Covenant on Economic, Cultural, and Social Rights and its Covenant on Civil and Political Rights (Hannum 1997). The narrower meaning, sometimes referred to as trade union rights, focuses attention on the rights of working people universally to a collective voice in the establishment of

[78] HUMAN RIGHTS, LABOR RIGHTS, AND INTERNATIONAL TRADE 13-95 (Lance Compa & Stephen F. Diamond, eds., 1996); Kevin Kolben, *Labor Rights as Human Rights*, 50 VA. J. INT'L L. 449 (2010); Mathias Risse, *A Right to Work? A Right to Leisure? Labor Rights as Human Rights* (July 6, 2008), *available at* http://www.hks.harvard.edu/fs/mrisse/Papers/Papers%20-%20Philosophy/LaborRightsHumanRights.pdf (last visited Oct. 3, 2010).

[79] *See, e.g.*, RICHARD P. MCINTYRE, ARE WORKER RIGHTS HUMAN RIGHTS? (2008). *See also* Hoyt N. Wheeler, *Employee Rights as Human Rights*, 28 BULL. COMP. LAB. REL. 9 (1994).

[80] Roy J. Adams, *Labor's Human Rights: A Review of the Nature and Status of Labor Rights as Core Human Rights* (Univ. of Denver Human Rights & Human Welfare Working Paper No. 36), *available at* http://www.du.edu/korbel/hrhw/workingpapers/2006/36-adams-2006.pdf (last visited June 8, 2011). *See also* HUMAN RIGHTS AT WORK: PERSPECTIVES ON LAW AND REGULATION (Colin Fenwick & Tonia Novitz eds. 2010). This collection of essays examines the issues of translating fundamental human rights as labor rights. HUMAN RIGHTS AT WORK: PERSPECTIVES ON LAW AND REGULATION, WorldCat, http://www.worldcat.org/title/human-rights-at-work-perspectives-on-law-and-regulation/oclc/501398359 (last visited June 22, 2011).

the conditions under which they work (Ewing 2000). Although advocacy of some worker rights such as the right to equal treatment at work regardless of sex, religion, or ethnic origin is shared by many human rights organizations, advocacy of the right to organize and bargain collectively has, until very recently, been left largely to labor unions (Leary 1996; Adams 2001).

Freedom of association and its manifestation in the realm of employment as the right to organize and bargain collectively preceded the establishment of the contemporary worldwide human rights regime. Human rights as a focus of global attention traces its heritage to the Universal Declaration of Human Rights, which appeared in 1948. Freedom of Association, on the other hand, was clearly recognized as a universal right in the 1944 Declaration of Philadelphia, which reaffirmed the mission and status of the International Labor Organization. Indeed, the Philadelphia Declaration is considered to have provided inspiration and guidance for the later Universal Declaration.

. . . .

Bringing About Compliance with International Human Rights Norms

The range of rights identified in the International Bill of Rights that might be considered worker rights is quite large. The five "core labor rights" identified in the International Labor Organization's 1998 Declaration of Fundamental Principles and Rights at Work as human rights are all mentioned in either or both of the Covenants making up the Bill. Those five rights are the "negative" rights to freedom from discrimination, child labor, and slavery and other forms of forced labor and the positive rights to freedom of association and the right to organize and bargain collectively. Although the last two rights are frequently combined and presented as a single right, the result produces ambiguity and conflict about their meaning and the duties of states and other actors in complying with them and thus they are enumerated here as five rights.

Additional rights that are identified in the International Bill of Rights are the right to remuneration that provides fair wages and a decent living, safe and healthy working conditions, paid holidays and reasonable working hours, the right to social security, the right of mothers to paid leave during pregnancy, and the right to strike.

Other rights that might be considered worker rights in appropriate circumstances are freedom from cruel, inhumane, or degrading treatment or punishment and freedom from being imprisoned for failing to fulfill a contractual obligation. Both of these freedoms are often offended in conjunction with forced and child labor. The right to peaceful assembly is closely associated with the right to strike. The range of labor standards, a category of entitlement less fundamental than human rights, established by the ILO is even larger (Leary 1997).

. . . .

Conclusion

At the international level, those expert in labor and human rights issues have reached a strong consensus that core labor rights are fundamental human rights on which all of the world's people should be able to rely. In addition, the human rights character of core labor rights has a strong foundation in philosophy and religious theory. Not only states but also individuals and corporations and other units of society have a moral and political responsibility to honor those rights. As a result of the activity that has been taking place over the last few decades, that consensus is being diffused into society more generally. However, there is still a long road to travel before aspiration and reality align.

. . . .

Labor Laws in the Vortex of Human Rights Protection[81]

David Ziskind

. . . .

The Universal Declaration (1948) capped a progression of prior pronouncements in which an effort was made to enshrine fundamental rights that had often been denied and that needed authoritative affirmation. England issued the Magna Charta (1215), France, the Declaration of the Rights of Man and Citizen (1789), the United States, The Bill of Rights in the 1st ten amendments to its constitution (1791). Other national constitutions followed which incorporated the older freedoms and added a list of social, economic and cultural rights. Exemplified by the Weimar Republic (1919) and Mexico (1917), this century's parade of new nations proclaimed many human rights. The first worldwide consensus upon such rights was in the United Nation's Universal Declaration of Human Rights.

This declaration has been followed by two U.N. covenants, the Covenant on Civil and Political Rights and the Covenant on Economic, Social, and Cultural Rights, which are more specific and which commit signatory countries to abide by their provisions. In a legalistic sense, these may be said to detail the acknowledged human rights. However, since there remains a great gap between the Declaration and its legal implementation, I prefer to use the Universal Declaration as the more widely recognized compendium of human rights. In considering labor laws as human rights, it seems advisable to look first at their relationship to the full panoply of rights set forth in the Universal Declaration.

The Universal Declaration is a comprehensive document. It consists of an eight paragraph preamble and thirty articles. Were one to itemize each and every right implicit in the words of the Declaration, the list would run to several hundred distinguishable rights. For simplicity of reference, the enumerated human rights have been grouped in various ways. One of the most concise groupings is composed of only three categories.

1. The right to be free from governmental violations of the integrity of the person, (torture, cruel and inhuman punishment, arbitrary arrest, denial of fair public trial, invasion of home);
2. The right to the fulfillment of vital needs (such as food, shelter, health care and education);
3. The right to enjoy civil and political liberties (speech, press, assembly, religion), to participate in government and to travel freely.

[81] David Ziskind, *Labor Laws in the Vortex of Human Rights Protection in*, CONCERNING HUMAN ASPIRATIONS: ESSAYS IN COMPARATIVE LABOR LAW ch. 2, at 6-23 (1985) [hereinafter Ziskind].

These highlight essential characteristics and serve well to give meaning to the human rights in their entirety. However, to discern the place of labor laws in the constellation of human rights, a much more detailed listing of the rights in the Universal Declaration will prove fruitful. A grouping of rights, somewhat as they have been in the Covenants – as Civil, Political, Economic, Social, and Cultural – and correlated with Duties – follows:

1. Economic Rights

All persons are entitled to:

a. No slavery or slave trade (Art. 4);
b. Right to own property alone and with others (Art. 17);
c. No arbitrary deprivation of property (Art. 17);
d. Right to social security (Art. 22);
e. Realization, in accord with State resources, of rights indispensible to dignity and free development of personality (Art. 22);
f. Right to work (Art. 23);
g. Free choice of employment (Art. 23);
h. Just and favorable conditions of work (Art. 23);
i. Protection against unemployment (Art. 23);
j. Equal pay for equal work (Art. 23);
k. Just and favorable remuneration ensuring worker and his family human dignity, supplemented if necessary by other means of social protection (Art. 23);
l. Right to form and join trade unions for protection of interests (Art. 23);
m. Rest and leisure, reasonable limitation of hours, and periodic holidays with pay (Art. 24);
n. A standard of living adequate for health and well being including food, clothing, housing, medical care, and necessary social services (Art. 25);
o. Security in the event of unemployment, sickness, disability, widowhood, old age, or other lack of livelihood beyond one's control (Art. 25);
p. Special care and assistance for motherhood and childhood (Art. 25);
q. Protection of moral and material interests of author of scientific, literary, or artistic production (Art. 27).

All of these Economic Rights have been the subject of what has traditionally been regarded as labor legislation. The interest of employees and employers and their organizations in each of these is obvious. The Declaration sets forth standards for private and government action to secure terms and conditions of work and income. These take concrete form and become legal norms through labor laws.

2. Social Rights

All persons are entitled to:

a. Rights and freedoms without distinction (Art. 1);
b. Right to marry and found a family (Art. 16);
c. Equal rights as to marriage, during marriage, and at its dissolution (Art. 16);
d. Protection of the family by society and the State (Art. 16);

e. Special care and assistance for motherhood and childhood (Art. 25);
f. Same social protection for children born in or out of wedlock (Art. 25);
g. A social and international order in which rights and freedoms can be fully realized (Art. 28);
h. Action toward one another in a spirit of brotherhood (Art. 1).

Some of the Social Rights, such as those pertaining to marriage, divorce, and the protection of illegitimate children, may have very slight relationship to labor laws; yet the assistance and support of family life have been incorporated into minimum wage laws and laws for the special protection of female and child labor. The Social Rights seeking a spirit of brotherhood and a social and international order in which rights and freedoms can be fully realized have a special pertinence, even if only a prophetic one, to the improvement of labor standards by law.

3. Cultural Rights

All persons are entitled to:

a. Freedom of thought, conscience, and religion (Art. 18);
b. Freedom to teach, practice, worship, observe or change religion or belief (Art. 18);
c. Freedom of opinion and expression (Art. 19);
d. Freedom to receive and impart information and ideas in any media and regardless of frontiers (Art. 19);
e. Peaceful assembly and association (Art. 20);
f. No compulsion to belong to an association (Art. 20);
g. Free development of personality (Art. 22);
h. Right to education (Art. 26);
i. Elementary education free and compulsory (Art. 26);
j. Technical and professional education available; higher education accessible on merit (Art. 26);
k. Education directed to the development of personality and strengthening respect for human rights; and to promote understanding, tolerance, and friendship; and maintenance of peace (Art. 26);
l. Parents' right to choose the kind of education they wish for their children (Art. 26);
m. Participate in cultural life of community, enjoy arts, and share in science (Art. 27).

The Cultural Rights mentioned in the Universal Declaration are also basic to the adoption of labor legislation. Labor laws are usually on the threshold of public debate and opinion. Without a free exchange of thought, all innovation and progress in labor laws would be stifled. Even religious thought, non-secular in character, has inspired labor movements in the advocacy of certain labor laws. Without freedom of association, power to press for such laws would be sapped. The development of one's personality has been the objective of much labor legislation. Education, even apart from vocational instruction and safety and health training, has been an essential ingredient in the process of elevating labor standards and the expectations expressed in labor laws. Participation in the cultural life of a community and the enjoyment of the arts and benefits of science has been a goal sought through labor laws.

4. Civil Rights

All persons are entitled to:

a. Freedom and equality in dignity and rights (Art. 1);
b. All rights and freedoms without distinction of any kind, such as race, color, sex, language, religion, political, or other opinion, national or social origin, property, birth, or other status (Art. 2);
c. Right to life, liberty, and security of person (Art. 3);
d. No torture, cruel, inhuman, or degrading treatment or punishment (Art. 5);
e. Recognition everywhere as a person before the law (Art. 6);
f. Equal protection of the law (Art. 7);
g. Protection against discrimination or incitement to discrimination (Art. 7);
h. Effective remedies for violation of fundamental rights (Art. 8);
i. No arbitrary arrest, detention, or exile (Art. 9);
j. Fair and public hearing of criminal charge by independent and impartial tribunal (Art. 10);
k. Presumption of innocence until proved guilty (Art. 11);
l. No ex post facto crime or penalty (Art. 11);
m. No arbitrary interference with privacy, family, home, or correspondence (Art. 12);
n. No attacks upon honor or reputation (Art. 12);
o. Freedom to move, reside, leave country, and return (Art. 13);
p. Foreign asylum from persecution (Art. 14);
q. No arbitrary denial of nationality or change (Art. 15).

The rights labeled Civil assure equality in the application of labor laws and protect labor activists from government persecution or individual abuse. Discrimination is the bane of all law enforcement; but it particularly stultifies the interpretation and the effectiveness of labor standards. The protections against arbitrary arrest, unjust criminal charges, and unfair trials are also designed for all situations, but have constant relevance to the enforcement of labor laws. Freedoms of asylum and nationality are more remotely associated with labor activities; yet freedom of movement within and across national boundaries is the subject of many labor laws. Civil rights are all encompassing and there are none which have not been crucial historically to the protection of persons engaged in activities regulated by labor law.

5. Political Rights

All persons are entitled to:

a. Right to take part in government (Art. 21);
b. Equal access to public service (Art. 21);
c. Authority through the will of the people, expressed in elections (Art. 21);
d. Universal and equal suffrage, secret vote, or equivalent procedure (Art. 21);
e. No distinction in rights or freedoms based on political, jurisdictional, international status, or limited sovereignty of one's country (Art. 2).

The rights characterized as Political are not confined to employers and employees, but they cover them as well as all other members of society. They seek to create a governmental atmosphere under which the parties to the labor relationship may function freely. They affect, directly and pervasively, the enactment and administration of labor law. The extent to which trade unions and employer associations are political varies greatly. In some industrial countries and in most of the less developed countries, trade unions operate primarily as interest groups seeking government action; and their political rights are the parameters of their effectiveness. In all countries, labor and management have special interests in the outcome of political action. Labor law flourishes or falters in proportion to the latitude permitted by a country's political rights.

6. Rights and Duties

Everyone has:

a. Duties to the Community making full development of personality possible (Art. 29);
b. Rights subject only to limitations of law for due recognition of rights of others and for morality, public order, and general welfare in democratic society (Art. 29);
c. No exercise of rights contrary to purposes and principles of the U.N. (Art. 29);
d. No right to aim at the destruction of any rights and freedoms (Art. 30).

Such duties have been implicit in the enactment of most labor laws. Economic conditions and market forces have generally exacted duties in the employment relationship. Additionally, in the legislative process, there has customarily been a balancing of the rights and obligations of employees and employers, and some consideration of the interests of society or third parties.

Labor law has occupied a central position in the exercise of human rights. This has been innately so. In a world of limited resources, differences of opinion over the division of available goods and services are unavoidable. The rewards for work are constantly being considered and rearranged. Labor laws clarify, define, and establish such arrangements. Even with the best of good will in idealized societies, and certainly in societies suffering economic stringency, the striving for human betterment through labor laws goes through a process of trial and error, with criticism, dissent and protest. In freer societies, labor laws are deliberately subjected to scrutiny and amendment, and even in highly controlled societies, labor laws are constantly being reexamined. In either situation, rising expectations upset every equilibrium. Progress in standards of labor, as expressed in labor laws, inherently and inevitably requires the protection of human rights in their broadest aspects.

. . . .

QUESTIONS

1. Discuss practical implications, if any, of an overly broad definition of labor rights that embrace human rights. Which human rights , if any, do the labor laws address?

2. Does "economic dependency" change the nature of the right as a human or labor right or is their status independent of their environment?
3. List three rights that are clearly labor rights and three that are clearly human rights.
4. Should workers have the same or fewer rights inside the workplace than as citizens?
5. Is the right to engage in a labor strike a labor right or a human right? Why, and based on what source?

e. Comparative Biases

Cultural biases come easily when dealing comparatively with foreign laws and methods of regulating labor and employment. The primary obstacles are ignorance, prejudice, and parochialism. The particular pitfalls arise in differences of language, political and ideational factors, and legal systems. For example, what is "law; what are its sources; what is local legal culture"; what are the differences between "legal rules, a legal system, and legal structures"? All should be understood to best deal with and within a foreign jurisdiction.

As one evaluates foreign labor and employment laws, there are certain guidelines that can be used to diminish biases and reach a more objective assessment. These can provide a reality check on whether the comparisons made are real and whether concepts are transferable (e.g., union's duty of fair representation). There is a human tendency to be parochial or look at the wording of the law, but not at its practical application. These concepts are explored in the following essay.

Cultural Bias in Labor Law[82]

David Ziskind

Comparison

....

That men in all cultures, throughout the ages, have claimed, "We are civilized, others are barbarians," merits serious consideration. It is not merely egotistical trumpeting. Such universality contains a touch of truth as well as the blemish of human fallibility. And the more true it is, the greater the problems it presents. For persons engaged in the comparison of labor laws, such cultural bias, whether extreme or slight, is an anomaly that calls for solution.

The term, bias, is ordinarily used in a pejorative sense, as a form of distortion, a limitation on the ability to think clearly, a blind spot in the observer, a discoloration of reality. To augment the problem, people may be unaware of their biases or may seek to

[82] *Id.*, ch. 8, at 118–33.

conceal them; and the discovery or disclosure of their biases may not be accomplished easily. In a great many instances, all these disturbing qualities are present; in other instances, however, there may be nothing wrong with a particular bias. It is a distinctive characteristic of thought, in labor law as in other social institutions. It may be merely a style or an orientation that differentiates one person or a people from others who share the same or similar form of social behavior. It may even be a conceit of personal identification with an idea or a practice; yet that conceit may be justifiable.

Bias is inherent in all thought. Thinking is a process of cumulative experience. It is embedded in neural patterns that may be modified from time to time but that remain in the cortex of the brain; and ideas and actions emerge when those past patterns are activated. Even innovative thinking utilizes and is dependent upon past accumulations of experience. That body of prior knowledge is a built-in cultural bias. The conditioning of individual experiences by social interaction tends to form similarities in bias, or many cultural biases, characteristic of the different groups in society. These take expression, as patterns, themes, or styles.

Because bias is built up out of past experience, and it is generally shared by the members of one's in-groups, there is a tendency to cling to it and to resist change, or even questioning. In that situation, labor law comparison may be of help. Comparison leads to questioning merely because differences exist and the comparative effort to define and distinguish stimulates questioning.

Bias is not necessarily a defect to be obliterated. Try as hard as any individual comparatist can to compensate for his own biases, he may still be unable to eliminate the biases of others. All too often, when he dislodges one bias, another takes its place. The comparatist does well to recognize the existence and effects of all cultural biases in the field of his study. That is indispensable to a full understanding and critical evaluation of labor laws. How that can be done in labor law comparison is the burden of this essay.

I shall offer a few suggestions as to how to identify and describe biases, and how to counteract those biases that impede the accomplishment of stated objectives. There are several promising aids to the location of bias and to the avoidance of its pitfalls. The latter, I shall discuss separately with respect to the comparatist himself and to the sources of his information.

. . . .

Biases in the Materials

Many biases protrude noticeably; many are obscure or hidden. We frequently accept those with which we are familiar, without comment. Some biases are immaterial; but before deciding that a bias does not matter for the purposes of a given study, it should be noted and assessed. To facilitate that process in the comparison of labor laws, I propose the use of several techniques or devices.

One is a check list of possible sources of bias. Areas that need to be observed and considered may be enumerated, and specific questions may be posed under each of them. I suggest the following:

1. Language. What linguistic novelties or ambiguities encountered in labor legislation, legal treatises, and court decisions require clarification?

2. Legal Systems. What attitudes and instrumentalities characteristic of legal systems impinge on the labor law under review?
3. Economic Factors. What economic factors underlie the labor problems dealt with by the laws studied?
4. Political Factors. What political influences are involved in the labor laws considered?
5. Ideational Forces. What philosophical and religious ideas pertaining to labor prevail in the countries involved?

Answers to questions such as these will probably produce recognition of most of the cultural biases relevant to labor laws.

. . . .

I shall endeavor to illustrate the importance of the above mentioned lines of inquiry with respect to specific labor laws.

Language

Every language is a cultural expression. Despite the fact that all languages convey common meanings, they are intelligible only to those who can read the language (or can have it translated), and most languages have words unique to themselves and have forms of grammar that affect meaning in idiosyncratic ways. Since the official publication of laws appears in more than 60 languages, few if any comparatists can read the legislation of all countries in their original printing. Translations are indispensable, but they are not infallible. Words in common usage and correctly translated may carry varying meanings in different countries. For instance, in certain European countries the term "civil rights" means the rights designated in a Civil Code, which may be those applicable to employer–employee relationships; whereas in the United States the term "civil rights" connotes only the freedom of speech, press, and assemblage, or rights to racial equality. The contexts and implications under which that term is used must be explained if confusing language bias is to disappear. Another example is found, even within the English language, in the British assertion that the rights of employers and unions are not contractual (although the parties have agreed upon a rule book). That concept is alien to Americans, who use the same term "contractual" to signify that an agreement has been reached between parties. Upon further explanation that the British use of the term refers to the unavailability of suit to enforce a rule book, the matter is clarified. Language bias is not apparent in certain expressions; and comparative understanding can be established only when the bias is revealed.

Greater difficulty, still not insuperable, is encountered with foreign terms for which there is no domestic equivalent. The German term "beamte" is not translatable into the English "public employee". The Spanish terms "latifundia", "colonato", and "pongueaje" and the Indian term "begar" refer to labor relations in systems of agriculture, and other countries have no such words. They require descriptions of the persons and situations to which they refer. Many countries have no words like the American "featherbedding" and "hot cargo". The concept of "filamparo" in Latin American countries is somewhat similar to, yet different from, "habeas corpus" in the United States and when the terms are applied, as they frequently are, to court relief sought by strikers arrested in labor disputes, much more explanation is required.

Words denominating social institutions and behavior, such as employment, strikes, and collective bargaining, are ordinarily clear; they point to conditions that differ among countries and become proper subjects for comparison without special difficulty. Other terms, similarly of general comprehension, such as forced labor, right to work, equal pay, full employment, and freedom of association have cultural overtones that require more careful distinction and definition. Their meanings are not only ambiguous within a single country, but they have become subjects of political criticism and controversy among nations. They involve deep, emotional biases that cannot be ignored. As difficult as it may be to attain objectivity in comparing those legal concepts and practices in competing and contentious countries, the task must be tackled.

Language is thus the embodiment of bias as well as one of the tools for explaining or overcoming it.

Legal Systems

Legal systems are forms of bias that permeate labor laws. Although there are several classifications of legal systems that are acceptable, I prefer that of Rene David, who grouped legal families of nations as Romano–Germanic, Common Law, Socialist, Muslim, Hindu, Jewish, Far East, African, and Customary. In some countries, these are coupled or intermingled, and each has variants; yet all contain identifiable biases. Each has a characteristic technique for formulating laws, a special classification of laws, and a method of reasoning in the interpretation of laws. Labor laws arise and take effect somewhat differently under these systems. Although appearing to set the same norms, a labor law under one system may be regarded as a mandate to be respected regardless of its effect; under another system, as a rule to be followed only in essence, and under another system, as a rule to be observed only to the extent that harmony is promoted thereby among all the persons affected. In one system, laws are interpreted by courts in accordance with established precedents; in another, laws are interpreted by priests, notaries, or executive officers according to their own guiding principles. Labor law comparison must not overlook these distinctions.

By way of more specific illustration, consider laws regulating strikes. A common prohibition against disturbing the peace or undermining national security assumes significant differences when in one legal system a strike leader is presumed to be innocent until proven guilty, and under another system (after an investigation and accusation by a procurator) he is presumed to be guilty until the contrary is established. Consider also the recourse of an employee wrongfully discharged. In one system he has a right to reinstatement to his former position and in another system he is limited to monetary damages. Such systemic biases exist even though legal documents do not spell out the differences.

In the Romano-Germanic system, rights and responsibilities flow from the social or occupational status of a person, whereas in the Common Law system they arise only from contracts voluntarily made (except where aspects of each system have infiltrated into the other). Labor law comparatists have noted these distinctions, but a conscious effort to answer the question, "What attitudes and instrumentalities characteristic of the legal systems impinge upon the labor laws under consideration?" would help disclose biases that cause significant differences.

Economic Factors

Labor relationships, and the laws governing them, are an essential part of the economic system; hence they are directly affected by the basic qualities of existing economic systems. This applies not only to differences between capitalist systems of private ownership and market competition and socialist systems of public ownership and controlled markets. The state of economic development in each nation, whether in the East/West, North/South, or Third World blocs, may be the most compelling influential factor. Labor laws also reflect the characteristic aspects of subsystems for agriculture, mining, manufacturing, services, and government. In labor law comparison, it is important to observe the biases in each.

For instance, hours and safety laws are customarily tied to the kind of work done in particular industries. Employment and social security laws are related to business cycles and trade balances. Labor disputes over the redistribution of income are regulated differently as the economic system stresses centralized or local control, economic planning or market competition, private enterprise or public ownership. Every aspect of an economy bears some influence upon labor relations and tends to develop biases pertinent to the problems involved. The selection of factors important for a comparison of labor law requires investigation of specific economic conditions and attitudes associated with them.

Political Factors

Politics may be defined as the art of asserting bias. Those who are successful in the field acquire the power to enact laws in the image of their own desires or the desires of their supporters. The modern lawmaking process is a weighing and mingling of interests; and labor law is the treacle that emerges from the political mill. Why certain labor laws exist and others do not, or why they contain certain provisions and exclude others, why pensions are given to public employees or the military and not to agricultural workers, or why hours of work are regulated in one industry and not another, cannot be fully explained without considering the political forces at work. In some countries, the political system involves an ongoing commitment to enact or to improve labor laws in every legislative session, and the progression of laws and amendments (such as follows the enactment of a law providing compensation for work related injuries) attests to that continuous political process. Occasionally, a change in political administration alters or reverses the direction of labor legislation, and political forces become extremely significant. At times, statutes remain the same, but their administration is radically transformed. Labor codes tend to be comprehensive and similar in content, yet with subtle distinctions that can be explained politically. The comparatist dealing with labor law will find, in political biases, much to explain what the laws signify and how they are to be evaluated.

Ideational Factors

Insofar as many people are moved by ideas, values, or goals, a comparison of labor laws should take into account prevailing ideologies.

Religions have set standards for human relationships and some of them have been applied to labor laws. A seventh day of rest and holidays are obvious examples. Laws for cash family allowances have also had strong support from organized religion. The extent to which the social values of religious groups have taken form in labor law, or the degree to which the rivalries of adherents to certain faiths have caused the enactment of laws against discrimination, is a matter that comparatists need to note.

Secular philosophies have been more specific in their espousal or repudiation of labor laws; and the assessment of laws by comparatists unavoidably involves philosophical concepts. Labor laws frequently proclaim such concepts as "Labor is not a commodity" "Labor is the source of all value"; and "Labor is a right and a duty". Others talk of "Industrial democracy", "the exploitation of man by man,"; "co-determination,", "workers participation in management,"; "from each according to his ability, to each according to his need"; "social partners"; and "the provider of employment". All are heavily biased terms with philosophical implications and all require clarification by comparatists.

It is obvious that the uncovering and identification of biases is not simple; and particularly troublesome, as will appear below, is the neutralization of distorting biases. Many comparative studies do not assume that burden because of the time and difficulty involved. I see no remedy for the situation that can be accomplished by mere legerdemain. There are, however, further guides and methods that can help.

A Scheme for Labor Law Comparison

Help in labor law comparison can be obtained from the use of a checklist of items that appear in nearly all labor legislation. Fortunately, it is feasible to formulate a classification scheme of the essential elements found in most substantive labor laws. This may serve as a set of compartments into which to slot provisions, to be held for eventual comparison.

I have found helpful this classification of legislative provisions.

1. The declared purposes of the legislation;
2. The coverage of the act (industry, workers, and geographic areas included or excluded);
3. Relationships exempted from the act;
4. The standards of behavior required by the act;
5. The benefits to be dispensed or qualified;
6. The agencies authorized to administer and enforce the act;
7. The sources and amount of funds made available for carrying out the act;
8. Remedies available to persons aggrieved; and
9. Penalties that may be imposed for violations of the act.

Under these headings, the substance of the laws can be made evident not only for literal comparison, but also for examination of cultural bias. Some biases stand out clearly, while some are only intimated; and the scheme is a device for holding them up to review.

The Evaluation Process

Every intelligent person has a set of values of which he cannot fully divest himself. Writers who have insisted that social science research should be value free have demonstrated merely that it should take deliberate steps to counteract or minimize the values that impair judgment.

That is what I suggest for the treatment of cultural bias. All too often, papers on comparative labor law seem designed to indicate only that the laws in the comparatists' culture are praiseworthy; and papers from small countries merely call to the attention of persons in more prominent countries that they too have laws of the highest order. It might be more useful for the writers to elaborate on the problems and benefits that have been experienced in their countries so that others may make applications to their countries as may be appropriate. The temptation to express or preach values may be irresistible (lessons need to be pointed out); but the comparatist would do well to separate fact-finding from value judgment and to indicate clearly which is which.

A problem-solution approach. A technique, especially suited to the differentiation of facts from values in labor law, is what has been called the "problem-solution approach." That poses a common labor problem and then observes to what extent the laws of each country solve that problem. Whether the problem be the adequacy of earnings, the persistence of work-related injuries, provision against the risks of unemployment, the settlement of labor disputes, or another, it can be found in most countries. The satisfaction of the needs of workers raises similar questions the world over. Labor laws seek solutions to those problems. The manner in which the laws work and the degree to which they succeed can be explored and compared. That is the essential essence of all law; and it offers a relatively simple and convenient basis for labor law comparison.

Labor laws may be likened to a set of social genes from which growth in labor relations takes place. What promotes or impedes that process is socially critical. Defining a labor problem and observing how solutions are sought and effected is a pattern and test for comparison and evaluation.

Data selection. To make a proper evaluation of labor law, much data must be accumulated, sorted out, and screened for relevance to the needs of society. To guard against errors due to bias, the comparatist should record the claims of participants and other observers in the area under study. No matter how far-fetched or erroneous the opinions of others may be, if they exist among nationals subject to the laws studied, they must be considered, for the nature of labor law is inseparable from the attitudes and observances of all persons affected. If any data are to be rejected on the ground that the informants were mistaken or represented an insignificant minority or a misguided majority, that requires explanation.

Consider laws for codetermination or workers' participation in management. There is a wide gamut of relevant attitudes and practices, ranging from conscientious and persistent efforts inspired by a belief in the system as a social and practical ideal, to an unwillingness to be bothered with something for which the particular worker has no expertise or interest. If the comparatist desires to cast light on what legal provisions may be emulated or discarded in worker participation (as in other labor laws), he must do more than quote statutes and regulations; he must at least report experiences observed by him or related to him, including all indications of cultural bias. The final report should indicate what information he acquired before editing and an explanation of how the data received were evaluated and utilized.

. . . .

For labor law analysis, I shall, somewhat arbitrarily, categorize labor laws as (1) laws seeking to protect workers from perils and abuses in the employment relationship, (2) laws seeking to elevate standards of living, and (3) laws designed to settle disputes concerning employment relationships and the distribution of income. The objectives are, of course, intermingled in pieces of legislation; but there is value in viewing them as distinct entities.

In the area of laws seeking worker protection, I would group laws ordinarily dealing with child, woman, domestic, migrant, and other special classes of workers, laws on hours of work, laws on wage collection and payment, and laws on industrial safety and health. With respect to such laws, only minimal conflict or inconsistency results from capitalist and communist biases. There are differences in rationale and style, and differences associated with degrees of economic development or transient political and social possibilities. At what ages children are permitted to work, or whether women are expected to engage in night work, or how aluminum or bamboo scaffolds should be constructed, or how new industrial chemicals are to be tested for safety, are not determined by the above mentioned cultural biases of communist and capitalist countries. Local customs or the availability of resources will determine how those laws read or how they are applied. Cross-cultural comparisons (recognizing the involvement of minor cultural biases, readily susceptible of easy modification or accommodation) can concentrate on the improvement of such laws.

In the areas of labor law that seeks to advance standards of living, I would include laws for minimum wages, employment, pensions, and other fringe benefits. . . . Comparative labor law studies in this area of labor law aid in the clarification of alternative legal techniques and promote a rivalry or vying among nations for the advancement of standards of living. Attention to cultural biases may highlight and subject different philosophical assumptions to review, even though they are left un-reconciled.

In the areas of labor law that seek to supply institutions and methods for settling disputes over personal employment relationships or the allocation of income among workers, I would distinguish between laws that facilitate the creation and activity of unions and employer organizations from laws on methods of accommodation. Laws on unionization, collective bargaining, and strikes are affected by cultural biases differently than laws on mediation and arbitration. . . .

. . . .

QUESTIONS

1. What is and how real is the "Eastern" versus "Western" perspective on the issue of human rights? Is it a bias or a cultural distinction or neither? Explain?
2. What are ways in which inappropriate biases may adversely affect the labor lawyer's legal advice?
3. How aware is a lawyer of potential bias and is there a checklist or protocol that can be used to limit it or expose it?

2. *Different Legal Systems*

a. Western Law and Legal Traditions

Western legal traditions are found in a large family of nations and encompass about seventy percent of the world's population and sixty-two percent of its legal systems (see map below).[83] Non-Western legal traditions can be found in Islamic, Jewish, Hindu, and other secular-based communities.

[83] *See* University of Ottawa, *JuriGlobe*, http://www.juriglobe.ca/eng/index.php (last visited Sept. 23, 2010). The map has been slightly modified so as to highlight the common and civil law jurisdictions.

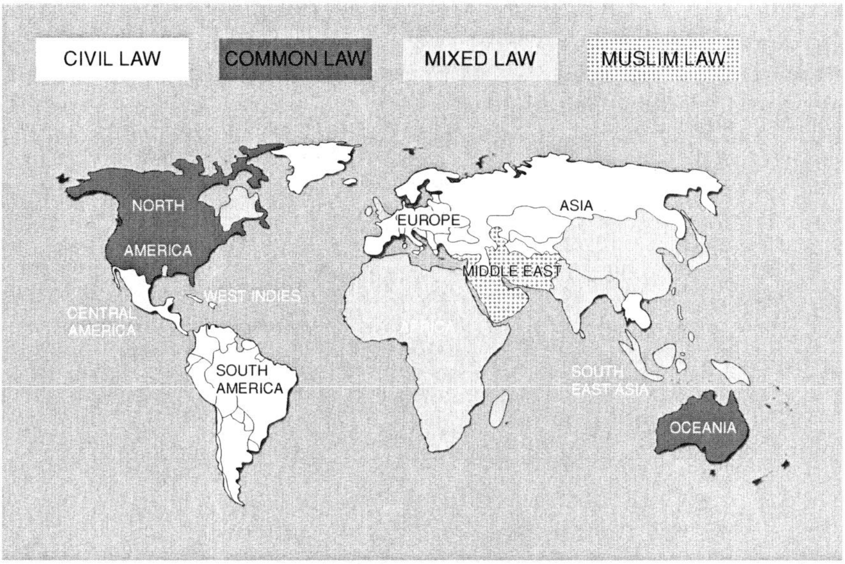

University of Ottawa World Legal Systems (© University of Ottawa, JuriGlobe)[84]

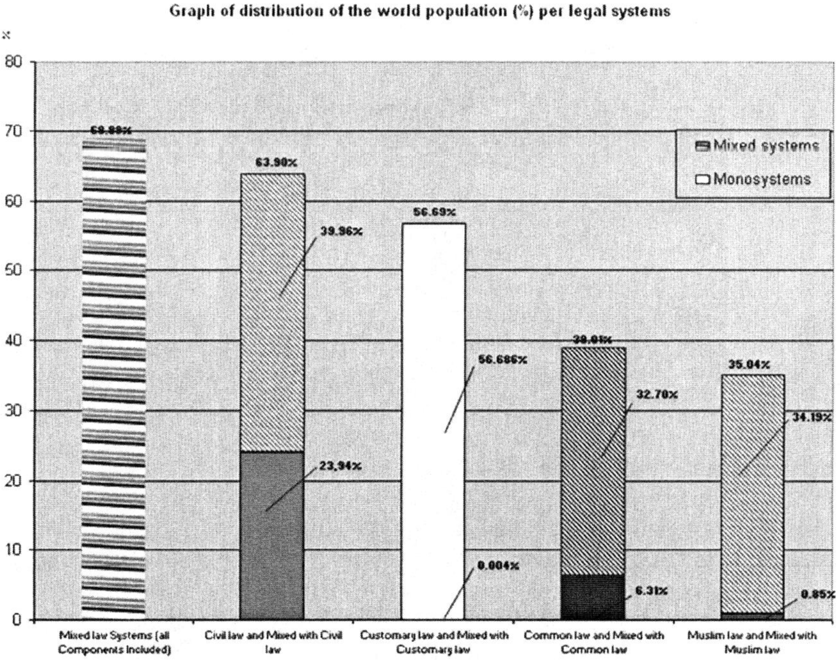

Demographic Distribution per Legal System. (© University of Ottawa, JuriGlobe)

. . . .

[84] *Id.*

JuriGlobe – World Legal Systems Introductory Remarks[85]

Five categories were selected for the creation of this Website on World Legal Systems: Civil law, Common law, Customary law, Muslim law, and Mixed law systems, the latter referring not to a single system but to a combination of systems. This categorization – and the admittedly imperfect classification of political entities resulting therefrom – calls for a few preliminary remarks.

The term "political entities" encompasses member States of the United Nations, as well as the few independent territories which are not part of it.

. . . .

As for religious law systems, we have included only Muslim law because of its permanent, broadly based nature. However we referred once to Jewish law to take into account the particularities of Israel's mixed legal system. Furthermore, some initially religious law systems have since lost their character and distinct status due to the fact that a number of their components have more or less been absorbed into customary or other legal systems.

Also, it must be pointed out that canon law is not a religious law *system*: it is a law inspired by religious dogma, but it is human in origin and belongs unquestionably to the Civil law family.

Customary law, which category also includes what is known as "Aboriginal laws," have [sic] not been highlighted in cases where, even though they may be used for certain means, they do not represent a key characteristic of the relevant political entity's legal system.

Upon reflection, we have ruled out the category of "Socialist law" whose inclusion, in the past, was unavoidable in certain classifications. True, despite recent political upheavals, Marxist-Leninist thought still plays a sometimes significant role in the legal organization of certain countries. But the criterion which governed the creation of a category of "Socialist law", as opposed to western law, was a material one, whereas on the whole we have given greater importance to the methodological and technical aspects of the legal systems, to legal concepts and to methods of developing and expressing law, without confining ourselves to superficially formal criteria.

Furthermore, you will note that the headings in the chapter entitled "Classification of Legal Systems and Corresponding Political Entities" refer to the legal systems in the plural rather than in the singular form (e.g. Civil law systems, Common law systems, Muslim law systems, Customary law systems and of course mixed law systems). Thus we wanted to account for the fact that each legal system (as a classification category) tends to acquire particular characteristics according to the territories and populations it serves. Need we be reminded that, despite their affiliation to the same legal family, there are significant differences between the positive laws of the United States, the United Kingdom and Australia, for example (Common law countries) and that the differences between the positive laws of France, Germany, and Chile, for example (Civil law countries) are no less substantial!

. . . .

---

85 *Id.*

b. Common Characteristics of Civil and Common Law

Western legal traditions have long been documented,[86] but the more useful generalizations come from comparing the common characteristics in the Civil and Common-Law families and the resulting hybrid characteristics. Western legal traditions and systems are established in a separate body of law (independent of church) – administered by legal professionals, not church clerics, whereas by contrast, non-Western legal systems usually are all-encompassing and include social, private, state, and church involvement.

Many of these characteristics can be identified in the legal traditions of particular countries, such as China, Japan, or South Korea, and assist in understanding how and why the law works as it does.

1. Characteristics of Western Legal Traditions:
   a. Legislation (including various government edicts) and case law
   b. Includes Civil, Common, and Socialist Law
   c. Supremacy of law (over politics); and legislation preempts case law and is Supreme (legislative supremacy), unless constitutional limits per Judiciary in some, but not all, states.
   d. Variables include functions and roles of legal actors and institutions; legal education; legal culture; courts; lawyers; judges.
2. Civil Law Characteristics
   a. Law is organized by primary codes: [Civil Law (Private) and Public Law, Commercial Law, Penal, and Civil and Criminal Procedure Laws] – with separate courts administering various areas; there are many and dramatic variations (e.g., Roman, French, German), as well as in China, Japan, and South Korea.
   b. "Inquisitorial" questioning by judges is used frequently versus the "adversarial" method.
   c. Decision making by courts applying codes, not precedents.
   d. Prior decisions are nonbinding, but provide internal guidance.
   e. Judges apply (not make) the law.
   f. Judges apply the law by "judicial" review but therein do not undertake "legislative review" to interpret or determine the validity of legislation.
3. Common-Law Characteristics
   a. Categories of law – Civil-Criminal division and court divisions thereunder may vary.
   b. Decision making: judicial interpretation of cases and legislation including the validity of legislation (and case interpretations of legislation).
   c. Tradition of applying "precedents" and using "stare decisis."
   d. Adversarial system used.
4. Differences, even within Systems

[86] Harold J. Berman, Law and Revolution: The Formation of the Western Legal Tradition (1983).

a. Cultural influences provide local variations, as exemplified by the contrasts in England, Australia, Canada, and Singapore.
b. In England, the Courts' role in judicial review is limited to application only, versus validity, whereas in the United States, courts may also review the validity. England, for many years had no Constitution, which gave rise to an issue of whether without it can there be a rule of law?
c. In Asia's former "colonized" countries (e.g., Malaysia and Singapore), the common-law system may vary because it has been "imposed" rather than having "evolved."

5. "Socialist" Law Characteristics
    a. Similarities with Civil Law legal system – codes; organization of law, courts, etc.
    b. Ideology is a strong component.
    c. Some enforcement of labor laws by trade union.
    d. Supremacy of controlling political party.
    e. Appearance of "parliamentary" system (e.g., UK Labor Party), but political party control.
    f. Transition from socialist to market economy may retain vestiges of socialist system of industrial relations. (e.g., China and its state-owned enterprises, bureaucratic administration, and political party influence).

Comparative Legal Traditions – Introducing the Common Law to Civil Lawyers in Asia[87]

Margaret Fordham

I. The Historical Role of Civil Law and Common Law in Asia

The two predominant legal traditions in the world – the civilian and common law systems – are to be found operating side by side in Asia. In an age when cooperation and mutual understanding are core aims, there is a strong impetus for lawyers from each system to be familiar with, and to be able to function within, the other. And while a formal legal grouping similar to the European Union may remain a distant dream in Asia, the fact that the E.U. has been able to bring together a large number of civil and common law traditions under a single legislature shows that the two systems are by no means as incompatible as they might at first appear.

[87] Fordham, Margaret (2006), *Comparative Legal Traditions – Introducing the Common Law to Civil Lawyers in Asia*, Asian Journal of Comparative Law: Vol. 1: Iss. 1, Article 11. DOI 10.2202/1932-0205.1013, *available at* http://www.bepress.com/asjcl/vol1/iss1/art11. Berkeley Electronic Press © 2006 [Footnotes omitted].

The two systems were, of course, introduced in Asia largely through colonization. Common law was introduced in countries colonized by the British, and it applies today in territories such as India, Malaysia and Singapore. Civil law was spread through colonizers such as the French and the Dutch to territories like Indochina and Indonesia. In addition, even without the civilian tradition being imposed through colonization, several major jurisdictions (notably China, Japan, South Korea and Thailand) chose to adopt systems which were based, either purely or predominantly, on civil law. There are a number of important differences between the two systems – ranging from the way in which judges are appointed (common law judges are drawn from within the legal profession, while civilian judges are specially trained for their roles) to the role of academic writing (which is very influential in civil law courts but of far less significance in common law ones). There is also the very important fact that civilian jurisdictions adopt an inquisitorial approach to deciding cases, in contrast to the adversarial approach of common law countries – which often operates, particularly in criminal matters, in conjunction with the jury system. But probably the most fundamental difference between the two systems lies in the fact that while civil law jurisdictions have comprehensive written codes which are designed to cover every area of law, common law systems are based on judge-made law, which is developed on a case by case basis. Even though, particularly in technical areas, legislation plays an increasingly important role, it is the weight given to judge-made law which really separates the common law world from its civilian counterpart.

II. The Challenges in Introducing a Civilian to the Common Law

The main challenges facing a civil lawyer who wishes to understand and function within a common law system thus relate to the role and structure of legislation and the overwhelming significance of case law.

A. *Legislation*

Legislation is the paramount source of law in both civilian and common law jurisdictions. However, there the similarities superficially end. For while in civilian systems jurisprudence plays a secondary role to codes (which govern the law primarily in the area of private law) and statutes (which predominate in public law matters), in common law jurisdictions case law was historically – and still, at least in theory, is – the backbone of the system, with legislation enacted only in certain areas. Civilians, both in Asia and elsewhere, are used to codes which offer a sequential view of the law in a given area, moving from first principles to specifics within a clear framework. Codes are written at a high level of abstraction, and are based on principles derived from the scientific study of legal data, thus offering an exhaustive overview of the law. On the other hand, most statutes in common law systems address only selective areas of the law, although they normally cover these areas in depth. They are thus also exhaustive, but in a different sense, since they do not normally offer a global snapshot or overview of a particular area of the law, but instead tend to provide comprehensive rules with respect to specific matters within that area. The complexity of many (particularly newer) common law statutes invites reference to other materials in order to gain a more complete understanding. But here the civil lawyer has to be introduced to the historical reluctance – at least within the English common law tradition – to make use of extrinsic aids, something which can seem bafflingly self-defeating.

The difficulties experienced by civilians in understanding legislation in common law jurisdictions should not, however, be overstated, and the differences between the two systems are often in practice more apparent than real. As has already been observed, civil law systems make extensive use of statutes as well as codes, particularly in the public law arena, and so civilians are quite familiar with their form and content, while many common law countries have long codified certain areas of law. And in an era when legislation has come to play a more prevalent role in common law jurisdictions, it seems likely that the line dividing the two systems will, in this respect at least, become ever fainter.

B. *Jurisprudence*

Perhaps the most striking aspect of the common law system lies in the hugely influential role of judges. In civil law systems, judges – at least in theory – have a purely interpretative role, within which doctrinal guidance leaves little room for individual discretion. In common law systems, however, judges play a pivotal role, molding and changing the law through case-by-case development.

Among the qualities of the common law are the fact that its case-by-case nature allows for both gradual development and timely response to the changing requirements of society. The system does, of course have its critics, and a civilian may well discover that, at least initially, he finds it easier to relate to criticisms of common law systems than to extol their virtues. The first response of many civil lawyers is to see judge-made law as somewhat inefficient, given that the development of the common law is dependent on particular fact patterns coming before the courts. Civilians often find the idea of the law being framed only when disputes arise to be odd and even somewhat crude and unsophisticated. Although in time many come to appreciate the benefits of a system which provides for response to changing social circumstances, some are never converted to the system and find its fluidity, and the inevitable gaps in the law to which it gives rise, incompatible with their idea that law must be predictable and certain.

In fact, the extent to which certainty is valued in the civil and common law traditions is what really lies at the heart of the differences between them. For while in civilian jurisdictions certainty is the fundamental goal, common law systems regard flexibility as equally important. Under the common law, a judge bears major responsibility for ensuring certainty and stability, but also for exercising the discretion to change and develop the law, with certainty being achieved through the rules of *stare decisis*, or binding precedent.

The rules of *stare decisis* – under which a lower court must follow decisions of courts above it in the judicial hierarchy, thus preventing a multiplicity of inconsistent rules developing in any given area – are fundamental to the common law system. However, they can prove very problematic for civilians. This is not so much because civil law jurisdictions do not recognize the significance of prior decisions (in practice, civilian judges are, of course, influenced by the decisions in earlier cases) but rather because the application of *stare decisis* necessitates a detailed analysis of often complex decisions in order to determine whether or not an earlier case *must* be followed. Under the rules of *stare decisis* only the *ratio decidendi* of a case – *i.e.*, the decision on the facts, is binding.

Obiter dicta – *i.e.*, observations which are not crucial to the decision, are not binding, even if they are statements by the most eminent judges in the highest courts. It is therefore critical within the common law process to determine the *ratio* of every case. But this can be a very difficult task, both because it is uncommon for a court to spell out the *ratio* of its decision and because common law judgments are often long and discursive (thus differing from judgments in civil law jurisdictions, where judges are trained to adopt a concise and formalistic approach).

. . . .

C. The Increasing Significance of Legislation and Its Effect on the Role of Jurisprudence

The increasing importance of statutes within common law jurisdictions sometimes leads civilian observers both to question the continued primacy of jurisprudence and to complain about the inconsistency of the sources of law. The common law can, as has already been observed, only develop in response to circumstances, since it is dependent on disputes being brought before the courts. In modern society, the growing need to anticipate problems before they develop, particularly in areas involving the use of new or complex technology, has led in recent years to an exponential increase in both the role and the volume of legislation. The common law – based as it is on the values of the community and on general societal norms and expectations – can offer valuable guidance with respect to the acceptable parameters of legislation. But it is inevitable that those with the task of drafting legislation in common law jurisdictions will be influenced by a plethora of additional concerns, often resembling those which face civil lawmakers. For this reason, as the volume of legislation within common law jurisdictions grows, so too does the number of areas in which the law has a greater civilian feel. The result for the civil lawyer is a somewhat bemusing mix in which, while some fields remain governed by rather unfamiliar, judge-made law, others are now governed entirely by the relatively familiar mechanism of legislation. Moreover, since purely judge-made law tends to predominate in older, more established, 'low-tech' areas, while legislation is almost endemic in newer and more technologically sophisticated areas, civilians may feel that jurisprudence as a source of law is on the wane, and that common law systems are slowly espousing a framework which more resembles that of the civil law.

III. Shared Values and Increased Mutual Understanding between Civil Law and Common Law Jurisdictions

Despite all the technical differences between the civilian and common law systems, there are a large number of similarities, the most important of which are, of course, the shared aspirations of regulating society, resolving disputes and meting out justice in as even-handed a manner as possible. And even in technical matters, such as those relating to procedure, there are areas of similarity. For example, in private law issues, civil law countries, like their common law equivalents, frequently rely on the parties to disputes to initiate actions, which are then decided on the basis of evidence brought before the court. Conversely, judges in normally adversarial common law jurisdictions on occasion adopt an inquisitorial stance, for example in family disputes, and particularly those involving the needs and interests of children.

In addition, many of the apparent differences in fact relate more to form than to substance. A civilian who becomes familiar with a particular area of common law may well, for example, find that if he transcribes the relevant law into a civil law format, there is a surprising degree of similarity between the two. And while civil law is supposedly more complete and coherent, in practice civilian judges face many of the same challenges as those faced by common law judges. Since civilian codes tend to be written at a high level of generality, judges have to base their judgments on general principles, and are frequently called on to draw analogies in order to fill in gaps or reconcile apparently conflicting provisions. Moreover, through legislation which often delegates powers to courts through general clauses, civilian judges also have the ability – albeit within a framework less obviously tailored to judicial law making – to adapt the law to meet changing social conditions and to assist in its evolution.

For similar reasons, the differences between the principles underlying the concept of separation of powers in common law and civilian jurisdictions are these days also acknowledged to be more apparent than real. In common law countries, the judicial role has traditionally been seen as balancing the power of other branches of government, whereas in civilian jurisdictions it has been seen as applying law which is made by the legislature. However, just as it is these days recognized that common law judges make law (with few, if any, proponents of the declaratory theory left to argue that common law judges may only find law which is waiting to be discovered), it is also recognized that, even without the formal system of *stare decisis*, jurisprudence plays a significant role in most civil law countries, and that the role of judges is more creative than the nature of the system might suggest. It can also be argued that, just as the increase in legislation in common law countries brings them closer to the position of their civilian equivalents, so too the increasing reliance on precedents in civil law jurisdictions indicates a greater empathy with the common law world. It is certainly true that there is more exchange between the systems than was historically the case, as is evidenced by the growing willingness of common law judges to refer to the position under civilian codes. In addition, in both systems a historical lack of clarity with respect to the most appropriate approaches to statutory interpretation has been resolved by preference for a purposive approach over the plain meaning or literal rule.

IV. Increasing Exposure to the Common Law within Asia

Historically the physical distance between Asia and major common law jurisdictions such as the United Kingdom and the United States meant that (unlike civil lawyers in Europe and South America) civilians in Asia were both physically and psychologically removed from common law cultures. This increased the obstacles faced by Asian civil lawyers in understanding and gaining access to the common law. Universities in Asia generally taught law as a narrow – and largely domestic – discipline, and law practices were confined within the same territorial boundaries. As a result, many Asian countries were unfamiliar even with the legal systems of their civilian neighbours, and had little if any knowledge of legal systems outside their own sphere. This hindered both pan-Asian legal development and, albeit less directly, economic growth and co-operation.

There has, however, been considerable progress in recent years in addressing this somewhat isolationist attitude. Cultural and legal influences are spreading, and we are beginning to see far greater willingness to look outside our own legal heritage. At an academic level, the introduction of more comparative law courses – and even specialized courses on the common law – within Asian universities means that aspiring lawyers within the region now have opportunities to learn about and understand other legal systems. Such courses are often taught by lawyers from the common law world, and thus offer the advantage of exposing students not only to the common law as a subject of study but also to the practical insights of those who have trained and worked within the system. Due also to a general increase in academic exchanges with countries such as the United Kingdom, the United States, Canada, and Australia – both at staff and student levels – there is now far better understanding of the common law world and a more relaxed attitude towards the differences between the civil and common law systems.

At a more practical level, the increasing number of common law legal practices which have established offices in Asia, particularly in the major business hubs, has also created opportunities to obtain experience of the common law.

This has fostered a level of understanding and acceptance unheard of only decades ago. Many Asian lawyers now enjoy the opportunity to work in foreign practices, both in their home countries and in overseas postings, and thus to acquire hands-on experience of the common law. Trans-national deals also expose them to the demands of negotiating with parties from common law systems, thus helping to remove much of the mystique which formerly surrounded the common law.

Thus through ease of communication, a more flexible approach to the teaching of law, and working conditions which are increasingly international in flavour, the differences between predominantly civilian Asia and the major common law jurisdictions are becoming ever less significant. The legal world is now, in a practical sense, a smaller and less disparate place, and the huge advances which continue to be made in terms of movement within, and access to, one another's systems suggest that integration of the world's two great legal cultures is likely to increase exponentially in the coming years.

. . . .

An example of a former "socialist" law system emerging into a clearer civil law-appearing legal system is exemplified in China, as discussed next.

China's Uniform Provisions of Evidence of the People's Court and the Convergence of Civil Law and Common Law[88]

John Capowski

. . . .

While the civil and common law judicial systems are moving towards harmonization, the historical distinctions in judicial roles, the manner in which evidence is both

[88] John Capowski, *China's Uniform Provisions of Evidence of the People's Court and the Convergence of Civil Law and Common Law*, Widener L. Sch. Legal Stud. Res. Paper Series no. 09-10 *available at* http://papers.ssrn.com/sol3/papers.cfm?abstract_id=1431505## (last visited Sept. 23, 2010) [Footnotes omitted].

developed and introduced, and the place of precedent in the two systems will give the two classifications continued force.

III. China's Character as a Civil Law System

I have suggested a binary classification of judicial systems into the common law and the civilian, but many scholars argue that socialist legal systems make up a third and separate category. Scholars who support this view describe socialist systems as fundamentally different from both civil and common law systems because, for example, "... a single political party dominates," public law is preeminent, law is "subordinated to creation of a new economic order," and "law is prerogative instead of normative."

While I claim to have no dog in this fight between those who suggest three as opposed to two major legal systems, I am inclined to classify socialist systems as a subclass of civil law. First, socialist systems exist in countries that have civil law traditions. Second, socialist systems are not unique in having a single or dominant party. Countries that are paradigms for the civilian have also existed under monarchies and single party dictatorships. Third, while socialist systems emphasize public law, the line between public and private is often a hazy one, and even in the most socialist/public law oriented countries significant elements of private law remain. Perhaps most importantly, socialist countries should be classified as a part of the civil law family because of their "inquisitorial style of trial, the reliance on codes, [and] the division of law into its civil law categories...."

If one accepts a binary classification, China fits squarely within the civilian. First, China, as do other civil law countries, has a system in which judges dominate the litigation and trial process. It was not until recently that Chinese law moved towards lessening the court's burden of producing the evidence and placed it more squarely upon the parties.

Second, in addition to the strong role of judges in China's trial process, the process is characteristic of civilian trials. Rather than the common law norm of a single proof taking event and the admission of all evidence at that event, China allows judges to accept evidence at various stages of the proceeding and in that way models the civil law process of admission of evidence over a period of time. And rather than having an elaborate set of common law exclusionary rules and heavily relying upon oral testimony, China mirrors the "free evaluation principle" and has limited exclusion of evidence – both characteristics of civilian law.

Third, the limited role of the court in relationship to the legislature places China's judicial system within the civil classification. Analogous to the limited powers of the highest courts of civilian countries, The Supreme People's Court does not have the power to review either legislation or government policy for constitutionality. Instead, the PRC Constitution and the Resolution on Strengthening the Legal Interpretation of Laws grants to the Standing Committee of the National People's Congress exclusive authority to interpret the Constitution. Similarly, the courts have no official authority to determine whether administrative rules and regulations are valid.

In addition to the traditionally civilian limits on the Supreme People's Court, *stare decisis* is not a principle of China's jurisprudence. But as is the case with other contemporary civil law countries, lower courts follow the decisions of the country's highest court, the Supreme People's Court.

....

---

c. Convergence and Divergence?[89]

There are strong signs that the legal systems are in many ways converging toward more "uniformity," and yet at the same time, in many ways, they remain quite diverse, as is seen within each system. Listed next are some of the factors influencing convergence.

1. Rise of legislation: common law has less need for judge-made law; civil law has less need for primary codes;
2. Emergence of administrative law wherein agencies resolve many formerly judicial disputes;
3. Rise of public law (e.g., employment law, ranging from freedom of contract to workers' compensation, minimum wages, etc.);
4. Use of precedents
5. Common law – less reliance on precedents: less reasoning in judges' decisions; multiple opinions in decisions; and
6. Civil law – increasing use of "binding guidance"; "model cases;" "review, but don't cite" the precedent in Japan and China.

QUESTIONS

1. What impact does the existence of a civil versus a common law legal system have, if any, on a country's labor laws?
2. How might each of the six factors listed above affect a country's labor laws?
3. Is one legal system more or less friendly to labor unions or business? If so how; if not how not?
4. How would the difference in legal systems affect, if at all, a U.S. lawyer's supervision of a foreign lawyer regarding a U.S. client's investments in the foreign country?

[89] See discussion in Charles H. Koch, Jr., *The Advantages of the Civil Law Judicial Design as the Model for Emerging Legal Systems*, 11 IND. J. GLOBAL LEGAL STUD. 139 (2004) and Charles H. Koch, Jr., *Envisioning a Global Legal Culture*, 25 MICH. J. INT'L L. 1 (2003).

II

Global Legal Standards

A. ILO CORE LABOR STANDARDS AND THE INTERPLAY OF DOMESTIC, INTERNATIONAL, AND FOREIGN LABOR LAWS

Regulating cross-border transactions can fall within the responsibility of domestic, foreign, or international laws, and sometimes it can involve all three, as discussed subsequently. International *law* regulating labor is scarce and guidance usually comes from international labor *standards* that are promulgated by the ILO or UN (e.g., covenants on "human rights") and incorporated or linked into domestic legislation involving cross-border trade or adopted (and adapted) into foreign law. The *laws*, unlike the *standards*, are actually enforceable in local courts or regulatory agencies. Treaties are another source of international obligation. Private codes of conduct incorporating ILO standards are of questionable legal enforceability.[1]

Indirect factors can also obligate countries to ILO standards, such as the World Bank's International Finance Corporation (IFC), the Bank's private-sector lending arm, which in February 2006 adopted a new loan performance standard on labor rights and working conditions. All companies that borrow from the IFC will be required to abide by the core labor standards of the International Labor Organization (ILO). These standards, among other things, prohibit discriminatory practices and require recognition of freedom of association and the right to collective bargaining. Additional obligations impose duties on basic conditions, including health and safety standards, protection for contract workers, and a policy for reductions in employment.

There are several themes that can be observed globally in labor law development. The ongoing social compact between capital and labor continues to be negotiated

[1] Doe v. Wal-Mart Stores, Inc., 572 F.3d 677 (9th Cir. 2009). The Ninth Circuit concluded Wal-Mart had no duty arising under its Code of Conduct or in common law negligence to monitor or protect the workers of its subcontractors in foreign locations from substandard working conditions.

globally, nationally, and locally with capital arguably increasing its prominence in recent times, although to be sure there is some progress shown by labor.

Perhaps because of this alignment, conflicts through work stoppages have decreased (although not necessarily workplace *disputes* per se), and "mechanisms of cooperation" have been put into place at the same time as union membership declines. Due both to opportunity and lack of effective union resistance, employers have increased their use of contingent workers and offshore workforces. International competitive pressures, it is argued, have resulted in *developed* countries, like *developing* countries, "racing to the bottom" to achieve the lowest costs; and often, the costs involve labor interests.

Since WTO's refusal in recent years to include labor standards in its mandate, the International Labor Organization (ILO) has moved ahead into the area with its core labor standards. Certainly there are now in place increasingly sophisticated international labor standards, largely emanating from United Nations covenants and ILO Conventions. Debate on the practical usefulness of these consensus standards centers on enforceability issues when a country doesn't ratify them, or does ratify them – but fails to meaningfully implement and enforce them.

While the debate on enforceability of ILO standards continues, some countries such as the United States have unilaterally imposed restrictions or granted benefits to U.S. companies that deal with other countries that adhere to the core ILO labor standards (e.g., U.S. Trade Act, Overseas Private Investment Corporation Act). In recent years there has been increasing discussion, emanating from the International Confederation of Free Trade Unions (ICFTU, which is now the International Trade Union Confederation [ITUC]), for the acceptance and use of a "labor clause" in trade agreements – the so-called "*social clause*."[2] Shenzhen, China, has worked on guidelines in this area, which would be implemented through use of the Shenzhen Stock Exchange.

Of the 183 ILO member states, 157 have ratified 6 or more of the 8 core labor standards (including Japan); and 130 have ratified all 8 (including France, Germany, and the United Kingdom).[3] China and South Korea have ratified 4 core standards and the United States has ratified 2 core standards.[4] Of course, ratification or not, the key is to have meaningful and enforceable domestic labor legislation. Whether

[2] Stephen S. Golub, *International Labor Standards and International Trade* (IMF Working Paper No. 97/37, 1997), *available at* http://papers.ssrn.com/sol3/papers.cfm?abstract_id=882280 (last visited Oct. 3, 2010).

[3] ILO, *Ratifications of the Fundamental Human Rights Convention by country*, ILOLEX (Jan. 6, 2011) (on file with author), *available at* http://www.ilo.org/ilolex/english/docs/declworld.htm (last visited June 1, 2011). [hereinafter Ratifications]. *See also* Philip Alston, *Core Labor Standards and the Transformation of the International Labor Rights Regime*, 15 Eur. J. Int. Law 457–521 (2004).

[4] Ratifications, *supra* note 3. *See also* Mary Jane Bolle, *Overview of Labor Enforcement Issues in Free Trade Agreements*, Congressional Research Service (CRS) Rep. & Issue Briefs, Feb. 29 2008, *available at* http://digitalcommons.ilr.cornell.edu/cgi/viewcontent.cgi?article=1497&context=key_workplace (last visited Oct. 3, 2010) [Footnotes omitted].

and how the domestic laws of individual East Asian countries measure up against these standards, and if there are Free Trade Agreements (FTA) in place, and what labor standards are required, are discussed at p. 118 of this book. The ILO "core (fundamental) labor standards" are listed below , followed by the ratifications by ILO members, including Japan, South Korea, and China. The United States has ratified Conventions 105 and 182.

---

1. *ILO Core Labor Standards*

ILO Core Labor Standards[5]

1. Convention 87 – Freedom of Association and Protection of the Right to Organize Convention, 1948
2. Convention 98 – Right to Organize and Collective Bargaining Convention, 1949
3. Convention 29 – Forced Labour Convention, 1930
4. Convention 105 – Abolition of Forced Labour Convention, 1957
5. Convention 100 – Equal Remuneration Convention, 1951
6. Convention 111 – Discrimination (Employment and Occupation) Convention, 1958
7. Convention 138 – Minimum Age Convention, 1973
8. Convention 182 – Worst Forms of Child Labour Convention, 1999

Ratifications of the Fundamental human rights Conventions by country[6]

Conv. 87		Conv. 98	Conv. 29	Conv. 105	Conv. 100	Conv. 111	Conv. 138	Conv. 182
Freedom of association and collective bargaining			Elimination of forced and compulsory labor		Elimination of discrimination in respect of employment and occupation		Abolition of child labor	
Total of 183	150	160	174	171	167	169	154	171

Ratifications by China, Japan, and South Korea follow.[7]

---

[5] ILO, *Conventions and Recommendations*, http://www.ilo.org/global/What_we_do/InternationalLabourStandards/Introduction/ConventionsandRecommendations/lang – en/index.htm (last visited Sept. 23, 2010).

[6] Ratifications, *supra* note 3.

[7] Ratifications, *supra* note 3.

	Conv. 87	Conv. 98	Conv. 29	105	Conv. 100	Conv. 111	Conv. 138	Conv. 182
China					02:11:1990	12:01:2006	28:04:1999	08:08:2002
Japan	14:06:1965	20:10:1953	21:11:1932		24:08:1967		05:06:2000	18:06:2001
Rep. of Korea					08:12:1997	04:12:1998	28:01:1999	29:03:2001

The ILO explains its role as follows:

About the ILO[8]

The International Labour Organization (ILO) is devoted to advancing opportunities for women and men to obtain decent and productive work in conditions of freedom, equity, security and human dignity. Its main aims are to promote rights at work, encourage decent employment opportunities, enhance social protection and strengthen dialogue in handling work-related issues.

. . . .

Origins and history

The ILO was founded in 1919, in the wake of a destructive war, to pursue a vision based on the premise that universal, lasting peace can be established only if it is based upon decent treatment of working people. The ILO became the first specialized agency of the UN in 1946.

. . . .

Tripartism and social dialogue

The ILO is the only 'tripartite' United Nations agency in that it brings together representatives of governments, employers, and workers to jointly shape policies and programmes. This unique arrangement gives the ILO an edge in incorporating 'real world' knowledge about employment and work.

International labour standards

The ILO is the global body responsible for drawing up and overseeing international labour standards. Working with its Member States, the ILO seeks to ensure that labour standards are respected in practice as well as principle.

Working out of Poverty

Poverty remains deep and widespread across the developing world and some transition countries, with an estimated 2 billion people in the world today live on the equivalent

[8] ILO Home, *About the ILO*, http://www.ilo.org/global/About_the_ILO/lang – en/index.htm (last visited Sept. 23, 2010).

of less than USD 2 per day. In the view of the ILO, the main route out of poverty is work.

....

International Labour Standards[9]

....

What are they?

The core labour standards reflected in the ILO Declaration on Fundamental Principles and Rights at Work represent only a part of the Organization's standard-setting activity. Since 1919, the ILO and its tripartite structure, encompassing governments of member States and employers' and workers' organizations, have built up a system of international standards in all work-related matters. These ILO standards take the form of international labour Conventions and Recommendations. ILO Conventions are international treaties, subject to ratification by ILO member States. Recommendations are non-binding instruments – often dealing with the same subjects as Conventions – which set out guidelines orienting national policy and action. Both forms are intended to have a concrete impact on working conditions and practices around of the world.

By the end of June 2003, the ILO had adopted over 180 Conventions and over 190 Recommendations covering a broad range of subjects: freedom of association and collective bargaining, equality of treatment and opportunity, abolition of forced and child labour, employment promotion and vocational training, social security, conditions of work, labour administration and labour inspection, prevention of work-related accidents, maternity protection, and the protection of migrants and other categories of workers such as seafarers, nursing personnel or plantation workers. More than 7,000 ratifications have been registered so far. International labour standards play an important role in the elaboration of national laws, policies and judicial decisions, and in the provisions of collective bargaining agreements. Whether or not a country has ratified a particular Convention, the standards provide guidance for the operation of national labour institutions and mechanisms, and good labour and employment practices. Thus, international labour standards have an impact on both national law and national practice, which goes well beyond simply adapting legislation to the requirements of a ratified Convention.

ILO supervisory mechanisms

The application of international labour standards is subject to constant supervision by the ILO. Each member State is required to present periodically a report on the measures taken, in law and practice, to apply each Convention it has ratified. At the same time, it must send copies to employers' and workers' organizations which also have a right to submit information. The Governments' reports are first examined by the Committee of Experts on the Application of Conventions and Recommendations, a body of twenty eminent figures in the legal and social fields who are independent of governments and appointed in their personal capacity. The Committee submits an annual report to the International Labour Conference, where it is closely examined by

[9] *Id.*

the Conference Committee on the Application of Conventions and Recommendations, a tripartite committee of government, employer and worker members.

In parallel with these regular supervisory mechanisms, employers' and workers' organizations can initiate contentious proceedings, called "representations", against a member State for its alleged noncompliance with a Convention it has ratified. If the representation is judged receivable by the ILO Governing Body, it appoints a tripartite committee to study the question. This committee subsequently submits a report containing its conclusions and recommendations to the Governing Body.

Moreover, any member country can lodge a complaint with the International Labour Office against another member State which, in its opinion, has not ensured in a satisfactory manner the implementation of a Convention which both of them have ratified. The Governing Body has the option to establish a Commission of Inquiry to study the question and present a report on the subject. This process may also be set in motion by the Governing Body itself for following a complaint by a delegate to the International Labour Conference. If necessary, the Commission of Inquiry formulates recommendations on measures to be taken. If governments do not accept these recommendations, they may submit the question to the International Court of Justice.

....

QUESTIONS

1. Can cross-border transactions be regulated by ILO standards? If not, what is their function?
2. What is the ILO and how did the "core labor standards" evolve?
3. What is the significance of "ratification" of an ILO Convention by a country?

2. *Linking Trade and Labor Standards*

Should Labor Standards Have a Role in U.S. Trade Agreements?

International labor standards, though not mandated by law, may be generated within an organization (e.g., ILO or OECD) or be imposed in international business activities through their incorporation into trade agreements (NAFTA; KORUS FTA) or other U.S. legislation. Domestic legislation in the United States has provided for "fast-track" authority to negotiate trade agreements under the Trade Promotion Authority (TPA) until 2007 when it ended.[10] In the congressional debate whether or not to renew the authority, policy questions arose as how best to include the ILO

[10] The U.S. Congress formally established a framework for U.S. trade negotiations as part of Bipartisan Trade Promotion Authority (TPA) (renewal of fast-track authority) under the Trade Act of 2002, Pub. L. No. 107–210, 116 Stat. 993 (codified as 19 U.S.C. §§ 3801–3813 (2010). Trade promotion authority refers to presidential authority to negotiate trade agreements that Congress then considers without amendment and under limited debate (most recently in Title XXI of the *Trade Act of 2002*, P.L. 107–210). A new bill, the "Trade Reform, Accountability, Development, and Employment Act of 2009" or the "TRADE Act of 2009," is proposed that would include labor standard

labor standards under the Free Trade Agreements (FTAs) – by requiring them to be met or by requiring the trading partner to enforce its own labor law standards?

An analysis of the usefulness of inclusion of labor provisions is discussed next,[11] followed by a research analysis as to how labor standards may fit into FTAs.[12] Their usefulness may be in the form of future labor reforms.

———

Trade Promotion Authority (TPA) Renewal: Core Labor Standards Issues: A Brief Overview[13]

Mary Jane Bolle

. . . .

Summary

This report is a brief overview of key issues addressed in CRS Report RL33864, *Trade Promotion Authority (TPA) Renewal: Core Labor Standards Issues*. Trade Promotion Authority (TPA), formerly known as "fast-track" authority, is scheduled to expire July 1, 2007. With it will expire the President's authority to negotiate trade agreements that Congress will then consider without amendment and with limited debate. For the 110th Congress, a likely issue in this debate is whether to include *enforceable core labor standards* as a principal negotiating objective in trade agreements. Accordingly, this report (1) identifies key labor provisions in the current TPA law and how they have translated into free trade agreements negotiated under it; (2) presents some legislative options, and summarizes arguments for and against listing enforceable core labor standards as a principal negotiating objective; and (3) looks at possible outcomes and implications of the legislative options. This report will be updated as events warrant.

Introduction

. . . .

requirements. *Landmark New Fair Trade Legislation: The TRADE Act*, OREGON FAIR TRADE CAMPAIGN, http://citizenstrade.org/orftc-tradeact.php (last visited Oct. 3, 2010).

11 Mary Jane Bolle, *Trade Promotion Authority (TPA) Renewal: Core Labor Standards Issues: A Brief Overview*, CONGRESSIONAL RESEARCH SERVICE (CRS) REP. & ISSUE BRIEFS, Feb. 21, 2007, *available at* http://digitalcommons.ilr.cornell.edu/cgi/viewcontent.cgi?article=1026&context=crs (last visited Oct. 3, 2010) [hereinafter Bolle]. For a general discussion on TPA renewal, see J. F. Hornbeck & William H. Cooper, *Trade Promotion Authority (TPA): Issues, Options, and Prospects for Renewal*, CRS REP. FOR CONGRESS, Dec. 5, 2006, *available at* http://fpc.state.gov/documents/organization/78415.pdf (last visited Oct. 3, 2010).

12 Kimberly Ann Elliott, *Labor Standards, Development, and CAFTA*, INT'L ECON. POL'Y. BRIEFS (2004), *available at* http://www.iie.com/publications/pb/pb04-2.pdf (last visited Sept. 23, 2010) [hereinafter Elliott]; *see also* KIMBERLY ANN ELLIOTT & RICHARD FREEMAN, CAN LABOR STANDARDS IMPROVE UNDER GLOBALIZATION? (2003).

13 Bolle, *supra* note 11. For a more historic summary, see Robert A. Rogowsky & Eric Chyn, *U.S. Trade Law and FTAs: A Survey of Labor Requirements*, 1 J. INT'L COM. & ECON. 113 (2007), *available at* http://www.usitc.gov/publications/332/journals/trade_law_ftas.pdf (last visited Sept. 23, 2010) [Footnotes omitted].

Currently, the Administration is negotiating a number of trade agreements that may not be completed before TPA is set to expire. If these activities are to continue, TPA renewal may be a central issue in the 110th Congress. Within the debate, a major issue is expected to be whether to include as a principal negotiating objective in trade agreements, "enforceable core labor standards."

The current TPA is contained in the *Bipartisan Trade Promotion Authority Act of 2002* (Title XXI of the Trade Act of 2002, P.L. 107–210). A total of nine free trade agreements (FTAs) have been negotiated under this authority. They are with Chile, Singapore, Australia, Morocco, Bahrain, Oman, the Dominican Republic and Central America, Peru, and Colombia. The last two await congressional consideration. The labor issue in these trade agreements is how key provisions in each reflect two principal negotiating objectives in TPA.

The first TPA principal negotiating objective is: "to ensure that a party *does not fail to enforce its own labor laws* through a sustained or recurring course of action or inaction, in a manner affecting trade between the parties." All nine FTAs track this principal negotiating objective by providing: that countries shall "not fail to enforce their own [labor] laws . . . in a manner affecting trade between the Parties" – popularly called the "enforce-your-own" provision. The second TPA principal negotiating objective is: "to seek dispute settlement and enforcement provisions *that treat U.S. principal negotiating objectives equally* with respect to the ability to resort to dispute settlement, the availability of *equivalent* dispute settlement procedures, and the availability of *equivalent* remedies." In what labor advocates see as a "departure" from the TPA provision, procedures for labor disputes differ in several respects from those for commercial disputes and include a cap on monetary penalties (while those for commercial disputes do not.)

Key Players and Their Positions

Those calling for expanded or strengthened labor provisions fault labor protections in the nine FTAs, arguing that they (1) lack the enforceability of commercial provisions; (2) fail to meet some congressional negotiating objectives and barely comply with others; (3) represent a "big step back" from both the U.S.–Jordan FTA and U.S. unilateral trade preference programs such as the Generalized System of Preferences (GSP); and (4) "completely exclude obligations for governments to meet such international standards as worker rights." These advocates further argue that in order to strengthen FTA provisions, the blueprint for their negotiation – the TPA language – needs to be strengthened. Advocates of strengthened labor provisions, in promoting enforceable core labor standards, appear to have two objectives. The first objective could be characterized as humanitarian: to promote the protection of workers around the world, particularly those in developing countries where protections are weak and/or poorly enforced. The second objective could be interpreted as economic: to help "level the playing field" between U.S. and foreign workers so that U.S. workers can compete on a more equitable basis.

Opponents respond in support of the current TPA, noting that labor provisions in the nine FTAs negotiated under it: (1) are the strongest labor provisions attached to FTAs to date; (2) are the product of bilateral negotiation; and (3) both depend on and reflect mutual agreement by negotiating countries; (4) treat U.S. principal negotiating objectives "equally" in that the principal remedies for labor and commercial disputes are "equivalent;" and (5) are preferable to enforceable core labor standards because the latter could raise sovereignty issues. Opponents have, as one key objective, promotion of U.S. investment. They often represent the viewpoints of businesses and investors, developing country governments, and the current Administration.

Many business groups support the passage of TPA in order to facilitate the expansion of U.S. multinational corporations abroad – their most important avenue for continued growth. In fact, both TPA and trade agreements typically include many protections for investors. Developing countries care about protecting their ability to attract investment, and are concerned about anything that might jeopardize that ability. In the World Trade Organization (WTO), developing countries have long resisted U.S. proposals to study the relationship between worker rights and trade, concerned that such a study could lead to enforceable labor standards that could undercut their comparative advantage in low-cost labor. However, as with businesses and investors, their flexibility to compromise on the issue of enforceable core labor standards seems to be related to the strength of their desire to have an FTA with the United States.

Major Legislative Options and Arguments

Major legislative options for treatment of labor standards as principal negotiating objectives *if TPA were to be renewed*, include the following:

Option 1: No enforceable labor standards provisions. This option would likely be viewed as a step back from the expiring TPA;

Option 2: Renewal of the current "enforce-your-own" provisions aiming:

(1) to ensure that a party *does not fail to enforce its own labor laws*; and (2) to seek dispute settlement provisions that treat U.S. principal negotiating objectives *equally*; and

Option 3: "Enforceable core labor standards" as reflected in H.R. 3019, introduced in 2001 by Representative Charles Rangel which aimed: (1) to ensure that a party does *not fail to enforce core labor standards*; and (2) to provide that violation of these standards would be subject to enforcement under a *single set of dispute settlement procedures* that would be *applicable to all disputes* under an FTA. The term *core labor standards* has been defined in two ways by two different sources: the International Labor Organization (ILO) which calls them "core labor standards," and U.S. trade law which refers to them as "internationally recognized worker rights." Both definitions are almost identical and share four standards or rights: (1) the right to organize, (2) the right to bargain collectively, (3) prohibition of forced labor, and (4) protections for child labor including the "worst forms of child labor." They differ on the fifth standard. U.S. law identifies it as: (5) labor standards pertaining to minimum wages, maximum hours, and occupational safety and health. ILO conventions define it as: (5) freedom from employment discrimination.

Should Enforceable Core Labor Standards Be Included as a Principal Negotiating Objective? General Arguments

For Enforceable Core Labor Standards. Those in favor of principal negotiating objectives that call for enforceable core labor standards include the AFL-CIO, Human Rights Watch, and the International Labor Rights Fund. Labor advocates traditionally argue: (1) that enforceable core labor standards help guard against a "race to the bottom," as workers all over the world compete against each other for scarce jobs; and (2) that labor standards do not interfere with natural comparative advantage in developing countries because labor standards are only one basis for comparative advantage. Others include abundance, skills, and education of available workforce; infrastructure; level of technological development of the country; and natural resource base.

Against. Opponents typically argue that (1) the enforce-your-own standards model provides a more direct, less encumbered path to economic growth; (2) most developing countries have few resources to devote to labor standards enforcement; (3) once a developing country is more economically developed and relatively near full employment, labor standards and their enforcement begin to rise on their own; and (4) imposing core labor standards on developing countries too soon could interfere with their comparative advantage in abundant and inexpensive labor, and amount to protectionism.

Arguments Related to U.S. Workers

For Enforceable Core Labor Standards. Supporters argue that a principal negotiating objective calling for enforceable core labor standards could help level the playing field for U.S. workers and make them more competitive internationally. *Against.* Some opponents argue that the need or desire to earn a living is often incentive enough to encourage displaced workers to find new employment. Others argue that there are better ways to help U.S. workers than trying to level the playing field, which, at best, may only slow the offshore movement (or technological elimination of) of some U.S. jobs. A better way, some argue, would be to expand adjustment assistance benefits, educational benefits, or other training and retraining programs to cover all displaced workers – whether the job loss results from trade or technology – and help them transition into new careers.

Arguments Related to Foreign Workers

For Enforceable Core Labor Standards. Advocates of strengthened labor standards argue that enforceable core labor standards can help foreign workers share in the gains of increasing productivity and economic expansion, and thereby become consumers in their own right.

Against. Opponents argue that real gains in standard of living in developing countries come from rising productivity, not from artificially imposed labor standards including minimum wages. In addition, they argue, some workers do not want enforceable core labor standards because these could limit their ability to maximize their earnings by working overtime.

Sovereignty Issues

For Enforceable Core Labor Standards. Those in favor of enforceable core labor standards as a principal negotiating objective could argue that the ILO already requires that countries comply with ILO core labor standards as a condition of continued membership in good standing, even if those countries do not formally approve the ILO conventions. Therefore, incorporating enforceable core labor standards into trade agreements does not add much more to this requirement.

Against. Opponents might respond that enforceable core labor standards interfere with national sovereignty in a way that ILO membership does not, since enforcement powers of the ILO are limited to consensus and persuasion.

If So, What Should Be the Definition of Core Labor Standards?

Arguments on the Definition of Core Labor Standards

For Enforceable ILO Core Labor Standards. If "enforceable core labor standards" is adopted as a principal negotiating objective for trade agreements, the AFL-CIO is strongly in favor of using the ILO definition over the U.S. definition because it is more current. Human Rights Watch, while not arguing for either definition specifically, stresses that the definition of core labor standards must include prohibitions against employment discrimination (which is in the ILO but not the U.S. definition).

Against. If the ILO definition were adopted, opponents point out, foreign governments could hold existing U.S. labor laws up to scrutiny, arguing that they don't totally comply with ILO core labor standards. This is because the United States has ratified only two conventions (one on forced labor and one on the worst forms of child labor). Accordingly, the U.S. Council for International Business (USCIB) argues that many U.S. labor laws would need to be changed to come into compliance with the ILO definition of core labor standards, especially in such areas as forced labor, minimum age for employment, and employment discrimination.

Possible Outcomes and Implications

Whether TPA is renewed, and whether the negotiation of enforceable core labor standards is included in any such renewal, international trade is likely to continue to expand in both volume and complexity. The economic effects on trade, investment, and labor markets of including enforceable core labor standards as a principal negotiating objective in TPA renewal could be relatively limited. They would likely depend on a number of factors including (1) the extent to which enforceable core labor standards were adopted and implemented in trade agreements; (2) the number of trade agreements affected; (3) the magnitude of U.S. trade with countries under such agreements; and (4) the extent of actual enforcement of those standards in trade agreements. In addition, the effects from any of these four factors could be dwarfed by shifts in the value of the dollar that might occur relative to other currencies.

If enforceable core labor standards were adopted as a principal negotiating objective in TPA legislation, whether or not the United States would need to make changes to its labor laws could depend on how the legislation defined the term "core labor standards." If TPA is not renewed, or if it should be renewed without enforceable core labor standards, a number of ways might be available to promote labor standards and protect worker rights. These include enforceable standards currently incorporated into U.S. trade preference laws; continuing efforts of the ILO to promote core labor standards; the efforts of various labor advocates and international labor "watchdog" groups; economic development forces in various countries which eventually lead to rising international demand for protections of the rights of workers; codes of conduct guiding the actions of corporations in protecting the rights of international workers; and U.S. government "trade capacity building" grants which help to improve labor standards in developing countries.

. . . .

Union Perspective on Labor Standards and Trade[14]

Trade agreements must include enforceable protections for the ILO core labor standards to ensure that companies and countries cannot gain an unfair competitive advantage by denying workers their basic human rights. Workers in the U.S. have an interest in seeing these rights enforced worldwide, and our government can and should show leadership in making this vision a reality. First, Congress must require the administration to include enforceable workers' rights in the core of every trade agreement it signs. The Baucus-Grassley Track bill falls far short of this standard, and proponents of the bill have responded to criticism by attacking the very idea of enforceable protections for core labor standards. Some common questions about the topic are answered below.

1. ISN'T IT UNFAIR FOR THE U.S. TO IMPOSE LABOR STANDARDS ON DEVELOPING COUNTRIES?
   The core labor standards were not unilaterally designed by the U.S. or modeled on our laws. The core labor standards are based on international human rights law and have been repeatedly reaffirmed by the entire international community, including developing countries. This consensus is evident in the Universal Declaration of Human Rights and other core human rights conventions, the UN Social Summit, and the ILO's 1998 Declaration on Fundamental Principles and Rights at Work and its corresponding conventions. The Declaration lists the core labor standards – freedom of association and the right to bargain collectively, the elimination of forced labor, the abolition of child labor, and the elimination of discrimination in employment – and states that all members, regardless of their level of development, must respect these standards. These standards are qualitative, not quantitative; they express the fundamental rights that all human beings have in the workplace, they do not set a global minimum wage or maximum hours. Compliance with these standards is not only morally right, but has been found to support stable and equitable economic development and to strengthen political democracy.
2. AREN'T ILO MEMBERS ALREADY REQUIRED TO ENFORCE THESE STANDARDS? By virtue of their membership, all ILO member countries are obligated to respect, promote, and realize the core labor standards enumerated in the Declaration, even if they have not ratified the relevant conventions that give content to these core standards. Unfortunately, since the ILO has no real enforcement power, many member countries' labor laws still violate the core labor standards. Thus, it is simply not sufficient to ask these same countries to commit in trade agreements to do nothing more than enforce their existing laws. For example, in the Americas alone the ILO has found that laws in Argentina and Brazil violate ILO standards by requiring collective bargaining agreements to win government approval or conform with the national interest in order to come into effect; El Salvador's labor laws infringe upon the right to organize by establishing excessive administrative requirements to register a union; Peru's labor laws do not allow workers to fully exercise their right to bargain collectively; Bolivia, Honduras, and Paraguay exclude all agricultural workers from legal protections

[14] AFL-CIO, *Common Questions About ILO Core Labor Standards and Trade*, Fast Track 2002, *available at* http://www.aflcio.org/mediacenter/resources/upload/commonquestionsonfasttrackilo.pdf (last visited Sept. 23, 2010).

for the right to organize; and El Salvador and Venezuela have overly restricted the rights of public sector workers to organize. Other ILO members' laws are even more egregious: in China, Cuba, Sudan, Vietnam and a number of Arab states all independent trade unions are simply outlawed, and Bangladesh and Pakistan explicitly exclude workers in export processing zones from protection under their labor laws.

3. WHY NOT JUST STRENGTHEN THE ILO IF ENFORCEMENT IS THE PROBLEM? The labor movement has long been a proponent of strengthening the ILO, even as the current administration has proposed cutting funding for international labor programs in half. Labor strongly supports increasing financial assistance and improving ILO technical assistance to help countries improve their labor standards. But in some cases this type of assistance is not enough, especially when individual governments have a direct economic or political interest in continuing to violate workers' rights and suppress independent trade unions. In these cases, the ILO cannot enforce core labor standards on its own; all international organizations, especially international economic organizations such as the WTO, IMF, and World Bank, must play a supporting role. Unfortunately, today these organizations are obstructing improvement in workers' rights more than they are contributing to it. For example, many countries have refused to act on the ILO's recent recommendation that members impose sanctions on Burma for the country's continued and systematic use of forced labor, citing fears that such sanctions would violate WTO rules (Burma is a WTO member). Until the WTO incorporates enforceable provisions for core labor standards into its rules, the ILO's efforts to remedy even the most blatant violations of workers' rights will continue to be isolated and ineffective.
4. AREN'T TRADE PANELS UNQUALIFIED TO RESOLVE LABOR DISPUTES? Proponents of linking trade and labor standards recognize that existing dispute resolution bodies must be reformed. Panels must have access – perhaps through collaboration with the ILO – to panelists with expertise on labor issues and professional neutrality, as well as the power to authorize trade sanctions if necessary. Disputes should be open to the public and should include some mechanism, such as *amicus curiae* briefs, for taking into account the views of interested parties, especially of trade unions in countries affected by the dispute. These same principles of expertise, neutrality, transparency, and public participation should apply to all trade disputes, and have always been an integral part of trade union demands for reform of the international trading system.
5. ISN'T USING SANCTIONS TO ENFORCE LABOR STANDARDS PROTECTIONIST? First of all, there is no intellectual basis for distinguishing between enforcing business interests – such as intellectual property rights and investor rights – with trade sanctions and enforcing workers' rights with trade sanctions. The only difference is that business interests are already an important part of our trade law, and workers' rights are much less so. Second, most obligations that carry the threat of trade sanctions do not actually result in many sanctions being imposed. The credible threat of sanctions is often enough to guarantee compliance, as can be seen in the history of the WTO and our other trade agreements, where the actual imposition of sanctions is very rare. Ideally, trade sanctions will work the same way for workers' rights: they will encourage countries to comply

with international standards, to accept financial and technical assistance when they have trouble enforcing these standards effectively, and to remedy any violations complained of by other countries. Third, a multilateral dispute resolution system that is neutral, expert, transparent, and equally accessible to all parties is probably the best way to ensure that the power to impose trade sanctions is not captured by narrow, domestic interests. It is just such a system that the international trade union movement has argued for, and that Congress should require the President to create.

On May 10, 2007, Congress and the administration agreed to the Bipartisan Agreement on Trade Policy, which included a new labor template for bilateral trade agreements.[15] That template has since been incorporated into a number of FTAs and changes the previous obligation of "enforce your own laws" standard to an obligation to meet ILO core labor standards. Under these standards, parties must agree to adopt, maintain, and enforce five core labor standards as listed in a 1998 ILO Declaration on Fundamental Principles and Rights at Work – freedom of association; the right to collective bargaining; elimination of all forms of forced labor; abolition of child labor; and elimination of discrimination in employment. In addition, there is an obligation to provide "acceptable conditions of work."[16] Violations of these obligations will potentially subject either country to trade sanctions, which differs from the fines to be imposed under the earlier obligations.[17]

QUESTIONS

1. What is "fast-track authority" and what are its advantages and disadvantages?
2. What is the preferable linkage option from the U.S. point of view? Would the European view differ?
3. Without a trade law linkage, what other enforcement avenues are available, if any?

---

15 Peter Tillman, *Partisanship and U.S. Trade Policy*, POL'Y INNOVATIONS (Jan. 23, 2008), *available at* http://www.policyinnovations.org/ideas/briefings/data/000024 (last visited Sept. 23, 2010) [hereinafter Tillman]. The obligations of this agreement, as they relate to the ILO, refer only to the 1998 ILO Declaration on Fundamental Principles and Rights at Work (core labor standards). *See also* Kimberly Ann Elliott, *Trading Up: Labor Standards, Development, and CAFTA* (May 28, 2004), *available at* http://www.cgdev.org/content/publications/detail/2849/ (last visited Oct. 3, 2010).

16 Claude Barfield, *The Grand Bipartisan Trade Deal*, N.Y. SUN, May 17, 2007, *available at* http://www.nysun.com/opinion/grand-bipartisan-trade-deal/54690/ (last visited Sept. 23, 2010).

17 Tillman, *supra* note 15. The U.S Korea FTA became law in the U.S. on October 21, 2011. *See* Congress Ends 5-Year Standoff on Trade Deals in Rare Accord, *available at* www.nytimes.com/2011/10/13/trade-bills-near-final-chapter.html? *See* President Obama signs 3 trade deals, biggest since NAFTA, *available at* http://www.nola.com/politics/index.ssf/2011/10/president_obama_signs_3_trade.html. On November 22, 2011 South Korea's parliament approved the FTA. See KORUS FTA in the News, *available at* www.koreauspartnership.org/news/index.htm.

3. Coordinating Domestic, International, and Foreign Labor and Employment Laws and HRM

Employment and Labor Law Considerations in International Human Resource Management[18]

Ronald C. Brown

Introduction: The Legal Aspects of Global Labor Management

The CEO had just returned from the new overseas project. Among the waiting list of phone calls for him to return were several to the company's labor lawyer. Although he had been gone only two weeks, a spate of messages stated that the overseas activities had already generated personnel questions under U.S. law and under foreign law. Specifically, management in the overseas operation reported that a sexual harassment complaint would soon be filed by an employee who held a U.S. "green card," and it wanted to know whether U.S. Equal Employment Opportunity (EEO) laws applied to those operations.

Also, the overseas management is about to hire a number of local employees in preference to U.S. based employees (who had requested to transfer per contractual seniority rights) because of its inability to obtain a sufficient number of visas to permit the transfer. The U.S. union is claiming this would violate the seniority and transfer provisions of its collective bargaining agreement. Additionally, the overseas operation reports that local authorities claim that under local law these newly hired local employees could not easily be terminated or have their employment rights modified by a negotiated settlement or arbitration.

And finally, the overseas management reports that news stories are suggesting that its operations and its suppliers are involved in using prison labor to keep down the labor costs. It is asking whether this is only a P.R. problem or whether it has legal implications.

These questions are real and involve such companies as Sears, United Airlines, and Sheraton Hotels; however, the kinds of legal questions arising under international human resource decisions are even more varied and can affect any size company involved in an overseas operation.

Employers increasingly are establishing operations and relationships throughout the world and looking to make international HRM decisions so as to remain globally competitive. The answer by affected employees, such as in a United Airlines case in which the employer allegedly gave hiring preference to Paris-based employees over U.S.-based employees with greater seniority rights under a collective bargaining agreement, was to go to court to enjoin the hiring decision. The union leadership stated "[W]e will continue to pursue all available avenues – whether in the courts, arbitration, at the bargaining table or in a political arena – to ensure that United's global desires do not provide an excuse for exporting jobs and depriving flight attendants of their legal rights."

Global competition drives business into every reach of the world. Choices made by foreign direct investors are often influenced by labor costs and government regulations. International human resource managers are increasingly confronted by foreign

[18] Ronald C. Brown, *Employment and Labor Law Considerations in International Human Resource Management, in* GLOBAL PERSPECTIVES OF HUMAN RESOURCE MANAGEMENT 37 (Oded Shenkar ed., 1995).

regulations that apply to their expatriate and local employees, as well as the U.S. labor regulations, which may bind them even in the overseas operations.

Just as U.S. labor laws are an important factor in operating a business in the United States, the increasing legalization occurring overseas, particularly in Asia, also affects operations on foreign soil. This blend of business necessity and legal requirements and legal issues generated by global management decisions are discussed in this chapter. Within the legal framework of international human resource management there are recurring employment and labor relations issues that managers must identify and address. In this chapter, employment and labor relations regulations in the United States are considered as they apply to HRM policies of U.S. and foreign companies operating overseas and in the United States. Foreign labor regulations involved in FDI, particularly in Asia, include illustrations from Japan, South Korea, and the Peoples' Republic of China.

Businesses operating in the United States know very well the numerous labor laws and regulations that shape and influence human resource management decisions here. However, when these businesses are part of global operations – even in just one foreign country – these same issues can multiply potential legal concerns by a factor of at least four or five times. For example, the U.S.-based company must know and comply with (1) the U.S. labor laws; (2) the foreign laws as they may apply to U.S. citizens working on foreign soil; (3) the foreign laws as they may apply to foreign employees working for the parent and/or the foreign-based company; (4) the U.S. labor laws applied extraterritorially to U.S. citizens working for foreign operation; (5) and finally, management must consider the applicability of the labor laws to its U.S.-based employees [versus those] working for the foreign-based operation. The 1991 Civil Rights Law's extension to extraterritorial locations and its provision for damages (including punitive damages) highlight the types of legal and management issues of increasingly vital concern to managers of international human resources.

. . . .

However, meeting the requirements of foreign laws first necessitates assessment of how the parent company's global personnel policies and decisions are established and how they will be administered, so as to meet U.S. labor laws as they apply to foreign-based employees and how that relates to home-based employees' rights and benefits. For example, coordinating staffing opportunities, compensation, and benefits to induce and retain the "right" employees to work overseas may well have an impact on personnel at home operations, as will be discussed. The fact that the male manager of a Chrysler plant in Beijing makes 25 percent more than a female manager in Newark should be reviewed before the EEO office makes an inquiry.

Therefore, going global requires knowing the United States and foreign labor environment and how business decisions invoke legal regulations, whether their source is domestic, international, or foreign. Knowing these laws raises issues that affect HRM decisions. Informed international human resource managers understand that these legal considerations can be factored into the business decisions to provide fairness and to avoid unnecessary litigation in the United States and overseas. The key is to be informed, know the legal issues that need to be addressed, and to accommodate the law with the needs of boards of directors, management, employees, labor unions, and foreign governments.

. . . .

U.S. Labor and Employment Law Applied to Global Operations

To identify items of legal importance under foreign law when doing business overseas, a brief overview of U.S. labor and employment law is described in three parts: (1) U.S. labor regulatory system applicable to U.S. businesses; (2) the regulatory system's application to foreign direct investors in the United States; and (3) the extraterritorial application of U.S. labor laws applied to U.S. companies doing business overseas.

. . . .

Extraterritorial Application of U.S. Labor Laws

Although some U.S. labor laws extend to certain global operations and provide legal rights and obligations for employees and employers operating in foreign locations, most do not. Generally speaking, most U.S. laws regulate only the U.S. operations of the U.S.-based parent company, although, as a practical matter they may strongly direct the human resource managers to coordinate and create generally parallel employment packages for its employees at home and abroad, particularly if overseas employees rotate back into the parent company's operations. For example, the National Labor Relations Act requires unionized employers to bargain over management decisions to relocate and shift work from U.S. locations when such shifts substantially displace U.S. workers. In addition, the 1988 Work Adjustment and Retraining Notification Act (WARN) requires advance notification to affected employees of U.S. plant closures. This again under scores the legal significance of whether the overseas connection is part of the global U.S. employer's operations or merely a foreign corporation with whom it is doing business.

Notable exceptions exist in the area of antidiscrimination legislation that is extended extraterritorially. Laws that prohibit discrimination on the basis of age, race, color, sex, handicap, national origin, or religion are applicable to certain employees working in global operations. In 1984, the Age Discrimination Employment Act (ADEA) defined employee to include citizens of the United States employed by an employer in a workplace in a foreign country. Employer was defined to include (1) a U.S. firm, (2) a foreign branch of a U.S. firm, or (3) a foreign corporation controlled by a U.S. firm. Furthermore, where an employer controls the foreign corporation, even the acts of the foreign incorporated entity are deemed to be the acts of the employer.

This legislation thus seeks to prevent the American parent company from circumventing the law by incorporating its subsidiaries in foreign countries. In determining whether the U.S. company controls the foreign entity, tests for common law control are used including (1) interrelationship of operations, (2) common management, (3) centralized control of labor relations, and (4) common ownership or financial control. An interesting legal question is whether a complaining employee can directly sue not only the U.S. firm but also the controlled foreign entity, either solely or as a codefendant. The law on this point does not provide obvious guidance or limits.

Congress did, however, place limits on the law's extraterritorial application by limiting it to U.S. citizens (though, arguably, noncitizen employees can be counted for purposes of attaining the required minimum number of employees for the law's application). Also, its application is limited if compliance would violate the laws of the country in which the workplace is located.

The primary U.S. labor law extended extraterritorially is the Civil Rights Act of 1991 (CRA) and also the Americans with Disabilities Act of 1990 (ADA). Overturning a recent

U.S. Supreme Court case that did not extend Title VII of the Civil Rights Act of 1964 (as amended), the law, by Section 109, explicitly paralleled the ADEA and applied the law to citizen-employees working in extraterritorial locations for the covered "employer," including foreign companies controlled by the U.S.-based company. It too is limited in its application where compliance would violate local laws. Perhaps the point of greatest interest to global employers is that these laws explicitly permit an increased scope of remedies including attorney fees, expert witness costs, and punitive damages.

A final substantive implication of the extraterritorial application of U.S. discrimination laws is its impact on U.S.-based operations. Because the laws apply to both locations, there is the obvious need to approach international HRM decisions in an evenhanded way and to have documentary reasons for selection and assignment of personnel to foreign locations. Also, there must be justifications for compensation disparities between employees at the U.S. location versus the overseas location. The legal issues thicken as one considers the impact of U.S. legal obligations on foreign operations when disparities are created with host country nationals in terms of selection, opportunity, or compensation. Does this create violations under foreign law? Can U.S. citizen employees also sue under the foreign laws? How does one decide whether the foreign law will be violated by compliance with the U.S. labor law? And finally, when will the U.S. law be excused when there is "compliance" with the foreign "law?"

. . . .

International Labor and Employment Law Affecting Global Operations International Labor Law and Labor Standards

. . . .

In addition to these local sources of foreign law, there are also international and regional sources of law, labor standards, and influences affecting global operations. The primary sources of international labor law standards, in addition to treaties, are those emanating from the International Labor Organization (ILO), a specialized agency of the United Nations (UN), and the United Nations itself, which has established basic human rights covenants applicable to all member nations.[19]

. . . .

U.S. Laws Enforcing Internationally Recognized Labor Standards

U.S. laws that grant or deny trade preferences, guarantee overseas investment, permit trade sanctions and import restrictions conditioned on local recognition and observance of internationally recognized labor standards, clearly and directly affect the global operations of private overseas business investors.

. . . .

[A] . . . law promoting and supporting international development through overseas investment is the Overseas Private Investment Corporation Amendment Act of 1985 which created OPIC, an autonomous federal corporation that provides assistance, financial incentives and guarantees, and political risk insurance to overseas investors. The law prohibits OPIC assistance to investors in countries whose governments fail to adopt and

[19] Discussed earlier in II. A. 1.

implement internationally recognized labor standards. . . . Also in an effort to meet the concerns of U.S. unions and to curb "capital flight" and loss of employment opportunities in the United States, the law further limits the availability of assistance in several instances: if the overseas investment is likely to cause a significant reduction in the number of employees in the United States or if it is likely to cause the investor to significantly reduce the number of its employees in the United States because of effective replacement of domestic production with foreign production of substantially the same product for the same market. Those limitations are of obvious concern in global operations and are an additional agenda item for overseas investors seeking financial support under OPIC. The limitations also raise a host of possible labor-related legal issues under the law as to their applicability and enforceability.

Other U.S. laws and agencies involved in enforcing internationally recognized labor standards that can affect overseas investors in global operations include the Export-Import Bank of the United States (Eximbank), an independent federal corporation that assists exports of U.S. origin or manufacture by providing financial aid (loans, credits, guarantees) to foreign buyers (governments or private entities of certain products). Restrictions on assistance include prior certification by the U.S. State Department of a country's compliance with, or movement toward, certain internationally recognized labor standards.

In sum, international labor standards [under domestic legislation] must be taken into account when operating under a foreign jurisdiction. Foreign investment can be significantly affected not only by local laws and conditions, but also those locally favorable business conditions may be used as a reason for U.S. laws to intervene to undermine and cut off investment services, loans, and guarantees under OPIC or Eximbank, or cause tariff preferences to be lost – all because of failure of the foreign country to meet the international labor standards.

Role of the Host Country's Laws: Foreign Laws

The most important law to consider in deciding whether to locate operations overseas is the law of the host country. Legal requirements imposing financial obligations for employee hiring, layoffs, or plant shutdowns; restrictions on management decisions on hiring, disciplining, and firing staff; and the difficulties of immigration laws permitting expatriates from the home country to work on foreign soil – all are important labor law considerations in successfully establishing operations in a foreign location.

. . . .

Legal Issues and Agenda Items of International HRM

Recruitment and Selection. Finding the right personnel for foreign assignments involves several issues depending on the variables of size, nature of operations, and so on, as well as the type of foreign country – industrialized, developing, and the like. For example, FDI in the PRC likely will take advantage of cheaper labor costs, and a local work force may be hired with an emphasis on a largely local supervisory staff. To establish a representative trading operation, an FDI in Japan may involve more management personnel from the home country.

. . . .

Of course, foreign employees can be brought in by the locally based enterprise, but regulations normally require a work permit and appropriate immigration status. The importation of foreign employees can be a sensitive local issue, and it is often an area covered in initial negotiations under the appropriate business entity law and resulting contracts.

In local operations in Japan, recruitment and staffing issues must first fit into the global management's decisions regarding business entity and coordination with parent company policies. However, in implementing those decisions within the obligations of local labor laws, some differences in approach from those used in China will be required. For example, open recruitment by newspaper ads may be regarded as only "inviting strangers." Emphasis on word-of-mouth referrals, hiring only men, or recruiting on the right college campuses might be the local practice. The ultimate selection may necessitate background checks and determinations about attitudes of potential employees regarding work habits, unions, family plans, and so on.

Most of these approaches are common in Japan and do not violate Japanese labor laws.

. . . .

Personnel choices are often divided into management and labor; the latter are usually hired locally. An important number of home country management staff may need to be recruited depending on business requirements, but how those choices are made, the incentives provided, and the compensation awarded are all governed by U.S. labor laws. Whether local customs regarding choices of personnel, such as religious, racial, or sexual preferences may be considered, may also depend on the foreign law (as a possible defense to U.S. law) and the extent to which it mandates discrimination of this kind. If expatriates are to be used, requirements of foreign immigration law must be met. Also, some executives and professional staff may be exempted from certain foreign labor laws under treaty provisions, such as the Friendship, Commerce, and Navigation Treaty (FCN) discussed earlier.

When promotions, transfers, and other benefits, including travel, compensation, and the like, are held out in the recruitment process as available to all "employees," considerations must be given to the U.S. EEO laws, as well as local laws, at least applied to the U.S. citizen employees. When overseas relocation of operations adversely affects the level of employment in the home-based operations, certain U.S. labor laws may be triggered, such as those of the NLRA and WARN.

When hired employees – U.S. and foreign – work side by side doing similar work, questions can be raised as to which country's legal standards apply. These issues are resolved by examining the laws and by determining how the employment relations are structured. That is, who is the "employer" and who are "employees" under the various applicable laws?

Managers of international operations obviously are trying to select the best qualified people on the basis of non-legal considerations of personality, ability, family situation, compensation need, and proper mix and interface with host country nationals. However, it should be underscored that there are monetary as well as moral incentives to give legal considerations to staff selection (e.g., the Civil Rights Law of 1991 permits far-reaching remedies, including punitive damages).

Performance Evaluation. An integral part of HRM is performance evaluation, and coordination of domestic and foreign employment policies is required. The key to understanding the legal issues in this area involves performance standards and uses of the evaluations based on the standards, both in the foreign location and in comparison with home-based operations. Again, ultimate decisions will depend on legal definitions of "employer" and "employee."

The legal issues raised by standards for performance evaluations depend on *whose* standards are applied *where*? Does the foreign operation use its own standards, those of the home company, or a global operations standard? And to whom are they applicable – home country versus foreign nationals, management versus workers? The main factors to be used, from a legal point of view, are those of fairness and defensibility. That is, are there legitimate, provable reasons upon which standards are based and used? When productivity of managers is not measured by merit because of local conditions, are the same or similar criteria used at the U.S. plant locations? And, if not, are the differences justifiable?

In foreign countries, customs regarding age, seniority, and sex of employees may affect labor pools and the selection process and may become a factor in evaluation, especially when foreign managers are used. One must determine the degree to which U.S. and local laws control those employees. The effect of any decisions taken under those laws on other employees located in both the host country and the United States must be considered.

Performance evaluation can also raise legal issues, largely under EEO laws, when one uses the results of performance ratings to see who needs training, discipline, compensation increases or decreases, and qualification for promotions or transfers. These business choices can affect basic interests and rights of employees. If favoritism or unfairness is perceived, disputes will arise under local and U.S. labor laws.

Therefore, who establishes the standards and who evaluates them can be legally significant. Employment tests in the United States under civil rights laws may need to be validated if there are adverse effects on legally protected employees. Are the same or different tests to be used overseas? What role, if any, is played by the home office or the local labor union in creating standards or using them? Are there local legal limitations, and is there an employment contract or labor union agreement that affects their use? Does a local government labor bureau perform the testing function before an applicant is referred to the employer?

An example of how such legal concerns can appear and possibly be bypassed by overriding business considerations is as follows. A global company has operations in several overseas locations to enhance its flexibility and competitive advantage. Because of declining sales, cutbacks in operations are called for, and a choice must be made about whom to lay off. If laws, regulations, and contracts in one country require large severance payments or unemployment compensation benefits, the employer may well choose the cheapest alternative, notwithstanding performance evaluations of the respective work forces. Does that violate any local legal requirements? If employees have strong unions and are likely to strike, labor relations considerations will also play a role.

Where individual cutbacks are required, performance standards, seniority, and legal requirements will all play a part in the decision, with possible legal issues arising along the way. For example, what are the legal obligations of the U.S.-based parent "employer" when a Beijing "employee" of a subsidiary in a PRC-based joint venture argues that she was laid off because of her gender?

Training and Development. A number of variables affect management's choices regarding training and development programs. Basic among them are whether the overseas programs will be integrated with or separate from that of the parent company. There will be questions about career development opportunities and techniques of training, about who does the training, who receives the training and where, and who pays for it. The important point here, from a legal perspective, is that training and development programs almost always create expectations, rights, and benefits. When expectations are frustrated, legal demands may be made.

First, one must decide how to coordinate or separate training "tracks" for personnel. U.S.-based personnel who are "rotating in" may have needs different from those of "borrowed" third-country nationals from another subsidiary operation or those of host country nationals who are performing the same job functions but who may have different future expectations and who there have different training needs. Local host country employees will be concerned how trainees are chosen and who gets the opportunity. For example, if it turns out those management trainees are predominantly of one gender and of one ethnic background, does that raise questions under either local or U.S. law? The answer is yes. And, to know which obligations to meet the global employer must take care in setting up the employment relationship so as to carefully define "employer," "employee," and "parent-subsidiary" relationships.

As for the content of training programs, in addition to work performance training, it is also useful to educate personnel about pertinent legal requirements – local and United States – regarding EEO, safety and health, dispute resolution, and the like. Properly trained personnel, both management and staff, is still the best way to deter legal problems.

A large practical issue with legal implications involves labor relations and how to dovetail these training programs into existing relationships with labor unions, contracts, and involved government agencies (e.g., immigration, if training will occur in the United States).

Lastly, another legal issue can arise with selected jobs. For example, there may be requirements for licenses or for locally required training or certification. From skilled workers, such as electricians, to accountants and lawyers, there may be special restrictions that must be met and perhaps, in the case of skilled workers, that could be integrated into training programs or linked with existing local programs.

Compensation. Money most easily attracts the interest of personnel. Financial discrimination that is, or is perceived to be, unfair can trigger legal claims under U.S. and local laws. Although the uses of salaries and fringe benefits to attract and retain needed employees are well known, in the global context, the legal ramifications are more complex. For example, if a global company brings into Beijing, China, managerial staff from Singapore and the United States, how may one justify any comparative compensation differentials or the fringe benefits, including housing and travel?

There are many business explanations that will determine and perhaps justify compensation differentials – but will they satisfy applicable law; United States or local – and not just the tax laws but also the labor laws? Foreign managers can often point to local laws or joint venture or contract obligations in seeking some parity in compensation and fringe benefits. Questions again arise – whose "employees" are they and what legal obligations apply? Legal concerns under U.S. EEO laws can also be raised regarding justification for compensation differentials while employees are overseas and upon their return, when higher (comparatively) compensation levels are maintained. Clever and appropriate uses of "overseas allowances" can usually lessen legal concerns.

With respect to the foreign-based work force, compensation-related opportunities and benefits, including training, travel, bonuses, vacations, housing, and other "fringes," can raise EEO issues and questions whether there has been compliance with local legal requirements regarding social insurance, job security, severance, and layoff funds or procedures, worker injuries, housing subsidies, redundancy, and so forth. Questions recur about who is the "employer" with the obligation – the local joint venture, the respective subsidiaries who have joined, or their parent companies – and who are the "employees" who are entitled to such benefits? Understanding and complying with these laws and coordinating them, to the extent necessary, with U.S. laws, is a tedious but necessary task. Global employers usually deal with these issues when first going into a foreign location, but changing and ongoing relationships with local suppliers, contractors, or partners often requires constant monitoring.

Labor Relations. No area of HRM is more important than the labor relations environment of the foreign location. This area more than ever crosses lines and mixes practical realities with legal requirements. The key to success in this area is twofold: preparation and execution. The employer must know and understand the history and the socioeconomic factors at work, primarily the current power bases and players of the government, business, and labor unions. The employer must then use this knowledge in executing and implementing his goals with the local rules and within the local power balances.

The specific factors to consider are as follows. In first formulating employment policies, a decision must be made as to the coordination and the allocation of decision-making authority over labor relations between the U.S.-based parent and the foreign-based subsidiary. Is it delegated, centralized, or handed over to local control? This has practical as well as legal significance on the potential extraterritorial application of U.S. civil rights laws. Important attention is paid to the control factor in assessing employer status. The extent to which local managers are empowered to make real decisions also affects the applicability of various labor laws concerning employment status, for purposes of coverage or non-coverage.

The type of employment relations and the manner in which they are derived is significant. Are wages, terms, and conditions fixed by statute, by collective negotiation, or on an individual basis? What role does a labor union have, if any? Are there rights of collective bargaining? Can a union be ignored? Would a strike be legal? Can replacement employees be found and used? What alternatives for dispute resolution are permitted and used?

All of these aspects of employee relations raise a myriad of legal questions upon which local law must be consulted and understood. Here, also, a practical understanding of how the law is used and enforced is absolutely required. If management under the law has a right to determine bonuses and their method of distribution, it may not want to use its right if local custom and a powerful local union have a tradition of making those determinations within employee committees and the labor union. Under such circumstances, it may be unnecessary and foolish to blindly adhere to legal "rights."

Such an example may be true in the PRC. On the other hand, even where legal rights of employees exist, such as the right to strike, knowing the likely local reaction of law enforcement officials may guide the employer in its legal deliberations.

Finally, it is obvious that employee relations are complex and vary with local conditions. Even in a location with certain government attitudes toward worker protections or lax enforcement thereof (e.g., in health or safety standards), there may be some other areas of great concern, such as payment of workers, social insurance, and other legally required worker subsidies. Balancing legal requirements with the practical realities of labor relations requires much attention by human resource managers.

Japan provides an illustration. Much of the mystery about Japan has been lifted by U.S. presence and involvement in Japanese business and society for the past fifty years. To many it remains a truism that the United States and Japan labor laws are about 96 percent alike, yet different in almost every way. The laws and bureaucratic institutions are often similar (e.g., the U.S. labor law, the Wagner Act, is also closely reflected in Japanese law), but their administration and the law and practices under them are different.[20]

The difference in operation and application of similar-appearing laws is due to the pervasive influence of culture on a rather homogeneous country and the degree of economic and "legal" control and guidance the government and related organizations exert over Japanese companies. Thus, the very close cooperation and the more than an implied social covenant among government, business, and labor unions have given rise to the stereotypical designation of Japan, as "Japan Inc." This is a useful aid in understanding Japan, at least as it connotes the heavy coordination undertaken by government, labor, and business and its acceptance by society. It should also alert the foreign investor to the clear fact that "outsiders" will probably remain just that. When foreign business locates in Japan, there is little doubt that to succeed it must accommodate local requirements, whether they are laws, culture, or human resource management practices.

In conclusion, legal implications abound in most decisions in labor relations, not only in the United States, but also on foreign soil. Decisions in international HRM covering all the areas of recruitment and selection, performance evaluation, training and development, compensation, and labor relations raise complex legal issues that can be largely eliminated by key legal planning. Careful consideration can be given to structuring "employer" and "employee" status which, if business values permit, can affect the applicability of laws. Careful assessment of the local legal requirements in foreign locations can result in employer policies compatible with U.S.-based policies that go a long way in complying with the law and practical realities. Clearly, as in all personnel situations, United States or foreign, no amount of planning can eliminate every legal dispute; but by anticipating them, they can be dealt with under a designed plan while also maintaining the global employer's business interests.

. . . .

---

[20] See discussions in Ronald C. Brown, *Faces of Japanese Labor Relations and the Emerging Legal Issues Under U.S. Labor Laws*, 15 SYRACUSE J. INT'L L. & COM. 231 (1988–1989). An argument is also working its way through the courts whether the NLRA should be applied extraterritorially. *See* John B. McDonald. Note. *Don't Cross That Line! The Case for the Extraterritorial Application of the National Labor Relations Act.* 64 U. MIAMI L. REV. 369–395 (2009).

Thus, it can be seen that the legal agenda concerning the potential applicability of U.S. labor laws, the possible interplay of international labor obligations and foreign law, and the foreign labor law itself all provide a significant area of concern affecting business choices and international human resource management.

QUESTIONS

1. Explain how a domestic U.S. law can have enforcement implications overseas.
2. How is it possible to comply with foreign law while at the same time violating U.S. domestic law?

B. ENFORCEMENT: CODES OF CONDUCT, U.S. LAWS, AND LITIGATION

1. *Codes of Conduct as Self-Regulation*

Strategies of monitoring labor and employment conditions in overseas locations vary from corporate codes of conduct by individual corporations, within industries, or by organizations such as the OECD. Likewise, there may be "framework" agreements between individual or international unions and individual corporations or MNCs. The common factor in almost all of these is that they are a form of self-regulation that is voluntary, not binding or enforceable. So what good are they? Certainly they may provide for good public relations for consumers of the manufactured or assembled products; additionally, they may provide monitoring and exposure of labor conditions in violation of standards, and in certain industries, for example, those falling under the OECD Guidelines, there may be other consequences.

Issues arise as to whether providing for third-party monitoring can take self-regulation, with its internal corporate controls, outside the corporation and provide for independent monitoring. Critics still say that even in this case, sanctions and external publicity to consumers are usually lacking. Another aspect, pointing up the difficulties of enforcement, even by self-regulation, is that a common business practice for many corporations is to operate with contractors and possibly multiple subcontractors. Although some corporations have added codes of conduct to monitor their subcontractors, it is often the case that much of the monitoring of these standards is left to purchasing agents and other untrained personnel.

These issues, and the question of whether self-regulation can work to protect workers, even with some sanctions being a possibility, are explored further in the following articles.

Codes of Conduct for Multinationals[21]

Concept

Codes of conduct or guidelines for multinational corporations do not have any fixed definition. However, it is important to make a distinction between *corporate codes of conduct* and *codes of conduct for multinational corporations* [emphasis added]. Corporate codes of conduct are individual company policy statements that define a company's own ethical standards, while codes of conduct for multinationals are externally generated and to some degree imposed on multinationals. These codes are not of the companies' own making, nor are they agreements between companies and the entities which create the codes. In some cases, however, multinationals are involved in the drafting process. The fact that these codes are externally established standards while other corporate codes of conduct are of a voluntary and internal nature has important implications when considering their implementation in corporate practice.

Codes of conduct for multinational corporations must also be distinguished from framework agreements, which are concluded between trade union organizations and individual companies regarding the companies' international activities. There are two types of framework agreements. First, there are written understandings between multinational corporations and international trade union organizations (such as an ITS), which may cover any subject. Examples of such framework agreements include those establishing information and consultation arrangements, as mandated by the European Works Council Directive. Second, there are framework agreements between trade unions and companies concerning the labour practices of the company, or of its suppliers and subcontractors in other countries. Such provisions may also be included in collective agreements that are recognized under national law.[22]

In relation to multinationals, codes of conduct for multinationals are recommendations. Even if the codes have been agreed by a number of sovereign states, or such other entities as have been granted international personality by sovereign states, they do not have a status of international law, which would set a binding effect on multinationals operating in those states which have adopted or joined the code. Hence, codes of conduct for multinationals impose no legal, but only moral, obligations on companies, and they are not capable of enforcement by the application of external sanctions. For multinationals, the commitment to the codes is voluntary. But some organizations have placed the acceptance of their code as a condition to their membership or licensing agreements.

Anyone may introduce codes of conduct for multinational corporations. Besides governments and intergovernmental organizations, codes have been introduced by trade union organizations; employers' organizations; various environmental, consumer,

[21] Codes of Conduct for Multinationals, 2002, http://actrav.itcilo.org/actrav-english/telearn/global/ilo/guide/main.htm (last visited Sept. 30, 2010). Copyright © 2002 International Labor Organization.

[22] For further reading on framework agreements, see International Confederation of Free Trade Unions (ICFTU), *Labor and Business in the Global Market*, http://actrav.itcilo.org/actrav-english/telearn/global/ilo/guide/icftuart.htm (last visited Sept. 30, 2010).

investor, religious, ethical and other organizations; and by various groups protesting certain international phenomena. Some of the codes have been adopted multilaterally, some unilaterally.

Codes of conduct for multinationals may address any issue relevant to their activities. Codes have in fact addressed a wide variety of issues, including: relations between multinationals in world markets (e.g. with regard to advertising, marketing, sponsorship, and competition in general); labour matters (e.g. terms and conditions of work and equality); environmental standards (e.g. emissions, waste or safety in production and transportation); and health and safety issues related to individual products (e.g. toys, baby milk substitutes, and other products).

Codes of conduct for multinationals can take various forms. Their credibility depends on three main factors – the governments that have adopted them or companies that have subscribed to them (e.g. in number, size or internationality); the nature of the substantive provisions of the code; and any related monitoring mechanisms (such as investigation methods, reporting of investigation results, and dissemination of reports).

. . . .

United States

The Clinton Administration has been very active in preparing guidelines for multinationals. The United States Department of Labor has sponsored sectoral codes, such as the White House Textile and Apparel Partnership on Sweatshops and Child Labor involving companies, NGOs, and trade unions. The agreement was adopted in April 1997. Its Workplace Code of Conduct has provisions on child labour (under the age of 15), worker abuse, safety and health, discrimination and harassment, freedom of association and collective bargaining, as well as wages, benefits, and hours. In addition, its Principles of Monitoring has provisions for independent monitoring. In 1995, Clinton Administration created its Model Business Principles which call for "fair employment practices, including avoidance of child and forced labour and avoidance of discrimination based on race, gender, national origin or religious beliefs; and respect for the right of association and the right to organize and bargain effectively".

In the apparel industry, a number of codes adopted by employers' organizations and trade unions have emerged since 1995. In June 1995, two New York locals of the International Ladies' Garment Workers' Union (ILGWU) and three industry associations signed a three-year code of conduct on workers' rights for employers' overseas contractors and subcontractors. The union and industry parties agreed to a "Code of Conduct for Overseas Vendors" (see summary) that touches upon key human rights issues covered by conventions of the ILO, including the right to freedom of association. Two organizations that bring together the bulk of United States apparel producers and retailers – the American Apparel Manufacturers Association (AAMA) and the National Retail Federation (NRF) – have also developed codes of conduct. (For codes of conduct in the apparel industry and corporate codes of specific apparel companies, see United States Department of Labour, The Apparel Industry and Codes of Conduct.)

. . . .

Summary of OECD Guidelines for Multinational Enterprises[23]

Scope

Addressed by	Governments of OECD Member countries
Addressed to	Entities of multinationals which operate in OECD Member countries and domestic enterprises of OECD countries.
Definition of multinationals	Multinational enterprises usually comprise companies or other entities whose ownership is private, state or mixed, established in different countries and so linked that one or more of them may be able to exercise a significant influence over the activities of others and, in particular, to share knowledge and resources with the others. The degrees of autonomy of each entity in relation to the others varies widely from one multinational enterprise to another, depending on the nature of the links between such entities and the fields of activity concerned. For these reasons, the Guidelines are addressed to the various entities within the multinational enterprise (parent companies and/or local entities) according to the actual distribution of responsibilities among them on the understanding that they will co-operate and provide assistance to one another as necessary to facilitate observance of the Guidelines. The word "enterprise" as used in these Guidelines refers to these various entities in accordance with their responsibilities.

The labor relations content of the code

Freedom of association	• Right of the employees to be represented by trade unions and other bona fide organizations of employees; • Observation of industrial relations not less favourable than those observed by comparable employers in the host country.
Collective bargaining and agreement	• Enable authorised representatives of their employees to conduct negotiations on collective bargaining or labour management relations issues with representatives of management who are authorised to take decisions on the matters under negotiation; • Engage in constructive negotiations, either individually or through employers' associations, with such employee organizations with a view to reaching agreements on employment conditions, which should include provisions for dealing with disputes arising over the interpretation of such agreements, and for ensuring mutually respected rights and responsibilities;

[23] The Organization for Economic Cooperation and Development (OECD) carried out a survey of 246 voluntary codes of conduct and prepared a chart of the various elements they encompassed. Summary with comments in Stacy Mosher, *Global Codes of Conduct – A Summary*, China Rights Forum, May 2003, 43, *available at* http://www.ir2008.org/PDF/initiatives/Social/GlobalCodes1.2003.pdf (last visited Sept. 30, 2010); *see also* OECD, *Codes of Corporate Conduct: Expanded Review of their Contents*, Working Papers on Int'l Inv. (2001), *available at* http://www.oecd.org/dataoecd/57/24/1922656.pdf (last visited Sept. 30, 2010).

- Provide such facilities to representatives of the employees as may be necessary to assist in the development of effective collective agreements;
- In the context of bona fide negotiations with representatives of employees on conditions of employment, or while employees are exercising a right to organize, not threaten to utilise a capacity to transfer the whole or part of an operating unit from the country concerned nor transfer employees from the enterprises' component entities in other countries in order to influence unfairly those negotiations or to hinder the exercise of a right to organize.

Disclosure of information

- Provide to representatives of employees information which is needed for meaningful negotiations on conditions of employment;
- Provide information which enables them to obtain a true and fair view of the performance of the entity or, where appropriate, the enterprise as a whole;
- In considering changes in their operations which would have major effects upon the livelihood of their employees, in particular in the case of the closure of an entity involving collective lay-offs or dismissals, provide reasonable notice of such changes to representatives of their employees, and where appropriate to the relevant governmental authorities and co-operate with the employee representatives and appropriate governmental authorities so as to mitigate to the maximum extent practicable adverse effects.

Terms and conditions of work

- Observe standards of employment not less favourable than those observed by comparable employers in the host country;
- In their operations, to the greatest extent practicable, utilise, train and prepare for upgrading members of the local labour force in co-operation with representatives of their employees and, where appropriate, the relevant governmental authorities;
- Implement their employment policies including hiring, discharge, pay, promotion, and training without discrimination unless selectivity in respect of employee characteristics is in furtherance of established governmental policies which specifically promote greater equality of employment opportunity.

Implementation

Acceptance

- OECD Member countries adopted the code.
- All enterprises concerned are recommended to indicate publicly their acceptance of the Guidelines, preferably in their annual reports.

Reporting and monitoring

- Member Governments shall set up National Contact Points for undertaking promotional activities, handling inquiries and for discussions with the parties concerned on all matters related to the Guidelines so that they can contribute to the solution of problems which may arise in this connection. The business community, employee organizations and other interested parties shall be informed of the availability of such facilities.

- National Contact Points in different countries shall co-operate if such need arises, on any matter related to the Guidelines relevant to their activities. As a general procedure, discussions at the national level should be initiated before contacts with other National Contact Points are undertaken.
- The Committee on International Investment and Multinational Enterprises (hereinafter called "the Committee") shall periodically or at the request of a Member country hold an exchange of views on matters related to the Guidelines and the experience gained in their application. The Committee shall be responsible for clarification of the Guidelines. Clarification will be provided as required. The Committee shall periodically report to the Council on these matters.
- The Committee shall periodically invite the Business and Industry Advisory Committee to OECD (BIAC) and the Trade Union Advisory Committee to OECD (TUAC) to express their views on matters related to the Guidelines. In addition, exchanges of views with the advisory bodies on these matters may be held upon request by the latter. The Committee shall take account of such views in its reports to the Council.
- If it so wishes, an individual enterprise will be given the opportunity to express its views either orally or in writing on issues concerning the Guidelines involving its interests.
- The Committee shall not reach conclusions on the conduct of individual enterprises.
- This Decision shall be reviewed at the latest in six years. The Committee shall make proposals for this purpose as appropriate.

Conflict settlement

- Member countries may request that consultations be held in the Committee on any problem arising from the fact that multinational enterprises are made subject to conflicting requirements. The Member countries concerned shall give prompt and sympathetic consideration to requests by Member countries for consultations in the Committee or through other mutually acceptable arrangements, it being understood that such consultations would be facilitated by notification at the earliest stage practicable. Member countries concerned will co-operate in good faith with a view to resolving such problems, either within the Committee or through other mutually acceptable arrangements.
- The Committee will continue to serve as a forum for consideration of the question of conflicting requirements, including, as appropriate, the national and international legal principles involved.

. . . .

III. Developing Codes of Conduct with Independent Monitoring Systems to Improve Labor Rights Enforcement[24]

Pharis J. Harvey

. . . .

[24] Pharis J. Harvey et al., *Developing Effective Mechanisms for Implementing Labor Rights in the Global Economy* (May 10, 2000), *available at* http://www.laborrights.org/files/developing_mechanisms.pdf

Introduction and Background

[A] number of private enforcement initiatives directed at corporations, rather than governments, have been proposed in recent years as alternatives or complements to bilateral labor rights clauses in trade agreements and regional social charters. These initiatives attempt to address directly the problem of employer violations of labor rights worldwide.

Corporate codes of conduct and mechanisms to enforce them provide a means to identify and address worker rights violations using consumer pressure, without directly relying on either individual government or international legal enforcement mechanisms. However we recognize that approach is limited to certain consumer-oriented MNCs with high profile brand names. Ultimately, therefore, the approach cannot be a substitute for the broader project of enhancing international labor standards and their enforcement.

In response to a flurry of exposés about inhumane conditions in the production of big name consumer items – especially garments, footwear, and toys – a number of MNCs which have significant elements of their corporate value tied up in name identification have turned to the strategy of adopting and publicizing corporate codes of conduct. Typically, such codes stress the company's commitment to good environmental practices, to prohibiting forced labor and child labor, to fair and safe working conditions for employees, variously defined, and to nondiscrimination for reasons of gender, race, or other factors not relevant to the performance of work. A few of these corporate codes go further, attesting to the company's commitment to recognize their employees' right to form trade unions and to bargain collectively. Nevertheless, codes of conduct and independent monitoring initiatives can play an important role in breaking new ground on labor rights enforcement, and thus paving the way for proposed mechanisms outlined

(last visited Oct. 3, 2010) [Footnotes omitted]. The following suggestion has been proposed to move MNCs closer to adherence of core labor standards. "We offer 'Ratcheting Labor [RLS] Standards' (RLS) as a regulatory strategy that does just this; rather than devising institutions that attempt to constrain the rapidly changing forces and processes of globalization, RLS attempts to redirect some of these energies toward the advancement of social ends. . . . RLS would systematize this competition and extend it in several ways. First, it would require *every* firm in a regulated sector (e.g., apparel or footwear) to adopt *some* certified provisions for monitoring their labor standards performance. The array of monitoring options already available includes corporate-centered efforts such as the supplier qualification and management programs of NIKE and Reebok, social monitoring firms accredited under SA8000 and similar bodies, and more independent inspections conducted by community-based NGOs. Second, RLS monitoring agents such as these would be required to make their inspections, improvements, and analyses transparent and independently verifiable. Transparency requires them to submit both their methodologies and measurements to a centralized and publicly accessible knowledge base, perhaps resembling the Toxics Release Inventory (TRI) or the NGO-sponsored Scorecard project (www.scorecard.org). Verifiability requires that firms and their monitors agree to allow independent inspection (perhaps by NGO or governmental entities) of facilities whose reported social performance seem dubious." Sabel, O'Rourke, & Fung, *Ratcheting Labor Standards* (2000), *available at* http://www.archonfung.net/papers/rls21.pdf. For a different perspective on this proposal, see Jill Murray, *The Sound of One Hand Clapping? The 'Ratcheting Labor Standards' Proposal and International Labor Law*, 14 AUSTL. J. LAB. L. 306 (2001). For an example of a somewhat specialized corporate ADR program that addresses complaints that management violated the company's corporate social responsibility policy and its commitment to the right of its employees to unionize, see, William B. Gould IV, *Using an Independent Monitor to Resolve Union-Organizing Disputes Outside the NLRB: The First Group Experience*, DISP. RESOL. J. 46 ((May/July 2011).

in the previous section. In particular, they have played a useful role in mobilizing large numbers of consumers and workers to fight for better implementation of international labor standards.

. . . .

B. Model Initiatives

The biggest issue facing advocates for a code of conduct approach today is that of implementation. How can it be ensured that companies or industries are obeying their own codes? What kinds of sanctions can be applied for failure to implement? Below are a few examples of specific initiatives to address the implementation issue. While each of the examples below has its own unique history and problems, overall they may provide a basis for development of a broader implementation strategy.

Rugmark. Reports of bonded child labor amounting to virtual slavery in the carpet industries of India and Pakistan were displayed in shocking detail on European television in the mid-1980s. This news caused an immediate and potentially disastrous loss of sales of carpets from India in Europe, especially in Germany, the largest market for oriental carpets in the world. Alarmed at the prospects of losing an important source of foreign exchange, Indian non-governmental organizations, together with export promotion agencies linking Germany to India, began to discuss appropriate means to market good corporate behavior in the making of rugs. A number of labeling programs grew out of these discussions, including the Rugmark program. The program was later implemented in Nepal, as well. Rugmark is a private, voluntary certification program founded in September, 1994. It is administered as a foundation. The program aims to reduce the use of child labor in the industry and thereby avoid consumer boycotts. It also seeks to improve the long-term prospects of children who are removed from jobs in the industry. The program administers two systems of licensing, one for manufacturers and exporters and the other for importers and retailers in consuming countries. Licensed parties are required to pay a licensing fee, which is used to cover inspections and monitoring, administrative costs, issuance of Rugmark labels and to provide funds to establish educational programs for children removed from carpet work.

Inspections are carried out by professional Rugmark inspectors, and representatives of local NGOs are permitted to accompany inspectors at any time. When child labor is detected, licensees are given one warning before they are sanctioned. Once carpets are completed and ready for export, a carpet identification number is issued on a label affixed to the carpet, which allows the carpet to be traced back to the actual loom on which it was produced.

As of December 1999, the Rugmark program had succeeded in licensing more than 180 manufacturers and exporters in India, and had certified the export of one and a half million carpets from India and several thousand from Nepal. Most of these were shipped to Germany, with smaller numbers reaching the United States, U.K, Italy, Spain, Switzerland, France, the Netherlands and Japan. The Rugmark program had also succeeded in establishing seven schools in Nepal and India to rehabilitate former child workers. A Rugmark Pakistan program has recently become operational.

FIFA Code of Conduct/ILO Sialkot Monitoring Program. The soccer ball industry, centered around the city of Sialkot in Pakistan, has come under fire in recent years for employing child workers. Public attention to this issue led to the model Code of

Labor Practice adopted in September, 1996 by the International Federation of Football Associations (FIFA), the world regulatory agency for soccer.

. . . .

SA8000. Another response to the welter of demands for greater corporate accountability has been the Center for Economic Priorities' development of a code and monitoring system based on the ISO series of quality standards. Called SA8000, this code to measure "Social Accountability" is an effort to provide standards that can be monitored by professional accounting firms to declare individual factories or work sites as socially accountable, so that multinational firms can contract with them in the assurance that they have been declared acceptable. The terms of the code are similar to others, and in some instances superior. For example, the code calls clearly for payment of a "living wage" and for reparations or rehabilitation funds to be paid to children who are laid off by companies in order to comply with the standards.

A detailed analysis of the program by Janneke van Eijk of the European Clean Clothes Campaign noted several of the program's flaws. Among issues raised were the fact that monitoring cannot simply be conducted on a periodic "spot check" basis, but must involve the establishment of reliable, permanent mechanisms through which workers can report problems and grievances; such mechanisms are lacking in the SA8000 plan.

Another problem noted by van Eijk is the program's focus on individual factories, rather than on retailers. A participating MNC can apply for certification of a single factory, or handful of factories, and receive such certification even if the vast majority of its facilities or suppliers remain uninspected. A company might thus choose to spotlight a model facility under the program, and receive the public benefit of such inspection, even when the vast majority of its production takes place under unregulated conditions. While the program's spokespeople have responded by noting that they provide certification only to factories, not to retailers, the overall "report card" approach of the Center for Economic Priorities may nevertheless convey to consumers the suggestion that a company has received, as a whole, a clean bill of health.

A final flaw of the program is that monitors must pay a fee to receive accreditation from the program, a process that many local NGOs may find prohibitive. Although the program is in theory open to any sort of organization that may wish to be accredited as a monitor, to date monitoring has been carried out by a small handful of MNCs with expertise in financial auditing or the area of customs inspection, principally *Societe Generale de Surveillance*.

The SA8000 scheme is likely to win some support among MNCs as being a consistent and relatively easily implementable approach. However, treating labor rights as a "quality control" issue similar to other ISO standards is unlikely to appease critics of corporate behavior from the trade union and NGO communities. Unlike verification of the quality of a product, independent monitoring of codes requires the establishment of relationships of trust between monitors and workers, as shall be described in the Issues section below.

. . . .

Monitors for Hire

During the past two years a number of companies have developed labor auditing services, provided to companies on a for-profit basis. These companies include accounting firms Ernst and Young and Price Waterhouse Coopers. The problems with for-profit auditing initiatives are discussed in the next section. An independent non-profit organization,

Verite, has also been established to provide labor auditing services to companies on a paid, contractual basis.

Issues to be Resolved

Initiatives to promote codes of conduct and independent monitoring and verification systems have made great strides in recent years. While these initiatives have garnered far more widespread attention and support from employers, consumers, and trade unions than any previous such efforts, and have achieved notable success in pushing the discussion on corporate responsibility forward, nevertheless there remain several outstanding issues under debate.

Below we review the most significant of these questions and outline our position on each.

1. Do Codes Undermine Collective Bargaining?

Although unions and union federations have been prominent participants in the promotion of, and creation of bodies to monitor, codes of conduct, nevertheless many activists in the trade union movement both in the United States and elsewhere have expressed fears that codes of conduct, if implemented, may obviate the need for trade unions to negotiate collective bargaining agreements on behalf of an enterprise's workforce. They fear that monitors will most likely be appointed from the NGO community, and, in handling grievances, take over the function of democratically-elected union leadership, thus removing the democratic right of workers to have a direct say in their own wages and working conditions.

The experience of the Independent Monitoring Group of El Salvador highlights the relevance of such fears. GMIES emerged as a response to a particular situation, that of the mass dismissal of independent trade union activists at the Mandarin plant. It succeeded in its original goal to compel the company to re-hire the fired activists. However, subsequently the group was saddled with the larger responsibility of monitoring overall company compliance with The Gap's code of conduct, a task for which it was unprepared, and which it undertook in a vacuum of coordinated guidance or oversight.

GMIES's role shifted away from one of supporting the independent union, and toward one of investigating and handling complaints of company non-compliance with labor standards in its code. By early 1998, the group had adopted a "neutral" stance *vis à vis* the conflict between the original, independent union and the company union. Superior resources and friendly relationships with management had allowed the company union to win widespread support among workers, whereas the independent union had dwindled to a small handful of supporters.

While the GMIES experiment did not lead to the establishment of a vibrant, independent trade union in the factory, it did serve to neutralize some of the factors that had previously made union organizing impossible, and to assist fired trade unionists to regain employment. This may reflect more broadly an important role for NGO monitors: they may serve as a check on employer behavior to prevent workers from exercising their right to associate. While this role is a limited one, given the severe restrictions on workers' right to associate today, particularly in the garment and other light manufacturing industries, monitoring may play a very useful role in strengthening nascent trade union activity.

We note that in most developing countries, employers are free to employ a wide variety of union-busting techniques at the slightest sign of independent organizing activity. The International Confederation of Free Trade Unions (ICFTU) has estimated that 300 to 500 workers are killed *each year* for their organizing activities. Thousands more are arrested, beaten, or intimidated. There are between 65,000 and 75,000 cases of union leaders reported to be fired for their activities each year. Many thousands more cases go unreported. Those who suggest that independent monitors will prevent independent unions from forming are to some extent ignoring the far more significant impediments that exist to independent union formation, such as employers' ability to enlist the support of police or other local authorities to arrest or intimidate workers, and the near-impossibility of resolving unfair terminations in a timely manner through local judicial systems.

One of the most important roles a monitoring group can play, particularly in closed polities such as China, where information flow on labor issues is carefully restricted, will be to collect information about such terminations and to pressure employers to act immediately to rehire these workers. This is an area in which immediate pressure from Western consumers and advocacy groups is far more likely to be effective than recourse to local judicial processes. The practice is also likely to act as a deterrent to any future such firings, thus removing a significant obstacle to union organizing.

Where independent unions exist, monitors within the workplace should be delegates of the union itself. In many if not most light manufacturing enterprises in developing countries, however, independent unions have not been able to form. In such a context, monitors may also serve a useful role in simply providing information to workers about their rights under a company's code. In this way, non-union monitors can and should become allies to union activists, not replacements for them.

Codes may help promote development of trade unions, provided they contain protections for workers' rights to associate and form unions, and to bargain collectively. By and large, the protections listed in codes of conduct do not vary significantly from protections contained in most countries' labor laws. Abuses occur because governments fail to enforce these laws. One area in which the problem is not enforcement, but weak legislation itself, is that of trade union activity. Many developing countries have consciously adopted a strategy of suppressing or heavily regulating all trade union activity. The links between such strategies and governments' desires to attract foreign investment, particularly in the manufacturing sector, are exemplified by the additional restrictions placed on labor organizing in export processing zones. In short, the "race to the bottom" has been as much a race to weaken trade union and bargaining rights as it has been a race to provide cheap wages. Codes of conduct have the potential to play a critical role in the promotion of free trade unions in such places, provided they contain language protecting workers' rights to associate and form unions and to bargain collectively. By pressuring MNCs not only to adopt but to honor such language, worker advocates may be able to create a context within which free trade unions can develop even under restrictive legal frameworks.

2. *Who Should Monitor Companies' Compliance with their Codes?*

Companies have experimented with three types of monitoring of codes: internal, external and independent. These definitions are taken from the report, "The Apparel Industry and Codes of Conduct: A Solution to the International Child Labor Problem?" produced by the US Department of Labor's Bureau of International Affairs in 1996. The definitions themselves are the subject of debate. Some feel that external monitoring is, in fact, independent monitoring while others feel it more closely resembles internal monitoring. This paper retains the DOL definitions in order to distinguish between monitoring performed on contract to the company and that which is not. For the purposes of the discussion below, internal monitoring is that conducted by representatives of the company (either the MNC or the supplier) itself. External monitoring is conducted by a third party, a monitor-for-hire, under contract to the company on a for-profit basis. Independent monitoring (also referred to as independent verification) is that which is performed by a group which does not have a direct or exclusive relationship with the company; usually some level of public reporting is a part of independent monitoring.

Internal Monitoring

Internal monitoring is that conducted by employees or representatives of the retailer itself or of its supplier. Its advantages are that monitors may be allowed free access to all information relevant to the production process without risk of jeopardizing any privileged information, such as trade secrets. The basic problem with internal monitoring is that it relies on the "good faith" of the company itself. The premise of consumer pressure is removed because even those companies with the best of intentions will have no incentive to reveal their own bad practices to the public. Where the company has a genuine desire to be a good corporate citizen, or to improve its labor practices for reasons of improved efficiency, stability, or to avoid negative publicity, individuals entrusted with monitoring may be able to enforce real compliance with standards. Where, however, the monitoring is being done merely to placate a hostile consumer audience, efforts to monitor may be restricted to a mere exercise in public relations. Under such circumstances, information presented by the company to the public cannot be relied upon.

An example of such an exercise in "bad faith" was the advertising campaign launched by Guess? Inc. in December, 1997. In previous years, Guess? had been the target of consumer campaigns to publicize the company's labor abuses. In December, the company took out full-page ads in the *New York Times* and other regional newspapers advertising its jeans as "sweat free" and stating that the company had been given a clean bill of health by the U.S. Department of Labor. In fact the Department of Labor had cited Guess? suppliers in the United States for labor violations earlier in the year, and insisted that the company remove the claim from its advertisements. The Guess? strategy illustrates the problems consumers might face if their only source of information were companies themselves.

External Monitoring[25]

External monitoring is monitoring contracted out by the company itself to a third party. Nike International provides an example of a company using external monitoring. For the

[25] [Author's note] See, e.g., SA 8000, which is a global social accountability standard "that aims to meet universal code of decent working conditions for workers. The Social Accountability 8000 is administered by Social Accountability International (SAI) and is responsible to maintain suitable employment practices in favor of the workers." SA 8000 *Social Accountability*, CONSTRAACH, http://www.constraarch.com/SA800.htm (last visited June 21, 2011).

past few years the corporation has hired the accounting firm Ernst and Young to provide labor audits of its plants in Southeast Asia. In 1997, Nike also contracted Goodworks International, a nonprofit led by former U.S. Ambassador Andrew Young, to inspect its plants in China and Southeast Asia.

External monitoring carries an information flow problem similar to that of internal monitoring. Since the external monitor is on contract to the company, the monitor is not free to disseminate information publicly. Instead, a confidential report is issued to the company which the company itself may or may not disseminate. This was a problem which arose in the Nike/ Ernst and Young example. The company discovered serious health and safety hazards at Nike producing facilities in Vietnam, but was precluded from publicizing this information. Despite its findings, Ernst and Young nonetheless certified that Nike was in compliance with its code. Nike chose not to correct the violations, and continued to assert publicly that the audits were assisting suppliers to improve their labor conditions. An independent NGO representative discovered and publicized the violations uncovered by Ernst and Young, to the company's embarrassment.

Another criticism leveled against external for-profit monitors is that they may not have the expertise or sensitivity necessary to conduct accurate interviews with workers. This criticism operates on two levels. First is the suggestion that an accounting firm or otherwise inexperienced group may simply not know what questions to ask. This problem can be overcome by a system to train and accredit monitors, a subject to be discussed in the following section. Second is the suggestion that workers may be afraid to provide external monitors, whom they perceive as company representatives, with accurate information. This was the criticism leveled against Andrew Young, who conducted his tour of Nike factories accompanied by factory management and made no attempts to interview workers in a confidential setting.

Independent Monitoring/Verification

Independent monitoring is that conducted by a third party not on exclusive contract to the company itself. Independent monitoring may use monitors-for-hire or may use local organizations, including labor, religious, human rights or other community-based groups, to conduct labor investigations in zones where such groups are located. This approach is exemplified by the Independent Monitoring Group of El Salvador, described earlier in this section. In theory monitoring by a firm such as Ernst and Young may be considered independent if the monitor is not acting as an agent of the company it is monitoring, or is not subject to a conflict of interest caused by the fact it may have or seek other commercial relationships with the company. For example in the Nike/Ernst and Young case, Ernst and Young could not be considered independent, even if their labor audits were paid for by a source other than Nike, because they have a separate commercial relationship with Nike to conduct the company's financial audits and a consequent disincentive to be overly, or even appropriately, critical of labor practices, since the other financial interest outweighed the social auditing program incentive.

Monitoring cannot work without a reliable, confidential reporting procedure. Workers in most developing countries know that they are vulnerable to being fired without cause, and that legal redress, if it is available at all, may take years in process. Rather than lose their jobs, most individual workers will exercise caution in criticizing their employer or airing their grievances publicly, or even confidentially. The most trustworthy interviewers will inevitably be those who arise from the ranks of the workers themselves, or from their communities. Local organizations are also best equipped to deal with language and other locale-specific barriers, since they possess the cultural knowledge necessary both to frame questions appropriately and to interpret answers accurately.

Independent trade unions, led by representatives elected directly by an enterprise's workers, are the organizations best equipped to set up a monitoring and reporting process within a factory.

. . . .

How Should Monitoring be Regulated?

Whether independent monitoring is conducted by international or by local groups, there is a need to regulate the monitors themselves in order to ensure that information to be provided to consumers is consistent and accurate. Initially, monitors should be accredited by a body that is recognizable and trusted by consumers. After accreditation, groups should be provided with guidance as to the types of information they are expected to provide. If the strategy of using local organizations is adopted, companies and worker advocates in consuming countries may wish to develop a training program to teach such organizations how to gather the relevant information and how to present it in a standard format that can be used easily by companies and consumer advocates. An essential function of an accreditation body would be to revoke accreditation from monitors who are found to be unreliable or otherwise substandard.

. . . .

The ILO may be able to play a useful role in the area of standardization of monitoring and reporting, by sharing through training or informational programs its own measures or benchmarks for compliance with ILO conventions. Such an exchange might also facilitate convergence of different private initiative toward a globally applicable labor rights monitoring framework.

3. *Who Should Pay for Monitoring?*

The possible sources of funding are, in essence, corporations, governments, and worker/consumer advocates (trade unions and other civic organizations). Various mixes of funding from these entities may provide for monitoring to take place and to remain independent.

The critical issue here is not who provides the funding, but what steps are taken to ensure that monitors may retain their independence from any single party and are not biased by the source of funding. Direct financial relationships between the monitor and company are not precluded, as long as the public interest is protected by measures that include transparency of monitoring contracts, some form of public access to results of audits, and protections against side payments or other improper transactions between the contracting parties.

The Rugmark example provides one workable funding scenario: companies wishing to utilize the services of monitors pay a licensing fee to an independent overseer (in this case, the Rugmark Foundation) and that overseer in turn provides inspection services. Since inspectors are not paid directly by their clients they are able to maintain their objectivity.

The Rugmark program also institutes other safeguards to ensure that inspectors are not vulnerable to bribery or other possible compromises of their integrity.

The Independent Monitoring Group of El Salvador in its first year used another model of funding, one in which the company itself and a worker advocate, the National Labor Committee, contributed equally to its upkeep. The group's independence from each funder was thus assured. However, The Gap's failure to provide a second year of funding is indicative of problems with this approach that might best be addressed if funding were to be channeled through a neutral body with ongoing oversight responsibility.

4. *Do Codes Undermine Efforts to Strengthen National and International Labor Standards?*

Some have expressed concern that by functioning independently of any country's legal system, codes of conduct and independent monitoring may palliate local desire to improve legal standards. In fact we feel codes and independent monitoring provide an important, complementary mechanism to augment enforcement of existing legal systems, and may foster greater desire to improve those systems. By adopting a code, a corporation also acknowledges its responsibility to abide by local labor laws. In most cases, local labor laws even in developing countries offer adequate protections for workers, conforming to at least minimum international standards on subjects such as working hours, overtime compensation, forced labor and child labor.

However, abuses occur because governments lack adequate enforcement budgets, or are offered multiple incentives to protect the interests of elites and capital rather than enforcing these laws. For example, in both China and Indonesia, partnerships between top military officials and investors have been documented. Such alliances give the military in both countries every incentive to safeguard their investments by participating in labor repression. If monitored, codes may improve enforcement of local labor laws. The codes approach recognizes that in many developing countries, workers may be unaware of existing legal protections. Even where they have information about such laws, workers may hesitate to involve corrupt or unsympathetic labor officials in their grievances. Through monitors, workers may gain access to information not only about a company's code of conduct but also about local labor laws and legal protections. Furthermore, if effective monitoring mechanisms can be established, it may be easier and less intimidating for a worker to use such mechanisms than to bring problems to the attention of local officials or courts. The development of such alternate dispute resolution mechanisms for MNCs with codes of conduct may provide officials in developing countries with incentives to better enforce existing labor laws, in order to preserve their own jurisdiction. At the very least such an approach provides some workers with another option to seek redress for grievances. This approach may ultimately have a spillover effect from MNCs that adopt and comply with codes to local employers, as workers share information between enterprises. Workers in local enterprises are ultimately unlikely to tolerate dual systems of enforcement.

The codes approach may also create incentives for some MNCs to become allies in the movement for harmonized labor standards and consistent enforcement of those standards. By initially creating an environment of greater accountability for MNCs with codes, it puts them at a competitive disadvantage to MNCs in the same industry without codes producing in the same countries. The approach may therefore convince companies that in order to compete effectively, they too have an interest in advocating for uniform adoption and implementation of labor legislation.

5. *Should Codes Define a Living Wage?*

The basic content of most codes of conduct does not vary significantly from the internationally-recognized worker rights called for in debates for a social clause in international settings. An exception to this generalization is local laws regulating trade union activity, discussed above. Insofar as this is true, the standards represent a broad international consensus on fundamental worker rights which has been generated by advocates in both developed and developing countries. The list of generally agreed-upon standards includes elimination of forced labor, elimination of child labor, decent wages and working conditions, decent health and safety standards, non-discrimination, the right to organize and bargain collectively. Most industry and company codes incorporate all of these standards. One issue that remains unresolved is the debate on wages. The AIP and ETI codes call for employers to pay either minimum or prevailing wages in the countries where they produce, and to recognize the need for those wages to meet workers' basic needs. Critics of this provision note that in most developing countries, the minimum or prevailing wages are insufficient to provide a basic market basket of goods to most workers. These critics call for the establishment of criteria to define what a living wage would be in each country, and call on companies to agree to pay this amount rather than minimum wage.

The debate on living wages has been a contentious one, in no small part because, unlike other rights covered by corporate codes, the definition of a living wage has yet to be clearly established by any international convention. Nor do economists or other social scientists agree on a cross-country definition of a standard market basket of goods. Since international consensus on this issue is lacking, consumer country advocates for a living wage clause have been particularly susceptible to the argument that they are acting out of protectionist rather than humanitarian motivations.

It is our position that the living wage issue cannot be resolved without (a) substantial further research and the development of a reasonable and widely acceptable cross-cultural index to measure basic needs; and (b) substantial effort by developed country advocates of a living wage to engage in open dialogue on this issue with trade unions and NGOs in developing countries.

. . . .

Conclusion

The codes of conduct approach offers a valuable means to create and foster dialogues between developed world and developing world advocates for labor and consumer rights. The strategy is, in effect, an extension of an older, proven strategy to mobilize consumer support for workers: the boycott. Threats of boycott action have helped turn the tide in labor/management battles in the United States and other developed countries on numerous occasions. Codes of conduct help to extend consumer awareness of labor's problems and battles in less-developed parts of the world. Exposés of labor rights abuses, whether child labor in the soccer ball industry or trade union harassment in El Salvador, were made possible by the creation of alliances between developed world and developing world advocates.

Consumers in the US and other developed countries have become increasingly aware that many of the goods they consume are produced under inhumane or substandard conditions in locales such as Pakistan and Guatemala. As this awareness increases, so too does the awareness of citizens of developed countries that they live in a global economy, and that trade relations between countries do affect their day to day lives.

. . . .

Business Ethics in the Textile, Clothing, and Footwear (TCF) Industries[26]

Jean-Paul Sajhau

The Codes of Conduct of the Major Retail Networks

The major retail networks are playing an increasingly important role in the TCF sectors and in particular in textiles. With their large number of sales outlets, sometimes established in several countries, they are tending to replace the traditional manufacturers and to have their TCF articles with their own logo manufactured by subcontractors. Since these enterprises generally cater for the mass market, their sourcing policies are extremely diversified although always governed by a search for low production costs. In order to maintain a good public image, without foregoing the possibility of stepping up their trade relations with subcontractors producing in the developing countries, the major retail networks have become aware of the importance of adopting a responsible ethical behaviour. They have thus adopted codes of conduct similar to those of their counterparts in the manufacturing sector. We have chosen to highlight four of the most developed of these codes: those of Wal-Mart, J. C. Penney, Sears, Roebuck and Company, and Woolworth.

Wal-Mart, which recently experienced some difficulties of an ethical nature in the Kathie Lee Gifford affair, attributes its continued commercial success since its establishment in 1962 to the respect of three principles which form the basis of its business ethics. These principles are: to provide value and service to its customers by offering quality merchandise at low prices; corporate dedication to a partnership between employees, ownership and management; a commitment to the United States (reflected in the "Buy American commitment" campaign in which Wal-Mart undertakes to sell as far as possible products manufactured in the United States) and the communities in which its stores and distribution centres are located. In order to develop these values within the context of globalization, in 1993 Wal-Mart established a detailed code of conduct in the form of Standards for Vendor Partners, in particular those located outside the United States territory. The code is summarized below. Each business partner is required to sign a contract accepting the standards contained in the code.

[26] Business ethics in the textile, clothing, and footwear (TCF) industries, 2000, ILO Working Paper No. SAP 2.60/WP.110, *available at* http://www.ilo.org/public/english/dialogue/sector/papers/bzethics/index.htm (last visited Oct. 3, 2010). Copyright © 2000 International Labor Organization.

TABLE VII. *Wal-Mart – Code of conduct for suppliers and subcontractors*

Keywords	Standards for Vendor Partners
Human rights	Non-derogation of basic human rights
Child labour	Prohibited. Obligatory reference to: – national legislation; and – Wal-Mart definition: children are defined as persons: – under the age of 15; – under the compulsory schooling age of the country. Wal-Mart supports apprenticeship education programmes for young persons.
Forced or prison labour	Prohibited
Non-discrimination	No discrimination on the basis of race, colour, national origin, gender, religion, disability, sexual orientation or political opinion in recruitment.
Conditions of work	The minimum Wal-Mart standards are: – adequate medical services; – emergency exits; – safety equipment; – well-lit workstations; – clean rest-rooms; – adequate living quarters where necessary; – prohibition of any mental or physical disciplinary practices.
Hours of work and overtime	– In accordance with national legislation. – In accordance with local industry standards if higher. – Maximum of 60 hours a week plus one day of leave: annual leave.
Remuneration/wages	– In accordance with national legislation. – In accordance with prevailing industrial standards if higher.
Legal requirements	– For all activities compliance with national legislation is the minimum standard. – Preference given to trade partners respecting prevailing local industry standards. – United States legislation is applicable concerning: – import requirements into the United States; – the protection of intellectual property rights; – indication of the country of origin; – transport of the merchandise; – information on the merchandise transported.
Environment	In accordance with the principles of the three "Rs": reduce, reuse and recycle.
Application	– Wal-Mart or a third party appointed by Wal-Mart will take concrete measures to implement and monitor its standards. The plants of business partners are inspected four times a year. – Wal-Mart has established a certificate of compliance with its ethical standards which suppliers/subcontractors must obtain to do business with Wal-Mart (the Wal-Mart vendor partner inspection and certification form).
Sanctions in the event of violation	Termination of any business relationship between Wal-Mart and a trade partner which fails to respect the code.

The case of Sears, Roebuck and Company (SR) deserves special attention. This major retail group has, in its search for supply sources at the lowest cost, established a number of trade relations with China. Given the assumptions about the non-respect of human rights which affect this country, SR believed that it would be desirable to create a specific code of conduct concerning forced labour which would be applicable to its Chinese partners. Thus the ethical approach of SR is characterized by the juxtaposition of two codes of conduct, a set of Import-Buying Policy and Procedures, along with an additional code on forced labour applicable to China. These two codes are summarized below.

Comparative analysis of the codes of conduct

There is a constant feature in all the different elements which make up these codes: the reference to a variable number of principles concerning human rights at work. It is therefore on this fundamental aspect of the ethical codification of trade relations within the context of globalization that we have focused the first part of the comparative analysis, in relation to fundamental ILO standards. On the basis of the information available (which has not always been very exact), we have then proceeded to a comparison between the different methods for the application of these codes.

References to fundamental ILO standards

Although the codes of the selected enterprises do not make specific reference to ILO Conventions, it is clear that the content of the texts concerning the respect of human rights at work is directly inspired by the pertinent ILO Conventions. This is particularly the case as regards the elements of the codes detailing with child labour, forced labour and the principles of non-discrimination, which appear in many of these texts.

On the other hand, few codes contain specific provisions detailing with freedom of association or the right to organize and collective bargaining. This absence, which is regrettable given the importance of these fundamental rights, can be explained in various ways. First of all, some codes stipulate that trade partners must exercise their activities in accordance with national legislation. In most countries, the right to organize and freedom of association are recognized in the Constitution and stipulated in labour legislation, which moreover establishes the methods of collective bargaining.

However, it is well known that some countries provide for exceptions to these general principles. Free zones in particular have a special legal status which, in some cases, restricts, in a derogation of national legislation, certain trade union freedoms and limits the right to collective bargaining. Since a large number of subcontractors in the apparel and footwear sectors operate in these free zones, the mention, in a code of conduct, of the principles contained in Conventions Nos. 87 and 98 could cause difficulties to both the enterprise placing the orders and the subcontracting enterprise.

. . . .

Methods of monitoring the application of the codes

In order to be credible, the codes of conduct must be applied in a way which leaves no doubt in the minds of observers outside the enterprise. This means that the application

TABLE VIII. *Sears, Roebuck and Company – Codes of conduct*

Keywords	Import-Buying Policy and Procedures	Policy on Goods Made by Forced in China
Basic principles	Strict adherence to local laws governing working conditions and production methods and to applicable United States laws (for United States trade partners).	Prohibition of forced or convict labour.
– Conditions of work – Child labour – Wages	In accordance with local legislation or United States legislation (for United States subcontractors).	
Forced labour (legal requirements)		Compliance with United States legislation concerning the import of merchandise manufactured on the basis of forced labour.
Application		
Contractual clauses	– Reference to the code in all international purchasing agreements.	– Inclusion of a clause in all contracts with Chinese subcontractors concerning the non-use of forced labour.
Inspection	– Periodical visits to plants abroad by foreign buying office personnel.	– Carrying out of unannounced inspections of the plants of Chinese subcontractors.
Reporting obligation	– Reporting of any violation of national or United States law to the competent authority.	– Reporting of violations to the United States Customs Service.
Communication	– Distribution of a copy of the code to all Sears' employees and its trade partners.	– Copies of the Import Buying Policy and Procedures must be supplied to all Sears' subcontractors in China.
Information specific to relations with China		Sears' buying office in Hong Kong, responsible for its activities with China, must: – supply a list of all Chinese subcontractors to Sears' trading partners and make this list available to shareholders: – draw up a list, which must be as comprehensive as possible, of all Chinese enterprises which use forced labour and to compare it with the above-mentioned list.
Sanctions in the event of deliberate violation	Termination of business relations with suppliers who do not respect the code.	Termination of trade relations with any supplier using forced labour.

TABLE IX. *J.C. Penney – Code of conduct applicable to its business partners*

Keywords	Foreign sourcing requirements
Child labour	Prohibited.
Indentured labour	Prohibited.
Forced or prison labour	Prohibited.
Legal requirements	JCP will seek suppliers who conform to the legislation applicable within the framework of their activities.
Application	
– Factory visits	Carried out by JCP associates and buying agents. The latter are required to report to headquarters any conduct which infringes the code.
– Country of origin labelling	JCP will not knowingly import merchandise which does not bear a label indicating the country in which it has been manufactured.
– Producer's certificate	Any merchandise from a foreign country must be accompanied by a certificate indicating the factory at which it was manufactured.
Sanctions in the event of violations	– Cancellation of orders. – Prohibition for suppliers to use subcontractors which do not respect the code. – Termination by JCP of any business relationship with the suppliers/subcontractors who do not respect the code.

of the codes must be supervised by competent persons specially trained for this purpose and whose integrity cannot be questioned.

As regards the general principles making up the ethics of major multinationals, internal methods of supervision, combined with external sources of pressure, can generally be seen as guaranteeing their application within the parent company. Within the enterprise, the human resources policy established by the personnel department must take account of the ethical policy of the enterprise if it wishes to win the support of staff representatives; those responsible for the different technical departments must be made sensitive to the determination of the enterprise to preserve its image as a responsible employer with, if necessary, the general management intervening to prevent any loss of control or dispute. Outside the enterprise, trade union representatives are vigilant and pressure groups remain active, whether in the form of associations, through the media or as individual consumers. On the other hand, the effective implementation of the codes of conduct by suppliers and subcontractors is more difficult. Multinational enterprises (producers and distributors) in the TCF sectors make use of a number of intermediaries and subcontractors in a large number of countries, some of which are located far away.

TABLE X. *Woolworth Corporation – Code of conduct*

Basic principles	Prohibition of: – forced labour as well as prison labour; – child labour.
Legal requirements	– Merchandise must be in conformity with United States legislation applicable to imported articles. Requirement included in Woolworth's standard purchase order. – Business partners must respect the national legislation applicable within the framework of their manufacturing and marketing activities.
Application	– Distribution of the code to all business partners, including United States suppliers selling imported products to Woolworth. – Woolworth's buyers and other representatives regularly visit the enterprises of suppliers/subcontractors. Woolworth has established a training programme for officials visiting enterprises abroad to familiarize them with the application of the code of conduct in the context of different national legislations. – Before any payment, Woolworth requires the supplier to obtain a certificate of compliance with the application of the code. This requirement has been extended to all foreign subcontractors.

The logistics required to ensure the respect of the codes are considerable and few enterprises have the necessary human means. As can be seen from the following table, it would appear, on the basis of the piecemeal information available, that most enterprises entrust their local buying agents and quality control representatives with the task of monitoring respect of the codes of conduct. Unfortunately, in a very large number of cases there is a lack of information on the specific training of these agents in the sphere of labour legislation and, more generally, human rights at work. Furthermore, although some enterprises require their suppliers to sign a document in which they undertake to apply the code of ethics of the enterprises for which they are working, this is a moral undertaking rather than a genuine method of supervision.

Frequent use is made in the apparel industry of the practice of multiple subcontracting, whereby an enterprise which receives an order from a multinational enterprise in turn contracts out all or part of the order to other enterprises. In such cases, it becomes extremely difficult to try and control the entire subcontracting chain and the chances of non-respect of the elementary rights of workers increase as use is made of increasingly smaller and less structured enterprises. Attempts, albeit positive, to monitor the application of the codes must therefore be treated with all due caution and inspiration should be sought from the best organized enterprises which have trained their staff accordingly and which, because of their position in a specific market, cannot risk being accused of failing to implement their ethical principles. Recourse to external monitoring of the type introduced by The Gap in El Salvador, although difficult and expensive to implement, could also be an avenue worth exploring.

TABLE XI. *Methods of application of codes of conduct by trade partners*

Enterprise	Methods of application	Sanctions in the event of violation
Levi Strauss	In three stages: **1. Terms of engagement evaluation** Evaluation carried out by a Levi Strauss team made up of members of several technical departments – each team includes one of the 50 inspectors trained by the enterprise in this particular task. A 20-page evaluation document reviews practices in production and working conditions. The assessment is also based on opinions about the enterprise by trade union officials and local associations. Workers are also directly concerned and unannounced visits to enterprises are sometimes carried out. **2. Terms of engagement monitoring** Selected suppliers/subcontractors are subject to periodical inspections (at least once a year; sometimes every three months), the objective of which is to resolve points of difficulty, on a partnership basis, before they become real problems. **3. Training–Sensitivization** The enterprise conducts a policy of permanent training and sensitivization to its ethical criteria. This training is provided in the first instance for inspectors responsible for the application of the code of conduct but it is also available to other employees in the group who, at one level or another, have working relations with external suppliers.	Termination of relations with business partners failing to respect the terms of engagement.
The Gap	**Internal methods:** – The plants of subcontractors are selected and inspected by a representative of the management of The Gap and/or by a commercial representative responsible for purchasing. A plant inspection certificate is issued, which is a necessary condition for the payment of merchandise. – Business partners must sign a vendor compliance agreement under which they must apply the same subcontractor selection criteria as The Gap. The Gap does not purchase foreign products from importers who have not signed this agreement. – The choice of countries with which The Gap has trade relations is approved by a sourcing committee which meets four times a year to update and publish a list of approved countries.	Termination of trade relations with supplier/subcontractors who do not respect the code of conduct.

Enterprise	Methods of application	Sanctions in the event of violation
	External methods: An independent monitoring working group set up in cooperation with: – The Interfaith Center on Corporate Responsibility – Business for Social Responsibility – The National Labor Committee works towards the improvement of the codes and proposes solutions. The initial aim is the improvement of working conditions in the international subcontractor "Mandarin International" in El Salvador.	Termination of trade relations with supplier/subcontractors who do not respect the code of conduct.
Reebok (R)	**Internal methods:** – R carries out supervision in accordance with its charter, in the form of factory inspections. No information is available on the internal structure established for this supervision. – R applies its charter for the protection of human rights in the selection of its trade partners and ensures that the latter apply the charter. – R seeks partners who provide complete information on the production means used and the conditions of recruitment and work.	No information on trade sanctions in the event of a violation of the code of conduct.
Nike (N)	**Internal methods:** – For each plant, a representative of N is responsible for the day-to-day application of the Memorandum. – Obligation for suppliers/subcontractors to retain and to make available to N all documentation concerning ethical criteria contained in the Memorandum. – The Memorandum is posted up in all the plants of N's subcontractors. – Reference to the code in all international purchasing contracts. **Methods independent of the enterprise:** – N reserves the right at all times to have an independent monitoring carried out of the plants of suppliers/subcontractors.	In the event of non-respect of the Memorandum, N may insist that the situation is redressed or it may cancel its trade commitments.
Sara Lee	The supervision of the application of the code by subcontractors is entrusted to the purchasing and quality control officials of Sara Lee.	No information on sanctions in the event of violation.
Phillips-van Heusen	No information is available on the internal structure set up for supervising the application of its code.	Termination of trade relations with suppliers/subcontractors who do not respect the code of conduct.

(*continued*)

TABLE XI *(continued)*

Enterprise	Methods of application	Sanctions in the event of violation
J.C. Penney (JCP)	**Internal methods:** – The inspection of plants of suppliers/subcontractors is carried out by purchasing agents. The agents carrying out these inspections report any failure to respect the code to the general management which takes appropriate measures. – JCP does not knowingly import goods which are not accompanied by a manufacturer's certificate indicating the manufacturing plant and certifying that the products have not been made by children or through forced labour. All merchandise must also include a certificate of origin indicating the country of manufacture.	– Termination of trade relations with subcontractors not respecting the code. – Prohibition for any supplier to use the sanctioned subcontractor.
Sears, Roebuck & Co.	**Internal methods:** – Periodical and unannounced visits to the plants of suppliers by the staff of the foreign purchase office. – Distribution of a copy of the code to all Sears employees and its business partners. – Reference to the code in all international purchasing contracts. In the case of a Chinese enterprise, inclusion in the contract of a clause on forced labour. – Reporting to the competent authorities of any violation of national United States legislation.	Termination of trade relations with suppliers/subcontractors who do not respect the code if the violation is deliberate.
Wal-Mart (W-M)	**Internal enterprise methods:** – WM or a representative appointed by WM carries out inspections on the application of ethical standards. – The plants of subcontractors are inspected four times a year. Plants which comply with the standards receive the Wal-Mart Vendor Partner Inspection and Certification Form.	Termination of trade relations with suppliers/subcontractors who do not respect the code.
Woolworth (W)	**Internal methods:** – W agents regularly inspect the plants of foreign subcontractors. – Before payment of goods, the supplier/subcontractor must provide a certificate certifying compliance with the code of conduct. – W intends to: – distribute its code to all suppliers/subcontractors; – establish a training programme for buyers and other persons visiting foreign plants to ensure that they understand the code in the context of the applicable local legislation; – ensure that the code of conduct is applied by United States importers which supply the company.	No information available on sanctions in the event.

QUESTIONS

1. Discuss why codes of conduct have evolved and how effective they are. Do they strengthen or undermine international labor standards?
2. What is the difference between a corporate code of conduct and an industrial code of conduct? Is one likely to be more effective than the other? If so, why; if not, why not?
3. What type of sanctions or enforcement methods could be built into the codes that might satisfy the trade unions? Are anti-retaliation provisions common?
4. Do these types of codes support or undermine trade unions? Provide examples of both situations.
5. Who should monitor the codes of conduct? Would the demands of the foreign workers and their union differ from those of the American workers and their union?
6. What is the relationship of codes of conduct to the laws regulating labor relations?

2. *Enforcement of Labor Standards through Litigation*

a. Codes of Conduct: Wal-Mart Case

Code or Contract: Whether Wal-Mart's Code of Conduct Creates a Contractual Obligation between Wal-Mart and the Employees of Its Foreign Suppliers[27]

Katherine E. Kenny

I. Introduction

On September 13, 2005, workers from China, Bangladesh, Indonesia, Swaziland, and Nicaragua sued Wal-Mart in Superior Court in Los Angeles for breach of contract as third-party beneficiaries to Wal-Mart Stores, Inc.'s supply contract with garment factories located in those respective countries. The suit, brought by the International Labor Rights Fund ("ILRF"), makes the novel claim that Wal-Mart's Standards for Suppliers Agreement, also known as the Code of Conduct, created contractual obligations between it and potentially hundreds of thousands of workers employed by Wal-Mart's foreign suppliers who had agreed to comply with the Code of Conduct.

Wal-Mart's Code of Conduct sets forth five standards relating to compliance with applicable law and practices, employment conditions, workplace environment, concern for environment, factory inspection, and Wal-Mart's gift and gratuity policy. Wal-Mart's supply contract requires that the foreign suppliers in the identified countries producing

[27] Reprinted by special permission of Northwestern University School of Law, *Northwestern Journal of International Law and Business*. Katherine E. Kenny, *Comment, Code or Contract: Whether Wal-Mart's Code of Conduct Creates a Contractual Obligation Between Wal-Mart and the Employees of Its Foreign Suppliers*, 27 NW. J. INT'L L. & BUS. 453 (2007).

goods for Wal-Mart adhere to Wal-Mart's Code of Conduct as a direct condition of supplying merchandise to Wal-Mart. In addition, Wal-Mart asks suppliers to sign the Code of Conduct for Wal-Mart's records and to display a poster version of the Code of Conduct in the local language and English in each production facility servicing Wal-Mart. The suit alleges that Wal-Mart was in turn "obligated to ensure supplier compliance with its Code of Conduct, and adequately monitor working conditions in supplier factories."

Workers claim that because Wal-Mart failed to leverage its "economic position and actual control over supplier factories," the workers were subject to employment conditions that violated the Code of Conduct. The suit outlines eight causes of action brought on behalf of the foreign workers: (1) Breach of Contract for Denial of Minimum and Overtime Wages, (2) Breach of Contract for Forced Labor, (3) Breach of Contract for Denial of Fundamental Right to Freely Associate, (4) Negligence and Recklessness, (5) Negligence Per Se, (6) Negligent Hiring and Supervision, (7) Unjust Enrichment and Violation of Business, and (8) Professions Code § 17200. The ILRF, who brought the suit on behalf of the workers, outlines the workers' demands. According to the ILRF, the workers demand that Wal-Mart enforce its Code of Conduct, create a dispute resolution system by which workers could air their grievances, reform its pricing practices to ensure that the prices provided to suppliers would still allow workers to receive the benefits of Wal-Mart's Code of Conduct, and provide workers with restitution and a commitment to sourcing from union shops and worker co-ops worldwide.

In recent years, the apparel and garment industry has experienced increased criticism and scrutiny due to allegations of sweatshop labor conditions, unfair wages, unreasonable hours, unsafe working conditions, and physical or mental abuse of workers. Some of these criticisms resulted in lawsuits brought against multiple garment manufacturers, including J. Crew, Gap, Tommy Hilfiger, and Wal-Mart. Wal-Mart settled a 1999 lawsuit brought by workers in the Northern Mariana Islands out of court for an undisclosed amount. For many multi-national corporations, internally created codes of conduct are seen as a way not only to self-regulate, but also to bolster their image and reputation among consumers and shareholders with respect to foreign business practices as a means to counter such criticisms and lawsuits.

Although "[i]ndividual corporate codes of conduct vary from brief, value policy statements to comprehensive guidelines . . . the uniform policy behind them is to show the [multi-national corporation's] support for the labor rights of workers." Historically, the main criticism levied against codes of conduct stems from the prior notion that they are self-imposed and voluntary, and thus lack a hard enforcement mechanism. According to Terry Collingsworth, ILRF's general counsel, the premise of the current lawsuit against Wal-Mart "is that Wal-Mart and many other companies issued these codes of conduct as public relations devices.[28] They never expected that someone would take the codes

[28] A class-action lawsuit filed in California on September 13, 2005, uses the code of conduct that Wal-Mart imposes on overseas suppliers against Wal-Mart itself. Complaint, Doe v. Wal-Mart Stores, Inc., No. BC339737 (Cal. Super. Ct. L. A. County, Sept. 13, 2005), (on file with author), *available at* http://docs.google.com/fileview?id=0B5vm9beLyq1sNmE4YmMzMTgtMTAxMS00NjdhLWIxM2MtOGRlYjQ3YWExNWYz&hl=en (last visited Sept. 28, 2010). The Wal-Mart plaintiffs are a purported class of Bangladeshi, Chinese, Indonesian, Nicaraguan, Swazilander, and U.S. workers suing for alleged violations of Wal-Mart's code of conduct. Multinationals that impose codes of conduct on offshore suppliers (or service providers) should reexamine their strategy in light of this new case.

seriously and use it as an affirmative tool to actually make them do what they promised to do." As a result, this case is likely to cause alarm among MNCs, which have increasingly "relied on codes of conduct to assert their commitment to socially responsible behavior without incurring legal liability."

This comment examines whether corporate codes of conduct and more specifically, Wal-Mart's Code of Conduct, are binding contracts between foreign suppliers and their employees or whether they are voluntary and non-contractual devices. An analysis of U.S. law and the text and implementation of Wal-Mart's Code of Conduct reveals that the Code should not be interpreted as a contract binding on foreign suppliers and their employees for the breach of contract for denial of minimum and overtime wages, the breach of contract for forced labor, and the breach of contract for denial of the fundamental right to freely associate.

The comment goes on to discuss the ramifications of this type of suit and other possibilities for bringing about the successful reform of labor conditions for foreign workers. This comment concludes that the best means for reform is not litigation but legislation. Part II of this comment discusses the historical origins of corporate codes of conduct and the role that they currently play within MNCs. Part III discusses how courts in the United States have interpreted corporate codes of conduct. Part IV analyzes the text and implementation of Wal-Mart's Code of Conduct and determines whether it should be interpreted as a contract or mere guidelines in light of recent court rulings. Part V analyzes the impact of the lawsuit and discusses the appropriateness of other possible means for reforming foreign working conditions. Part VI draws conclusions with respect to the most effective means of impacting workers' conditions, such as grassroots efforts.

II. Historical Origins of Internal and External Corporate Codes of Conduct and Their Role within Multinational Corporations

MNCs use "corporate codes of conduct" to set out ethical standards in their conduct. For the most part, MNCs that adopt codes of conduct voluntarily create a written pledge or establish standards to respect labor rights outlined in the code. Underlying these codes is a fundamental premise: that "corporations, due to their dominance as global institutions, should address the social and environmental problems affecting humankind."

. . . .

III. How Courts Interpret Corporate Codes of Conduct

In order to determine whether or not Wal-Mart's Code of Conduct could be interpreted as establishing a contractual obligation to employees of foreign suppliers, it is necessary to evaluate how codes of conduct are interpreted. Recently, a federal district court in the Northern District of Illinois laid out a framework under which employer codes of conduct would be considered contractually binding. The court determined that in order for an employee handbook or other employment policies, such as a code of conduct, to create enforceable contractual rights, the language of the policy must conform to the traditional requirements of contract formation. Therefore, the code of conduct must:

First, contain a promise clear enough that an employee would reasonably believe that an offer has been made. Second, the statement must be disseminated to the employee in such a manner that the employee is aware of its contents and reasonably believes it to be an offer. Third, the employee must accept the offer by commencing or continuing to work after learning of the policy statement.

In determining that the disputed Code of Conduct, from the company Weber Shandwick, was not a contract, the court pointed out that the Code of Conduct did not contain clear promissory language. Rather, the Code's use of the phrase "may result in disciplinary action" was just a general statement of company policy or practice and was therefore too indefinite to create a binding contractual obligation. Because Weber Shandwick's Code of Conduct contained general statements of company policy and guidelines for employer–employee conduct, it did not constitute a binding contract. The court concluded that if the language had been more precise to include phrasing like "will result in disciplinary action," it would have been considered precise enough. The court argued that "language that merely gives examples of the kinds of conduct that subject an employer to discharge does not amount to a contractual promise." Furthermore, when the purpose of a handbook or code of conduct is not to confer rights, but to warn employees about conduct that could result in termination or adverse action, the language does not constitute a contract.

Similarly, the Court of Appeals for the Ninth Circuit expressed the importance of looking at the specific language of the code of conduct when determining whether or not it was a contract. In order for statements in employment manuals and codes of conduct to be binding, the court ruled, in an unreported case that they must "constitute promises of specific treatment in specific situations, not merely policy statements." As a result, the court ruled that the statement contained in the manual, "Honeywell will make every effort in terms of counseling employees whose work is unsatisfactory," did not constitute a specific promise because it did not provide "detailed or specific procedure to be followed prior to terminating an employee." In determining that the language was too vague, the court focused on the specific term "make every effort" to infer that under some circumstances "every effort" might mean that there is still nothing that can be done to prevent termination.

The Ninth Circuit also laid out a framework by which employers can escape contractual obligations for their employee codes of conduct. Employers can avoid contractual obligations if they "specifically state, in a conspicuous manner that nothing contained therein is intended to be part of the employment relationship and are simply general statements of company policy." However, if an employer promises specific treatment in specific circumstances and an employee is induced thereby to remain on the job and not actively seek alternative employment, those promises are enforceable as contracts. In the specific instance, the court concluded that the employer was not bound by statements in an employment manual because the Code of Conduct stated specifically that it was not "to be construed as limiting [the employer's] right to terminate without cause."

Although the courts have not specifically addressed a case where an implied contract modified an at-will employment relationship, court opinions still provide a framework from which inferences can be drawn to decide whether an implied contract modified an at-will employment relationship. Even if a worker cannot prove that an express contract existed, a worker may be able to prove that a code of conduct established an implied contract. This possibility might give some insight into how a court would interpret whether a code of conduct created an implied contract with an employee. To determine whether there is an implied contract, courts will look at: (1) length of service; (2) actions or communications by the employer reflecting assurances of continued employment; (3) the employer's personnel policies and practices; (4) whether the employee gave independent consideration for the employer's promise; and (5) practices in the industry in which the employee is engaged.

Although the Ninth Circuit has ruled that statements must contain promises of specific treatment for specific instances in order for a contractual relationship to be created from employer codes of conduct, some court decisions indicate that when an employer puts forth formal personnel policies and procedures in codes of conduct, those policies and procedures will be viewed as contractually binding. In Guz v. Bechtel National, Inc., the California Supreme Court held that "when an employer promulgates formal personnel policies and procedures in handbooks, manuals and memoranda disseminated to employees, a strong inference may arise that the employer intended workers to rely on these policies as terms and conditions of their employment." In Guz, the company's written personnel documents were seen as contractually binding and therefore modified the original conditions of the employee's contract.

In addition to rulings in the United States, a 2005 ruling in Wuppertal, Germany by a local labour court offers some insight into whether codes of conduct should be seen as contractually binding overseas. The court found that the Code of Conduct given to Wal-Mart's employees in Germany, which is similar to the one implemented in stores in the United States, violated German labor laws. In February 2005, Wal-Mart's German workers were given a thirty-three-page Code of Conduct attached to their pay checks. In addition, all store managers were provided with a special poster regarding the company's Code of Conduct. This poster was supposed to go on permanent display in German Wal-Marts' Human Resources departments. The guidelines on ethics forced Wal-Mart's employees to adhere to rules about behavior and their private and sexual relationships. One of the provisions of the company's Code for employees forbids intimate relationships among co-workers and requires employees to inform Wal-Mart via a telephone hotline if they suspect violations. The German workers' council filed the suit against Wal-Mart Germany in protest of the controversial provisions. The Local Labour Court of Wuppertal ruled in favor of the employees. The Court ruled that provisions in the Code violated the German Constitution and more specifically German law, which says that anything regulating the personal lives of employees should first be agreed upon between employers and workers.[29] In addition, the Court ruled that the Code breached the right of co-determination because it required staff to report Code violations via a so-called ethics hotline. In order for the provisions to pass constitutional muster in Germany, the "works council" would have to agree upon the provisions.

Even though the ruling was in Germany and not the United States, let alone California where the complaint was filed, the ruling is important because it shows that Wal-Mart considers its Code of Conduct to be binding on employees. Thus, a violation of that Code can result in termination of employment. For Wal-Mart employees in Germany, as well as the United States, the Code of Conduct is not merely a suggestion, but a binding obligation of employees when they accept the job. This obligation gives insight into Wal-Mart's intent in creating a code of conduct for suppliers. This case is also relevant because it shows a tendency for courts to see codes of conduct, particularly ones that are distributed and displayed to employees, as having some binding force on those employees. In addition, codes are held to be illegal if they contain a clause that violates local law.

[29] [Author's comment] This also could be the likely outcome in China under its new Labor Contract Law, discussed under IV.C, although in China, the union or workers have only a right to consult on such matters before the employer's code can be implemented.

IV. Should Wal-Mart's Code of Conduct Be Interpreted as a Contract or Merely as Guidelines?

In order to determine whether Wal-Mart's Code of Conduct for foreign suppliers should be viewed as contractually binding, an analysis of the text and implementation of Wal-Mart's Code of Conduct in light of recent court rulings must take place. Based on recent court rulings, it seems that the contractual determination will hinge on whether Wal-Mart's Code of Conduct (1) made a promise clear enough for an offer; (2) was disseminated in a manner that employees knew of its contents and reasonably relied on it; and (3) whether employees accepted the offer either by commencing or continuing to work.

Based on Wal-Mart's own admissions, it appears that the Code of Conduct was disseminated in such a manner that employees knew of its contents and reasonably relied on it. Wal-Mart's own "Supplier's Responsibilities" make clear that Wal-Mart requires that a poster version of the Supplier Standards in the local language and English be placed in each production facility serving Wal-Mart. The poster version has already been translated into twenty-five languages. The filed complaint alleged that all "plaintiffs either saw posted in the supplier factory or were otherwise made aware of Wal-Mart's Code of Conduct and understood that the worker rights protections contained therein . . . were for their direct benefit." Specifically for the Indonesian plaintiffs, the complaint alleges that Wal-Mart's Code of Conduct is posted on the walls of factories in Indonesia, and that one of the plaintiff's supervisors provided him a copy of the Code of Conduct to "distribute to the employees for whom he served as foreman." Even if the argument can be made that some of the workers did not see the poster or were not provided with a copy of the Code of Conduct, by Wal-Mart's own admission the Code was supposed to be distributed to all employees. Therefore, it seems likely that the requirement for contract formation was satisfied.

Similarly, because the plaintiffs in the complaint all continue to work at Wal-Mart, it appears that there can be little debate about whether the employees actually ever accepted their offer. Because they maintained their employment, it seems that if the court rules that Wal-Mart indeed made an offer, then acceptance was also made.

The primary issue in this case will likely center on whether Wal-Mart's Code of Conduct was a promise clear enough to constitute an offer. As courts have analyzed codes of conduct for general or specific terms, the court will likely find that Wal-Mart's Code of Conduct is not a contract, as long as the Code merely contains general statements of company policy and guidelines for employer–employee conduct. Wal-Mart's Code of Conduct says that Wal-Mart "reserves the right to make periodic, unannounced inspections" and that "Wal-Mart will favor suppliers who meet such industry practices." Such language seems analogous to the language in Shandwick where the court ruled that the code of conduct did not create a contract because it was too general and seemed only to be a general statement of company policy.

. . . .

Most likely, the foreign workers will still assert that the Code creates an implied contract with workers because it is visibly displayed in the factory and personally distributed to each individual worker, and therefore Wal-Mart intends for it to be binding upon workers. The code, however, makes no guarantees of enforcement to workers. The Code states, "[a]ny person with knowledge of a violation of any of these practices by a Supplier, factory, or a Wal-Mart associate should call the appropriate number."

. . . .

Even if foreign workers assert that the Code of Conduct creates an implied contract, their claim would likely fail because the court would look at the practice in the industry. As noted in Part II, *supra*, MNCs have historically adopted codes of conduct voluntarily, using them as guidelines for suppliers, employees, and executives. Until now, employees of foreign suppliers had not alleged that a code of conduct created a contractual obligation. Therefore, it is highly unlikely that the Wal-Mart Code of Conduct created an implied contract, because it is unreasonable to think that the practice in the industry is for codes of conduct to be contractually binding.

Ultimately, because the wording in Wal-Mart's Code of Conduct is too vague and merely gives examples of the type of conduct that could result in disciplinary action by Wal-Mart rather than confers a right on workers, Wal-Mart's Code of Conduct for foreign suppliers does not create a contractual obligation with the employees of Wal-Mart's foreign suppliers.

V. The Impact of the Lawsuit and Appropriateness of Other Means for Reforming Foreign Working Conditions

Although a California court will eventually answer the debate over whether corporate codes of conduct can be contractually binding, the question remains as to what the most effective means are for bringing about positive changes in the working conditions of foreign workers. In recent years, foreign workers have been successful using civil litigation against MNCs to bring about changes in workers' conditions.

. . . .

VI. Conclusion

Although Wal-Mart is not likely to be found liable for breach of contract in the present matter, the relevance of this suit goes beyond any court ruling.[30] As globalization increases and MNCs increasingly expand their operations into foreign countries, they are more, not less, likely to face similar suits from labor groups, NGOs, and foreign workers who want to force corporations to be accountable for what takes place on foreign soil. Although MNCs like Wal-Mart may be able to avoid some suits, they will not be able to avoid them all. Ultimately, MNCs will have to be proactive with their own enforcement and monitoring mechanisms if they wish to avoid the perpetual onslaught of public criticism.

. . . .

Workers for Foreign Suppliers Lose in Suit against Wal-Mart[31]

Susan Bisom-Rapp

The Doe v. Wal-Mart decision is in, with the Ninth Circuit ruling against all the claims asserted by workers of Wal-Mart's foreign suppliers in Bangladesh, China, Indonesia,

30 [Author's note] In 2009, the Ninth Circuit agreed and decided there was no enforceable contract. Doe v. Wal-Mart Stores, Inc., 572 F.3d 677 (9th Cir. 2009).

31 Susan Bisom-Rapp, *Workers for Foreign Suppliers Lose in Suit against Wal-Mart*, WORKPLACE PROF BLOG (Jul. 15, 2009), http://lawprofessors.typepad.com/laborprof_blog/2009/07/susan-bisom-rappthomas-jefferson-provides-us-with-this-post-about-last-weeks-decision-by-the-ninth-circuit-in-doe-v-wal-m.html (last visited Sept. 28, 2010).

Nicaragua, and Swaziland. . . . Based on Wal-Mart's Code of Conduct, which provided that the company or a third party would undertake on-site inspection of suppliers' production facilities to monitor supplier compliance with local laws and labor standards, the workers sought to tie the suppliers' routine violation of those standards to Wal-Mart.

Four legal theories were asserted to hold Wal-Mart liable for adverse working conditions flourishing in its global supply chain. First, the workers argued that they were third party beneficiaries of Wal-Mart's supply contracts and were owed compensation for breach of contract. Next, they argued that Wal-Mart was their joint employer and thus liable for the substandard conditions in which they worked. Third, the workers asserted that Wal-Mart was negligent in carrying out its duty to monitor workplace conditions and protect the workers. Finally, they claimed the company was unjustly enriched at the workers expense. Rejecting each claim in turn, the Ninth Circuit concluded Wal-Mart had no duty arising under the Code of Conduct or in common law negligence to monitor or protect the workers from substandard working conditions. Wal-Mart is not the workers' joint employer, noted the court, and the relationship between the parties too attenuated to support an unjust enrichment claim.

When filed in 2005, the case attracted media notice as a test case to determine whether voluntary codes of conduct are enforceable. While given the right factual circumstances a code might constitute a legally binding contract, Doe v. Wal-Mart indicates courts considering such claims will apply common law principles very narrowly. Nonetheless, Doe v. Wal-Mart is an example of creative, though in this case unsuccessful, transnational advocacy aimed at holding TNCs responsible for the conditions from which they profit. For employers, the case represents both the promise and perils of corporate self regulation.

Jane Doe et al. v. Wal-Mart Stores, Inc.[32]

GOULD, Circuit Judge:

. . . .

I

Plaintiffs are employees of Wal-Mart's foreign suppliers in countries including China, Bangladesh, Indonesia, Swaziland, and Nicaragua. Plaintiffs allege the following relevant facts, which we take as true for purposes of this appeal:

In 1992, Wal-Mart developed a code of conduct for its suppliers, entitled "Standards for Suppliers" ("Standards"). These Standards were incorporated into its supply contracts with foreign suppliers. The Standards require foreign suppliers to adhere to local laws and local industry standards regarding working conditions like pay, hours, forced labor, child labor, and discrimination. The Standards also include a paragraph entitled "RIGHT OF INSPECTION":

To further assure proper implementation of and compliance with the standards set forth herein, Wal-Mart or a third party designated by Wal-Mart will undertake affirmative measures, such as on-site inspection of production facilities, to implement and monitor said standards. Any supplier which fails or refuses to comply with these standards or does

[32] Doe, 572 F.3d.

not allow inspection of production facilities is subject to immediate cancellation of any and all outstanding orders, refuse [sic] or return [sic] any shipment, and otherwise cease doing business [sic] with Wal-Mart. Thus, each supplier must acknowledge that its failure to comply with the Standards could result in cancellation of orders and termination of its business relationship with Wal-Mart. Wal-Mart represents to the public that it improves the lives of its suppliers' employees and that it does not condone any violation of the Standards. However, Plaintiffs allege that Wal-Mart does not adequately monitor its suppliers and that Wal-Mart knows its suppliers often violate the Standards. Specifically, Plaintiffs claim that in 2004, only eight percent of audits were unannounced, and that workers are often coached on how to respond to auditors. Additionally, Plaintiffs allege that Wal-Mart's inspectors were pressured to produce positive reports of factories that were not in compliance with the Standards. Finally, Plaintiffs allege that the short deadlines and low prices in Wal-Mart's supply contracts force suppliers to violate the Standards in order to satisfy the terms of the contracts. Plaintiffs filed a class action lawsuit in California Superior Court in 2005 and Wal-Mart removed the case to federal court based on diversity of citizenship. Plaintiffs then filed an amended complaint in federal court, which is the complaint relevant here. Wal-Mart filed a motion to dismiss under Federal Rule of Civil Procedure 12(b)(6) for failure to state a claim. The district court granted the motion in a written order, and judgment was entered on March 27, 2008. 2 Plaintiffs timely appealed.

. . . .

III

Plaintiffs present four distinct legal theories, all of which aim to establish that the Standards and California common law provide substantive obligations that can be enforced by the foreign workers against Wal-Mart: (1) Plaintiffs are third party beneficiaries of the Standards contained in Wal-Mart's supply contracts; (2) Wal-Mart is Plaintiffs' joint employer; (3) Wal-Mart negligently breached a duty to monitor the suppliers and protect Plaintiffs from the suppliers' working conditions; (4) Wal-Mart was unjustly enriched by Plaintiffs' mistreatment. Applying California law, we address each claim in turn.

A.

[1] We first address Plaintiffs' third-party beneficiary theory. The common law in California and elsewhere establishes that, as recited in the applicable Restatement (Second) of Contracts: "A promise in a contract creates a duty in the promisor to any intended beneficiary to perform the promise, and the intended beneficiary may enforce the duty." Restatement (Second) of Contracts § 304 (1981). However, the Restatement also explains that a beneficiary is only "an intended beneficiary if recognition of a right to performance in the beneficiary is appropriate to effectuate the intention of the parties. . . ." Restatement (Second) of Contracts § 302(1).

Contract interpretation is a question of law that we review *de novo*. *See Milenbach v. Comm'r of Internal Revenue*, 318 F.3d 924, 930 (9th Cir. 2003).

Plaintiffs argue that Wal-Mart promised the suppliers that it would monitor the suppliers' compliance with the Standards, and that Plaintiffs are third-party beneficiaries of that promise to monitor. Plaintiffs rely on this language in the Standards: "Wal-Mart will undertake affirmative measures, such as on-site inspection of production facilities, to implement and monitor said standards." We agree with the district court that this language does not create a duty on the part of Wal-Mart to monitor the suppliers, and does not provide Plaintiffs a right of action against Wal-Mart as third-party beneficiaries.

[2] The language and structure of the agreement show that Wal-Mart reserved the right to inspect the suppliers, but did not adopt a duty to inspect them. The language on which Plaintiffs rely is found in a paragraph entitled "Right of Inspection," contained in a two-page section entitled "Standards for Suppliers." And after stating Wal-Mart's intention to enforce the Standards through monitoring, the paragraph elaborates the potential consequences of a supplier's failure to comply with the Standards – Wal-Mart may cancel orders and cease doing business with that supplier – but contains no comparable adverse consequences for Wal-Mart if Wal-Mart does not monitor that supplier. Because, as we view the supply contracts, Wal-Mart made no promise to monitor the suppliers, no such promise flows to Plaintiffs as third-party beneficiaries. . . .

[3] Plaintiffs alternatively argue that they are third-party beneficiaries of the suppliers' promises to maintain certain working conditions, and that Plaintiffs may therefore sue Wal-Mart. This theory fails because Wal-Mart was the promisee vis-à-vis the suppliers' promises to follow the Standards, and Plaintiffs have not plausibly alleged a contractual duty on the part of Wal-Mart that would extend to Plaintiffs. . . .

[4] Plaintiffs' allegations are insufficient to support the conclusion that Wal-Mart and the suppliers intended for Plaintiffs to have a right of performance against Wal-Mart under the supply contracts. *See* Restatement (Second) of Contracts § 302(1). We therefore conclude that Plaintiffs have not stated a claim against Wal-Mart as third-party beneficiaries of any contractual duty owed by Wal-Mart, and we affirm the district court's dismissal of the third-party beneficiary contract claim.

B.

We next address Plaintiffs' theory that Wal-Mart was Plaintiffs' joint employer, such that they can "sue Wal-Mart directly for any breach of contract or violation of labor laws." We conclude, to the contrary, that Wal-Mart cannot be considered Plaintiffs' employer on the facts alleged.

[5] The key factor to consider in analyzing whether an entity is an employer is "the right to control and direct the activities of the person rendering service, or the manner and method in which the work is performed. . . . "

Here, Plaintiffs' allegations do not support the conclusion that Wal-Mart is Plaintiffs' employer. Plaintiffs' general statement that Wal-Mart exercised control over their day-to-day employment is a conclusion, not a factual allegation stated with any specificity. We need not accept Plaintiffs' unwarranted conclusion in reviewing a motion to dismiss. . . .

Plaintiffs allege specifically that Wal-Mart contracted with suppliers regarding deadlines, quality of products, materials used, prices, and other common buyer–seller contract terms. Such supply contract terms do not constitute an "immediate level of 'day-to-day'" control over a supplier's employees so as to create an employment relationship between a purchaser and a supplier's employees. *Vernon*, 10 Cal. Rptr. 3d at 132. Plaintiffs also allege that Wal-Mart exercised control over their employment through Wal-Mart's promise to monitor the DOE v. WAL-MART 8621 suppliers and Wal-Mart's system for monitoring.

However, we have already concluded that Wal-Mart undertook no duty to monitor the suppliers and the monitoring and inspections by Wal-Mart were performed to determine whether suppliers were meeting their contractual obligations, not to direct the daily work activity of the suppliers' employees.

[7] Plaintiffs have provided no persuasive support for finding a common law employment relationship between a purchaser and its suppliers' employees on the facts of this case. We conclude that the joint employer theory should here be rejected, and we hold that Wal-Mart is not Plaintiffs' employer.

C.

We next address Plaintiffs' negligence claims, which Plaintiffs bring under four distinct theories: third-party beneficiary negligence, negligent retention of control, negligent undertaking, and common law negligence. Whichever theory is invoked, however, we conclude that Wal-Mart did not owe Plaintiffs a common-law duty to monitor Wal-Mart's suppliers or to prevent the alleged intentional mistreatment of Plaintiffs by the suppliers. Without such a duty, Plaintiffs' negligence theories do not state a claim.

. . . .

[8] Plaintiffs' "third-party beneficiary" negligence theory relies on the assumption that Wal-Mart owes Plaintiffs a duty under Wal-Mart's supply contracts. Because we have already determined that no legal obligation flows from Wal-Mart to Plaintiffs under Wal-Mart's supply contracts, Plaintiffs do not state a claim for third-party beneficiary negligence.

[9] In order to state a claim for "negligent retention of control and supervision," Plaintiffs must allege facts that, if proven, would show that Wal-Mart exercised significant control over Plaintiffs and that "exercise of retained control *affirmatively contributed* to the employee's injuries." *Hooker v. Dep't of Transp.*, 38 P.3d 1081, 1083 (Cal. 2002) (emphasis in original). We have already determined that Wal-Mart is not Plaintiffs' employer because Wal-Mart exercised minimal or no control over the day-to-day work of Plaintiffs in the suppliers' foreign factories. Accordingly, we hold that Wal-Mart did not owe Plaintiffs a special duty to protect Plaintiffs from the suppliers' alleged intentional misconduct.

[10] Plaintiffs' "negligent undertaking" theory relies on the assumption that Wal-Mart undertook to protect Plaintiffs, and therefore Wal-Mart had to exercise reasonable care in monitoring the suppliers. *See Delgado v. Trax Bar & Grill*, 113 P.3d 1159, 1175 (Cal. 2005) (stating that one who "undertakes to provide protective services to another" must exercise a duty of care). This theory fails because, as we have already concluded, Wal-Mart did not undertake any obligation to protect Plaintiffs. "[T]he scope of any duty assumed depends upon the nature of the undertaking," *id.*, and here Wal-Mart merely reserved the right to cancel its supply contracts if inspections revealed contractual breaches by the suppliers. Any inspections actually performed by Wal-Mart were therefore gratuitous, and do not independently impose a duty on Wal-Mart to protect Plaintiffs. *Id.*

[11] Plaintiffs' "common law negligence" claim provides no additional ground for finding a duty on the part of Wal-Mart. Wal-Mart had no duty to monitor the suppliers or to protect Plaintiffs from the intentional acts the suppliers allegedly committed. Thus, Plaintiffs' theories sounding in negligence do not state a claim. *See Paz*, 994 P.2d at 980–81.

D.

[12] We turn finally to Plaintiffs' claim of unjust enrichment. Plaintiffs allege that Wal-Mart was unjustly enriched at Plaintiffs' expense by profiting from relationships with suppliers that Wal-Mart knew were engaged in substandard labor practices. Unjust enrichment is commonly understood as a theory upon which the remedy of restitution may be granted. *See* 1 GEORGE E. PALMER, LAW OF RESTITUTION § 1.1 (1st ed. 1978 & Supp. 2009); Restatement of Restitution § 1 (1937) ("A person who has been unjustly enriched at the expense of another is required to make restitution to the other."). California's approach to unjust enrichment is consistent with this general understanding: "The fact that one person benefits another is not, by itself, sufficient to require restitution. The person receiving the benefit is required to make restitution only if the circumstances are such that, as between the two individuals, it is *unjust* for the person to retain it." *First Nationwide Sav. v. Perry*, 15 Cal. Rptr. 2d 173, 176 (Cal. Ct. App. 1992) (emphasis in original).

[13] The lack of any prior relationship between Plaintiffs and Wal-Mart precludes the application of an unjust enrichment theory here. *See Smith v. Pac. Props. & Dev. Corp.*, 358 F.3d 1097, 1106 (9th Cir. 2004) (noting that a party generally may not seek to disgorge another's profits unless "a prior relationship between the parties subject to and benefitting from disgorgement originally resulted in unjust enrichment"). Plaintiffs essentially seek to disgorge profits allegedly earned by Wal-Mart at Plaintiffs' expense; however, we have already determined that Wal-Mart is not Plaintiffs' employer, and we see no other plausible basis upon which the employee of a manufacturer, without more, may obtain restitution from one who purchases goods from that manufacturer. That is, the connection between Plaintiffs and Wal-Mart here is simply too attenuated to support an unjust enrichment claim. . . .

IV

In sum, we conclude that Plaintiffs have not stated a claim against Wal-Mart. Wal-Mart had no legal duty under the Standards or common law negligence principles to monitor its suppliers or to protect Plaintiffs from the suppliers' alleged substandard labor practices. Wal-Mart is not Plaintiffs' employer, and the relationship between Wal-Mart and Plaintiffs is too attenuated to support restitution under an unjust enrichment theory.

Because we have determined that Plaintiffs did not state a claim under state law, we need not address Wal-Mart's additional contentions that United States domestic law does not apply and that foreign affairs preemption bars application of state law.

AFFIRMED.

. . . .

QUESTIONS

1. What is the employment relationship, if any, between Wal-Mart and plaintiffs? Would it make a difference if plaintiffs worked for Wal-Mart directly?

2. Given the right factual circumstances, might a code of conduct constitute a legally binding contract? If so, how? Is a third-party beneficiary argument available?
3. What would be an appropriate remedy for breach?
4. How might an employer draft its code of conduct, delineating between promise and policy?
5. What is the likelihood that employment contract laws in East Asian countries will be interpreted the same as in the U.S. courts?
6. Do you agree that even a failing lawsuit has benefits for the plaintiffs? Why or why not?

---

b. Alien Tort Claims Act

The Alien Tort Claims Act (ACTA) was enacted in 1789 to combat piracy on the high seas. It provided federal courts with jurisdiction over all causes where an alien sues for a tort "only in violation of the law of the nations."[33] Although it remained in relative disuse until the twentieth century, it has since been used by human rights proponents to fight murder, torture, and similar abuses. In recent years, attempts have been made through litigation to find those human rights abuses, such as forced labor, which may overlap with labor rights.[34] This American law is used only by the United States, and other jurisdictions will have very different approaches.

In 2004, the U.S. Supreme Court held, on a jurisdictional issue, that the ACTA was more than jurisdictional, thus leaving open the door for federal courts to enforce violations of international norms, albeit, not those committed by private individuals.[35] Thus with the door still open, advocates began litigating cases, some against private companies that were arguably in league with foreign governments.[36] Whether some labor rights embodied in ILO labor standards satisfy "the law of the nations" has yet to be decided.

---

[33] Judiciary Act of 1789, ch. 20, § 9(b), 1 Stat. 73, 77 (1989), 28 U.S.C. § 1350 (2002) [hereinafter ATCA].

[34] *See* JAMES ATLESON ET AL., INTERNATIONAL LABOR LAW: CASES AND MATERIALS ON WORKERS' RIGHTS IN THE GLOBAL ECONOMY 571–668 (2008) [hereinafter ILL]; *see generally* Terry Collingsworth, *Symposium, Separating Fact from Fiction in the Debate over Application of the Alien Tort Claims Act to Violations of Fundamental Human Rights by Corporations*, 37 U.S.F. L. REV. 563, 586 (2003).

[35] Sosa v. Alverez-Machain, 542 U.S. 692 (2004).

[36] ILL, *supra* note 34, at 589–623; Marisa Anne Pagnattaro, *Enforcing International Labor Standards: The Potential of the Alien Tort Claims Act*, 37 VAND. J. TRANSNAT'L L. 203 (2004). The author documents cases brought against multinational corporations and argues that U.S. courts should recognize that the Alien Tort Claims Act's (ATCA) protection against violations of "the law of nations" can include torts committed in connection with core labor rights' freedom of association, the right to collective bargaining, prohibitions on child labor, and discrimination.

The Key Human Rights Challenges: Developing Enforcement Mechanisms[37]

Terry Collingsworth

. . . .

At this point in time, the ATCA, despite its limitations, remains the only current vehicle for direct enforcement of human rights norms. Until human rights are given the same priority as property rights, incidents of torture, murder, kidnapping, and sexual assault will continue to be shocking, but routine, consequences of a lawless global economy. If the ILRF and other organizations are successful in getting large judgments against corporations using ATCA litigation, other companies will be deterred from violating human rights out of a fear of substantial legal liability. Successful litigation might also provide an incentive for some companies to join the dialogue about alternatives to litigation, including adoption of a social clause to add enforceable human rights norms to trade agreements.[38]

The ATCA will no doubt prove to be a useful tool for enforcing human rights norms, but this approach has major limitations and should not be viewed as an ultimate solution to the non-enforcement issue. First and foremost, the ATCA is limited to cases that can be brought in the U.S. federal courts against defendants over which there is federal jurisdiction. Thus, in the Unocal case, there was jurisdiction over the Unocal defendants because they are incorporated in the U.S. and have a principal place of business in the country. However, Unocal's joint venture partner, the French oil giant Total, was held not to be subject to federal jurisdiction.[39]

A second limitation to ATCA litigation is the necessarily narrow scope of the "law of nations." While the law of nations is evolving and expanding, we are far from international consensus on many issues crucial to human rights concerns such as a living wage, minimum health and safety standards, maximum hours, and sexual harassment. The ATCA presents the potential to address claims involving intentional physical or mental harm, but is not likely to reach less extreme but much more common claims, including abominable working conditions.[40]

The other major limitations are simply practical. By definition, ATCA cases involve human rights violations in countries that allow such things to happen; in most cases, the government itself is involved in the wrongful acts. Victims in these cases are often terrified of making claims, and are not likely to have access to lawyers unless they are discovered by local organizations with U.S. connections. . . . Finally, the costs and time involved in bringing an ATCA case require that it be viewed as an extraordinary remedy, not lightly undertaken. The Unocal case is in its sixth year, and attorneys for plaintiffs have donated millions of dollars in legal fees to date, in addition to spending several hundreds of thousands of dollars in costs. These are unusually expensive test cases because

[37] Terry Collingsworth, *The Key Human Rights Challenges: Developing Enforcement Mechanisms*, 15 Harv. Hum. Rts. J. 183 (2002), *available at* http://www.law.harvard.edu/students/orgs/hrj/iss15/collingsworth.shtml (last visited Sept. 28, 2010) [Footnotes omitted] [hereinafter Collingsworth].

[38] *Id.* at 203.

[39] *Id.* at 202.

[40] *Id.*

they require substantial travel and large expenditures of time to address novel legal issues.[41]

. . . .

QUESTIONS

1. What is the likelihood of applying this law to the types of labor conditions complained of in the typical "race to the bottom" situation? Why or why not?
2. Are labor conditions in Japan, China, or South Korea likely to be of that nature to invoke the Alien Torts Claim Act? Would an American company contracting directly or indirectly with a government prison for products made by prison labor, be subject to this law?

---

c. Litigating ILO Standards: U.S. Illustration

Beyond Soft Law? An Assessment of International Labour Organisation Freedom of Association Complaints as a Means to Protect Collective Bargaining Rights in the United States[42]

Andrew J. Ziaja

. . . .

Introduction

Put broadly, this article examines the effectiveness of International Labour Organisation Complaints as a means to protect workers' ability to bargain collectively in the United States. It focuses, as a case study, on an ILO Committee on Freedom of Association ("CFA") report that was issued in 2007.

Two years prior, in 2005, The United Electrical, Radio, and Machine Workers of America ("UE") filed an ILO complaint alleging that a North Carolina statute, which prohibited any public entity from entering into a collective bargaining agreement with a trade union, violated international law and the United States' treaty obligations under the ILO regime. The CFA agreed and recommended that the statute be repealed. The Committee also remarked in its report ("UE Report") that "[d]omestic courts in the United States have not yet ruled on the validity of the Statute in the context of its compliance with principles of international law and treaties to which the United States is a party." The question here, accordingly, is how a district court would rule were UE or

[41] *Id.*

[42] Ziaja, Andrew J. (2009), *Beyond Soft Law? An Assessment of International Labor Organization Freedom of Association Complaints as a Means to Protect Collective Bargaining Rights in the United States*, GLOBAL JURIST: Vol. 9: Iss. 2 (Topics), Article 1. DOI: 10.2202/1934-2640.1299, *available at* http://www.bepress.com/gj/vol9/iss2/art1 (last visited May 13, 2011). Berkeley Electronic Press © 2009 [Footnotes omitted; some formatting altered]. The U.S. Supreme Court has construed an ILO convention as a self-executing treaty and allowed a citizen to use it to obtain redress. *See* Warren v. United States, 340 U.S. 523 (1951).

another union to challenge North Carolina's statute as a violation of the United States' treaty obligations while attempting to enforce the UE Report as a binding declaration of those obligations.

The statute at issue in the UE Report was North Carolina General Statute ("NCGS") § 95-98. NCGS § 95–98 is titled "Contracts between units of government and labor unions, trade unions or labor organizations concerning public employees declared to be illegal." It provides that any agreement, or contract, between the governing authority of any city, town, county, or other municipality, or between any agency, unit, or instrumentality thereof, or between any agency, instrumentality, or institution of the State of North Carolina, and any labor union, trade union, or labor organization, as bargaining agent for any public employees of such city, town, county or other municipality, or agency or instrumentality of government, is hereby declared to be against the public policy of the State, illegal, unlawful, void, and of no effect.

While technically public employees in North Carolina may still join unions, the CFA concluded that "the right to bargain freely with employers... constitutes an essential element in freedom of association, and trade unions should have the right, through collective bargaining or other lawful means, to seek to improve the living and working conditions of those whom the trade unions represent." The CFA declared the United States to be in violation of freedom of association principles and called for the repeal of NCGS § 95–98, accordingly.

UE or any other union that relied on the CFA's report to challenge NCGS § 95–98 in federal court as a violation of the United States' treaty obligations would face numerous obstacles. Precedent upholding NCGS § 95–98 under federal constitutional free association doctrine could pose an initial challenge. In addition, while it may be clear that NCGS § 95–98 violates a number of ILO documents, it is less clear that these documents bind the United States, and equally unclear upon which of them the CFA relied in its report. The UE Report may imply that prohibiting collective bargaining violates a preemptive norm of international law, but making a convincing case on this point before a federal court would be challenging, moreover. The Supreme Court's recent opinion in *Medellín*, furthermore, casts doubt on the domestic enforceability of the UE Report and the rights enshrined by the entire ILO regime.

This article addresses these obstacles in turn. Part I discusses the UE Report in relation to domestic precedent upholding NCGS § 95–98 under United States constitutional law. Part II examines the legal basis of the UE Report under international law, including whether the right to bargain collectively is a preemptory norm. Part III, finally, considers the domestic enforceability of ILO treaty law and the UE Report under *Medellín*.

I. The UE Report and Domestic Precedent on the Question of Free Association

This section presents the substantive reasoning of the UE Report against the background of domestic precedent – Atkins v. City of Charlotte and Winston-Salem/Forsyth County Unit of the North Carolina Association of Educators v. Philips – upholding NCGS § 95–98 under United States constitutional law.

Comparing the reasoning of the UE Report to domestic law serves both practical and theoretical purposes. The practical implication is that any attempt to enforce the UE Report as a legally binding document in United States court could run afoul of established domestic precedent; the UE Report concludes that NCGS § 95–98 violates the right of free association whereas domestic federal courts have explicitly held that it does not. The theoretical implication is that the UE Report and domestic precedent present two starkly different and irreconcilable visions of the right of free association. This theoretical difference also presents a practical edge: If a district court decided that the question was not controlled by domestic precedent, it presumably would be because the UE Report dealt with free association under the ILO treaty regime while *Atkins* and *Winston-Salem/Forsyth County* dealt with the concept under the United States Constitution. A district court might, therefore, hold that free association under the ILO treaty regime and the United States Constitution are legally distinct concepts and an opinion as to one would have no bearing as to the other. The best case scenario for a plaintiff union challenging NCGS § 95–98 would, accordingly, be that *Atkins* and *Winston- Salem/Forsyth County* have no bearing on the question of the statute's legality under ILO treaty law. The worst case scenario would be for the court to hold that *Atkins* and *Winston-Salem/Forsyth County* would control the free association issue.

A. *Domestic Precedent:* Atkins *and* Winston-Salem/Forsyth County

NCGS § 95–98 survived domestic constitutional challenges in 1969 and 1974, respectively, in *Atkins v. City of Charlotte* and *Winston-Salem/Forsyth County Unit of the North Carolina Association of Educators v. Philips*. Together, these cases stand for precisely the opposite of the CFA's conclusion in the UE Report. The CFA concluded that collective bargaining "constitutes an essential element in freedom of association." The *Atkins* and *Winston-Salem/Forsyth County* courts together held that freedom of association, as defined in the United States Constitution, does not depend on the ability to bargain collectively. In *Atkins*, members of the City of Charlotte's Fire Department sought "a declaratory judgment and injunctive relief declaring unconstitutional and preventing enforcement of Sections 95–97, 95–98, and 95–99 of the General Statutes of North Carolina." These three statutes together formed a formidable firewall against any public sector union activity of any kind. NCGS § 95–97 provided that no employee of the State of North Carolina,... or any employee of a city, town, county, or other municipality or agency thereof, or any public employee or employees of an entity or instrumentality of government shall be, become, or remain a member of any trade union, labor union, or labor organization... which has as its purpose or one of its purposes, collective bargaining with any employer mentioned in this article with respect to grievances, labor disputes, wages or salary, rates of pay, hours of employment, or the conditions of work of such employees.

NCGS § 95–97 thus banned the mere act of being a union member. NCGS § 95–98, as quoted above, went further to bar public entities from entering into collective bargaining agreements. NCGS § 95–99 declared a violation of either NCGS 95–97 or 95–98 to be a misdemeanor. The prohibition against public sector unionism was airtight.

The *Atkins* court's holding split the concepts of free association and collective bargaining. It held NCGS § 95–97 to be "void on its face as an abridgement of freedom of association protected by the First and Fourteenth Amendments of the Constitution of the United States." Similarly, it voided NCGS § 95–99 because it "was an *in terrorem* provision intended to make certain that no employee of the State or its subordinate municipal corporations should so much as lift a finger to form or join a labor union."

Regarding NCGS § 95–98, however, it held that "[nothing in the United States Constitution . . . entitles one to have a contract with another who does not want it. . . . The right to a collective bargaining agreement, so firmly entrenched in American labor-management relations, rests upon national legislation and not upon the federal Constitution." NCGS § 95–98 did not prevent public employees from, among other things, organizing to influence the legislative process. It posed no threat to freedom of association as a result.

The *Winston-Salem/Forsyth County* court drove the wedge between freedom of association and collective bargaining yet deeper. The case arose when a North Carolina board of county commissioners unilaterally reduced the salaries of public school teachers. To that point, teachers had received a portion of the local property-based school tax to augment their wages. The teachers union attempted to engage the county commissioners in negotiations over the cut, but talks broke down once the county commissioners determined that NCGS § 95–98 would prohibit any agreement that resulted. The plaintiff union sued for declaratory and injunctive relief, renewing the argument raised in *Atkins* that the prohibition of public sector, collective bargaining agreements violated union members' free associational rights.

The *Winston-Salem/Forsyth County* rejected this premise even more emphatically than did the *Atkins* court. The court accepted that NCGS § 95–98 frustrated a union's ability to serve and retain its members but held that there was simply no intersection between the right to bargain collectively and free association: "[W]e cannot accept the premise that plaintiffs' alleged right of association requires that state governmental units negotiate and enter into contracts with them. The Constitution does not mandate that anyone, either the government or private parties, be compelled to talk to or contract with an organization." The court went further to note that the First Amendment and the right to free association guarantee only a group's right to speak at all – not the right to speak effectively.

. . . .

B. The UE Report

The CFA hewed its opinion from a grove of ILO treaty documents: ILO Conventions 87, 98, and 151; the ILO Constitution; and the ILO Declaration of Fundamental Principles and Rights at Work ("DFPRW"). Taken together, these documents provide robust protections for workers' rights, ranging in specificity from the right of public employees to negotiate over their terms of employment, to a right to organize, to a general right of free association. How these provisions factored doctrinally into the CFA's opinion, however, is not exactly clear. Sussing out the doctrinal workings of the UE Report is necessary in considering whether the issues it resolves are controlled by domestic precedent. It will further enable the discussion, *infra* section II, about whether the UE Report is based on any treaty law that binds and obliges the United States.

1. Relevant ILO Treaty Law

a. ILO Conventions. The CFA first referenced ILO Convention 87. The relevant provisions of Convention 87 are articles 8 and 11. Article 8 provides that member states may not create nor apply domestic law in such a way as to violate the rights established by the Convention: "The law of the land shall not be such as to impair, nor shall it be so applied as to impair, the guarantees provided for in this Convention." Article 11 provides that "Each Member of the International Labour Organisation for which this Convention is in force undertakes to take all necessary and appropriate measures to ensure that workers and employers may exercise freely the right to organise."

The CFA next referenced ILO Convention 98. Three provisions of Convention 98 are relevant here: articles 3, 4, and 6. Article 3 creates an affirmative obligation for member states to protect workers' ability to join unions: "Machinery appropriate to national conditions shall be established, where necessary, for the purpose of ensuring respect for the right to organise. . . . " Article 4 goes further to create an affirmative obligation to encourage collective bargaining: "Measures appropriate to national conditions shall be taken, where necessary, to encourage and promote the full development and utilisation of machinery for voluntary negotiation between employers or employers' organisations and workers' organisations, with a view to the regulation of terms and conditions of employment by means of collective agreements." Article 6 explicitly excludes high level public employees from the scope of Convention 98: "This Convention does not deal with the position of public servants engaged in the administration of the State, nor shall it be construed as prejudicing their rights or status in any way."

The final ILO Convention referenced by the CFA was Convention 151. Convention 151 applies specifically to public employees "to the extent that more favourable provisions in other international labour Conventions are not applicable to them." In article 4 it provides that "Public employees shall enjoy adequate protection against acts of anti-union discrimination in respect of their employment." Article 5, section 2 provides that "Public employees' organisations shall enjoy adequate protection against any acts of interference by a public authority in their establishment, functioning, or administration." Article 7 protects public employees' right to bargain collectively and requires that member states "promote the full development and utilisation of machinery for negotiation of terms and conditions of employment between the public authorities concerned and public employees' organizations. . . . " In Article 9, Convention 151 also broadly protects public employees' right to free association: "Public employees shall have, as other workers, the civil and political rights which are essential for the normal exercise of freedom of association. . . . "

b. ILO Constitution. The ILO Constitution states that a primary purpose of the ILO is to protect the rights of workers to freely associate. Its preamble envisions free association as part of an antidote to "such injustice hardship and privation to large numbers of people as to produce unrest so great that the peace and harmony of the world are imperiled;. . . . " The preamble states that "conditions of labour" are to blame for the world's imperilment and that the "recognition of the principle of freedom of association" is therefore "urgently required." The concepts of free association and collective action to improve working conditions are closely intertwined under the ILO Constitution, accordingly.

c. ILO Declaration of Fundamental Principles and Rights at Work. The ILO Declaration of Fundamental Principles and Rights at Work was passed by the ILO in 1981 and contains the most broad-reaching protection of the right of free association referred to by the CFA. Section (2)(A) declares that all Members, even if they have not ratified the Conventions in question, have an obligation arising from the very fact of membership in the Organization to respect, to promote, and to realize, in good faith and in accordance with the Constitution, the principles concerning the fundamental rights which are the subject of those Conventions, namely . . . freedom of association and the effective recognition of the right to collective bargaining. . . .

The plain language of the provision is clear: All members are obliged to uphold the right to free association. The Declaration of Fundamental Principles does not clearly define, however, its use of the term "freedom of association."

2. The Union's Arguments

The union, UE, raised a host of arguments. It argued that NCGS §95–98 straightforwardly violated ILO Conventions Nos. 87, 98, and 151. UE also attacked the reasoning of *Atkins* and *Winston-Salem/Forsyth County* by arguing that effects of NCGS § 95–98 went to the core of workers' free associational rights. The inability to bargain collectively produced ill effects: "miserable working conditions. . . . health and safety violations . . . unconscionable wages, unreasonable and unsafe hours of work, extreme understaffing, unreasonable forced overtime, favouritism, and disrespectful treatment from superiors" along with the loss of "the basic dignity associated with having a say in establishing one's conditions of work." More seriously, NCGS § 95–98 acted "as a state-mandated impediment to eliminating race and sex discrimination" by depriving workers of an essential tool to counteract existing racism and sexism in public workplaces. UE also posited a definition of "freedom of association" that hinged on the right to bargain collectively. The union argued that [w]hen workers lose the right to collectively negotiate and form agreements regarding terms of employment with their employers, they are denied the intended benefit of employee unions. Hence, their right to freedom of association becomes a hollow right. The undeniable interdependence of the right of freedom of association and the right to engage in collective bargaining was recognized in the preliminary work for the adoption of Convention No. 87. UE concluded by arguing that the United States, since it allowed NCGS § 95–98 to remain on the books, violated it obligations under the Declaration on Fundamental Principles and Rights at Work to uphold "the fundamental rights of freedom of association and the right to collective bargaining."

3. The United States' Arguments

The United States' counter-arguments were twofold: First, the inability to bargain collectively had not hindered workers' ability to join unions; second, even absent public sector collective bargaining, the United States remained in compliance with its ILO treaty obligations thanks to "a safety net of federal and state laws and practices that secure their right to be free from workplace discrimination, unsafe and unhealthful workplaces, and substandard pay and conditions of employment." In other words, the government's arguments amounted to the propositions that neither free association nor workers' rights generally depend on the ability to bargain collectively. The government argued this point emphatically and, though not explicitly, effectively argued that *Atkins* precluded any finding that NCGS § 95–98 violated workers' right to organize. The government framed the right to free association under the United States Constitution and the ILO regime as co-terminus with one another [b]ecause the US Constitution's provisions supersede conflicting state laws by virtue of the supremacy clause of article VI, North Carolina is not free to abridge this fundamental right by enacting contrary state legislation. As a practical matter, this means that the North Carolina law cannot and does not impede the rights of state and local government employees [under ILO Convention No. 87] to form and join unions or employee associations.

Citing to *Atkins* and *Winston-Salem/Forsyth County*, the government emphasized yet more that, under the United States Constitution, the right to free association does not in any way involve the right to bargain collectively. To the contrary, public sector collective bargaining impinges upon other citizens' right to advocate their interests to the government. Granting public employees the right to bargain collectively would give "one interest group special status and access to the decision-making process."

4. The CFA's Conclusion

The CFA's reasoning, taken at face value, was opaque. NCGS § 95–98 violates the United States' treaty obligations, but it is not at all clear which ILO treaty documents it meant. The CFA concluded that NCGS § 95–98 should be overturned because the right to bargain freely with employers, including the government in its quality of employer, with respect to conditions of work of public employees who are not engaged in the administration of the State, constitutes an essential element in freedom of association, and trade unions should have the right, through collective bargaining or other lawful means, to seek to improve the living and working conditions of those whom the trade unions represent. The public authorities should refrain from any interference which would restrict this right or impede the lawful exercise thereof. Any such interference would appear to infringe the principle that employers' and workers' organizations should have the right to organize their activities and to formulate their programmes. . . .

While the CFA recited UE's allegations that the government violated Conventions Nos. 87, 98, and 151 and its obligations under the ILO Constitution and Declaration on Fundamental Principles and Rights at Work, the CFA gave little guidance as to how these provisions factored into its reasoning. To the contrary, the CFA's assertion of its legal authority was elusive:

. . . .

In sum, the CFA's reasoning in the UE Report is a morass from which only two conclusions may be safely drawn. First, since none of the documents cited by the CFA can be isolated out as any more or less important than the others, a district court evaluating the CFA's reasoning with respect to the United States' treaty obligations would need to account for all of them: ILO Convention Nos. 87, 98, and 151 along with the ILO Constitution and the Declaration on Fundamental Principles and Rights at work. Second, in the ILO context, the rights of free association and collective bargaining are inextricably interconnected.

C. Comparative Analysis and Conclusion

Were UE or another union to attempt to enforce the UE Report in district court in order to invalidate NCGS § 95–98, the United States government would, in all likelihood, move for summary judgment arguing that *Atkins* and *Winston-Salem/Forsyth County* would bind the court as to the free association issue. Indeed, the government effectively made this argument before the CFA when it argued that, as a matter of law, NCGS § 95–98 could not violate the principle of free association since it survived domestic constitutional scrutiny. The plaintiff union would argue that, to the contrary, *Atkins* and *Winston-Salem/Forsyth County* dealt with a wholly separate right – free association under the Constitution – from that involved in the UE Report – free association under the ILO treaty regime which includes as an essential element the right to bargain collectively.

A district court would likely rule in favor of the challenging union. The CFA emphasized time and again that collective bargaining lay at the core of the ILO right to free association. The very holdings of *Atkins* and *Winston-Salem/Forsyth County* were that free association under the Constitution does not depend on the right to bargain collectively. In this way, what is otherwise bad precedent for the union in *Atkins* and *Winston-Salem/Forsyth County* actually works to the union's advantage in order to keep the issue alive. Were the district court to rule that the issues were identical and that *Atkins* and *Winston-Salem/Forsyth County* controlled, moreover, it would also concurrently rule by necessity that collective bargaining was not essential to the right to free association under the ILO regime, just as it is not essential to the right under the United States Constitution. This would force the court to either somehow distinguish the CFA's holding or to make a broad proclamation about the weight of authority to be given CFA reports (i.e., little or none) as a matter of first impression, which is to say that it would force the court between a rock and a hard place. The court could avoid all this by distinguishing the free associational rights discussed by the UE Report and *Atkins* and *Winston-Salem/Forsyth County* – on the one hand a treaty-based right and on the other a constitutional one. Refusing to allow *Atkins* and *Winston-Salem/Forsyth County* to control, moreover, would allow the court to reach the issue of whether NCGS § 95–98 really violates the United States' treaty obligations at all. Ruling in favor of the government, if the court is so inclined, would be much easier on this basis than performing the doctrinal acrobatics to cabin the UE Report as discussed above. This question is the subject of the next section, accordingly.

II. Whether NCGS § 95–98 Violates the United States' Obligations under International Law

A challenging union would likely also face on summary judgment the argument that, no matter whether NCGS § 95–98 violates some ILO provisions in the abstract, none of those provisions bind the United States and that, even if they do, they do not oblige the United States to overturn NCGS § 95–98. This argument would devastate much of the union's position. To shore up its position, the union could also argue that the right to collectively bargain has become a norm of customary international law. The United States' conduct in following the DFPRW might support this claim. However, a 2003 district court case addressing this argument, Villeda Aldana v. Fresh Del Monte Produce, Inc., resolutely rejected a similar argument. Though that case, as a parallel district court case, would not bind a district court in North Carolina, it would hold persuasive authority. Whereas Section I, *supra* mapped out the CFA's reasoning against the backdrop of United States domestic case law and attempted to identify which ILO documents formed the basis of the CFA's decision, this Section asks two questions: first, whether any of the ILO documents in play bind the United States; second, whether any of those documents create the obligations to which the CFA alluded.

A. *Whether the Authority Cited by the CFA Binds the United States*

1. ILO Conventions

UE argued before the CFA that the United States was obligated to uphold "workers' basic rights embodied in the fundamental international principles of freedom of association and the right to negotiate through collective bargaining . . . regardless of whether it has ratified Convention Nos. 87 and 98 [and 151]." Given that the United States has not ratified any of these Conventions, a fact which both UE and the CFA freely admit, no such obligation arises from them. All three Conventions contain an identical provision that expressly absolves any non-ratifying member from any of the obligations they create: "This Convention shall be binding only upon those Members of the International Labour Organisation whose ratifications have been registered with the Director-General." Despite the frequent references to the Convention Nos. 87, 98, and 151 of the UE Report, the conventions could not have formed the legal basis of its opinion on this account. The Conventions do not bind the United States.

2. ILO Constitution and DFPRW

The ILO Constitution and DFPRW, by contrast, most likely bind the United States. The United States coauthored the ILO Constitution in 1919 in the wake of World War I. The United States is and has remained an ILO member state. The ILO Constitution therefore presumably binds it.

The DFPRW presents a slightly more complex picture, though it also binds the United States. The ILO adopted the DFPRW as a body in 1998, so it is governed by the Vienna Convention on the Law of Treaties under article 5, which provides: "The present Convention applies to any treaty which is the constituent instrument of an international organization and to any treaty adopted within an international organization without prejudice to any relevant rules of the organization." Vienna Convention article nine, section two requires that "[t]he adoption of the text of a treaty at an international conference takes place by the vote of two thirds of the States present and voting. . . . " The ILO Constitution, in turn, requires that "a majority of two-thirds of the votes cast by the delegates present shall be necessary on the final vote for the adoption of the Convention or Recommendation, as the case may be, by the Conference." The DFPRW, passed under the ILO Constitution, thus satisfies the Vienna Convention and binds the United States.

A. *Whether the Authority Cited by the CFA Obliges the United States to Overturn* NCGS § 95–98

The remaining question is whether any of these provisions oblige the United States to overturn NCGS § 95–98. The ILO Conventions, assuming *arguendo* that they bind the United States, and the ILO Constitution present the easiest calls: yes and no, respectively.

The DFPRW once again presents the more complex analysis – one that points to a cautious yes.

1. The ILO Conventions and Constitution

Under the ILO Conventions, the relevant provisions are article 4 of No. 87; article 4 of No. 98; and articles 5, 7, and 9 of No. 151. Those provisions are presented *supra* at Section I.B.1.a. It is worth noting, in addition, that articles 4 and 7 of Convention Nos. 98 and 151, respectively, are nearly identical save for one provision: Article 7 of No. 151 concludes, "… or of such other methods as will allow representatives of public employees to participate in the determination of these matters." Article 1, however, also limits the applicability of No. 151 to public employees "to the extent that more favourable provisions in other international labour Conventions are not applicable to them."

Together, Convention Nos. 87, 98, and 151 oblige ratifying states to "take measures" to protect workers' ability to join unions and bargain collectively. This does not require that they all take the same "measures"; to the contrary, the Conventions limit themselves to steps "appropriate to national conditions" or only those that are "necessary and appropriate." It does, however, by inference require that they not take steps backwards to hinder collective bargaining. NCGS § 95–98 is obviously such a step backwards. The government would likely argue before a district court that the "safety net of federal and state laws" and the ability of public employees to advocate for their interests in the political process falls within No. 151's exception for "other methods as will allow representatives of public employees to participate in the determination of these matters." The entirety of No. 151 does not apply, however, when "more favourable provisions in other international labour Conventions" are available, and under the ILO regime the ability to bargain collectively clearly trumps the ability to advocate within the political process; the ILO regime gives special status to public sector labor organizations whereas under *Atkins* and *Winston-Salem/Forsyth County* the United States system expressly does not. This cannot be "more favourable" than the broad protections afforded by Convention No. 98. There is little doubt that NCGS § 95–98 violates the obligations created under the ILO Conventions. There is, however, also little likelihood, as discussed *supra* Section II.A.2, that a district court would hold the United States bound by Conventions, so this line of argument would be a long shot for a plaintiff union.

The ILO Constitution, meanwhile, creates no discernable obligations whatsoever as to the right of free association. As noted *supra* in section I.B.1.b., the Constitution only proposes "recognition of the principle of freedom of association" in the abstract as a solution to global imperilment. It does not refer to specific or even general measures that member states must take. It therefore straightforwardly establishes only background principles and not affirmative obligations.

2. The DFPRW

The DFPRW presents a more complex analysis because it uses a mix of the hard language of the Conventions and soft language similar to the ILO Constitution. Section (2)(a) of the DFPRW states that all Members, even if they have not ratified the Conventions in question, have an obligation arising from the very fact of membership in the Organization to respect, to promote, and to realize, in good faith and in accordance with the Constitution, the principles concerning the fundamental rights which are the subject of those Conventions, namely . . . freedom of association and the effective recognition of the right to collective bargaining. . . .

This provision meshes with the language of Conventions on several, though not all, points and a plaintiff union could argue that it simply obliges all member states to uphold the Conventions whether or not they have ratified them. The DFPRW, even more clearly creates an obligation than do the Conventions by its explicit use of the word "obligation." It furthermore imposes a duty of good faith and binds member states to a definition of fundamental rights that equally includes free association and collective bargaining. The DFPRW was passed, moreover, against the background of long-standing CFA precedent establishing that, under the ILO regime, the rights of free association and collective bargaining are intertwined. On this view, a plaintiff union would have a strong argument that the United States has obligations under the DFPRW.

The argument that NCGS § 95–98 violates those obligations is not as strong, however. While the Conventions require steps towards the establishment of "machinery" to effect certain purposes, the DFPRW requires the mere promotion of principles. The scope of measures a member state could take to discharge their obligation under the DFPRW is thus broader than under the Conventions. A plaintiff union could not, as a result, as easily argue that the DFPRW prohibits backwards steps, as argued *supra* in the Convention context in Section III.B.2; the DFPRW seems to only require vaguely defined promotion.

In this vein, the DFPRW does not prohibit member states from balancing their promotion of free associational and collective bargaining rights against other domestic interests, so long as their efforts are in "good faith." The *Atkins* and *Winston-Salem/Forsyth County* courts reasoned that the right to bargain collectively had to give way to concerns of equality in public democratic participation. No matter how thin the support for this proposition, a plaintiff union would be hard-pressed to show that the courts' reasoning was pretextual. The duty of good faith under the DFPRW thus also serves as an escape valve and lets out the steam of a plaintiff union's case that NCGS § 95–98 violated the United States' obligations under the DFPRW.

3. DFPRW as Customary International Law

A plaintiff union could also rely on the DFPRW to establish that the right to bargain collectively is part of a norm of customary international law that does not depend on any one specific treaty provision for enforcement.[43] The benefits to a union plaintiff would be threefold. First, it would provide an additional means by which to show that the United States is bound and obliged under international law to observe the right of free association. Second, it would allow the union to argue that the obligation under customary international law goes beyond the mere "promoting of principles" required under the DFPRW. Third, it would allow a union plaintiff to be more creative in defining the scope of the right.

The plaintiffs in *Villeda Aldana v. Fresh Del Monte Produce, Inc.*, a 2005 case, mounted a similar argument in a different context. The *Villenda Aldana* plaintiffs were a group of Guatemalan union officials who were allegedly kidnapped and tortured by Del Monte employees in order to quell union activity at Del Monte's Bobos banana plantation in Guatemala. The plaintiffs sued Del Monte in district court in Florida under the Alien

[43] [Author's note] See discussion in Jon M. Van Dyke, *The Role of Customary International Law in Federal and State Court Litigation*, 26 U. HAW. L. REV.361 (2004) [hereinafter Van Dyke].

Tort Claim Act ("ATCA") for a "whole host of violations of international law." Among the plaintiffs' claims was that Del Monte had violated their fundamental right to organize and associate, which derives from customary international law. The plaintiffs relied "heavily on the twin ILO Conventions [Nos. 87 and 98] in attempting to demonstrate that the core right, to establish and join an organization of one's choosing, is universally recognized." According to the court, "[c]lose inspection of their provisions, however, does not provide solid support for Plaintiffs' claimed universal rights" because the Conventions only bind ratifying states and "roughly less than one-third of the ILO signatory countries have ratified the conventions." The court did not consider the impact of the DFPRW.

Under the same analysis, the DFPRW provides ample support to declare the right to free association, as defined under the ILO regime, as customary international law. It binds and is endorsed by all ILO member states by virtue of their ILO membership. It was passed by the ILO by an "overwhelming majority" of the member states. The DFPRW therefore cures the defect in the "widespread acceptance" prong in the *Villena Aldana* plaintiffs' argument. The *Villena Aldana* plantiffs fared better on the second prong: The existence of *opinio juris* as to the right of free association as defined under the ILO. The plaintiffs asserted that no country has expressly disputed that the norm exists, citing as an example the aftermath [of] the Tiananmen Square events in China, where in its response to an ILO complaint, the Chinese government did not contest that it was obligated to support freedom of association – rather, it denied the specific act as charged.

While the court found this insufficient under the heavier burden imposed by the ATCA, it noted plaintiff's argument approvingly. Furthermore, as the CFA noted, the United States has continued to voluntarily comply with the reporting requirements under the DFPRW, which offers even more weighty support that *opinio juris* exists as to the right of free association.

A union challenging NCGS § 95–98 would thus stand a fair chance at establishing the right free association as a norm of international customary law. The union would still need to establish the substantive scope of the norm and the ensuing arguments would assuredly rehash those outlined above regarding the scope of the obligations created by the ILO Conventions, its Constitution, and the DFPRW. The chief difference is that the union, and government for that matter, would be able to look beyond just the ILO texts to establish the scope of the right. Despite the fact that it seems doctrinally possible, it is hard to imagine a district court in North Carolina declaring that free association is a norm of customary international law, however, given that it would then face the enormous question of whether to declare an international law-based right to free association that is more expansive than that protected by the United States Constitution.

III. The Domestic Enforceability of ILO Treaty Law and the UE Report under *Medellín*

In the wake of the United States Supreme Court's recent opinion in *Medellín v. Texas*, it is now clear that to be enforceable in a United States federal court, international law must be self-executing. The *Medellín* Court drew a "distinction between treaties that automatically have effect as domestic law, and those that – while they constitute international law commitments – do not by themselves function as binding federal law." The Court explained further that "while treaties may comprise international commitments . . . they are not domestic law unless Congress has either enacted implementing statutes or the treaty itself conveys an intention that it be 'self-executing' and is ratified on these terms."

. . . .

A. Prong One: The Text of the ILO Conventions, Constitution, and DFPRW

Convention No. 87 and the DFPRW wilt under the first prong of the *Medellín* analysis. Convention No. 87 uses the same fatal magic words quoted by the *Medellín* Court: "Each Member of the International Labour Organisation for which this Convention is in force *undertakes to take* all necessary and appropriate measures to ensure that workers and employers may exercise freely the right to organise." Once again, the DFPRW presents a more complex analysis. It provides: "[]ll Members . . . have an *obligation...* to respect, to promote, and to realize, in good faith and in accordance with the Constitution, the principles [of] . . . freedom of association and the effective recognition of the right to collective bargaining. . . . " At first blush, the use of the phrase "have an obligation" would self-execute; mere membership gives rise to the obligation. The problem is that, as the *Medellín* Court acknowledged, "treaties may comprise international commitments . . . [but] they are not domestic law unless Congress has either enacted implementing statutes or the treaty itself conveys an intention that it be 'self-executing' and is ratified on these terms."

. . . .

Little analysis is needed to determine that the ILO Constitution's preamble discussing freedom of association is not self-executing; preambles by definition are non-executing portions of a legal document.

B. Prong Two: The Mechanisms for Enforcement and Remedying Noncompliance

The CFA's mechanisms for enforcement and remedying noncompliance fare as woefully as can be imagined under the *Medellín* analysis. Once a charging party initiates a complaint, the CFA reviews the matter. If the CFA finds no violation, it takes no action. If the CFA finds a violation, it makes recommendations and "requests [that the] government to keep it informed."

The analysis could stop here; the CFA refers its decisions to the Governing Body just as the ICJ refers its decisions to the U.N. Security Council for enforcement. Its decisions are not automatically enforceable. What follows adds insult to injury. In the event of noncompliance, the Governing Body has two options: It can refer the matter back to the CFA for follow-up or, if the member state has ratified the conventions in play, it can refer it to the Committee of Experts. Since the United States has not ratified Convention Nos. 87, 98, or 151, the matter would simply go back to the CFA. All of this is punctuated by the fact that the CFA has power only to render recommendations, rather than binding judicial decisions, in the first place.

Conclusion

While attempting an objective analysis, this article has demonstrated that, ultimately, seeking to enforce an ILO CFA report in general, and the UE Report in particular, in United States district court would be dismally ineffective. The maneuver is rife with obstacles at every intersection where domestic and international law meet: differing interpretations of "freedom of association;" severe doubts as to whether the United States is bound by any of the key treaty documents, most especially the Conventions; vaguely defined treaty obligations; and the devastating impact of Medellín. This total drubbing begs the question why the United States is involved in the ILO at all, given that the United States disagrees with one of the ILO's fundamental principles. It further calls into question the efficacy and legitimacy of the ILO, given that when pressed to defend one of its fundamental principles it has no teeth with respect to the United States, which was one of the drafters of the ILO constitution. This is not to say that there is no value at all in obtaining CFA decisions declaring the United States to be out of step with international law.

The UE Report seems to have served as a platform and focal point to allow unions to build solidarity across international boundaries. There have been, furthermore, attempts to repeal NCGS § 95–98 in North Carolina's legislature and gaining the support of the ILO might aid the effort politically. One could also argue, however, that – in an era in which the United States has blissfully ignored international law in executing prison inmates, until recently executing minors and the mentally disabled, torturing its military captives, and starting unprovoked wars – the right to bargain collectively is just another log for the fire. In sum, the ILO regime provides United States workers with little beyond soft law to help their cause.

Perhaps helpful in understanding the possible enforcement of international obligations is to consider how the World Trade Organization (WTO) deals with the matters through certain agreed-upon provisions. The U.S. has agreed to certain national obligations under the WTO. In the process of resolving trade disputes, the findings of a WTO dispute settlement panel cannot force the U.S. to change its laws. Only the United States determines exactly how it will respond to the recommendations of a WTO panel, if at all. If a U.S. measure is found to be in violation of a WTO provision, the United States may decide to change the law; compensate a foreign country by lowering trade barriers of equivalent amount in another sector; or do nothing and possibly undergo retaliation by the affected country in the form of increased barriers to U.S. exports of an equivalent amount. But the U.S. retains full sovereignty in its decision of whether or not to implement a panel recommendation.

Congress has comprehensively dealt with the legal effect of World Trade Organization (WTO) agreements and dispute settlement results in the United States in the Uruguay Round Agreements Act (URAA), P.L. 103–465, which provides that domestic law prevails over conflicting provisions of WTO agreements and prohibits private remedies based on alleged violations of these agreements. As a result, WTO agreements and adopted WTO rulings in conflict with federal law do not have domestic legal effect unless and until Congress or the executive branch, as the case may be, takes action to modify or remove the statute, regulation, or regulatory action at issue. State laws may be withdrawn by the state or, in rare circumstances, invalidated through legal action by the federal government.[44]

---

[44] Jeanne J. Grimmett, *WTO Decisions and Their Effect on U.S. Law*, CRS Rep. for Congress, Jan. 2, 2008, *available at* http://www.nationalaglawcenter.org/assets/crs/RS22154.pdf (last visited Sept. 28, 2010).

QUESTIONS

1. How likely is it that a U.S. court would hold that free association under the ILO Convention is a legally distinct concept from the treaty regime and constitutional analyses and an opinion as to one would have no bearing as to the others?[45]
2. Are the ILO Conventions binding on the United States absent their ratification?[46]
3. In the discussion earlier, which ILO Convention, if any, appears to have been violated? Why?
4. Assuming the right to bargain collectively is recognized in either customary international law or under the DFPRW, is such a right enforceable in the domestic courts of the United States?[47]
5. Consider whether a trade dispute involving a WTO decision against the United States will be treated differently in the courts from a labor dispute case involving an ILO decision against the United States, due to a violation caused by an inconsistent state law? How is this explained?

3. *Enforcement of Labor Rights in FTAs, OECD Guidelines, and Trade Legislation*

Overview of Labor Enforcement Issues in Free Trade Agreements[48]

Mary Jane Bolle

Summary

Since 1993, the Administration has negotiated and Congress has approved 10 Free Trade Agreements (FTAs) that contain labor provisions with different degrees of enforceability. Three more (with Colombia, Peru, and South Korea) await congressional consideration. This report identifies two types of enforcement issues: (1) those that relate to the FTA

[45] Compare Medellín v. Texas, 552 U.S. 491, 128 S. Ct. 1346 (2008), where the U.S. Supreme Court discussed whether an international treaty obligation can be binding and self-executing and enforced in the domestic courts of the United States, absent separate implementing legislation, and whether in that case a private cause of action was authorized. Contrast that with *Warren v. United States*, 340 U.S. 523 (1951), where the U.S. Supreme Court construed an ILO convention as a self-executing treaty and allowed a citizen to use it to obtain redress.

[46] *See* Warren, 340 U.S. See discussion in Van Dyke, *supra* note 43. How would a court hold in the following case, *ILO Upholds TWU Complaint, finds NY Strike Ban Violates Workers Human Rights*, *available at* http://www.twu.org/international/article/1081/. The decision is at, http:www.twu.org/wrhr-newsletter/jrae/newsletter_37_images/ILO_CFA_Decision_re_Taylor_Law.pdf.

[47] For a full text of the Convention, see NGO Committee on Education, *Declaration on Fundamental Principles and Rights at Work and Follow-up to the Declaration*, UN Documents: Gathering a Body of Global Agreements, http://www.un-documents.net/dfprw.htm (last visited Sept. 28, 2010).

[48] Mary Jane Bolle, *Overview of Labor Enforcement Issues in Free Trade Agreements*, Congressional Research Service (CRS) Rep. & Issue Briefs, Feb. 29 2008, *available at* http://digitalcommons.ilr.cornell.edu/cgi/viewcontent.cgi?article=1497&context=key_workplace (last visited Oct. 3, 2010) [Footnotes omitted].

provisions themselves, including their definitions and their enforceability, and (2) those that relate to executive branch responsibilities, such as resource availability and determining dispute settlement case priorities. This report will be updated as events warrant.

....

Labor Enforcement in U.S. Free Trade Agreements

Since 1993, the United States has negotiated 13 FTAs that include 19 countries. These are, chronologically, the North American Free Trade Agreement (NAFTA) with Mexico and Canada; bilateral agreements with Jordan, Chile, Singapore, Australia, Morocco, Bahrain, and Oman; a regional agreement known as CAFTA-DR, with the Dominican Republic and the five Central American Countries (Costa Rica, El Salvador, Guatemala, Honduras, and Nicaragua); and bilateral FTAs with Peru, Colombia, Panama, and South Korea. The last four agreements reflect a bipartisan compromise on labor language as delineated in the *New Trade Policy With America*. Jointly agreed to by the leadership in Congress and the Administration on May 10, 2007, this policy calls for, among other things, two key labor provisions in FTAs: The first is a fully enforceable commitment that FTA countries will adopt, maintain, and enforce in their laws and practice, the basic international labor standards as stated in the 1998 *ILO Declaration*. The second is the use of identical enforcement provisions for labor and commercial disputes.

Labor and enforcement provisions in these various trade agreements can be categorized into four different models.

Model 1. For *NAFTA*, labor provisions are included in the *North American Agreement on Labor Cooperation (NAALC)*, a side agreement, rather than in the main agreement. Under NAALC, countries agree to enforce their own labor laws and standards. However, under NAALC, the only provision enforceable with sanctions is a Party's "persistent pattern of failure . . . to effectively enforce its occupational safety and health, child labor or minimum wage technical standards," where that failure is trade-related and covered by mutually recognized labor laws (Article 29). By comparison, all provisions relating to commercial operations are enforceable under the *NAFTA*. Furthermore, the labor side agreement has different enforcement procedures than does the main agreement, and places limits on monetary enforcement assessments, with suspension of benefits for noncompliance. There are no monetary assessments under the *NAFTA*.

Model 2. In the *U.S.–Jordan Free Trade Agreement*, labor provisions and commercial provisions share the same dispute resolution procedures. The agreement incorporates a number of labor provisions, including that a Party agrees to "not fail to effectively enforce its labor laws . . . in a manner affecting trade" (Article 6.4). Under the *Jordan* agreement, labor laws are defined as U.S. *internationally recognized worker rights*. Technically under the agreement, all labor provisions and commercial provisions are equally enforceable. If the dispute is not resolved under procedures specified in the agreement, the affected Party shall be entitled to take "any appropriate and commensurate measure" (Article 17.2(b)). However, in an exchange of letters between the USTR Robert Zoellick and Jordanian Ambassador Marwan Muasher before Congress considered the implementing legislation in 2001, the governments reportedly agreed to resolve any potential disputes without resorting to trade sanctions.

Model 3. Seven trade agreements with 12 different countries (Chile, Singapore, Australia, Morocco, Bahrain, Oman, and the six CAFTA-DR countries) include only one enforceable labor provision: each country "shall not fail to effectively enforce its labor laws . . . in a manner affecting trade between the Parties." The agreements define *labor laws* as "a Party's statutes or regulations . . . that are directly related to" the list of U.S. *internationally recognized worker rights*. All provisions in these agreements relating to commercial operations are enforceable. The seven trade agreements share many of the same procedures for labor and commercial disputes. Procedures for labor disputes place limits on monetary penalties, whereas those for commercial disputes do not. Suspension of benefits is a "last recourse" option for both types of disputes.

Model 4. On May 10, 2007, the Democratic leadership in Congress and the Administration agreed to a *New Trade Policy for America*. It included four enforceable labor concepts, which pending free trade agreements (with Peru, Colombia, Panama, and South Korea) would be amended to include. These are (1) a fully enforceable commitment that Parties to free trade agreements would adopt and maintain in their laws and practices the *ILO Declaration*; (2) a fully enforceable commitment prohibiting FTA countries from lowering their labor standards; (3) new limitations on "prosecutorial" and "enforcement" discretion (i.e., countries cannot defend failure to enforce laws related to the five basic core labor standards on the basis of resource limitations or decisions to prioritize other enforcement issues); and (4) the same dispute settlement mechanisms or penalties available for other FTA obligations (such as commercial interests).

The four concepts have been inserted into all four agreements as "template language" – that is, language that was specifically agreed to by the Administration and leadership in Congress and was then inserted into all four agreements in virtually identical form. The template language makes an important change from item (1) in the *New Trade Policy*, described above. The template language states that each Party shall adopt and maintain in its statutes, regulations, and practices, the *rights* as stated in the *ILO Declaration and its Follow-Up*. However, a footnote in each trade agreement limits obligations of Parties to those specified in the *ILO Declaration* (i.e., without also including the *Follow Up*, which, as mentioned, calls for annual reports by countries that have not ratified one or more Conventions, on the status of implementing the core labor standards). Another footnote requires that a party seeking to challenge violations is required to demonstrate that the failure to adopt or maintain *ILO core labor standards* has been "in a manner affecting *either* trade *or* investment between the two countries," (Article 17, footnote 1 of the FTA with Peru.) In Model 4 agreements, there are no caps on penalties. Only the agreement with Peru has been approved by Congress at this time (P.L. 110–138, December 14, 2007).

Enforcement Issues

Based on these different provisions, policy issues can be divided into two categories: enforceability issues relating to the FTA provisions (addressed in issues 1–3 below), and issues relating to the agencies charged with enforcement (addressed in issues 4 and 5 below).

1. *Only some provisions are enforceable*. One issue relating to the enforcement of labor provisions in trade agreements is that only certain labor provisions in some trade agreements are enforceable, whereas all commercial provisions in trade agreements are fully enforceable. More specifically, under Model 1, the model for the *NAFTA*, the labor side agreement, *NAALC*, as mentioned, includes only certain enforceable

provisions – that a country must enforce its labor standards relating to child labor, minimum wages, and occupational safety and health. Not enforceable is the requirement that a country enforce its laws relating to the most basic core labor rights: to organize and bargain collectively. These two labor standards account for 16 out of the 21 labor submissions filed with *NAALC*.

Under the FTAs described by model 3, as mentioned, only one labor provision is enforceable: Each country must enforce its own labor laws (defined as "a Party's statutes or regulations directly related to the list of U.S. *internationally recognized worker rights*") in a manner affecting trade between the Parties.

2. *Different enforcement procedures for and caps on penalties for labor provisions.* For labor and commercial disputes, Model 1 has separate and dissimilar enforcement provision procedures from Model 3. However, both place caps on potential maximum monetary penalties for labor disputes, but place no caps on penalties for commercial disputes.

3. *Limits placed on scope of definition of a term in labor provisions.* Labor provisions in Model 4 agreements are "fully *enforceable*" through the same dispute-resolution procedures as are available for commercial disputes. As mentioned under the description for Model 4, the template language in the trade agreements includes a footnote saying, "The obligations set out in Article 17.2, as they relate to the ILO, refer only to the ILO Declaration." This would suggest that trading Partners could be held to the principles of the Declaration, but not the details of the Conventions. *The House Committee Report on the U.S.–Peru Trade Promotion Agreement Implementation Act*, H. Rept. 110–421, is silent on the issue. The U.S. Council on International Business (USCIB), the American Affiliate of the International Chamber of Commerce, argues that if trading partners were held to the details of Conventions supporting the core labor standards, a number of U.S. labor laws could need to be changed to comply with the *ILO core labor standards* as defined and clarified by the various conventions.

4. *Differentials in federal resources available for labor as compared with commercial disputes.* In the U.S. government, there is a large differential between support available to enforce labor provisions and support available to enforce commercial provisions in preparing any petition for enforcement to be submitted to the USTR. The U.S. government's monitoring and enforcement activities for non- agricultural commercial issues are primarily centered in the Office of the USTR and U.S. Department of Commerce (DOC). The DOC Trade Compliance Center (TCC) Web page describes the TCC as being "the U.S. Government's focal point for monitoring foreign compliance with trade agreements to see that U.S. firms *and workers* get the maximum benefits from these agreements" (emphasis added). None of the related links on the page, however, leads the viewer specifically to labor compliance assistance. The DOC receives complaints about compliance with trade agreements from the TCC "hotline," industry groups, trade associations, Congress, U.S. Foreign Commercial Service officers, the USTR *National Trade Estimates Report*, and other sources. It uses its many resources to conduct research on a compliance case. If a case is not resolved short of the dispute resolution process, it may be referred to the Office of the USTR.

The Department of Labor (DOL) is less directly involved in researching issues of labor noncompliance. Petitions for enforcement of a trade agreement are typically researched and prepared by an outside interested party, such as a labor union. That petition is then reviewed by the Trade Agreement Administration and Technical Cooperation Division, within the Department of Labor's Office of Trade and Labor Affairs at the Department of Labor.

5. *Priorities for disputes to be pursued by the USTR.* To date, no labor dispute under any of the free trade agreements has reached the USTR. Therefore, this discussion is purely hypothetical. Should a case not be resolved short of dispute resolution, the USTR must decide which cases it will pursue based on priorities. The USTR is a small operation. Entering into the dispute resolution process is a lengthy, involved, expensive process in terms of both personnel and resources. The USTR typically chooses cases to pursue based on a number of factors. These may include cases that could showcase or clarify particular issues, strengthen support of U.S. positions, and/or be cases the USTR believes it can win.

Labor disputes could be more difficult to resolve than commercial disputes. This is because the labor principles in the *ILO Declaration* against which foreign actions could be compared are less detailed and specific. Moreover, under model 4, the USTR may not wish to pursue the enforcement of these principles because if Conventions were to enter the cases as definitions for the principles, this could possibly, as the USCIB argues, subject a number of U.S. labor laws to challenge.

. . . .

Using Trade as a Lever for Improved Enforcement of Labor Rights[49]

Pharis J. Harvey

A. The Trade–Labor Rights Linkage

. . . .

The basic rationale for linkage is that poverty eradication and improved conditions for workers should be the focus of and primary objective of trade, not incidental, "trickle down" byproducts of an exploitive system that provides lopsided benefits to a few MNCs. The initial development goal stated in the GATT preamble and echoed in the ILO's Constitution and the Declaration of Philadelphia has been substituted with a raw form of laissez faire capitalism that surpasses in cruel effects the last experiment in trickle-down economics early in this century. The ideology of trade policy has been captured by the MNCs, the one interest group that should be the subject of regulation, rather than the drafter of the rules.

It is essential to any understanding of the need for a new trade policy that there is no such thing as "free trade." The final draft concluding the Uruguay Round of negotiations and creating the WTO is several hundred pages of regulations setting the rules of trade and protecting market access for MNCs. A 32-page Annex I C deals only with protecting intellectual property rights, and the U.S. government has pursued aggressively the claims of such companies as Microsoft, which charged the Chinese government with failing to enforce its laws on copyright piracy. That this system exists, which values computer

[49] Pharis J. Harvey et al., *Developing Effective Mechanisms for Implementing Labor Rights in the Global Economy* (May 10, 2000), *available at* http://www.laborrights.org/files/developing_mechanisms.pdf (last visited Oct. 3, 2010) [Footnotes omitted].

codes more than children and young people who make CDs in sweatshops, reflects the concentrated power of MNCs to impose regulations that protect their interests, and to resist regulations that might cut into their enormous profits. There is no defensible distinction for allowing regulations in a "free trade" regime to protect property but not people. This distortion will remain until advocates for worker rights and social justice unify to counterbalance the power of MNCs in setting the rules of the global economy. Economic evidence to support the assertion that trade has resulted in increasingly skewed income distribution rather than broad-based development is continuing to accumulate.

....

B. History of Trade–Labor Rights Linkage in U.S. Trade Law

Labor rights advocates in the U.S. have been quite successful in legally mandating the link between labor rights and trade on a unilateral basis in U.S. law. A series of laws have been passed that certain trade benefits on compliance with labor rights:

(1) The Generalized System of Preferences Act ("GSP"), which grants developing countries duty free status on many exports to the U.S. conditioned on compliance with "internationally recognized worker rights," thus providing a substantial comparative advantage in U.S. markets. The worker rights conditionality was added to GSP in 1986. The idea was that the U.S. was spending billions of dollars on direct foreign assistance that was having little permanent impact on solving the underlying problems of poverty. The theme of GSP was "trade not aid," meaning that it would be a better policy to give benefits that helped economies to develop and grow so that countries could become self-sustaining and direct foreign aid could be phased out;

(2) The Caribbean Basin Economic Recovery Act (CBERA), which is virtually identical to the GSP program but focuses on the Caribbean basin.

(3) Overseas Private Investment Corporation ("OPIC"), which provides financing and insurance to U.S. companies investing in developing countries provided that the host country is in compliance with "internationally recognized worker rights";

(4) The Omnibus Trade and Competitiveness Act, passed in 1988, which amended section 301 of the Trade Act of 1974, which applies to all U.S. trading partners and makes failure to comply with "internationally recognized worker rights" an unfair trading practice and subjects the offender to a wide range of sanctions. Compliance with this law ensures that a developing country will not be subject to trade sanctions;

(5) The 1992 Amendment to the Foreign Assistance Act of 1961, which restricts funding of U.S. AID programs that contribute to the denial of "internationally recognized worker rights";

(6) The 1994 Amendment to the Foreign Assistance Act, which provides that "the Secretary of Treasury shall direct the United States Executive Directors of the International Financial Institutions ... to use the voice and vote of the United States to urge the respective institution ... to adopt policies to encourage borrowing countries to guarantee internationally recognized worker rights;" and

(7) The 1997 Sanders Amendment to Section 307 of the Trade Act of 1930, which clarified that the ban on importation of products made with "forced" labor applied to products made with "forced or indentured child labor."

All of these laws incorporate the five factor definition of "internationally recognized worker rights" from the GSP provision: (A) the right of association; (B) the right to organize and bargain collectively; (C) a prohibition on the use of any form of forced or compulsory labor; (D) a minimum age for the employment of children; and (E) acceptable conditions of work with respect to minimum wages, hours of work, and occupational safety and health.

These U.S. experiments in trade–labor rights linkage have not been very successful for a number of reasons, but they do demonstrate the conceptual premise that trade conditionality can be an effective tool for regulating worker rights. These models also offer insight into the problems that will be encountered in seeking to develop an enforceable labor rights clause as part of the rules of trade. The most significant problem in realizing the objective of improved labor rights enforcement is that a combination of conservative U.S. governments and powerful lobbying by the MNCs has prevented any real enforcement of the laws. The administrations of Presidents Reagan, Bush, and Clinton have consistently used their discretionary authority to decline to enforce the worker rights provisions of the various laws.

The concerned bureaucracies at the U.S. Trade Representative and the Departments of State, Commerce, Labor, and Treasury opposed rigorous enforcement of the worker rights provisions, ultimately resulting in litigation brought by the ILRF to challenge the non-enforcement of the law. Likewise, the ILRF is currently pressuring the Treasury Department to comply with its obligation to require respect for worker rights as a condition to U.S. support for international financial institutions. To date, the Clinton Administration has been hostile to pursuing worker rights at the IMF or the World Bank. This experience demonstrates that any future solution requires a mandatory and transparent process, not easily undermined by bureaucratic hostility or inertia. Most recently, efforts by ILRF to require the U.S. Customs Service and the Department of Treasury to enforce the child labor provision of section 307 of the Trade Act of 1930 have met with extreme bureaucratic resistance. For outside observers of this process, it is crucial to understand that there is not any homogenous "U.S. view." Advocates for workers pushed for legislation that provided tools to work to improve enforcement of internationally recognized worker rights. The U.S. government and corporate interests disagreed with the policy and have worked to undermine it. That advocates for workers want stronger language and a multilateral mechanism does not change this fundamental dynamic.

The U.S. approach of linking trade to worker rights, while never enforced adequately, drew considerable criticism for being unilateral. This reflects a basic suspicion in the South, and in Europe for that matter, of anything that is perceived as U.S.-initiated action. However, the critics have failed to understand that the U.S. government, as represented by the Executive branch, never wanted the laws, never enforced the laws, and resisted any effort to introduce social policy into trade policy. The entire process was an effort by labor rights advocates, with allies in the U.S. Congress, to force the U.S. government to treat labor rights as a priority in its trading relations. These advocates also pressed Congress to pass a law that required the U.S. government to push for inclusion of a social clause in the GATT.

The preferred solution remains a multilateral provision that firmly links labor rights to the trading regime. However, the combination of lackluster U.S. advocacy for the policy, and the absence of any strong allies in the multilateral discussions, resulted in the ratification of the Uruguay Round document without any social clause. At the first World Trade Organization (WTO) Ministerial, the WTO managed to sidestep a renewed call for a social clause by refusing to discuss the addition of a social clause and renewing a commitment to observe the Conventions of the ILO, an alternative all concerned knew meant there was no prospect of any enforcement threat since the ILO has no power to impose any penalty for non-compliance. Thus, U.S. advocates for labor rights are left in a bind: they are criticized for pursuing unilateral measures, but got little support in efforts to persuade other governments to join the U.S. in pushing for a social clause at the WTO. Again, any ultimate solution requires a unified effort by labor rights advocates on a global basis. This requires recognition that labor rights advocates in the U.S. are struggling to force the U.S. government to incorporate worker rights into its global trading agenda; the U.S. government is largely a hostile and unwilling partner in this effort, or, at its best, a divided and ambivalent ally.

———

C. Regional Trade Agreements: Experiments with Multilateral Labor Rights–Trade Linkage

A firm labor rights–trade linkage with an enforcement mechanism has not been established at a multilateral level. With more than 100 member countries each, the two principal multilateral institutions, the WTO and the ILO, each possess one-half of an enforcement mechanism. The WTO allows economic sanctions against countries that violate GATT rules, but has so far refused to adopt rules on labor rights, insisting that labor issues belong in the ILO. For its part, the ILO can investigate and determine violations of international labor standards, but has no sanctioning power. Another multilateral institution, the 29-member OECD, has "guidelines" for multinational corporations in their dealings with unions, "and a forum for consultation on alleged violations." However, the OECD does not contemplate sanctions as a remedy.

. . . .

OECD as an Enforcement Tool?

In addition to the possible enforcement of labor provisions in free trade agreements, another approach is through the requirements of organizations such as the OECD and its Guidelines.[50] The issue is whether and how "guidelines" are "enforced." In an optimistic critique, it is suggested that recent enforceability of OECD guidelines provide a basis to suggest "the MNE Guidelines are beginning to serve as the focal point for the construction of an autonomous transnational governance system that is

[50] Reprinted with permission by the International Labor Organization. Codes of Conduct for Multinationals, 2002, http://actrav.itcilo.org/actrav-english/telearn/global/ilo/guide/main.htm (last visited Sept. 30, 2010). Copyright © 2002 International Labor Organization; *see also* OECD Guidelines for Multinational Enterprises (2008), *available at* http://www.oecd.org/dataoecd/56/36/1922428.pdf (last visited Sept. 28, 2010). The Guidelines were updated in May, 2011 without significant changes in relevant areas. See, OECD Guidelines for Multinational Enterprises (2011), *available at* www.oecd.org/dataoecd/43/29/48004323.pdf (last visited October 7, 2011).

meant to serve as the touchstone for corporate behavior in multinational economic relationships."[51]

> The enforcement framework for the OECD's Guidelines for Multinational Enterprises has long been the subject of criticism, especially by representatives of private and public actors. But two recent cases have suggested that enforcement actions arising from civil society efforts to utilise the national contact points complaint system may be slowly influencing the emerging discourse of corporate behaviour in ways that will have substantial effect. Beyond providing evidence of a more muscular institutional transnational enforcement structure for soft law codes, the cases serve to outline a framework for the interaction of transnational and national systems of corporate regulation. The multilateral system for governing multinational corporate behaviour will affect not only that behaviour, but also the rules through which corporations may be governed as to their internal affairs and with respect to the character of their legal personality. The cases illustrate the way in which advances in governance issues are being crafted, step-by-step, from out of a system that, while formally non-binding, is increasingly developing the characteristics of a binding governance system.[52]

On the other hand, unions generally have less optimism on the nonenforceable Guidelines, as stated in the following article.

The OECD Guidelines for Multinational Enterprises[53]

What are the OECD Guidelines?[54]

They are standards and principles for responsible business conduct, developed by the Paris based Organisation for Economic Co-operation and Development (OECD) and adopted by the member governments already in 1976. They have been revised several times since. The latest review was concluded in June 2000 and resulted in major improvements in the Guidelines such as the strengthening of the implementation procedures, the coverage of corporate activities outside the OECD area, the inclusion of all core labour standards, and their extension to suppliers and sub-contractors.

[51] Larry C. Backer, *Rights and Accountability in Development 'Raid' v. Das Air and Global Witness v. Afrimex; Small Steps Towards an Autonomous Transnational Legal System for the Regulation of Multinational Corporations*, 10 MELB. J. INT'L. L., 258 (2009), *available at* http://papers.ssrn.com/sol3/papers.cfm?abstract_id=1427883 [Footnotes omitted]; *see also* United Kingdom National Contact Point (UK NCP), Final Statement by the UK National Contact Point for the OECD Guidelines for Multinational Enterprises: Afrimex (UK) Ltd (Aug. 28, 2008), *available at* http://www.berr.gov.uk/files/file47555.doc (last visited Sept. 28, 2010) [hereinafter Afrimex]; UK NCP, Statement by the United Kingdom National Contact Point (NCP) for OECD Guidelines for Multinational Enterprises: DAS Air (July 21, 2008), *available at* http://www.berr.gov.uk/files/file47346.doc (last visited Sept. 28, 2010) [hereinafter DAS Air].

[52] DAS Air, *supra* note 51 at 258 (2002).

[53] OECD GUIDELINES FOR MULTINATIONAL ENTERPRISES, *supra* note 50.

[54] *Id.* at 2.

The Guidelines are government recommendations addressed to corporations based in those countries that adhere to them. These include the 30 OECD countries, plus Argentina, Brazil, Chile, Estonia, Israel, Latvia, Lithuania and Slovenia. Enterprises are, however, expected to abide by the Guidelines in their business operations worldwide. The Guidelines include prescriptive chapters covering most aspects of company behaviour: disclosure of information, employment and industrial relations, environment, combating bribery, consumer interests, science and technology, competition and taxation. Though not binding in a legal sense, they are not optional for corporations, which cannot pick and choose among the provisions of the Guidelines nor subject them to their own interpretations. Their application does not depend on endorsement by companies. They are the only multilaterally endorsed and comprehensive rules that governments have negotiated, in which they commit themselves to help solve problems arising in corporations.

National Contact Points

Although the Guidelines are not legally binding, every government that has adopted them is legally obliged to establish an NCP to promote and implement them. When a company is believed to be in breach of the Guidelines, a trade union, an NGO or another interested party can raise this as a case with the appropriate NCP. If the violation has occurred in a country that has adhered to the Guidelines, the case should be raised with the NCP of that country. If, on the other hand, the problem has arisen in a non-adhering country, the case has to be submitted to the NCP in the country where the company is headquartered. Thus, if a French company was believed to infringe the Guidelines in a non-adhering country such as Malaysia, the case would have to be filed with the French NCP. If it was a Japanese company breaking the Guidelines in its operations in Malaysia, the case would have to be presented to the NCP of Japan.

When an NCP receives a case, it is responsible for trying to resolve the issue, through a range of available options that include offering a forum for discussion for the parties concerned, allowing conciliation or mediation. In deciding what course of action to take, the NCP is required to make an initial assessment as to whether the case "merits further examination." It must then respond to the party that raised the case. If the NCP decides that the issue does not merit further consideration, it must give reasons for its decision. Ultimately, if no agreement can be reached, the NCP is required to issue a public statement on the case. It could also make recommendations to the parties on how the Guidelines apply to the case. NCPs may, therefore, inform a corporation that its activities violate the Guidelines. Although the Guidelines do not provide for sanctions against companies that do not respect them, the mere fact that the conclusions of NCPs should be in the public domain can have an impact and affect company behaviour. Moreover, the purpose of the procedure is to find solutions to problems rather than to "punish" companies that have failed to live up to the Guidelines. Governments are free to organise their NCPs in the way they see fit. Consequently, NCPs structures are heterogeneous. Most governments have located their NCP either in the Ministry of Economies or the Ministry of Foreign Affairs. Some involve a single government agency, while others are multi-agency (involving several ministries). Some are tripartite (government, labour and business), e.g., in Belgium, France and Sweden, or quadripartite (government, labour, business and NGOs) in Chile and Finland, but governments are ultimately responsible for decisions taken. Whatever the form, representatives of labour, business and NGOs must be informed of the availability of the NCP, which is also expected to develop and maintain relations with these groups.

Introduction[55]

Among the first cases raised under the revised OECD Guidelines for Multinational Enterprises concerned the operations of two Czech subsidiaries of the German companies Siemens and Bosch.

In June 2001, the Czech National Contact Point (NCP) received two submissions from the Czech-Moravian Confederation of Trade Unions (CMKOS) alleging violations of the Guidelines. In the Siemens case, the management refused to negotiate with the union, while in the Bosch case the workers struggled to establish a union. The Bosch subsidiary also threatened to move and dismiss workers if a trade union was created. The Czech NCP examined the cases and summoned the companies and the unions to a number of meetings in order to discuss the issues and try to resolve them. The role of the NCP consisted of facilitating the discussions and assisting in the negotiations. It also consulted the German NCP and informed the German Embassy of the situation. In addition, the parent companies were involved in the process. After six months, the dispute at the Siemens plant was resolved. It took however another five months for the parties involved in the Bosch case to reach an agreement. After a change in management at the Bosch subsidiary, the workers were able to form a trade union and negotiate a collective agreement. The CMKOS was pleased with the outcome and the action taken by the NCP.

. . . .

Trade Union Cases

Trade unions have raised more than 50 cases with NCPs since the 2000 review. A number of cases have also been raised by NGOs. Most of the cases submitted by trade unions refer to violations of trade union rights. Closures or transfers of companies or parts of companies are also common issues. Almost half of the cases concern corporate conduct in non-adhering countries.

About half of the cases have been closed. This means that they have either been resolved, or not accepted by the NCPs or finalised without an agreement between the parties involved. Some of the issues treated include the closure of Marks and Spencer in France and Belgium, violations of trade union rights in Guatemala by the Korean company Choi Shin, union busting activities by a US subsidiary (Brylane) of Pinault-Printemps-Redoute (PPR), the transfer of a plant in Brazil owned by Parmalat and the withdrawal of British American Tobacco from Burma.

Half the cases raised at the time of writing are still pending. Two recent cases have been raised concerning the operations of Bata in Sri Lanka and Ryanair in Europe. Other more prolonged cases regard the anti-union behaviour of Saint-Gobain in the United States and the Korean company Kiswire Sdn Bhd in Malaysia. Both cases were submitted in 2003, and it appears that the U.S. and Korean NCPs have done little to resolve the issues.

[55] *Id.* at 1.

On average, it takes NCPs about 10 months to deal with a case. TUAC has repeatedly criticised governments for not handling cases in an efficient and timely manner. The NCP procedure needs to be faster. Considering, however, that the aim of the procedure is to negotiate a joint solution, it goes without saying that it may be a process that takes time. Nevertheless, some NCPs barely react to cases. A few cases that were raised already in 2002 are still pending and there are also several cases submitted in 2003 which have yet to be concluded. Clearly, some NCPs are not fulfilling their mandate. They are reluctant to set up tripartite meetings to try to resolve the problems and appear to be afraid to criticise corporate conduct not compatible with the Guidelines. Besides, although the Guidelines are not legally binding, some NCPs take a legalistic approach in searching for loopholes that allow them to turn down cases.

This being said, there are also NCPs that are functioning properly and are seriously examining cases that may not be straight forward. Despite the fact that not all NCPs are performing adequately, trade unions are still using the Guidelines. When part of a negotiating strategy or a campaign, the Guidelines become an additional instrument to put pressure on a company. In some of the cases concerning restructuring, the Guidelines have been used to obtain a better result in the negotiations with the employer. The Guidelines, however, cannot prevent a company from closing down a plant. The Brylane/PPR case is an example of a Guidelines case being part of a campaign against a company, which ended successfully with the union gaining recognition. A few of the cases have been withdrawn as the mere submissions of cases have made companies more inclined to negotiate and find solutions to the problems. At some occasions, the social partners managed to reach an agreement on an issue because the company management was informed of the union's intention to raise a case. One reason for this outcome is that these so called cases involved responsible parent companies that were willing to intervene with the local management. The problem is that local trade unions do not always have access to the management at company headquarters.

Conclusions

Nearly five years after the revision, the Guidelines are becoming increasingly used by trade unions and NGOs. This period has served as a kind of trial and error period for all those involved with the Guidelines. NCPs have taken the time to establish procedures to handle cases. Some NCPs are now operating effectively, while others have a long way to go to meet acceptable standards. Furthermore, a considerable number of NCPs have yet to deal with their first case. It should be recognised that trade unions and NGOs have not always presented the best cases. We have been trying to find out under which circumstances it is useful to raise a case under the Guidelines. It is clear, however, that for the Guidelines to become an effective instrument, governments must strengthen their efforts to ensure that they have properly functioning NCPs. Based on our experiences with the Guidelines, we would draw the following lessons. First, a trade union must be clear over the goal when raising a case. What does it want to achieve by raising a case? What is the likely outcome? Before putting time and resources into a case, the union should be aware of the possibilities and not have unrealistic expectations. The Guidelines are not the ultimate solution, but they can play a role in addressing corporate malpractice. Secondly, cases must be well prepared. Although the implementation procedure is not juridical, cases should be well documented. A submission should explain how the Guidelines have been violated. Thirdly, we need to improve inter-trade union co-operation when raising cases. It is important that relevant national and international organisations, notably the Global Union Federations, are informed and that cases that concern several countries are coordinated. Fourthly, the Guidelines are essentially a tool for social dialogue. They could be used more proactively in contacts with companies. Two framework agreements currently refer to the Guidelines. Fifthly, the Guidelines need to be linked to other strategies. They should form minimum requirements for corporate conduct. Governments should ensure that the Guidelines are respected in public procurement and only companies that observe the Guidelines should be eligible for public subsidies.

In 2010, TUAC held its first meeting on the Update of the Guidelines. The meeting was attended by representatives from TUAC affiliates, the Global Union Federations (GUFs), the ITUC, and the Council of Global Unions, as well as from the OECD, the UN Special Representative of Business and Human Rights (SRBHR) and OECD Watch. Key points from the trade union discussion are excerpted next.[56]

3.1 Trade Union Use of the Guidelines

. . . .

8. Trade unions identified the following as reasons for using the Guidelines:
   - To gain access to the company;
   - As part of a campaign strategy: in many cases companies do not know the Guidelines;
   - As a central plank of a national CSR strategy;
   - As a fact-finding tool;
   - As an instrument of last resort;
   - In specific contexts: for example, restructuring in the current crisis.
9. The discussions also focused on why trade unions are not making greater use of the Guidelines:
   - Lack of government promotion of the Guidelines;
   - Lack of trade union promotion of the Guidelines;
   - Low awareness among trade unions/works councils;
   - Greater effectiveness of domestic industrial relations processes: 'why not go to Court'?
   - Delays due to parallel legal proceedings;[57]

[56] The OECD Guidelines for Multinational Enterprises – Update of the OECD Guidelines for Multinational Enterprises Paris, February 16, 2010, Background Paper, *available at* http://www.tuac.org/en/public/e-docs/00/00/06/F5/telecharger.phtml?cle_doc_attach=2308 (last visited June 1, 2011). For a list of cases under these Guidelines and the case status, *see* TUAC OECD MNE Guidelines, *available at* http://www.tuac.org/OECDMNEGuidelines.htm. The Guidelines were updated in May, 2011 without significant changes in relevant areas. *See*, OECD Guidelines for Multinational Enterprises (2011), *available at* www.oecd.org/dataoecd/43/29/48004323.pdf (last visited October 7, 2011).

[57] The Japanese NCP reports that parallel proceedings are a problem for the Japanese NCP as "the company involved tends to avoid commitment to the operation of the NCP." The OECD Guidelines

- Long timescales;
- Poor functioning of many NCPs.

11. The discussions also highlighted the following obstacles as impeding the performance of the NCP:
    - Limited knowledge/capacity in the NCP's start-up phase (Brazil, Peru);
    - Inappropriate structure of the NCP, and in particular conflicts of interest arising from the location of an NCP in a single Ministry;
    - Lack of a common supportive position on parallel legal proceedings;
    - Lack of resources (Austria, Sweden, United States);
    - Lack of training of NCPs, in mediation, for example;
    - Lack of experience/knowledge of industrial relations;
    - Lack of transparency, both internally within the NCP process and as regards the publication of information;
    - Insufficient promotion of the Guidelines by NCPs/the OECD;
    - Lack of common understanding on the role of the NCP;
    - Lack of cooperation by companies;
    - Inability of the NCP to ensure the cooperation of companies;
    - Lack of sanction of companies for failure to cooperate in the process or comply with the recommendations;
    - Lack of follow-up on cases;
    - Lack of a right of review/appeal;
    - Long timescales: even though these have been reduced, several months is a long time for a worker involved in a dispute;
    - The difficulty for NCPs in meeting the burden of proof;
    - The lack of resources for fact-finding on complex cases.
12. The discussions led to agreement on a number of points:
    - Role of the NCP: the importance of mediation for trade unions and the need to clarify the role of the NCP in line with the proposal made by OECD Watch – to move to adjudication only if there is no mediation. This provides an incentive for companies to participate in mediation;
    - Incentives/Sanctions: related to the above, the need to put in place incentives for companies to cooperate and sanctions for those who fail to cooperate/comply with NCP recommendations;
    - Transparency: the value of the procedural guidance setting out standards of transparency for internal proceedings between parties, as well as for public information;
    - Follow-up and Right to Appeal: the need for the procedural guidance to provide for follow-up procedures;
    - Parallel proceedings: the importance of common guidance from the OECD on parallel legal proceedings, based on the UK NCP approach. There must be a right of review.

. . . .

for Multinational Enterprises 2010 'Update' TUAC Submission to the OECD Investment Committee, Paris, October 7, 2009, *available at* http://www.tuac.org/e-docs/00/00/05/89/telecharger.phtml?cle_doc_attach=1850 (last visited June 1, 2011).

3.3. Substantive Issues: Priority Issues

13. The discussion on substantive issues highlighted the following priorities.

The first five issues are closely inter-related:

- Investment nexus: remove the requirement for an investment nexus;
- Supply chains: strengthen application to the supply chain and the full range of business relationships taking into account changing employment relationships;
- Changing working relationships: ensure the Guidelines apply in the context of declining direct, permanent employment and the increasing use of sub-contractors often for the purposes of avoiding union recognition and limiting the applicability of the ILO Conventions. This issue relates to the need to remove the requirement for an investment nexus, which would mean that a transport company servicing one multinational company would fall outside the scope of the Guidelines;
- Living wage: the Guidelines should be updated to include provisions on a living wage in line with other international standards;
- Due diligence: this is a vast area and the subject of on-going work by the SRBHR;
- Private equity: ensure that the description of enterprises covered under the Guidelines captures private equity;
- Investment agreements.

14. In addition, it was noted that neither of the terms collective bargaining or Decent Work is present in the current text of the Guidelines.

. . . .

In 2004 and 2006, the AFL-CIO unsuccessfully attempted to have the Bush administration file a Section 301 unfair trade practice petition against China under the U.S. Trade Act of 1974, claiming China's treatment of labor provided a trade barrier and gave it an unfair trade advantage. This request was twice rejected. The union's argument is next.

Section 301 Petition against the Chinese Government[58]

Executive Summary

Mark Barenberg

Introduction

The AFL-CIO has filed a Section 301 petition charging that the Chinese government persistently and systematically denies workers' rights, hurting U.S. workers and

[58] Mark Barenberg, Section 301 Petition Against the Chinese Government, executive summary prepared for the Executive Council, AFL-CIO, and Members of Congress, *available at* http://www.aflcio.org/issues/jobseconomy/globaleconomy/upload/china_execsum.pdf (last visited Sept. 28, 2010). Section 301 cases can be self-initiated by the U.S. Trade Representative (USTR) or as the result of a petition filed by a firm or industry group. If USTR initiates a Section 301 investigation, it must seek to negotiate a settlement with foreign country in the form of compensation or elimination of the trade barrier. For cases involving trade agreements, the USTR is required to request formal dispute proceedings as provided by the trade agreements.

communities, while also preventing Chinese workers from exercising their internationally recognized rights at the workplace. Under Section 301 of the U.S. Trade Act, this egregious repression of workers' rights is considered an unfair trade practice, and the President has the authority to impose trade sanctions or take other action to induce the Chinese government to cease its violation of the rights of its own workers.

Two years ago, the AFL-CIO filed a similar petition, which the United States Trade Representative (USTR) refused to investigate. The USTR did not dispute the overwhelming evidence presented in the petition, but asserted that alternative actions by the President would advance workers' rights in China. There have been no such effective actions, and workers in China and the U.S. continue to bear the brunt of our nation's failure to act. The new Section 301 petition, filed by the 9-million member AFL-CIO, again documents how the Chinese government and multinational corporations persistently violate the rights of China's factory workers. The petition also shows, through four methodologies, that the Chinese government's systematic repression of the human rights of its factory workers contributes to the loss of more than a million jobs in the United States.

In China, millions of child workers and forced laborers produce goods and services, many of them for export. Workers who protest or seek to form independent unions are fired, beaten, and imprisoned. China's labor market bears no resemblance to a free, competitive market. Millions of migrants from the countryside are denied the basic rights of urban residents in manufacturing towns and cities. They are so powerless that the average worker is simply not paid two or three months of earned wages. Meanwhile, corporations are reaping huge profits at the expense of China's factory workers who are paid wages as low as 15 to 50 cents per hour.

The Chinese government's violation of internationally recognized workers' rights constitutes an unfair trade practice, as defined by Section 301 of the U.S. Trade Act. The AFL-CIO calls on the USTR and the President to immediately take action to ensure that the Chinese government complies with internationally recognized workers' rights.

. . . .

QUESTIONS

1. Can there ever be an argument about "labor conditions" constituting a Section 301 unfair "trade" practice?
2. Are the OECD Guidelines a sensible avenue for labor unions to pursue workers' labor rights? If so, why; if not, why not?
3. What are the weaknesses in the use of FTA enforcement as a means of protecting workers' labor rights? What are its strengths?

III

Agenda Items

Criteria, Alternatives, and Evaluative Standards

A. REGULATORY SOURCES, STRUCTURES, AND ADMINISTRATION

1. *Diverse Approaches Addressing Common Issues*

The structural and administrative alternatives of operation, regulation, and enforcement of labor and employment laws are of course embedded in local traditions. Regulations are varied and many, but the issues they address are often common. Most often, the regulatory schemes reflect the interplay among the mixtures of capital, labor, and government, with the government's role ranging from employer-dominated laissez-faire to that of referee to that of strict regulation with strong union influence. From this composition flows the extent of the laws' reach, the level of its enforcement, the strength of labor unions and their use of economic weapons, the quantum and quality of labor rights, and the availability and efficacy of dispute-resolution methods.

As in most comparative law contexts, the sources, structures, and administration of labor laws may appear strikingly similar, yet operate quite differently in application. Also, understanding a country's economic position (e.g., developing, developed, etc.) often provides insight into understanding the practical aspects of a regulatory system.

Labor Relations and the Law[1]

D. Wollett and B. Aaron

The processes of industrialization create similar, sometimes identical problems wherever in the world they take place. The persistence of such problems suggests that they are

[1] LABOR RELATIONS AND THE LAW 1030–34 (Donald H. Wollet & Benjamin Aaron eds., Little Brown 2nd ed. 1960); although somewhat dated, the variety of labor issues and regulatory approaches raised remain current. For general discussion, see DAVID ZISKIND, *Standards for Evaluating Labor Legislation, in* CONCERNING HUMAN ASPIRATION: ESSAYS IN COMPARATIVE LABOR LAW 146 (1985).

inevitable by-products of industrialization and the system of large enterprises (whether private or public) which accompanies it. A fair accommodation in the labor market appears to be one of the critical needs of the free society. Efforts elsewhere to achieve this accommodation, and the laws *which those* efforts induce, reveal similarities corresponding to the efforts and laws of the United States. Yet there are perhaps equally significant differences in their experiences. To look briefly at a few examples of these parallels and particulars of experience is to realize (1) that the developments in the other democracies have a helpful relevance as we continue in this country the search for firmer "labor law" concepts, but (2) that glib transplantations of one country's approaches and solutions to another may prove unworkable because of the close and mutually interacting relationship between a country's industrial and labor institutions and its labor laws.

Right to, and extent of, unionization. The development of labor law in various countries has been closely related to the checkered history of the development of the right to associate together and to engage in collective action. The law has wavered between prohibition, permission, and protection of these rights, somewhat as it has in the case of business combinations. As in the United States, the trend has been toward positive governmental protection of the right of employees to associate in labor unions, with considerable differences as to the date when this step was taken. The trend has not, however, been a steady one. Thus, for example, the right to operate free labor organizations was virtually obliterated during the Hitler regime in Nazi Germany.

It is difficult to generalize about the extent of union organization and union membership in the various countries of the world. In some highly industrialized states it is comparable to that in the United States, and may in some exceed the percentage here. The extent of unionization and the nature and general orientation of the labor movement of any country obviously have a significant impact upon the character of the labor relations law of that particular country.

Statutory as opposed to contractual regulations. A major difference between our system and that of most European countries is the extent to *which the* unions in those countries are politically oriented and have accomplished their objectives through political and legislative activities. This has resulted in statutes which define and control in great detail aspects of labor relations which in the United States are usually controlled by the collective bargaining agreement. These include, for example, such details as vacation pay, conditions for discharge, severance pay, holidays, pensions, and sick leave. The rights of employees, including in some instances even the right to continued employment, rest upon legislative enactment rather than upon contract.

This has tended to reduce greatly the significance of the collectively negotiated agreement. Not only do many European collective bargaining agreements fail to include many provisions found in American contracts because the matters are governed by statute, but the clauses which they do contain, such as wage terms, frequently merely play the role of establishing floors or minima for the industry which are supplemented by individual contracts between employers and employees. Thus it may be said that the admixture of legislative regulation (in the form of protective labor legislation and social insurance) and contractual regulation (as a result of collective bargaining) varies greatly in the labor relations systems of various countries.

Works Councils and labor courts. One striking difference between a number of European countries and the United States is that the European unions rarely participate, as such, in any procedures for the handling of the intimate day-to-day relations with the employer, including the handling of what we call grievances. In Europe some of these functions are performed by statutory Works Councils, which in some cases must be elected by the employees. These are bodies quite independent of the trade-union. This makes the typical European Union more remote from the worker than is the union in the United States. This remoteness also reflects the greater political orientation of the European labor movement.

Similarly, there are in many countries of Europe special systems of courts to handle complaints of workers concerning grievances or breaches of contracts or statute. These appear to perform the functions of our grievance procedure, and of voluntary arbitration as the final step in that procedure. Cases before these courts are limited to legal claims under statutes and contracts. These courts have no jurisdiction to fix terms of employment; they are thus to be distinguished from industrial courts in Australia and New Zealand which will be mentioned below and which have this much broader function.

One important consequence of this labor court system is to give the employee a much greater ease of individual enforcement of his rights than he would have in the United States. Here his claims must normally be pressed through, and with the aid of, his union, by means of the grievance procedure. Our approach gives the union a degree of control over the individual's claim which it does not have in Europe; the employee can go to court easily and freely there. (This freedom is somewhat akin to the freedom of an individual here to file a charge of an unfair labor practice with the National Labor Relations Board.)

Statutory extensions of collective agreements. A feature of European labor law completely unknown to our system is the phenomenon of statutory extension of collective bargaining contracts reached between some employers and unions, for their workers, to other portions of the industry which may not be unionized. This has been done quite generally in some European countries, and occasionally in Great Britain. Practices have varied from time to time and from country to country. Sometimes these extensions have been automatic. Sometimes they have been optional. Always they have been subject to government approval.

A similar phenomenon is the extension, which has been worked out most carefully in West Germany, of the duration of a contract which prevents its termination. Even though the termination date has arrived, the contract cannot expire. It continues until replaced by some other agreement.

Compulsory arbitration. Some countries have a wide or virtually universal use of compulsory arbitration for the settlement of what we would call contract or interest disputes, i.e., disputes over the terms of new or modified collective agreements. This practice was pioneered and has attained its widest use in Australia and New Zealand [since, discarded]. The only analogous phenomenon in the United States would be the comprehensive regulation of wages and other contract terms which we have utilized during [national] emergencies.

....

Nationalized industries. Interesting questions of law and policy as to labor relations arise in countries where there is extensive nationalization of industries. Technically, workers in such industries become government employees and their rights to organize, to engage in collective bargaining, and to strike, may as a matter of political theory be subject to curtailment. We face this problem in this country in connection with civil servants – most critically when groups such as policemen are involved.

....

Union security. With respect to the union security issue, which generates so much controversy in our country, it is of some interest to observe that the policies of other countries range over a spectrum from absolute prohibition, as in Denmark and Belgium, to permissive policies as in Great Britain, Switzerland, Norway, and Sweden. There is in fact no wide use of such clauses even in those countries where they are permitted; and yet, in practice, the very large percentage of workers are union members. New Zealand provides for statutory compulsory union membership in certain instances. Intermediate solutions, such an allowing obligatory membership for employees hired subsequent to the effective date of a collective agreement, are utilized in some countries. This approach would be analogous to maintenance-of-membership clauses of the type innovated by our War Labor Board during World War II.

Picketing and the boycott. Picketing has not been an important subject of litigation in most foreign countries. Peaceful picketing in connection with strikes has increasingly achieved lawful status, without presenting problems of particular significance, as the high incidence of union membership renders picketing largely unnecessary in many countries. The boycott, particularly in Europe, has enjoyed greater toleration than typically has been true in the United States. This is probably attributable to the lack of an antitrust tradition hostile to economic combinations generally, whether of business groups or of labor groups. Thus the boycott by either has tended to be viewed as a legitimate device of competitive economic conflict. It is too early to assess the impact on this of the post World War II anti-cartel movement which has sprung up in Europe.

Exclusive representation by a single union. A striking contrast between our labor relations law and the systems found elsewhere is the unique use in our country of the device of the exclusive bargaining representative in an appropriate unit. The situation abroad will vary, depending upon the structure of a particular country's labor movement. Thus an employer may deal with a single union where the country's labor movement is so unified that in the particular industry only one union exists. On the other hand, an employer may frequently deal with several unions simultaneously or with committees of unions – and not always, the same unions – each of which represents its own members. This situation may prevail because the labor movement of a country is divided, along political or religious lines, or both, or because unions have organized along trade or craft lines. That the union–shop issue has tended to be less controversial and jurisdictional disputes rarer in Europe than in the United States is probably traceable to this absence of exclusive powers of representation in bargaining relationships. Whether these considerations are outweighed by the advantages gained under our system is an intriguing problem of labor relations and collective bargaining. . . .

. . . .

Understanding one country's system of labor regulation can facilitate identifying common issues in the workplace and act as a foil or backdrop against which diverse approaches to labor regulation can be contrasted and compared and comparative advantages can be ascertained. These comparisons are organized in the following materials under four "agenda items" that seek to make categories related to the major issue areas of labor and employment law in any country, allowing easier comparisons of similar issues. Although the regulatory approaches may vary, the real-life situations in the workplace arising from national and local cultures, regarding wages, working conditions, and labor disputes and their resolution, will be similar.

2. *U.S. Illustration as Context*

In this text, the U.S. system of labor law regulation is used as a context and as a frame of reference to introduce all four agenda items, beginning with the first agenda category – regulation and administration. This category includes the range of subjects regulated and the institutions administering the laws. The other three agenda items – workers' rights and benefits, trade unions, and dispute resolution – are also introduced, within the discussion of ILO core labor standards, so as to provide that context and act as a "snapshot" of labor and employment laws in one country, in this case, the United States.

From an international point of view, it is sometimes argued that the United States is an outlier in international, and especially Western, labor regulation in that it has a relatively low union role, high resort to litigation rather than interest coordination, relatively weak substantive labor rights, and so on.[2]

Summary of the Major Laws and Administrative Enforcement Agencies of the U.S. Department of Labor[3]

The Department of Labor (DOL) administers and enforces more than 180 federal laws. These mandates and the regulations that implement them cover many workplace activities for about 10 million employers and 125 million workers.

[2] An example of differences in approach can be found in employment contracts. *See* Leah F. Vosko, *Legitimizing the Triangular Employment Relationship: Emerging International Labour Standards from a Comparative Perspective*, 19 COMP. LAB. L. & POL'Y J. 43 (1997). This article discusses "[t]he rise of the triangular employment relationship[,] . . . characterized by a fixed-term contract [contrasted with the American bilateral relationship, often with 'at-will' rather than term contracts used]. . . ." *Id.* at 43. In acknowledging that "states are beginning to recognize that the triangular employment relationship creates a serious tension within prevailing regulatory regimes associated with the standard employment relationship . . . [this] article examines Convention No. 181 and, to a lesser extent, the emerging instrument on Contract Labor in light of the growth of the triangular employment relationship." *Id.* at 44–45. For a brief introduction to labor laws in the European Union, see Dublin Chamber of Commerce, *EU Labour Law* (July 24, 2009), *available at* http://www.dublinchamber.ie/Uploads/EU%20Labour%20law.pdf. A report by ITUC on July 6, 2011 reported shortcomings in labor laws in EU member states, including insufficient protection from anti-union discrimination, unreasonable restrictions on the the right to strike, and European Court of Justice rulings that it claims erodes fundamental workers' rights. ITUC, *New Report Reveals Labor Law Shortcomings in Europe*, ITUC CSI IGB (July 6, 2011), http://www.ituc-csi.org/new-report-reveals-labour-law.html.

[3] U.S. Dep't of Labor (DOL), Summary of the Major Laws of the Department of Labor, at http://www.dol.gov/opa/aboutdol/lawsprog.html (last visited December 1, 2011) [Some formatting altered] [hereinafter "Foreign Labor Trends"]. Some of the statutes and regulations enforced by agencies within the Department of Labor require that posters or notices be posted in the workplace. The DOL provides electronic copies of the required posters and some of the posters are available in languages other than English.

Following is a brief description of many of DOL's principal statutes most commonly applicable to businesses, job seekers, workers, retirees, contractors, and grantees.

. . . .

- Wages & Hours
- Workplace Safety & Health
- Workers' Compensation
- Employee Benefits
- Unions & Their Members
- Employee Protection
- Uniformed Services Employment and Reemployment Rights Act
- Employee Polygraph Protection Act
- Garnishment of Wages
- The Family and Medical Leave Act
- Veterans' Preference
- Government Contracts, Grants, or Financial Aid
- Migrant & Seasonal Agricultural Workers
- Mine Safety & Health
- Construction
- Transportation
- Plant Closings & Layoffs

Department of Labor Organizational Chart[4]

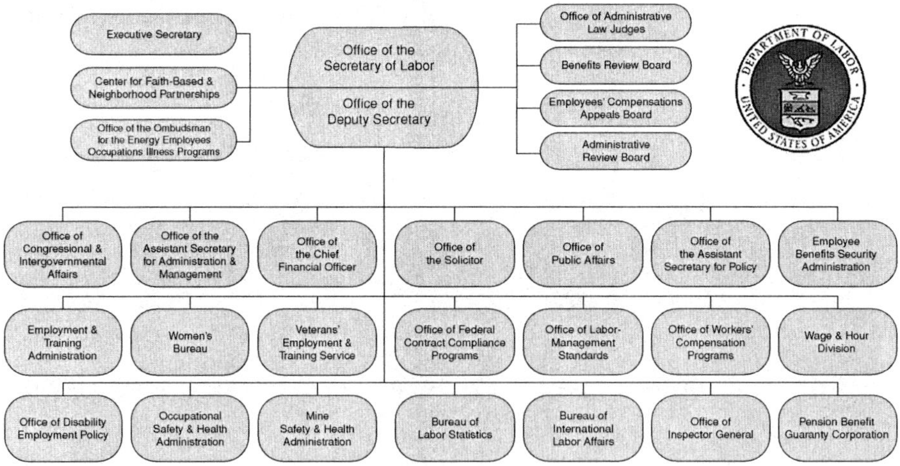

See DOL, *Poster Page: Workplace Poster Requirements for Small Businesses and Other Employers*, http://www.dol.gov/oasam/programs/osdbu/sbrefa/poster/matrix.htm (last visited Sept. 30, 2010).

4 DOL, *Organizational Chart*, http://www.dol.gov/dol/aboutdol/orgchart.htm (last visited Sept. 30, 2010).

Other federal agencies besides the Department of Labor enforce labor and employment laws and regulations that affect the employment relationship, e.g., the National Labor Relations Board (NLRB).

Statutes that ensure non-discrimination in employment are generally enforced by the Equal Employment Opportunity Commission (EEOC).

The Taft-Hartley Act regulates a wide range of employer–employee conduct and is administered by the National Labor Relations Board (NLRB).

United States Labor Profile 2007[5]

. . . .

Human Resources

The United States Workforce

The United States has a population of over 302 million. According to the Bureau of Labor Statistics (BLS), the U.S. civilian workforce – the number of persons working or looking for work – in 2007 was 153.1 million and is projected to reach 164.2 million in 2016. The female workforce in 2007 was 71.0 million. The U.S. workforce has four particular assets: education, high productivity, flexibility, and mobility. According to the 2007 Key Indicators of the Labor Market (KILM) report by the International Labor Organization (ILO), the United States leads the world in productivity as measured by output per person employed per year and is second only to Norway in output per hour worked. According to BLS, U.S. nonfarm business productivity grew at an annual rate of 2.7 percent from 2000 through 2006. The U.S. labor market just recorded the longest uninterrupted period of job growth in the 68 years that monthly job records have been kept. Between August 2003 and December 2007, the U.S. enjoyed 52 consecutive months of job gains, totaling over 8 million jobs.

. . . .

Unions

Most unionized workers in the United States are represented by unions affiliated with one of two organizations. The American Federation of Labor-Congress of Industrial Organizations (AFL-CIO) was formed by the merger of the two then separate organizations in 1955. It currently includes 55 national unions, organized by craft or industry, and claims about 10 million members. The Change to Win Federation was formed by a group of seven unions that withdrew from the AFL-CIO in 2005. It claims about six million members. In addition, there are a number of non-affiliated national unions.

[5] Foreign Labor Trends, http://www.dol.gov/ilab/media/reports/flt/2007USLabor.pdf (last visited Dec. 8, 2011). By 2010, the Change to Win Union had lost some of its key members – Carpenters, Laborers, and UNITE HERE; see, Carl Horowitz, *Laborers to Leave Change to Win, Rejoin AFL-CIO* NATIONAL LEGAL AND POLICY CENTER (October 17, 2010), http://www.nlpc.org/stories/2010/08/17/laborers-leave-change-win-rejoin-afl-cio. The coalition currently consists of four member unions: The International Brotherhood of Teamsters (IBT); Service Employees International Union (SEIU); United Farm Workers (UFW); and United Food and Commercial Workers (UFCW). *See* WIN, http://www.changetowin.org (last visited Dec. 1, 2011).

The largest of these is the National Education Association (NEA), which represents public school teachers, and claims over three million members. The United Brotherhood of Carpenters and Joiners of America, with 512,000 members, and the Fraternal Order of Police (FOP), which claims over 312,000 police officer members, are among the other large independent organizations. In 2007, BLS estimated that 12.1 % of employed wage and salary workers were unionized, up from 12.0 % a year earlier. Most of the growth in union membership over the last several years has taken place in the public sector, while private sector unions have declined in membership in percent and absolute terms.

The national labor federations generally do not directly engage in collective bargaining, but provide services and support to their affiliated organizations, and engage in political activities. Most collective bargaining is carried out by the national unions or local unions.

Unionization and collective bargaining for most private sector workers in the United States is regulated by the National Labor Relations Act (NLRA) passed in 1935. The law is administered and enforced by the National Labor Relations Board (NLRB), an independent agency that is not part of the Department of Labor. Unionization and collective bargaining in the railroad and airline industries are regulated by the Railway Labor Act (RLA) which is administered and enforced by the National Mediation Board.

Unions usually win the right to represent workers either through voluntary recognition by the employer or through a vote overseen by the NLRB in which the majority of workers vote for union representation. Once the union has won the support of a majority of the bargaining unit and is certified in a workplace, it has the exclusive authority to negotiate the conditions of employment on behalf of all workers in the bargaining unit.

Labor relations in the public sector are regulated by federal or state laws, depending on the identity of the government employer. Federal workers have the right to organize and bargain collectively, but may not strike and are restricted in the scope of bargaining, with wages and working hours established by law and regulation. Labor-management relations in the federal government are overseen by the Federal Labor Relations Authority, which is governed by Title VII of the Civil Service Reform Act of 1978, also known as the Federal Service Labor-Management Relations Statute.

Public sector worker unions at the state and municipal levels are governed by labor laws in each of the 50 states. Many states typically model their laws and boards after the NLRA and the NLRB, though in some states, public workers do not have the right to seek representation by a union or bargain collectively.

Employer Organizations

Among the largest organizations representing business are the National Association of Manufacturers (NAM), the U.S. Chamber of Commerce, and the U.S. Council for International Business (USCIB).

The NAM is an important voice for American industry. The NAM does not engage in collective bargaining. Its lobbying efforts are organized to inform Congress and the Administration how proposed changes in laws and regulations would be helpful or harmful to manufacturers and the jobs which they provide. In general, NAM represents the interests of larger employers.

The U.S. Chamber of Commerce is a leadership and service organization that works on national and international business-related issues in addition to local and state concerns.

The Chamber plays a leading role in many coalitions that bring together other business groups to work on specific issues. It also has set up a Congressional Action Network, consisting of Congressional Action Committees across the country, to activate member grass-roots support on legislation before Congress. Compared to NAM, the Chamber generally represents the interest of medium and smaller employers.

The USCIB was founded in 1945 to promote an open system of world trade, investment, and finance. The Council represents U.S. employers before the International Labor Organization. The USCIB has a membership of multinational companies, law firms, and business associations and is the U.S. affiliate of the International Chamber of Commerce, the Business and Industry Advisory Committee to the Organization for Economic Cooperation and Development and the International Organization of Employers. It formulates policy positions through many committees and working groups composed of business representatives and facilitates international trade policy through harmonization of commercial practices.

....

U.S. Labor Laws and Standards

Responsibility for protecting workers is divided between the federal government and the states. The federal government may act to regulate commerce among the states; and the states may set conditions applicable to commerce within their own borders. Many states have adopted laws dealing with labor standards.

The NLRA and the RLA govern the labor-management relationship between most private employers and their employees.

The Fair Labor Standards Act (FLSA) of 1938, as amended, provides for minimum wage, overtime, and child labor restrictions for covered employees. The Occupational Safety and Health Act of 1970 (OSH Act) protects the workplace safety and health of employees. In addition, state labor laws supplement the federal occupational health and safety law where not preempted by federal law, or where a state obtains federal approval to administer its own program. The Federal Mine Safety and Health Act of 1977 (Mine Act) protects the workplace safety and health of miners.

The Right of Association

Freedom of Association is protected under the First Amendment of the U.S. Constitution, which has been interpreted by the courts to include an employee's right to form and join a union. The NLRA guarantees employees the right to self-organization, to form, join, or assist labor organizations; to bargain collectively through representatives of their own choosing; and to engage in other concerted activities for the purpose of collective bargaining or other mutual aid or protection. The NLRA also provides that it is an unfair labor practice, and therefore a violation of the law, for an employer or union to restrain or coerce employees in the exercise of these rights.

The NLRB is an independent federal agency created by Congress in 1935 to administer and enforce the NLRA. The statute guarantees the right of employees to organize and to bargain collectively with their employers or to refrain from such activity. Generally applying to all employers involved in interstate commerce – other than airlines, railroads, agriculture, and government – the Act implements the national labor policy of assuring free choice and encouraging collective bargaining as a means of maintaining industrial peace. Through the years, Congress has amended the Act and the Board and courts have developed a body of law drawn from the statute.

The NLRB has two principal functions: (1) to conduct secret ballots, in appropriate circumstances, in order to determine whether workers wish to be represented by a union in dealing with their employers and if so, by which union; and (2) to prevent and remedy unlawful acts, called unfair labor practices, by either employers or unions. Unfair labor practices are various actions that impede workers or employers from exercising their rights under the NLRA, for example, the dismissal or intimidation of workers who attempt to organize a union. The agency does not act on its own motion in either function. It processes only those charges of unfair labor practices and petitions for employee elections that are filed with the NLRB in one of its 51 Regional, Sub-regional, or Resident Offices.

In the railroad and airline industries, the RLA protects the freedom of association and self-organizing rights of employees and provides a mechanism to ensure the peaceful resolution of collective bargaining disputes in these industries. A three-member, presidentially appointed National Mediation Board mediates disputes over wages, hours, and working conditions that arise between rail and air carriers and organizations representing their employees; investigates representation disputes; and certifies employee organizations as representatives of crafts or classes of carrier employees.

The Right to Organize and Bargain Collectively

Though the government regulates certain conditions of employment – such as the minimum wage, job safety and health, pensions, and hiring practices – the principal method for determining overall working conditions for unionized workers is through collective bargaining. Negotiations are usually decentralized, covering a single plant, corporation, or region, though in some instances, large parts of an entire industry may be covered. Union members or their representatives generally have the final say on whether to ratify collective bargaining agreements since most union constitutions require members to vote approval before agreements can be signed.

The NLRA grants collective bargaining rights to most private sector employees, but it excludes from coverage railroad and airline employees, independent contractors, domestic workers, agricultural workers, employees of small businesses, supervisory or managerial employees, and employees of federal, state, and local governments. The NLRA provides that it is an unfair labor practice for an employer or union to restrain or coerce employees in the exercise of their right to self-organization; their right to form, join, or assist labor organizations; their right to bargain collectively through representatives of their own choosing; and their right to engage in other concerted activities for the purpose of collective bargaining or other mutual aid or protection of these rights. Further, the NLRA guarantees that a representative designated or selected by the majority of the employees in an appropriate unit will be the exclusive representative of all the employees in the unit for purposes of collective bargaining.

Under the NLRA, collective bargaining expressly encompasses the mutual obligation of the employer and the representative of the employees to meet at reasonable times and confer in good faith with respect to wages, hours, and other terms and conditions of employment, and the execution of a written contract incorporating any agreement reached if requested by either party. Virtually all collective bargaining agreements provide for grievance arbitration, by which disputes arising under the terms of the agreement are submitted to third-party arbitrators for resolution.

Workers can obtain union representation by organizing a majority of their coworkers to designate a union as their representative. They can then either persuade their employer to voluntarily recognize the union, or they can request the NLRB to hold an election. The NLRB will conduct an election if at least 30 percent of the workers in the workplace show an interest in being in a union. The union gains exclusive representation if a majority of the workers vote in favor of the union. If more than one union seeks to be the exclusive representative, the Board may conduct an election in which workers vote to determine whether they want to be represented by either of the competing unions or want no representation. If one union receives a majority of the votes cast, that union is certified as the exclusive representative. If no choice receives a majority, a runoff among the choices that received the most votes in the first election is held.

Exclusive representation is a unique feature of U.S. labor law. The union that becomes the collective bargaining agent is required to represent all workers in the bargaining unit, whether they are union members or not. The employer, for its part, may not bargain with workers individually or with any other organization. Another union can challenge the incumbent bargaining agent, but is generally barred from doing so during the year following the Board's certification of the results of an election making the incumbent the exclusive representative and the year following the period of a valid contract of three years or less.

An unfair labor practice case is initiated under the NLRA when an individual, union, or employer files a charge with an NLRB regional office. The charge is investigated by the regional office on behalf of the NLRB's General Counsel to determine whether there is reasonable cause to believe that the NLRA has been violated. If the Regional Director (RD) concludes that the charge has merit, the RD will seek first to remedy the apparent violation by encouraging a voluntary settlement by the parties. Most cases are voluntarily settled.

If a case is not settled, a formal complaint is issued and a hearing is held before an Administrative Law Judge (ALJ). Following the hearing, and after the parties have prepared briefs regarding the issues, the ALJ issues a decision containing proposed findings of fact and a recommended order. Any party may appeal the ALJ's decision to the five-member, presidentially appointed Board, which may adopt, modify, or reject the findings and recommendations of the ALJ. If no exceptions are filed to the ALJ decision, that decision and recommendation automatically become the decision and order of the Board. The Board has authority to order an employer to reinstate an employee with or without back pay among other remedies.

If a party fails to comply with the Board's order voluntarily, the NLRB's Office of the General Counsel files an enforcement petition in the appropriate U.S. Court of Appeals. Similarly, any "person aggrieved," (which may include either the respondent or the charging party (or both), by a final order of the Board may seek to have the order reviewed and set aside by filing a petition with the appropriate U.S. Court of Appeals.

The Railway Labor Act (RLA), which regulates labor relations in the railroad and airline industries, contains mediation and conciliation procedures that are more elaborate than under the NLRA. The RLA also provides for arbitration in the event of employees' disputes arising under the terms of a collective bargaining agreement.

In the federal sector, the Civil Service Reform Act (CSRA) generally provides employees the right to bargain collectively on such matters as personnel policies, grievance procedures and other working conditions. The CSRA established the Federal Labor Relations Authority to conduct union representation elections among federal employees, to protect federal employees' rights to organize and bargain collectively, and resolve unfair labor practice claims. Strikes by employees in federal agencies are illegal, and major economic issues such as wages, hours, and pensions are excluded from bargaining except in the Postal Service, which is covered by a separate law.

In state and local governments, the rights of public employees vary. Many of the states have relatively comprehensive bargaining laws, and some permit strikes under some circumstances. A number of states have laws requiring binding arbitration of disputes involving public employees, particularly for police and fire services and sanitation workers.

The Federal Mediation and Conciliation Service (FMCS), created in 1947, is an independent agency whose mission is to preserve and promote labor-management peace and cooperation. For over 50 years, FMCS has promoted sound and stable labor-management relations by providing mediation assistance in contract negotiation disputes between employers and their unionized employees. Headquartered in Washington, D.C., with two regional offices and more than 70 field offices, the agency provides mediation and conflict resolution services to industry, government agencies, and communities.

Prohibition of Forced or Compulsory Labor

The Thirteenth Amendment of the U.S. Constitution prohibits involuntary servitude except as punishment for a person convicted of a crime. In support of the Thirteenth Amendment, U.S. criminal statutes prohibit forced labor and peonage, a form of involuntary servitude based upon real or alleged indebtedness. In addition, the Trafficking Victims Protection Act of 2000 and its subsequent amendments prohibit human trafficking and provide protection for trafficking victims. The United States is signatory to ILO Convention No. 105 concerning the Abolition of Forced Labor.

Child Labor Laws

The FLSA sets the minimum age for employment at 16 for most non-farm employment and at 14 for most farm work. Children 14 to 16 years of age may perform non-hazardous non-farm work in various non-manufacturing, non-mining jobs, with limitations on the time of day and the number of hours they are permitted to work. Children 14 to 16 years old may perform non-hazardous farm work, outside of school hours. Children 12 to 14 years old may perform non-hazardous farm work, outside school hours, on farms that also employ their parent(s) or with written parental consent. Children 16 and 17 years old may perform any non-hazardous non-farm work without regard to restrictions on hours worked. Children who are 16 years old may perform all farm work with no restrictions under the child labor laws. Civil enforcement of the child labor provisions of the FLSA is done by the U.S. DOL's Employment Standards Administration (ESA), Wage and Hour Division (WHD), and criminal enforcement is led by the U.S. Department of Justice. The United States has ratified ILO Convention No. 182 on the Worst Forms of Child Labor.

Discrimination in Employment

There are several federal statutes and executive orders as well as a number of state statutes that prohibit private and public employer discrimination based on, among other things, race, color, religion, ethnic origin, gender, age, political affiliation, and disability. The following is a list of some of the major federal statutes and executive orders that apply:

- Title VII of the Civil Rights Act of 1964 (Title VII) prohibits employment discrimination on the basis of race, sex, color, religion, or national origin.
- The Americans with Disabilities Act of 1990 (ADA) prohibits private employers with 15 or more employees, employment agencies, labor unions, and state and local governments, from discriminating against qualified individuals with disabilities in all aspects of employment.
- Executive Order 11246, as amended by Executive Order 11375, prohibits all non-exempt government contractors and subcontractors from discriminating in employment and requires them to take affirmative action to ensure that employees and applicants for employment are treated without regard to race, color, religion, gender, or national origin.
- The Civil Service Reform Act (CSRA) of 1978 prohibits federal employers from discriminating on the basis of race, color, creed, national origin, sex, age, preferential and non-preferential civil service status, political affiliation, marital status, or handicapping conditions.
- The Age Discrimination in Employment Act (ADEA) of 1967 protects applicants and employees 40 years of age and older from discrimination on the basis of age in hiring, layoffs, promotion, compensation, or any other terms, conditions or privileges of employment.
- The Equal Pay Act of 1963 prohibits discrimination on the basis of gender in wages or benefits, where men and women perform work of substantially equal skill, effort, and responsibility for the same establishment under similar working conditions.
- The Uniformed Services Employment and Reemployment Rights Act (USERRA) of 1994 prohibits discrimination against any person because of his or her service in the military, and sets forth the employment and reemployment rights of persons who leave their employment to perform military service.

The Equal Employment Opportunity Commission (EEOC) enforces Title VII, the Equal Pay Act, the ADEA, Title I and Title V of the ADA, and Sections 501 and 505 of the Rehabilitation Act of 1973, which prohibits employment discrimination against federal employees with disabilities. EEOC also provides oversight and coordination of all federal equal employment opportunity regulations, practices, and policies.

USDOL's ESA's Office of Federal Contract Compliance Programs (OFCCP) enforces Executive Orders 11246 and 11375 with respect to equal employment opportunity (EEO) requirements of federal contractors and subcontractors. Approximately 200,000 contractor-employers are covered by these requirements. USDOL's Veterans' Employment and Training Service (VETS) administers USERRA.

Acceptable Conditions of Work

Wages: Minimum wages are fixed by both federal and state laws in the United States. For employees covered by the FLSA, the U.S. minimum wage is . . . $7.25 by the summer of

2009. Individual states are free to establish higher minimum wages than those provided by the FLSA for covered employees. . . . Minimum wage rates established by the FLSA may not be abated by collective bargaining agreement or individual agreement. The minimum wage is adjusted at irregular intervals by legislation that includes consultations with interested parties in the legislative process. The federal minimum wage is enforced by the WHD or by employees through private suit.

Hours of Work: Hours of work in the United States are established by employer policy, by individual agreement between employers and employees, or by collective bargaining between employers and labor organizations. An employee covered by the FLSA's overtime provisions is generally entitled to pay not less than one and a half (1.5) times the employees' regular rate of pay for all hours worked in excess of 40 hours per week. The FLSA's overtime provisions are enforced by the WHD or by employees through private suit.

Vacations/Holidays: Vacations and holidays in the United States are established by employer policy, by individual bargaining between employers and employees, or by collective bargaining between employers and labor organizations. The Family and Medical Leave Act of 1993 (FMLA) requires establishments with 50 or more employees to provide up to 12 weeks of unpaid, job-protected leave per year for employees to care for a newborn, a newly adopted child, or a newly placed foster child; to care for a child, a spouse, or parent who has a serious health condition; or to treat one's own serious health condition. To be eligible, an employee must have worked for the employer for at least 1,250 hours during the months prior to the start of the FMLA leave.

. . . .

The *Employment Standards Administration (ESA)* is an enforcement and benefit delivery agency, composed of four major divisions/programs/offices: the Wage and Hour Division (WHD), the Office of Federal Contract Compliance Programs (OFCCP), the Office of Workers' Compensation Programs (OWCP), and the Office of Labor-Management Standards (OLMS). In addition to enforcing the FLSA's minimum wage, overtime pay, record keeping, and child labor requirements, the WHD enforces the FMLA; the Migrant and Seasonal Agricultural Worker Protection Act (MSPA); the Employee Polygraph Protection Act (EPPA); field sanitation and migrant farm-worker housing standards under the OSH Act; the worker protection provisions of the Consumer Credit Protection Act; and a number of employment standards and worker protections provided in the Immigration and Nationality Act (INA). Additionally, WHD administers and enforces the prevailing wage requirements of the Davis-Bacon Act, the Service Contract Act of 1965, and other statutes applicable to federal contracts for construction and for goods and services.

In addition to enforcing the equal employment opportunity (EEO) requirements of federal contractors and subcontractors in *Executive Orders* 11246 and 11375, the OFCCP enforces the provisions of the Vietnam Era Veterans' Readjustment Assistance Act (VEVRAA) that require affirmative action in employment of protected veterans. OFCCP also assists in the enforcement of some provisions of the INA and Title I of the ADA. The OWCP mitigates the financial burden on certain workers, or their eligible dependents or survivors, resulting from work-related injury, disease, or death, by providing wage replacement and cash benefits, medical treatment, vocational rehabilitation, and other benefits. The Federal Employees' Compensation Act (FECA) provides income and medical cost protection and return-to-work services to civilian employees of the federal government, and to certain other designated groups injured at work. OWCP also administers two programs under federal statutes that provide private sector employees with similar benefits paid for, mostly by their employers. The Longshore and Harbor Workers' Compensation Act (LHWCA) requires covered employers to provide benefits to workers engaged in certain maritime and related employment. The Black Lung Benefits Act (BLBA) provides benefits to the nation's coal miners who are totally disabled by pneumoconiosis or to certain of a miner's survivors if the miner dies due to pneumoconiosis. The Energy Employees Occupational Illness Compensation Program Act (EEOICPA) delivers benefits to eligible employees and former employees of the Department of Energy, its contractors and subcontractors or to certain survivors of such individuals, as provided in the EEOICPA as a result of illness or death from exposure to toxic substances at covered facilities. EEOICPA also provides benefits to certain beneficiaries of Section 5 of the Radiation Exposure Compensation Act (RECA).

Workers' Compensation. Workers' compensation laws have two aims: to reimburse workers for lost wages, medical and rehabilitation expenses; and to limit employers' liability. State laws govern specific conditions for reimbursement. Some states limit coverage to certain occupations or even to types of injuries. With the exception of certain federal programs such as EEOICPA and LHWCA, workers' compensation benefits for employees who experience work related injuries, occupational diseases, or death while employed by private companies or state and local government agencies are provided by workers' compensation systems established by individual states rather than the federal government. While state workers' compensation plans vary, generally, an employer is obligated to provide limited compensation to workers whose injuries, illnesses or death arise out of and in the course of his employment, regardless of fault. In exchange, an injured worker relinquishes the right to sue his employer for negligence, and an employer's liability is thereby reduced. At the federal level, as discussed above, the OWCP administers workers' compensation programs that provide wage replacement benefits, medical treatment, vocational rehabilitation and other benefits to federal employees, longshore and harbor workers, and coal miners.

. . . .

Social Security: The Social Security Act of 1935 is administered by the Social Security Administration (SSA). Social Security pensions may begin at age 62, but the minimum age for receiving full social security pension payments is being increased in increments to age 67 over the period of 2000–2027. Amounts are adjusted annually in line with changes in the cost of living index. Additionally, payments are made for surviving spouses and minor or invalid children of deceased beneficiaries. In 2000, Social Security recipients aged 65 to 69 were allowed to continue to earn income without a reduction of social security benefits. In 2004, Social Security benefits accounted for 38.6 % of the aggregate income of the elderly population. In addition to the pension payment programs administered by SSA, the SSA administers two programs that provide income to individuals who have a disability. Social Security Disability Insurance pays disability income to individuals and certain members of their families if the individual is "insured," meaning that the person worked long enough and paid Social Security taxes. Supplemental Security Income (SSI) pays benefits based on financial need and not prior work. SSI is a Federal income supplement program funded by general tax revenues (not Social Security taxes) that provides benefits to people with limited income and resources who are disabled, blind, or age 65 or older in order to help them meet basic needs for food, clothing and shelter.

Pension Benefit Guaranty Corporation

The Pension Benefit Guaranty Corporation (PBGC) protects the retirement incomes of nearly 44 million American workers in 30,330 private sector defined benefit pension plans. A defined benefit plan provides a specified monthly benefit at retirement, often based on a combination of salary and years of service. PBGC was created by the Employee Retirement Income Security Act of 1974 to encourage the continuation and maintenance of private-sector defined benefit pension plans, provide timely and uninterrupted payment of pension benefits, and keep pension insurance premiums at a minimum. PBGC is not funded by general tax revenues, but collects insurance premiums from employers that sponsor insured pension plans, earns money from investments and receives funds from pension plans it takes over. PBGC pays monthly retirement benefits, up to a guaranteed maximum, to about 612,000 retirees in 3,683 pension plans that have ended. PBGC is responsible for the current and future pensions of about 1,271,000 people. The maximum pension benefit guaranteed by PBGC is set by law and adjusted yearly. For plans ended in 2007, workers who retire at age 65 can receive up to $4,125.00 a month ($49,500.00 a year). The guarantee is lower for those who retire early or when there is a benefit for a survivor. The guarantee is increased for those who retire after age 65.

Medical Insurance. Medicare is a federal health insurance program overseen by the U.S. Department of Health and Human Services (HHS) Agency on Aging that provides medical insurance for over 43 million people who are elderly or disabled. It pays for most of the care in hospitals and related services, and since January 1, 2006, provides prescription drug coverage. At a small cost to pensioners, medical insurance also pays for part of the doctor's bills and related services. Medicare is financed, in part, by a portion of the payroll taxes paid by workers and their employers and in part by monthly premiums deducted from Social Security checks. Medicaid is also overseen by the U.S. Department of HHS's Agency on Aging. Medicaid was established in 1965, at the same time as Medicare, under Title XIX of the Social Security Act. It is a jointly -funded, federal-state health insurance program for certain low-income and needy people. Medicaid also covers certain individuals who fall below the federal poverty level. It covers hospital and doctor's visits, prenatal care, emergency room visits, drugs and other treatments. Medicaid also provides coverage for low-income children under age 6, low-income pregnant women, Supplemental Security Income recipients, adopted or foster children, specially protected groups, children under age 19 whose family income is below federal poverty level, some Medicare beneficiaries and other groups, as determined by each state. In 2004, it covered 37.5 million individuals including children, the aged, blind, and/or disabled, and people who are eligible to receive federally assisted income maintenance payments. In private industry, about 80 % of full-time employees participate in medical insurance programs that are at least partly financed by their employer, and the same proportion participates in life insurance programs. About 60 % of full-time workers participate in retirement programs which employers help pay.

. . . .

Dispute Resolution

Resolution of labor disputes can occur in the following ways: mediation, arbitration, or litigation. In some instances processes can be used in that order; other times they may overlap, and/or preclude each other. Administrative agencies can resolve statutory labor rights claims, but not individual or collective contracts, which are usually resolved in litigation or in grievance arbitration machinery, respectively. Private labor arbitrators have been enabled by U.S. Supreme Court rulings to decide individual contract and statutory labor rights. However, this right under collective contracts extended only to contract and not statutory rights until 2009. In 14 Penn Plaza, LLC v. Pyett, the U.S. Supreme Court held contractual *and statutory labor rights* can be resolved through private labor arbitration. That is, the arbitration forum may be substituted for the judicial forum. This holding is summarized next.

---

14 Penn Plaza, LLC v. Pyett[6]

129 S. Ct. 1456, 556 U.S. __ (2009)

Facts of the Case:

A group of employees brought this action following a job transfer they believed to be based on age discrimination. The employees filed a grievance with their union, including the age discrimination issues but also asserting that the transfer violated their collective bargaining agreement. The union pursued the employees' collective bargaining claim through Penn Plaza's arbitration system; however, the employees themselves pursued their age discrimination claim in federal court under the Age Discrimination in Employment Act (ADEA). Penn Plaza argued that the arbitration clause included in the employment contract, stating that all age discrimination claims must be pursued through arbitration, prevented the employees from bringing the claim in federal court. The district court ruled in favor of the employees, holding the arbitration clause unconscionable and therefore unenforceable.

The U.S. Court of Appeals for the Second Circuit affirmed the ruling, relying on its previous decisions holding that arbitration clauses with respect to statutory claims, such as the ADEA, are unenforceable.

Question:

Are arbitration clauses in employment contracts – waiving an employee's right to bring statutory claims in federal court – enforceable?

Conclusion:

Yes. The Supreme Court held that a provision in a collective bargaining agreement that clearly and unmistakably requires union members to arbitrate ADEA claims is enforceable as a matter of federal law. With Justice Clarence Thomas writing for the

6 Reprinted with permission from the Oyez Project *available at* www.oyez.org. 14 Penn Plaza, LLC v. Pyett, Summary, Oyez, *available at* http://www.oyez.org/cases/2000-2009/2008/2008_07_581 (last visited Sept. 30, 2010).

majority and joined by Chief Justice John G. Roberts and Justices Anthony G. Scalia, Anthony M. Kennedy, and Samuel A. Alito, the Court reasoned that, here, the arbitration provision was a "bargained-for exchange" in the collective bargaining agreement and thus should not be interfered with by the courts. The Court went on to state that because the ADEA itself did not mandate such interference, the arbitration provision should be enforced.

Justice John Paul Stevens wrote a separate dissenting opinion. He noted that the majority opinion was a departure from Supreme Court precedent with respect to arbitration clauses in collective bargaining agreements. He went on to state that it was Congress' responsibility to reassess the policy arguments favoring arbitration rather than for the Supreme Court to decide. Justice David H. Souter also wrote a separate dissenting opinion and was joined by Justices Stevens, Ruth Bader Ginsburg, and Stephen G. Breyer. He reemphasized that Supreme Court precedent did not preclude the pursuit of an ADEA claim because of an arbitration provision in a collective bargaining agreement, as in this case.

. . . .

---

3. *Evaluation of U.S. Labor and Employment Laws on Core Labor Standards*

To provide a more balanced perspective and perhaps some practical insight on how well a country's laws are working in practice, a critique from the International Trade Union Confederation (ITUC) is provided for each of the three East Asian countries. It is organized under the ILO's core labor standards. Below is a critique of the United States.

International Union Perspective[7]

Executive Summary

The United States has ratified only two of the eight core ILO labour Conventions. In view of restrictions on the trade union rights of workers and continuing problems of child labour, determined measures are needed to comply with the commitments the US accepted at Singapore and Doha in the WTO Ministerial Declarations over 1996–2001, and in the ILO Declaration on Fundamental Principles and Rights at Work.

The US has not ratified the ILO core Convention on the Right to Organise and Collective Bargaining, nor the Convention on Freedom of Association and Protection of the Right to Organise. There is insufficient protection against anti-union discrimination. The right to strike and the right to collective bargaining are severely restricted, in particular for public sector workers and for certain groups of private sector workers.

[7] ITUC, *Report for the WTO General Council Review of the Trade Policies of the United States* (June 9 & 11, 2008), *available at* http://www.ituc-csi.org/IMG/pdf/US_report_cls_2008.FINAL.pdf (last visited Oct. 3, 2010) [Footnotes omitted]; *see also* ITUC, *Annual Survey of Violations of Trade Union Rights* (2008), http://survey08.ituc-csi.org/survey.php?IDContinent=2&Lang=EN (last visited Oct. 3, 2010).

The US has not ratified the core ILO Convention on Equal Remuneration nor the Convention on Discrimination. Discrimination in employment is prohibited by law but does occur in practice. Legislation requires equal pay for work of equal value but wage differences continue to exist between men and women and among different ethnic groups.

The US has ratified the ILO core Convention on the Worst Forms of Child Labour, but not the Convention on Minimum Age. Child labour remains a problem in the US, in particular in agriculture where fewer regulations apply and where children continue to be exposed to hazardous working conditions, pending new legislation.

The US has ratified the Convention on the Abolition of Forced Labour but not the Convention on Forced Labour. Forced labour exists in such forms as forced prostitution (trafficking of women and girls), forced agriculture and domestic work, and in the garment industry within the US territories.

Internationally Recognized Core Labor Standards in the United States

Introduction

. . . .

The ITUC affiliate in the US is the American Federation of Labor and Congress of Industrial Organizations (AFL-CIO). 12.2% of the labour force is unionised (15.7 million workers).

. . . .

Freedom of Association and the Right to Collective Bargaining

The US has not ratified Convention No. 87 on the Freedom of Association and Protection of the Right to Organise, nor Convention No. 98 on the Right to Organise and Collective Bargaining.

Trade Union Rights in Law

The National Labor Relations Act (NLRA) is the primary federal labour law in the United States, and is binding on the states. The NLRA guarantees the right of freedom of association, the right to bargain collectively, and the right to join trade unions to private sector employees. However, in addition to excluding public sector workers, the statute excludes many categories of private sector employees from its scope, including agricultural and domestic workers, supervisors, and independent contractors. In 2002, the U.S. General Accounting Office found that some 25 million private civilian workers, as well as 6.9 million federal, state and local government employees, did not have the right under any law to negotiate their wages, hours or employment terms. Since then, even more workers have been denied coverage.

In the private sector, the law requires proof of majority status in order for a union to become the exclusive representative of employees within a bargaining unit. The National Labor Relations Board (NLRB), the administrative agency that enforces the NLRA, will only certify a union that obtains a majority vote during a Board-supervised election although voluntary recognition agreements are also legal.

Employers have a statutory right under the NLRA to express their views during a union campaign so long as they do not interfere with their employees' free choice. In practice, however, employers have a legal right to engage in a wide range of anti-union tactics that chill the exercise of freedom of association. For example, employers have the right to hold "captive audience" meetings, which they use to make anti-union presentations. Under the law it is perfectly legal for employers to discipline or even fire workers for failing to attend these meetings. The law also allows employers to "predict" (though not "threaten") that a workplace will shut down if workers vote for the union.

Section 2(3) of the NLRA excludes "supervisors" from the definition of employees who have the right to organise and collective bargaining under the Act. Section 2(11) of the NLRA defines supervisors as "any individual having authority, in the interest of the employer, to hire, transfer, suspend, lay-off, recall, promote, discharge, assign, reward or discipline other employees, or responsibly to direct them". However, in 2006 the NLRB expanded the interpretation of "supervisor" under the NLRA. The employer can classify or reclassify as "supervisors" employees with minor or sporadic oversight over co-workers even when such oversight is far short of genuine managerial or supervisory authority. This authority only needs to be applied on a "regular and substantial" basis, with "regular" meaning according to a set schedule and "substantial" at least 10-15% of the employee's work time. This amendment would clearly deprive many workers of their organising and collective bargaining rights. The AFL-CIO has filed a complaint with the ILO Committee on Freedom of Association.

In the public sector, approximately 40 per cent of all workers are still denied basic collective bargaining rights. While the Federal Labor Relations Act covers over two million employees of the federal government, the statute outlaws strikes, proscribes collective bargaining over hours, wages, and economic benefits, and imposes extensive management rights that further limit the scope of collective bargaining.

Collective bargaining for state employees varies from state to state. Only a little more than half of the states allow for collective bargaining in the public sector; several more allow it only for narrow categories of workers. Even where public sector workers have the right to bargain, they generally do not have the right to strike. In North Carolina all public employees are denied collective bargaining rights, which is in violation of workers' fundamental rights as determined by the ILO (Case No. 2460).

The NLRA and judicial decisions interpreting the law place limitations on the ability of workers to engage in "concerted activity," such as intermittent strikes, secondary boycotts and other forms of aid. The law allows employers to replace striking workers permanently. Permanent replacement workers can vote in a decertification election to eliminate union representation.

The NLRA, anti-discrimination laws, and wage and hour standards apply to employees regardless of their immigration status. However, the U.S. Supreme Court ruled in 2002 that undocumented workers are not entitled to back pay as a remedy for unfair labour practices under the NLRA, and they are not entitled to reinstatement. These restrictions have made it difficult to enforce trade union rights on behalf of the millions of undocumented workers in the United States. The ILO's Committee on Freedom of Association recommended in November 2003 that the government should amend the legislation to bring it into line with freedom of association principles but the United States has not done so.

. . . .

Trade Union Rights in Practice

An entire USD $4 billion union-busting industry exists in the United States with the objective of undermining trade union organising through coercion and intimidation. A recent study found that 82 per cent of employers hire these high-priced, union-busting consultants to fight organising drives. Consultants employ a wide range of tactics, including many that skirt the law.

According to a 2005 survey by the University of Illinois commissioned by American Rights at Work, 91 per cent of employers, when faced with employees who want to join together in a union, force employees to attend closed-door meetings to hear anti-union propaganda. In 70 per cent of organising campaigns in the manufacturing sector, employers threaten to move the plant if the union wins. Thirty percent of employers fire pro-union workers. Unions frequently establish initial majority support among a workforce, only to see it erode under employer threats. According to the survey, in 91 percent of the union recognition petitions filed with the NLRB as a prerequisite to an election, a majority of employees indicated they wanted a union. However, unions were victorious in only 31 percent of these campaigns. In addition, employers often challenge the results of union elections, which can delay union representation and contract negotiations for several years.

Even after a trade union becomes certified as the exclusive representative of the workers, employers often engage in bad-faith bargaining in order to prevent the union from winning a first contract. As a result, 45 per cent of all attempts at winning a first contract fail.

Remedies for intimidation and coercion such as the illegal firing of workers who seek to form unions and bargain collectively are both limited and ineffective. According to a recent study, as of the end of fiscal year 2006 the cases identified by the NLRB as raising significant labour law issues took an average of 1,312 days to decide, while other cases took 824 days. Many employers who violate labour laws are never punished. Even when they are, the penalties are too weak to deter them from doing it again. According to Human Rights Watch, "Many employers have come to view remedies like back pay for workers fired because of union activity as a routine cost of doing business, well worth it to get rid of organising leaders and derail organising efforts". According to Cornell University research, one quarter of private sector employers fire at least one worker during union organising campaigns. A study published in 2007 by the Center for Economic and Policy Research (CEPR) on illegal firings during union election campaigns estimated that "almost one-in-five union organisers or activists can expect to be fired as a result of their activities in a union election campaign."

In 2007 the NLRB further narrowed the NLRA coverage by withdrawing protections and weakening its already ineffective remedies. In September 2007 the Board issued 61 decisions, most of which reflected an anti-union and anti-collective bargaining bias. These decisions included ones that make it harder for workers who were illegally fired or denied employment to recover back pay; made it a certainty that employers who violate the Act will incur only the slightest monetary loss and be required to undertake as little remediation as possible; made it harder for workers to achieve union recognition without being forced to endure the hostile, divisive, delay-ridden NLRB representation process; made it easier for employers to deny jobs to workers who exercised their legal right to strike; made it easier for employers to file lawsuits in retaliation for protected union activities and to punish workers and their unions for lawful, protected conduct; made it easier for employers to discriminate against employees and job applicants who are also union organisers, even though the US Supreme Court had specifically held that such workers are employees entitled to the Act's protections.

. . . .

Conclusions

Workers have the right to organise, form trade unions, and engage in collective bargaining, but large groups of workers are excluded from this right such as public sector workers, agricultural workers, domestic workers and independent contractors. The right to strike is recognised but restricted. Many of the anti-union tactics used by employers are allowed by law, and even when employers act illegally, the penalties are too weak and the judicial system too ineffective to deter them. Consequently, an anti-union climate has continued to increase.

II. Discrimination and Equal Remuneration

The US has not ratified Convention No. 100 on Equal Remuneration nor Convention No. 111 on Discrimination (Employment and Occupation).

Title VII of the Civil Rights Act is the principal federal statute governing discrimination in the US and prohibits discrimination on the basis of race, colour, religion, sex, or national origin. The Age Discrimination in Employment Act (ADEA) prohibits discrimination on the basis of age, and the Americans with Disabilities Act (ADA) prohibits discrimination against persons with disabilities. In addition, the principle of equality of opportunity and treatment, including in the field of remuneration is recognised in the United States. Equal pay for equal work is recognised in the Equal Pay Act of 1963. The Equal Pay Act, which is part of the Fair Labor Standards Act of 1938 (FLSA), prohibits sex-based wage discrimination between men and women in the same establishment who are performing under similar working conditions. Notably, section 6 of the FLSA (29 USC §206) reads:

> (d) (1) No employer having employees subject to any provisions of this section shall discriminate, within any establishment in which such employees are employed, between employees on the basis of sex by paying wages to employees in such establishment at a rate less than the rate at which he pays wages to employees of the opposite sex in such establishment for equal work on jobs the performance of which requires equal skill, effort, and responsibility, and which are performed under similar working conditions.
>
> . . . .

Statistics from 2005 show that labour force participation rates for women by race were 61.6% for Black women, 58.9% for White women, 58.2% for Asian women, and 55.3% for

Hispanic women. The labour force participation rates for men were 80.1% for Hispanic men, 74.8% for Asian men, 74.1% for White men, and 67.3% for Black men. The largest percentage of women worked in management, professional, and related occupations (38%), and sales and office occupations (35%). 59.3% of all women were in the labour force in 2005.

Unemployment rates in 2005 were 4.4% for White women and men, 9.5% for Black women, 10.5% for Black men, 5.4% for Hispanic women, 6.9% for Hispanic men, 3.9% for Asian women, and 4.0% for Asian men.

....

An AFL-CIO fact sheet (2007) shows that in 2006, median weekly earnings for women were 80.8% those of men. For most women of colour, the earnings gap was even larger. African American women earned 70% of male earnings in 2006. Hispanic and Latina women earned just 59% of male earnings. Asian American women's earnings were 94% that of all men. However, they earned 79% of Asian American male earnings. The wage gap was also higher for older women. In 2006, women over 25 earned 79% that of men in the same age group while women aged 16–24 earned 95% that of men in that age group.

....

From 2000 to 2004, suits alleging discrimination on the basis of sex ranged from 30% to 43.5% of suits filed each year by the EEOC. Harassment was the most frequent complaint, in 75.6% of cases. In 2007, the EEOC received 24,826 charges of sex-based discrimination. The EEOC resolved 21,982 sex discrimination charges in 2007 and recovered $135.4 million in monetary benefits for charging parties and other aggrieved individuals.

Roughly 15% to 21% of the suits filed each year alleged race discrimination while allegations of national origin discrimination were present in approximately 7% to 13% of all suits filed. Harassment was the most frequently alleged issue in suits with national origin as a basis (62.1%) followed by discharge (48.6% of the suits).

....

Conclusions

Discrimination in respect of employment and occupation is prohibited by law. However, there is still a wage gap between men and women and between different ethnic groups. Women are also disproportionately represented in several occupations.

III. Child Labour

The US ratified Convention No. 182, the Worst Forms of Child Labour Convention in 1999. The US has not ratified Convention No. 138, the Minimum Age Convention.

ILO statistics show 7,114,000 economically active children in the US aged between 16-19 years in 2004, which is an activity rate of 43.9%. The National Institute for Occupational Safety and Health estimates that 200,000 adolescents are injured in the workplace every year and more than 100 are killed on the job. Net primary school enrolment/attendance is 95%. According to estimates, as many as two million American children are schooled at home, with the number growing as much as 15 to 20% per year.

Under the Fair Labor Standards Act (FLSA) federal law, 16 is the minimum age for nonagricultural employment, but 14- and 15-year-olds may be employed for certain periods that are considered not to interfere with their schooling, in jobs that the Secretary of Labor has determined will not interfere with their health and well-being. With regard to agricultural employment, Federal law states that a child working in agriculture on a farm owned or operated by his or her parent is exempted from Federal agricultural child labour provisions. Young farm workers who are not the children of the farmer employing them are subject to Federal child labour provisions that differ by age. Children aged 14 or 15 may perform any non hazardous farm job outside school hours. Children aged 12 or 13 may be employed outside school hours in non hazardous jobs, but only on the farm on which their parent works or with the written consent of a parent. Children under 12 may be employed outside school hours in non hazardous jobs on farms not subject to the Fair Labor Standards Act (FLSA) minimum wage if their parent also is employed on that farm, or with parental consent. Overtime pay is not required for agricultural work (either for children or adults), unlike most other occupations.

The American Federation of Teachers in its publication on child farmworkers in the US "In Our Own Backyard" estimates that the number of child farmworkers is around 500,000, although figures are disputed and vary from 150,000 to 1.2 million, according to the report. The Association of Farmworker Opportunity Programs (AFOP) estimates that 85% of migrant and seasonal farm workers are racial minorities, many of them Latino, up to 99% in some communities. The children work on average 30 hours per week, even during school periods and half of them do not graduate from high school.

Health and safety standards for child farm workers are severely lacking. Some 20% of all farm fatalities concern children. According to Human Rights Watch, child farm workers account for 8% of all working children but suffer 40% of work-related fatalities among children. Many of these children work long hours in hot weather and are exposed to pesticides and dangerous equipment. Often they only earn as little as US$2 per hour, much less than the minimum wage. Girls are also subject to sexual harassment. There is often a lack of toilet, washing and drinking water facilities.

. . . .

In 2005, the Department of Labour's Wage and Hour Division (which enforces the federal child labour laws) conducted 1,784 child labour investigations. This is a drastic 31.5 percent decline from the 2,606 child labour investigations conducted in fiscal year 2004 and represents the lowest number of child labour investigations in at least 10 years.

. . . .

Conclusions

Child labour in the US is a serious problem in the agricultural sector in particular. Child labour in agriculture is the least protected form of child labour in the US and the most hazardous one. There is also a serious lack of labour inspection and enforcement of the legislation on child labour.

IV. Forced Labour

The US ratified Convention No. 105, the Abolition of Forced Labour in 1991. It has not ratified Convention No. 29, the Forced Labour Convention. Forced labour is prohibited in the US but does occur in practice. Trafficking of persons for the purpose of forced labour and forced prostitution also occurs, despite stricter regulations.

New legislation regarding trafficking has been enacted, the Trafficking Victims Protection Reauthorization Act (TVPRA) of 2003 and the Trafficking Victims Protection Reauthorization Act of 2005. Both Acts created new federal crimes, including a "forced labour" crime in a new section 1589 inserted in Title 18 of the United States Code, and which also strengthened penalties for trafficking-related offences and afforded new protection and expanded services to trafficking victims.

The ILO CEACR Direct Request of 2006 notes "from the documents appended to the Government's report, the findings of the United States Congress: that 'Approximately 50,000 women and children are trafficked into the United States each year'". The primary source countries for the United States are Thailand, Vietnam, China, Mexico, Russia, Ukraine, and the Czech Republic. Most are employed in prostitution, domestic and cleaning work (in offices, hotels, etc), sweatshops and agricultural work. The highest incidence is in prostitution and sex services.

In the domestic services sector, U.S. citizens and foreign nationals bring domestic workers into the country where many suffer abuses. Domestic workers have few legal protections and there is a high demand for cheap, docile and exploitable household labour. Under an employer visa scheme, migrant domestic workers can come to the US. There are reported cases of physical abuse, severe restrictions on freedom of movement and working conditions that are close to slavery. Many are paid less than the minimum wage and, under the terms of their visa, face deportation if they leave their employer to escape from these oppressive conditions. Diplomats have been involved in several cases of extreme abuse and exploitation. However, due to their diplomatic immunity it has not been possible to hold them responsible for these practices.

There are reports of forced labour in agriculture. In some cases migrant workers are forced to work without pay or below the minimum wage, under threat of violence. There have been reports of trafficking in at least 20 different states, with most reported cases occurring in New York, California, Texas and Florida. Reports on slavery and abuse of workers on tomato fields in Florida have found that migrants are not only forced to work in sub-human conditions but mistreated and forced into debt, locked up at night and have to pay for sub-standard food. The Coalition of Immokalee Workers (CIW) estimates that some 5% of farm workers in the US are subjected to forced labour. The majority of the people affected are from Mexico, Guatemala and Haiti. The workers are trafficked into the US indebting themselves before they start to work and subsequently are forced to pay off their debts by working 12–14 hours per day, seven days per week. Deductions are made from their wages for transport, accommodation, food, work equipment and supposed tax and social security payments, and often workers are not paid at all. Workers are under constant surveillance and subject to verbal and physical abuse.

A report by the University of California, Berkeley (2004) looked at specific cases of forced labour in the US. Researchers found that at any given time, some 10,000 people in the United States are forced to work against their will under threat of violence. The victims of forced labour came from at least 38 countries, but most from China, Mexico and Vietnam. Some were born in the United States.

. . . .

Conclusions

Forced labour is prohibited by law but does occur in the US in the form of trafficking for forced prostitution, forced domestic labour, and forced prison labour. There is also forced labour in agriculture as well as in garments in the US territories.

Final Conclusions and Recommendations

There is a need for legislation to provide for adequate protection, with sufficiently effective and dissuasive penalties, against acts of anti-union discrimination for trade union membership or activities and against acts of interference by employers or their organisations in trade union affairs. The Government has to ratify Convention No. 87, bring legislation in line with the Convention and ensure its enforcement. In particular, the Employee Free Choice Act needs to be enacted with the shortest possible delay.

1. The government has to ratify Convention No. 98 and bring legislation in line with the Convention in order to extend the right to collective bargaining and the right to strike to all workers, including federal or state government employees, agricultural workers, supervisors, independent contractors and household workers.
2. Wage inequalities and inequalities in access to employment still exist between men and women and between different ethnic groups, despite progress that has been made to diminish inequalities. The Government should focus more on reduction of inequalities in certain occupations, such as managerial, professional and sales functions. The Government should increase training and education for ethnic minorities and improve security, especially in certain sectors like agriculture, construction and manufacturing.
3. More progress has to be made with the effective elimination of hazardous forms of child labour in agriculture. Increased control and protection are needed as well as higher penalties. The CARE Act needs to be ratified and implemented.
4. There is a need for the effective elimination of forced prostitution and trafficking of women and children. A stronger enforcement of the law is needed as well as effective cooperation with the countries the women and children come from. The government needs to make serious efforts to enforce legislation and to end forced domestic work, forced agriculture work and forced labour in overseas territories.
5. With regard to compulsory prison labour, the government should take effective measures to bring legislation in line with Convention No. 105, in particular at the state level.
6. Large differences exist between states with regard to labour legislation and enforcement. The Federal Government should make efforts to achieve more harmonisation of legislation with regard to core labour standards among the different states.
7. There is an overall need for increased labour inspection and enforcement of the legislation. In line with the commitments accepted by the United States at the Singapore and Doha WTO Ministerial Conference and its obligations as a member of the ILO, the Government of the United States should therefore provide regular reports to the WTO and the ILO on its legislative changes and implementation of all the core labour standards.

8. The WTO should draw to the attention of the authorities of the United States the commitments they undertook to observe core labour standards at the Singapore and Doha Ministerial Conferences. The WTO should request the ILO to intensify its work with the Government of the United States in these areas and provide a report to the WTO General Council on the occasion of the next trade policy review.

QUESTIONS

1. Why doesn't the administration of all federal labor laws fall under the authority of the Department of Labor?
2. How does the U.S. system utilize administrative agencies and statutory prohibitions?
3. Would you expect "employees" to be defined and classified the same way under all labor laws? If there is diversity, is this preferable to a universal definition and coverage?
4. Do these labor statutes provide worker protections of labor rights arising under both collective and individual labor contracts?
5. Are *statutory* dispute resolution mechanisms available to both statutory and contractual labor rights?
6. Is *private* labor arbitration available to resolve both statutory and contractual labor rights?
7. Do U.S. labor laws exceed ILO standards, notwithstanding the previous criticisms? If so, how; if not, why not?
8. How is the disparity between laws and practice in the United States explained?
9. Is the United States justified in telling other countries to adhere to the ILO's core labor standards, when it has not ratified all of them itself? Explain.

B. WORKERS' LABOR RIGHTS AND BENEFITS

1. *Definitions, Sources, and Coverage: The Dilemma of Underregulation*

a. Employees Defined

Inasmuch as labor and employment law protections are often provided to workers whose status is that of "employee," some consideration should be given to its definition, its exceptions, and its exemptions under those laws. It is not uncommon for U.S. labor laws to look like "Swiss-cheese" with the many exceptions to coverage, thus excluding many workers from the protections of the laws.

An Employee by Any Other Name?[8]

Ronald C. Brown

What's in a name? That which we call a rose by any other name would smell as sweet.
– William Shakespeare

I. Introduction: Who is an "Employee"?

Can an "employee" by any other name still be an employee? An individual tells you, "I'm working for Microsoft." So, he's employed by Microsoft as an "employee?" Not necessarily. Under a variety of contractual and statutory definitions he might be categorized as casual, temporary, part-time; independent contractor, or a number of other exclusionary terms that render him ineligible for full or more than partial "employee" rights and benefits under a variety of laws. Microsoft was saving tens of millions of dollars by classifying a large number of workers as independent contractors who, since they were not "employees", were not eligible to participate in employee contractual benefits. Then, unexpectedly, the workers were found by the court to be "employees" and it cost Microsoft more than its illusory savings when the courts determined these workers had been misclassified and thus eligible for and due these employee benefits.[9]

While that case involved a contract benefit, more often it is statutory rights and benefits that are attached to "employee" status. In the U.S. there are wide variances in definitions among federal labor laws and even more among the 50 states' definitions. In the European Union (EU), with 27 countries and as many languages, definitional consistency becomes even more problematic.

The dilemma may be three-fold: (1) substantively, arising from the changing employment relationships that are replacing many of the traditional "regular" employees with those who have a more tenuous employment relationship, often referred to as "contingent" or "atypical" employees; (2) varied and inconsistent definitions under a variety of labor and employment laws; and (3) from lingual variances arising from translations or applications of the "employee" term in different jurisdictions. Contingent employees typically have fewer labor rights and benefits than the former. Employers know this distinction and take advantage of it by employing increasing numbers of these contingent employees so as to attain flexibility, lower labor costs, and competitive advantage. How to classify an individual worker, therefore, becomes a task for employers with significant legal and economic consequences.

One can ask: does the legislative language capture the intended substance of the legislation? Were the laws written to allow a bifurcation and diversification of employee status or did that occur through the translations, interpretations, and applications of the laws? In classifying workers as "employees" entitled to all or fewer rights and benefits, is it possible for the laws to use words that clearly guide and bind employers so as to avoid the evasive mischief of misclassification or outright denial of rights and benefits? Is this a

[8] Ronald C. Brown, *An Employee By Any Other Name?*, *in* Attivit'a transnazionali. Sapere giuridico e scienza della traduzione, 107, 107–23 (Michele Faioli & Pasquale Sandulli eds., 2011); *see also* PRECARIOUS EMPLOYMENT: UNDERSTANDING LABOUR MARKET INSECURITY IN CANADA (Leah F. Vosko ed., 2006).

[9] Viscaino v. Microsoft Corp., 120 F.3d 1006, 1009–10 (9th Cir. 1997).

question of substance (policy decisions of lawmakers) or the use of language that surfaces differently in the applications and translations of the applied laws? It has been said that language must have more than mere clarity.

"It is still not enough for language to have clarity and content . . . it must also have a goal and an imperative. Otherwise from language we descend to chatter, from chatter to babble and from babble to confusion." Rene Daumal[10]

In attempting to avoid confusion and to provide fair and consistent coverage under different laws and in different jurisdictions, there are two questions that must be answered before classifying a worker: (1) what is the *legal* significance of not being an "employee" under an array of laws (federal and state) and common-law contract definitions; and, (2) what legal test(s) is used to determine the status of an individual? In the U.S., the *economic* significance of not being an "employee" is to remove from the employer numbers of legal and financial obligations to pay social security, health insurance, etc. as well as removing many countervailing rights of workers. With such economic incentives for employers to misclassify employees, it is too often not accidental, but rather viewed by some businesses as a business risk. The U.S. Government Accounting Office (GAO) estimated that nearly $2.7 billion per year (in 2006 dollars) is lost in tax revenues from misclassified employees.[11] However, for many employers, what makes the "employee" classification *unexpected* is the maze of laws and varying legal tests under a variety of employment and labor laws that must be met before an employer can decide how to categorize an individual worker. The same "employee" status has different meanings under different federal and state labor laws.

In deciding how to categorize an individual in the employment relationship, many variables in the workplace must be considered. These variables may (a) involve working hours; (b) duration of employment; (c) location of work; or, (d) nature of employment. These may translate into the following employment arrangements and worker classifications: (1) *regular* employees; or (2) *contingent* or *atypical employees* (the latter is sometimes referred to as *alternative employment arrangements*).[12]

[10] *Rene Daumal Quotes*, BRAINY QUOTES, *available at* http://www.brainyquote.com/quotes/authors/r/rene_daumal.html (last visited May 13, 2011).

[11] GAO, *Employment Arrangements, Improved Outreach Could Help Ensure Proper Worker Classification* 7 (July 2006), *available at* http://www.gao.gov/new.items/d06656.pdf (last visited Sept. 30, 2010) [hereinafter "Employment Arrangements"].

[12] *See generally* MICHAEL S. HORNE ET AL., THE CONTINGENT WORKFORCE: LEGAL AND BUSINESS STRATEGIES (2000); *see also* RESTATEMENT (THIRD) EMPLOYMENT LAW § 1.01 (2009).

§ 1.01 General Conditions for Existence of Employment Relationship:

(1) [A]n individual renders services as an employee of an employer if
  (a) the individual acts, at least in part, to serve the interests of the employer,
  (b) the employer consents to receive the individual's services, and
  (c) the employer's relationship with the individual effectively prevents the individual from rendering the services as part of an independent business.

(2) An individual renders services as part of an independent business when the individual in his or her own interest exercises entrepreneurial control over the manner and means by which the services are performed.

(3) Entrepreneurial control over the manner and means by which services are performed is control over important business decisions, including whether to hire and where to assign assistants, whether to purchase and where to deploy equipment, and whether and when to service other customers. *Id.*

The U.S. Government Accounting Office (GAO) in its study on contingent workers categorized the following employment relationships under the term "contingent employee: agency temporary workers; contract company workers; direct-hire temporary workers; on-call workers; self-employed workers; standard part-time workers."[13]

. . . .

The United Nations Statistical Commission approved in 1958 the following classification of "employee", which has been used by the ILO: "a person who works for a public or private employer and receives remuneration in wages, salary, commission, tips, piece-rates or pay in kind."[14]

[13] Employment Arrangements, *supra* note 11.

TABLE 3.1. *Contingent workers and the total employed workforce (February 1995, February 1999, February 2005)*

Worker Category	February 1995		February 1999		February 2005	
	Estimated numbers of workers (in thousands)	Estimated percentage of the workforce	Estimated numbers of workers (in thousands)	Estimated percentage of the workforce	Estimated numbers of workers (in thousands)	Estimated percentage of the workforce
Contract company workers	652	0.5	769	0.6	813	0.6
Agency temps	1,181	1.0	1,188	0.9	1,217	0.9
On-call workers/day laborers	2,014	1.6	2,180	1.7	2,736	2.0
Direct-hire temps	3,393	2.8	3,227	2.5	2,972	2.1
Self-employed workers	7,256	5.9	6,280	4.8	6,125	4.4
Indep. contractors	8,309	6.7	8,247	6.3	10,342	7.4
Standard part-time workers	16,813	13.6	17,380	13.2	18,360	13.2
Subtotal: contingent workers	39,618	32.2	39,271	29.9	42,567	30.6
Standard full-time workers	83,589	67.8	92,222	70.1	96,385	69.4
Total workforce	123,207	100.0	131,493	100.0	138,952	100.0

[14] Reprinted with permission from the United Nations. United Nations Statistical Office, *Supplementary principles and recommendations for population and housing censuses*, Statistical Papers (doc. ST/ESA/STAT/SER./M/67/Add.1) (1990); ILO, *International Classification by Status in Employment*, LABORSTA Internet, http://laborsta.ilo.org/applv8/data/icsee.html (last visited Sept. 30, 2010). Employees are all those workers who hold the type of job defined as "paid employment jobs" (*cf.* paragraph 6*[see later]). Employees with stable contracts are those "employees" who have had,

II. The American Experience

"Employees" Protected Under Labor and Employment Laws

In America, as elsewhere, there are changing employment relationships which affect the rights of workers.[15] The usual employment relationship is controlled by common-law (non-statutory) principles. As there is no statutory requirement for labor contracts and relatively few written employment contracts, the tenure of workers is severely limited by the "at-will" doctrine which allows employers to terminate the relationship for no reason or any reason that is not illegal, regardless of any definition of "employee." This often leaves the employee with only the statutory rights. While some benefits may be provided to all employees under handbooks or employer policies, these are not the rights which protect workers in the way statutory rights protect employees.

In the U.S., statutory protections under various labor and employment laws are accorded to workers under the legislatively-prescribed status of "employee". Under the Fair Labor Standards Act (FLSA) an "employee" is entitled to minimum wages and overtime; and, under the National Labor Relations Act (NLRA), an "employee" is provided the right to join a union and collectively bargain.[16] To the great dismay of employers in the U.S., when workers are determined by a court or administrative agency to be "employees" under one statute, the "domino effect" may kick in where employees and government agencies quickly follow up under other statutes for monies owed due to the misclassification that may also lie there.[17]

and continue to have, an explicit (written or oral) or implicit contract of employment, or a succession of such contracts, with the same employer on a continuous basis. "On a continuous basis" implies a period of employment that is longer than a specified minimum determined according to national circumstances. (If interruptions are allowed in this minimum period, their maximum duration should also be determined according to national circumstances.) *Regular employees* are those "employees with stable contracts" for whom the employing organization is responsible for payment of relevant taxes and social security contributions and/or where the contractual relationship is subject to national labor legislation. Paid employment jobs are those jobs where the incumbents hold explicit (written or oral) or implicit employment contracts that give them a basic remuneration that is not directly dependent upon the revenue of the unit for which they work (this unit can be a corporation, a nonprofit institution, a government unit, or a household). Some or all of the tools, capital equipment, information systems, and/or premises used by the incumbents may be owned by others, and the incumbents may work under direct supervision of, or according to strict guidelines set by the owner(s) or persons in the owners' employment. (Persons in "paid employment jobs" are typically remunerated by wages and salaries, but, may be paid by commission from sales, by piece rates, bonuses, or in-kind payments such as food, housing, or training.)

15 These changes are detailed in KATHERINE V. W. STONE, FROM WIDGETS TO DIGITS: EMPLOYMENT REGULATION FOR THE CHANGING WORKPLACE (2004).

16 For a list of labor and employment laws and their coverage of "employees," see Employment Arrangements, *supra* note 11, at Appendix V. *See, e.g.*, Sec'y of Labor v. Lauritzen, 835 F.2d 1529 (7th Cir. 1987) (applying test for employee under the Fair Labor Standards Act); *see also* 29 U.S.C. § 152(11) (supervisor exclusion under NLRA); Wojewski v. Rapid City Reg'l Hosp., Inc., 450 F.3d 338 (8th Cir. 2006) (holding that worker as an independent contractor cannot bring claim under Title VII); Nationwide Mut. Ins. Co. v. Darden, 503 U.S. 318 (1992) (using a multifactor test for employee classification under the Employee Retirement Income Security Act).

17 For example, a California court found many of FedEx Home Package System drivers to be "employees" under a wage law, see Teamsters for a Democratic Union, *FedEx Truck Drivers are Employees, not Independent Contractors* (Aug. 15, 2007), http://www.tdu.org/node/1370 (last visited Sept. 30, 2010).

It soon became apparent that not all workers are "employees" under the different labor laws. Certain "manager-employees" are "*exempted*" from the FLSA overtime requirements and "supervisor-managerial – employees" are "*excluded*" from the "employee" definition providing the protection of the NLRA, and the list goes on and on. These exclusions are explicitly provided by the labor laws. Often the facts are unclear whether an individual is a manager or a supervisor or an "employee." In these cases a legal test, particular to each labor law (federal or state) must be applied to determine whether the individual is an "employee" under a particular law.

At first, most of these legal issues dealt with "regular employees" and questions focused on titles, functions, responsibilities, etc. Soon, however, changing employment relationships spawned more and more "contingent" or "atypical" workers where more variables were introduced. The employer found using these contingent employees gained it more flexibility and economy as they often fell outside the "employee" definition and its protections.[18]

Contingent "Employees"[19]

In 2005, the GAO reported that 42.6 million workers in the U.S. economy were participating in some form of contingent employment, such as temporary or part-time

"The IRS challenged the classification of FedEx Ground workers, and imposed fines and penalties of $319 million (for 2002 alone). FedEx could face over one billion dollars after the IRS completes its investigation. The IRS and various State taxing agencies are also challenging FedEx's independent contractor business model." Contingent Law, *Independent Contractor Law Center*, http://www.contingentlaw.com (last visited Sept. 30, 2010). By contrast, under the NLRA, the court found FedEx home delivery workers to be independent contractors and not "employees[.]" FedEx Home Delivery v. NLRB, 563 F.3d 492 (D.C. Cir. 2009).

[18] A 2006 GAO Report found employers hire contingent workers for a variety of reasons: to "accommodate workload fluctuations, fill temporary absences, employees' requests for part-time hours, screen workers for permanent positions, and save on wage and benefit costs." Employment Arrangements, *supra* note11.

[19] The 2006 GAO Report states "contingent work" refers to work arrangements that are not long-term, year-round, full- time employment with a single employer. For example, an employer may hire workers when there is an immediate and limited demand for their services, without any offer of permanent or even long-term employment. Temporary workers, independent contractors, and part-time workers are examples of contingent workers. *Id.* at Appendix I provides the following chart of its categories of workers the GAO considered contingent:

Agency temporary workers (temps) Individuals who work for temporary employment agencies and are assigned by the agencies to work for other companies ("client firms"), such as temporary workers supplied to companies to fill in for full-time workers who are on vacation or to work on special projects

Contract company workers Individuals who work for companies that provide services to other firms under contract, such as security, landscaping, or computer programming services

Day Laborers Individuals who get work by waiting at a place where employers pick up people to work for the day, such as low-skilled construction workers

Independent contractors Temporary workers hired directly by companies to work for a specified period of time, such as seasonal workers and workers hired to work on special projects

Direct-hire temps Individuals who obtain customers on their own to provide a product or service (and who may have other employees working for them), such as maids, realtors, child-care providers, and management consultants

work.[20] Between 1995 and 2005, an additional 3 million contingent workers were added to the workforce, although their proportion remained relatively constant at about 30 percent, with a high percentage (particularly part-time workers) being women.[21] The GAO stated many of the contingent workers are "excluded from key worker benefits and protections such as the guarantee of workers' rights to safe and healthful working conditions, a minimum hourly wage and overtime pay, freedom from employment discrimination, and unemployment insurance."[22] The Internal Revenue (IRS) estimates that 15 percent of employers in past years misclassified 3.4 million workers as independent contractors, costing the government $2.6 billion in lost tax revenues in 2006 dollars.[23]

When Are Contingent Workers "Employees"?

In the U.S., definitions of employees and the legal tests used vary among the labor and employment laws; and, ultimately government agencies and the courts determine the legal nature of an individual employment relationship. Illustrative descriptions of some of the key labor laws designed for workers' protection and their applicability to members of the contingent workforce is provided below.

The language of the labor laws typically distinguish between "employees" and independent contractors and self-employed workers, with only employees being protected.[24] The legal tests used to distinguish them are either (1) the traditional common law test of "right of control how the work is performed"; or (2) the "economic realities" test which examines whether the worker is economically dependent upon the principal or is in business for him or herself.

But what about contingent workers; how do they fit inside or outside the definitions? The number of jobs for *temporary* employees in recent years has grown more than ten times faster than that for jobs in the workforce generally[25] and the number of individuals affected is nearly 5 million.[26] These temporary jobs include agency work, employee leasing, in-house temps, and on-call workers and individuals in each job category raise issues of whether labor rights and benefit legislation are available.[27]

On-call workers Individuals who are called to work only on an as-needed basis, such as substitute teachers and construction workers supplied by union hiring halls

Self-employed workers Self-employed workers who are not independent contractors, such as doctors and restaurant owners

Standard part-time workers Individuals who regularly work less than thirty-five hours a week for a particular employer and are wage and salary workers.

20 GAO, *Contingent Workers: Incomes and Benefits Lag Behind Those of Rest of Workforce* (June 2000), *available at* http://www.gao.gov/archive/2000/he00076.pdf (last visited Sept. 30, 2010) [hereinafter "Contingent Workers"].

21 Employment Arrangements, *supra* note 11, at 3.

22 *Id.* at 1, 3.

23 *Id.* at 2.

24 A detailed list of labor laws and legal tests for determining employee status is provided in *id.* at Appendix IV.

25 *Id.* at 16.

26 DOL, *Contingent and Alternative Employment Arrangements*, Table 8 (February 2005), *available at* http://www.bls.gov/news.release/conemp.nro.htm (last visited Sept. 23, 2010) [hereinafter "DOL"].

27 Katherine V. W. Stone, *Legal Protections for Atypical Employees: Employment Law for Workers Without Workplaces and Employees Without Employers*, 27 BERKELEY J. EMP. & LAB. L. 251 (2006) [hereinafter "Stone"].

Statutory labor rights and benefits for temporary employees are not consistent among federal or state laws. Eligibility under some laws is foreclosed for temporary employees working too few hours in the qualifying period (Family Medical Leave Act (FMLA) and Unemployment Compensation (UI). Some laws allow temporary employees to be explicitly excluded from benefit plans or found ineligible for vested rights due to work of short duration (Employment Retirement Security Act [ERISA]) and denied benefits for "voluntarily" leaving a job that was temporary (UI). Sometimes dispatched temporary employees are singled out, such as under the National Labor Relations Act (NLRA), and are precluded from joining the union where they work, but rather must join the union of the agency (employer) that is sending them for temporary work and their "co-workers" to other employer locations.[28]

Independent contractors are another category of workers, some of whom may function as atypical or contingent employees. Of the over 10 million independent contractors, who by most labor laws, are excluded from coverage, over 3 million are likely in the category of "*dependent*" independent contractors who have little autonomy and depend on another business for their livelihood.[29] While the traditional independent contractors run or work for an independent business and contract their labor services, the atypical independent contractor, working as an individual or as a member of a crew, may work for an employer in an on-going or project-based employment relationship in construction, agriculture, manufacturing or transportation sectors.[30]

The legal consequence of being classified or misclassified as an independent contractor is clear: these employees are not necessarily covered or protected by the laws on minimum wage, unemployment insurance, workers' compensation, collective bargaining, anti-discrimination laws, occupational safety and health, etc.[31]

Therefore, the issue comes down to how the proper definition gets determined. The legal tests of control or economic realities will be used by the government agencies and the courts, but the initial choice by the employer how to classify the employee will be the subject matter of the legal case. And if an employer misjudges or misclassifies its workers, it may end up like Microsoft paying millions of dollars for its choice.[32] Many employers look to the Internal Revenue Service guide on how to classify employees so as to avoid tax liabilities in addition to any consequences of labor law violations.[33]

[28] For further discussion, see Stephen F. Befort, *Revisiting the Black Hole of Workplace Regulation: A Historical and Comparative Perspective of Contingent Work*, 24 Berkeley J. Emp. & Lab. L. 153, 165 (2003) and Stone, *supra* note 27.

[29] Stone, *supra* note 27.

[30] DOL, *supra* note 26.

[31] The true independent contractor, as an employer, may have some or all protections, depending on the size of the business and eligibility under the coverage provisions of the labor laws; many small companies and certainly individuals will likely not be covered by federal labor laws, but may have some state law protections.

[32] Viscaino v. Microsoft Corp., 120 F.3d 1006, 1009–10 (9th Cir. 1997).

[33] IRS Independent Contractor Test.The IRS formerly used what has become known as the "Twenty Factor" test. Under pressure from Congress and from representatives of labor and business, it has recently attempted to simplify and refine the test, consolidating the twenty factors into eleven main tests, and organizing them into three main groups: behavioral control, financial control, and the type of relationship of the parties. IRS, *Employer's Supplemental Tax Guide*, Publication 15-A, at 6 (2006), *available at* http://www.irs.gov/pub/irs-prior/p15a – 2006.pdf (last visited Sept. 30, 2010).

III. Question of Language or Substance in Integrating Contingent Employees into Protected "Employee" Status?

. . . .

Language of Law: Form or Substance?

There is a well-known quote from Alice-in-Wonderland that underpins the issues of language.

> "When I use a word," Humpty Dumpty said in rather a scornful tone, "it means just what I choose it to mean – neither more nor less." "The question is," said Alice, "whether you can make words mean so many different things." "The question is," said Humpty Dumpty, "which is to be master – that's all."[34]

"Employee" may be one of those words; each jurisdiction can make that word mean just about anything it wants it to be – either directly by legislation, by use of legal tests, or by exemptions and exclusions. Solutions to fair and substantive definitions harmonizing the laws with a common vocabulary will clearly state who an employee is. The vehicle used will of course be language. One language is difficult enough as can be seen in the practices of the U.S. Translating the true meaning of employee into multiple languages and having it survive multiple interpretations is a challenge indeed.

There would seem to be two thresholds to cross: (1) providing substantive reform to inclusively embrace workers who are true employees and according them their legal rights and benefits provided by labor and employment laws; (2) finding and using appropriate choice of language to diminish variances in interpretations and applications. To accomplish the first requires political will and courage and a determination it is unfair to do less. The second, to implement the first, can be achieved by simple, straightforward language that perhaps adds a common source of reference through a list of factors to be used in all cases of applying or interpreting the word "employee".

For example, in the U.S. case of independent contractors, absent an over-arching specific law (such as the Independent Contractor Classification Act), the clear meaning of "employee," distinguishing it from "independent contractor" could be referenced in all cases (absent explicit legislation to the contrary excluding certain categories of "employees", e.g., "supervisors" under NLRA) to the IRS Code definition.[35] This could provide a legal presumption of coverage and has the advantage of discouraging misclassifications and discovering "unexpected employees." Importantly, it provides meaningful and consistent enforcement by a single government agency whose laws all employers must follow. The same single government-enforced standard definition could be

34 *Alice in Wonderland Quotes*, Lenny's Alice in Wonderland site, http://www.alice-in-wonderland.net/books/alice-in-wonderland-quotes.html (last visited Sept. 30, 2010).

35 Another proposal suggests using a simple two-part test: where there are subordination and dependence, a person should be treated as an employee and given employment protections. *See* Brian A. Langille & Guy Davidov, *Employed or Self-Employed? The Role and Content of the Legal Distinction: Between Employees and Independent Contractors: A View from Canada*, 21 Comp. Lab. L. & Pol'y J. 7 (1999).

formulated and referenced for the contingent employees, allowing for explicit exclusions of subcategories.[36]

....

---

b. Coverage

What are the labor rights that are protected? Who is covered and who is not? Which status is protected – race, sex, health, legal immigrant, etc.; what type of discrimination is prohibited? How do the laws deal with the following inquiries?

1. May an employer discriminate because of an employee's health condition?
2. May an employee be fired only for cause?
3. What is the coverage of labor laws?
4. Can employees join a union, collectively bargain, and strike?
5. Can employees have pregnancy leave?
6. Can the employer deduct breakage at work from an employee's paycheck?
7. Can employees insist on safer working conditions without risk of discipline?
8. How is entitlement to unemployment insurance determined?
9. How do I qualify for workers' compensation?
10. Is there a right to redress if an employer provides a bad reference?

An Untouched Majority[37]

David Ziskind

The vast majority of all human beings who work for their living are not reached by labor legislation. It is known who they are, where they are, and how they contribute to the

[36] A suggested definition standardizing the term "employee" has recently been advanced in the United States in RESTATEMENT (THIRD) EMPLOYMENT LAW § 1.01 (2009).

§ 1.01 General Conditions for Existence of Employment Relationship

(1) [A]n individual renders services as an employee of an employer if
  (a) the individual acts, at least in part, to serve the interests of the employer,
  (b) the employer consents to receive the individual's services, and
  (c) the employer's relationship with the individual effectively prevents the individual from rendering the services as part of an independent business.
(2) An individual renders services as part of an independent business when the individual in his or her own interest exercises entrepreneurial control over the manner and means by which the services are performed.
(3) Entrepreneurial control over the manner and means by which services are performed is control over important business decisions, including whether to hire and where to assign assistants, whether to purchase and where to deploy equipment, and whether and when to service other customers. *Id.*

[37] DAVID ZISKIND, *An Untouched Majority*, *in* CONCERNING HUMAN ASPIRATIONS: ESSAYS IN COMPARATIVE LABOR LAW 1, ch. 1, at 1–5 (1985); *see also* Judy Fudge & Fiona Macphail, *The Temporary Foreign*

well-being of the world. Governments are aware of their needs and problems; but they have not extended to them the protection and assistance of labor laws.

Modem labor legislation was a response to transformed work relationships brought on by the Industrial Revolution. As its new forms of energy led to excessive exploitation of human resources, compassionate concerns stimulated adjustments by law. Further technological changes continued, always outrunning the social adaptations. Today we look forward to an on-coming micro-electronic revolution that bodes numerous dislocations in work patterns. We expect to cope with these new difficulties; yet there is little realization that the majority of workers are still not the beneficiaries of our old legal techniques for improving conditions of labor.

The absence of aid is most noticeable in agriculture but there are voids in industry, commerce, and service trades as well.

Despite the great drift from farms to urban centers, most workers are still in agriculture; and by and large, agricultural workers have been left out of the purview of labor legislation.

. . . .

Almost nowhere is there a legal requirement of minimum wages or maximum hours for farmworkers even though their earnings are extremely low and their hours very long. The family farm system, which tends to support a livelihood for all kin, also promotes excessive woman and child labor; and for the males in the family it shields under-employment or under-utilization of their productive capacity. Large-scale, mechanized farming has benefited by some labor regulation, primarily confined to the promotion of safety and health. Additional labor standards have been formulated for plantation work; but they have not been adopted widely. Adding inertia to weakness, nowhere in the world has a country provided adequate funds for the administration of laws that may be applicable to agricultural labor.

In industry, also, gaps leave many workers unprotected. The labor laws germinated by the Industrial Revolution started with simple rules to eliminate a few abuses, and progressed slowly, step by step. Agriculture was side-stepped because the concentrated, industrial workers suffered more visible and disturbing hardships, and they were dealt with more easily. Nonetheless, most labor laws in industrial nations have also been restricted in their coverage. Sometimes limited to specified industries or establishments of large size, they have excluded substantial numbers of workers. Even in the comprehensive labor legislation of the United States of America there are voids. Under the federal Fair Labor Standards Act, executive, administrative, and professional personnel are exempted, and approximately one-fifth of the nonsupervisory employees are not subject to its minimum wage provisions (prior to 1966 amendments, two-fifths were excluded). Under the Social Security Act there is no coverage for a large number of domestic employees, self-employed and employees of nonprofit or local government agencies that do not elect to come under the Act. Similar laws in other countries have excluded even larger portions of the

Worker Program in Canada: Low-Skilled Workers as an Extreme Form of Flexible Labor, 31 COMP. LAB. L. & POL'Y J. 5 (2009). In "focus[ing] on the legal regime that regulates the entry and exit of low-skilled temporary foreign workers and these workers' rights and terms and conditions of employment while in Canada[,]" this article offers a "preliminary . . . assessment of the impact of the [Temporary Foreign Worker Program] on the Canadian labor market and evaluate[s] whether or not the employment rights of the workers who are admitted under it are protected." *Id.* at 6–7.

industrial labor force. Rarely has any labor law embraced all the industrial workers in a country. Reasons for this neglect are not difficult to find.

The problems of workers change constantly and they seem to defy solution. Legislation customarily deals with only a portion of a problem at any one time. Until experience is gained, that may be a matter of sound judgment or it may be pragmatically unavoidable. After legislation has proved itself, all too often, attention has been preempted by new problems and old endeavors remain unfinished.

. . . .

The ILO has a world-wide, all encompassing viewpoint; but it has been ever conscious of and restricted by the political limitations imposed upon its work. It functions through a governing body of employer, worker, and government representatives; and its activities are dependent upon a broad endorsement. ILO Conventions and Recommendations call for government action and frequently find it necessary to spell out certain limits beyond which implementation is not required. The result is often the exclusion of a great many workers. Some principles (such as the right of workers to organize) are considered by the ILO to be universal and they are demanded even of nations that have not ratified pertinent Conventions. However, most workers have not been educated to know and to seek the benefits of ILO protective principles. Except as they have shared standards elevated by ILO influences in their communities at large, masses of untutored and leaderless workers have not been gathered under the wings of the ILO.

I appreciate also the ripple effect of labor legislation that spreads the economic pattern of a law beyond its explicit provisions. In a few, exceptional, countries, wage laws specify that once standards are set for certain organized workers they shall become applicable to all workers. The lag in such social extension of labor standards is significant and many workers never experience the embrace.

To some readers, the foregoing may appear to state merely what everyone has or should have known. It is that; but like the absence of the emperor's clothes, it still needs mentioning. Even scholars of labor law have difficulty in learning about the laws of countries other than their own, and in their preoccupation with laws as written and administered, they at times overlook the great number of workers who are not even mentioned. The true significance of society's efforts to improve conditions and standards of work must be measured by our shortfall as well as by our reach. Those who are strangers to labor law are not invited to sit at the table of society and to share in its blessings. Viewed from a world-wide perspective, a majority of all workers are so untouched.

QUESTIONS

1. Is it possible to draft a universal definition of "employee" for use under the labor and employment laws of one country or of several (e.g., the European Union or East Asia)? By what guideposts would you proceed? Does that make sense in view of the varied purposes of labor statutes?
2. In addition to agriculture, what are other areas of unregulated or underregulated work regarding labor rights and protections?
3. What are the arguments why exceptions and exemptions are needed?
4. How might the answer to the previous question vary in developing versus developed countries?

---

2. *Labor Rights: Sources and Illustrations*

Labor rights are many and varied, and derive from a myriad of sources. Questions continually arise whether alleged rights are legally cognizable and in what forum; for example, whether it is a human right, a health or safety right, a compensation right, or even a legal right at all. Possible types and classifications of labor/human rights are suggested by UN covenants and declarations, provided below.

a. Illustrative Sources[38]

- Germany Sources of Law
  - German Civil Code
  - Directives and regulations of the EU
  - Decisions of the European Court of Justice
  - European Court of Human Rights
  - ILO treaties
  - Domestic legislation required by the Organization for Economic Cooperation and Development
  - Supplementary Protocol to the UN Convention on the Elimination of All Forms of Discrimination Against Women
- China Sources of Law
  - Labor Laws of the People's Republic of China, Central and Local
  - State Council Regulations;
  - Supreme People's Court's and Supreme People's Procuratorate Pronouncements
  - Ministries' Rules
- Japan Sources of Law
  - Constitution
  - Criminal, Civil, Commercial Codes
  - Labor Standards Law
- South Korea Sources of Law
  - Constitution
  - Labor Legislation
  - Court Decisions
  - Administrative Interpretation

. . . .

---

[38] *See, e.g.*, 1 INTERNATIONAL LABOR AND EMPLOYMENT LAWS 4-2-4 (Germany); 31-3-5 (China), (A.B.A., William L. Keller et al. eds., 2d. ed. 2004); 2 INTERNATIONAL LABOR AND EMPLOYMENT LAWS 26-6-11 (Japan); 26-6-11 (South Korea), (A.B.A., William L. Keller et al. eds., 2nd ed. 2004).

Labor Laws in the Vortex of Human Rights Protection[39]

David Ziskind

Labor laws mark progress in the survival of human rights.... For the purposes of this essay it will be assumed that human rights are those rights mentioned in the Universal Declaration of Human Rights and the U.N. Covenants based thereon.

....

The Universal Declaration is a comprehensive document.... One of the most concise groupings is composed of only three categories.

1. The right to be free from governmental violations of the integrity of the person, (torture, cruel and inhuman punishment, arbitrary arrest, denial of fair public trial, invasion of home);
2. The right to the fulfillment of vital needs (such as food, shelter, health care and education);
3. The right to enjoy civil and political liberties (speech, press, assembly, religion), to participate in government and to travel freely.

These highlight essential characteristics and serve well to give meaning to the human rights in their entirety. However, to discern the place of labor laws in the constellation of human rights, a much more detailed listing of the rights in the Universal Declaration will prove fruitful. A grouping of rights, somewhat as they have been in the Covenants, including Economic, Social, Cultural, Civil, Political, and Rights and Duties follows:

1. Economic Rights

All of these Economic Rights have been the subject of what has traditionally been regarded as labor legislation. The interest of employees and employers and their organizations in each of these is obvious. The Declaration sets forth standards for private and government action to secure terms and conditions of work and income. These take concrete form and become legal norms through labor laws.

2. Social Rights

Some of the Social Rights, such as those pertaining to marriage, divorce, and the protection of illegitimate children, may have very slight relationship to labor laws; yet the assistance and support of family life have been incorporated into minimum wage laws and laws for the special protection of female and child labor. The Social Rights seeking a spirit of brotherhood and a social and international order in which rights and freedoms can be fully realized have a special pertinence, even if only a prophetic one, to the improvement of labor standards by law.

[39] David Ziskind, *Labor Laws in the Vortex of Human Rights Protection*, *in* Concerning Human Aspirations: Essays in Comparative Labor Law ch. 2, at 7–13 (1985).

3. Cultural Rights

The Cultural Rights mentioned in the Universal Declaration are also basic to the adoption of labor legislation. Labor laws are usually on the threshold of public debate and opinion. Without a free exchange of thought, all innovation and progress in labor laws would be stifled. Even religious thought, non-secular in character, has inspired labor movements in the advocacy of certain labor laws. Without freedom of association, power to press for such laws would be sapped. The development of one's personality has been the objective of much labor legislation. Education, even apart from vocational instruction and safety and health training, has been an essential ingredient in the process of elevating labor standards and the expectations expressed in labor laws. Participation in the cultural life of a community and the enjoyment of the arts and benefits of science have been goals sought through labor laws.

4. Civil Rights

The rights labeled Civil assure equality in the application of labor laws and protect labor activists from government persecution or individual abuse. Discrimination is the bane of all law enforcement; but it particularly stultifies the interpretation and the effectiveness of labor standards. The protections against arbitrary arrest, unjust criminal charges and unfair trials are also designed for all situations, but have constant relevance to the enforcement of labor laws. Freedoms of asylum and nationality are more remotely associated with labor activities; yet freedom of movement within and across national boundaries are the subject of many labor laws. Civil rights are all encompassing and there are none which have not been crucial historically to the protection of persons engaged in activities regulated by labor law.

5. Political Rights

The rights characterized as Political are not confined to employers and employees, but they cover them as well as all other members of society. They seek to create a governmental atmosphere under which the parties to the labor relationship may function freely. They affect, directly and pervasively, the enactment and administration of labor law. The extent to which trade unions and employer associations are political varies greatly. In some industrial countries and in most of the less developed countries, trade unions operate primarily as interest groups seeking government action; and their political rights are the parameters of their effectiveness. In all countries, labor and management have special interests in the outcome of political action. Labor law flourishes or falters in proportion to the latitude permitted by a country's political rights.

. . . .

QUESTIONS

1. How would you define a "labor right"? What categories of rights would you include under its protection?
2. How important are international definitions? Why?

b. Safety and Health

Safety and Health: An Elusive Quest[40]

David Ziskind

. . . .

Striving for occupational safety and health has been much like the search for a holy grail. Prayers have not sufficed. Good deeds have been found lacking. A relentless reaching for relief has gone on, driven by human misery and faith in the ultimate survival of good over evil. The processes of law have been a reckoning with reality.

The magnitude of occupational accident and disease has never been negligible, and it has grown monstrously – ever emerging in new places and new forms. The Industrial Revolution may have caught people unawares. But the increasing complexity of machines, the discovery of novel and mighty sources of energy, the invention of new toxins and explosives, and the daily manufacture of substances with unknown properties bring on dangers with which we are little prepared to cope. For more than a century, the experts of society – chemists, physicians, engineers, educators and law makers – have been engaged in a race against the risks of modern technology. They understand the problem. There is almost universal agreement upon what can or should be done about it. Yet we have failed to eradicate occupational accidents and diseases, and we seem resigned to the burden of struggling with them forever. Laws constitute our plan of battle.

Legal Doctrines

Some inviolability of the human body has been inherent in all legal systems. Even slaves were protected from mutilation and murder; and free workmen have had the rights of all men to recover damages for tortious injury to life or limb. In the area of occupational injury, however, the rights of the injured have been diminished by countervailing rights of employers.

Common Law concepts of the right to redress wrongs were completely inadequate to deal with occupational accidents and diseases. The law involved an underlying search for fault or negligence, and an assessment of damages against a person responsible for the injury. An employer was charged with an obligation to remain free from personal negligence and with the further obligation to make reasonable provision for a safe place of work; but he was generally not held responsible for accidents that he did not cause.

There evolved three (or four) doctrines that made it virtually impossible for an injured employee to recover compensation for his pain and financial loss. These were the doctrines of (1) contributory negligence, (2) fellow servant negligence (known in Europe as the common employment rule), (3) assumption of ordinary risks, and in certain jurisdictions, (4) assumption of known extraordinary risks. Contributory negligence defeated all recovery if the negligence of the injured employee contributed to the accident in any degree. The fellow servant doctrine denied recovery for accidents caused by the negligence of others employed by the same employer. Assumption of risk assumed that

[40] David Ziskind, *Safety and Health: An Elusive Quest*, *in* Concerning Human Aspirations: Essays in Comparative Labor Law, ch. 4, at 54–71.

the worker accepted the ordinary risks of his occupation and gave up any right to recover damages for injuries attributable to ordinary actions or conditions of the trade. This was a defence that could be invoked by the employer, without proof that the worker knew the risks ordinarily involved. And in some jurisdictions, if the employer was able to show that the employee had knowledge of extraordinary circumstances and dangers he could raise the defence that the employee had assumed the extraordinary risks as well. With the impersonal causation of many industrial accidents and the imposition of these defences, not to mention the costs and delays of litigation, an injured worker found little recourse under the Common Law.

Civil Law doctrines, applied on the European continent, similarly stifled relief. The concept of vicarious liability which was applied to a limited extent in Anglo-American law (and the law of Denmark and Norway) was not part of the Roman law, and was rejected by Germany, Sweden, and other civil law countries. The employer's liability in tort (or in contract) was effectively minimized by presumptions of freedom from negligence, by rules setting burdens of proof and by some form of the "unholy trinity" of defenses – contributory negligence, voluntary assumption of risk and common employment. It took a revolution in the law to correct this situation. The element of fault or negligence was discarded by workmen's compensation legislation.

Law makers recognized that the tremendous burden of industrial accidents and diseases fell upon those persons least able to bear it. To do equity and to assist the crippled and the infirm, statutes were enacted that would compensate for disability, and loss of earnings, regardless of cause. The early statutes took the form of compulsory health insurance with cash benefits and in time they added medical and hospital care and rehabilitation assistance. Germany initiated its insurance plan in 1884, Great Britain in 1897, France in 1898. The United States did not adopt a workmen's compensation law until 1910. Some form of workmen's compensation is now the predominant legislation assuring payment for loss of income, and medical care to workers sustaining work related injuries.

Common law and civil law doctrines still remain where workmen's compensation statutes have not been made all inclusive; but the earlier doctrines have been modified to make relief more available. Prevailing philosophies seeking to care for the poor and the afflicted have been transformed into public policies identifying society with the needs of all human beings, and the law has broadened its horizons. Legal doctrines of individual fault and responsibility have been supplemented by doctrines of social assistance for all persons subject to occupational accidents and disease.

A Comprehensive Safety and Health Program

From the inception of social concern over occupational safety and health, it was recognized that the problem required many approaches. The earliest legislation sought to overcome the excesses of child labor, work by women after child birth, and long hours of work for women and children. Such laws have remained an on-going effort to protect and prolong life. Accident legislation as such started with designated trades, deemed especially dangerous, and went on to cover all industry. Public health laws, designed primarily to avoid epidemics, have also been extended to all areas of health. Workmen's compensation laws, considered a replacement for inadequate doctrines of tort law, have been joined (and in certain respects may be supplanted) by social security programs devised to cover many risks of life including the risks of disability and some of the salient problems presented by occupational safety and health legislation.

1. A *statement of objectives or desired public policies*. There is little difficulty with drafting a statement that the preservation of safety and health or the eradication of occupational accident and disease is a matter of public policy. Problems may arise, however, with the definition of the concepts involved. Does occupational health include the absence of all disease? How is the illness to be related to the work performed? A perplexing clarification was posed recently by a draft convention proposed for consideration at the International Labour Office Conference of 1981. The draft Convention Concerning Occupational Safety and Health and the Working Environment stated, The aim of the policy shall be to prevent accidents and injury to health *(including well-being)* arising out of, linked with or occurring in the course of work by minimizing, so far as is reasonably practicable, the causes of hazards inherent in the working environment.

At the Conference in Plenary Sitting, the employers' adviser from the United States stated that the reference to "well-being" raised some interesting but vexatious questions and would create problems if the employer had to meet such responsibilities. He said this was a vague, ill-defined, concept and he urged very strongly that the concept be reconsidered. A workers' delegate from the Netherlands suggested that maybe a better wording could be found for "well-being". A government member from the United Kingdom requested clarification. In the final action on the proposed Convention 155, the parenthetical clause "(including well-being)" was omitted. The extent to which mental or emotional disturbance might be deemed a matter of health was left unresolved. Public policy statements have been customarily phrased in terms general enough to permit the broadest interpretation found feasible by administrators.

2. *The delineation of a manageable portion of the problem to be dealt with*. Since occupational accidents and illnesses are quite pervasive and are linked with wide-spread environmental conditions, it is frequently found necessary to restrict the scope of the legislation in some manner.

Ordinarily there is a pre-determination as to whether the statute will deal exclusively or primarily with the prevention of accidents and diseases, or with the care and treatment of the injured and infirm, or with death. All of these legal efforts have been essential ingredients of a comprehensive occupational safety and health program.

There has been a great shift in the emphasis of safety and health law, from compensation for occupational injury to the prevention of accidents and disease. Occupational health is being viewed as part of public health, the working environment as part of the entire human environment. The elimination of work related accidents and diseases is seen as the preservation of human resources, and as part of a program to improve the quality of work life. That calls for many separate endeavors involving the participation not only of employers and employees and public servants but also of scientists, engineers, educators and many other imaginative persons in all parts of society. To martial their many talents and focus them on occupational safety and health requires special measures.

Although the so-called occupational safety and health statute is only one of the many laws now dealing with the maintenance of safety and health in the workplace, if well designed, it can interface with and take advantage of many of the social efforts that support or reinforce its objectives. I shall attempt to demonstrate some of the potentials and problems involved by noting them under a hypothetical outline of a comprehensive occupational safety and health statute.

Most social legislation follows a pattern of topics. It usually includes (1) a statement of objectives or desired public policies, (2) a delineation of a manageable portion of the problem it is to deal with, (3) a prescription of norms of conduct it seeks within its area of regulation, (4) the creation of an administrative agency with powers designed to attain the desired normative conduct, (5) a specification of penalties for deviation, and (6) a provision of funds for administration and enforcement.

Sometimes at the beginning of an approach to a problem, legislators have spoken timidly, in hortatory terms, hoping that the standards they set forth would be accepted. Later, they have branched out on small portions of the problem, for the accumulation of regulatory experience. In time the broader reaches of the problem have been broached, new goals and techniques ventured, and more attention given to positive administrative action and enforcement. Such development, characteristic of nearly all social legislation, has been the course of legislation on occupational safety and health.

I shall follow the outline of topics I have just indicated to discuss the provision of financial assistance to the victims and their families. And the law may be drafted as a single purpose or an omnibus measure.

Nonetheless, adequate coverage is a mark of good legislation. In principle, it is desirable to cover all industries and all workers. Some areas of economic activity, however, have been historically singled out for special attention, and it may be advisable not to disturb existing regulation. Conditions of work in manufacturing, agriculture, service trades, fishing and mining are so diverse, there may be some advantage to specialized agencies or laws. Limited public funds or the availability of private industry resources also may make it practicable to exclude certain areas, industries or occupations from coverage – at least temporarily. The recent ILO convention on Safety and Health and the Working Environment permits the exclusion of particular branches of economic activity, such as maritime shipping or fishing, with a provision for progressively wider application. Whenever coverage must be limited, provision should also be made for expansion.

This has been particularly apparent in dealing with occupational diseases. Many early statutes have confined coverage to a schedule of designated diseases. Experience has demonstrated, however, that the inclusion of all work related illnesses costs little more and results in a much more satisfactory program.

Other threshold questions relate to how much the government should be involved or how much the government may depend upon private activities to address the problem, how much regulation should be centralized or decentralized, and to what extent general standards should be tailored to specific conditions at an enterprise level. Policy decisions on such questions are usually best considered separately under each of the several topics comprising the whole statute.

3. *The prescription of desired norms of conduct.* This is the substantive mentality and message of safety and health laws. It defines and specifies the kinds of action that are expected to accomplish safety and health. The types of regulation and the details of each may be left, within general legislative guidelines, to the discretion of an administrative agency; or the statute itself may indicate what is to be required in greater or lesser detail.

In either case, there are several outstanding issues concerning how safety and health are to be safeguarded.

. . . .

The factors pertinent to safety and health are innumerable. Statutes may specify those to be considered such as work place cleanliness, ventilation, lighting, sanitary facilities, temperature, humidity, noise and vibration; equipment speed, force, accessibility and protective covering; contact and inhalation of noxious fumes and particulate matter; fire, electric shock and explosion; physical and mental stress; monotony and attention span; protective garments; first aid and medical facilities. All of these items change from time to time. The basic statute therefore must provide for a continuous proliferation of standards or norms of safe conduct.

Education and training in these matters must be provided – not only for the workers involved but also for employers, supervisory personnel and care takers. The more effective the educational process, the less other enforcement is needed.

In acknowledgement of the practical inevitability of occupational accidents and diseases, a comprehensive safety and health program goes beyond prevention and provides for after care, for a restitution of the financial losses involved and for the rehabilitation of the injured. First aid is ordinarily required by a safety and health law; whereas provisions for medical treatment, hospital care and rehabilitation must often be considered in conjunction with workmen's compensation, social security, and public health statutes. Compensation for pain and suffering and for loss of earnings is also frequently the subject of other statutes. These provisions are generally based upon social sharing and public facilities, though private responsibilities are also taken into consideration. The creation of a comprehensive national health plan, with its many possible variables is obviously of crucial significance to a safety and health program.

The prescription of norms of conduct to assure occupational safety and health reaches into many areas of activity, nearly all of which seem essential to an effective system of legal regulation. In countries that have works councils, they too are utilized.

4. *The creation of administrative agencies to carry out a safety and health program.* Because of the great multiplicity of things that should be done, it is foolhardy to expect an occupational safety and health program to be self-executing. The problem is how to decide what can best be accomplished by government agencies, by employers, by employees, by private organizations, and by special committees or representatives. No one agency is sufficient. The optimum seems to lie in a coordination of many administrative agents, with the least duplication of effort or without the neglect of any effective instrumentality.

. . . .

The key to the adequacy of government safety law enforcement is the number of inspectors available. Only through inspectors is it possible to detect infractions of the law, to educate managers and employees as to the requirements of regulations, and to cite willful or serious violators. It is cost prohibitive to inspect every work place or to inspect the places of major employment with frequency. Sampling is unavoidable, and concentration on places or occupations found most likely to be unsafe is commonplace. Proper administration, however, depends upon an ample staff of inspectors.

In countries where workers are organized, there is use of trade union representatives, usually called safety delegates, or safety and health committees, or joint labor-management safety committees. In countries that have works councils, they too are utilized. Safety and health laws can promote and protect the contributions of such administrative agents.

In many advanced industrialized countries, there are private organizations devoted to the formulation of safety standards, and many physical and social scientists whose research has contributed significantly to the understanding of accident causation and human safety motivation. Though they function largely on private resources, their work can be integrated into the work of public agencies and their findings do find their way into laws.

The immediate participant in occupational activity – the worker – should be the person most interested in his safety and health, and though he may be impotent to detect many hazards or to prevent many accidents, he can be a vital agent in the administration of safety and health laws. His instruction and his continuing motivation to maintain safe practices are extremely important elements of safety legislation. Though the employer and his supervisors may be a step farther removed from accidents, they, because of their power to control the working environment and to order work conduct, must also be treated as primary parties in the administration of safety and health laws.

The allocation of responsibilities to see that the law is carried out is necessarily many faceted.

5. *The punishment of deviants.* Fines and imprisonment are the normal forms of punishment for law violators. Administrative authorities may develop expertise in the fair and just imposition of fines. Ordinarily only courts of law may order imprisonment and because of the difficulties of proving causation or personal knowledge of the unlawful practice, jail sentences in accident cases are often rare. However, the possibility of both punishments is deemed essential to a deterrent effect.

The punishment of workers as well as employers who knowingly violate safety regulations is also provided by some laws.

The amount of fines (as well as the damages assessed against employers found willfully or grossly negligent in accident suits) has often been insufficient to induce employers to install costly new equipment or protective devices. The cost balance has frequently been weighted heavily against the adoption of safe equipment and practices. Administrative agencies may enable manufacturers to pool such costs or to spread them over time so that they can be met. The saving of human lives and the avoidance of human misery resulting from occupational accidents and diseases cannot be equated with the cost of safe equipment and practices, and the law must so provide.

6. *The budgeting of appropriations for safety and health.* The cost of social welfare programs is perhaps their greatest nemesis, and the cost of a multi-pronged safety and health program is a very serious consideration. Unfortunately there are many social needs and the question of national budget priorities is not easily answered. At times when nations rate national defense over occupational safety and health, there does not seem to be enough money for both of them. More casualties occur in work places than in war, and appropriations for occupational safety and health save lives for more production and wealth.

7. *An overall observation on legislation.* Given the peculiarities of all countries, it is difficult to evaluate the relative merits of their safety and health laws. Occupational fatality statistics, even when available, are not comparable. All countries are committed to safety and health. The techniques they use are applied to different situations with different results. It is possible, however, for any country to find apparently successful practices in other countries and to discern in them suggestions for improving their own laws. I have indicated some of those practices and some policy questions they raise.

Constitutional Commitments

A new element of law affecting occupational safety and health has been introduced by modern constitutions. Many of the countries that have incorporated social and economic rights in their constitutions have spelled out a right to safety and health for workers. A few prohibit work in unhealthful places, for women and minors. All of these countries and more also have constitutional provisions for public health. Some provide for a free national health plan and others for social security covering disability and death. These basic commitments have yielded a diversity of laws and regulations for occupational safety and health, reflecting differences in industrialization, political philosophy and government structure. Nonetheless, these constitutions attest to the modern acknowledgement of the safety and health problem and a universal desire to seek a solution.

International Efforts to Promote Occupational Safety and Health

1. *Historical antecedents.* A conference of eleven European countries held in Berlin in 1890, adopted a series of resolutions on child labor, woman labor and work in mines. They merely expressed the desirability of measures ("*voeux*") that would protect the health of workers. Though regulatory legislation did not follow immediately, the unofficial International Association for Labor Legislation was instrumental in calling three labor conferences in Berne (1905, 1906 and 1913). The second conference adopted two specific conventions, one respecting Prohibition of Night Work for Women and one on the Prohibition of the Use of White (Yellow) Phosphorous in the Manufacture of Matches. Although these had primarily a moral effect, they were followed by the adoption of safety and health laws in a number of countries.

2.*The ILO.* By far, the most influential international force in the promotion of occupational safety and health has been the International Labour Office. Though known primarily for its development of standards in Conventions and Recommendations adopted by member states, it has made direct and practical contributions through its studies and research, tripartite meetings, exchanges of information and experience, and technical cooperation. From 1921 on, the ILO promulgated 23 Conventions and 22 Recommendations on safety and health, mostly on special hazards but culminating in 1981 in a comprehensive policy Convention 155 Concerning Occupational Safety and Health and the Working Environment. Each of these has been ratified by many countries, which have taken further implementing action. ILO Conventions and Recommendations have served as a catalyst to regulatory action around the globe.

List of instruments concerning occupational safety health and the working environment adopted by the International Labour Conference since 1919

Year	Convention	Recommendation
1921	13. White Lead (Painting)	
1929	27. Marking of Weight (Packages Trans-	
1937	62. Safety Provisions (Building)	53. Safety Provisions (Building)
1946	73. Medical Examinations (Seafarers)	79. Medical Examination of Young Persons
	77. Medical Examination of Young Persons (Industry)	
	78. Medical Examination of Young Persons (Nonindustrial Occupations)	
1947	81. Labour Inspection	81. Labour Inspection
		82. Labour Inspection (Mining and Transport)
1949	92. Accommodation of Crews (Revised)	
1953		97. Protection of Workers' Health
1958		105. Ships' Medicine Chests
		106. Medical Advice at Sea
1959	113. Medical Examination (Fishermen)	112. Occupational Health Services
1960	115. Radiation Protection	114. Radiation Protection
1963	119. Guarding of Machinery	118. Guarding of Machinery
1964	120. Hygiene (Commerce and Offices)	120. Hygiene (Commerce and Offices)
	121. Employment Injury Benefits	121. Employment Injury Benefits
1965	124. Medical Examination of Young Persons (Underground Work)	
1967	127. Maximum Weight	128. Maximum Weight
1969	129. Labour Inspection (Agriculture)	133. Labour Inspection (Agriculture)
1970	133. Accommodation of Crews (Supplementary Provisions)	140. Crew Accommodation (Air Conditioning)
		141. Crew Accommodation (Noise Control)
	134. Prevention of Accidents (Seafarers)	142. Prevention of Accidents (Seafarers)
1971	136. Benzene	144. Benzene
1974	139. Occupational Cancer	147. Occupational Cancer

[*Updates include the following.][41]

41 [Author's note] Report III (Part 1B) from the International Labor Conference, 98th Session, 2009, *available at* http://www.ilocarib.org.tt/portal/images/stories/contenido/pdf/OccupationSafetyandHealth/survey155engpdf.pdf (last visited Sept. 23, 2010). Published by the International Labor Organization. *See* Official titles of the Conventions adopted by the International Labor Conference (2010), *available at* http://www.ilo.org/ilolex/english/conventions.pdf (last visited Sept. 30, 2010); *see also* Official titles of the Recommendations adopted by the International Labor Conference (2010), *available at* http://www.ilo.org/ilolex/english/recommendations.pdf (last visited Sept. 30, 2010).

1977	148	Working Environment (Air Pollution, Noise, and Vibration)	156	Working Environment (Air Pollution, Noise, and Vibration)
1979	152	Occupational Safety and Health (Dock Work)	160	Occupational Safety and Health (Dock Work)
1981	155	Occupational Safety and Health	164	Occupational Safety and Health
1985	161	Occupational Health Services	171	Occupational Health Services
1986	162	Asbestos	172	Asbestos
1988	167	Safety and Health in Construction	175	Safety and Health in Construction
1990	170	Chemicals	177	Chemicals
1993	174	Prevention of Major Industrial Accidents	181	Prevention of Major Industrial Accidents
1995	176	Safety and Health in Mines	183	Safety and Health in Mines
2001	184	Safety and Health in Agriculture	192	Safety and Health n Agriculture
2002			194	List of Occupational Diseases
2006	187	Promotional Framework for Occupational Safety and Health	197	Promotional Framework for Occupational Safety and Health

The ILO has also produced codes of practice and guides on many safety subjects, and published studies in an Occupational Safety and Health Series. More spectacularly, it has conducted a computerized International Occupational Safety and Health Information Center (CIS) which abstracts annually over 2000 journal articles, laws, conference reports, books, films, bibliographies, translations, and other publications, and makes them available to computer terminals throughout the world.

. . . .

The ILO has truly been a world-wide force to combat occupational accidents and diseases, utilizing representatives of government, management, and labor from every country. It may be credited with stimulating a universal awareness that occupational safety and health must be supported by practical measures and with a view to the entire working environment.

United Nations. The U.N. has voiced the concern of the world over safety and health, and the International Covenant on Economic, Social, and Cultural Rights, now ratified by 63 countries, pledges to observe "the right of everyone to the enjoyment of just and favorable conditions of work which ensure, in particular... safe and healthy working conditions" and to take steps for "the improvement of all aspects of environmental and industrial hygiene; the prevention, treatment, and control of occupational and other diseases." U.N-. affiliated agencies have taken such steps.

The World Health Organization. In 1976, the WHO formulated a workers' health program and its 1980–81 budget supports occupational safety and health activities – emphasizing health control for underserved working populations in small industries, agriculture, and mining, and care for vulnerable working groups including migrant workers; generating a body of knowledge on simplified and feasible methods to control occupational hazards; and providing guidance for workers' participation and the motivation of employers and health officials.

WHO has held scientific conferences on the health problems of migrant workers and has sponsored research on exposure to toxic substances and the permissible limits for pesticides and other solvents. It has established regional occupational health centers in Botswana and Zambia, Sri Lanka and Thailand. Its International Agency for Research on Cancer at Lyon has produced many monographs on carcinogenic risks encountered at work. WHO's educational work has increased an awareness of health problems attending industrialization in developing countries so that the ILO and many nations have been better able to prescribe codes of safe practice.

The United Nations Environment Programme (UNEP) has collaborated with agencies concerned with occupational health by keeping an international record of potentially dangerous chemical substances.

The International Atomic Energy Agency (IAEA) has prepared Safety Standards for Radiation Protection. Its code of practice on Radiation Protection in the Mining and Milling of Radioactive Ores has been developed cooperatively with the ILO, and the WHO.

. . . .

The Organization of Economic Cooperation and Development OCED (now embracing all countries in the European Community plus Australia, Austria, Canada, Finland, Iceland, Japan, New Zealand, Norway, Portugal, Spain, Sweden, Switzerland, Turkey and the USA) has concerned itself with economic growth, including better conditions of work. In seeking a set of indicators measuring the quality of life, it has researched fatal accidents and diseases and the potentially harmful effects of chemicals. Among its publications are standards for noise abatement and safety tests of agricultural equipment.

Private Professional Organizations. There are several international associations of experts in the field of occupational safety and health that have contributed significantly to the knowledge and activities of governmental agencies and technicians in industry. *The International Social Security Association* (ISSA) has a Permanent Committee on the Prevention of Occupational Risks, and International Sections which hold meetings and publish materials on prevention of accidents in particular industries. It has held world congresses in Rome, Bucharest, and Amsterdam, and regional congresses in Mexico and Algiers. *The International Organization for Standardization* (IOS) surveys nationally and globally to obtain consensus among manufacturers, consumers and governments on safety standards, such as acoustics and mechanical vibration and shock. *The International Electrochemical Commission* plays a similar role in the field of electro-technology. *The International Association of Labour Inspection* organizes international symposia for labor inspectors. Most of these organizations cooperate with the ILO as well as maintain direct contact with their own members in many countries.

Occupational accidents and diseases are universal, and even though legal regulations are national and regulations must be applied to local undertakings, varying very widely in customs and facilities, innumerable benefits have been derived from international cooperation.

. . . .

Concluding Observations

Much has been done to secure occupational safety and health.

Much more remains to be done. The law has been remolded from tort doctrines based on fault to doctrines of social welfare. The main legal concern has shifted from compensation for injury to prevention of accidents and illnesses. This has enlisted scientific research, inspection, education, and training. At the same time, health care has gone public and social security programs have extended monetary assistance to the disabled as well as to others suffering loss of income. New programs for improving the quality of work life have suggested pleasant alternatives to stultifying and dangerous work patterns. Legal techniques to progress along these many roads have been devised and are available to all who would use them. Despite problems of inertia and cost, we have made headway and know how to proceed further.

Most of the attention to occupational safety and health has been directed toward conditions in industrialized countries. Yet many developing countries have committed themselves to the patterns of control found feasible in more advanced economies. By constitutional pronouncement, by approval of ILO conventions, and by the enactment of far sighted statutes, they have affirmed progressive policies. Unfortunately it has often been impossible to carry out those policies where there has been a lack of medical facilities and an extreme shortage of funds for inspection, education, and training. The predominance of agriculture in the less developed countries has also presented special problems. Nonetheless, there has been no dearth of understanding and knowledge of the steps that should be taken.

. . . .

QUESTIONS

1. Discuss and distinguish labor legislation that prevents versus compensates workers for workplace injuries. Which does lax enforcement affect the most, prevention or compensation? Are diseases covered?
2. What types of penalties are needed to prevent or inhibit employer violations? If not used, what explanation can there be?
3. Is safety equipment required; and, if so, should the employer or worker pay for it? Should failure to use this equipment affect liability? If so, how and why?

c. Equality and Discrimination

Questions arise as to who is protected; what is "discrimination;" and how is it proven? In a recent call for papers in a conference on the issues of discrimination, some of the facets of the term "discrimination" are highlighted as are the breadth and depth of regulation.

Introduction[42]

Hiroya Nakakubo and Takashi Araki

. . . .

What are the recent developments in employment discrimination law in your country? How do the newer types of discrimination differ from the "traditional" ones such as race and sex?

In Japan, the Equal Employment Opportunity Act was amended in 2006 for the second time since its enactment. By shifting from a ban on "discrimination against women" to "discrimination on the basis of sex," and by adopting the concept of indirect discrimination in certain areas, the amendment marked a significant development in Japanese sex discrimination law. In addition, in June 2007, other statutes were amended (1) to mandate that employers give equal opportunity regardless of age at the time of recruitment and hiring of workers and (2) to prohibit wage and benefits discrimination against part-time workers who are equivalent to regular workers in certain aspects. It appears that these measures are aimed at achieving broader employment-policy goals as well as vindicating equality rights of individual workers. While Japan has yet to prohibit discrimination because of disability, a new era of employment discrimination has certainly begun.

The same may be true of the European Union member states. The Framework Directive on Equal Treatment (2000/78/EC) added age, disability, and sexual orientation, among others, to the prohibited grounds, and the legislative body of each country has acted upon it. It is interesting to see how such new types of discrimination law operate along with the preexisting ones in achieving equality in the workplace. Meanwhile, in the U.S., where a federal statute has prohibited age discrimination in employment since 1967, the Supreme Court took the position in 2005 that prohibition of age discrimination is targeted at protection of older workers. Does this mean age discrimination is somewhat different from race or sex discrimination? And why don't we hear about discrimination against part-time employees in the U.S.? In other countries as well, employment discrimination is an area experiencing remarkable developments in recent years and we believe it presents fascinating issues for comparative discussion.

Proposed Outlines

Based on such an idea, we asked the participants to cover the following issues in their national papers.

1. General description of employment discrimination law in your country
    - Please present a brief historic overview of employment discrimination law. Have there been notable developments in recent years?

[42] Reproduced with the permission of Wolters Kluwer Law & Business from Hiroya Nakakubo & Takashi Araki, *Introduction*, New Developments in Employment Discrimination Law, © 2009, *available at* http://www.jil.go.jp/english/events_and_information/documents/clls08_intro.pdf (last visited May 18, 2011).

- Do you have statutes to prohibit discrimination on the following grounds?
  - race/ethnicity
  - sex
  - religion/beliefs
  - age
  - disability
  - sexual orientation
  - employment status (such as part-time and fixed-term contract). Are there any other grounds for discrimination prohibited by law?
- Do they cover all aspects of employment? Do you have special laws regarding wages, such as equal pay between men and women?
- Does your Constitution offer a basis for antidiscrimination statutes?
- What are the most typical cases of employment discrimination?

2. Structure of proof and remedy of employment discrimination
   - Taking the example of race and/or sex discrimination, what constitutes illegal discrimination and what are justifiable grounds for distinction or disparity?
   - Does your law mandate prohibition of so-called indirect discrimination? If yes, how are the courts applying the theory?
   - How do you compare newer types of discrimination (e.g., age, disability, employment status) with traditional ones (e.g., race, sex) in terms of definition and proof of discrimination?
   - Are there any particularly important issues of remedial procedure regarding employment discrimination cases?
3. Relationship between employment discrimination law and employment policy considerations
   - Did (or would) prohibition of age discrimination affect employment practices of your country? What about prohibition of employment-status discrimination?
   - Do you have measures to promote employment of elderly or disabled people? How do they relate to prohibition of discrimination because of such traits?
   - What are the merits and demerits of addressing employment issues from the standpoint of "discrimination"?
4. Finally, please identify the most important issue of employment discrimination in your country today and give your opinion as to its future direction.

Papers and the Discussion

The national papers presented at the seminar are contained in the following pages. They are all informative, and readers will find it interesting to see various developments of antidiscrimination laws in each country. While the growing importance of this area is commonly observed, there are differences in specific grounds covered by law and in legal and societal contexts in which they came to be addressed. It is impossible to summarize the contents of the papers here, but a word or two would be appropriate for each county by way of introduction.

In the United States, which led the history of employment discrimination law with the enactment of Title VII of the Civil Rights Act of 1964, the search for substantive equality is still in progress under a complex body of statutes and judicial interpretations, and the issue of contingent workforce is becoming serious.

In the United Kingdom, since the seminal Sex Discrimination Act of 1975, so many antidiscrimination statutes have been enacted under the influence of both the

U.S. law and the EC law that an effort is being made to streamline them, and there was a remarkable increase of litigation recently regarding equal pay.

In Germany, a comprehensive statute called the General Equal Employment Act, which prohibits discrimination based on race or ethnic origin, gender, religious or secular belief, disability, age, or sexual identity, was enacted in 2006 to comply with EC Directives, and the issue of age discrimination is raising particularly difficult problems.

In France, the legal framework to deal with EC Directives was adopted by a similarly comprehensive statute, the statute law of November 16, 2001, although it is only recently that the judicial court acknowledged the doctrine of indirect discrimination, and in 2006 the use of anonymous CV was mandated for larger employers.

In Australia, anti-discrimination laws developed relatively early with the adoption of the Racial Discrimination Act of 1975, followed by prohibition of sex discrimination in 1984, disability discrimination in 1992, and age discrimination in 2004, but their individual complaints-based model is showing its limits in promoting equality.

In Korea, prohibition of sex discrimination has been strengthened considerably in recent years through amendments of the Equal Employment Opportunity Act of 1987, and new laws were enacted to prohibit discrimination against fixed-term and part-time employees in 2006 and to prohibit disability discrimination in 2007.

In Taiwan, the Employment Service Act of 1992, a comprehensive statute prohibiting discrimination based on race, religion, country origin, sex, and disability, among others, was expanded in 2007 to cover age and sexual orientation, and another statute was enacted in 2002 to specifically deal with gender discrimination.

In Japan, despite the 2006 amendment of the Equal Employment Opportunity Act and the new legal provisions regarding age and part-time status mentioned above, anti-discrimination laws are still modest, leaving the stage of hiring largely unregulated, with a trend toward the approach of employment policy rather than human rights.

After presentations of these national papers, there was a general discussion among the participants. The issues include whether and in what respect the newer types of employment discrimination are different from the traditional "core;" the relationship between employment policy considerations and human rights aspect of equality; the position of employment discrimination law, especially its relation to the traditional labor law; and the role of the courts and the parties involved in the application of employment discrimination law. Naturally, there were no specific conclusions, but all the participants enjoyed the lively discussion and deepened their understanding of the theme.

Concluding Remarks

Before bringing the readers to the national papers, we would like to make three short points regarding employment discrimination law. Firstly, prohibition of employment discrimination is a valid cause. Nobody will doubt the evils of invidious discrimination, and law can and should play an important role in combating them. Secondly, on the other hand, anti-discrimination law is a powerful tool in that it condemns the violating employer as the discriminator. While such an effect is absolutely necessary in some areas, the legislature may choose to avoid it in other areas. Thirdly, even under anti-discrimination legislation, substantive equality is not an easy goal to achieve. Employment discrimination law may need to develop new tools and ideas in addition to negative rights of employees. It may also be necessary to improve general labor and employment laws so as to form the basis for substantive equality.

There is no ready-made recipe. Each country has to pursue the best portfolio of measures in view of its own conditions. However, it is definitely necessary and beneficial to learn from the systems and actual experiences of other countries. . . .

The problem of continuing widespread discrimination across the globe is described below in an ILO Report on Changing Patterns in the World of Work, notwithstanding longstanding ILO Conventions prohibiting discrimination, also listed below.

Discrimination in Employment and Occupation[43]

Juan Somavia

. . . .

Poverty and discrimination: A vicious cycle

96. Discrimination in employment and occupation often exacerbates or perpetuates poverty, while poverty furthers discrimination at work in a vicious cycle. Lack of work or work that is unproductive, insecure and unprotected are the main causes of the material deprivation and vulnerability that poor people experience. Discrimination in the labour market, by excluding members of certain groups from work or by impairing their chances of developing market relevant capabilities, lowers the quality of jobs to which they can aspire. This, in turn, enhances their risk of becoming or remaining poor, which further reduces their ability to obtain jobs that can lift them out of poverty.

Awareness increasing of discrimination as an abuse of rights and a waste of human capabilities

97. Discrimination in the world of work not only constitutes an abuse of fundamental principles and rights at work but is of huge cost to society. It deprives not just the individuals and communities concerned of the full benefits of their capabilities but also society as a whole. A global assessment of whether discrimination is increasing or decreasing is well beyond the scope of this Report and would in any case be very difficult to measure. However, it is perhaps possible to say that awareness of discrimination and the damage it does is increasing along with action to counter it.

Some signs of progress in the long struggle against gender discrimination in the world of work . . .

98. Throughout this Report, the gender dimensions of trends in the world of work have been identified. While the last 15 years have seen increasing female labour force participation rates and economic activity, a look at female employment by status, sector

[43] Juan Somavia, *Changing Patterns in the World of Work*, Int'l Labor Conference 9th Session 2006, *available at* http://www.ilo.org/public/english/standards/relm/ilc/ilc95/pdf/rep-i-c.pdf (last visited Sept. 23, 2010). Published by the International Labor Organization (2006) [Footnotes omitted]. (Juan Somavia is Director General of the ILO).

and wages or earnings reveals that: women are still less likely than men to be in regular wage and salaried employment; women continue to contribute more to household work than men; and women are more likely to earn less than men for the same type of work, even in occupations that are "traditionally female". Although the gender pay gap in manufacturing is still high in practically all countries, it has been narrowing in a number of countries. Some of the countries with the largest differences in female and male earnings are also those where the growth in female employment has been the fastest, such as Chile, China, Republic of Korea and Singapore.

In a number of countries, the key ILO Conventions – the Equal Remuneration Convention, 1951 (No. 100), the Discrimination (Employment and Occupation) Convention, 1958 (No. 111), the Workers with Family Responsibilities Convention, 1981 (No. 156), and the Maternity Protection Convention, 2000 (No. 183) – have influenced legislative measures to promote gender equality ... *but it remains deeply entrenched.*

99. But women still face many obstacles to equal integration in the labour market. Across nearly all occupations they still do not get equal pay for work of equal value or balanced benefits that would ensure equality with men. An overview of women in the world of work shows that they are still overwhelmingly segregated in occupations that tend to be at the lower end of the wage scale. In the United Kingdom, 60 per cent of women workers are employed in ten occupations, with the majority concentrated in "the five 'Cs': caring, cashiering, catering, cleaning and clerical. Women still also generally receive lower levels of education, making it much more difficult for them to get more productive and better-paid jobs. A further struggle for women today is to break through the "glass ceiling"; that is to gain access to opportunities for positions with decision-making authority and power. Women are also more likely to be engaged in the informal economy than are men and now represent nearly half of all international migrants.

Racial discrimination widespread

100. In the world of work, "racial discrimination" refers to arbitrary barriers to the advancement of members of linguistic communities or minorities whose identity is based on religious or cultural characteristics or even national origin. Ethnic minorities, indigenous and tribal peoples, "coloured" people and migrant workers are common victims of racial discrimination in employment and occupation. Patterns of racial discrimination against migrant workers, second and third generations of migrants and citizens of foreign origin have changed considerably with the intensification of global migration. Although nationality is what often leads to discrimination against non-nationals, race, colour and perceived religion are also factors. It is the perception of these workers as foreigners that may explain discriminatory behaviour against them. Throughout the world, migrant labour today is a vital asset in many sectors, including agriculture, construction, labour-intensive manufacturing, domestic work and the sex sector. This has, in some cases, led to competition between nationals – particularly in the marginal segments of the labour force – and migrant workers who are willing to work under inferior conditions. This, in turn, has reinforced sentiments of racism against the newcomers. Often, however, migrants take jobs that the locals refuse.

Risks of religious and cultural discrimination

101. The intensification of domestic and international migration has revealed the difficulty of reconciling social cohesion and inclusion with respect for religious and cultural

diversity. Particularly in the past decade, discrimination based on religion appears to have acquired greater significance. The present urgency of countering and preventing terrorism has fuelled sentiments of mutual fear and discrimination between Muslims and non-Muslims. It is clear, however, that any strategy aimed at tackling conflicts of interest should respect religious freedom; denying the basic right to follow a religion of one's choice can destabilize societies and generate violence. The fight against religious discrimination in employment and occupation, and concrete demonstrations that religious discrimination can be eliminated in the workplace, constitute a useful pathway to encourage religious tolerance in society. The dynamics and manifestations of religious discrimination in the workplace have not been researched as much, and as well, as other forms of discrimination. This is related in part to the difficulty of discussing a topic that is seen as pertaining to the private sphere and to the broader question of freedom of conscience.

Another constraint, as in the case of national origin or political opinion, deals with the legal prohibition in many countries on requesting or gathering information about religion. In practice, detecting and distinguishing religious discrimination from discrimination based on race or national extraction is often problematic because religion, race, and national extraction are closely intertwined; indeed, they are frequently perceived as together defining distinct cultural or ethnic identities.

Multiple discrimination highlights importance of a life-cycle approach to equality of opportunity

102. People experience discrimination in the labour market differently. The intensity or severity of the disadvantages they may confront depends on the number and interplay of the personal characteristics that generate discrimination against them. For example, a person may be different in race/colour, e.g., black; a black person may be a woman; a woman may have a physical disability; a person with a disability may be old; and one person can have all these characteristics, e.g., be an older, disabled, black woman, and therefore experience very complex forms of discrimination. Furthermore, discrimination has clear life-cycle dimensions. If no remedial action is taken, disadvantages tend to accumulate and intensify over time, with negative repercussions on life after work – and on society more generally. For example, gender inequalities in social protection reveal the perverse consequences of direct and indirect forms of discrimination against women throughout working life. Women's interrupted careers, lower pay, and fewer contributions, as well as earlier retirement records, mean that social protection benefits are, on average, lower for women than they are for men.

. . . .

The ILO has had a convention on discrimination since 1958. It prohibits any distinction, exclusion, or preference made on the basis of race, color, sex, religion, political opinion, national extraction, or social origin. As seen earlier, it has taken even the developed countries many years to get to the place they now are in – which is by no means free from employment discrimination on prohibited grounds. In addition to the ILO Convention, an example of national prohibition is illustrated by the U.S. regulations, both of which are detailed next.

Discrimination (Employment and Occupation) Convention, 1958 (No. 111)[44]

Adopted on 25 June 1958 by the General Conference of the International Labour at its forty-second session

Entry into force: 15 June 1960, in accordance with article 8

The General Conference of the International Labour Organisation,

Having been convened at Geneva by the Governing Body of the International Labour Office, and having met in its forty-second session on 4 June 1958, and

Having decided upon the adoption of certain proposals with regard to discrimination in the field of employment and occupation, which is the fourth item on the agenda of the session, and

Having determined that these proposals shall take the form of an international Convention, and

Considering that the Declaration of Philadelphia affirms that all human beings, irrespective of race, creed or sex, have the right to pursue both their material well-being and their spiritual development in conditions of freedom and dignity, of economic security and equal opportunity, and

Considering further that discrimination constitutes a violation of rights enunciated by the Universal Declaration of Human Rights,

Adopts this twenty-fifth day of June of the year one thousand nine hundred and fifty-eight the following Convention, which may be cited as the Discrimination (Employment and Occupation) Convention, 1958:

Article 1

1. For the purpose of this Convention the term "discrimination" includes:
   a. Any distinction, exclusion or preference made on the basis of race, colour, sex, religion, political opinion, national extraction or social origin, which has the effect of nullifying or impairing equality of opportunity or treatment in employment or occupation;
   b. Such other distinction, exclusion or preference which has the effect of nullifying or impairing equality of opportunity or treatment in employment or occupation as may be determined by the Member concerned after consultation with representative employers' and workers' organisations, where such exist, and with other appropriate bodies.
2. Any distinction, exclusion or preference in respect of a particular job based on the inherent requirements thereof shall not be deemed to be discrimination.

[44] United Nations, *Discrimination (Employment and Occupation) Convention, 1958 (No. 111)*, http://www2.ohchr.org/english/law/employment.htm (last visited Sept. 30, 2010).

3. For the purpose of this Convention the terms "employment" and "occupation" include access to vocational training, access to employment and to particular occupations, and terms and conditions of employment.

Article 2

Each Member for which this Convention is in force undertakes to declare and pursue a national policy designed to promote, by methods appropriate to national conditions and practice, equality of opportunity and treatment in respect of employment and occupation, with a view to eliminating any discrimination in respect thereof.

Article 3

Each Member for which this Convention is in force undertakes, by methods appropriate to national conditions and practice:

(a) To seek the co-operation of employers' and workers' organisations and other appropriate bodies in promoting the acceptance and observance of this policy;
(b) To enact such legislation and to promote such educational programmes as may be calculated to secure the acceptance and observance of the policy;
(c) To repeal any statutory provisions and modify any administrative instructions or practices which are inconsistent with the policy;
(d) To pursue the policy in respect of employment under the direct control of a national authority;
(e) To ensure observance of the policy in activities of vocational guidance, vocational training, and placement services under the direction of a national authority;
(f) To indicate in its annual reports on the application of the Convention the action taken in pursuance of the policy and the results secured by such action.

Article 4

Any measures affecting an individual who is justifiably suspected of, or engaged in, activities prejudicial to the security of the State shall not be deemed to be discrimination, provided that the individual concerned shall have the right to appeal to a competent body established in accordance with national practice.

Article 5

1 Special measures of protection or assistance provided in other Conventions or Recommendations adopted by the International Labour Conference shall not be deemed to be discrimination.

2 Any Member may, after consultation with representative employers' and workers' organisations, where such exist, determine that other special measures designed to meet the particular requirements of persons who, for reasons such as sex, age, disablement, family responsibilities or social or cultural status, are generally recognised to require special protection or assistance, shall not be deemed to be discrimination.

Article 6

Each Member which ratifies this Convention undertakes to apply it to non-metropolitan territories in accordance with the provisions of the Constitution of the International Labour Organisation.

Article 7

The formal ratifications of this Convention shall be communicated to the Director-General of the International Labour Office for registration.

Article 8

1. This Convention shall be binding only upon those Members of the International Labour Organisation whose ratifications have been registered with the Director-General.
2. It shall come into force twelve months after the date on which the ratifications of two Members have been registered with the Director General.
3. Thereafter, this Convention shall come into force for any Member twelve months after the date on which its ratification has been registered.

Article 9

1. A Member which has ratified this Convention may denounce it after the expiration of ten years from the date on which the Convention first comes into force, by an act communicated to the Director-General of the International Labour Office for registration. Such denunciation shall not take effect until one year after the date on which it is registered.
2. Each Member which has ratified this Convention and which does not, within the year following the expiration of the period of ten years mentioned in the preceding paragraph, exercise the right of denunciation provided for in this article, will be bound for another period of ten years and, thereafter, may denounce this Convention at the expiration of each period of ten years under the terms provided for in this article.

Article 10

1. The Director-General of the International Labour Office shall notify all Members of the International Labour Organisation of the registration of all ratifications and denunciations communicated to him by the Members of the Organisation.
2. When notifying the Members of the Organisation of the registration of the second ratification communicated to him, the Director-General shall draw the attention of the Members of the Organisation to the date upon which the Convention will come into force.

Article 11

The Director-General of the International Labour Office shall communicate to the Secretary-General of the United Nations for registration in accordance with Article 102 of the Charter of the United Nations full particulars of all ratifications and acts of denunciation registered by him in accordance with the provisions of the preceding articles.

Article 12

At such times as it may consider necessary the Governing Body of the International Labour Office shall present to the General Conference a report on the working of this Convention and shall examine the desirability of placing on the agenda of the Conference the question of its revision in whole or in part.

Article 13

1. Should the Conference adopt a new Convention revising this Convention in whole or in part, then, unless the new Convention otherwise provides:
   (a) The ratification by a Member of the new revising Convention shall ipso jure involve the immediate denunciation of this Convention, notwithstanding the provisions of article 9 above, if and when the new revising Convention shall have come into force;
   (b) As from the date when the new revising Convention comes into force this Convention shall cease to be open to ratification by the Members.
2. This Convention shall in any case remain in force in its actual form and content for those Members which have ratified it but have not ratified the revising Convention.

Article 14

The English and French versions of the text of this Convention are equally authoritative.

The foregoing is the authentic text of the Convention duly adopted by the General Conference of the International Labour Organisation during its forty-second session, which was held at Geneva and declared closed the twenty-sixth day of June 1958.

In faith whereof we have appended our signatures this fifth day of July 1958.

. . . .

Equal Employment Opportunity is THE LAW[45]

[U.S.]Private Employers, State and Local Governments, Educational Institutions, Employment Agencies and Labor Organizations

Applicants to and employees of most private employers, state and local governments, educational institutions, employment agencies and labor organizations are protected under Federal law from discrimination on the following bases:

[45] Equal Employment Opportunity is THE LAW (Nov. 2009), *available at* http://www.dol.gov/ofccp/regs/compliance/posters/pdf/eeopost.pdf (last visited Sept. 30, 2010).

Race, Color, Religion, Sex, National Origin
Title VII of the Civil Rights Act of 1964, as amended, protects applicants and employees from discrimination in hiring, promotion, discharge, pay, fringe benefits, job training, classification, referral, and other aspects of employment, on the basis of race, color, religion, sex (including pregnancy), or national origin. Religious discrimination includes failing to reasonably accommodate an employee's religious practices where the accommodation does not impose undue hardship.

Disability
Title I and Title V of the Americans with Disabilities Act of 1990, as amended, protect qualified individuals from discrimination on the basis of disability in hiring, promotion, discharge, pay, fringe benefits, job training, classification, referral, and other aspects of employment. Disability discrimination includes not making reasonable accommodation to the known physical or mental limitations of an otherwise qualified individual with a disability who is an applicant or employee, barring undue hardship.

Age
The Age Discrimination in Employment Act of 1967, as amended, protects applicants and employees 40 years of age or older from discrimination based on age in hiring, promotion, discharge, pay, fringe benefits, job training, classification, referral, and other aspects of employment.

Sex (Wages)
In addition to sex discrimination prohibited by Title VII of the Civil Rights Act, as amended, the Equal Pay Act of 1963, as amended, prohibits sex discrimination in the payment of wages to women and men performing substantially equal work, in jobs that require equal skill, effort, and responsibility, under similar working conditions, in the same establishment.

Genetics
Title II of the Genetic Information Nondiscrimination Act of 2008 protects applicants and employees from discrimination based on genetic information in hiring, promotion, discharge, pay, fringe benefits, job training, classification, referral, and other aspects of employment. GINA also restricts employers' acquisition of genetic information and strictly limits disclosure of genetic information. Genetic information includes information about genetic tests of applicants, employees, or their family members; the manifestation of diseases or disorders in family members (family medical history); and requests for or receipt of genetic services by applicants, employees, or their family members.

Retaliation
All of these Federal laws prohibit covered entities from retaliating against a person who files a charge of discrimination, participates in a discrimination proceeding, or otherwise opposes an unlawful employment practice.

QUESTIONS

1. Which statuses should be protected against discrimination? Does ILO Convention No. 111 circumscribe the types of statuses protected? If so, why? If not, why not?
2. How may "equality," "discrimination," and "affirmative action" be explained, distinguished, and reconciled under antidiscrimination laws?
3. Should unlawful discrimination include "unintentional," but indirect discrimination? Explain.
4. Should legal standards of protection vary, depending on which protected status is involved?
5. To what extent might cultural or political mores shape the approaches in antidiscrimination laws? Provide an example.
6. May these antidiscrimination prohibitions be waived by contract? If so, how; if not, why not? Is there a difference between a waiver and a substitution of forum to the arbitration forum or other forum?
7. Is there a difference in the U.S. and Civil Law approach to prohibiting discrimination?

C. LABOR UNIONS

1. *Global and International Labor Unions*

Global Unions, Frequently Asked Questions[46]

Global Unions is a term used to describe international trade union organizations that share many of the same traditions and values that includes the belief that trade unions must be free and independent and controlled by their members rather than by political parties, governments or employers.

Global Unions, in their constitutions, structures, and practices adhere to the principles of democratic governance. They are autonomous organizations controlled by their affiliated trade unions or trade union confederations. They all have periodic Congresses that set policy and elect governing bodies.

The International Trade Union Confederation (ITUC) and the Trade Union Advisory Committee (TUAC) to the OECD formulate policy and represent the trade union movement with larger society and with intergovernmental organizations. Their memberships and role are different although they have much in common.

Global Unions also include Global Union Federations (GUFs) that group national trade unions by sector or occupation and two organizations that are composed of national confederations of unions.

[46] *See generally* Global Unions, *Frequently Asked Questions*, http://www.global-unions.org/spip.php?rubrique2 (last visited December 9, 2011) [hereinafter "Global Unions FAQ"]; Global Union Primer, http://www.global-unions.org/IMG/pdf/GlobalUnionsPrimer.pdf (last visited Sept. 22, 2010) [hereinafter "Global Union Primer"].

The ITUC, with its worldwide union network, is based in Brussels, Belgium and has more than 230 affiliated union federations in 152 countries representing 150 million workers.[47]

The Trade Union Advisory Committee (TUAC) to the OECD is a forum for trade unions with the OECD. It is an international trade union organization which has consultative status with the OECD and its various committees.[48]

Together with the ITUC and the Trade Union Advisory Committee to the OECD, there are global union federations (GUFs), listed below, which are the international representatives of unions organizing in specific industry sectors or occupational groups.

Global Union Federations (GUFs)[49]

- EI – Education International
- BWI – Building and Wood Workers International
- IAEA – International Arts and Entertainment Alliance
- ICIEM – International Federation of Chemical, Energy, Mine, and General Workers' Unions
- IFJ – International Federation of Journalists
- IMF – International Metalworkers' Federation
- ITGLWF – International Textile, Garment, and Leather Workers' Federation
- ITF – International Transport Workers' Federation
- IUF – International Union of Food, Agricultural, Hotel, Restaurant, Catering, Tobacco, and Allied Workers' Associations
- PSI – Public Services International
- UNI – Union Network International

GUF's have negotiated more than sixty International Framework Agreements (IFAs) with multinational corporations.[50] IFAs are agreements on how a MNC will operate and are an alternative to codes of conduct, which are developed without the input of workers. IFAs, on the other hand, are the product of negotiations between MNCs and labor and as such more closely represent the interests of workers.[51] These agreements

47 *See also* INTERNATIONAL TRADE UNION CONFEDERATION, http://www.ituc-csi.org/ (last visited Sept. 22, 2010) [hereinafter "ITUC"].

48 TRADE UNION ADVISORY COMMITTEE TO THE OECD, TUAC, *About TUAC*, http://www.tuac.org/en/public/tuac/index.phtml (last visited Dec. 9, 2011) [hereinafter "TUAC"].

49 Global Union Primer, *supra* note 46. Global Unions FAQ, *supra* note 46.

50 *See* generally Global Unions, *Framework Agreements*, http://www.global-unions.org/spip.php?rubrique70 (last visited Sept. 30, 2010); Renee-Claude Drouin, *Promoting Fundamental Labor Rights Through International Framework Agreements: Practical Outcomes and Present Challenges*, 31 COMP. LAB. L. & POL'Y J. 591 (2010). *See also* Michael Fichter et al., *Regulating Labor Relations in Global Production Networks: Insights on International Framework Agreements*, INTERNATIONALE POLITIK UND GESELLSCHAFT (INTERNATIONAL POLITICS AND SOCIETY) no. 2 at 68 (June 2011).

51 The International Metalworkers' Federation (IMF) has created a "model IFA." A group consisting of equal numbers of employers and employees is set up in some IFAs to monitor implementation.

can facilitate worker representatives working closely with counterparts in developing countries to ensure the MNC is respecting the rights of all workers.[52] IFAs allow GUFs to get MNCs to agree in advance to bargain collectively with workers wherever they may be located; and, there is a clause in the IMF model IFA that allows the ILO, or a neutral third party agreed upon by both labor and employer representatives, to arbitrate disputes.[53]

There are also regional organizations organized under the ITUC including the Regional Organization for Asia and Pacific (ITUC Asia Pacific), originally founded in 1951. It is a regional organization of the International Trade Union Confederation representing trade unions from countries in Asia and Oceania. It has forty-eight affiliated organizations in twenty-eight countries, including South Korea and Japan, and claims a membership of seventeen million people.

The AFL-CIO is affiliated with the International Trade Union Confederation (ITUC) – the worldwide union network. Currently, the AFL-CIO president serves on the Steering Committee and Executive Board of the ITUC and also serves as the president of the Trade Union Advisory Committee to the Organization for Economic Cooperation and Development.

ITUC and TUAC formulate policy and represent the trade union movement with larger society and with intergovernmental organizations. Their memberships and role are different although they have much in common.

Further detail on the organizational structures and functions of these global unions, including GUFs, is provided next.[54]

International Trade Union Confederation (ITUC)[55]

The ITUC's primary mission is the promotion and defense of workers' rights and interests, through international cooperation between trade unions, global campaigning and advocacy within the major global institutions. The Programme Document adopted at

Owen E. Herrnstadt, *Are International Framework Agreements a Path to Corporate Social Responsibility?*, 10 U. PA. J. BUS. & EMP. L. 187 (2007).

52 *See* STEFAN RUB, SOCIAL MINIMUM STANDARDS IN MULTINATIONAL GROUPS: ARGUMENTS AND PRACTICAL HELP TO INITIATE AND IMPLEMENT AN INTERNATIONAL FRAMEWORK AGREEMENT (2004), *available at* http://www.fh-fulda.de/fileadmin/Fachbereich_SK/FG-Arbbez/IGM-Handlungshilfe_IFAs_englisch2004.pdf (last visited Sept. 30, 2010).

53 International Metalworkers' Federation (IMF), *IMF Model International Framework Agreement*, *available at* http://www.imfmetal.org/files/05051023014 87/ifamodel_total_english.pdf (last visited Sept. 30, 2010).

54 Global Union Primer, *supra* note 46; ITUC, *supra* note 47; WORLD FEDERATION OF TRADE UNIONS (WFTU), http://www.wftucentral.org (last visited June 7, 2011).

55 *See* TUAC, *About Us*, http://www.ituc-csi.org/about-us.html (last visited December 9, 2011).

the ITUC founding Congress sets out the Confederation's overall policy framework. Its main areas of activity include: trade union and human rights; economy, society and the workplace; equality and non-discrimination; international solidarity.

The ITUC adheres to the principles of trade union democracy and independence, as set out in its Constitution. It is governed by four-yearly world congresses, a General Council and an Executive Bureau.

. . . .

The ITUC has close relations with the Global Union Federations and the Trade Union Advisory Committee to the OECD (TUAC), working together through the Global Unions Council.

The ITUC works closely with the International Labor Organization. It maintains contacts with several other UN Specialized Agencies.

Along with its Regional Organizations and their sub-offices, the ITUC has offices in Amman, Geneva, Moscow, New York, Sarajevo, Vilnius and Washington DC.

Trade Union Advisory Committee (TUAC) to the OECD[56]

The Trade Union Advisory Committee (TUAC) to the OECD is an interface for trade unions with the OECD. It is an international trade union organization which has consultative status with the OECD and its various committees.

TUAC's origins go back to 1948 when it was founded as a trade union advisory committee for the European Recovery Programme – the Marshall Plan. When the OECD was created in its current form in 1962 as an intergovernmental policy making body, TUAC continued its work of representing organized labor's views to the new organization. TUAC's role is to help ensure that global markets are balanced by an effective social dimension. Through regular consultations with various OECD committees, the secretariat, and member governments TUAC coordinates and represents the views of the trade union movement in the industrialized countries. It is also responsible for coordinating the trade union input to the annual G8 economic summits and employment conferences.

TUAC's affiliates consist of over 58 national trade union centres in the 30 OECD industrialized countries which together represent some 66 million workers. It is they who finance TUAC activities decide priorities and policy and elect the TUAC officers.

The large majority of TUAC affiliates' are also affiliated to the International Trade Union Confederation (ITUC). Most European affiliates also belong to the European Trade Union Confederation (ETUC). TUAC also works closely with Global Union Federations to ensure effective trade union input to OECD sectoral work such as education, public sector management, steel, or maritime transport.

TUAC operates through a small secretariat, based in Paris, of 5 policy staff and 3 administrative staff. John Evans is the General Secretary of TUAC.

---

[56] TUAC, *About TUAC*, http://www.tuac.org/en/public/tuac/index.phtml.

Global Union Federations GUFs (Sectoral)
What Do the Global Union Federations (GUFs) Do?[57]

Just as the roles of the ITUC and TUAC correspond to the policy and representation responsibilities of their national affiliates, the GUFs are the extensions of their national respective affiliates. The GUFs that have a primarily private sector membership group unions in sectors, but also, increasingly, inside common employers or supply/production/service chains. This role has assumed greater importance with the integration of the global economy and global production.

Global Union Federations have negotiated over 60 international framework agreements with major multinational enterprises. IFAs are a visible sign of growing contact and relations of GUFs with their corporate counterparts. Nearly all GUFs group several sectors and are structured in a way that accommodates sectoral differences. Greater detail is provided in descriptions of specific GUFs.

There are GUFs that represent mainly public sector workers. They also focus on specific sectors within their membership and seek to reinforce the rights and influence of their affiliates. They provide services and, like the ITUC and the TUAC, focus a great deal on public policy issues that affect public service and governance. The major, predominantly public service GUFs are PSI and EI although many other GUFs have public sector membership.

How do Global Unions help workers organize and bargain?

The roles of TUAC and ITUC on the one hand and GUFs on the other are complementary and overlap to some degree in the areas of organizing and collective bargaining. The ITUC and TUAC in the context of their respective mandates TUAC seek to create an enabling environment for organizing and bargaining. Organizing and bargaining depend on a legal framework that protects those rights and credible enforcement that makes them real. The fundamental rights in those areas are reflected in conventions of the tripartite (worker, employer, and government representation) International Labor Organization, including, but not limited to conventions 87 on freedom of association and the right to organize and convention 98 on the right to collective bargaining.

In addition to using the standards and procedures of the ILO, work and intervention with other international bodies, including the World Bank and the OECD (in the case of TUAC) is often designed to put pressure on governments and/or companies to respect the rights to organize and bargain. GUFs are also often involved with or associated with this action, initiate them or, in some cases, act on their own.

Much of the work of GUFs, including in their campaigns and relations with multinational enterprises, focuses on improving the organizing and industrial relations strength of their affiliates. It is in that connection that they often work with ITUC and TUAC. Although the contents of IFAs vary, they all contain language related to the respect of principles contained in the key conventions of the ILO and many go beyond that to more specifically address the problem of employer opposition to efforts by workers to form independent trade unions.

[57] Global Unions FAQ, *supra* note 46.

How and why do they co-operate?

Trade unions join together for the same reason that workers do, to be in a stronger position to defend their interests and to act. This is true for the international trade union organizations as well. Industrial strength often effectively combines with political strength to enhance the overall influence of the trade union movement.

However, most of the co-operation among Global Unions involves a limited number. To give one example, in recent years, several international framework agreements have been negotiated and signed with companies by more than one GUF.[58]

In January of 2007, the Council of Global Unions was created. It is composed of GUFs, the ITUC, and TUAC. Its role is to stimulate co-operation in agreed, priority areas and to reinforce work already being carried out by Global Unions.

. . . .

Further Illustrations of Global Unions: UNI Global Union[59]

UNI Global Union provides a voice and a platform for workers at the international level in jobs ranging from the night janitor in your office block to the big-time Hollywood director of your favorite movie. With 20 million workers in 900 unions worldwide UNI fosters international solidarity and provides a voice at the international level for all its members.

UNI is focusing on Global Agreements to achieve power and parity for workers at multinational corporations. In the age of globalization this is more important than ever. The global economy is in crisis and workers are bearing a disproportionate part of the burden. The solution to the crisis must include a global employment strategy that creates sustainable well-paying employment with bargaining rights.

As part of its Organize and Recognize campaign, UNI works with its member unions to ensure that union organizing and bargaining rights are enshrined in law. In countries where these laws do not exist, UNI is joining the fight to get them on the books. Where these laws do exist, UNI works with unions, the International Labor Organization and other groups to ensure that they are enforced. UNI also works in developing countries to build trade unions where there are none and to offer training and capacity building to its members.

UNI was created on January 1, 2000, by members of The Communications International, FIET (the white collar and services global union), the International Graphical Federation and the Media and Entertainment International.

58 For further discussion on international framework agreements, *see*, Michael Fichter et al., *Regulating Labor Relations in Global Networks: Insights on International Framework Agreements*, Internationale Politik & Gesellschaft (INT'L POL. & SOC'Y), June 2011, at 68–86.

59 UNI GLOBAL UNION, About Us, http://www.uniglobalunion.org/Apps/iportal.nsf/pages/20090122_jh47En; for Global Partners, *see* http://www.uniglobalunion.org/Apps/iportal.nsf/pages/20090202_vb8yEn (last visited Dec. 9, 2011). http://www.uniglobalunion.org/Apps/iportal.nsf/pages/homeEn (last visited Sept 30, 2010).

Global Partners

Development cooperation requires a genuine partnership between:

- national trade unions and workers organizations
- UNI and its regional organizations
- UNI affiliates in donor countries, and
- funding organizations.

This chain of partnership is important because it makes us stronger to create synergies in the exchange of experience and understanding of other people's living and working conditions in a global economy. It provides the opportunity to improve education and training of union members, to develop union management and administration and to advance recruitment and organizing strategies.

An important element in the partnership is . . . affiliates in donor countries which are involved in project work and contribute financially and with human resources to the success of projects. UNI is a multi-sector global union federation. It is vital for UNI and its integration at a global, regional and national level that along with sector-specific projects there are also projects covering all affiliates representing a number of sectors in one country, as well as cross-sector regional projects. Where more than one affiliate is involved in one country the project work should be done through a joint liaison committee. For the bulk of the development and regions' department projects UNI relies on finance from funding organizations. As a rule, direct relations with funding organizations are only maintained by the development and regions' department at Head Office.

. . . .

International Arts and Entertainment Alliance (IAEA)[60]

This Global Union Federation comprising FIM, FIA and UNI-MEI is a truly independent and representative body, recognized by ITUC and, with respect to its European activities, by ETUC. Recent activities have included workshops in Latin America through the regional coordination of IAEA (CREA) to promote the rights of workers in film production. Alliance members are recognized by WIPO, UNESCO and the ILO and the Council of Europe and the European Union. Additionally, FIM holds observer status with the International Organization of the Francophonie.

The International Federation of Actors (FIA) was set up in 1952 by the French performers' union and its sister organization in the UK and currently represents more than 100 performers' unions, guilds and professional associations in over 75 countries.

The International Federation of Musicians (FIM), founded in 1948, is the only international organization representing musicians worldwide. It has member unions in over 70 countries.

UNI-MEI, the media and entertainment section of Union Network International represents broadcasting workers, film and theatre technicians and staff, specific creative

[60] Global Unions, *IAEA*, http://www.global-unions.org/international-arts-and,60.html (last visited June 7, 2011).

and professional groups (writers, screenwriters, directors, visual artists), other arts and entertainment workers, as well as workers in sports and a variety of related groups.

. . . .

QUESTIONS

1. Explain the relationships of a global union and a GUF.
2. What is the nature and functions of the previously listed unions in their interaction with employers?
3. Are global unions significant in the protection of workers' rights; if so, why and how?
4. Explain a framework agreement.

---

2. *National Labor Unions*

Membership: East Asian Trade Union Federations (Selected Countries and U.S.)[61]

Country	Trade union federations	Membership	Website
China PRC	*All-China Federation of Trade Unions* (ACFTU) 中华全国总工会 *Zhōnghuá Quánguó Zǒnggōng Huì*	134 million	*ACFTU*
Japan	*Japanese Trade Union Confederation* (JTUC-RENGO) 日本労働組合総連合会 *Nihon Rōdōkumiai Sōrengōkai National Confederation of Trade Unions* (Zenroren) 全国労働組合総連合 *National Trade Union Council* (Zenrokyo)	6.6 million (RENGO) 846,362 (Zenroren) 139,424 (Zenrokyo)	*RENGO* *Zenroren* *Zenrokyo*
Korea ROK	*Korean Confederation of Trade Unions* (KCTU) 전국민주노동조합총연맹 *Jeon-guk Minju Nodong Johap Chongyeonmaeng Korean Federation of Trade Unions* (KFTU) 한국노동조합총연맹 *Hanguk Nodong Johap Chongyeonmaeng*	682,418 (KCTU) 740,308 (FKTU)	*KCTU* *KFTU*
United States of America USA	American Federation of Labour-Congress of Industrial Organizations (AFL-CIO) Change to Win Federation (CTW) Industrial Workers of the World (IWW)	9,000,000+ (AFL) 6,000,000 (CTW) 2,000 (IWW)	*AFL* *CTW* *IWW*

---

[61] *List of federations of trade unions*, WIKIPEDIA, http://en.wikipedia.org/wiki/List_of_federations_of_trade_unions (last visited June 7, 2011).

The South Korean KFTU and the KCTU and the U.S. AFL-CIO are used as illustrative national centers and are listed next, with self-described responsibilities.

Korean Federation of Trade Unions (KFTU)[62]

The Korean Federation of Trade Unions (KFTU) was formed in 1961 after a military coup, and the dissolution of the General Federation of Korean Trade Unions and its affiliates. The KFTU was placed under the guidance of the military authorities.

The KFTU was the sole legal trade union center in South Korea until the Korean Confederation of Trade Unions was finally recognized in November, 1999.

The KFTU is affiliated with the International Trade Union Confederation and in 2007 had 740,308 members.[63]

Structure of KFTU[64]

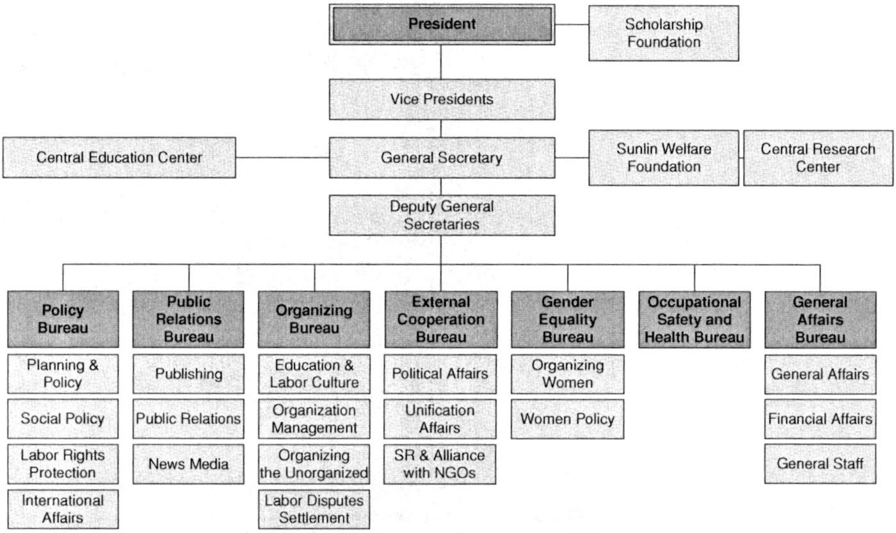

FIGURE 1. Federation of Korean Trade Unions

. . . .

Korean Confederation of Trade Unions (KCTU)[65]

The Korean Confederation of Trade Unions (KCTU) is a national trade union centre officially established in 1995 as an independent alternative to the Korean Federation of

[62] FEDERATION OF KOREAN TRADE UNIONS (FKTU), http://www.fktu.or.kr/ (last visited June 7, 2011).

[63] FKTU, *Affiliates*, http://www.fktu.or.kr/about/affiliates.asp (last visited June 7, 2011) [hereinafter "Affiliates"].

[64] *Id.*

[65] Korean Confederation of Trade Unions, *This is KCTU*, http://kctu.org/kctu (last visited May 18, 2011) [hereinafter "KCTU"].

Trade Unions. With 682,418 members in 2007, the KCTU accounted for 40.6% of trade union members in South Korea. The KCTU has more than 1,200 affiliated enterprise level trade unions. It is the second largest union with 682,418 members in 2007.

The Birth

On November 13, 1994, the Preparatory Committee for Korean Confederation of Trade Unions was launched to build on the work of the previous body. Its main task was to prepare and facilitate the reorganisation of individual unions into various industrial federations and the formation of the Confederation. After one year, the Korean Confederation of Trade Unions (KCTU, Minju Nochong) was officially established on November 11, 1995, with 862 enterprise unions and a total membership of 418,000. As of June 1997, the Korean Confederation of Trade Unions has increased its membership to over 526,300 in 1,144 unions. In less than two years since the establishment, KCTU has emerged, not only as the representative organisation of Korean workers and the trade union movement, but a leading force for democratisation. . . .

. . . .

Commitment to International Solidarity: KCTU's growth and success in making demands on the government are significantly attributable to international support, as seen in full force for the first time during the General Strike. To strengthen the capability of workers' movements around the world, KCTU is actively participating in organisations internationally and in the Asia-Pacific region, including the ICFTU and ITSs. KCTU rejects state-unionism and any unionism controlled by employers, and fully supports democratic trade union movements across borders through joint activities in education, policy development, and campaigns. In order to engender greater international worker solidarity, KCTU is also committed to supporting workers' fighting abuse by Korean companies abroad and struggling for their trade union rights.

. . . .

KCTU Structures[66]

Decision-Making Bodies
National Congress (statutory session once a year in January)
Central Committee (statutory sessions 4 times a year)
Executive Bodies
Central Executive Committee (statutory sessions once a month)
Standing Executive Commitee (weekly)
Permanent Committee
Women's Committee
Industrial Relations Taskforce Committee
Social Security Committee
Reunification Committee
Political Empowerment Committee
Education Committee
Special Committee for Dismissed Workers

66 *Id.*

Special Committee
Trade Union Movement Development Strategy Committee
Regional Councils
14 Province level regional councils with district level offices in each of the councils
Regional councils have their own decision making structures and elects their own leaders
Regional councils are at the same time extension of the National Secretariat
Secretariat

U.S. National Center[67]

The American Federation of Labor and Congress of Industrial Organizations (AFL-CIO) is a voluntary federation of 57 national and international labor unions. The AFL-CIO was created in 1955 by the merger of the AFL and the CIO.

The AFL-CIO union movement represents 11.5 million members, including 3 million members in Working America, its community affiliate. We are teachers and miners, firefighters and farm workers, bakers and engineers, pilots and public employees, doctors and nurses, painters and plumbers – and more.

Governance[68]

The AFL-CIO is governed by its members, who meet in a quadrennial convention. Each member union elects delegates, based on proportional representation. The AFL-CIO's state federations, central and local labor councils, constitutional departments, and constituent groups are also entitled to delegates.

The delegates elect officers and vice presidents, debate and approve policy, and set dues.

Executive Council

The AFL-CIO has three executive officers: president, secretary-treasurer and executive vice president. The executive vice president is the most recently established office; it was created by constitutional amendment in 1995. Each officer's term is four years, and elections occur at the quadrennial convention.

. . . .

The AFL-CIO membership also elects 43 vice presidents at each convention, who have a term of four years. Election is by plurality, with the top 43 candidates with the highest votes winning office. Article VI, Sec. 5, of the AFL-CIO constitution permits the president of the federation to appoint up to three additional vice presidents during the period when the convention is not in session, in order to increase the racial, gender, ethnic and sexual diversity of the executive council.

[67] *Global Unions*, AFL-CIO, http://www.aflcio.org/aboutus/globalunions (last visited Sept. 30, 2010) [hereinafter AFL-CIO Global Unions].
[68] *Id.*

The three officers and the vice presidents form the executive council, which is the federation's governing body between quadrennial conventions. It is required to meet twice a year, and in practice meets four or five times a year. It passes resolutions, directly oversees AFL-CIO's legislative program, and has other duties. In 2005, the AFL-CIO constitution was changed to permit the executive council to form "Industrial Coordinating Committees" based on geography, employer, occupation, or other appropriate subdivisions to coordinate the organizing and collective bargaining work of the member unions.

Executive Committee

An executive committee was authorized by constitutional change in 2005. The executive committee is composed of the president, vice presidents from the 10 largest affiliates, and nine other vice presidents chosen in consultation with the executive council. The other two officers are non-voting ex officio members. The executive committee governs the AFL-CIO between meetings of the executive council, approves its budget, and issues charters (two duties formerly discharged by the executive council). It is required to meet at least four times a year, and in practice meets on an as-needed basis (which may mean once a month or more).

General Board

The AFL-CIO also has a General Board. Its members are the AFL-CIO executive council, the chief executive officer of each member union, the president of each AFL-CIO constitutional department, and four regional representatives elected by the AFL-CIO's state federations. The General Board's duties are very limited. It only takes up matters referred to it by the executive council, but referrals are rare. However, because of the sensitive nature of political endorsements and the advisability of consensus when making them, the General Board traditionally is the body that provides the AFL-CIO's endorsement of candidates for president and vice president of the United States.

State and Local Bodies

Article XIV of the AFL-CIO constitution permits the AFL-CIO to charter and organize state, regional, local and city-wide bodies. They are commonly called "state federations" and "central labor councils" (CLCs), although the names of the various bodies varies widely at the local and regional level. Each body has its own charter, which establishes its jurisdiction, governance structure, mission, and more. Jurisdiction tends to be geopolitical: Each state or territory has its own "state federation." In large cities, there is usually a CLC covering the city. Outside large cities, CLCs tend to be regional (to achieve an economy of scale in terms of dues, administrative effectiveness, etc.). State federations and CLCs are each entitled to representation and voting rights at the quadrennial convention.

The duties of state federations differ from those of CLCs. State federations tend to focus on state legislative lobbying, statewide economic policy, state elections, and other issues of a more over-arching nature. CLCs tend to focus on county or city lobbying, city or county elections, county or city zoning and other economic issues, and more local needs.

Both state federations and CLCs work to mobilize members around organizing campaigns, collective bargaining campaigns, electoral politics, lobbying (most often rallies and demonstrations), strikes, picketing, boycotts, and similar needs.

Although the AFL-CIO constitution requires that all state and local unions affiliate with the appropriate state and local AFL-CIO body, in practice this is not enforced. Many unions do not affiliate with their state federation or CLC, or affiliate only a portion of their membership, leaving state feds and CLCs chronically short of funds.

Interestingly, the AFL-CIO constitution permits international unions to pay state fed and CLC dues directly, rather than have each local or state fed pay them. This relieves each union's state and local affiliates of the administrative duty of assessing, collecting and paying the dues. International unions assess the AFL-CIO dues themselves, and collect them on top of their own dues-generating mechanisms or simply pay them out of the dues the international collects. But not all international unions pay their required state fed and CLC dues.

. . . .

As of January 2007, there are six AFL-CIO constitutionally mandated departments:

- Building and Construction Trades Department, AFL-CIO
- Maritime Trades Department, AFL-CIO
- Metal Trades Department, AFL-CIO
- Department for Professional Employees, AFL-CIO
- Transportation Trades Department, AFL-CIO
- Union Label Department, AFL-CIO

Constituency Groups

"Constituency groups" are nonprofit, nonpartisan organizations chartered and funded by the AFL-CIO to enhance the representational effectiveness of various under-represented groups. Usually they serve as a means to enhance the organizing of new members and as voter registration and mobilization bodies.

. . . .

Allied Organizations

"Allied organizations" are nonprofit, nonpartisan organizations chartered and funded by the AFL-CIO to serve certain policy goals of the federation.

. . . .

The current three allied organizations are all self-sustaining. Their boards are interlocking with the AFL-CIO executive council.

As of January 2007, there are three allied organizations:

- American Center for International Labor Solidarity
- International Labor Communications Association
- Working for America Institute

Allied groups

"Allied groups" are organizations that have more informal relationships to the AFL-CIO. Some, like the Labor and Working-Class History Association, are truly independent organizations that wish to work very closely with the AFL-CIO and promote its mission and goals. Others, like American Rights at Work, are independent in name only; they are nonprofit, nonpartisan organizations with their own articles of incorporation, charter, governance structure, etc., but are funded largely by the AFL-CIO, and their boards are dominated by its directors.

. . . .

International policy

The AFL-CIO is affiliated to the Brussels-based International Trade Union Confederation, formed November 1, 2006, and incorporating the member organizations of the International Confederation of Free Trade Unions, of which the AFL-CIO had long been part. The ITUC is the most representative international labor grouping.

History

For the history of the AFL-CIO prior to and including the merger see American Federation of Labor and Congress of Industrial Organizations and Labor unions in the United States.

In 2003, the AFL-CIO began an intense internal debate over the future of the labor movement in the United States with the creation of the New Unity Partnership (NUP), a loose coalition of some of the AFL-CIO's largest unions. This debate intensified in 2004, after the defeat of labor-backed candidate John Kerry in the November 2004 U.S. presidential election. The NUP's program for reform of the federation included reduction of the central bureaucracy, more money spent on organizing new members rather than on electoral politics, and a restructuring of unions and locals, eliminating some smaller locals and focusing more along the lines of industrial unionism.

In 2005, the NUP dissolved and the Change to Win Federation formed, threatening to secede from the AFL-CIO if its demands for major reorganization were not met. As the AFL-CIO prepared for its 50th anniversary convention in late July, three of the federations' four largest unions announced their withdrawal from the federation: the Service Employees International Union (SEIU), the International Brotherhood of Teamsters (The Teamsters) and the United Food and Commercial Workers International Union (UFCW). The Laborers' International Union of North America and the United Farm Workers remain members of both the AFL-CIO and Change to Win Federation.

Change to Win Union

It was founded in September 2005 by seven unions and six million workers devoted to building a movement of working people with the power to provide workers a paycheck that supports a family, universal, affordable health care, a secure retirement, and dignity on the job. Change to Win's primary focus is to unite the 50 million workers in Change to Win affiliate industries whose jobs cannot be outsourced and who are vital to the global economy – but who are not given a chance to reach the middle class. We are uniting workers in industries such as hospitality, construction, retail, food processing, health care, trucking, and transportation among others. The seven affiliated unions are: International Brotherhood of Teamsters, Laborers' International Union of North America, Service Employees International Union, UNITE HERE, United Brotherhood of Carpenters and Joiners of America, United Farm Workers of America, and United Food and Commercial Workers International Union. [Author: By 2010, three of these unions, the Carpenters, Laborers, and UNITE HERE, had withdrawn their membership and returned to the AFL-CIO.]

. . . .

---

3. *Roles of Unions*

Unions operate differently in each country, although usually there are many common characteristics. Each has its own constitution that orders its administration. At the national level, unions are typically established under a constitution with subordinate regional and local affiliates often around occupational or industrial lines, agreeing to abide by the national constitution and to financially contribute to the national union. In return, the national union provides support to its regional and local affiliates. Some are seen as independent from the government, such as the AFL-CIO and its affiliates in the United States; others have a close alignment with the government, such as the All China Federation of Unions (ACFTU) in China.

Functions of the unions also vary. For example, in the United States the union is perceived to be the champion of the worker and to protect worker rights and increase their wages and benefits – a singular role obtained through collective bargaining and enforcement of the resulting agreement and under pertinent labor laws. In Japan, an added role of the unions, under its enterprise union system, is to also look out for the economic welfare of the employer – a dual role. In China, the union, the All China Federation of Trade Unions (ACFTU), has multiple roles, including the role to guard and promote the government's agenda and that of the Chinese Communist Party – a triple or quadruple role. It appears to be slowly disengaging from its role as the enforcer of employer interests to the extent they are separable from the preceding roles.

Another contrast is the use of strikes. In the United States, they are used as an economic club by the unions, or as a threat of the same, to get the employer to give concessions. In China, strikes are not outlawed and do occur, but the union by law is responsible for bringing the employer and workers back together, rather than calling for or supporting a strike. In Japan, unions would not usually call a strike; rather "strikes" traditionally take the form of working while wearing armbands in protest of employer positions. In South Korea, strikes are hard-fought battles, often erupting in disturbances.

---

4. *Alternatives to Unions*

European Works Councils[69]

European Works Councils (EWCs) are standing bodies providing for the information and consultation of employees in Community-scale undertakings and Community-scale groups of undertakings as required by the 1994 European Works Council Directive (Directive 94/45/EC). EWCs are highly significant in terms of European industrial relations since they represent the first genuinely European institution of interest representation at enterprise level. They reflect a growing recognition of the need to respond to the 'europeanisation' of business emerging from the Single European Market by supplementing existing national channels of information and consultation, a goal which was expressed in the Social Charter of 1989 and the accompanying Social Action Programme.

In this context, information refers to the transmission by the employer to the employee representatives of data in order to enable them to acquaint themselves with the subject matter and to examine it. Consultation is a process of exchange of views and establishment of dialogue between the employee representatives and the employer.

A requirement for the provision of information in the enterprise and consultation in the enterprise with employee representatives was introduced by Council Directive 2002/14 establishing a framework for informing employees and consulting with them in the European Community. It applies to all undertakings employing at least 50 employees or EU establishments employing at least 20 employees. The directive is estimated to cover fewer than 3% of all companies, yet these represent about half of all employees in the EU. Member States were obliged to implement the directive into national law by 23 March 2005.

The practical arrangements for information and consultation are to be determined by Member States, which can entrust management and labour to make voluntary agreements, including different arrangements, 'while respecting the principles set out in Article 1. For example, Article 1(3) requires that:

> When defining or implementing practical arrangements for information and consultation, the employer and the employees' representatives shall work in a spirit of cooperation and with due regard for their reciprocal rights and obligations, taking into account the interests both of the undertaking or establishment and of the employees.

The practical arrangements which Member States are required to determine for information and consultation incorporates a process of nine sequential stages:

- transmission of information/data (Article 2(f));
- acquaintance with an examination of data (Article 2(f));
- conduct of an adequate study (Article 4(3));
- preparation for consultation (Article 4(3));
- formulation of an opinion (Article 4(4)(c));

[69] European Foundation for the Improvement of Living and Working Conditions, *European Works Councils*, http://www.eurofound.europa.eu/areas/industrialrelations/dictionary/definitions/europeanworkscouncils.htm (last updated May 26, 2009).

- meeting (Article 4(4)(d));
- employer's reasoned response to opinion (Article 4(4)(d));
- exchange of views and establishment of dialogue (Article 2(g));
- discussion (Article 4(4)(b)) 'with a view to reaching an agreement on decisions' (Article 4(4)(e)).

Previous EC law has provided for the information and consultation of employees in specific circumstances, such as collective redundancy or transfer of an undertaking, or over issues like health and safety. The 1994 Directive on European Works Councils provided for information and consultation on certain matters in multinational companies and groups. Directive 2002/14 is highly significant since it is the first EC law stipulating a general obligation to inform and consult employees. Arguably, it establishes a European social model of mandatory employee representation and mandatory information and consultation of employee representatives.

The extent of the changes required by the directive to existing systems of information and consultation and workplace representation has varied considerably between countries. According to a report published by the European Foundation for the Improvement of Living and Working Conditions (Eurofound), it is possible to distinguish three broad groups among the EU Member States. In the first group of countries, characterised by 'continental' statutory works council systems, existing arrangements were considered as meeting the directive's requirements, following only minor amendments. In the second group, mostly new Member States and Nordic countries, some changes to the respective countries' information and consultation systems were required to conform to the directive, but not radical change. The third group consists of countries characterised by a voluntarist industrial relations tradition, the primacy of trade unions as a representation channel or the relatively recent adaptation of industrial relations systems to Community law. These countries have had to make major changes in response to the directive.

In the resolution of 19 February 2009 on the implementation of the directive, the European Parliament acknowledges that there is a need for a more effective transposition of the directive. Given that in the past some Member States have failed to take account of certain groups – young workers, women working part-time, or workers employed for short periods on fixed-term contracts – the European Parliament urged the Member States to ensure that the calculation of thresholds is always based on the actual number of workers. Furthermore, the Parliament calls on the Member States to define precisely the term 'information', leaving no scope for alternative interpretations. Finally, the Parliament emphasises the importance of effective, proportional and dissuasive sanctions against employers who fail to comply with the obligations laid down in the directive

The thresholds required for an enterprise to be covered by the directive are, for a Community-scale undertaking, 'at least 1,000 employees within the Member States and at least 150 employees in each of at least two Member States' (Article 2(1)(a)). It is left to Member States to decide on the mechanism for determining the selection of employee representatives, 'in accordance with the principle of subsidiarity'.

Essentially, the aim of the directive is to promote voluntary agreements on the constitution and operation of EWCs. This operated in two ways. First, the directive allowed multinational companies (MNCs) and groups covered by the directive to reach voluntary agreements with employee representatives on the establishment of EWCs before the directive actually came into force on 22 September 1996. These so-called 'Article 13 agreements' were exempt from the provisions specified in the directive, for the lifespan of the agreement, as long as they covered the entire workforce of the group within the scope of the directive.

Second, since 22 September 1996, negotiations to establish EWCs have been governed by the procedures under Article 6 of the directive, which requires the formation of a special negotiating body (SNB). Crucially, it is up to the undertaking's central management and the SNB to agree on the precise form and function of their EWC. This includes, for example, the signatory parties; coverage, composition, numbers and seat allocation; the terms of office; functions and procedure; venue, frequency and duration of meetings; financial and material resources; duration of the agreement and the procedure for its renegotiation; issues for information and consultation; experts; confidentiality; select committee operations; employee-side pre-meetings; rules on deputies to employee representatives; languages policy and interpretation provided; procedure for agreeing the agenda; procedure for drawing up minutes or other records; and communication to employees generally. Only if there is a failure to agree between the parties, or if they so choose, is the 'fallback position' triggered of the provisions detailed in the Annex to the Directive.

By no means have all MNCs established EWCs. According to the European Trade Union Institute (ETUI) EWC database, some 881 EWCs in 858 multinational companies were active in 2008, representing 15.6 million workers. These represent only a third of all companies concerned. This is due to the fact that the introduction of EWCs is not automatic but requires either the initiative of central management or 'the written request of at least 100 employees or their representatives in at least two undertakings or establishments in at least two different Member States' (Article 5(1)).

. . . .

Chinese Workers' Representative Congresses[70]

China has introduced a "workers' representative congress" for the workplaces. In some respects it has the appearance of the European works councils, though it operates differently. In 2008, the ACFTU, drawing upon earlier regulations, issued a new call for use of workers representative congresses and promulgated draft regulations for review by the State Council.[71] The draft Regulations for the Democratic Management of

[70] For comprehensive discussion, *see* Zhu Xiaoyang & Anita Chan, *Staff and Workers' Representative Congress: An Institutionalized Channel for Expression of Employees' Interests?*, 37 Chinese Soc. & Anthropology 6 (Summer 2005). English translation copyright © 2005 by M.E. Sharpe, Inc. Reprinted with permission. All Rights Reserved. Not For Reproduction.

[71] Ronald C. Brown, Understanding Labor And Employment in China 46–47 (2010). "Apart from the Constitution itself, there are two laws which refer to democratic management in general and SWRCs in any detail. There are also a crucial set of administrative regulations that set out a detailed procedural framework for SWRCs in publicly owned enterprises (state and collective), their relationship with trade unions and the rights and duties of worker's representatives. The two laws are the Labor Law (1995) [and now the 2008 Labor Contract Law)] and Trade Union Law (2001), and the regulations are entitled Regulations on SWRCs in public-owned enterprises (hereafter Regulations). Also important is Article 20 of the Bankruptcy Law (Trial Implementation) 1988, which stipulates that the views of the staff and workers' congress must be actively listened to prior to a formal declaration of bankruptcy.... It should be noted that worker representation either on the company board or

Enterprises indicate that companies with at least 100 employees may be required to establish employee representative congresses – collective employee representation bodies that meet once or twice a year to discuss employee-related matters.[72] The 2008 Labor Contract Law further empowered the workers representative congress to be consulted before an employer may implement rules or rule changes.[73] "Shanghai is reportedly introducing a new 'Guiding Opinion' to increase the power of 'Staff and Workers' Representative Congresses' (or simply 'workers congresses') in the city. 'Workers' congresses' are similar to Western European 'works councils' and, at least in principle, ensure representatives of ordinary workers a voice in enterprise decision-making. Precursors of today's congresses were created as far back as 1949 and the system was revived during the early reform era (. . .)."[74]

. . . .

QUESTIONS

1. Discuss how the purposes and roles of national unions in South Korea and the United States are similar and dissimilar.
2. How effective are the global unions, in your opinion? What positive functions do they serve?
3. Are worker councils likely to replace trade unions in East Asia? Why or why not?
4. What are the differences between Europe's works councils and China's workers' congresses?
5. How do the labor activities of South Korean unions differ from those in China?
6. In China, how are workers' congresses likely to work with the trade union; are workers better off with or without a workers' congress?

shareholders' committee is mentioned fairly extensively in the Company Law (1993, amended 1999) and is a topic worthy of further research by trade unions. In theory, SWRCs are one of the vehicles through which workers can give concrete expression to their status as "masters of the country." At the same time, democratic management is not an institution through which workers decide on enterprise policy – as has historically been the case under the aforementioned "workers' councils" – but rather a channel through which workers can, in certain carefully defined and regulated circumstances, veto or reject management decisions. SWRCs give form to the expression of such rights." *Staff and Workers Representatives Congress under Chinese Labor Law*, IHLO, http://www.ihlo.org/LRC/ACFTU/000804.html (last visited June 16, 2011) [Footnotes omitted] (The IHLO is the Hong Kong Liaison Office of the international trade union movement, founded in 1997, shortly after Hong Kong's reunification with China).

72 Phil Taylor, *Employment: Unions increase the pressure*, China L. & Prac., Dec. 9, 2009, *available at* 2009 WLNR 26474605; Andreas W. Lauffs & Jeffrey Wilson, *Draft Regulations Propose Compulsory Employee Representative Congresses*, Int'l L. Off., (2008), *available at* http://www.ilonewsletters.com/newsletters/detail.aspx?g=0097643e-c352-442d-ad39-61b102a1c8eb (last visited Sept. 30, 2010).

73 Labor Contract Law, art. 4 (2008) (P.R.C.).

74 Shanghai presently has workers congresses in 7,479 state-owned enterprises, of which 6,088 or 81.4 percent are carrying out "democratic evaluations." Manfred Elfstrom, *New Guidelines for Shanghai Staff and Workers Representative Congresses*, Labor Is Not A Commodity (July 23, 2008), http://laborrightsblog.typepad.com/international_labor_right/china/page/2/. (last visited Nov. 29, 2011).

7. What are the pros and cons of national unions, such as the ACFTU and AFL-CIO, having a close or independent relationship with government?
8. What is the basic difference between the role of KFTU and the KCTU and the AFL-CIO in their functions in local bargaining and relationship with the local union?

D. DISPUTE RESOLUTION

1. *Alternative Procedures*

Alternative Dispute Resolution[75]

The term "alternative dispute resolution (ADR)" means any procedure, agreed to by the parties of a dispute, in which they use the services of a neutral party to assist them in reaching agreement and avoiding litigation. Types of ADR include arbitration, mediation, negotiated rulemaking, neutral fact-finding, and mini-trials. With the exception of binding arbitration, the goal of ADR is to provide a forum for the parties to work toward a voluntary, consensual agreement, as opposed to having a judge or other authority decide the case.

In addition to serving as a potential means of avoiding the expense, delay, and uncertainty associated with traditional litigation, ADR also is intended as a vehicle for improving communication between the parties. ADR provides a forum for creative solutions to disputes that better meets the needs of the parties.

The Possibilities of Alternative Dispute Settlement Schemes[76]

Rebecca C. Chato

The possibilities of Alternative Dispute Settlement Schemes in labor are endless. All of us are one in saying that its time has come, in fact, not just now but a long time ago.

But allow me to put into context my discussion of ADR by briefly going over considerations such as: (1) nature of the labor disputes; (2) the existing means and procedures of dispute settlement; (3) problems encountered; and (4) finally, the guidepost.

Nature of Labor Disputes

A labor dispute is any controversy or matter affecting or concerning terms or conditions of employment or the association or representation of persons in negotiating, fixing, maintaining, changing, or arranging the terms and condition of employment. . . .

[75] See generally, Arnold M. Zack, *The Regulation of ADR* (2005), *available at* http://www.law.harvard.edu/programs/lwp/people/staffPapers/zack/The%20Regulation%20of%20ADR-ABA%207th%20conference.pdf. Arnold M. Zack, John T. Dunlop and John Thomas Dunlop, MEDIATION AND ARBITRATION OF EMPLOYMENT DISPUTES (1997).

[76] Rebecca C. Chato, The Possibilities of Alternative Dispute Settlement Schemes (2005) (on file with author). Copyright © Rebecca C. Chato.

Labor disputes may involve violations of labor standards, labor relations, and welfare and social laws.

1. Labor Standards Disputes include non-payment or under-payment of wages and wage-related benefits and violations of health and safety standards and violations of minimum standards.
2. Labor Relations Disputes include employee discipline or dismissals, unfair labor practices, disputes arising from the right of unions to represent employees for purposes of bargaining, bargaining deadlocks, strikes and lockouts, contract administration, and personnel policy disputes. Inter-union dispute refers to any dispute arising from union representation for purposes of collective bargaining, affiliation, and disaffiliation. Internal union dispute refers to any dispute arising from any violation of or disagreement over any provision of the Constitution and By-laws of union including any violation of the rights and conditions of union membership provided for in the Labor Code.
3. Welfare and Social Legislations Disputes refer to claims arising from failure of the employer to comply with its social and welfare obligations under the law, such as remittance of . . . premiums and . . . contributions, or failure to pay social benefits including maternity pay, Medicare and disability compensation. A labor dispute may be between: (1) the employer and its employees or employees' organizations;. . . . Dispute settlement, on the other hand, refers to the modes and systems prescribed by law to settle labor disputes concerning the employers and their workers on terms and conditions of employment or inter- and internal union disputes.

The Present Dispute Settlement Procedures

As presented in the paper, the present regime of dispute settlement provides different means and procedures as prescribed by the [Philippines] Labor Code, as amended. These modes of settling employee-management disputes are:

1. Collective Bargaining – a process by which representatives of a company and its employees discuss and negotiate the various phases of their relationships with the view of arriving at a mutually acceptable labor agreement
2. Grievance Machinery – a process or mechanism wherein grievances or matters arising from the implementation or interpretation of a collective bargaining agreement (CBA) and those arising from the interpretation or enforcement of company personnel policies. (In many jurisdictions a complaint may also arise from an alleged breach of contractual or statutory duty.)
3. Conciliation – a process whereby a third party (conciliator) brings the parties together, encourages them to discuss their differences, and assists them in developing their own solutions.
4. Mediation – a process whereby a third party (mediator) is more active in assisting parties reach acceptable solutions to the problem/s and help the disputing parties develop or come out with an acceptable solution. He [or she] can even submit his own proposal/s for the settlement of disputes.

5. Arbitration – a process whereby a third party (individual arbitrator), a board of arbitrators, or an arbitration court, is empowered to make a decision which disposes of the dispute. [In many jurisdictions this may be private or governmental arbitration].
6. Voluntary Arbitration – a method of settling dispute/s by submitting the "controversy" before an arbitrator or panel of arbitrators chosen by both parties. The voluntary arbitrator shall render a decision after proper hearing of the issues. The decision of the arbitrator shall be final and binding on the contending parties.
7. Compulsory Arbitration – a method [primarily used only in the public sector] resorted to when the dispute has become hardened and irreconcilable and remains unresolved after exhausting all the available remedies under existing laws and procedures.

. . . .

Conciliation of Disputes over International Labor Standards[77]

Arnold M. Zack

. . . .

In the decades between the Second World War and the current era of globalization and free trade, those of us in the labor relations world functioned nationally within our borders working with a prescribed set of laws and practices, which we viewed as difficult enough without having to add an international dimension to that mix. Despite the fact that the International Labor Organization since 1919 has promulgated 184 International Conventions on a wide range of workplace inequities, most countries have operated with scant regard for, let alone adoption of those Conventions.

In each of our countries we have applied our own domestic mix of law and practice to channel union, management, employment disputes into established procedures which were able to achieve resolution of those disputes whether through the use of law and the judicial system, or special labor courts, or through private dispute resolution systems. Even though none of our systems of dispute resolution has been perfect, they have usually been successful in forestalling greater conflict and unrest over unresolved claims of worker rights or workplace justice. We have had a distinct roster of players, a prescribed legal structure for resolving anticipated disputes and players who were usually committed to the resolution of their disputes and the continued operation of the economy in which they worked. In the United States the dispute resolution system does not include works councils, industry councils, labor courts, or multiple unionism. Rather we have a system, which provides trade union representation to a scant 12 % of the work force.

The remainder of our 125,000,000 workers operates under the doctrine of termination at the employers' option, with resort to the traditional legal and judicial system only on

77 Arnold M. Zack, *Conciliation of Disputes Over International Labor Standards*, Fifth Asian Regional Congress of the International Industrial Relations Association (2004), *available at* http://www.law.harvard.edu/programs/lwp/people/staffPapers/zack/ArnoldZack_korean_paper.pdf (last visited Sept. 30, 2010) [hereinafter Conciliation].

issues involving allegations of statutory violation. The parties traditionally use mediation and arbitration as the standard procedures for bringing resolution to collective bargaining disputes. Non-unionized employers often develop their own internal mediation and arbitration structures for resolving employee complaints with or without employee option on access to the courts. Nevertheless, in our system as in yours, the established metes and bounds of our formal and informal structures have generally minimized industrial unrest and conflict, hopefully with an eye to protecting fairness in the workplace. Throughout this period we had little more than perhaps academic concern as to work practices in other nations.

---

2. *Settlement of Disputes over Labor Rights*

A classic description follows delineating the distinction and significance of labor *rights*. This is the subject of most labor disputes resolved and is contrasted below with labor *interests*, which are dealt with in other ways. These labor rights are further classified into individual and collective labor rights. This is followed by the illustration of Japan's relatively new labor tribunal system and how it deals with resolving labor rights issues.

. . . .

Settlement of Disputes over Rights[78]

Alan Gladstone

I. Classification of Disputes and Systems for Their Resolution

1. Industrial relations systems the world over differ in the manner in which labour disputes are classified, indeed if they are classified at all. Nevertheless, the intrinsic nature of one or another labour dispute falls into a certain category, whether intended or not, and regardless of the procedures and mechanisms foreseen for their resolution. This being said, the classification of labour disputes into a given category will dictate, in many industrial relations systems, the particular mechanism employed in an effort to resolve the dispute.

2. The most common sets of classifications are first, interest disputes (sometimes referred to as economic or bargaining disputes) as opposed to rights disputes (sometimes referred to as legal or juridical disputes); and, secondly, collective disputes as opposed to individual disputes. Interest disputes arise out of a failure of the parties (normally a trade union and an employer or employers' grouping) to agree in collective bargaining on the establishment of new, or the renewal or modification of existing, norms.

[78] Reproduced with the permission of Wolters Kluwer Law & Business from R. Blanpain & C. Engels, *Settlement of Disputes over Rights*, Comparative Labour Law and Industrialized Market Economies, 595–622, copyright © 1993 [Footnotes omitted].

3. In regard to disputes over rights, the subject of this chapter, one may envisage a limited (and probably not exhaustive) number of general or specific grounds that give rise to such disputes. These include, from the point of view of an aggrieved worker: claimed violation or non-application of legislative or regulatory norms, of the provisions of a collective agreement, of the provisions of works rules or unilateral firm policies, including disciplinary rules, and of provisions of an individual contract of employment. All of these grounds involve an assertion by or on behalf of the aggrieved worker that he/she has not been treated in accordance with what is due to him/her, that is that his/her *rights* or entitlements have not been respected. There may also be situations, as will be seen below, in which employers may claim that their *rights* have not been respected in the collective employment situation. It might be helpful to look more closely at some of the above grounds for disputes over rights.

. . . .

4. Examples of complaints by workers concerning violations or non-application of statutory or regulatory norms fall largely into three groups: claims that the employer has not met legal obligations to the worker as to terms and conditions of employment prescribed by law or regulations; or that the employer has violated legal norms concerning workers' freedom of association rights (e.g. discriminatory discharge for reasons of trade union activity or membership) where these are inscribed in law; or that the employer has acted contrary to legal rules respecting other types of discrimination in the employment situation (race, religion, sex, age, etc.).

Similarly, *where* collective agreements are legally binding (the usual rule in the great majority of the countries concerned), the worker may seek to vindicate his/her *rights under* the agreement through legal or legally recognized procedures. For instance, if the worker concerned believes that he/she has not been paid wages in accordance with the applicable scales of the collective agreement, he/she would have a legally recognized remedy to pursue. Complaints for breach of a legally binding collective agreement can also be brought by an employer. This is not infrequently the case where trade unions are party to an agreement strike in violation of a no-strike clause in the agreement.

Rights disputes may also arise concerning individual contracts of employment where the worker maintains that the employer with whom he/she has a contract has not met his/her obligations under the said contract. (The employer may of course also bring an action for alleged breach of contract but the more usual employer reaction is to take disciplinary action against the worker concerned.)

The non-application of employer promulgated works rules (and related directives) as valid grounds for a dispute over rights may give rise to some debate, specifically regarding whether such rules confer rights on employees. Employee 'rights' arising out of works rules might depend on whether the rules are considered to be, by implication, a part of the individual contract of employment or considered to have achieved the status of 'acquired rights'. However, a more likely scenario regarding works rules is disciplinary action by the employer against workers for alleged breach of such rules.

5. It perhaps should be reiterated that the above descriptions of various types of disputes over rights are meant to serve as illustrations of the varied nature and characteristics of such disputes. Also, while some emphasis is quite naturally placed on disputes in which employees or their representatives are the initiating party, employers may also activate the resolution machinery, as mentioned above, in cases of alleged violations of their

rights (and this particularly with regard to industrial action (strikes) taken contrary to law or to the provisions of a collective agreement). It may further be emphasized that, in general, we are dealing with rights disputes and methods for their resolution in the private sector of industrialized market economies.

6. As regards the mechanisms for resolving disputes over rights, these generally fall into four categories: the regular court system, labour courts, quasi-judicial administrative agencies, and arbitration. Each of these will be treated below.

7. However, mention should also be made of mediation and conciliation procedures. These are means of assisting the parties to the dispute, through third party intervention, to reach a mutually agreed settlement of the conflict. While mediation and conciliation are usually identified more with interest disputes (. . .) than with disputes over rights, they nevertheless are frequently resorted to in the latter as a precursor to adjudication or arbitration, either as an independent mechanism or as a part of the adjudicatory or arbitral procedure. Sometimes this is done quite informally and as an ad hoc measure, and sometimes it is an obligatory feature of the system for resolution of rights disputes. There has in the past been some controversy regarding the use of formal or informal conciliation or mediation in rights disputes. These procedures are often identified with compromise and, in the view of certain commentators, there is no room for compromise as between the parties in a question concerning rights. One either has an entitlement or does not have it. This however seems to be a rather short-sighted view for two reasons. First, there are certainly many issues, particularly of a collective nature, which may well be subject to compromise. An example would be the interpretation of a vague clause in a collective agreement. Secondly, the conciliation/mediation process may well serve the purpose of better informing the parties of their respective rights and obligations and hence obviate the need for litigation. An example would be the existence, applicability or interpretation of the relevant legislative provisions.

8. In addition to conciliation/arbitration as a possible precursor to adjudication or arbitration, mention should also be made of internal (usually) bilateral procedures within the enterprise or, possibly, the industry, which may be utilized in an effort to resolve rights disputes typically, but not necessarily, of an individual nature. Such grievance procedures, implicitly or explicitly, reserve to the employer the final decision prior to possible recourse to adjudication or arbitration. At times the exhaustion of grievance procedures (as with conciliation/mediation) may be a prerequisite to resolution through adjudication or arbitration.

9. In the discussion below, we shall group together labour courts and those administrative agencies of a quasi judicial nature, mainly in the United States, Great Britain, Japan, and Canada, although these agencies frequently exercise a quite limited and specific jurisdiction in terms of specific rights disputes. They may also be subject to a wider area of judicial review by the regular courts than would be the case in respect of labour courts. And we group together under the heading of regular or ordinary courts both those courts where absolutely no provision is made for any kind of special handling of labour disputes over rights and those in which there is, within the regular court system, some measure of special dealing. No effort is made to make any distinctions with regard to the various

fora on the basis of their place within or without the regular judiciary, or on the basis of hierarchical or administrative reporting arrangements within a given system.

II. Ordinary Courts

In General

In a number of the countries concerned there is no special juridical or quasi-judicial procedure to which appeal can be made where a labour dispute over rights arises. Such differences are treated in exactly the same manner and by exactly the same judicial organs as any legal dispute under civil law. After all, it is argued, a contract dispute is no different whether it concerns an employment contract or a collective contract or a commercial or other contract. And a generally qualified judge is competent to apply the law – statutory or common law —regardless of the context. This argument is of course contrary to the very idea on which labour court (and, indeed, other specialized court) systems are grounded. And, as we shall see later, one of the criticisms of certain labour court (and arbitration) systems is precisely that they rely overly on procedures and attitudes reminiscent of the regular courts.

11. This being said, there are only a small number of countries (Germany and Israel, to mention two of these) with which we are concerned in which the labour courts have a very general competence and in which the regular courts are not involved in any significant labour cases.

12. Countries in which the ordinary courts play the major (and often exclusive) role in the resolution of disputes over rights include the Netherlands and Italy. And even with this very limited number of countries, Italy, as we shall see, does accord a degree of special treatment to cases relating to rights disputes. Japan may also be included among those countries where competence over rights disputes lies virtually exclusively with the regular judiciary, although disputes relating to unfair labour practices will be heard by special commissions under a system somewhat similar to that in the United States. This being said, it is worth noting that traditionally in Japan rights disputes have not frequently found their way to the courts.[79] Furthermore, even those countries with labour court or arbitration systems, as alluded to above, may still rely on the regular courts to handle many rights disputes. Thus, for example, in the Nordic countries the labour courts are competent only in cases involving alleged noncompliance with collective agreements. Similarly, in the United States, the regular civil courts will deal with breaches of individual contracts of employment (and can be involved in damage actions based on certain breaches of collective agreements). And it must be remembered that in that country the 'grievance/ arbitration' system applies only to the approximately 20% of the workforce [now near 12 percent] covered by collective agreements (some 95% of which contain arbitration clauses). In Great Britain, apart from the specialized tribunals handling complaints under the laws concerning termination of employment

[79] See following discussion of Japan's new labor tribunal system that is within the court system.

and employment discrimination, breaches of individual employment contracts and of certain other legislated protection for workers would be heard by the regular courts.

13. Thus, in the vast majority of the countries with which we are dealing, the regular courts continue to play a significant role in the resolution of disputes over rights. Given the fact that Italy and the Netherlands reflect the predominant role of the ordinary courts, and that Italy presents a somewhat unusual case in this context, while the Netherlands represent a traditional approach, we shall take a somewhat closer look at these two countries, as well as Japan.

. . . .

III. Labor Courts and Similar Institutions

A. *In General*

In the industrialized market economies, labour courts and similar institutions as vehicles for adjudicating labour disputes over rights have become quite prevalent. At the same time it is clear that the range of competence and the types of cases treated by the various fora are often quite different.

Indeed, interest in the administration of industrial justice through instituting systems of labour courts has heightened in recent years as it becomes increasingly evident, in certain of those remaining countries where rights disputes are referred to the ordinary courts, that these courts are not always in a position to render such justice in an adequate manner. But it should also be noted that much of the pressure for introducing a system of labour courts in countries where such system does not exist comes from academic circles, and rarely from members of the judiciary. There is still the belief abroad among many judges that, as mentioned earlier in this chapter, any competent judge is qualified to deal with any legal dispute or, at least, any contractual or torts dispute.

29. Why labour courts? Traditional theory holds that the resolution of industrial disputes, in this case rights disputes, requires, in order to ensure social justice, that cases be heard and decided rapidly, at no or with a minimum of cost to the litigants, with a relative lack of formality and judicial trappings, and by bodies with a specialized capability in labour matters. Whether in the present situation labour courts in all of the industrialized market economies in which labour courts exist substantially meet these criteria is an open question. However it is generally recognized that in respect of most of the elements mentioned, labour courts are more user-friendly than the ordinary courts. This is so in spite of the fact that complaints are quite widely heard that labour courts, in their operation if not in theory, have become overly formal, particularly in terms of legal procedures (e.g. rules of evidence) and atmosphere of hearings. Complaints are also heard that from a substantive point of view, there may be too much reliance on precedents. It would be in order to have a closer look at certain of the criteria mentioned above.

30. Rapidity in deciding cases is of importance in adjudication in any area of law, but can often be crucial in respect of labour law. Let us take two types of cases as examples, cases which in certain jurisdictions constitute significant percentages of the work load of labour courts (and which will be discussed further below).

First, that of a challenge by an employee (or his/her trade union) to his/her dismissal: In virtually all of the countries with which we are concerned, a dismissal can be contested on the grounds of insufficient cause. Such protection is most often based on legislative standards, or otherwise on provisions of collective agreements barring unjustified dismissals. Dismissal being industrial capital punishment, it would be unconscionable to require, particularly in a situation of a tight employment market, that a dismissed employee suffers the delays that are common to ordinary court procedures, delays which can run into years. The repercussions on the employee and his/her family's well being are patent.

The importance of relative rapidity in resolving conflicts is often reflected in cases involving the application or interpretation of collective agreements. Here the possible negative impact on the individual and, particularly, the collective labour-management relationship and the decline in morale resulting from the frustrations of the parties where decisions in cases involving important personnel and labour relations matters are not forthcoming in a timely manner may compromise the economic well-being of the enterprise (or industry).

31. Labour courts differ in many respects in the many industrialized market economies where they have been established. As already noted, they differ in their competence, i.e. the types of cases over which they exercise jurisdiction. They also differ in their composition (tripartite, bipartite or unipartite), the choice and role of lay judges or assessors in tripartite courts, the use of pre-trial procedures (conciliation of one sort or another), remedial powers and a host of other characteristics. To have a better idea of these differences as well as of the functioning of labour courts, a number of examples are described briefly hereafter.

. . . .

VII. Remedies in Rights Disputes: Two Examples

83. This chapter is meant to deal principally with procedures and mechanisms for resolving conflicts of rights. However, there are two areas of particular substantive interest when considering the handling of rights disputes through certain, if not all, of the procedures and institutions discussed in this chapter. These are remedies in cases of unjustified termination of employment of workers at the initiative of the employer and, secondly, remedies, particularly temporary or interim relief, for employers in cases of allegedly unlawful strikes. In the case of termination of employment, this is the preponderant item on the case load for a great many of the courts, boards, tribunals, commissions, etc. Moreover, dismissals can involve situations that threaten either the morale of the workplace or the possibility of maintaining sound labour-management relations. In the case of the delicate area of strikes, the economic implications for the enterprise or industry are apparent.

A. *Termination of Employment*

84. Either legislative or collectively bargained protection against unjust dismissal is provided in virtually all industrialized market economies. Where this protection results from the provisions of collective agreements, then protection is obviously limited to those employees covered by the agreement. A major point of contention has been the

nature of the remedy for unjust dismissals, particularly since the remedy must serve the double purpose of indemnifying the employee concerned and deterring such dismissals. Criminal penalties excluded, the two remedies available are reinstatement (and back pay) or compensation.

85. In Germany, Sweden (as well as in Denmark and Norway), and the United Kingdom, for example, the judges have a certain discretion as between the two possible remedies. However in some of these countries, such as Sweden, the reinstatement remedy will not be awarded if the employer objects or, as in the case of Germany, if the labour court finds that it is unreasonable to assume that the parties can cooperate in the future. In Britain reinstatement will be awarded unless it is 'inappropriate'. In such cases, compensation will be awarded. In other countries, save in exceptional cases, compensation would be the rule. Where reinstatement is granted, it is usually accompanied by a monetary award to make up for lost wages and, where appropriate, restoration of seniority is ordered.

86. Arbitral practice in North America, as well as that of the NLRB and the Japanese labour relations commissions, is to award reinstatement almost automatically, in cases where the dismissal is found to be unjustified or an unfair labour practice. Even in the European and Australian contexts where compensation might be the more usual remedy, it is common to award reinstatement in cases of dismissal for reasons of trade union membership or activity. In these cases the concern is to preserve the integrity of trade union centered industrial relations and to prevent employers from ridding themselves, for a price, of trade union elements they find annoying. In the eyes of many commentators, the existence and utilization of the reinstatement remedy is key to a real protection of workers against unjust dismissal.

B. *Remedial Measures for Illegal or Unlawful Strikes*

87. In some industrialized market economies no strike would be illegal, unlawful. or enjoinable, either because of constitutional or legislative dispositions. However in most of the countries concerned, resorting to strike action contrary to the provisions of industrial peace obligations (dictated by agreement, legislation, or jurisprudence) or without fulfilling prior procedural requirements (e.g., notice periods, exhaustion of conciliation procedures, etc.) would be illegal or unlawful. Here we will limit our consideration to the role of labour courts and their jurisdiction to rule in questions of strikes, and we will stress the use of interim or provisional measures, i.e. temporary injunctions. This is a vital but problematical sphere of action since the courts (or other bodies) can determine, by the position they take, the ultimate outcome of what is essentially an economic and not a juridical conflict. This is because where even temporary relief is granted and the strike is later found to be lawful or legal, the injunction may well have broken the strike by stifling the momentum that had built up and discouraging the workers concerned. It is very difficult in most cases to simply resume the strike at a later stage. Thus judges generally do, or should, approach applications for injunctions with caution and circumspection.

88. Interim measures may be applied for in many countries. This would not be the case for Finland where the labour court is barred from entertaining such applications. However, in practice the court will hear the case expeditiously and finally decide on

the legality of the strike in a question of four to six days. Given that many strikes last only a few days and can be effective in that limited period, there is some discussion in Finland aimed at reviewing the ban on interim injunction orders. The situation is not dissimilar in Norway where it is felt that interim measures may be superfluous since the labour court will deal with the matter definitively within 48 hours. In other countries, as a matter of judicial policy, temporary injunctions are available but, for the reasons mentioned above, are rarely used.

89. Where they are used, the court will normally make its decision balancing the various interests at stake. This would mean, in particular, weighing the degree of damage to the employer, enterprise or industry in question (including, possibly, a consideration of the capacity of the trade union to respond in damages should the strike be illegal) if the preliminary injunction is refused, as against the effect on the position of the trade union and the workers involved should the injunction be granted and the strike later be found legal. This is frequently a very delicate balancing act, made more difficult for the court by the fact that a decision must be taken almost immediately.

90. The above examination of labour disputes concerning rights can only be considered cursory at best. The differences in treatment of such disputes both in terms of the forums available (often multiple) and the conceptual limits and diversity of the very notion of rights disputes, not to mention the varied substantive treatment of such disputes in legislation and by the various courts, tribunals, boards, commissions, etc. which deal with them, are certainly the subject of a far longer and more comprehensive comparative effort than is reflected in this chapter.

. . . .

The *process* by which the labor rights dispute is resolved also varies widely between private and government institutions, industrial tribunals, arbitration commissions, and court arbitration and adjudication. The following excerpt shows Japan's use of arbitration in the courts utilizing judges and laymen.

The Birth of the Labor Tribunal System in Japan: A Synthesis of Labor Law Reform and Judicial Reform[80]

Kazuo Sugeno

I. Introduction

. . . .

Judicial reform attained an important innovation in labor dispute resolution through the introduction of the Labor Tribunal System. According to the Labor Tribunal Law,

[80] Kazuo Sugeno, *The Birth of the Labor Tribunal System in Japan: A Synthesis of Labor Law Reform and Judicial Reform*, 25 Comp. Lab. L. & Pol'y J. 519 (2005), *available at*, http://www.law.uiuc.edu/publications/CLL&PJ/archive/vol_25/issue_4/SugenoArticle25-4.pdf (last visited Sept. 30, 2010) [Footnotes omitted].

enacted in April 2004, either party in an employment relationship can bring a dispute of rights arising from employment relations under this procedure in the district court. A tribunal composed of one career judge and two part-time experts in labor relations first makes mediation efforts, and, if such efforts fail, renders a decision clarifying the merits of the case and specifying measures to resolve the case. The decision is not binding, and if either party objects, the case is automatically transferred to an ordinary civil procedure. The Law requires the tribunal to dispose of the case within three sessions, and is premised upon the cases lasting a few months. This measure to reform the labor dispute resolution system was introduced recently to cope with the drastic increase in employment disputes since the collapse of the bubble economy.

. . . .

III. The Increasing Worker Grievances in the Post-Bubble Years

Since the early 1990s, the number of disputes involving employment relations has increased sharply. Over the last thirteen years, the number of civil litigations at district court involving labor relations tripled, while the number of entire civil litigation in the same court has grown 1.5 times. The major types of civil actions involving labor relations are claims for unpaid wages (including retirement benefits) and claims contesting termination of employment. They are followed by claims challenging the validity of disadvantageous alteration of working conditions and disadvantageous transfers. Claims for damages for excessive inducement of resignation and sexual harassment are also on the increase.

Labor administrative agencies also received an increasing number of complaints within their jurisdiction. The labor standards inspection offices in the Ministry of Labor received more than 20,000 complaints annually regarding violations of labor protection statutes in the mid-1990s. These complaints concern mostly non-payment of wages and dismissals without the mandatory thirty-day notice, both violations of the Labor Standards Law. The labor relation offices of prefecture governments also received an increasing number of individual workers' grievances. The offices of the Tokyo Metropolitan Government, for example, received about 45,000 cases in 1996, as compared to about 31,000 cases annually in 1989–91. The Tokyo government offices attempted to settle 1,200 cases in 1996, of which 40–50% involved termination of employment and 20–30% concerned non-payment of wages.

. . . .

IV. The Necessity for the Reform of Employment Dispute Resolution System

In light of the rapid increase in employment disputes, taken against the backgrounds of structural changes in the corporate management and the labor markets, it became obvious that the dispute resolution system was in need of a major reform.

. . . .

VII. The Profile of the Labor Tribunal System

The Labor Tribunal System is a procedure instituted in the district court. It has jurisdiction over employment relationships. Dismissals, terminations of employment, disciplinary measures, transfers, demotions, and unpaid wages or retirement benefits are typically the subjects of such disputes. Either party in an employment relationship can file a complaint to the district court having jurisdiction over the localities where the other party resides or the employment is carried out. The claimant must submit a written complaint indicating both the specific claims he or she seeks against the other party (the respondent) and the legal grounds justifying such claims. The complaint must also specify the status of negotiations made between the parties regarding the claim as well as any major evidence that the claimant can submit.

Upon receiving the complaint, the court organizes a labor tribunal to handle the case. The tribunal is composed of three members: one career judge and two experts in labor relations (one from labor and one from management). The career-judge member presides over the procedure, and labor and management members add their expertise into the procedure. Labor and management members are appointed beforehand at each district court and serve on a part-time basis when they are assigned to a particular case. They participate in decision -making on equal footing with the career judge member. They must be fair and impartial in the handling of the case.

The tribunal sends a copy of the complaint to the respondent urging him or her to submit a written response within an indicated period. This response must state a position with regard to the claim and the legal grounds thereof. It must also describe the status of negotiations between the parties and any major evidence the respondent can submit. The tribunal also notifies each party as to the date of the first hearing requesting their attendance.

Hearings are held informally and are not open to the public, although the panel may allow the observers deemed necessary or desirable. In order to make the tribunal procedure expeditious, the Law prescribes that the panel must, in principle, dispose of the case within three sessions of hearing, expecting that the procedure will last three to four months at the longest. Typically, the panel will clarify the issues in the case and the evidences to be examined in the first session. It will also ascertain the status of negotiations between the parties, to assess the feasibility of mediating the dispute. In the second session, the panel will investigate the facts by interviewing witnesses and examining documents in front of the parties. The panel may also inquire as to the desires of the parties for resolving the case through mediation. In the third session, the panel will make supplementary inquiries of both facts and desires for mediation, and then makes a mediation proposal. If both parties agree with this proposal, the agreement is written into the record of the court, putting an end to the dispute.

However, if either party rejects the proposal, the panel closes the hearing and makes a judgment on the merits of the complaint. Based on such judgment and taking the desires of the parties into account, the panel specifies the measures that would realistically resolve the dispute. The panel renders a decision stating such judgment and measures, either orally at the end of the third session or in writing within a number of days thereafter. The measures to be adopted by the panel include confirmation of the rights, execution of obligations and direction of the monetary payments. The decision is not binding on the parties. Either side can notify the court in writing and reject the decision within two weeks after the notification. If rejected, the decision loses its effect, and the case is automatically transferred to a regular civil procedure, to be pending in the same district court retroactively from the date when the complaint was submitted. On the other hand, if both parties accept the decision or do not submit a notice of rejection, the decision is binding on the parties. The measures specified in the decision will be enforceable in accordance with the Civil Execution Law.

The Labor Tribunal System is a new court procedure added to the conventional labor dispute resolution systems. It does not replace or repeal any existing procedures or mechanisms. It is a part of a menu of dispute resolution services along with the regular civil process, the provisional disposition procedure, the Welfare and Labor Ministry counseling and mediation services, the Prefecture Government counseling and mediation services described in the first section. Parties in employment relationships can make use of these services respectively, simultaneously, or accumulatively.

As foreign observers will easily understand, the new Labor Tribunal System borrows ideas from the European labor court systems, and creates an expeditious court procedure with the participation of expert lay judges. But even though it includes features common to foreign procedures, the System is still uniquely Japanese especially in the respects that it is set up within the ordinary court, closely coordinated with ordinary civil procedure. The three sessions of hearing and an integrated mediation procedure may also be unique aspects. From the perspective of American law, the System may also be regarded as a non-binding arbitration procedure set up within the court as a prior stage of the ordinary civil procedure. The great wave of Judicial Reform and the rising demand of the reform of the labor dispute resolution system combined to generate such an ingenious system. The Labor Tribunal procedure is expected into a central scheme of labor dispute resolution systems in Japan, along with the Ministry of Welfare and Labor counseling and mediation services. With the prompt and informal procedure strengthened by expert participation, parties will make frequent use of the Labor Tribunal System, and mediation proposals or decisions handed down by the System will be highly persuasive to the parties. However, for such expectation to come to pass, a few conditions must be met in its implementation.

The first and most important condition is to organize high quality experts in labor relations to be appointed as panel members. Such experts should have a wealth of experiences in labor management relations in order to provide useful insight. They should also have sufficient legal backgrounds to discuss cases with career judges. In addition, they should also possess the ethics to be fair and impartial. It is estimated that at least 500 such experts are needed each from labor and management in order to start the new system. Exploration and selection has been first entrusted to national organizations of labor and management. The court will review the candidates recommended by these organizations. There will be intensive training programs for such experts to work through both before and after the appointment.

Second, the Labor Tribunal System is designed to be an informal procedure to be easily accessible by ordinary workers. Therefore, the court must see to it that workers are able to make use of this procedure without the assistance of lawyers. However, in order to make the System more effective and expeditious, it is much more desirable that the complainant (and also the respondent) be represented by lawyers with expertise in labor law. One of the key factors for the success of the new system will be whether the Bar and the associations of labor and management lawyers will be able to organize a sufficient number of lawyers with relevant expertise to assist the parties with reasonable expenses. The expansion of legal profession under the Judicial Reform will hopefully enable the provision of such legal services.

....

QUESTIONS

1. How do ADR functions differ, if at all, among arbitration, industrial/labor tribunals, administrative agencies, and industrial/labor courts?
2. Who are the decision makers in the above forums and will their qualifications likely differ; if so, how?
3. Is there a choice of alternatives or a required sequence of ADR processes; and, if so, are there procedural obstacles to be aware of in those processes, especially if ultimately seeking final adjudication in a court?
4. Typical employee discipline cases invoke what type of dispute resolution procedures?
5. How do ADR approaches differ, if at all, between labor/employment disputes arising under domestic law and international standards?

---

3. *Settlement of Disputes over Labor Interests*

Settlement of Disputes over Interests[81]

Alvin Goldman

I. Overview of Models for Interests Disputes Settlement

1. To a considerable degree, the processes of notice, information exchange and consultation, discussed in earlier chapters, serve to avoid disputes over interests. This chapter examines and compares seven basic models for the resolution of such disputes when they do arise. These models are:

(a) Acquiescence in Unilateral Action;
(b) Governmental Fiat;
(c) Political Discipline;
(d) Adjudication;
(e) Voting;
(f) Negotiation; and
(g) Conciliated Negotiation.

Each of these dispute resolution models has variations in structure. Though each model at times is used independently to resolve an interests dispute, at other times two or more

[81] Reproduced with the permission of Wolters Kluwer Law & Business from R. Blanpain & C. Engels, *Settlement of Disputes over Interests*, Comparative Labour Law and Industrialized Market Economies, 623–48, copyright © 1993 [Footnotes omitted].

are involved either simultaneously or sequentially in dispute settlement. In broad terms, these models can be described as follows.

A. *Acquiescence in Unilateral Action*

2. Some might argue that Acquiescence in Unilateral Action is not a model for interests dispute settlement but rather represents the absence of such disputes. However, the failure of a party to assert displeasure concerning employment interests does not necessarily mean that that party is satisfied with the nature, level, or distribution of those interests. Acquiescence in Unilateral Action occurs if the acquiescing party either does not have a way to influence the resolution of those differences or does not wish to exercise its power to influence the result. Accordingly, the differences do not go unresolved; they are resolved, but the resolution results from one side submitting to the other's dominance or accepting the other's initiative.

B. *Governmental Fiat*

3. An essential characteristic of every social unit is the ability to establish, alter, and enforce behavioural norms. Societal units have greater ability than do individuals or informal groups to achieve adherence to norms because, in addition to inducements, social units generally can legitimately resort to a variety of coercive techniques including manipulating psychological ties of group loyalty. When all members of a social unit are committed to conformity with a particular behavioural norm, we can speak of that norm as a law or a rule of governance.

4. The norms established and maintained by social units sometimes are the product of prior exercises of individual autonomy to which others have acquiesed and which have developed into a generally imitated pattern of behaviour. Such patterns are known as customs or tradition. Other norms are determined at the discretion of those who control the prerogatives of the societal unit. For our purposes, the establishment or modification of a social unit's behavioural norms constitute the Governmental Fiat model for conflict resolution, when they are imposed by those responsible for exercising the unit's prerogatives.

C. *Political Discipline*

5. In some political systems, the coercive power of the state treats nonconformity with the controlling political party's doctrine as a crime against the state itself. The political party thereby wields the power of Governmental Fiat. Even in pluralist political systems, a prevailing political party asserts influence to the extent that it can offer economic opportunities. Generally, such patronage benefits are available to the party in power with respect to at least some government jobs. Also, some employment opportunities with government-owned, controlled, or influenced enterprises often are reserved for members of the dominant political party.

Opportunities to do business with the government similarly may be reserved for loyal supporters of the party in power. Generally, beneficiaries of such patronage are relied on to comply with the dictates of those who control the party. The party's influence over its members also may be enhanced by the psychological and ideological ties of its supporters. Whatever the source of that influence, the party's ability to control its members' conduct constitutes its power of Political Discipline.

D. *Adjudication*

6. Adjudication is the model by which one or more individuals having no direct personal interest in a dispute impose a resolution upon the interested parties on the basis of settled principles.

7. Employment disputes over interests are adjudicated by a variety of entities including courts of justice, specially structured labour courts, administrative agencies, and arbitrators. The latter term describes a process in which, typically, the impartial tribunal that decides the dispute is selected either by or with the participation of the disputing parties.

E. *Voting*

8. Voting is a format for collective self-determination by which each interested participant makes an unequivocal choice from among specific alternatives. Essentially, it is a fact-finding method for recording individual preferences. Because Voting requires that the issue be defined before the choices are made, it almost always is utilized in conjunction with other models of interests dispute resolution.

F. *Negotiation*

9. Negotiation is the process by which two or more parties through some form of communication mutually resolve to alter, or refrain from altering, the relationship between or among themselves or their relationship with respect to an object or group of objects. The process involves clarification of issues, exchanging information, exploring alternative settlements, examining the consequences of not settling, persuasion, and mutual accommodation. It covers a broad range of formats. In Germany, for example, the term 'bargaining' is used to connote a settlement reached under pressure of a work stoppage. Clearly, though, this process is Negotiation. The term 'co-determination' is used in Germany to connote settlements reached through the deliberations of works councils and of supervisory boards having joint representation. However, applying our description of the dispute resolution model, it is clear that these institutions, too, largely rely on the Negotiation process in reaching their decision.

10. As previously noted in this book, there is an uncertain line between consultation and negotiation. In its pure form, consultation aims at dispute avoidance. It accomplishes this through the exchange of information and persuasion that results in unilateral acts of accommodation. However, if that exploration fails to avoid the dispute, and if the issue is not reserved for unilateral resolution, consultation is readily transformed into negotiation.

G. *Conciliated Negotiation*

11. When negotiating parties are unable to agree, neutral third parties sometimes try to assist the negotiators in reaching a settlement. The resulting Conciliated Negotiation can involve the third party serving as a communications conduit or can involve the more

active role of the third party making fact findings or suggesting formulas for agreement. In the area of disputes concerning employment interests, government agencies often offer or mandate the aid or mediators or conciliators.

12. Before comparing applications of the foregoing models for settling interests disputes, two points are worth reiterating. The first is that each model has its variations. The second is that the basic models for interests dispute settlement can operate simultaneously or sequentially. For example, if the legislative branch of government imposes a solution to the parties' differences based upon its objective collective judgment respecting fair balancing of the parties' competing equities, the dispute is resolved through the simultaneous application of the Adjudicative and Governmental Fiat models. An example of the sequential operation of interests dispute settlement models would be where the Negotiation model is used by the parties' representatives to reach an agreement but the completion of that agreement is contingent upon approval by the parties' constituents using the Voting model.

QUESTIONS

1. Explain how labor interest disputes between an employer and an employee are generally resolved.
2. Are there any limits on an employer's authority to decide labor interest disputes? If so, what are they?
3. Discuss the pros and cons of using mandatory settlement approaches to interest disputes. When, if ever, might there be justifications? Is there a difference between private and government employees' disputes? If so, how and why?
4. Is there a difference between mandating use of procedures versus mandating outcomes? Explain.
5. What is the difference, if any, between the operations and functions of an administrative and judicial determination?
6. Explain the difference, if any, of a "waiver" of labor rights and a "substitution of forum" from administrative/judicial to arbitration.
7. Can there be an "adjudication" of labor interest disputes; if so when and how? Which is the preferable forum – arbitration, administrative, or judicial – and why?

IV

East Asian Labor Law Regimes

For direct investors to determine comparative and competitive advantages of establishing business operations in a foreign country, many factors must be considered, including labor and employment issues and costs. To know, for example, whether termination of employees is easy, difficult, or expensive, a certain level of understanding of law is necessary as to the labor law requirements and practices in the countries being considered. The following sections delineate the basics of the labor law regimes of Japan, South Korea, and China to further that understanding; brief overviews of Hong Kong and Taiwan are also provided. They are discussed in general terms under the four agenda items, identified and discussed earlier in Chapter III.

A. JAPAN

Japanese labor law is principally set forth in the Constitution, international treaties, statutes, regulations, and, to a lesser extent, cases. Work rules also constitute an important source of labor rights. The Labor Standards Law and the Trade Union Law, respectively, include the most comprehensive coverage of labor and union rights. Labor law is administered under the Ministry of Health, Labor, and Welfare (MHLW) and several subordinate bureaus and departments.

Labor rights in Japan arose in the wake of industrialization in the late nineteenth century and began expanding significantly after World War II. Key worker rights include freedom of association (as it pertains to union participation); freedom of contract in the employment context; equal protection, privacy, minimum wage, and hour standards; the right to receive leave, a pension, and other benefits; protection from coercive deployment; and the right to a reasonable dismissal and the right to terminate the employment contract with sufficient notice. Recent changes in the laws have expanded gender equality and privacy rights.

Trade unions in Japan can be divided into labor federations, trade unions, and enterprise unions. More than ninety percent of unionized workers are associated with enterprise unions. Unions are primarily engaged in collective bargaining, although such activities have been increasingly preempted by the spread of joint labor–management consultation bodies, which often work out the terms of bargaining subjects before conflicts of interest arise. Strikes, lockouts, and slowdowns are uncommon.

There are separate avenues for dispute resolution depending on whether the dispute is between labor and management or between an individual worker and a company. In either case mediation, conciliation, arbitration, and litigation are legitimate paths to a remedy, although each may have a different binding effect on the parties. Additionally, these processes are not necessarily mutually exclusive.

1. *Regulatory Sources, Structures, and Administration*

Japan is a civil law country. Legislative enactments and administrative regulations have served as the foundation of jurisprudence rather than case law, although case law is appearing more regularly as nonbinding guidance. Res judicata is not recognized, although case law has persuasive authority, particularly the decisions of the appellate bench. The principal sources of labor law are included in the following section.

Constitution

The current constitution was ratified in 1947 and was drafted during the American occupation under the supervision of the Supreme Commander of Allied Powers. Several labor provisions are included. Article 25 provides that the state has a duty to "maintain minimum standards of wholesome and cultured living."[1] Article 27 sets forth the right and duty to work; requires the state to develop standards for wages, hours, rest, and other working conditions; and prohibits the exploitation of children.[2] Article 18 prohibits involuntary servitude except as punishment for crime.[3] Article 28 guarantees the right of workers to organize and to bargain and act collectively.[4] Article 14 prohibits discrimination based on race, creed, social status, or family origin.[5]

International Law

Article 98, Section 2 of the Constitution states that "treaties concluded by Japan and established laws of nations shall be faithfully observed"[6] and the Japanese

[1] Nihonkoku Kenpo [Kenpo][Constitution], art. 25 (Japan).
[2] *Id.* at art. 27.
[3] *Id.* at art. 18.
[4] *Id.* at art. 28.
[5] *Id.* at art. 14.
[6] *Id.* at art. 98, para. 2.

government and the courts have consistently held that treaties have the force of law in Japan under Article 98.[7] Japan has ratified forty-eight International Labor Organization (ILO) conventions, forty-one of which remain in force including: No. 87 (Freedom of Association and Protection of the Right to Organize), No. 100 (Equal Remuneration), No. 138 (Minimum Age Convention), No. 182 (Worst Forms of Child Labor Convention), and No. 29 (Forced Labor Convention). Japan has not ratified Nos. 105 (Abolition of Forced Labor Convention) and 111 (Discrimination (Employment and Occupation) Convention).[8]

Civil Code

The Civil Code has a few labor provisions that remain in effect such as freedom of either party in an employment contract to terminate the contract. Such general provisions remain on the books but have been largely superseded by newer labor laws and court decisions.

Other Laws and Regulations

Individual employment relationships between employers and employees are governed by the Labor Standards Law of 1947 (LSL), and any contract provision that establishes working conditions below the standards required under the LSL are void and automatically replaced with the minimum requirements under the LSL.[9] In 2008, a new Labor Contract Law came into effect, providing specific guidance on employment agreements.[10] Other relevant laws have been in place for some years. The Trade Union Law of 1949 governs collective bargaining and union relations. The Labor Relations Adjustment Act covers dispute settlements, and the Labor Tribunal Law was added in 2006 that applies to individual labor disputes. The Labor Contract Succession Law of 2000 facilitates employer–employee relationships in the context of a corporate reorganization. The Minimum Wage Law of 1959 regulates minimum wages. The Industrial Safety and Health Law of 1972 and corresponding regulations govern workplace safety standards.

Work Rules

Under the LSL, employers with ten or more continuous employees are required to draft work rules specifying wages, hours, rest periods, and other working conditions;

[7] Yuji Iwasawa, International Law, Human Rights, and Japanese Law 31 (1998).

[8] ILO, *List of Ratifications of International Labor Conventions, Japan*, http://webfusion.ilo.org/public/db/standards/normes/appl/appl-byCtry.cfm?CTYCHOICE=0350&&hdroff=1%E2%8C%A9=EN (last visited Sept. 29, 2010).

[9] Labor Standards Law (LSL), Law No. 49 of Apr. 7, 1949, as amended through Law No. 107 of June 9, 1995, art. 13, *available at* http://www.ilo.org/dyn/natlex/docs/WEBTEXT/27776/64846/E95JPN01.htm (last visited Sept. 29, 2010).

[10] The Japan Institute for Labor Policy and Training, Labor Contract Act (Dec. 5, 2007), *available at* www.jil.go.jp/english/laborinfo/library/documents/llj_law17.pdf (last visited June 7, 2011).

file the rules with the local Labor Standards Inspection office; and post them in a conspicuous place in the workplace or furnish them to employees.[11] Employers primarily satisfy these notification requirements by creating work rules. Work rules must meet or exceed the minimum standards established by the LSL and other labor laws and constitute contract provisions enforceable under the Civil Code.[12]

Regulation and Administration of Labor

The Ministry of Health, Labor, and Welfare (MHLW) was established in 2001 following the merger of the Ministry of Labor and the Ministry of Health and Welfare.[13] The Director-General for Policy Planning is in charge of labor management relations. The Equal Employment, Children and Families Bureau, and the Worker's Life Department handle worker discrimination and sexual harassment, child labor, and family-leave issues. The Industrial Safety and Health Department and Workers' Compensation Department fall under the Labor Standards Bureau. Other bureaus include Employment Security, Human Resources Development, and Pensions. The Labor Relations Commissions, responsible for administrative adjudication of labor disputes, are considered external organs of the MHLW. Workplace safety standards are set by the MHLW in consultation with the Central Labor Standard's Standing Committee on Safety and Health.

The International Affairs Division of the Minister's Secretariat handles the responsibilities associated with Japan's participation in the ILO, the OECD, and the Asia Pacific Economic Cooperation (APEC) forum. To facilitate its international work, the Ministry is aided by Labor Attaches assigned to Japanese Embassies around the world.

The MHLW also supervises the activities of government-affiliated corporations, including the Labor Welfare Projects Corporation, which implements welfare projects related to workers' compensation; the Foundation for Employment and

[11] *Id.* at art. 89.

[12] Under a new Labor Contract Act (Act No.128, Dec. 5, 2007), effective in 2008, "[C]hanges to Labor Contracts are subject to the mutual agreement of the employee and the employer; provided that the employer may change work rules unilaterally if such change is reasonable in the sense of necessity of such change, appropriateness of the terms after such change, manners of negotiation with the union, etc. (Article 10). The terms and conditions of a Labor Contract that are unfavorable to an employee and which are contrary to the work rules are invalid (Article 12)." Lawrence Carter et al., *New Japanese Labor Law*, DLA Piper Newsletter, March 2008 (On file with author). [Formatting altered] [hereinafter "New Japanese Labor Law"].

[13] Nat'l Inst. of Population and Soc. Sec. Research, Social Security in Japan, Table 1.2, Organization Chart of the Ministry of Health, Labor, and Welfare (2001), *available at* http://www.ipss.go.jp/s-info/e/Jasos2001/p2-6.html (last visited Sept 29, 2010). *See also* Ministry of Health, Labor, and Welfare, *Organization of the Ministry of Health, Labor, and Welfare*, http://www.mhlw.go.jp/english/org/detail/index.html (last visited Sept. 29, 2010).

Human Resources Development, which provides vocational training; and the Japan Institute of Labor, which promotes labor education and research.

The Ministry of Health, Labor, and Welfare

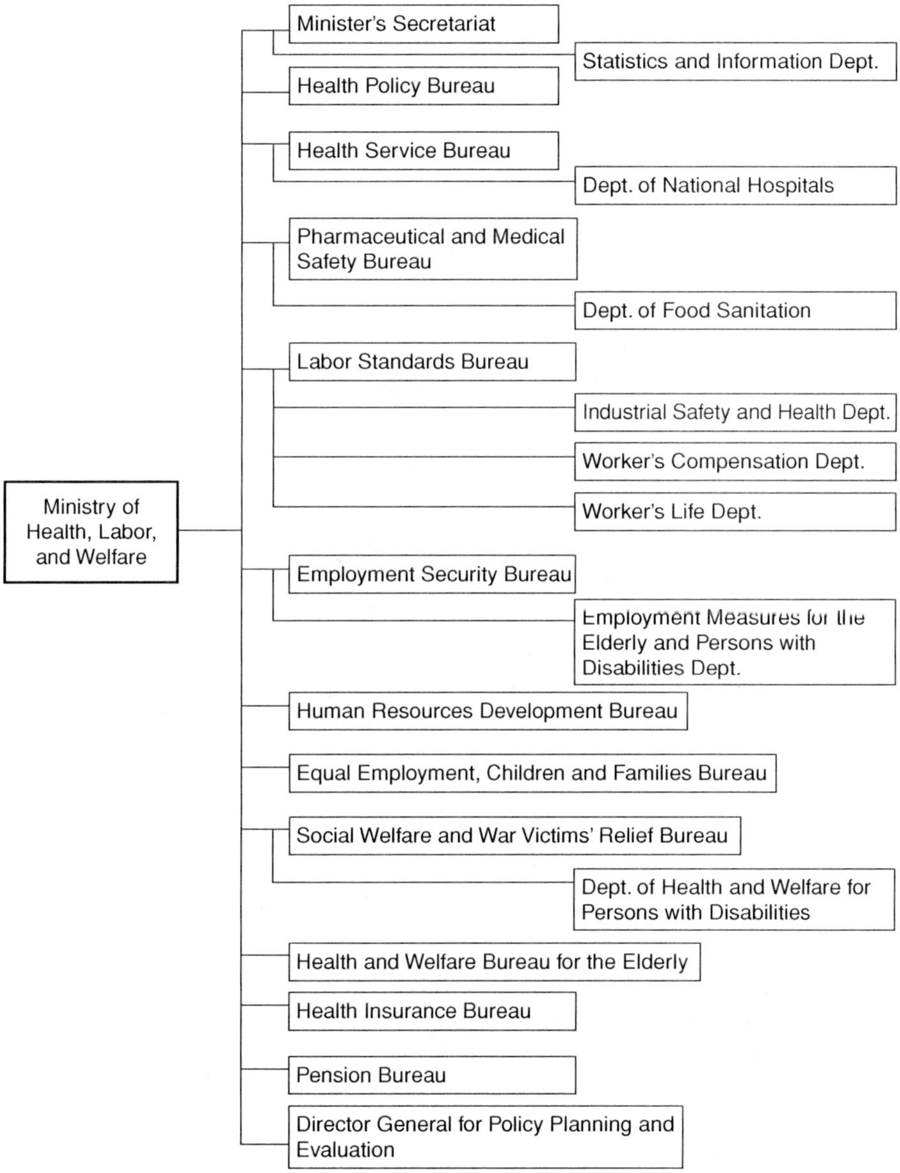

QUESTIONS

1. Do the scope and structural layout of the Japanese labor laws and their administration parallel that of the United States? What are the similarities and differences?
2. Are there other supervising government labor law agencies outside the MHLW?
3. What are the differences of a civil-law-based labor law system versus a common-law-based system?

---

2. *Workers' Labor Rights and Benefits*

Japan's labor-related laws are listed next.

Labor Laws of Japan[14]

1. Labor Union Act (latest revision: 2005)
   Order for the Enforcement of the Labor Union Act
2. Labor Relations Adjustment Act (last revision: 2004)
   Order for the Enforcement of the Labor Relations Adjustment Act (last revision: 2006.2.1)
3. Labor Standards Act (last revision: 2004)
   Ordinance for Enforcement of the Labor Standards Act
4. Defined Contribution Pension Law (last revision: 2001.6.29)
5. Employment Insurance Law (last revision: 2007)
6. Employment Measure Act (last revision: 2009.7.15)
7. Employment Security Act (last revision: 2007)
   Ordinance for Enforcement of the Employment Security Act
8. Human Resources Development Promotion Act (last revision: 2006)
9. Labor Contract Act (Act No.128 of 2007.12. 5)
10. Minimum Wage Law (last revision: 2002.5.31)
11. Act on Promoting the Resolution of Individual Labor-Related Disputes (last revision: 2004)
12. Act on Securing, Etc. of Equal Opportunity and Treatment between Men and Women in Employment (last revision: 2006)
13. Act for Securing the Proper Operation of Worker Dispatching Undertakings and Improved Working Conditions for Dispatched Workers (last revision: 2006)
    Ordinance for Enforcement of the Act for Securing the Proper Operation of Worker Dispatching Undertakings and Improved Working Conditions for Dispatched Workers

[14] The Japan Institute for Labor Policy and Training (JILPT), *Labor Laws of Japan*, http://www.jil.go.jp/english/laborinfo/library/Laws.htm (last visited Mar. 24, 2011).

Order for Enforcement of the Act for Securing the Proper Operation of Worker Dispatching Undertakings and Improved Working Conditions for Dispatched Workers (last revision: 2007)

14. Security of Wage Payment Law (last revision: 2002.5.31)
15. Law concerning Stabilization of Employment of Older Persons (last revision: 2004.6.11)
16. Act on the Succession to Labor Contracts upon Company Split (last revision: 2005)
    Ministry of Labour Ordinance No. 48
    Ministry of Labour Announcement No. 127
17. Act on the Welfare of Workers Who Take Care of Children or Other Family Members Including Child Care and Family Care Leave (last revision: 2004)
18. Act on Improvement, etc. of Employment Management for Part-Time Workers (last revision: 2007)
19. Industrial Accident Compensation Insurance Law (last revision: 2007)
20. Industrial Safety and Health Act (latest revision: 2006)
21. Working Environment Measurement Law (latest revision: 1999.12.22)

National Labor Law Profile – Japan[15]

Liliane Jung

. . . .

Labour Law

Fundamental labour standards are granted in the Constitution. Those are:

- the right and the obligation to work (Art. 27 para. 1)
- a ban on child labour (Art. 27 para. 3) and
- the freedom of workers' association – the worker's right to organize, to bargain and to act collectively (Art. 28).

Concerning individual labour law, it is stipulated that wages, hours, rest, and other working conditions be fixed by law (Art. 27 para. 2).

Japanese labour law is established within this constitutional framework. It is elaborated by acts, ordinances, collective agreements, and work rules. The Civil Code adopted on 27 April 1896, gives a basic definition of employment contracts. Labour laws must additionally meet constitutional demands by setting minimum labour standards. There are three major labour laws, namely:

- the Labour Standards Law (LSL),
- the Trade Union Law (TUL), and
- the Labour Relations Adjustment Law (LRAL).

[15] Liliane Jung, *National Labor Law Profile: Japan*, http://www.ilo.org/ifpdial/information-resources/national-labour-law-profiles/WCMS_158904/lang–en/index.htm (last visited December 3, 2011). Copyright © International Labor Organization.

The LSL regulates firstly working conditions and secondly the workplace safety and hygiene. The TUL guarantees the worker's right to organize and to bargain collectively, whereas labour management adjustments and means of dispute settlement are specified in the LRAL. . . . [16]

The acts apply to Japanese employees of the private sector, with the exception of seafarers, and may also include foreign workers possessing a visa with a work permit. Concerning those employees who work in publically owned enterprises, only the LSL is applicable. Labour relations of public employees are governed mainly by special provisions according to the relevant category. Labour legislation is often supplemented by ordinances, which are issued by the Ministry of Health, Labour and Welfare (prior to 6 January 2001, this role had been fulfilled by the Ministry of Labour) and the appropriate Labour Relations Commission. The latter body consists of representatives coming equally from the workers' and employers' ranks as well as from the general public. Labour legislation also tends to be rather abstract and therefore often needs to be interpreted by ordinary courts, since there are no special labour courts in Japan, and by the Labour Relations Commission.

The second strongest legal norm is the collective agreement, which in practice, for the most part, is enterprise based, because it is mainly the enterprise trade union and the respective employer who draw up agreements. Collective agreements affect primarily those workers of the firm who are trade union members. According to custom, they tend to be put in writing only as far as is legally required. Further provisions of the agreement, which must of course be in line with the law, are often simply agreed to verbally. The written part of the agreements might therefore be simple or vague.

This fact gives more importance to work rules, which stipulate common working conditions at the enterprise level. Any employer with more than 10 employees must draw them up in consultation with the trade union. Work rules must not infringe upon the applying collective agreement. Then, they fix the elements of the labour contracts within the company, independently of whether the individual worker is a trade union member or not. According to the amended Art. 15 of the LSL and its Enforcement Ordinance, contractual matters like wages, working hours, and working conditions must be put in writing, when the labour contract is concluded. In practice, vague contract provisions are nevertheless preferred by the parties so as to have the contract always in line with the work rules and the collective agreement.[17]

. . . .

Contract of Employment

The Permanent and Fixed Term Contracts of Employment

Japanese employment practice . . . [was] traditionally founded on lifetime employment. The employee usually remain[ed] with one company for his/her entire working life. The employment period is thus not stipulated and the post is assured until mandatory

[16] [Author's note.] The TUL was adopted on June 1, 1949, and last amended November 12, 1993. The LRAL was adopted on September 27, 1946, and last amended June 14, 1988.

[17] [Author's note.] The texts (in English) of the Labor Standards Law (including amendments until 1995), Trade Union Law and Labor Relations Adjustment Law are available from NATLEX, the database of national labor, social security, and related human rights legislation maintained by the ILO's International Labor Standards Department.

retirement age, which is usually somewhere between 55 and 60 years. Such a regular employee normally does not have special skills when he/she enters but tends to be trained within the company by being rotated between different jobs and departments. [This is greatly changed in most companies in the current labor market].

. . . .

Fixed term contracts are therefore permitted under the restriction of Art. 14 of the LSL.[18] No objective reason for the limitation is necessary, but the legal period of validity must not be extended. In general, labour contracts of a fixed term must not be longer than one year. In some exceptional cases, the maximum period is three years. Such cases are labour contracts with highly skilled or experienced workers who are necessary for either the development of new products or temporary need of the business. The employment of workers who are at least 60 years can also be limited up to three years.

Equal treatment of fixed term and permanent contractors is not legally mandated. Nevertheless, Art. 2 of the LSL provides for a determination of working conditions by workers and employers on an equal basis. De facto, such determination is strongly influenced by trade unions through collective agreements and work rules, but most of the fixed term contractors are not trade union members and therefore not necessarily covered. Thus, also the unlawful prolongation of the fixed term contract by repeated renewals does not establish an indefinite-term contract as of a regular employee.

Probation

Any labour contract may specify a probation period at the beginning of the employment contract. The probation time is not legally limited. Its renewal is also not prohibited

[18] [Author's note.] In 2008, a new labor contract law was passed. A brief summary follows:

> The new Labor Contracts Law is short and relatively simple, consisting of only 19 Articles. It does not contain any significant new obligations on employers or rights for employees. Rather, it can be said to be a modification of labor law principles that have been developed over time. The key provisions, which are generally restatements of existing principles, include that:
>
> - Labor Contracts need to be executed or amended by mutual agreement of the employee and the employer who are in equal position (Article 3). Note that "Labor Contracts" include reasonable work rules that are known to the employees.
> - Labor Contracts must be confirmed in writing to the extent possible (Article 4.2).
> - Changes to Labor Contracts are subject to the mutual agreement of the employee and the employer; provided that the employer may change work rules unilaterally if such change is reasonable in the sense of necessity of such change, appropriateness of the terms after such change, manners of negotiation with the union, etc. (Article 10).
> - The terms and conditions of a Labor Contract that are unfavorable to an employee and that are contrary to the work rules are invalid (Article 12).
> - A secondment order is invalid if such order is considered an abuse of the employer's right with respect to the necessity of the secondment and the selection of the employee and other circumstances (Article 14).
> - Dismissal and disciplinary action are invalid because it is an abuse of employer's right when such dismissal/disciplinary action is unreasonable and socially inappropriate (Articles 15 and 16).
> - A fixed-term employment contract may not be terminated during its term without a compelling reason (Article 17.1).
> - Employers will give due consideration to the purpose of employment and may not continually renew short-term employment contracts (Article 17.2).

New Japanese Labor Law, *supra* note 12.

by law. A protection against dismissal is nevertheless assured. After the first 14 days of the probation time, the employer is legally forced to consider the normal notice period of 30 days when giving notice (Art. 21 of the LSL). According to court rulings, the employer's freedom to dismiss is also only merely extended during the probation time.

Special Contracts of Employment

Temporary work (dispatched work) is governed by the Worker Dispatching Law (WDL) adopted 5 July 1985, and last amended 30 June 1999. In this employment situation, the worker has an employment contract with a worker dispatching agency but works under the direction of a client company which has concluded a dispatching contract with the dispatching agency. The agency may hire the dispatch worker on a permanent basis. However, most workers are only registered at the agency and then employed for a period according to the request of a client company. This latter type of business requires permission from the Ministry of Health, Labour and Welfare.

Dispatched work is prohibited mainly in port transport, construction and guard services (Art. 4 para. 1). In all other cases, the worker can be dispatched but in principle only up to one year (Arts. 35.2 and 40.2 para. 1). Exceeding the one year limitation the client company will be recommended but not forced by the government to hire the temporary worker as its own employee.

The one year limitation does not apply to the following three cases (Art. 40 para. 1 No. 1–3):

- the dispatched worker has one of the 26 types of listed special skills
- the worker is needed for additional business of a limited duration, or
- the worker taking maternity or child care leave needs to be replaced.

Administrative guidance nevertheless advises against but does not prohibit the dispatching of a worker to the same post for longer than three years.

A *dispatched* worker can report any violation of the WDL to the Ministry of Health, Labour and Welfare (Art. 49). However, his/her legal protection is comparatively weak. For example, there is no obligation to enroll the worker in a social and labour insurance program. Privacy is nonetheless secured considerably in the WDL (Arts. 24–26). *Part-time work* is governed by the Part Time Work Law (PTWL), which came into force 18 June 1993. In the year 2000, 14.7% of all employees worked part-time. Most of them (91.8%) were women. The number is increasing (*Source*: Ministry of Public Management, Home Affairs, Posts, and Telecommunication).

Part-time workers are defined as workers whose scheduled working hours per week are shorter than those of regular employees in the same workplace (Art. 2). De facto, also quasi part-time workers exist. They are part-time workers only in name and in law but work long hours. Part-time workers are considered to be non regular workers, like the fixed term contractors. Regular pay hikes, bonus payment, and retirement allowances thus actually do not apply to them. However, a protection of part-time workers is intended by the PTWL. Part-time workers' abilities, for example, should be used effectively and working conditions should be balanced with those of regular employees (Art. 3 para.1). This is after all no obligation to the employer who is asked only to endeavour. The only obligation laid down in the PTWL applies to the state, e.g. the promotion of the part-timers' welfare by the Ministry of Health, Labour and Welfare (Art. 5).

Vocational training contracts concluded by employers and young employees do not exist in Japan. Instead, young employees are hired on the basis of a normal labour contract and then trained on the job.

Suspension

Many enterprise-based collective agreements and work rules establish suspension periods. A suspension period is a period, during which the labour contract continues to be in force, but the worker has no duty to work and the employer is partly or even completely released from paying wages.

A worker may be suspended firstly as a form of punishment and secondly while a punishment is decided upon, provided that the worker is prosecuted for a severe crime and the court has not yet decided. In any case, each suspension with a possible wage decrease or even cut needs to be appropriate to the situation. Suspension also often occurs, if the employee is on sick leave, becomes a full-time union official, or attends full-time training. The amount of wages to be paid in these cases is determined at the enterprise level with no minimum set by law. However, if the suspension is for reasons attributed to the employer (e.g., temporary layoff), the employer must pay an allowance equal to at least 60% of the worker's average wage (Art. 26 of the LSL).

. . . .

Hours of Work

The average working time as stipulated in Article 32 of the LSL is 40 hours per week and 8 hours per day. These limits may be relaxed for a definite period, which is defined by agreement of the employer and the enterprise trade union or, if such union does not exist, a worker representing a majority of workers. There may be different forms of a flexible working time, which are confined by ordinances. In any case, the average working time during the agreed period must not exceed 40 hours per week (Art. 32–34 of the LSL). The employer must also provide at least one rest day per week as well as rest periods during working hours, at least 45 minutes after 6 working hours and one hour after 8 working hours (Arts. 34 and 35 of the LSL). Night work against increased wages is legally permitted but cannot be ordered to those workers who are raising a child and request to be excepted.

Overtime work may also be stipulated by agreement of the employer and the trade union. Increased wages must then be paid within a range of no less than 25% and no more than 50% over the normal wage per working hour (Art. 37 of the LSL). On the numbers of hours worked overtime, there is no statutory limit, except for female workers responsible for the care of children and senior workers who must receive special protection. The Ministry of Labour, however, is entitled to set a standard limit, by which employers and trade unions shall endeavour to abide. In fact, the number of hours worked overtime is decreasing.

. . . .

The exceptional case of a discretionary work scheme applies to legally specified professionals including highly qualified white collar workers. For the application of this scheme, means of accomplishment and allocation of time must be left largely to the discretion of the employee (Art. 38–34 of the LSL). No overtime premium is paid and the number of working hours is stipulated by the above mentioned agreement regardless of any legal limitation.

Paid Leave[19]

Annual leave with pay of the average wages is granted in Art. 39 of the LSL. The worker can claim it, only if he/she reported for work on at least 80% of the total working days. The number of annual leave days is related to the time the worker has already been employed in the enterprise counting only those years, in which the worker reported sufficiently for work. Upwards of 6 months of continuous employment, the worker can claim 10 days of annual leave. In the following two years, one day per year is added. Being employed for at least two and a half years the worker is guaranteed two days added for each additional year of continuous service. However, the total number of annual leave days does not become more than 20 days. Provided that the vacations do not prevent business from operating adequately, they can be taken whenever the employee decides to do so. In Japan, there are also 14 national holidays a year, which are not legally binding for the private sector.

Maternity Protection and Maternity Leave

Maternity protection is regulated by the LSL. During pregnancy and up to one year after childbirth, a ban is put on heavy physical work and on work with dangerous materials (Art. 64–65). Upon request, the expectant or nursing mother has the right to refuse overtime or night time work and may ask for light work as well.

Maternity leave is secured by Art. 65 of the LSL, which does not include any payments during this period. Upon request, a woman is excused from work within 6 weeks up to childbirth and in case of a multiple birth, within 14 weeks up to giving birth. Within 8 weeks after childbirth, there is in principle a ban on work, but the mother may return to work after 6 weeks, if upon her request and a doctor's approval.

Other Leave Entitlements

The Child Care Leave Act provides for child care leave, which a female as well as a male worker may take in order to care for her/his child who is less than one year old. This right does however not apply to fixed term contractors (Art. 2 No.1). A child care leave benefit is paid according to the Employment Insurance Law (Arts. 61–4 and 61–5). The employee receives a child care leave basic benefit and a reengagement benefit from employment insurance. Social security premiums for health insurance and welfare pension insurance can be exempted on the worker's request.

The employee is also entitled to leave in order to care for a family member according to the Child Care and Family Care Leave Act. The family member, who might be the spouse, the child, the parents, or even the grand-parents, needs to be in a condition requiring continuous care (Art. 2). Such leave must not exceed three months and can, except for certain circumstances, be exercised only once per person (Arts. 15 and 11).[20] The employee does not get any payment during this period.

[19] [Author's note.] *See also* Rebecca Ray & John Schmitt, *No-vacation nation USA – a comparison of leave and holiday in OECD countries*, European Economic and Employment Policy Brief, at 11 (2007), *available at* http://www.law.harvard.edu/programs/lwp/papers/No_Holidays.pdf (last visited Sept. 29, 2010).

[20] [Author's note.] The Child Care and Family Leave Act of 1991 as amended in 2005 allows employees to request leave up to one year to care for a child up to one and a half years old, under-school-age children up to five days per year, or up to three months to care for a family member who

Sick leave as described under *Suspension* is not ruled by law. It may be established by work rules (Art. 89 par. 1 of the LSL). Work rules can also stipulate assistance for injury or illness (Art. 89 para. 8 of the LSL). However, the employee must be given time off to carry out official duties (Art. 7 of the LSL). During menstrual periods, female employees can also request days off (Art. 68 of the LSL).

Minimum Age and Protection of Young Workers

The Constitution puts a ban on child labour (Art. 27 para. 3). This is elaborated in the LSL. Children under 15 full years must not be employed, except for those working for motion picture production and theatrical performances (Art. 56). Children under age 18 may be employed outside of school hours in light labour that is not dangerous or harmful. Underground work is also forbidden.

Equality

Discrimination on the basis of race, creed, gender, social status, or family origin is banned already by the Constitution (Art. 14). This prohibition is elaborated in the LSL (Arts. 3 and 4) and in view of gender also by the Equal Employment Opportunity Act (EEOA).[21] Female and male employees are subject to the same regulations in terms of overtime, night work, and rest days. With respect to wages, gender discrimination is prohibited by the LSL (Art. 4). Discriminatory recruitment, hiring, assignment, and promotion are prohibited on the basis of the EEOA (Arts. 5 and 6). Any violation may be publicized by the Ministry of Health, Labour and Welfare (Art. 26 of the EEOA). The EEOA also prohibits sexual harassment and its observance must be supervised by the employer (Art. 21 para.1).

The Anti-Age Discrimination Law was enacted in 2007.[22] Employees also have a right to privacy regarding the disclosure of personal information. The Personal Information

requires constant care for two or more weeks due to disability. *See* Act on the Welfare of Workers Who Take Care of Children or Other Family Members Including Child Care and Family Care Leave, Law No. 76 of 1991, amendment Law No. 160 of 2004, *translated by* JILPT, *available at* http://www.japaneselawtranslation.go.jp/law/detail/?id=81&vm=04&re=02 (last visited Sept. 29, 2010). Toshiko Kanno, *Act on the Welfare of Workers Who Take Care of Children or Other Family Members Including Child Care and Family Care Leave*, *available at* http://www.jil.go.jp/english/JLR/documents/2007/JLR15_kanno.pdf (last visited Sept. 29, 2010).

21 [Author's note.] Equal Employment Opportunity Act (EEOA) (1986, as amended). *See also The Cabinet Office White Paper on Gender Equality 2009* (May 2009), *available at* http://www.gender.go.jp/whitepaper/ewp2009.pdf (last visited Sept. 29, 2010). The Basic Law for a Gender Equal Society ("Basic Law," Law No. 78 of 1999) calls for the prevention of sexual discrimination and for the creation of equal opportunities for men and women in the workplace. The Basic Law also nullified regulations preventing female employees from working overtime, at night, and on holidays and allows the names of companies that practice sexual discrimination to be publicized. Gender Equality Bureau, Cabinet Office, Government of Japan, *The Basic Law for a Gender-equal Society*, Women and Men in Japan 2009, http://www.gender.go.jp/english_contents/pamphlet/women-and-men09/index.html (last visited Sept. 29, 2010).

22 [Author's note.] Ryoko Sakuraba, *The Amendment of the Employment Measure Act: Japanese Anti-Age Discrimination Law*, 6 Japan Lab. Rev. 56 (2009), *available at* http://www.jil.go.jp/english/JLR/documents/2009/JLR22_sakuraba.pdf (last visited Sept. 29, 2010).

Privacy Law went into effect in 2005 and requires employers to obtain employee consent before collecting or processing the employee's information or before transferring such information to a third party].[23]

Pay Issues

The Japanese wage system is highly dependent on the number of years served with the same company, the employee's level of education and the age also being taken into consideration. Wages are defined as any payment to the worker from the employer, including salaries, allowances and bonuses (Art. 11 of the LSL). In fact, the employee's economic situation is often not only determined by the basic wage but also by added allowances, which may be paid according to particular work rules, e.g., housing allowance or retirement allowance (Art. 89 paras. 3 and 4 of the LSL)....

However, a minimum wage is guaranteed to any employee, as stipulated in Art. 28 LSL and the Minimum Wage Act. The minimum amount is not specified in legislation but set and frequently adjusted by the Ministry of Health, Labour and Welfare in consultation with the Minimum Wage Deliberation Commission. This commission has a national and a local level and is composed of three delegations from among workers, employers, and the public.

The payment of wages is additionally safeguarded, in the case of bankruptcy, with priority being given to wage claims in the paying off of debts.

....

> The Employment Measure Act, which was enacted in 1966 and proclaimed the general principles of Japan's labor market policies, was revised in 2007.... Article 10 stipulates that firms must provide equal opportunities to workers in relation to recruitment and hiring irrespective of age, thereby making a former 'duty to endeavor' into a 'legal duty.' As a result, job offers with age limits may be rejected by employment placement organizations and discriminated workers may claim damages in tort suits.
>
> However, there are some doubts as to the effectiveness of Article 10 due to its broad exemptions, including hiring only 'new graduates.'... Regulations on age-based treatment appear to be merely a patchwork rather than a conclusive anti-age discrimination law.
>
> Apart from the anti-age discrimination provision, in order to improve the employment management of youth and foreigners, the 2007 revision added an obligation of employers to report to Public Employment Security Offices in the event of the employment and separation of foreign workers. It also adopted 'duty to endeavor' provisions and guidelines, both of which recommended employers to take various measures, such as the introduction of a recruitment process for old graduates, employment of youth as regular workers, support of foreign workers in claiming for workers' compensation benefits, and so forth. This paper provides an analysis that though these measures based on 'duty to endeavor' have only weak legal effects, they seem an appropriate means to attain their policy objectives while not giving rise to the issues of 'reverse discrimination' or 'intrusion into freedom of contracts.'

Id.

[23] [Author's note.] World LII Privacy Law Resources, Act on the Protection of Personal Information (Japan) – (2005), http://www.worldlii.org/int/other/PrivLRes/2005/1.html (last visited Sept. 29, 2010). Article 13 of the Constitution provides the basis of privacy rights in Japan. In an employment context, this may limit an employer's right to search an employee's private areas without a reasonable justification. NIHONKOKU KENPO [KENPO][CONSTITUTION], art. 13.

Social Safety Net[24]

Unemployment Benefits[25]

Established in 1947, the employment insurance system is overseen by the MHLW but is administered by the local authorities. The system covers all employees, with the exception of seasonal workers, seamen, and government employees. Coverage is voluntary for employees in firms with fewer than five workers. . . . Employees [and employers] are required to contribute [a] percent of the salary to the employment insurance system. . . . To be eligible for benefits, an individual must have been insured and working for at least six months prior to becoming unemployed. Unemployed workers receive 60 percent to 80 percent of their previous daily wage. The duration of benefits is between 90 to 300 days; depending upon the number of years they have been insured and their age.

Occupational Safety and Health[26]

The MHLW administers the Industrial Safety and Health Law, as well as other laws and regulations governing occupational safety and health. Standards are set by the MHLW and issued after consultation with the Standing Committee on Safety and Health of the Central Labor Standards Council. Japan has Labor Standards Inspection Offices, whose staff carry out safety inspections and accident investigations and provide judicial punishment for serious violations of the law.

Worker's Compensation[27]

Participation in the Worker's Compensation Insurance System is mandatory for all firms in industry and commerce, with the exception of the Government and seamen. It is voluntary for agriculture, forestry, and fishery establishments with less than five workers. Coverage also is open to the self-employed and to workers sent overseas by their employers. . . . All medical expenses are paid for injured workers. After a three-day waiting period, workers receive 60 percent of their daily wage per each missed workday for up to 18 months. In addition, disabled workers are given a temporary disability supplement. . . . Commencing in the 19th month, the severely disabled receive the Injury and Disease Compensation Pension. . . . Permanently disabled individuals are entitled to receive a pension . . . or they can obtain lump-sum compensation . . . if they are less seriously disabled. The permanently disabled also qualify for . . . constant care . . . [and] for part-time care. Survivor benefits include a pension. . . . If no survivors

[24] Bureau of Int'l Labor Affairs, U.S. Dept. of Labor, *Foreign Labor Trends: Japan* (2002), *available at* http://webharvest.gov/peth04/20041102060017/http://www.dol.gov/ILAB/media/reports/flt/japan-2002.pdf (last visited Oct. 2, 2010) [hereinafter "Foreign Labor Trends"].

[25] *See* Employment Insurance Law, Law No. 116 of Dec. 28, 1974, *translated by* The Japan Institute of Labor (JIL), *available at* http://www.jil.go.jp/english/laborinfo/library/documents/llj_law11.pdf (last visited Sept. 29, 2010). For availability of benefits for foreigners, see Nagoya International Center, *Unemployment Insurance*, http://www.nic-nagoya.or.jp/en/e/2010/09/09/unemployment-insurance-3/ (last visited Sept. 29, 2010).

[26] Foreign Labor Trends, *supra* note 24, at 16. Japan National Institute of Occupational Safety & Health (JNIOSH), http://www.jniosh.go.jp/en/index.html (last visited Sept. 29, 2010).

[27] *See* Ministry of Health, Labor, and Welfare, *Worker's Compensation Department*, http://www.mhlw.go.jp/english/org/policy/p19.html (last visited Sept. 29, 2010).

meet the specified age and disability requirements, compensation is given in a lump-sum payment . . . [and] . . . a funeral grant.

. . . .

Health Insurance[28]

Japan has a universal health insurance system, under which all citizens can receive medical attention if they become ill or injured. Businesses with at least five workers must provide their employees and their families with government-managed health insurance or comprehensive insurance obtained from a health insurance association. . . . The National Health Insurance programs cover the self-employed, farmers, employees of small businesses, and the unemployed. Foreign residents of Japan may receive national health insurance if permitted by the local government. . . . Government workers, instructors at private schools, and senior citizens are all covered by insurance from mutual aid associations. . . .

National Pension Program[29]

The Japanese pension system consists of a public pension plan and corporate pension funds.[30] Japanese citizens between the ages of 20 and 59 must be enrolled in the public pension plan, which comprises national pensions, employee pensions, and mutual aid pensions. Farmers and the self-employed contribute a fixed premium . . . per month to the national pension plan and may also subscribe to a supplemental national pension fund. In March 2000, students were given a 10-year grace period from participating in the national pension plan. The Government and government workers equally contribute [a] percent of the worker's monthly salary into the Mutual Aid Pension plan. Employers and employees in the private sector also pay [a] percent of the monthly salary to the Employees' Pension Insurance (EPI), as well as [a] percent on bonuses.

The three pension plans begin paying basic benefits between the ages of 60 and 65. Beginning at age 65, retirees under the national pension plan receive a monthly allotment. . . . Both the Mutual Aid Pension plan and the EPI pay proportional benefits in addition to the national pension benefits; the age at which payments begin is being gradually increased over time from age 60 to age 65 in accordance with the 2000 Public Pension Reform legislation. . . . The national pension plan and the EPI also provide basic pensions to the disabled, as well as pensions to the families of deceased beneficiaries.

. . . .

---

[28] *See* Michael Tanner, *The Grass is Not Always Greener: A Look at National Health Care Systems Around the World*, Policy Analysis, Mar. 18, 2008, at 15–17, *available at* http://www.cato.org/pubs/pas/pa-613.pdf (last visited Oct. 2, 2010).

[29] *See* David Rajnes, *The Evolution of Japanese Employer-Sponsored Retirement Plans*, 67 Soc. Sec. Bull. (2007), *available at* http://www.ssa.gov/policy/docs/ssb/v67n3/v67n3p89.html (last visited Sept. 29, 2010).

[30] In addition to the public pension plan, private-sector employees contribute to the Employee's Pension Insurance; government workers contribute to the Mutual Aid Pension. The three government pension programs are supplemented by corporate pensions, although most retirees prefer to receive a lump sum upon retirement in lieu of pension payments. Individual retirement accounts were introduced in 2001 to supplement the previously mentioned plans.

QUESTIONS

1. What are the strengths and weaknesses in the scope of Japan's labor laws?
2. Which plays a more significant role in Japan in regulating labor – the law or collective agreements? Why?
3. Based on the comprehensive coverage of the labor laws, what assessment can be made whether or not there is meaningful, consistent enforcement of the labor rights?
4. What is the status of contingent workers, part-timers, foreign workers, and women in the Japanese workforce?

3. *Labor Unions and Industrial Relations*

Industrial Relations in Japan

The industrial relations setting in Japan, within which employers and trade unions operate, and which provides the underpinnings of the implementation of the labor law system, is laced with familiar Japanese characteristics and traditions, and even stereotypes. Some are common to Asia, while others are more uniquely Japanese. Some of the dominant features of these Japanese characteristics of labor–management relations are discussed next, followed by a description of labor unions in Japan.

The Three Pillars of Japanese Industrial Relations: Realities and Myths[31]

Ronald C. Brown

....

The Japanese have incorporated the traditional attributes of their personnel management relations, such as a cooperation and working for the common good of the enterprise, into their more recent industrial relations policies. These policies, the so-called "three pillars" of Japanese industrial relations, are lifetime or permanent employment (*shushin koyo*), wage-seniority policies (*nenko*), and enterprise unionism.

Loyalty and cooperation are encouraged by the first two policies because of the job security provided by the policy of permanent employment and by the assurance given to the more senior workers under the wage-seniority policy that even though their wages will be lower initially, the less senior workers generally will not pass them in wages or rank. This protection of a worker's "status" is further supported by a common, related policy of "promoting from within" the company, rather than through a lateral hiring. Over the years there has been low employee mobility as employers seemed reluctant

[31] Ronald C. Brown, *Faces of Japanese Labor Relations and the Emerging Legal Issues Under U.S. Labor Laws*, 15 SYRACUSE J. INT'L L. & COM. 231, 237–39 (1988–1989) [Footnotes omitted].

to hire mobile employees, especially at a lateral level, perhaps because their loyalty is suspect.

The third pillar, enterprise unionism, is a system where employees are organized on a plant-wide basis, rather than on an industrial or craft basis. Also, Japanese unions, while having vertical affiliations, differ from those in the U.S. in that the relationship does not usually provide "international union muscle" at the local enterprise level, but rather performs other functions. The local enterprise union has autonomy over its decisions and rules. Inasmuch as the enterprise union in Japan has the dual function of protecting workers and productivity, it finds itself in a position to be quite responsive to the local needs of the plant.

The face of labor relations portrayed by Japanese employers' use of these three pillars is marred, however, by the fact that these practices are minority practices riddled with exceptions. In fact, lifetime employment is provided to fewer than twenty-five percent [now at about 15 percent] of Japanese workers; pure wage-seniority is available to less than one percent; and enterprise unionism is more prevalent in the larger companies.

In fact, studies show Japanese employees work long work weeks, are noted for not taking their vacation time, and the Japanese employers have a history of under-employing women and minorities, and making great use of temporary workers – the so-called shock absorbers for business fluctuations – who do not qualify for the same benefits as permanent employees.

Critics of the Japanese system of labor relations contend that in addition to the statistical absence of the three pillars of industrial relations in Japan, there are other defects. For example, life-time employment may keep incompetent but loyal employees on the payroll, but if they are not producing, this cuts into efficiency.

The policy of wage-seniority is a method of deferred compensation that permits an employer to employ young workers very inexpensively and arguably inhibits their mobility as every year goes by.

The third pillar, enterprise unionism, is viewed by some as too weak a protection for workers. They argue that the union's loyalty is divided loyalty and their lack of effective affiliation at either a horizontal or vertical level renders the union too responsive to the needs of the employer at the expense of the workers.

Recent commentary about Japan suggests that work is long and hard in Japan, that labor mobility is on the rise, and that underneath the veneer of cooperation is a strenuous competition. This is the face of Japanese labor relations seen by some.

. . . .

Emerging Styles of Management and Labor Relations: Understanding the "New Labor Relations"[32]

Ronald C. Brown

. . . .

Management philosophies and industrial relations policies of Japanese employers generally contain five underlying principles.

[32] Ronald C. Brown, *Labor Law Issues Facing Multinational and Japanese Companies Operating in the United States and United States Companies Using Japanese-Style Labor Relations: Agenda Items under the "New Labor Relations,"* 8 U. Haw. L. Rev. 261, 267–272 (1986) [Footnotes omitted].

First, their primary concern is the continued existence and further development of their corporation. Second, they regard all company employees, including themselves, as members of the same corporate community. Third, they take an egalitarian view of income distribution between labor and management within the company. Fourth, they are crucially concerned with maintaining stability and peace in the company's industrial relations. In other words, they strive to avoid industrial disputes and strikes, often at any cost. Fifth, they tend to reject the intervention of outside labor groups in any negotiations over internal labor problems, an attitude that might be described as exclusionist.

These principles pervade the ["traditionally-perceived"] Japanese personnel management system, and although there are many similarities with the American system, one of the most apropos of the many comparisons made of American and Japanese management approaches is that "Japanese and American management is 95 percent the same and differs in all important respects." [The three dominant features are below].

a. Collectivism

Japanese notions of familism and collectivism, which are based on Japanese culture and the *amae* relationship merge individual interests with group interests. Japanese workers see themselves as contributing to a group effort rather than to an individual cause. These same principles are also evident in Japanese corporate structures. For example, the managerial structures of the zaibatsu, a pre-World War II Japanese conglomerate, was based on "familial principles of hierarchy, loyalty, and dependency" which were "essentially that of the hierarchical familism of traditional Japan." These principles seem to persist in modern Japanese corporations. The parent-child or lord-servant (*oyabun-kobun*) relationship is analogous to the parent (*oya-gaisha*) and subsidiary (*ko-gaisha*) company relationship. The parent maintains firm control over its subsidiary by providing managerial, technical, and financial support; the subsidiary, in turn, provides services and outreach for the parent.

Personnel practices are also based on a cultural background of familism. Two of the most significant management personnel practices are the tradition of cooperation between employer and employees and the system of seeking consensus before implementing decisions.

Japanese firms try to achieve cooperation by treating their employees as part of the family, thus humanizing employment relations. These efforts manifest themselves in policies which discourage layoffs and firings and which encourage retention and retraining rather than replacement of employees when new technology would otherwise displace them. The system of having supervisors, as "associates," working side-by-side with workers, de-emphasizes "management-worker" class distinctions. All levels of management attempt to mix with workers at the work place and at work-related social gatherings.

Cooperation is further manifested in company policy providing for joint consultation (*roshikyo giseido*) through committees and meetings between the employer and the workers. While Japanese law mandates some of these joint committees, or at least their subject matter, these committees also deal with issues involving terms and conditions of employment and seek to raise productivity and prevent industrial conflict.

An example of such joint consultation in Japan is collective bargaining. Three features characterize the Japanese collective bargaining system: "(1) it is practiced within the boundaries of each individual enterprise; (2) labor unions are concentrated in the large enterprises; and (3) both white- and blue-collar workers are members of and are represented by the same union." Joint consultation, regardless of form, is further facilitated by the sharing of information with employees, which in turn supports a necessary element of cooperation-trust.

Consensus decision making (*ringi* system) also flows from the continual meetings of quality control groups, joint consultation committees, and collective bargaining representatives. The workers and management, through a series of "orchestrated" meetings, contribute and exchange ideas as they strive for unanimity in the announcement of the final "decision," now accepted by all.

b. Job Flexibility

Another characteristic of Japanese management is job flexibility: the hiring, training, and utilization of employees for a variety of job functions within the employer's enterprise. Job flexibility permits greater managerial use of the worker to provide performance when and where it is needed without the encumbrances of job classifications, inadequate training, work rules, or contract restrictions. Thus, Japanese management emphasizes functional interdependence rather than job specificity, and group rather than individual performance. By reducing job categories and rotating workers within a plant, Japanese managers seek to "[broaden] an employee's job skills . . . improve employee morale and help nurture a holistic perspective regarding the firm's business and competitive posture."

The characteristics of job flexibility require that Japanese employers take great care in the recruitment of new employees "into the family" since they generally will be retained for their entire work career. Japanese recruiters emphasize not just the somewhat objective factor of the worker's ability to perform the work but also place great importance on subjective qualifications relating to personal and social characteristics, such as how well the worker will "fit in," his or her prior conduct, character, thought, and home environment. The use of these subjective factors in interviews, background checks, and testing may expose the Japanese employer to charges of racial and anti-union motivations in potential violation of American labor laws.

c. Conflict Avoidance[33]

Another dominant characteristic of Japanese personnel management relations is the use of pervasive, culture-based, conflict-avoidance techniques to resolve disputes. Cooperation and joint consultation procedures both work toward harmony in the workplace. Japanese labor dispute resolution has three distinguishing characteristics:

1. There is a "societal pressure towards consensus, which places a heavy responsibility on the parties to resolve a dispute by themselves and without resorting to overt conflict."
2. There is a "tendency for industrial action to be taken in demonstrative form."

[33] See discussion re: "saving face" in CONFLICT IN JAPAN 116 (Ellis S. Krauss et al. eds., 1984), relevant portions also available at http://books.google.com/books?id=pMebnnqB_eoC&lpg=PA377&ots=4vAqcorA-T&dq=CONFLICT%20in%20JAPAN%2C%20Ellis%20S.%20Krauss&pg=PA377#v=onepage&q&f=false .

3. The union, "being mindful of the extent to which its members' interests are bound up in the enterprise, is likely to refrain from any action likely to prejudice its long-term future: thus, harassment rather than damage is what is aimed at."

. . . .

Labor Unions in Japan

Unions in Japan are divided into labor federations, trade unions, and enterprise unions. The three national labor federations in Japan are the Japanese Union Confederation (Rengo), the National Confederation of Trade Unions (Zenroren), and the National Trade Union Council (Zenrokyo). These organizations serve as a voice for members in national politics.[34] Rengo is the largest of the three and represents almost two-thirds of union workers from seventy industry-level unions. Industry-level unions coordinate negotiating tactics and labor demands of workers across their respective industries. Of the more than sixty-seven thousand unions in Japan in 2000, over 90 percent were enterprise-based unions. Enterprise unions engage in collective bargaining directly with company management.

It has been noted "[T]he unionization rate in the world's second largest economy actually rose for the first time since 1975, according to the country's Ministry of Health, Labor, and Welfare. The estimated percentage of union members among all employees for 2009 was 18.5 percent, up 0.4 percent from last year. While the increase is marginal, it marks the first time in 34 years in which union membership showed consecutive yearly growth."[35]

Below is a self-described description of RENGO.

The National Center in Japan: RENGO[36]

Countries with strong national centers have strong trade unions! Japanese trade union organizations have a three-tier hierarchical structure: enterprise-based unions, industrial federations, and the national center at the top. There is also a wide-ranging network, with local organizations, called "Local RENGOs," set up in all of Japan's prefectures.

The enterprise-based unions utilize negotiations and labor-management consultations in the workplace to improve working conditions, monitor corporate activities, and provide services to their members.

The industrial federations for their part are composed of enterprise-based unions in the same industry. Their member unions exchange information on common working

[34] Foreign Labor Trends, *supra* note 24.

[35] Akito Yoshikane, *Uptick in Japan's Union Members Mirrors U.S. Trend*, WORKING IN THESE TIMES (Dec. 23, 2009), http://www.inthesetimes.com/working/entry/5351/uptick_in_japans_union_members_mirrors_u.s._trend/ (last visited May 19, 2011).

[36] Japanese Trade Union Confederation, *RENGO Updates*, http://www.jtuc-rengo.org (last visited Sept. 30, 2010).

conditions in the industry, discuss industrial policies and other problems, and strive to rectify these industry-specific problems.

RENGO itself is a national center, made up of these industrial federations. From the standpoint of "defending the employment and livelihoods of all working people," including of course RENGO union members, we work with the national government and employers' organizations on issues such as labor standards, tax systems, and social security, which cannot be settled at the industry or local level.

Further, the forty-seven Local RENGOs throughout the country serve as a foothold for working people in their local communities. They address a broad range of tasks, including consultation activities on issues of labor and employment. They also provide support for organizing efforts.

By bringing together the power of individual trade unions, the national center is able to raise the level of working conditions and living standards for all workers. Successes in these areas by the national center create, in turn, trust toward trade unions at the workplace level, contributing to strengthening enterprise-based unions and their industrial federations. In the past, Japan had several divided national centers, but efforts to enhance the power of trade unions resulted into the formation in 1989 of a unified national center, Japanese Trade Union Confederation, or RENGO.

. . . .

With regard to problems that should be solved at the national government and/or municipal government levels, the opinions of working people need to be reflected to help realize better policy solutions. These efforts are what we mean by institutional and policy-related demands. This is one of the areas where RENGO exerts its remarkable strength as the national center. We have made systematic demands in areas ranging from economic policy, tax reform, social security policy, employment and labor policy, reforms in welfare/political/administrative/judicial systems, and industry and energy policy, to gender equality and human rights, the environment, education, foreign policy, and measures for medium and small enterprises. In national and municipal advisory councils, where essential legislation and policy measures are debated, members nominated by RENGO have articulated the opinions of labor vis-à-vis new legislative bills and major amendments to existing laws.

The Spring Struggle for a Better Life

The Spring Struggle for a Better Life is an effort for the comprehensive improvement of living, with the specific goal of raising working conditions.

Typically, the new fiscal year in Japan starts from April. Most businesses take in fresh recruits, and carry out revisions of their wage rates, promotions, and transfers at this time. Therefore, in accord with this season of change, the "Spring Struggle for a Better Life" was launched in 1955, as a time for trade unions to file demands for wage hikes and improvements of working conditions to their employers and to conduct negotiations.

During the period of high economic growth, this Spring Struggle was very effective in pushing labor's demands. Industrial federations staged unified struggles focused on wage hikes. Their affiliates made their demands simultaneously, and asked their employers for sincere responses, sometimes using the threat of strikes. A system was built under which the contents of labor agreements won by major unions had an impact on the wage rates and other working conditions of smaller unions, nonunionized workers, and public employees whose trade union rights are unjustly restricted.

. . . .

RENGO Structures[37]

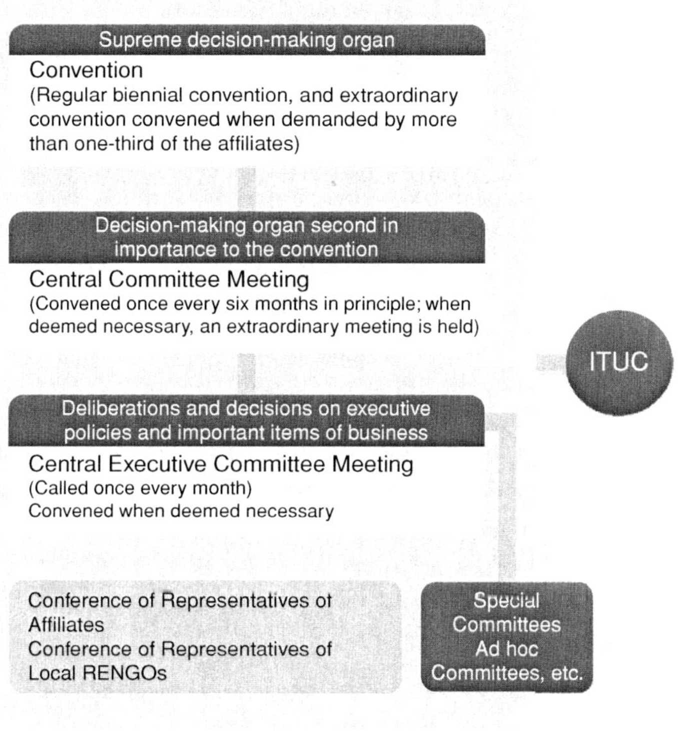

National Labor Law Profiles – Japan[38]

Liliane Jung

. . . .

Trade Unions

The freedom of workers' associations is granted in Art. 28 of the Constitution. Trade unions are regulated in the Trade Union Law (TUL) and defined as those organisations, which are formed autonomously and composed mainly of workers for the main purposes of maintaining and improving working conditions and raising the economic status of

[37] *Id.*

[38] Jung, *supra* note 15. *See also* Foreign Labor Trends, *supra* note 24.

workers (Art. 2).[39] Legally covered are all workers, except for those either with a supervisory position or working for welfare or political and social movements (Art. 2 paras. 1, 3, and 4). De facto, non-regular workers – temporary and part-time employees – are also mostly not unionized.

The trade union's constitution must inter alia include the members' right to participate in all affairs and prohibit the disqualification for union membership on the basis of race, religion, gender, social status, or family origin (Art. 5–2). Trade unions meeting all conditions are registered by the Labour Relations Commission and then they gain a legal personality as well as legal protection. This covers protection against unfair labour practices (Art. 7). Any discrimination because of trade union activities is forbidden, and the employer must not have any influence on the trade union's management. The employer is also not entitled to refuse to bargain collectively without proper reason.

Over 90% of the unions are formed within the limits of one company. These enterprise unions engage in activities and issues related to their members within the enterprise. However, most of the enterprise unions in the same industry are affiliated to industry federations such as the Confederation of Japan Automobile Workers and the Japanese Electronic and Information Union. Industry federations are generally constituents of the nationwide Japanese Trade Union Confederation (Rengo). Rengo, which was founded in 1989, absorbed rival national organisations and embraces now unions of the private as well as from the public sector. Its competitor of much smaller size and politically more to the left is the National Confederation of Trade Unions (Zenroren). The industry federations and also the nation-wide confederation are in charge with the discussion and the advice on general policies like wages or working conditions.

Employers' Association

Employers' organisations are not covered by the TUL, even though there are a number which impact on the role of employers. The Japanese Federation of Employers' Associations (Nikkeiren) plays a main role on behalf of employers in industrial relations. It has no direct part in collective bargaining but sets guidelines to employers and thus actually influences labour issues. It is also the official voice of Japanese employers in the International Labour Organisation (ILO).

Collective Bargaining and Agreements

According to Art. 14 of the TUL, parties to collective bargaining must be, on one side, a trade union and, on the other, either the employer or an employers' association.

[39] To enjoy the statutory rights and remedies afforded unions, the labor organization must satisfy four basic requirements: (a) the union must primarily be formed of workers; (b) the union must be independent; (c) purpose must be to maintain and improve working conditions and status; (d) union must be an organization or federation of an organization. In general, no union can claim to represent members of another union and the right to become a member extends to both public- and private-sector workers, although managers and certain staff representing employer's interest are ineligible for membership. In Japan, multiple unions may coexist within a single company. *See* Trade Union Structure and Recognition, Trade Union Law, art. 2 (last visited June 17, 2011). Takato Natsui, *Trade Union Law*, LINKS TO LAW OF JAPAN, http://www.isc.meiji.ac.jp/~sumwel_h/links/linkJ04.htm (last visited Sept. 29, 2010).

In practice, collective bargaining is mostly enterprise based. The employer must bargain with the appropriate trade union in good faith (Art. 7 para. 2 of the TUL). According to the Supreme Court's decision, this applies also in favour of a trade union representing dispatched workers, if it wants to bargain with the client company regarding dispatched work related working conditions (668 Rodo Hanrei 11; Sup.Ct. Feb. 28, 1995).

Further regulation of the collective bargaining process may be found in respective enterprise based collective agreements, which often oblige employers to consult the trade union. In Japan, consultation is regarded as a peaceful attempt to reach convergence, whereas collective bargaining is recognized as a confrontation. Often, collective bargaining can barely be distinguished from strike actions. Joint consultation may take place prior to collective bargaining or may replace it in management policies that do not provide for the possibility of bargaining. In some cases, even formal consultative committees are set up.

Wages are traditionally discussed each year in spring during the so called *spring offensive*. Enterprise unions submit claims for pay increases under coordination from Rengo and Zenroren as well as from the industrial federations. The employers respond under the guidance of Nikkeiren. As soon as the major enterprises of influential industries come to an agreement, a pattern is set for medium- and small-sized enterprises. However, circumstances of individual firms are always taken into consideration, because it is the enterprise union's own interest not to damage their own firm.

Written and signed collective agreements may have different terms of validity, but must not exceed three years (Art. 15 of the TUL). Only those agreements in which no term of validity is provided for can be terminated at either party's initiative at any time (Art. 15–3 of the TUL). A collective agreement, which had ended, is basically no longer effective, but the parties may agree that it should remain in force until a new collective agreement is concluded.

All collective agreements apply primarily to those employees who are trade union members. If in one workplace, three-fourths of comparable workers fall under a collective agreement, this agreement applies to all workers of the same kind within the workplace (Art. 17 of the TUL). A collective agreement may have general binding power even in a whole locality, which is actually an exception (Art. 18 of the TUL). This requires that the agreement applies to a particular locality, not only to a firm, and a majority of comparable workers is bound. Further, the Ministry of Health, Labour and Welfare must upon request of either party and pursuant to a resolution of the Labour Relations Commission declare the agreement as binding to all workers of the same kind.

Collective agreements have a normative effect on work rules and labour contracts. Work rules must not infringe upon the collective agreement (Art. 92 of the LSL) and any labour contract's provision that contravenes the standards set by the agreement is null and void (Art. 16 of the TUL). A majority interprets these rules not as the setting of minimum standards but as the establishment of a pattern, which should be followed in every respect.

Collective agreements additionally establish duties and rights to the contractual parties – mostly the employer and the enterprise trade union. The employer has always the obligation of executing what is to be understood as an obligation to provide conditions according to the collective agreement. In many cases, further duties are imposed like the employer's obligation to consult the trade union.

Workers' representation in the enterprise

Within the enterprise, workers are usually represented by an enterprise trade union organized by a majority of the workers. Its members are elected out of the own workers' ranks. The election as well as the term of office is ruled in the trade union's constitution. If such a trade union does not exist, the interest of the workers' majority must be represented by a single worker.

Workers' representation is of considerable importance in the drawing up of work rules, which the employer is obliged to do as soon as 10 or more workers are continuously employed (Art. 89 of the LSL). Before drawing up work rules the employer has to consult the trade union or the representing employee (Art. 90–1 of the LSL). The given statement then needs to be attached, when the employer submits the work rules to the Labour Standards Inspection Office (Art. 90–2 of the LSL).

. . . .

QUESTIONS

1. Discuss the strengths and weaknesses of the enterprise union system.
2. To whom does the union owe its loyalty? How is that accommodation possible? Is it a good model?
3. Is the protection of labor rights better protected by collective contracts or by statutory protections?
4. How do the Japanese union structures differ, if at all, from those in the United States?

---

4. *Dispute Resolution*

Labor disputes arise in many ways, including from discipline, termination, and contract violations. They may emanate from contractual or statutory labor rights and may involve an individual or collective labor right. The processes of dispute resolution vary in Japan, depending on whether the labor right is individual or collective.[40]

---

[40] "Labor conflict resolution machineries have concentrated on collective dispute settlement in Japan. Grievance procedures stipulated in labor contracts have not been working effectively. The center of gravity of labor-management relations has shifted from collective bargaining with labor unions to individual labor contracts with individual workers both in the unorganized sector and the nonunion members within the organized sector. Similarities and differences between Japan and the United States are examined. Vague demarcation between rights and interest disputes as well as between collective and individual disputes characterizes the dispute settlement machineries in Japan." Kazutoshi Koshiro, *Abstract to Formal and Informal Aspects of Labor Dispute Resolution in Japan*, 22 Law & Pol'y 353–367, *available at* http://www3.interscience.wiley.com/journal/119009813/abstract?CRETRY=1&SRETRY=0 (last visited Sept. 29, 2010).

a. Labor Disputes

National Labor Law Profile – Japan[41]

Liliane Jung

Termination of Employment

Termination of a labour contract at the worker's and the employer's initiative is governed by Art. 627 of the Civil Code, under which they are free to terminate the contract. In order to meet the demand of Art. 27 of the Constitution to promote job security as a public matter, the employer's dismissal is limited predominantly by the LSL, court rulings, and collective agreements. This restriction applies to unlimited labour contracts as well as to those contracts of a definite period which have continued for longer than the period prescribed by law.[42]

Notice must be given at least 30 days in advance before the dismissal takes effect (Art. 20 of the LSL). The number of days can be reduced, if the employer pays the average wage for each day by which the period is shortened. It is recommended by court rulings but not legally required to give notice in writing. Legal precedent further established the rule that the dismissal must be based on a reasonable cause. Without reasonable cause any dismissal is regarded as an abuse of the right to dismiss and thus considered null and void. For example, a dismissal for business reasons is allowed, if it satisfies all of the four requirements set by court:

- A personnel reduction is based on business necessity.
- Every possible measure to avoid layoffs is tried.
- The selection of employees to be dismissed is made on an objective and reasonable basis.
- The employer consults faithfully with unions or employees.

On the contrary, dismissals on the following grounds or during the following periods are regarded as null and void:

- reason of marriage, pregnancy or childbirth (Art. 11 para. 3 of the Act on Equal Opportunity and Treatment between Men and Women in Employment)
- requesting child care leave (Art. 7 of the Act Concerning the Welfare of Workers who take Care of Children or Other Family Members)
- trade union activities guaranteed by Art. 28 Constitution (Art. 7 of the TUL)
- the sex of the worker (Art. 8 para. 1 of the Act on Equal Opportunity and Treatment between Men and Women in Employment)
- during the absence of an employee because of work related illness and 30 days thereafter (Art. 19 of the LSL)
- during an employee's maternity leave and 30 days thereafter (Art. 19 of the LSL).

41 Jung, *supra* note 15.

42 Practical advice on worker rights in the government procedures is provided in the following. University Teachers Union Information (2008), http://nugw.org/utu/downloads/UTUInformation.pdf (last visited Sept. 29, 2010).

Giving notice in advance when dismissing an employee is not obligatory in two exceptional cases laid down in Art. 20 of the LSL:

> The continuance of the enterprise has been made impossible by a natural disaster or an equivalent inevitable reason.
>
> The dismissal is for reasons attributable to the worker.
>
> On the employee's request, the employer shall deliver a certificate stating reasons for dismissal without delay (Art. 22 of the LSL). In case of an illegal dismissal, the court orders the continuance of the labour contract and the employee is reinstated. The employee also may claim damages instead. . . .
>
> . . . .

Labour Disputes[43]

Article 28 of the Constitution guarantees the workers' right to act collectively, which includes labour disputes. Labour disputes are defined in the Labour Relations Adjustment Law (LRAL) as "a disagreement over claims regarding labour relations arising between the parties concerned with labour relations resulting in either the occurrence of acts of dispute or the danger of such occurrence" (Art. 6). For labour disputes, the trade union and its members are liable neither under civil law nor under penal law, as long as they act properly (Arts. 8 and 1 para. 2 of the TUL). This requires firstly that it is a legally registered trade union that acts and secondly that no violence is used (Art. 1 para. 2 of the TUL). Legally recognized are the acts of dispute mentioned in Art. 7 of the LRAL, such as strikes, slowdowns, and other acts hampering the normal course of work, like the order to all workers to take holiday on the same day or the posting of posters on the establishments premises. Also shutting down the flow of traffic through the gates is a legal form of labour dispute, as long as it is peaceful. All acts must additionally be for a lawful purpose, which is surely the achievement of better working conditions. The workers are paid no wages while striking.

Lock outs

The employer's right to lock out employees is not constitutionally and legally established. However, it is recognized as a right of defence by a majority, but the employer needs to gain first an injunction from the court.

> . . . .

---

[43] Jung, *supra* note 15. [Author's note] Industrial actions do occur in Japan. Strikes can be engaged in, but when they occur, they usually continue for only a short period of time; only defensive lockouts are permitted; picketing is a common practice, but cannot include physical force as this is considered illegal; handbilling is quite common both inside and outside of employer's premises, and slow-downs and sit-ins are not common in Japan.

INTERNAL GRIEVANCE MECHANISMS. A vast majority of unionized enterprises employ labor-management consultation systems to promote information exchange and mutual understanding between enterprise unions and management.[44] Firms without unions may have joint consultation systems.[45] Such systems may be leveraged to mitigate conflicting interests to head off disputes, provide an alternative to collective bargaining, give workers an ongoing voice in operations, and offer a forum for pre-collective bargaining consultations.[46]

Administrative Mediation, Conciliation, and Arbitration

TRADE UNIONS: COLLECTIVE RIGHTS. The Labor Relations Commission is a tripartite system under the Trade Union Law comprised of commissioners representing the public, employers, and workers. In order to bring a dispute before the Commission a union must qualify for recognition under Article 2 of the Trade Union Law. The procedures for the resolution of collective disputes are set forth in the Labor Relations Adjustment Act, which emphasizes voluntary settlement of disputes. If the prefectural Labor Relations Commission determines that an unfair labor practice has occurred, the Commission may issue a remedial order (such as reinstatement of an employee, ordering an employer to bargain in good faith, etc.). An employer may appeal the order of a prefectural Labor Relations Committee to the Central Labor Commission or seek judicial review. Mediation and conciliation results may be rejected by the parties. Arbitration awards are binding.

INDIVIDUAL RIGHTS. Under the Law to Promote Resolution of Individual Labor Relations Disputes,[47] an individual complainant (the law is reserved for individual rather than organized labor disputes) can file a grievance with Regional (Prefectural) Labor Office (of the Ministry of Health, Labor, and Welfare).[48] If there is a possible violation of employment law, the Labor Office will refer the matter to the Labor

44 KAZUO SUGENO, JAPANESE EMPLOYMENT AND LABOR LAW 554 (Leo Kanowitz trans., 2002). Individual labor grievance-arbitration provisions may also be used, see, e.g., RENGO Model Contract, but the arbitration must, under law, be advisory only since the two options available to an individual are civil proceedings or the Labor Tribunal. Labor Tribunal Law, art. 16 and based on 2011 author interviews with Judge Kazutaka Tanaka, Labor Tribunal, Tokyo District Court.

45 *Id.* at 555.

46 *Id.* at 554.

47 Kobetsu dōrō funsō no kaiketsu no sokushin kansuru hōritsu [Law to Promote Resolution of Individual Labor Relations Disputes], Law No. 112 of 2001, *available at* http://www.jil.go.jp/jil/laborinfo-e/docs/llj_law8.pdf (last visited Sept. 29, 2010) [hereinafter "Individual Labor Relations Disputes Law"].

48 Kazuo Sugeno, *The Birth of the Labor Tribunal System in Japan: A Synthesis of Labor Law Reform and Judicial Reform*, 25 COMP. LAB. L. & POL'Y J. 519, 520–21, 524 (2005), *available at* http://www.law.uiuc.edu/publications/CLL&PJ/archive/vol_25/issue_4/SugenoArticle25-4.pdf (last visited Sept. 30, 2010) [Footnotes omitted].

Standards Inspection Office for further investigation, which may in turn either issue a notice of recommendation (usually a request for an apology or other minor remedial action) to the respondent on behalf of the complainant, or refer the complainant and respondent to the Dispute Adjustment Commission for conciliation.[49] The Dispute Adjustment Commission is comprised of three to twelve commissioners serving two-year terms, part-time.[50] Mediators are typically practicing lawyers and law professors.[51] In 2003, out of approximately 170,000 cases handled by all of the national labor offices, about 4,500 were resolved with notices of recommendation and 5,000 cases were mediated.[52]

Judicial

TRADE UNIONS. Union cases begin and typically end with Labor Relations Commissions. Courts rarely play a role in the appeals process. Nonetheless courts tend to treat remedial orders from Labor Relations Commissions with deference.[53]

INDIVIDUALS. In addition to and without prior administrative conciliation, an individual worker may proceed with a civil claim under an individual or collective contract in district court. Upon hearing the complaint, the district court organizes a labor tribunal composed of a career judge, a representative from labor, and a representative from management.[54] Labor and management representatives are appointed to the district court on a part-time basis for a two-year term before they are assigned to individual cases.[55] The tribunal sends a copy of the complaint to the respondent and notifies both parties of their appearance date. Proceedings are informal and generally not open to the public.[56] To limit the time to a final decision, hearings are limited to three sessions intended to take no more than three to four months from start to finish.[57] At the third session the tribunal will propose a settlement.[58] If either party rejects this, the tribunal will issue a decision.[59] If neither party rejects the decision or if they mutually accept it, the decision becomes binding.[60] If both parties reject the decision, it is not binding and the matter will be

49 Individual Labor Relations Disputes Law, *supra* note 47, at art. 5, para. 1; *see also id.* at 525.
50 Individual Labor Relations Disputes Law, *supra* note 47, at arts. 6–8.
51 Sugeno, *The Birth of the Labor Tribunal System in Japan*, *supra* note 48, at 525.
52 *See id.* at 525–26.
53 *Id.*
54 *Id.* at 530.
55 *Id.*
56 *Id.*
57 *Id.*
58 *Id.* at 531.
59 *Id.*
60 *Id.*

returned to the district court where the parties may continue with civil litigation if so desired.[61]

---

b. Labor Dispute Resolution Processes

Japan has introduced a new process for resolving individual labor disputes, housed within the judicial system. Professor Kazuo Sugeno explains and summarizes the process in the below article. This is followed by an assessment of the new system by Professor Takashi Araki.

The Birth of the Labor Tribunal System in Japan: A Synthesis of Labor Law Reform and Judicial Reform[62]

Kazuo Sugeno

. . . .

II. The Conventional System: Infrequent Employment Disputes until the 1980s

Judicial reform attained an important innovation in labor dispute resolution through the introduction of the Labor Tribunal System. According to the Labor Tribunal Law, enacted in April 2004, either party in an employment relationship can bring a dispute of rights arising from employment relations under this procedure in the district court. A tribunal composed of one career judge and two part-time experts in labor relations first makes mediation efforts, and, if such efforts fail, renders a decision clarifying the merits of the case and specifying measures to resolve the case. The decision is not binding, and if either party objects, the case is automatically transferred to an ordinary civil procedure. The Law requires the tribunal to dispose of the case within three sessions, and is premised upon the cases lasting a few months. This measure to reform the labor dispute resolution system was introduced recently to cope with the drastic increase in employment disputes since the collapse of the bubble economy.

The Japanese labor law system established after World War II attached the highest importance to collective bargaining disputes, the rights for which are guaranteed by the Constitution and the Trade Union Law. Under this Law, Labor Relations Commissions were established as expert agencies to handle collective labor disputes through their mediation, conciliation, and arbitration procedures. Commissions were also endowed with power to adjudicate complaints of unfair labor practices prohibited under the Law. The expertise of the Commissions mainly derived from the assistance of labor and management members toward neutral members, who presided over procedures and decided on the cases.

Individual labor disputes arising from employment relations, on the other hand, were not regarded as significant enough to require a particular system for their resolution.

[61] *Id.*

[62] Sugeno, *The Birth of the Labor Tribunal System in Japan*, *supra* note 48.

Thus, the post-War labor law system did not prepare any special scheme to deal with disputes of rights in employment relations. Such disputes were entrusted to ordinary civil procedures.

Under this "conventional" labor law system, workers can claim rights guaranteed by the labor statutes, collective agreements, work rules, or employment contracts by filing lawsuits in the court. These suits are brought in an ordinary court that has jurisdiction of the first instance with regard to the case in accordance with the Civil Procedure Law. The judges presiding over procedures and making judgments are those who have developed a career in the judiciary after finishing legal education and passing the State Legal Examination. They do not specialize in labor law, but apply all fields of law as they are rotated to various courts or benches. Only certain district courts located in urban areas have the benches specializing in labor cases.

Besides such regular procedure, the Civil Temporary-Relief Law sets forth provisional procedures for giving temporary relief in civil actions. The most useful for cases involving employment relationships is a "provisional disposition procedure" by which a temporary order, named a "provisional disposition order," may be issued. To obtain such an order, the Law requires the claimant to establish prima-facie proof of the merits of the case and of the urgency for temporary relief. The Law also makes the provisional procedure more informal by releasing the claimant from the requirement of formal and adversarial hearings. With dismissals and other terminations of employment, there is usually an urgent need to give prompt relief to the workers. Accordingly, workers frequently use such procedures when seeking relief for employment terminations.

Since 1970, the annual number of newly filed lawsuits involving labor relations has numbered around 1,000, including both the regular and provisional procedures. As discussed in the next section, there has been a drastic increase in this number in the Post-Bubble period, but the figure is still extremely small in comparison to other industrialized countries such as the United States, Great Britain, Germany, and France.

The relative infrequency of employment litigation in industrial relations has been one aspect of the general non-litigiousness of Japanese society, which can be attributed to the difficulties ordinary citizens face in pursuing litigation. The shortage of lawyers, the financial and mental costs of litigation, the formalities of the court, and underdeveloped legal aid programs discourage citizens from using judicial procedures. Moreover, the government has made a distinct policy of channeling civil disputes toward administrative agencies rather than into the court.

This is also true in the field of labor relations. It has been the Labor Commissions, rather than the court, which have been given a major role in resolving labor disputes. When the Equal Employment Opportunities Law was enacted in 1985 to promote equality of gender in the workplace, the responsibility to enforce the Law was likewise placed on the Prefecture Women's Offices of the Ministry of Labor, and not on the court. Furthermore, parties in industrial relations established informal mechanisms to prevent labor disputes from occurring. Supervisors absorbed employee dissatisfaction through daily communication. Joint consultation mechanisms worked to execute disciplinary measures or employment adjustment smoothly. Above all, the mechanisms of firms' internal labor markets, based upon the long-term employment system, had created a community of interests between labor and management inducing both sides to avoid overt confrontation. All these factors contributed to the small amount of litigation arising from labor relations.

III. The Increasing Worker Grievances in the Post-Bubble Years

Since the early 1990s, the number of disputes involving employment relations has increased sharply. Over the last thirteen years, the number of civil litigations at district court involving labor relations tripled, while the number of entire civil litigation in the same court has grown 1.5 times. The major types of civil actions involving labor relations are claims for unpaid wages (including retirement benefits) and claims contesting termination of employment. They are followed by claims challenging the validity of disadvantageous alteration of working conditions and disadvantageous transfers. Claims for damages for excessive inducement of resignation and sexual harassment are also on the increase.

Labor administrative agencies also received an increasing number of complaints within their jurisdiction. The labor standards inspection offices in the Ministry of Labor received more than 20,000 complaints annually regarding violations of labor protection statutes annually in the mid-1990s. These complaints concern mostly non-payment of wages and dismissals without the mandatory thirty-day notice, both violations of the Labor Standards Law. The labor relation offices of prefecture governments also received an increasing number of individual workers' grievances. The offices of the Tokyo Metropolitan Government, for example, received about 45,000 cases in 1996, as compared to about 31,000 cases annually in 1989–91. The Tokyo government offices attempted to settle 1,200 cases in 1996, of which 40–50% involved termination of employment and 20–30% concerned non-payment of wages.

The increase in grievances of individual workers can be attributed mainly to restructuring and downsizing of enterprises and intensifying global competition during the decade long recession. Japanese economy entered a serious slump after the collapse of the bubble economy in the beginning of the 1990s, particularly after the mid-nineties. Firms experienced drastic devaluation of corporate property and asset portfolios caused by the decline in value of land and stock. The greatest hardship was caused by the paralysis of financial systems, due to massive amounts of bad loans left over from excessive lending and investment during the bubble years. In personnel management, firms suffered from extravagant hiring during the bubble economy. In this context, intensifying competition in the globalized market and, in particular, from rising Asian economies, pressured firms to exert fierce efforts to cut down costs.

. . . .

IV. The Necessity for the Reform of Employment Dispute Resolution System

In light of the rapid increase in employment disputes, taken against the backgrounds of structural changes in the corporate management and the labor markets, it became obvious that the dispute resolution system was in need of a major reform.

. . . .

> [T]he Ministry of Welfare and Labor drafted the Law to Promote Resolution of Individual Labor Relations Disputes, and obtained Parliamentary endorsement in 2001. The Law set forth a statutory scheme to provide counseling and mediation services at the local offices of the Ministry placed in each of forty-nine prefectures.

Under this scheme, the Regional Labor Office of the Ministry receives inquiries, grievances, or claims of either party of an employment relationship via telephone, the Internet, or visit on any employment relation subject. Nevertheless, 95% of the parties contacting the Office are workers. The Office begins by giving information or counseling, as requested by the party.

At this stage, if the Office finds the case involves a possible violation of labor statutes (such as the Labor Standards Law, the Minimum Wage Law, the Occupational Health and Safety Law), the Office refers the case to the labor standards inspection offices in the same locality. The parties using the Office service are frequently satisfied or relieved merely in understanding the merits or demerits of their case through counseling. However, if the case involves a dispute of employment rights, and if the party using the service desires to further pursue his or her legal claim, the Office can make efforts to resolve the case in two ways. First, they may issue a notice of recommendation to the other party regarding measures for resolving the dispute. The Office issues such a notice if it finds the merits in the complainant after making further investigation by collecting information from both parties. Otherwise, there is a mediation service offered by a mediation panel set up in each Office. The mediators are typically practicing lawyers and law professors serving on a part-time basis. The panel listens to the allegations of both parties and makes its mediation proposal within a few hours. The success rate of such expeditious mediation is about 40%.

. . . .

VII. The Profile of the Labor Tribunal System

The Labor Tribunal System is a procedure instituted in the district court. It has jurisdiction over disputes of rights arising from employment relationships. Dismissals, terminations of employment, disciplinary measures, transfers, demotions, and unpaid wages or retirement benefits are typically the subjects of such disputes. Either party in an employment relationship can file a complaint to the district court having jurisdiction over the localities where the other party resides or the employment is carried out. The claimant must submit a written complaint indicating both the specific claims he or she seeks against the other party (the respondent) and the legal grounds justifying such claims. The complaint must also specify the status of negotiations made between the parties regarding the claim as well as any major evidence that the claimant can submit.

Upon receiving the complaint, the court organizes a labor tribunal to handle the case. The tribunal is composed of three members: one career judge and two experts in labor relations (one from labor and one from management). The career-judge member presides over the procedure, and labor and management members add their expertise into the procedure. Labor and management members are appointed beforehand at each district court and serve on a part-time basis when they are assigned to a particular case. They participate in decision-making on equal footing with the career judge member. They must be fair and impartial in the handling of the case.

The tribunal sends a copy of the complaint to the respondent urging him or her to submit a written response within an indicated period. This response must state a position with regard to the claim and the legal grounds thereof. It must also describe the status of negotiations between the parties and any major evidence the respondent can submit.

The tribunal also notifies each party as to the date of the first hearing requesting their attendance.

Hearings are held informally and are not open to the public, although the panel may allow the observers deemed necessary or desirable. In order to make the tribunal procedure expeditious, the Law prescribes that the panel must, in principle, dispose of the case within three sessions of hearing, expecting that the procedure will last three to four months at the longest. Typically, the panel will clarify the issues in the case and the evidences to be examined in the first session. It will also ascertain the status of negotiations between the parties, to assess the feasibility of mediating the dispute. In the second session, the panel will investigate the facts by interviewing witnesses and examining documents in front of the parties. They may also inquire as to the desires of the parties for resolving the case through mediation. In the third session, the panel will make supplementary inquiries of both facts and desires for mediation, and then makes a mediation proposal. If both parties agree with this proposal, the agreement is written into the record of the court, putting an end to the dispute.

However, if either party rejects the proposal, the panel closes the hearing and makes a judgment on the merits of the complaint. Based on such judgment and taking the desires of the parties into account, the panel specifies the measures that would realistically resolve the dispute. The panel renders a decision stating such judgment and measures, either orally at the end of the third session or in writing within a number of days thereafter. The measures to be adopted by the panel include confirmation of the rights, execution of obligations, and direction of the monetary payments. The decision is not binding on the parties. Either side can notify the court in writing and reject the decision within two weeks after the notification. If rejected, the decision loses its effect, and the case is automatically transferred to a regular civil procedure, to be pending in the same district court retroactively from the date when the complaint was submitted.[18] On the other hand, if both parties accept the decision or do not submit a notice of rejection, the decision is binding on the parties. The measures specified in the decision will be enforceable in accordance with the Civil Execution Law.

The Labor Tribunal System is a new court procedure added to the conventional labor-dispute resolution systems. It does not replace or repeal any existing procedures or mechanisms. It is a part of a menu of dispute resolution services along with the regular civil process, the provisional disposition procedure, the Welfare and Labor Ministry counseling and mediation services, the Prefecture Government counseling and mediation services described in the first section. Parties in employment relationships can make use of these services respectively, simultaneously, or accumulatively.

VIII. Conclusion

As foreign observers will easily understand, the new Labor Tribunal System borrows ideas from the European labor court systems, and creates an expeditious court procedure with the participation of expert lay judges. But even though it includes features common to foreign procedures, the System is still uniquely Japanese especially in the respect that it is set up within the ordinary court, closely coordinated with ordinary civil procedure. The three sessions of hearing and an integrated mediation procedure may also be unique aspects. From the perspective of American law, the System may also be regarded as a non-binding arbitration procedure set up within the court as a prior stage of the ordinary civil procedure. The great wave of Judicial Reform and the rising demand of the reform of the labor dispute resolution system combined to generate such an ingenious system. The Labor Tribunal procedure is expected into a central scheme of labor dispute resolution systems in Japan, along with the Ministry of Welfare and Labor counseling and mediation services. With the prompt and informal procedure strengthened by expert participation, parties will make frequent use of the Labor Tribunal System, and mediation proposals or decisions handed down by the System will be highly persuasive to the parties. However, for such expectations to come to pass, a few conditions must be met in its implementation.

The first and most important condition is to organize high quality experts in labor relations to be appointed as panel members. Such experts should have a wealth of experiences in labor management relations in order to provide useful insight. They should also have sufficient legal backgrounds to discuss cases with career judges. In addition, they should also possess the ethics to be fair and impartial. It is estimated that at least 500 such experts are needed each from labor and management in order to start the new system. Exploration and selection has been first entrusted to national organizations of labor and management. The court will review the candidates recommended by these organizations. There will be intensive training programs for such experts to work through both before and after the appointment.

Second, the Labor Tribunal System is designed to be an informal procedure to be easily accessible by ordinary workers. Therefore, the court must see to it that workers are able to make use of this procedure without the assistance of lawyers. However, in order to make the System more effective and expeditious, it is much desirable that the complainant (and also the respondent) be represented by lawyers with expertise in labor law. One of the key factors for the success of the new system will be whether the Bar and the associations of labor and management lawyers will be able to organize a sufficient number of lawyers with relevant expertise to assist the parties with reasonable expenses. The expansion of legal profession under the Judicial Reform will hopefully enable the provision of such legal services.

Establishment of the Labor Tribunal System: Lay Judge Participation in Japanese Labor Proceedings[63]

Takashi Araki

1. Introduction: Participation in Labor Law

This paper explores the ways in which management and labor "participate" in Japanese labor law. Specifically, the paper firstly identifies the two patterns of participation: participation in norm establishment and norm enforcement. Second, focusing on the norm enforcement participation, it reviews the historical development of dispute resolution

[63] Takashi Araki, *Establishment of the Labor Tribunal System: Lay Judge Participation in Japanese Labor Proceedings*, http://www.j.u-tokyo.ac.jp/~sota/info/Papers/Araki%20Labor%20Tribunal%20final 080907.pdf (last visited Sept. 29, 2010).

systems in the postwar period. Third, it delineates the new Labor Tribunal Act which entrenches participation in innovative and promising ways. Finally, the significance of lay participation in dispute resolution system in labor law and more broadly its impact on the judiciary will be examined.

1.1. *Participation in Norm Establishment*

Norm establishment occurs across different levels. Most centrally, the highest level of participation is in the government's tripartite Labor Policy Council, which discusses and determines labor law and policy. The Council has a number of subcommittees. Both the Council and subcommittees adopt a tripartite membership involving representatives of labor, management, and the public interest. It is an established custom in Japan that deliberative councils (and their subcommittees) initially consider major legislative and policy initiatives. At a more decentralized level, namely the firm level, both parties participate in collective bargaining and joint labor management consultation processes. In the scholarship on Japanese-style corporate governance, the involvement of employees in corporate administrations is held out as one of the hallmarks of Japan's stakeholder-model governance that treats employee interests as highly – if not more so – than shareholder returns. Unlike European countries, however, sector-level or industry-level industrial negotiations are uncommon in Japan because more than 90% percent of labor unions in Japan are enterprise-specific.

1.2. *Participation in Norm Enforcement*

One of the features of Japan's labor dispute resolution procedures or the norm enforcement mechanism in labor law (see Figure 1) is that Japan does not maintain a separate court system for resolving labor disputes such as those found in many European countries. In the European system, labor disputes may be heard by lay judges representing the interests of management and labor. For instance, both the labor courts in Germany (*Arbeitsgerichts*) and the employment tribunals in the UK are tripartite organs whereas the labor courts in France (*conseil de prud'hommes*) have bipartite panels. However, since 1945 Japan has had a system of labor and management-participating dispute resolution bodies, the labor relations commissions. The labor relations commissions are the tripartite administrative bodies consisting of members representing public interests, labor, and management. These commissions have two major functions: (i) collective dispute resolution through mediation, conciliation, and arbitration; (ii) and quasi-judicial determination of cases involving allegations of unfair labor practices. The former function is not limited to norm enforcement; it also includes resolution of disputes that play a role in establishing work-related norms, such as collective bargaining culminating in strikes or lockouts. The latter function is directed at enforcing norms in the Trade Union Acts, namely the proscription of such unfair labor practices by employers as the disadvantageous treatment of union members, the unreasonable refusal to submit to collective bargaining, and attempts to control or interfere in the unions' formation and administration.

Labor relations commissions deal with collective labor disputes only. As for individual labor-related disputes, there were no dispute resolution mechanisms where labor and management participate.

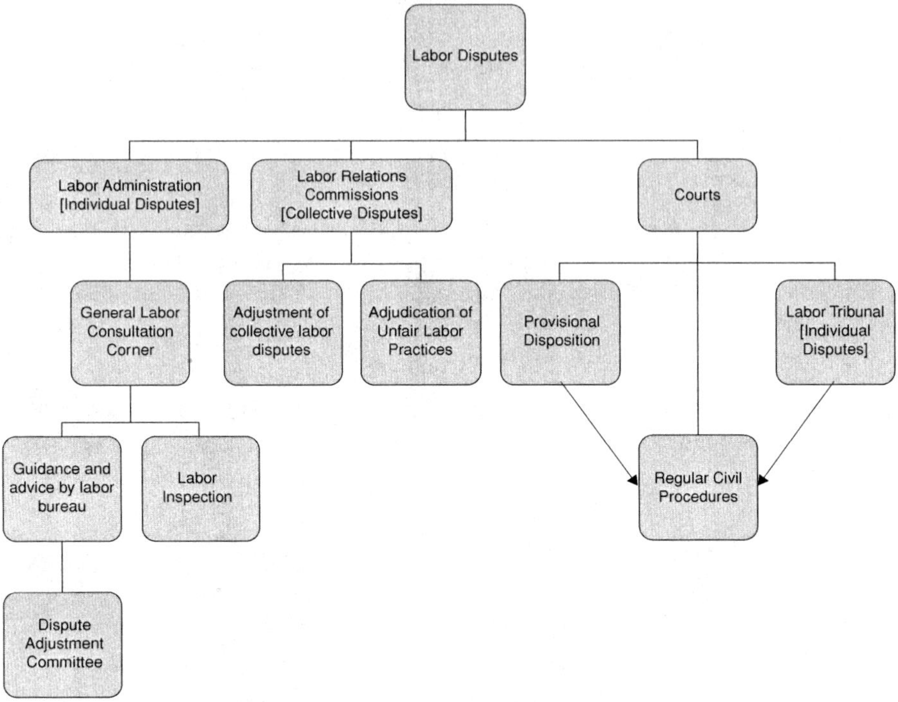

FIGURE 1. Overview of Labor Dispute Resolution Systems

In 2004, however, Japan enacted the Labor Tribunal Act which introduced a new dispute resolution body for individual labor-related disputes, namely, the Labor Tribunal (*Rodo Shinpan*). The Labor Tribunal is a *de facto* tripartite panel established in each district court adjudicating on cases of individual labor relations. The Labor Tribunal system commenced on April 1, 2006.

. . . .

2.3. *New Mechanism to Resolve Individual Labor Disputes*

The mentioned increase in individual labor cases and grievances arising from individual labor relations put Japan on notice that it needed new mechanisms to efficiently resolve individual labor disputes.

2.3.1. 2001 Act to Promote Individual Labor Dispute Resolution

In response to such surge of individual labor disputes, the government enacted the Act to Promote Resolution of Individual Labor Relations Disputes in 2001. The prefectural Labor Offices, which are the local offices of the Ministry of Health, Labor, and Welfare, started to provide counseling and mediation services. Since the Labor Offices launched such services, the number of complaints received by the Labor Offices has also been increased annually (see Figure 4). If necessary, the Head of the Labor Office may transfer the grievances to the mediation procedures of the Dispute Adjustment Committee

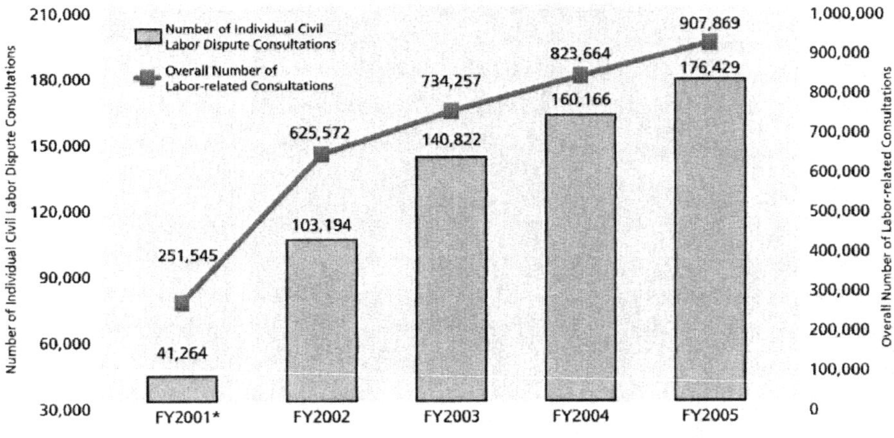

FIGURE 4. Number of Consultations at the Labor Offices

[*Funso Chosei Iinkai*] in the Labor Office. The Dispute Adjustment Committee can provide a mediation proposal but it is up to the parties whether or not to accept it.

2.3.2. Judicial Reform and the Proposal by the Labor Study Group

Until recently, Japan did not have labor courts. All labor related litigation had to be filed with the ordinary courts where all judges are professional jurists. Neither was there a special procedure for labor litigation. Partly because of this, the number of labor cases in Japan, although increasing, has remained extremely small compared to other countries.

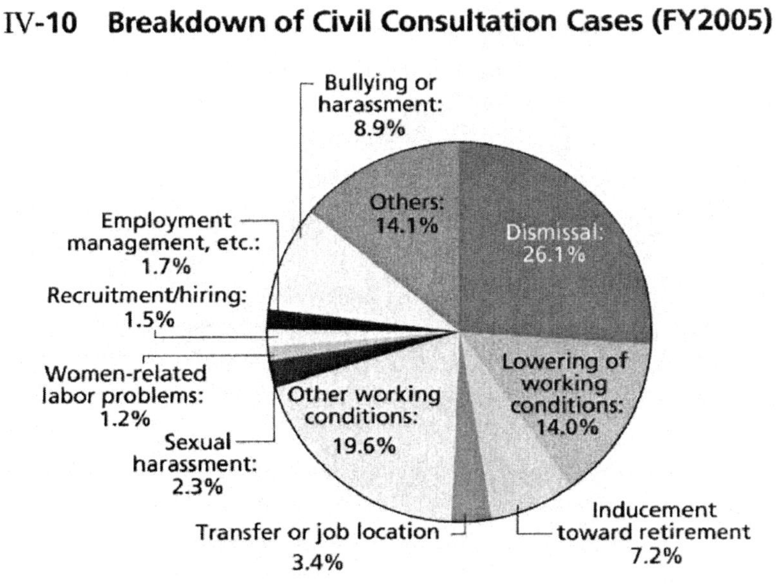

FIGURE 5. Breakdown of Civil Consultation Cases (FY 2005)

The number of labor-related cases newly filed in Japanese district courts (for instance) in 2002 was only about 3,000. This is an exceptionally small number compared with 90,000 in the Netherlands, 160,000 in France, 200,000 in the United Kingdom, and 600,000 in Germany. Labor cases in Japan were only one two-hundredth of those in Germany. . . .

. . . .

3. Labor Tribunal System

3.1. *Outline and Features of the Labor Tribunal System*

The Labor Tribunal System is a non-contentious procedure established in a district court to mediate and, if mediation proves unsuccessful, to adjudicate on individual labor disputes (see Figure 6). The judge who was charged with establishing the Labor Tribunal System characterized the new tribunal as providing "triple-S" justice: speedy, specialized, and suitable.

3.1.1. Speed

The first feature is the expeditiousness of the procedures. Since the new tribunal is in principle aimed at overcoming delays in labor litigation, the Labor Tribunal Committee (LTC) which hears the dispute must decide the case within three sessions (LTA Art. 15, Para 2), which means that a filed complaint will be disposed of within three or four months. Hearings are informal and not open to the public, although the LTC may allow observers if appropriate.

To dispose of the case within three sessions, the LTC will clarify the issues of the case and examine evidences in the first session. In the second and third session, the Committee seeks a solution through mediation (*Chotei*) while continuing to investigate the facts by interviewing witnesses and examining documents. If the parties to the case accept the mediation proposal by the LTC, the agreement shall be written into the record of the court, which has the same effect as a court settlement or a finalized court decision.

3.1.2. Specialty

The second important feature of the procedures is the participation of lay judges with specialist expertise, experience, or knowledge of labor relations. The Labor Tribunal Committee (LTC), thus, comprises one professional judge and two lay members, both of whom are experts in labor relations. Although these two experts are recommended by *Rengo* (Japanese Trade Union Confederation) and *Nippon Keidanren* (Japan Business Federation), in practice, they must be fair and impartial in the handling of the case. These experts participate in decision making on equal footing with the professional judge member.

3.1.3. Suitability

The third characteristic of the labor tribunal procedures is the flexibility and wide discretion given to the LTC to make such orders as are appropriate to resolve the dispute. If one of the parties rejects the mediation proposal, the LTC will hand down a labor tribunal decision (this decision is also called "*Rodo Shinpan*"). In the decision,

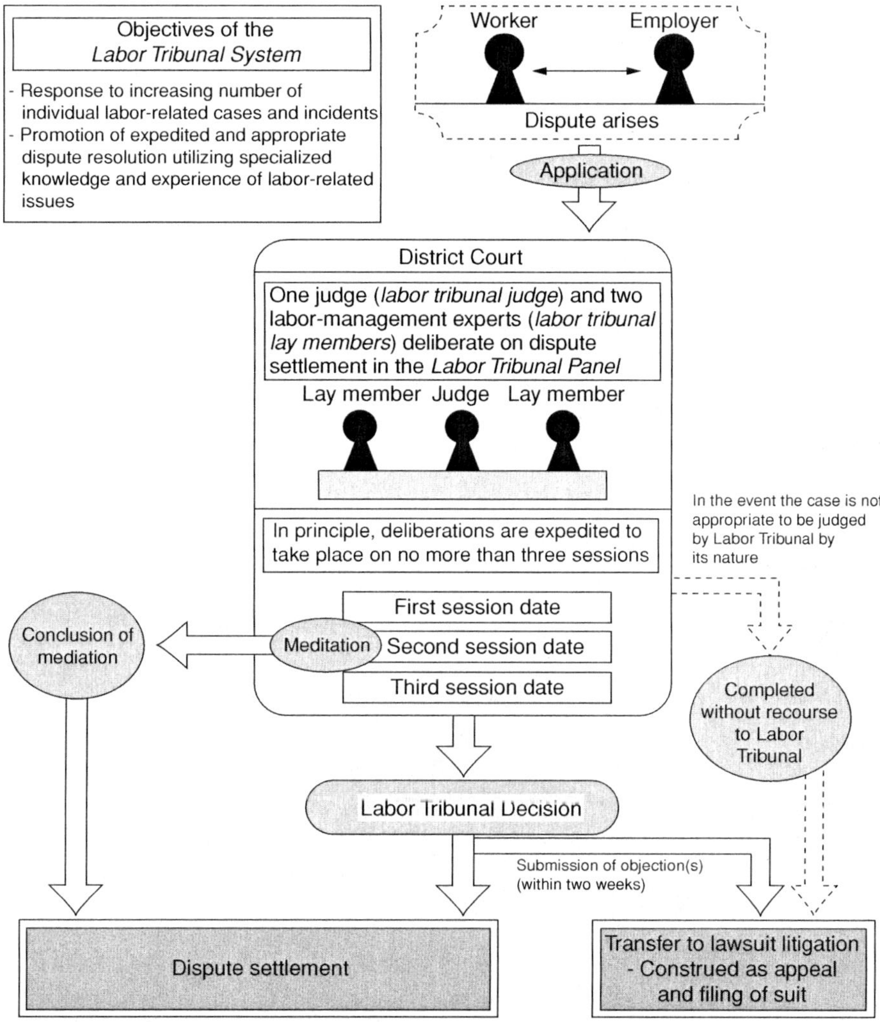

FIGURE 6. Overview of the Labor Tribunal System. *Source*: Japan Institute for Labor Policy and Training, Labor Situation in Japan and Analysis: General Overview 2006/2007, 78.

the LTC may confirm the rights between the parties, order payment or delivery of property, or specify the measures that would be "appropriate to resolve the dispute taking the judgment of the rights of the parties as well as the situations found in the labor tribunal procedures into account" (Art. 20, LTA). It is notable that the LTC is not limited to determining the merits of the complaints, but may also consider the broader circumstances of the case such as the parties' desires.

The LTC is not bound to determine the strict rights and obligation of each of the parties, but may order a decision more appropriate to resolve the dispute. For instance, it is possible for the LTC to order an employer who unjustly dismissed a worker to pay a certain amount of money rather than to nullify the dismissal. Such a monetary remedy is not available in the ordinary courts because, under current Japanese law, remedies for unjust dismissals are limited to nullifying dismissals, ordering reinstatement and payment for wages during the dismissed period. In other words, ordinary courts cannot order payment of money in exchange for the dissolution of the employment contract, but LTC can render such a decision.

3.1.4. Relationship with Regular Civil Procedures

Fourthly, the Labor Tribunal Procedures are connected to regular civil procedures. If either party does not notify the court of the rejection of the labor tribunal decision in writing within two weeks, it becomes binding on both parties in the same way as if it were a court settlement, and is thus enforceable under the Civil Execution Act. If either of the parties rejects the decision and makes a formal notification to that effect, the LTC decision has no effect.

However, if the decision is rejected, the case will automatically be transferred to the regular civil section in the same district court. The case is deemed to have been filed in the court retrospectively from the date when the complaint was filed to the Labor Tribunal. This connection with the regular procedures gives both parties an incentive to settle the case in the Labor Tribunal to avoid the time -delays and costs associated with regular civil procedures.

3.2. *Active Utilization of the Labor Tribunal System*

The Labor Tribunal System came into operation from April 2006. As expected, many cases were filed with it (see Figure 7). The Labor Tribunal enjoys a strong reputation for its services among litigants, lawyers, and members of labor tribunal committees. The average period for the hearing is less than 2.5 months (74.2 days). Therefore, the tribunal has achieved its aim of effecting speedy justice. Labor, management, and their lawyers have also approved these expedited procedures.

. . . .

Of the 877 cases filed to Labor Tribunals in the first year (from April 2006 to March 2007), 644 (70.1%) resulted in the acceptance of the mediation proposal and 162 (17.6%) reached the stage of a formal labor tribunal determination. Among the 162 cases resulting in labor tribunal decisions, 95 cases (58.6%) were subject to an objection by one or more of the parties and were transferred to the regular civil procedures, but the other 67 cases (41.4%) concluded with the tribunal decisions since no objection was raised. Considering other settled cases, such as those withdrawn prior to or during the hearing, nearly 80 % of the filed cases were resolved through the Labor Tribunal procedures.

All in all, the Labor Tribunal system has had a highly successful debut.

4. Significance of the Lay Judge Participation in the Labor Tribunal System

4.1. *High Reputation of Lay Judges*

Apart from family and civil in-court mediation services, lay judges are unprecedented in Japan. Therefore, professional judges were initially skeptical about their deployment, in particular in the field of labor relations where ideological conflicts are, they thought, conspicuous and irreconcilable. One judge, head of the Tokyo District Court, Labor Division, candidly stated: "Professional judges could not imagine the kind of people the Labor Tribunal Lay members would be before the implementation of the Labor Tribunal System. However, we have come to recognize that they are long on common sense and very industrious."

Because the lay members in Labor Tribunal are recommended by *Rengo* (Japanese Trade Union Confederation) and *Nippon Keidanren* (Japan Business Federation), they are or used to be officials of enterprise-based labor unions (on the labor side) and directors or officials in charge of labor relations or human resource management (on the management side). The concern whether they would be capable of serving as impartial, fair adjudicators proved unfounded. Practicing lawyers stated that, in the Labor Tribunal session, they could not recognize which member represented labor and which represented management since the seat arrangement were not fixed and they kept their neutrality and impartiality when questioning the parties.

Professional judges who worked with these lay members have highly evaluated their quality and ability to identify the facts and issues of the case, as well as find an appropriate resolution to the dispute.

4.2. *High Performance in Resolving Disputes*

As mentioned above, four out of five complaints filed have been resolved within the Labor Tribunal system. Such a high rate of resolution has largely been accomplished due to the effective utilization of lay members' expertise.

4.2.1. Expertise effective in Finding Key Facts and Issues of the Disputes

Since the LTC must dispose a filed case within the three sessions, finding the key points to solve the dispute is vitally important. The lay members have fully exerted their expertise in finding the crucial facts and issues which may have escaped the notice of the professional judge or even the representing lawyers. In one case, for instance, the employer contended that the firm had a briefing session for employees to explain that the introduction of the annual salary system would entail the change of open-ended labor contracts into fixed-term contracts. The lay member requested the submission of the handouts used at that briefing because it was unthinkable that such a meeting would be conducted without any handouts. Such practical common sense has functioned very effectively in uncovering crucial facts.

The same applies to clarification of the issues in the disputes and to forming an appropriate solution of the case.

4.2.2. Persuasiveness of the Mediation Proposals

An important factor that explains the high resolution rate of the labor tribunal cases is the persuasiveness of the mediation proposal. Almost all mediation proposals are unanimously agreed upon by the three members of the LTC. Such a proposal adopted by both labor and management sides is highly persuasive to the parties.

The content of such mediation proposals can be more flexible than a decision of an ordinary court and more responsive to the actual circumstances of the dispute.

In shaping such contextual proposals, lay members' knowledge and experiences are both helpful and useful.

Furthermore, lay members are adroit at persuading the parties to accept the mediation proposals.

4.3. *From "Precise Justice" to "Resolution-oriented Justice"*

The high resolution rate in the Labor Tribunal is not solely attributable to the lay member participation. The mechanism of the Labor Tribunal combined with the lay members' expertise has enabled such high performance of the Labor Tribunal System.

The third feature of the Labor Tribunal System, namely the flexible and wide discretion given to the LTC in rendering a labor tribunal decision, paves the way for the active utilization of the lay members' expertise and experience. Combined with the first feature, the speediness of the procedure, both the parties and LTC prioritize the resolution of the disputes ("resolution-oriented justice") over making precisely elaborate legal decision though technically precise, strictly formalized procedures ("precise justice"). The speediness of the procedure induces the parties to express their real intention (*hon-ne*) to resolve the dispute, rather than resorting to a legal position (*tatemae*).

This is especially true in dismissal cases. In ordinary civil procedures, a plaintiff or a dismissed worker must assert the invalidity of the dismissal and reinstatement, even if he or she does not want to be re-hired by the company. The respondent or the employer, in the same manner, must contend the validity of the dismissal, even though it may fully intend to pay compensation for the dissolution of the employment contract. In the Labor Tribunal, the LTC has a power to order a monetary settlement when both parties want to resolve the dispute in this way.

Another example of the resolution-oriented justice of the Labor Tribunal is the calculation of an unpaid overtime premium. Under ordinary civil procedures, precise calculation of unpaid wages is indispensable and it requires time-consuming procedures. By contrast, in the Labor Tribunal, if the Committee found a certain amount of unpaid overtime premium in a specific month, it can exercise its discretion by applying a similar calculation to the other period. The aim of the procedure is not to precisely clarify the right and obligations of each of the litigated parties but to seek an appropriate resolution of the dispute considering each party's rights and obligations.

Such a resolution-oriented justice introduced under the Labor Tribunal System combined with the work-site based common sense provided by the lay members seems to enable the effective functioning of the new dispute resolution system.

4.4. *Relationship between a Mediation Proposal and a Labor Tribunal*

Decision

In the second or third session, LTC will propose a mediation. This mediation proposal is not binding, and if one of the parties rejects the proposal, the LTC will hand down a labor tribunal decision. This decision is also not binding. If one of the parties submits an objection, the decision loses its effect and ordinary civil procedure will commence.

Why does the Labor Tribunal adopt these two, not-legally binding steps? Judge Nanba first deemed a mediation proposal to be an interim and conciliatory decision whereas the labor tribunal decision is adjudicative in nature. Thus, his committee handed down a labor tribunal decision different from the mediation proposal. It is natural that the party who thought the decision was unfavorably changed from the mediation proposal opposes the labor tribunal decision. Faced with these objections, Judge Nanba realized that three sessions in the Labor Tribunal would all be in vain. He then changed his mind and endeavored to make the mediation proposal and labor tribunal decision the same or similar, which decreased the parties' objections.

When parties know that a rejection of the mediation proposal will only result in the labor tribunal decision of the same purport and without too much prospect of a better outcome, they tend to settle the dispute at the mediation stage without requesting the tribunal decision. In fact, attorneys persuade the parties to accept the mediation proposal by explaining the implications of an objection. This practice explains the high acceptance rate of the mediation proposal (about 70%).

On the other hand, however, if one of the parties is not satisfied with the mediation proposal and the same content tribunal decision, he or she will reject both. In fact, among the 162 cases seeking for labor tribunal decisions, 95 cases (58.6%) were objected and transferred to the regular civil procedures.

Having said that, about 40% of the labor tribunal decisions are accepted. Most of them are estimated to be the same in effect as the rejected mediation proposals. Why do similar proposals result in different responses? Judge Nanba explains this by the difference in the psychological impact of the mediation proposal and labor tribunal decision on the parties. To make the mediation proposal effective, the parties must express their positive intention to accept the mediation proposal. It is not easy for the disputing parties to proactively express such an intention. By contrast, to make the labor tribunal decision effective, no action is needed. Even though the decision is identical to the rejected mediation proposal, the parties who deem the decision to be within acceptable limits tend to make no objection and accept the decision. This is a very interesting observation on the behaviors of disputing human beings.

4.5. Educational Effect of the Labor Tribunal System

The participation of lay members in the court judicial procedures has educational benefits for both lay members and professional judges.

First, most lay members are active union leaders and active personnel in charge of labor relations or human resource management. Therefore, their experience as a lay member enforcing labor law has a feedback effect on their activities in labor and employment relations. In other words, lay member participation in the court will further embed the rule of law in Japanese workplaces.

Second, professional judges also learn about worksite common sense through their involvement in labor tribunal activities. This will make their decisions handed down in the regular civil division more attuned to the realities of the modern workplace.

Furthermore, the expedited procedures and resolution-oriented justice experienced in the labor tribunal may have an impact on other court procedures.

5. Conclusion

This paper has analyzed labor and management participation in norm establishment process focusing on the newly created Labor Tribunal System with lay judges. The author would like to conclude this article by pointing out two impacts of the Labor Tribunal System.

First, the Labor Tribunal System has triggered the reconsideration of justice in employment relations. The Labor Tribunal System was needed to resolve increasing individual disputes swiftly and properly. Speediness is vital because slow justice is no justice. This is especially true of employment disputes. The two year experience of the Labor Tribunal has reconfirmed that speediness minimizes the loss for both labor and management sides and greatly facilitates dispute resolutions.

Thus, the three-session labor tribunal is welcomed by both sides to the dispute. Such expedited resolution has been made possible by utilizing lay members' expertise and worksite common sense, and also by giving the tribunal wide discretion in ordering decisions appropriate to resolve the dispute. Where appropriate, the tribunal may depart from a strict assessment of the rights and obligations of each of parties. This implies the change of the notion of justice at courts. This paper emphasized this by the shift from "precise justice" to "resolution-oriented justice."

The other point worth mentioning is the significance and impact that Labor Tribunal has had on traditional labor law and the substantive labor law.

Traditional labor law envisages two guardians for workers: labor inspectors and labor unions. The state establishes minimum labor standards and violations are inspected by the government or labor inspectors. More favorable working conditions than minimum standards have been expected to be established through collective bargaining between employers and labor unions. However, the governmental inspection system is inefficient and union density continues to decrease. Thus, the traditional labor law model has become dysfunctional. Individual workers need a mechanism to enforce their rights other than by relying on labor inspectors or labor unions. In this sense, the Labor Tribunal System and other individual labor dispute resolution systems have become the new guardians of working conditions and rights.

However, the establishment and strengthening of various dispute resolution systems have also exposed the lack of substantive law regulating individual labor relations. Of course, case law also provides rules governing individual labor relations, but unwritten case law rules have problems in transparency. Thus, in order to clarify the substantive rules governing employment relations, the Labor Contract Act was enacted in 2007 and put into force from March 2008. However, the current content of the Labor Contract Act is very poor because of political disagreement between labor and management. Therefore the development of both procedural and substantive labor law is an important challenge that the current Japanese law faces.

. . . .

QUESTIONS

1. Is the Labor Tribunal System a judicial or nonjudicial approach to resolving labor disputes?
2. Evaluate the effectiveness of the Labor Tribunal System. How, if at all, does the possible influence of the traditional Japanese culture of conflict avoidance contribute to the Tribunal's success?

3. What is the role and/or effect of utilizing lay judges in the arbitration process? Is it desirable to use lay judges?
4. Should the Tribunal's use be mandatory? Why or why not?
5. Is there a time when a Japanese worker can use the Labor Tribunal when the union cannot, even though the issue is over the same labor dispute? Explain.
6. Can you think of an example when a Japanese worker might wish to choose the court over the Labor Tribunal? Consider the following hypothetical situation proffered to the author by a judge in Japan's Labor Tribunal.

Hypothetical: A union and a company agreed in a collective-bargaining agreement to pay a summer bonus equivalent to three months' pay. The company didn't pay the bonus to the worker (Tanaka-San). Tanaka-san can take civil proceedings against the company. He can use not only an ordinary civil procedure, but also the Labor Tribunal System.

For example, if under the terms of his contract (individual or collective), he is owed a bonus in addition to salary, Tanaka-san can go to the Labor Tribunal to enforce the promise. On the other hand, the union cannot demand a confirmation of the agreement to the Labor Tribunal because then it is not an *individual* dispute but rather one between the union and the company.

Article 1 of the Labor Tribunal Act states, "[T]he purpose of this Act is to promote the prompt and appropriate resolution, adapted to their actual circumstances, of individual civil disputes between individual workers and business operators with respect to the existence or nonexistence of a labor contract and other matters concerning labor relationships." The Labor Union Act (Article 16) reads, "[A]ny part of an individual labor contract contravening the standards concerning working conditions and other matters relating to the treatment of workers provided in the collective agreement shall be void. In such a case, the invalidated part of the individual labor contract shall be governed by those standards. With respect to matters as to which the individual labor contract does not provide, the same shall apply. In this case the collective-bargaining agreement provides the enforceable promise.[64]

---

[64] However, the judge suggested it may not be advisable, for strategic reasons, to proceed in the Labor Tribunal or to accept a Tribunal's recommended decision in the case if the company couldn't pay the bonus, without facing bankruptcy. To use the Labor Tribunal System would be a waste of time. The company's lawyer must reject the Labor Tribunal decision. Therefore Tanaka-san's lawyer would use the ordinary civil procedure to get a *title of debt*. See discussion of title-of-debt (*saimu meigi*) in Section 11.01[4] Requirements for Execution [a] Enforceable Instruments-Titles-of-Debt and Execution Clauses (See Labor Tribunal Act §20-2). TAKAAKI HATTORI & DAN FENNO HENDERSON, CIVIL PROCEDURE IN JAPAN (1985). But, note well, can the Labor Tribunal order the same result as the court, raising the issue whether there really is a difference in fact? (See Labor Tribunal Act §20-2).

5. *Critique under International Labor Standards*

In addition to the previous overview description of Japan's labor and employment laws, there are other sources that "critique" those laws, emphasizing the purported "shortcomings" of the laws as measured against international core labor standards. Together, the overview and critique raise issues of how law works in practice and what issues need to be further addressed.

Internationally Recognised Core Labour Standards in Japan, Report for the WTO General Council Review of the Trade Policies of Japan[65]

Executive Summary

Japan has ratified six of the eight core ILO labour Conventions. In view of restrictions on the trade union rights of workers, determined measures are needed to comply with the commitments Japan accepted at Singapore, Geneva, and Doha in the WTO Ministerial Declarations over 1996–2001, and in the 1998 ILO Declaration on Fundamental Principles and Rights at Work. Japan has ratified the ILO core Convention on the Right to Organise and Collective Bargaining and the Convention on Freedom of Association and Protection of the Right to Organise. However many workers are excluded from the right to organise, the right to collective bargaining, and the right to strike, in particular public sector workers. In practice this right to organise and collective bargaining is further undermined by the increase in precarious contracts and an increase in the number of holding companies and investment fund companies. Japan has ratified the core ILO Convention on Equal Remuneration but not the Convention on Discrimination. Although progress has been made, discrimination between men and women in employment and remuneration continues, due to a concentration of women in part-time and temporary employment but also due to the two-track personnel administration system. Japan has ratified the ILO core Convention on the Worst Forms of Child Labour and the Convention on Minimum Age. Child labour does generally not occur in Japan and education is free and compulsory up to the age of fifteen. Japan has ratified the Convention on Forced Labour but not the Convention on the Abolition of Forced Labour. Forced labour is prohibited but there remain problems with trafficking of people into Japan for the purpose of forced prostitution and forced work, as well as forced labour practices among foreign workers and trainees.

. . . .

The ITUC affiliate in Japan is RENGO. 18.1% of the Japanese labour force was unionised in 2008.

[65] ITUC, Internationally Recognized Core Labor Standards in Japan, Report for the WTO General Council Review of the Trade Policies of Japan (Geneva, Feb. 18 & 20, 2009), *available at* http://www.ituc-csi.org/IMG/pdf/20090216163313-Microsoft_Word_-_Japan_draft_report_2009_final.pdf (last visited Sept. 29, 2010) [Some formatting altered]. *See also* U.S. Dep't of State, Bureau of Democracy, Human Rights, & Labor, *Overview of State Department's 2009 Human Rights Report* (March 11, 2010), http://www.america.gov/st/texttrans-english/2010/March/20100311150938eaifas0.6720087.html (last visited Sept. 29, 2010); ITUC, *Annual Survey of Violations of Trade Union Rights* (2011), http://survey.ituc-csi.org/+-Japan-+.html (last visited June 7, 2011).

I. Freedom of Association and the Right to Collective Bargaining

Japan ratified ILO Convention No. 87 on the Freedom of Association and Protection of the Right to Organise in 1965, and Convention No. 98 on the Right to Organise and Collective Bargaining in 1953.

The Constitution recognises the right to organise and the right to collective bargaining. However, this right is restricted in particular for civil servants and for employees of state-run companies and private companies that provide so-called essential services.

Three major labour laws govern the employment status of private sector workers. These are the Trade Union Law (TUL), which guarantees the right to organise and collective bargaining, the Labour Relations Adjustment Law (LRAL), which covers dispute settlements, and the Labour Standards Law (LSL), which deals with working conditions.

Workers have the right to bargain collectively and collective bargaining is widespread in Japan, but mainly at enterprise level.

Workers have the right to strike but those that are employed in the "essential services" have to give a ten day advance notice. These essential services include businesses involving electric power generation and transmission, transportation and railways, telecom, medical care and public health, and postal services.

In practice, organising in Japan has become increasingly difficult due to the growing number of precarious non-regular workers. One third of the Japanese employees are part-timers and other non-regular workers. Disguised contract labour, in particular in the manufacturing sector, has serious implications for working conditions and health and safety of workers.

Also, the practice of undertaking business through holding companies and an increase in the number of investment fund companies have led to difficulties for trade unions to conduct collective bargaining with such companies, which are not legally considered as employers.

The Industrial Training Programme (ITP) and the Technical Internship Programme (TIP), which provide three year visas to unskilled foreign workers for training, have been abused by employers. Work permits are required and while workers have the right to organise, that right is indirectly undermined, mostly through contracts between the trainees and trainee-sending agencies of the sending countries. Many of these workers end up in sweatshops where they are forced to work long hours, under dangerous conditions and below minimum wages. Employment agencies add to the abuse by providing inferior employment contracts.

In the public sector many restrictions are in place on the right to organise, the right to strike, and the right to collective bargaining. Public sector workers have the right to organise with the exception of members of the police force, fire fighting services, penal institutions, the maritime safety agency and the self-defence forces. However trade union registration for local public employees requires separate unions to be created in each municipality, which contradicts "freedom of association". Administrative and clerical workers do not have the right to bargain or conclude collective agreements at local or national level. Their wages are set by law and regulations.

Public sector workers do not have the right to strike. Under the National Public Service Law and the Local Public Service Law, trade union leaders who incite strike action in the public sector can be dismissed and fined or imprisoned for up to three years.

The ILO Committee of Experts on the Application of Conventions and Recommendations (CEACR) has made particular comments and requests with regard to the denial of the right to organise of fire fighters, the prohibition of the right to strike of public servants, and the right to organise of prison staff. According to the CEACR, fire fighters should have the right to organise. Civil servants who are not exercising authority in the name of the state and workers who are not working in essential services within the strict meaning of the term should be ensured the right to strike too. However, many of these ILO Committee recommendations regarding public sector workers have been ignored.

Some of the public agencies in Japan have been transformed into Independent Administrative Institutions (IAIs). There are specified IAIs and non-specified IAIs. All employees in IAIs have the right to organise and collective bargaining, however, only workers in non-specified IAIs have the right to strike. A plan for restructuring of IAIs was adopted in December 2007.

Conclusions

The right to organise, collective bargaining, and the right to strike are recognised in Japan but serious restrictions exist, in particular for civil servants and employees in state-run enterprises and essential services. In practice, the right to organise and collective bargaining is further undermined due to the increase in the number of non-regular workers as well as in the number of holding companies and investment fund companies.

II. Discrimination and Equal Remuneration

Japan ratified Convention No. 100 on Equal Remuneration in 1967 but has not ratified Convention No. 111 on Discrimination (Employment and Occupation).

The law prohibits discrimination on the basis of race, gender, disability, language, and social status. However, discrimination remains a problem in Japan.

Despite the existence of the Equal Employment Opportunities Law and a reduction in direct discrimination, indirect discrimination against women remains a problem in Japan. One of the causes is the "dual career ladder" system which encourages male employees along the professional career track and women towards the general or clerical track.

Women are underrepresented in senior and managerial posts. Discrimination against women in wages and employment occurs in almost all sectors, although less regarding specialists, professionals, skilled workers, and the like. The gender wage gap is highest among full time regular employees with women earning 67% of male wages in 2007. While the wage of women is 89% that of men among part-time, non regular employees, this somewhat small gap is explained mainly by the fact that part-time, non regular employees are mostly women.

The Japanese labour market is further characterised by a three-tier employment pattern with a small number of permanent managerial posts, a number of experts in certain fields, and a large group of non-permanent, part-time, or outsourced workers. Most women fall in this third category which is not addressed sufficiently by the Equal Employment Opportunities Law.

The law prohibits sexual harassment. However, sexual harassment remains a problem in Japan. In 2006, there were 11,102 reports of sexual harassment.

The law prohibits discrimination against persons with physical and mental disabilities in employment, education and access to health care. However, the effectiveness of the Disabled Persons Fundamental Law is unclear and, in reality, there exists discrimination against persons with disabilities. For example, the number of private companies which fulfilled the statutory employment rate for persons with disabilities remains low and stood at just 43.8% in 2007.

Conclusions

Discrimination in employment and remuneration is prohibited but widespread in Japan. There is a high gender wage gap, serious underrepresentation of women in managerial posts, and a high level of indirect discrimination. Sexual harassment is a problem as well.

III. Child Labour

The minimum age specified in the Convention is 15 years. Children under the age of 18 are not allowed to work in dangerous or harmful jobs. Children between the age of 13 and 15 are allowed to perform light work. Children under the age of 13 may be employed in the entertainment industry only. The law is well enforced and child labour does not generally occur. However, the law excludes from its application employment of children in family undertakings and domestic workers. Moreover, the law restricting hazardous work by children does not apply to children employed in family undertakings. Furthermore, a number of migrant children in Japan, mainly of Brazilian origin, have been found working in factories. Education is free and compulsory until the age of 15.

Conclusions

Child labour does not generally occur in Japan and legislation is well enforced.

IV. Forced Labour

Japan ratified Convention No. 29, the Forced Labour Convention in 1932 but has not ratified Convention No. 105, the Abolition of Forced Labour.

Forced labour is prohibited by law and does not generally occur. There are reports that some companies force foreign workers to work illegal overtime, control their movements and travel documents, and force them to make deposits in company controlled accounts.

The National Public Service Law and the Local Public Service Law, referred to in Section I above, provide that public employees who incite strike action can be fined or sentenced up to three years' imprisonment, or possibly dismissed, reprimanded with a pay cut, or disciplined. This is not in line with Convention No. 105, which prohibits penal servitude as a punishment for having participated in a strike.

Trafficking for the purpose of forced prostitution or forced labour is prohibited, however trafficking remains a problem. Japan is a destination and transit country for men, women, and children trafficked for the purposes of commercial sexual exploitation, pornography, and forced labour. The trafficked women and children for forced prostitution mainly come from China, South Korea, Southeast Asia, Eastern Europe, Russia, and, to a lesser extent, Latin America. Japan is also a transit country for persons trafficked from East Asia to North America. Forced labour also occurs through training programmes that are characterised by fraudulent terms of employment, debt bondage, restrictions on movement and withholding of salary payments.

Conclusions

Forced labour is prohibited and does generally not exist in Japan. However trafficking, mainly of women and girls, for sexual exploitation or forced work remains a serious problem. There are also abuses among foreign workers and trainees.

Final Conclusions and Recommendations

1. The government of Japan must ratify ILO Convention No. 111 on discrimination and ILO Convention No. 105 on the Abolition of Forced Labour, and implement measures to ensure an effective transposition into national law.
2. The government has to bring legislation in line with Conventions No. 87 and No. 98 and eliminate restrictions on the right to collective bargaining and the right to strike for public sector workers, including all administrative and clerical staff. The government has to adopt the recommendations of the ILO Committee on Freedom of Association and the Committee of Experts on the Application of Conventions regarding these issues.
3. The National Public Service Law and the Local Public Service Law, which stipulate that public servants who incite strike action can be imprisoned, must be amended.
4. Wage inequalities and inequalities in access to employment continue to exist between men and women. The government must implement affirmative actions to ensure equal representation of women in managerial and regular posts. The government has to take measures to address indirect discrimination and to extend protection to non-permanent workers. It must furthermore increase efforts and measures to ensure equal pay for work of equal value.
5. The government has to extend labour legislation (including on hazardous labour), inspection and enforcement to children employed in family undertakings and domestic work.
6. There is a need for increased labour inspection, enforcement of legislation and prosecution in the area of forced labour including trafficking of people for forced labour.
7. In line with the commitments accepted by Japan at the Doha WTO Ministerial Conference and its obligations as a member of the ILO, the Government of Japan should therefore provide regular reports to the WTO and the ILO on its legislative changes and implementation of all the core labour standards.
8. The WTO should draw to the attention of the authorities of Japan the commitments they undertook to observe core labour standards at the Doha Ministerial Conference. The WTO should request the ILO to intensify its work with the Government of Japan in these areas and provide a report to the WTO General Council on the occasion of the next trade policy review.

QUESTIONS

1. How do Japan's labor laws compare against ILO standards?
2. What areas of labor law could use improvement and why?
3. Are Japan's labor laws "business-friendly"?

B. SOUTH KOREA

1. *Regulatory Sources, Structures, and Administration*

Sources of Law

South Korea has a legal system that is a blend of civil law and common law. At the beginning of its judicial modernization, South Korea adopted the modern European civil law system; however, some laws began to model Anglo-American law systems because of the increasing influence of overseas countries. Thus, South Korea's legal system demonstrates a harmonization of both the European civil law system and the Anglo-American law system. Written laws (statutes, decrees, rules and regulations, and international agreements) are the primary source of law in South Korea. Court decisions are a secondary source of law that is only persuasive. There is no principle of stare decisis. The principal sources of labor laws are governed by statute, administrative decrees, and regulations.

The Constitution prevails over all other sources of labor law. Article 32 governs individual employment relationships. It guarantees the right to work, which is the constitutional basis for laws concerning employment security, minimum wage, unemployment insurance, and vocational training. It also provides for protective labor laws, requiring minimum standards for working conditions and special protections for working women and minors. Article 33 guides collective labor relations, providing for the right of workers to organize, bargain, and act collectively.

Rules established by labor legislation are the key source of various labor-related protections. Worker protection laws merely set minimum standards. Labor laws supersede individual employment contracts and collective agreements that do not provide minimum working condition standards established by law; yet, when individual contracts, collective agreements, or work rules exceed minimum standards, the private terms govern parties' relationship. The Labor Standards Act (LSA) is the most important law in this area; it is known as the bedrock of employment law in South Korea.[66]

Courts clarify general provisions of statutes and fill in gaps regarding matters left undecided by legislators. The Constitutional Court or general courts can make

[66] Jeong Han Lee, *South Korea: Key Limits on Employer Latitude in Structuring Workforce*, LABOUR AND EMPLOYMENT (Mar. 20, 2007), http://www.mondaq.com/article.asp?articleid=46866 (last visited Sept. 29, 2010).

decisions in the area of labor law; however, the decision of the Constitutional Court prevails over general courts. As mentioned earlier there is no principle of stare decisis or precedent in the Korean legal system. However, in practice, lower courts tend to follow the legal interpretations promulgated by the Supreme Court. Supreme Court decisions are secondary sources of law.

The Ministry of Labor or Ministry of Justice makes administrative interpretations that are binding on subordinate offices, but are not equivalent to a statutory provision and are merely persuasive on courts. Custom or established practice may be a source of law and is treated as if incorporated into an individual employment contract.

On international matters, the Constitution provides that treaties promulgated in accordance with the Constitution and generally recognized rules of international law have the same effect as the domestic laws. Ratified conventions of ILO are legally binding at the national level; thus, ILO conventions are legal sources of domestic labor law. Korea has ratified the core ILO conventions on Discrimination, on Equal Remuneration, on the Worst Forms of Child Labor, and on Minimum Age. In 2007, Korea entered into a Free Trade Agreement with the United States that contains some provisions on labor protections (in October, 2011 President Obama signed the agreement following congressional approval; South Korea approved it in the following month).[67]

[67] It was not until October 21, 2011 that it was enacted into law in the United States; South Korea approved it on November 22, 2011. United States-Korea Free Trade Agreement Implementation Act, H.R. 3080, 112th Cong. (2011) (enacted). President Obama signs 3 trade deals, biggest since NAFTA, *available at* http://www.nola.com/politics/index.ssf/2011/10/president_obama_signs_3_trade.html. *See* KORUS FTA in the News, *available at*, www.koreauspartnership.org/news/index.htm.

The United States and the Republic of Korea signed the United States–Korea Free Trade Agreement (KORUS FTA) on June 30, 2007. The U.S. Trade Representative's Office reported, "[a]s the first U.S. FTA with a North Asian partner, the KORUS FTA could be a model for trade agreements for the rest of the region, and underscore the U.S. commitment to, and engagement in, the Asia-Pacific region." However, the Labor Advisory Committee for Trade Negotiations and Trade Policy (LAC) concluded the FTA "does not contain enforceable provisions requiring that the government meet its obligations under the ILO core labor standards." Furthermore, it added, it:

> [D]oes not prevent Korea from 'weakening or reducing the protections afforded in domestic labor laws' to 'encourage trade or investment.' Under the agreement, Korea could roll back its labor laws without threat of fines or sanctions. It does not require that Korea effectively enforce its own laws with respect to employment discrimination, a core ILO labor right.

Office of the United States Trade Representative (USTR), The U.S.–Korea Free Trade Agreement: Report of the Labor Advisory Committee for Trade Negotiations and Trade Policy (LAC), at 7, *available at* http://ustraderep.gov/assets/Trade_Agreements/Bilateral/Republic_of_Korea_FTA/Reports/asset_upload_file698_12781.pdf (last visited Sept. 29, 2010).

Article 19 has a number of provisions, including Article 19.2, which provides "[E]ach Party shall adopt and maintain in its statutes and regulations, and practices thereunder, the following rights, as stated in the *ILO Declaration on Fundamental Principles and Rights at Work and its Follow-Up* (1998) (ILO Declaration)," but Art. 19.3.2 provides "for greater certainty, nothing in this Chapter shall be construed to empower a Party's authorities to undertake labor law enforcement activities in the territory of the other Party." USTR, Free Trade Agreement Between the United States of

Korea utilizes employer "rules of engagement" as a binding source of rights and duties, enforceable by law. Typically, they detail most working conditions, such as compensation, working hours, leave, rest periods, and so on. These provisions are usually unilaterally created by employers; but to be valid, the rules must be accepted by employees, explicitly or implicitly. These employer rules may not provide conditions worse than those specified by law or in collective agreements; if they do, they are null and void. However, these rules do override less favorable terms in individual employment contracts.

Current Labor Situation in Korea[68]

Overview

. . . .

Until the mid-1970s, industrial relations were not viewed as a major social and economic issue, but in the late 1970s, when the country came close to exhausting its labor supply, the problem of working conditions replaced that of job creation as the central social and economic issue of the day. A series of fierce labor disputes took place, which resulted in severe crackdowns at the hands of the government.

In the early 1980s, workers' awareness of their rights became widespread, especially with regard to claiming their fair share of the fruits of the economic growth achieved in the 1960s and 1970s. However, the Fifth Republic regime cracked down on the labor movement. As a result, in spite of the marked increase in the number of workers from 1980 to 1987 and the growing awareness of their rights, the number of unionized workers remained at the level of around one million.

In Korea, 1987 was the year when major political democratization was achieved and also when the Constitution was amended. After the June 29 Democratization Declaration, there was an explosive increase in labor disputes, and new trade unions were quickly organized. The government's labor policy underwent sweeping changes through the reduction of government intervention based on the principle of labor-management autonomy and the revision of the labor related laws to meet international standards.

The government also made efforts to actively promote the interests of workers with the institutionalization of the minimum wage system, the reduction of working hours, and the abolition of legal restrictions on strikes.

Since the massive strikes of the late 1980s, companies have attempted to build cooperative relations with employees, realizing that they cannot achieve profits under extremely confrontational labor conditions. Trade unions have also realized that they cannot achieve much from confrontation and violence.

However, with the sense of the looming economic crisis and the emergence of powerful and radical trade unions during the second half of 1989, the government's labor policy

America and the Republic of Korea ch. 19, at 1–7, *available at* http://www.ustr.gov/sites/default/files/uploads/agreements/fta/korus/asset_upload_file934_12718.pdf (last visited Sept. 29, 2010).

68 Korea International Labor Foundation (KOILAF), Current Labor Situation in Korea 2006 30 (2006), *available at* http://www.koilaf.org/KFupload/kfpublication_file/CLS2006.PDF (last visited May 20, 2011) [hereinafter "Current Labor Situation in Korea 2006"].

took a turn towards a harder line coupled with interventionist measures. Designation of guidelines for wage hike and severe crackdowns on illegal strikes are examples of such policy.

On the other hand, in the 1990s, the government made notable efforts to help improve labor-management relations. While making continuous efforts to draw a consensus among labor, management, and the government over the major labor issues, it revised labor laws to meet international standards in 1997 with the founding of the Labor-Management Relations Reform Committee and thereby achieved remarkable improvements in the area of basic labor rights. During this period, collective bargaining negotiations between labor and management were delayed because of disagreements over the revision of the labor law, but overall industrial relations in 1997 were deemed as the most peaceful since 1987, with a drastic cut in the number of days affected by labor disputes.

The Tripartite Commission was formed as the need to draw a national consensus for the sake of overcoming the economic crisis became clear after Korea was put under the IMF program in late 1997. A historic consensus was reached among labor, management and the government over structural reforms and burden-sharing in February 1998. On the basis of this consensus, many businesses could implement corporate restructuring measures, including employment adjustments and pay freezes.

Thanks to such efforts, the Korean economy recovered quickly, posting 10.7% growth in 1999. Industrial relations, however, worsened as workers' expectations ran high and more structural reforms got underway. The number of factors that contribute to labor-management conflicts, such as lay-offs, decrease in new hiring, larger number of non-regular workers, widening gap between labor and management positions on wage hikes, compensation and provisional seizure claims against strikers, etc., has been on the rise in line with worsening economic conditions since the second half of 2000.

Recently, the government has reinforced prevention and mediation of labor disputes to minimize social costs through labor-management conflict resolution, and worked to provide administrative and financial support, so that partnership based on trust can be established between labor and management. Furthermore, in the end of 2004, the government legislated the Civil Servants' Trade Union Act, establishing a framework to guarantee the basic rights of civil servants.

As employment stability rose as the core issue due to increasing uneasiness caused by long-term economic downturn, labor-management relations in 2005 saw widespread uncertainty among labor and management concerning the non-regular workers issue, the implementation of the 40-hour workweek in workplaces with not less than 300 and less than 1,000 employees, etc. Particularly, conflicts among labor, management, and government over legislation of the laws on non-regular employment have continued for a whole year. Moreover, the morality of unions was greatly damaged as bribery and other cases of corruption were discovered implicating certain leaders of the KFTU and KCTU. This caused a debate on the "crisis of the labor movement" and led to self-reflection and movements for inner innovation.

In 2006, there has been a continuous war of nerves between the government and labor concerning establishment of unions for public officials and the extent of basic labor rights to be allowed to such officials. Furthermore, the tug-of-war between labor and government over legislation of the laws on non-regular employment is still continuing. In the second half of 2006, conflicts among labor, management, and government are expected to elevate, with regard to the issues of allowing multiple unions in workplaces, prohibiting wage payment to full time union officials and the roadmap for industrial relations systems reform.[69]

. . . .

Regulation and Administration of Labor

Korea's Ministry of Labor (MOL) oversees and administers the labor laws. Its functions and organization are described next. The MOL is in charge of government labor policy. It primarily deals with the status of employment, employment insurance, and working conditions. The MOL is responsible for the general administration of industrial relations and international labor matters. Government agencies regulate employment and labor relations. The Labor Standards Act provides for labor inspectors to implement workers' protection requirements and to ensure employer compliance.

The Labor Relations Commission (LRC) is a tripartite body composed of an equal number of representatives of workers, employers, and public interest sector that administers labor laws and policies, and provides a forum for mediation of disputes. Labor disputes may also be settled by courts; but the LRC specializes in labor problems and is usually preferred over courts because it deals with labor problems more simply and rapidly than courts. Under the Labor Relations Commission Act (LRCA), the LRC is under the jurisdiction of the MOL, but is a quasi-autonomous body. Its independence enables it to make impartial decisions on labor matters.

Korea also has a Tripartite Commission that acts as an advisory body to the president. It is a consultative body composed of representatives from government, labor, business, and the public interest.

---

[69] [Author's note.] In 2006, the MOL sought to redress overuse of and discrimination against nonregular workers and drew up the Non-Regular Workers' Act to protect nonregular workers. Ministry of Labor Republic of Korea, *Employment and Labor Policy in Korea*, http://search.korea.net:8080/intro_korea2008/society/pdf/01_04.pdf (last visited Sept. 29, 2010). In 2008, the new government made a shift in labor policy by aiming to pursue growth and employment simultaneously by supporting economic revival and job creation and to this end, the Ministry of Labor set three labor policy goals: cooperative industrial relations, dynamic labor market, and customer-oriented labor policy. *Id.* at 9. One of the biggest issues in the labor relations in 2010 was the ban on wage payment by employers to full-time union officials. The Trade Union and Labor Relations Adjustment Act passed on January 1, 2010, banned wage payments for full-time union officials from July 1, 2010, and at the same time allowed union pluralism at the workplace level from July 1, 2011. KOILAF, Labor Situation in Korea 2010 54, (2010), *available at* http://www.koilaf.org/KFupload/kfpublication_file/Labor%20Situation%202010.zip (last visited Sept 29, 2010) [hereinafter "Current Labor Situation in Korea 2010"].

Ministry of Labor[70]

Purpose

The Ministry of Employment and Labor is responsible for labor standards, the adjustment of industrial relations and guidance for trade unions, occupational safety and health, employee welfare, employment policies, equal employment, employment insurance, vocational skills development training, industrial accident compensation insurance, and other labor affairs.

Functions

- Employment policy
- Resolving mismatch in the labor market through advanced employment service, providing employment security programs for unemployment prevention and employment promotion, and working to create more decent jobs by analyzing the labor market and implementing social job service programs
- Vocational training and qualification
- Creating a society with respect for technologies and skills and cultivating human resources by providing vocational training in knowledge-based occupational areas
- Equal employment
- Creating a culture of equality at work for women, the disabled, the aged, youths and minors, foreign workers, etc., and making a society based on the spirit of togetherness.
- Social insurance
- Making efforts to ensure the systematic management of employment insurance and industrial accident compensation insurance in terms of applying them and collecting their premiums
- Industrial relations
- Striving to coordinate labor relations and promoting cooperation between labor, management, and the government, finding the best examples of labor-management cooperation and providing support in many ways for the advancement of industrial relations
- Labor standards
- Supervising the various standards both workers and employers should comply with, such as for labor contracts, rest/holidays/leave, wages, retirement pay, employment relationships, dismissal, employment rules, etc.
- Occupational safety and health
- Making efforts to prevent industrial accidents by creating an accident-free, actively responding, and pleasant work environment
- International cooperation to international labor constituencies through overseas exchanges and cooperation

[70] Ministry of Employment and Labor, *Objectives*, http://www.molab.go.kr/english/about/purpose_function.jsp (last visited Sept. 29, 2010).

Ministry of Labor Organization Chart

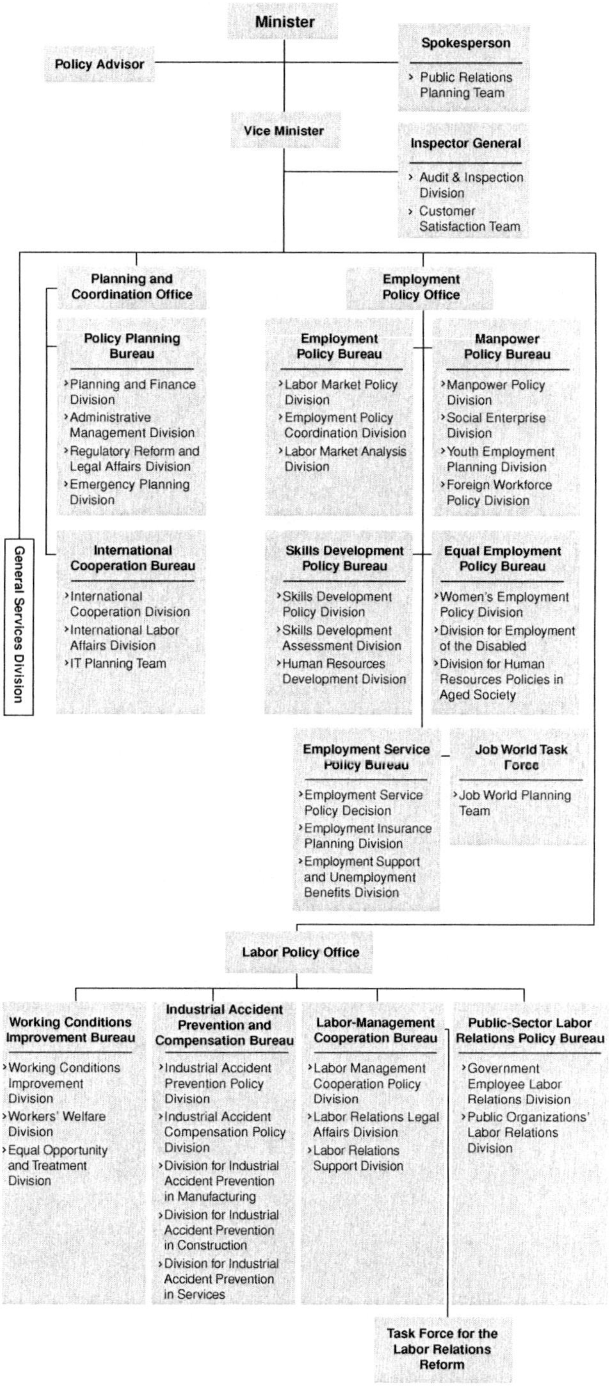

QUESTIONS

1. What is the extent of oversight by the MOL? What use is made of subordinate agencies?
2. In South Korea what is the role of judicial decisions, if any?
3. What are the legal obligations, if any, that flow from international agreements to which the Korean government is a party?

2. *Workers' Labor Rights and Benefits*

Labor Laws in Korea[71]

Korea's labor laws can be divided into three categories: individual labor relations laws such as the Labor Standards Act and the Minimum Wage Act; collective labor relations laws such as the Trade Union and Labor Relations Adjustment Act (TULRAA) and the Act on the Promotion of Worker Participation and Cooperation; and employment relations laws such as the Basic Employment Policy Act, the Employment Security Act, and the Employment Insurance Act. The most important labor laws are the Labor Standards Act and TULRAA. The Labor Standards Act was legislated in 1953 and TULRAA was legislated in 1997 by merging the former trade union law and the former labor disputes adjustment law.

- Individual labor relations laws regulate relations between workers and employers. These laws aim to provide legal criteria for signing a labor contract, its contents, and its change & termination in order to protect working conditions of workers.
- Collective labor relations laws regulate labor-management relations between trade unions or workers' representatives and employers. These laws support autonomous resolution of concerned matters between labor and management (labor-management autonomy) by guaranteeing workers' right to unite, who are economically and socially inferior to employers in terms of their position, so that they can have substantially equal relationship with employers. The law on the promotion of workers' participation is, due to its characteristics, called 'cooperative labor-management relations law.'
- Employment relations laws aim to contribute to striking a balance between supply and demand of the labor market, stabilizing workers' lives through employment security, and developing the national economy.

Individual Labor Relations Law

- Labor Standards Act
  The purpose of this act is to set the standards for the conditions of labor in conformity with the constitution, thereby securing and improving the living standards of workers and achieving a well-balanced development of the national economy.
- Employee Retirement Benefit Security Act
  The purpose of this act is to contribute to securing workers' stable livelihood in their old age by stipulating matters needed to establish and operate a retirement benefit scheme for workers.

[71] Current Labor Situation in Korea 2006, *supra* note 68, at 43–49.

- Wage Claim Guarantee Act
  The purpose of this act is to contribute to the stabilization of workers' livelihood by coming up with measures to guarantee the payment of overdue wages, etc. to workers who have retired having unpaid wages, etc. because his/her company cannot continue its business, or its business is unstable due to economic fluctuation, changes in industrial structure, etc.
- Minimum Wage Act
  The purpose of this act is to stabilize workers' lives and improve the quality of labor force by guaranteeing them a minimum level of wage and thereby contribute to the sound development of the national economy.
- Act on Equal Employment and Support for Work-Family Reconciliation
  The purpose of this act is to realize gender equality in employment in compliance with the idea of equality in the Constitution of the Republic of Korea by ensuring equal opportunity and treatment for men and women in employment, while protecting maternity and promoting women employment, as well as to contribute to improve the quality of life for all the people by providing support for the reconciliation of work and family life for workers.
- Act on the Protection, etc. of Fixed-Term and Part-time Workers
  The purpose of this act is to promote sound development of the labor market by redressing undue discrimination against fixed-term and part-time workers and strengthening the protection of their working conditions.
- Act on the Protection, etc., of Dispatched Workers
  The purpose of this act is to enhance the flexibility of supply and demand of manpower by proper operation of worker dispatch and setting up criteria such as working conditions for dispatched workers, thereby contributing to employment security and welfare promotion for dispatched workers.
- Occupational Safety and Health Act
  The purpose of this act is to maintain and promote the safety and health of workers by preventing industrial accidents and diseases through establishing standards on occupational safety and health and clarifying where the responsibility lies, and by creating a comfortable work environment.
- Industrial Accident Compensation Insurance Act
  The purpose of this act is to compensate workers rapidly and fairly for their work-related accidents by carrying out industrial accident compensation insurance activities, establishing and operating insurance facilities to promote the rehabilitation of accident victims and their return to society, thereby contributing to the protection of workers by preventing accidents and carrying out other projects for promoting workers' welfare.

Collective Labor Relations Law

- Trade Union and Labor Relations Adjustment Act
  The purpose of this act is to maintain and improve the working conditions and improve the economic and social status of workers by securing the workers' rights of association, collective bargaining, and collective action pursuant to the Constitution, and contribute to the maintenance of industrial peace and the development of the national economy by preventing and resolving labor disputes through the fair adjustment of labor relations.

- Act on the Promotion of Worker Participation and Cooperation
  The purpose of this act is to keep industrial peace and contribute to the development of the national economy by promoting the common interests of labor and management through their participation and cooperation.
- Labor Relations Commission Act
  The purpose of this act is to contribute to the security and development of labor relations by establishing the Labor Relations Commission and regulating matters as to the operation of the Commission in order to perform, in a prompt and fair manner, functions of adjudication and adjustment in labor relations.
- Act on the Establishment, Operation, etc., of Trade Unions for Teachers
  The purpose of this Act is to stipulate matters concerning the organization of trade unions for teachers in conformity with the proviso of Article 5 of the Trade union and Labor Relations Adjustment Act and to regulate special provisions necessary for the Trade union and Labor Relations Adjustment Act to be applied to teachers, notwithstanding Article 66(1) of the Government Employee Act and Article 55 of the Private School Act.
- Act on the Establishment, Operation, etc., of Public Officials' Trade Unions
  The purpose of this act is to stipulate matters concerning the establishment and operation, etc. of public officials' trade unions in accordance with the proviso of Article 5 of the Trade Union and Labor Relations Adjustment Act in order to guarantee public officials' basic rights prescribed in Article 33 (2) of the Constitution.

Employment Relations Laws

- Framework Act on Employment Policy
  The purpose of this act is to formulate and implement the employment policy comprehensively by the State and to contribute to employment security, improvement in economic and social status of workers, and balanced development of the national economy and society by helping the individual nationals develop and display their abilities to the maximum and by attaining enhanced efficiency in the labor market and balance in demand and supply of manpower.
- Employment Security Act
  The purpose of this act is to strive for the employment security of every worker, and to contribute to development of the national economy, by giving him an opportunity to find employment in which he may develop and display his own ability, and supporting an expansion of the workforce required for the industry.
- Employment Insurance Act
  The purpose of this act is, through the enforcement of employment insurance, to prevent unemployment, promote employment and develop and improve the vocational skills of workers, to strengthen the nation's vocational guidance and job placement capacity, stabilize the livelihood of workers and promote their job-seeking activities by granting necessary benefits when they are out of work, thereby contributing to the economic and social development of the nation.
- Act on the Collection, Etc. of Premiums for Employment Insurance and Industrial Accident Compensation Insurance
  The purpose of this act is to enhance the efficiency of insurance-related affairs by stipulating necessary matters concerning the establishment and termination of insurance relationships and payment and collection of insurance premiums, etc. for employment insurance and industrial accident compensation insurance.

- Act on Age Discrimination Prohibition in Employment and Aged Employment Promotion
  The purpose of this act is to prohibit employment discrimination based on age without a reasonable reason, and contribute to employment security of the aged and development of national economy by supporting and promoting their employment suited to their abilities.
- Act on Foreign Workers' Employment, etc.
  The purpose of this act is to achieve the smooth supply and demand of manpower and the balanced development of the national economy by systematically introducing and managing foreign workers.
- Social Enterprise Promotion Act
  The purpose of this act is to contribute to the integration of society as well as to the enhancement of the quality of the people's life by means of expanding social services which are not sufficiently provided in society and creating jobs.
- National Technical Qualifications Act
  The purpose of this act is to contribute to the development of vocational competency of human resources with skills, improvement of their social status, and development of the national economy by upholding qualifications systems needed for industrial demand and enhancing efficiency in operating the national technical qualifications system.
- Act on the Encouragement of Technical Skills
  The purpose of this act is to contribute to promoting economic and social status of people by acquiring technical skills so that they can be encouraged to acquire and improve technical skills and be committed to their areas with self-esteem and pride.
- Workers Vocational Skills Development Act
  The purpose of this act is to secure the employment of workers, raise their social and economic status, and improve the productivity of enterprises, thus contributing to social and economic development by promoting and supporting their skills development throughout their lives.
- Act on Employment Promotion and Vocational Rehabilitation for Disabled Persons
  The purpose of this act is to contribute to the employment promotion and vocational rehabilitation of disabled persons so that they can live a decent life undertaking jobs suited to their abilities.

E. Other Labor Relations Laws

- Act on the Tripartite Commission for Economic and Social Development
  The purpose of this act is to establish the Tripartite Commission for Economic and Social Development (ESDC) where workers, employers, and the government coordinate labor policies and related economic and social policies, etc. based on mutual trust and cooperation, have the Commission answer questions posed by the president, and prescribe necessary matters regarding the organization and its operation in a bid to promote industrial peace and to contribute to balanced development of the national economy.
- Basic Workers Welfare Act
  The purpose of this act is to improve workers' quality of life and contribute to the balanced development of the national economy by prescribing the matters necessary in establishing welfare policies for workers and carrying out welfare projects.

- Employee Welfare Fund Act
  The purpose of this act is to contribute to the stabilization of workers' living and promotion of their welfare, by making the employer establish, manage efficiently and operate an Employee Welfare Fund financed with a portion of the profits yielded from his/her business operation.
- Act on the Legislation of Workers' Day
  May the 1st is designated as Workers' Day, which is a paid holiday pursuant to 'Labor Standards Act'.

. . . .

Below is a chart correlating firm size with applicable labor laws[72]

TABLE 10. *Firm size and applicable labor laws*

Act		Number of Workers Employed	Remarks
Labor Standards Act		5 or more workers	- Selected provisions shall be applied to businesses with four or fewer workers. - Rules of employment have to be established in businesses with 10 or more workers.
Industrial Safety and Health Act	General	All workplaces are subject to this Act regardless of the number of workers employed.	- Selected provisions are applied to businesses with 4 or fewer workers and some selected types of businesses.
Industrial Safety and Health Act	Appointment of personnel in charge of safety and health management	100 or more workers	- Also applied to workplaces with fifty or more workers for some selected types of businesses
Industrial Safety and Health Act	Appointment of a safety and health supervisor	50 or more workers	- Not appliable to some selected types of businesses
Industrial Safety and Health Act	Industrial safety and health committee	100 or more workers	
Minimum Wage Act		All workplaces	

[72] *Id.* at 48–49; *see also* Current Labor Situation in Korea 2010, *supra* note 69, at 86.

Equal Employment Act	All workplaces	- Some selected provisions are not applied to businesses with four or fewer workers.
Industrial Accident Compensation Insurance Act	All workplaces	- Some selected types of industries, such as businesses with four or fewer workers in agriculture, forestry, and fishery, are excluded.
Act Concerning the Promotion of Worker Participation and Cooperation	Thirty or more workers	- Businesses with 30 or more workers should establish a labor-management council that includes members to handle grievances.
Trade Union and Labor Relations Adjustment Act & Employment Security Act	All workplaces	
Act on Employment Promotion and Vocational Rehabilitation for the Disabled	Fifty or more workers	- Employers should hire disabled workers to account for as much as 2% of their total regular workforce. Employers who fail to meet this requirement will be subject to penalites. On the other hand, incentives will be awarded to those hiring disabled workers that account for more than 2% of the total workforce. - Workplaces with less than 100 penalties will be exempt from the penalties. Workplaces hiring 200–299(100–199) workers will be subject to penalties from 2006(2007), but for the first five years of application, only 50% of the penalties will be charged.
Employee Welfare Fund Act	Workplaces interested in establishing the fund	
Aged Employment Promotion Act	All workplaces	- Workplaces with 300 or more workers should make efforts to employ old people more than the standard employment rate. - Standard Employment Rate: Manufacturing 2% / transportation, real estate and leasing, 6% / other industries, 3%
Employment Insurance Act	All workplaces	- Some selected types of industries, such as businesses with four or fewer workers in agriculture, forestry, and fishery, are excluded.

National Labor Law Profile: Republic of Korea (South Korea)[73]

Liliane Jung

Labour Law

The Constitution grants fundamental labour standards, such as:

- the right and also the obligation to work (Art. 32 paras. 1 and 2);
- the workers' right to freedom of association, collective bargaining, and collective action (Art. 33), with public officials and employees of important defence industries being excepted unless provided for by law;
- special protection for working children and working women including prevention of unjustified discrimination against women (Art. 32 paras. 4 and 5).

The Constitution also stipulates that the legislature make laws governing working conditions so as to guarantee human dignity (Art. 32 para. 3).

Within this constitutional mandate, labour law is determined by labour legislation, supplementary administrative decrees, collective agreements and work rules.

Labour legislation includes a number of acts, among which the following – all adopted on 13 March 1997 – may be considered as key acts:

- Labour Standards Act (LSA) last amended on 20 February 1998,
- Trade Union and Labour Relations Adjustment Act (TULRAA) last amended on 20 February 1998,
- Labour Relations Commission Act (LRCA), and
- Act Concerning the Promotion of Worker Participation and Cooperation (ACPWPC).

The LSA sets minimum standards for working conditions and includes regulations on enforcement measures. According to the LSA's aim and structural principle, working conditions are to be understood as all kind of contractual matters, particularly wages and working hours. The LSA applies to all employees except for domestic workers; seafarers are only covered by the LSA where they are not covered by the Seafarers' Act. Even though some articles may concern every workplace with at least one employee, the LSA entirely covers workplaces where ordinarily 5 or more workers are employed who are not relatives living together (Art. 10 paras. 1 and 2 of the LSA. . . .

The TULRAA regulates the formation of trade unions as well as collective bargaining and is supplemented by the LRCA, which aims to secure stable labour relations through the Labour Relations Commission, an independent administrative body under the Ministry of Labour. The workplace based Labour-Management Council, which is composed of workers' and employer's representatives, is subject to the ACPWPC.

Legislation is to an increasing degree subject to jurisprudence, which may, in some cases, be influenced by administrative interpretation issued by the Ministry of Labour or the Ministry of Justice.

[73] Liliane Jung, *National Labor Law Profile: Republic of Korea (South Korea)*, http://www.ilo.org/public/english/dialogue/ifpdial/info/national/kor.htm (last visited Sept. 29, 2010). Copyright © International Labour Organization. [Some formatting altered].

Collective agreements are also legally binding, if they do not fall short of limits set by legislation (Art. 33 para. 1 TULRAA and Arts. 2 of the LSA). In practice, they are mostly concluded by the enterprise trade union and the employer and are thus enterprise based. De jure and de facto, collective bargaining and freedom of association is still a developing issue.

Within any workplace with more than 10 employees, working conditions such as those enumerated in Article 96 of the LSA must be stipulated by work rules that must not run counter to legislation and collective agreements (Art. 99 of the LSA).

As a matter of fact, an applicable collective agreement regularly needs to be elaborated by the work rules, which are drawn up by the employer in consultation with the trade union or, as an alternative, with the Labour-Management Council (Arts. 96 and 97 of the LSA and Art. 19 para. 1 No. 11 of the ACPWPC). A report to the Ministry of Labour is also necessary. Any provision of the labour contract in conflict with the work rules is null and void (Art. 100 of the LSA). Labour contracts need not be drawn up in writing, even though a clear statement to the employee after the conclusion is legally demanded as far as contractual matters like remuneration and working hours are concerned (Art. 24 of the LSA). If the employee successfully claims that his actual labour conditions are unlawful, he/she is entitled to claim damages or to terminate the contract (Art. 26 of the LSA).

Contract of Employment

Permanent and fixed term contract of employment

The traditional system of lifetime employment, which was similar to that of Japan, has nearly vanished due to the deteriorating economic situation since 1997 and the LSA amendment in 1998, which recognized – under further conditions – an urgent managerial need as a justifying reason for dismissal.

According to the LSA, the term of a labour contract shall not exceed one year, except in cases where there is no term fixed or a term is fixed as necessary for the completion of a certain project (Art. 23). In case of any violation by the employer, he/she is punished by a fine not exceeding five million Won (Art. 115 of the LSA). It is, however, necessary that the worker report the violation to the Ministry of Labour or its subordinate offices (Art. 107 para. 1 of the LSA).

Equal treatment of permanent and fixed term contractors is not legally assured. Even in the LSA, fixed term contractors are treated less favourable in some regards, *e.g.* with reference to an advance notice of dismissal (Art. 35 of the LSA).

Probation

Any labour contract may specify a probation period at the beginning of the employment relationship. During the first three months of this term, the employee may be dismissed without advance notice (Art. 35 no. 5 of the LSA and Art. 12 of the Enforcement Decree). Precedent also sets lower standards for justifiable reasons, as far as dismissals of probationers are concerned.

Special contracts of employment

Temporary work (dispatched work) was legalized by the Act Relating to Protection, etc. for Dispatched Workers, which was adopted 20 February 1998 and entered into force the first of July the same year. In this employment situation, the worker has a labour contract with a temporary work agency but works under the direction of a client company, which has concluded a dispatching contract with the temporary work agency. The agency's operation needs a frequently renewed permit from the Ministry of Labour.

Temporary work is legally permitted for jobs requiring expertise, special skills, or experience selected by Presidential Decree (Art. 5 para. 1). In such circumstances, the dispatch period is limited to one year but can be extended to two years. After this time, the worker is entitled to be regarded as employed in the client company (Art. 6 para. 3).

However, temporary workers may be requested also for other occasional needs, in particular to replace regular employees who are absent due to maternity or illness. Such cases require a prior consultation of the enterprise trade union (Art. 5 para. 3), and the worker may not be dispatched to perform certain work like construction work, seafarer's activities, or dangerous activities (Art. 5 para. 2 no. 2). Furthermore, the dispatch period is more restricted: In cases of child birth and illness, the period is limited to the required term and in case of other occasional needs, to three months with the possibility of extension of another three months (Art. 6 para. 2).

For any dispatch work, the dispatching agency, as well as the client company, is regarded as employers with differing obligations towards the temporary worker, against whom discrimination is prohibited (Arts. 34 para. 1, 35, and 21).

Part-time workers are specifically protected by legislation since the last amendment to the LSA. They are defined as "employees whose contractual working hours per week are shorter than those of full-time workers engaged in the same kind of job at the pertinent workplace" (Art. 21 LSA). Those part-time workers "whose contractual working hours per week are less than fifteen hours on the average of four weeks", are for the most part excluded (Art. 25 para. 3 LSA and Art. 9 para. 2 Enforcement Decree). In 1999, 55.2% of the total of part-time workers were female.

. . . .

The working conditions of part-time workers are specified by Presidential Decrees within the limits of Art. 25 paras. 1 and 2 LSA. Wages need to be calculated on an hourly basis, and holidays as well as paid leave must be granted in an equivalent manner to those of full-time employees. Part-timers may work overtime but the limits must be stated in the labour contract. Apart from these standards set by legislation, the employer may establish work rules, which concern only part-time workers and thus may be less favourable than those of full-timers.

Vocational training is provided for throughout a worker's entire career and thus is not stipulated as a special labour contract (Art. 3 para. 1 of the Vocational Training Promotion Act). It receives, however, special protection in the LSA, which mandates that vocational trainees only perform work from which they acquire technical skills (Art. 77). Training methods and contract terms of long term training are even fixed by Presidential Decree (Art. 78 para. 1 of the LSA).

. . . .

Hours of Work

Pursuant to Art. 49 of the LSA, the statutory working time is not more than 44 hours per week and 8 hours per day excluding rest periods. A rest period of half an hour must be granted for every 4 working hours and of one hour for every 8 working hours (Art. 53 of the LSA). One day per week must be a holiday (Art. 54 of the LSA). Night work – 10 PM to 6 AM – is forbidden for female workers and minors (Art. 68 of the LSA).

The limits of the average working time may be relaxed with and without a written agreement of the employer and the enterprise trade union or the workers' representative. Without such agreement, the employer may ask the worker to work up to 48 hours in one week, provided that the average working hours in two weeks do not exceed 44 hours (Art. 50 para. 1 of the LSA). Having succeeded the required agreement the employer may request work of up to 56 hours in a specific week or 12 hours in a particular day, if the average weekly working hours do not exceed 44 hours within a period of one month (Art. 50 para. 2 of the LSA).

Apart from the normal or flexible working time, the employee may also work overtime of up to 12 hours a week (Art. 52 paras. 1 and 2 of the LSA). This, however, requires the agreement of the employer and the enterprise trade union as well as the payment of overtime compensation, at least 50% over the normal wage. In special businesses as stipulated in Art. 58 of the LSA *e.g.* transportation business, movie production or medical business, the employee may work overtime even in excess of 12 hours per week. In any case, it is prohibited by legislation that female workers do overtime work exceeding two hours per day, 6 hours per week and 150 hours per year (Art. 69 of the LSA).

The legislative limitation of working hours does not apply to employees of the following fields: agricultural and forestry work, cattle-breeding, sericulture and fishery business as well as surveillance or intermittent work (Art. 61 of the LSA).

Paid Leave

Apart from those employees mentioned under *Hours of work*, each employee may be entitled to monthly leave and annual leave, both with pay (Arts. 57 and 59 of the LSA). Monthly leave is one day and can be taken, only if the employee has been working all days during the preceding month (Art. 27 of the Enforcement Decree). It can be accumulated up to one year and then be taken at once. Annual leave is basically 10 or 8 working days, dependently of whether the employee has been working the entire year without absence or at least 90 % of the working days during the year. From the second year of consecutive employment, one day of annual leave is added each consecutive year of service. The number of guaranteed annual leave days, however, does not exceed 20 days, but normal wages may be paid for the number of days in excess of 20 days. Annual leave must be taken within the working year, unless the employee is prevented for reasons lying with the employer. In case of untaken monthly or annual leave, an additional ordinary wage for the relevant days must be paid.

Maternity Protection and Maternity Leave

Maternity is protected in the LSA, which also stipulates the employer's punishment in case of any violation. The pregnant employee must not work overtime and, upon request, she must be assigned to light and easy work (Art. 72 para. 2). This protection is supplemented by the requirement that night work by women is only accompanied by the worker's consent and the approval of the Ministry of Labor. In addition, maternity leave with pay is guaranteed (Art. 72 para. 1). The employee is obliged to take 30 days after childbirth, while she is legally entitled to ask for up to 60 days of maternity leave within the period before and after childbirth. During this period, she is protected against dismissal (Art. 30 para. 2).

Other Leave Entitlements

Sick leave is not provided for by legislation. Only a medical treatment because of an occupational injury or disease allows the employee to be absent from work (Art. 82 of the LSA). In this case, 60 % of the average wage is paid. Sick leave may, however, be granted by collective agreements or work rules.

Child care leave is governed by the Equal Employment Act adopted on 4 December 1987 and last amended 8 February 1999. It is a not paid leave and can be taken by either the mother or the father in order to care for the child who is less than one year (Art. 11 para. 1). The leave cannot be extended beyond the child's first birthday.

Female workers are also entitled to menstruation leave (Art. 71 of the LSA), and men are authorized to leave for mandatory military service.

Minimum Age and Protection of Young Workers

The constitutional provision protecting young workers has been implemented in the following way: The employment of children under the age of 15 is generally banned (Art. 62 para. 1 LSA). Individual cases may be exempted by permission of the Ministry of Labour, if compulsory education is not impeded (Art. 62 para. 2 of the LSA). Children under age 18 must not be employed at night or in dangerous or hazardous workplaces (Arts. 63 and 68 of the LSA). Further, the working hours are slightly reduced to 7 hours per day and 42 per week. However, they may be extended by mutual agreement of the employer and the minor by one hour per day and six hours per week (Art. 67 of the LSA).

Equality

Pursuant to Art. 5 of the LSA, the employer must not discriminate against workers by nationality, religion, social status, or gender [age has been added]. Gender equality is further addressed by the Equal Employment Act (EEA), which elaborates the constitutional demand for gender equality in terms of employment, wages, and working conditions. It applies inter alia the principle of equal wages for work of equal value in the same business (Art. 6-2 para. 1). However, it is fair to say that inequalities persist in Korean society. In 1999, female workers of the non-agricultural sector earned 63% of the male workers' income and in the manufacturing sector only 55% of the male workers' earnings (based on figures collected by the Ministry of Labour). The EEA also prohibits any provision of the employment contract that stipulates marriage, pregnancy, or child-delivery as a reason for retirement and thus revises a common practice in the Korean labour market (Art. 8 para. 2). In addition, sexual harassment is prohibited with responsibility residing with the employer (Art. 8-2 of the EEA). In order to safeguard gender equality, punishment of a fine of 10 million Won or imprisonment is imposed for any violation of the EEA.

Pay Issues

Wages are defined as "any payment to a worker from an employer as remuneration for work, regardless of the designation by which such payment is called" (Art. 18 of the

LSA). Wages thus may not only be comprised of the normal remuneration but also of allowances and bonuses. The individual wage level is usually determined by enterprise based collective agreements. In November 1999, 89% of all workplaces had concluded wage negotiations (based on figures collected by the Ministry of Labour). The enterprise based wage determination tends to create differences among the various firms, depending on the firm's size or other economic factors. However, a certain minimum level of wages is guaranteed in the Minimum Wage Act adopted on 31 December 1986. It is annually determined by the Ministry of Labour, which takes the cost of living, the wages of kindred workers and labour productivity into consideration and makes a division into different business categories (Art. 4 paras. 1 and 2 and Art. 8 para. 1). Upon permission of the Ministry of Labour, the following workers may be exempted from the Minimum Wage Act (Art. 7):

- workers on probation,
- workers with a very limited working capacity due to mental or physical handicap, and
- workers who receive basic training.

Wage claims are guaranteed on the basis of the Wage Claim Guarantee Act, which was adopted on 20 February 1998. In cases such as bankruptcy of the employer, the retired employee may claim wages of the final three months or retirement allowance of the final three years (Art. 6 I, II of the WCGA and Art. 37 II LSA). All payments are made out of a wage claims guarantee fund established and operated by the Ministry of Labor. The fund is mainly financed by employers with contributions not exceeding 0.2% of the wages paid to employees. However, employers are liable to reimburse money paid from the fund to their employees (Art. 7 of the WCGA).[74]

Social Insurances

Current Labor Situation in Korea[75]

Four major social insurances refer to the national pension, health insurance, industrial accident compensation insurance, and employment insurance. Such a four social insurance system was completed by introducing the employment insurance as of July 1995 and the four insurances are applied to all nationals and workers.

The National Pension Service (national pension), National Health Insurance Corporation (health insurance), and Korea Workers' Compensation & Welfare Service (industrial accident insurance and employment insurance) are the public agencies in charge of their mandatory operations. For the premium, national pension, health insurance, and employment insurance are equally shared between workers and employers, but in case of industrial accident insurance, employers bear the burden for all premiums. Currently, each premium is collected by the respective national insurance corporation but

[74] For a detailed listing of rights and duties under the various labor and employment laws, created by the MOL and updated by a law firm, see Sean Hayes, *Korean Labor Law Checklist for Employers and Employees*, The Korean Law Blog (Feb. 17, 2008), http://www.thekoreanlawblog.com/2008/02/korean-labor-law-check-list-for.html (last visited Oct. 2, 2010).

[75] Current Labor Situation in Korea 2010, *supra* note 69, at 46–49 [Formatting altered].

premiums of those four insurances will be integrated and collected by the National Health Insurance Corporation from 2011.

National pension

One of the most important social security schemes in Korea is the national pension system which was introduced in 1988. The scheme is aimed to secure a stable livelihood for Korean people by providing a certain amount of pension for life when they or their family members are in situations of not being able to sustain a livelihood after getting old or retired, or suffering due to unexpected accidents, diseases, or death. Subscription is allowed for people aged from 18 to 60 residing in Korea. However, public servants, soldiers, private school teachers who have their own schemes protected under the Public Servants Pension Act, Soldiers Pension Act, and Private School Teacher Pension Act, or other people designated by the Presidential decrees are excluded from its subscription.

In July 2007, the National Assembly passed a revised act on national pension, requiring 'contribute the same, but receive less'. Accordingly, 9% (4.5% for employee, and 4.5% for employer) of the insurance premium rate was kept unchanged, but pension benefit rate was reduced from the previous 60% to 50% in 2008. Furthermore, 0.5 percentage point of the benefit rate will be reduced every year from 2009, reaching 40% by 2028. In 2008, the Basic Pension for Aged People was introduced anew, which subsidizes 60% of the elderly people with 5% (amounting to 100,000 won) of monthly average income of all national pension subscribers every month. According to the Ministry of Health and Welfare, the national pension fund stands at 277,642 billion won as of the end of 2009, an increase by 42,209 billion won from the previous year.

Health insurance

Health insurance was introduced to improve people's health and social insurance by providing insurance payment for prevention, diagnosis, treatment, and rehabilitation against diseases, injuries, childbirth, and death. Health insurance, started in 1977 as an obligatory system for all people, was integrated in 1998 by the 1st phase of integration of regional medical insurance and government employees and teachers medical insurance. Then, in July 2000, workplace medical insurance was also merged to complete the process, which led to the launch of the 'National Health Insurance Corporation'. Currently, health insurance applies to all workplaces. Insurance premium is 5.08% of monthly standard wage. For this premium, the employer and worker equally share by 50%.

The National Health Insurance Corporation declared emergency management in March 2010 because of its alarming financial state and loss is expected for the year. Health insurance recorded 226.8 billion won loss as of the end of January 2010 with more expenditure (2,789 billion won) than income (2,562 billion won) in total. The corporation says, "Due to the moderation of wage level, premium revenue is likely to be flat while the insurance expenditure will continue to rise, resulting in a large deficit in 2010". The government and the corporation, therefore, are coming up with various solutions for sound financial state of the health insurance.

Employment insurance

Employment insurance, along with industrial accident compensation insurance, is a social insurance that acts as a social safety net. Employment insurance was introduced in

1995 with a view to preventing unemployment, promoting employment and enhancing worker's vocational skills development. In 2004, it started to apply to non-regular workers, such as daily and time-based employees who work more than 15 hours a week.

Korea's employment insurance is different from the unemployment insurance of other countries since it focuses on prevention of unemployment that goes beyond the supporting livelihood of the unemployed. It also serves as a core tool of active labor market policy which promotes re-employment and actively engages in vocational skills development and workforce demand & supply.

In order to accomplish these goals, the employment insurance is divided into different programs, including unemployment payment program, vocational skills development program, employment stability program, and benefits for child care leave and maternity leave. A worker who subscribed to the employment insurance shall receive 50 percent of his/her daily average wage before unemployment for 90 to 240 days in accordance with his/her age and period of subscription. However, a worker must have subscribed the insurance for more than 18 months and worked for more than 180 days before lay-off. In addition, it is applied to workers who were involuntarily laid off because of a managerial reason. Benefits of early re-employment and child care leave are also paid from the employment insurance to promote reemployment of the unemployed.

. . . .

Industrial Accident Compensation Insurance

Industrial accident compensation insurance, introduced in 1964, is a solid insurance system as much as it is the first social insurance system of the four major social insurances. The current Act on Industrial Accident Compensation Insurance defines an industrial accident as "on-duty accident" Industrial accidents can be classified into two categories: occupational accidents and occupational diseases. Occupational accidents refer to one due to slips, falls, and strictures, while occupational diseases refer to on-duty diseases and occupation-related diseases. One of the occupational diseases is poisoning by organic solvents. On-duty diseases include lumbago and muscular-skeletal disorders due to repetitive working. Insurance premium is paid all by employers.

The Act on Industrial Accident Compensation Insurance was extensively amended in 2008 and 2009. As of July 1st, 2008, workers under special-type working status like insurance salespersons, visiting private tutors, golf caddies, and ready-mix drivers, who were previously rejected from benefits due to their duplicate status as a worker and business owner, were now allowed to subscribe to the insurance. Moreover, from July 1st of 2009, construction machinery owner-truckers of 27 types including dump trucks, excavators, and bulldozers became eligible for this insurance. Workplaces with more than 20 permanent employees shall also be allowed to get premium discounts if industrial accidents do not occur.

. . . .

QUESTIONS

1. Do South Korea's current labor laws omit any area of labor and employment law; if so, what?

2. Is South Korean labor law more or less consistent with common-law legal systems; in what ways?
3. Are there any notable "South Korean or Asian characteristics" reflected in its labor and employment laws?

---

3. *Labor Unions and Industrial Relations*

National Labour Law Profile: Republic of Korea (South Korea)[76]

Liliane Jung

. . . .

Trade unions and Employers' Association

The worker's right to independent associations and to collective bargaining is constitutionally guaranteed. Public officials and employees of important defence industries are, however, excepted unless provided for by law (Art. 33 of the Constitution).[77]

Pursuant to the TULRAA, workers are free to establish a trade union, for which at least two employees are required who file a report with the relevant government office (Arts. 5 and 10). If the report is accepted, the union is established. A trade union is considered "an organization or associated organization of workers, which is formed in voluntary and collective manner upon the workers' initiative for the purpose of maintaining and improving working conditions or improving the economic and social status of workers" (Art. 2 No. 4 of the TULRAA).

Most trade unions are de facto enterprise based and each enterprise may legally only have one trade union. The principle of multiple unionism at enterprise level will be recognized from the year 2002 [postponed until 2011]. The enterprise based trade unions are affiliated with federations at industry level, which join federations on a national level. The two most important national federations are the Korean Federation of Trade Unions (KFTU) and the Korean Confederation of Trade Unions (KCTU). The latter was officially registered in November 1999, while the KFTU had been for many years the only authorized national organization. Trade union pluralism at industrial and national levels is legally permitted since May 1998.

Workers are free to join trade unions, which applies to dismissed workers only as long as they are still engaged in legal disputes because of the dismissal (Arts. 5 and 2 No. 4d of the TULRAA). In cases where a trade union is representing more than 2/3 of workers employed in the same business, the employee even may be forced to join the trade union, if such is provided in the enterprise based collective agreement (Art. 81 No. 2 of the TULRAA). Union members are guaranteed equal rights and duties to participate in all of the trade union's affairs, provided that the union dues are regularly paid. They also

[76] Jung, *supra* note 73.

[77] [Author's note.] One of such laws is the Act on the Establishment and Operation, etc. of Trade Union for Teachers. In the year 2000, 338,000 public servants out of a total of 930,000 were eligible to join workplace associations, which are not considered a trade union in terms of the TULRAA.

elect union officials who may be engaged as full-time officials (Art. 23 para. 1 and Art. 24 para. 1 of the TULRAA). As from January 2002, full-time union officials will be banned from being paid in part or in full by their employer (Art. 24 para. 2).

. . . .

———

Trade Union Profile[78]

In Korea, workers can organize a trade union with the purpose of improving working conditions and the economic and social status of workers. In principle, all workers excluding public service personnel are granted rights of organization, collective bargaining, and collective action.

All forms of trade unions – by company, by occupation type, by region, or by industry – are allowed. At present, however, most trade unions are organized at enterprise level and working conditions are determined through collective bargaining negotiations between labor and management of each company.

. . . .

- National Trade Union Federations

Most trade unions in Korea are affiliated with one of the two national organizations: the Korean Federation of Trade Unions (KFTU) and the Korean Confederation of Trade Unions (KCTU). It can be said that while KFTU takes a moderate rationalist stance, placing more emphasis on dialogue than on struggle, KCTU has been relatively struggle-oriented in its practice of labor movement. In recent years, however, as union density has declined and the labor movement has lost ground and influence in terms of social issues, both organizations are giving more weight to negotiations with the Government and employers' organizations in their efforts to resolve labor relations issues.

Union activities and labor movement in Korea have centered on the two national union organizations. Both have played a pivotal role, representing workers on important social issues such as protection and organization of the non-regular workforce – one of the hottest issues at present; the problem of employment insecurity caused by economic downturn and increased labor market flexibility; and the enactment and revision of laws and regulations concerning labor relations.

The KFTU dates back to the Korean Labor Federation for Independence Promotion (KLFIP), which was established under the initiative of President Rhee, Syngman in 1946, the year following national liberation from the Japanese rule. KLFIP was founded as a rightist labor organization, in opposition to the General Council of Korean Trade Unions, which was led by a group of leftists. Later, in 1960, KLFIP was renamed KFTU, its present name, and evolved into the only national organization of trade unions in Korea.

Up until the historic struggle of workers in July and August of 1987, which was the watershed of Korean democratization, KFTU had often been stigmatized as "yellow," because – due to its orientation toward labor-management cooperation – with its tradition

[78] Current Labor Situation in Korea 2006, *supra* note 68, at 33–37 [Formatting altered].

of rational moderation, has played a central role for development of the labor movement in Korea.

With regard to its membership, as of the end of 2005 KFTU includes 25 industry-level organizations and 16 regional organizations, which in turn cover about 780,000 unionists. The leading players of KFTU are: the Korean Financial Industry Union, the Federation of Korean Drivers' Unions, and the Federation of Korean Metal Workers Trade Unions. Overall, the trade unions of the traditional manufacturing sector and of small and medium-sized companies take up the majority of KFTU affiliates.

In an effort to realize its long-cherished objective to "create a political powerhouse of workers," KFTU inaugurated a political party named "Green Party of Socialist Democrats" and ran in the 2004 general election, but failed to get any seat in the National Assembly. The leaders of KFTU, holding itself responsible for the failure, all stepped down from their leadership posts.

KFTU has been representing workers at the Tripartite Commission, a three-way consultative body created in 1998, and thereby has contributed substantially toward the resolution of labor relations issues, by way of dialogue with other social partners. Additionally, each of KFTU's regional headquarters is intent on working together with its corresponding employer organization(s) to stimulate the local economy.

KFTU, which celebrated its 60th anniversary in 2006, is implementing a bold inner reform, through establishment of a new movement ideology called "participatory unionism of social solidarity for realization of an equal welfare society," and presentation of 3 major movement directions, namely building industry-wide unions, strengthening its struggle for social reform, and constructing a social dialogue system. The KFTU has also set a goal to reach a membership level of 2 million, equivalent to that of 1989, by 2010, and is focusing on building office workers' unions, establishing unions for public officials and teachers, and organizing unorganized workers as well as non-regular workers.

KCTU: 1987's great struggle by the workers led to an explosive increase in the number of trade unions and the establishment of regional and industrial organizations that disapproved of the existing KFTU and claimed to stand for autonomy and democracy. In the early 1990s, the National Council of Trade Unions, the Congress of Industrial Unions and the Large Plant Union Organization were founded; and later in 1993 these were merged into the National Council of Trade Union Delegates (Chon-no-dae) representing 420,000 union workers, which was the beginning of what is today the Korean Confederation of Trade Unions.

Since its inauguration in November 1995, KCTU has protested Government decisions on labor law revisions and other social issues, remaining non-statutory until it was legalized in 1998. Unlike KFTU, the other national union organization, KCTU has been more struggle-oriented and therefore in conflict with the Government in many cases. For instance, at the end of 1996 when the National Assembly forcibly passed a bill on labor law revisions allowing corporate layoffs, KCTU staged a general strike, jointly with KFTU, protesting the bill's passage, and succeeded in making the Government and the Assembly withdraw the bill.

As of the end of 2005, KCTU affiliates include 17 union federations and 16 regional organizations, representing 670,000 union workers. In general, the unions of large plants in the manufacturing sector have the strongest power in the operation of KCTU.

Unlike previous KCTU leaders who stood for militant corporatism, the former executives, including Lee Soo-Ho, and the incumbent executives, led by Cho Jun-Ho, have declared a new stance of "utilitarian corporatism," participating in tripartite representatives' meetings to negotiate with the government and employers, and working to combine dialogue and struggle in dealing with pending issues.[79]

In the meantime, thanks to the long preparations for a political force for workers, the Democratic Labor Party (established in 2000), which is led by KCTU, succeeded in winning 10 Assembly seats for its worker and farmer candidates in the 2004 general election.

As the Korean Government Employees' Union (KGEU), which is the largest organization of public officials with 140,000 members, joined the KCTU, the Confederation has become the largest trade union federation in Korea, with more than 800,000 affiliated members. Thus, the two major trade union centers are expected to see more intensive competition in increasing their influence.

. . . .

Current Labor Situation in Korea 2010[80]

According to MOL statistics, as of the end of 2004, the number of trade unions stood at 6,017, union membership at 1,536,843 (1,211,952 men and 324,891 women), and organization rate at 10.6%. Compared with the figures for 2003, the number of unions dropped by 240, and membership dropped by 13,106. Organization rate decreased by 0.4% compared to 11.0% in 2003. In terms of membership at the national confederation level, a total of 3,714 unions (43.5% of all unions) with 780,183 members (50.8% of all union members) were affiliated with the Federation of Korea Trade Unions (FKTU), while 1,256 unions (20.9% of all unions) with 668,136 members (43.5% of all union members) were affiliated with the Korean Confederation of Trade Unions (KCTU). 1047 unions with 88,524 members were not affiliated with any umbrella organization.

. . . .

According to '2008 State of the Korean Trade Unions,' trade union members total up to 1,665,798, which is 1.3% (21,984) lower than the level of 2007. Unionization rate of trade union is at 10.5%, a 0.3% point decrease from the last year. The rate in the private sector continued to decline from 9.2% to 8.8%, and that of the teachers' union lowered by 2.8% points to 21.5%. On the other hand, government employees unionized 8.2% points more to reach 75.3%, compared from the previous year. Rate of trade union recorded at 19.8 in 1989 and continued to fall afterwards: 12 level between 1997 and 2001, 11 level in 2002 and 2003, and 10 level since 2004 (see Table 18).

As for the state of umbrella organizations, the KFTU has 725,014 members, which takes up 43.5% of all unions, followed by the KCTU at 39.5% (658,118) and non-affiliates with 17.0% (282,666).... The KFTU has 2.1% less members than in 2007 while the number of members has kept on decreasing since 2000. The KCTU witnessed even larger decrease of 3.6%. The number of the KCTU members seemed to rise due to the

[79] [Author's note.] On April 26, 2011, it was reported the two unions will join forces to seek legislative labor reforms. "This is the first time the two major union federation heads have made a joint statement and embarked upon a joint struggle against the Korean government." *See KCTU-FKTU Cooperation Must Lead to Solution of Irregular Employment and Other Problems*, The Kyunghyang Shinmun, Apr. 26, 2011, *available at* http://english.khan.co.kr/khan_art_view.html?code=790101&artid=201104261439417.

[80] Current Labor Situation in Korea 2010, *supra* note 69, at 58.

TABLE 18. 2008 *State of trade union organization*

Category	Number of trade unions	Total	(Unit: number, person) number of trade unions Male	Female
Total	4,886	1,665,798	1,290,682	375,116
Unit Unions				
– Company (workplace)	4,526	784,521	626,053	158,468
– Regional Industrial Unions	254	94,856	90,665	4,191
– Industrial Unions	63	786,421	573,964	212,457
Federations				
– National Centers	2	–	–	–
– National Federations	41	–	–	–

* Unionization rate = Total number of trade union members (1,666 thousand)/number of targeted workers wage workers (16,189 thousands)-government employees who are not allowed to subscribe to trade unions (342 thousands) 100

* Number of union members: 1,668 thousand (2007) 1,666 thousand (2008) (A decrease by 22 thousand (1.3%)) *Industrial union: Unions of nation-wide reach under its name or union conventions

Source: 2008 State of the Trade Unions' Organization, Ministry of Labor (June 17, 2009)

new entrance of government employees' union but began to decrease again. On the other hand, non-affiliates rose by 6.6% compared to the previous year.

Looking into details of the unionization rate at the company level, the rate for companies having 300 and more employees is 45.4%, indicating that larger companies take higher influence of trade unions. Companies having 100 to 299 employees show 13.6% of the unionization rate, while those having 30 to 99 employees have only 3.1% of the rate. For companies having less than 30 workers, the rate stands only at 0.2%.

It is noteworthy that the number of non-enterprise level trade unions continues to grow. . . . The number of members to regional, national, and industrial trade unions stands at 881,277, accounting for 52.9% of all union members. This is 1.6% points increase compared to 2007, and such trend has been ongoing since.

. . . .

Unfair Labour Practice[81]

In principle, employment must be independent from the fact of joining a particular or no trade union. The discrimination against and the dismissal of trade union members is thus considered an unfair labour practice, as stipulated in Art. 81 of the TULRAA. Furthermore, the employer is prohibited from dominating or interfering with the formation or operation of a trade union. The refusal to conclude collective agreements as well as any wage payment to full-time union officials is likewise banned.

Any affected worker or trade union may file a complaint with the Labour Relations Commission within three months from the commitment of a possible unfair labour

[81] Jung, *supra* note 73.

practice (Art. 82 paras. 1 and 2 of the TULRAA). The Labour Relations Commission is a tripartite body, which exists as a local commission and as a central commission. The Local Labour Relations Commission investigates the case, by hearing witnesses if necessary, and then issues a decision. The defeated party may apply for review at the National Labour Relations Commission within the following 10 days. This application does not immediately suspend the former decision (Art. 86 of the TULRAA). The ruling of the National Labour Relations Commission is final, unless the party concerned files an administrative litigation (Art. 85 para. 2 of the TULRAA). Only in this case does the Civil Court take the final decision.

. . . .

Employers' association

Four large organizations represent the enterprises' interest: the Korea Chamber of Commerce and Industry (KCCI), the Korea Federation of Small Business (KFSB), the Federation of Korean Industries (FKI), and the Korea Employers' Federation (KEF). The latter association is in charge of the employers' interest on labour issues and is a merger of 16 industrial employers' organizations. Collective bargaining, however, takes place mostly at the enterprise level, while employers' associations may provide support.

. . . .

Current Labor Situation in Korea 2006[82]

Labor-Management Councils

Within the enterprise, workers are represented by the enterprise based trade union, if such exists, and the Labour-Management Council. The latter body consists of an equal number of representatives of employees and the employer and is governed by the Act Concerning the Promotion of Workers Participation and Cooperation (ACPWPC). Its power varies depending on the issue concerned. In quite a number of matters, as stipulated in Art. 19, the Labour-Management Council needs to be consulted, (*e.g.*, occupational safety and health measures and rules of employment). In other cases, a report to the council is required. Only a few items like welfare facilities or training plans need to be agreed by the council (Art. 20).

The Labour-Management Council must be established in any workplace that has 30 or more employees and shall be composed of more than three but fewer than 10 members (Art. 4 para. 1 and Art. 6 para. 1). The employees' representatives are appointed by the enterprise based trade union, if the majority of the workers are union members. In all other cases, they are directly elected by the employees. The members serve for three years, and reappointment or reelection is possible. The compensation for their services to the council is prohibited, but the time spent must be regarded as working time (Art. 9 paras. 1 and 3). The Labour-Management Council meets at least each three months.

The representatives of both, employees and the employer, should work together in good faith (Art. 23). In cases where the council cannot come to a legally necessary resolution, the issue may be referred to an internal arbitration panel or, as an alternative,

[82] Current Labor Situation in Korea 2006, *supra* note 68, at 27.

TABLE 8. *Key Agendas of Labor-Management Council*

Matters to be reported by the employer	o Matters concerning the general management plan and business performance o Matters concerning quarterly production plans and business performance o Matters concerning manpower plans o Economic and financial conditions of the enterprise
Matters subject to consultation between labor and management	o Improvement of productivity and profit-sharing o Recruitment, placement, education, and training of workers o Prevention of industrial disputes o Handling of employee grievances o Improvement of occupational safety and health measures and working conditions as well as the promotion of employee health o Institutional improvement for labor management o General rules of employment adjustment such as relocation, retraining, and dismissal for managerial or technological reasons o Administration of working hours and breaks o Institutional improvement of wage-payment method and wage structure o Introduction of new technology and machinery or streamlining of work processes o Establishment or amendment of work rules o Support for employee savings including ESOP o Matters concerning compensation for work-related inventions o Improvement of employee welfare o Other matters regarding labor-management cooperation
Matters subject to council resolution	o Establishment of basic plan for employee education/training and job-skill development o Establishment and administration of welfare facilities o Establishment of in-house employee welfare fund o Matters not resolved by the Grievance Committee o Establishment of various joint committees involving both labor and management

to the Labour Relations Commission in the function of an arbitrator (Art. 24 para. 1). The method of and the procedure for arbitration are regulated in by-laws, which have to be established by the council (Art. 17 of the ACPWPC and Art. 5 para. 1 No. 5 of the Enforcement Decree).

This council, composed of an equal number of management and labor representatives, should hold regular meetings on a quarterly basis to discuss general matters concerning the common interests of labor and management, such as the improvement of productivity, sharing of business profits, recruitment and dismissal of workers, employee safety and health, HR decisions, and management of labor affairs. [See agenda items above in Table 8].

Organization of the councils at enterprises had been slow until 1987, but the number of enterprises with such bodies rapidly increased after 1988, as the opportunities for participation and cooperation were greatly expanded following the frequent eruption of labor disputes and the extension of workers' rights.

The number of workplaces that have established labor-management councils, which stood at 6,775 in 1987, jumped to 12,473 in 1988 and rose steadily to 24,411 in 1997 and to 31,821 in 2003, with the establishment rate reaching 98.9% (32,188 workplaces eligible for establishment). In 2005, the number greatly rose to 35,968.

Even if a firm is unionized, it must also establish a labor-management council. When both a labor-management council and a labor union are established at an enterprise, union leaders usually become the workers' representatives in the former. With the recent expansion of the labor movement, it has become more difficult to differentiate between the functions of the two organizations. However, employers and the government have preferred to deal with issues inappropriate for collective bargaining at the labor-management councils.

From 2003, the government is operating a project to financially support autonomous labor-management cooperation programs. The government provides expenses needed for various cooperation programs such as workplace renovation, joint problem-solving by labor-management and improvement of industrial relations at enterprise, region, and industry levels.

. . . .

The relationship between collective bargaining and the Labor-Management Council is outlined in the below Table 21.[83]

TABLE 21. *Comparison between Collective Bargaining and Labor-Management Council*

	Collective bargaining	Labor-management council
Laws concerned	Trade Union and Labor Relations Adjustment Act	Act on the Promotion of Worker Participation and Cooperation
Purpose	To improve workers' status and working conditions	To increase common benefits for labor and management
Workplace	Workplace with a trade union	Workplace with thirty employees and more
Composition (party)	Trade union and employer (employers' organization)	Employee and employer council members of LMC
Activity	Bargaining and sign agreement on working conditions (wage, working hours)	Negotiate and determine on issues related to reporting matters of the enterprise management
Methods to use	If bargaining fails, strike is possible	A final decision is made by employer and even if workers disagree with employer, they cannot wage a strike.
Feature	Process of mutual reconciliation	Process of mutual understanding

Source: "Labor management manual for foreign investors" (Ministry of Labor, KOILAF).

Collective Bargaining and Agreements[84]

The workers' right to collectively bargain is constitutionally assured (Art. 33). The bargaining process may be determined by the previously applicable collective agreement. Pursuant to the TULRAA, the trade union's representatives are authorized to bargain with employers or employers' associations (Art. 29 para. 1). Wage negotiations take place traditionally every year in spring, like in Japan. In all cases of collective bargaining, no unjustified refusal or delay is permitted, and it applies the principle of bargaining in

[83] Current Labor Situation in Korea 2010, *supra* note 69, at 67.

[84] Jung, *supra* note 73.

good faith and sincerity (Art. 30 paras. 1 and 2 of the TULRAA). In practice, the system of collective bargaining still tends to be unstable, since trade unionists continue to remain subject to arrest and detention (ILO Committee of Experts, Report No. 320, Case No. 1856, year 2000).

Collective agreements must be in writing and are, in practice, mostly enterprise based. They are binding on the members of the relevant trade union but may apply also to those nonunion members who are employed in the same kind of job (Arts. 35 and 36 of the TULRAA). In case of an enterprise based collective agreement, this requires trade union membership of more than 50% of the workers employed in the enterprise. As far as a collective agreement concluded at the branch level are concerned, at least two-thirds of the workers within the same area must be trade union members for the collective agreement to be declared as general binding by the administrative authority in consultation with the Labour Relations Commission.

The collective agreement's term of validity must never be more than two years (Art. 32 para. 1 of the TULRAA). After the date of expiry, the agreement may, however, remain effective for a certain period. This period is three months if collective bargaining is engaged in to come up with a new collective agreement. It can be extended, if such is provided in the agreement.

There is no statutory regulation as to the subject matter of collective agreements. However, standards for all kinds of working conditions may be set, as long as the matter does not concern only one employee. Such standards must not be contradicted by work rules and contracts of employment; this is predominantly understood meaning that the agreement sets the minimum standard (Art. 33 para. 1 of the TULRAA). Collective agreements also establish the duties and rights of the contractual parties, such as the peace keeping obligation over the period of application and the duty to regulate the bargaining process.

. . . .

Current Labor Situation in Korea[85]

According to . . . the Ministry of Labor, there are four types of bargaining in Korea: enterprise-based bargaining, diagonal bargaining, group bargaining, and unified bargaining. Industry-based bargaining is similar to unified bargaining.

Enterprise-based bargaining is carried out between an enterprise union and its employer. Diagonal bargaining is a direct bargaining between a higher-level trade union or an industrial union and an employer of an individual enterprise. Group bargaining is a bargaining between higher-than-enterprise-level unions or industrial unions and a large number of their counterpart employers, which is carried out in the same place at the same time. Unified bargaining is the one between a high level union or an industrial union and an employers' organization. If there are no such employers' organizations, those who are entrusted with the bargaining authority from a number of individual employers are allowed to conduct the bargaining.

Industrial bargaining, like unified bargaining, intends to sign a collective bargaining that is to be applied to a large number of enterprises in the same industry. Korea's

[85] Current Labor Situation in Korea 2010, *supra* note 69, at 61.

representative industrial unions are Korean Metal Workers' Union (KMWU), Korean Health and Medical Workers' Union (KHMWU), mostly by nurses, and Korean Financial Industry Union (KFIU) of banking and other financial organizations' employees.

Among them, only KMWU carries out an industrial bargaining every year with an industrial employers' association that prescribes collective bargaining in its articles of association. In the cases of KHMWU and KFIU, they do not have their counterpart employers' organizations and, therefore, have held a collective bargaining with related associations that are trusted with the bargaining right (associations of hospitals and banks). In 2009, employers of health and medical industry organized Health and Medical Industry Employers' Council, but as they had difficulties in bargaining with trade union, the council was dismissed. Employers of financial industry organized Financial Industry Employers' Council which was registered as a corporation to the Ministry of Labor in January 2010. Hence, the industry bargaining in the financial sector is expected to be the one between industry trade union (financial trade union) and industry employers' organization (Financial Industry Employers' Council), for the first time in history.

In order to promote industrial bargaining, so-called 'double bargaining' issue needs to be resolved. In the case of the metal union, which is Korea's representative industrial union, it has a three-tiered bargaining system: central industrial bargaining; complementary bargaining at regional chapters; and complementary unit workplace-level bargaining. Employers of the metal industry are reluctant to participate in the industrial central bargaining due to increasing bargaining costs. That's why large corporations like Hyundai Motors and Kia Motors are yet to participate in the bargaining. The labor community also acknowledges such issue of cost increase.

Collective bargaining is valid mostly for two years. The current trade union law (article 32) states, "No collective agreement shall have a valid term exceeding two years. In cases where a collective agreement does not specify a valid term or have a valid term exceeding the period stipulated in paragraph (1), the valid term shall be two years." Therefore, most collective bargaining between labor and management in Korea are carried out every two years, whether it is enterprise-level or industry-level union. However, in the case of wage agreement, it is renewed every year by practice. Therefore, in one year, there are wage bargaining and collective bargaining at the same time and then in the next year, there is a wage bargaining only.

. . . .

QUESTIONS

1. What are the functional differences between the union's collective bargaining and the Labor Management Council's discussions? How do the discussion topics vary, if at all?
2. How do employees choose their union and bargaining representative?
3. What is the relative importance of South Korean labor unions in management decision making?

---

4. *Dispute Resolution*

Labor disputes can arise from asserted labor rights or labor interests and may be individual or collective. They may arise from alleged violations of statutes or contracts and be incident to individual disciplinary cases, such as suspension or termination; or they may involve collective interests that result in work stoppages. Different legal processes available to resolve these labor disputes are described next, following a discussion of the types of labor disputes that may arise, including an individual's suspension or termination, the union's strike, or the employer's lockout.

---

a. Labor Disputes

Current Labor Situation in Korea 2006[86]

. . . .

The number of labor disputes accompanied by work stoppages was fewer than 300 annually before 1987, but increased sharply to more than 3,700 in that year. The social instability caused by strained industrial relations for the next several years provided an opportunity for the government to have a close look at the labor situation, which led to improvements in hitherto oppressive labor policies and systems. As the nature of industrial relations, which have been marred with confrontation and conflict, changed to put more emphasis on participation and cooperation, labor, management and the government came to seek resolutions through dialogue and negotiation. As a result, industrial relations have been stabilized during the 1990s, with the number of industrial disputes dropping to 78 in 1997. However, the number of disputes again increased to 129 in 1998, to 198 in 1999, and to 250 in 2000 as the industrial relations became aggravated due to corporate restructuring and lay-offs. In 2001, the number of labor disputes dropped to 234 involving 88,548 workers, down 50.2% from a year earlier.

. . . .

Labor disputes decreased significantly in 2005, with 287 dispute cases and 117,912 workers involved in disputes. The total number of work days lost to strikes also decreased to 847,697.[87]

The characteristic of labor disputes in 2005 was that while the number of disputes was the lowest since 1997 at 17 (5.9%), the average length of continued disputes was 48.6 days, which was about twice as long as the disputes in 2004, which lasted 24.7 days on average.

. . . .

---

86 Current Labor Situation in Korea 2006, *supra* note 68, at 38.

87 The greatest cause of labor disputes was collective agreements, accounting for 82.2% of the cases, while wage hikes caused 12.5% of the disputes. By type of business, manufacturing saw the most disputes with 170 cases (59.2%), followed by social private service (53 cases, 22.3%), and transportation, warehousing, and communication (35 cases, 12.2%). By size of business, workplaces with 100~299 employees had the most dispute cases with 106 disputes (36.9%), while those with 50~99 employees experienced 53 cases (18.5%), those with fewer than 50 saw 40 cases (13.9%), those with 1,000 or more saw 38 cases (13.2%) and those with 500~999 had 30 cases (10.5%). *Id.*

Current Labor Situation in Korea 2010[88]

[In 2010,] labor disputes were reported to be on the decrease. (See Table 17.)

TABLE 17. *Labor Disputes in Recent Years*

Year	Cases of Disputes	Lost Working Days
2006	138	1,201,000
2007	115	536,000
2008	108	809,000
2009	121	627,000

Source: Labor statistics, website of Ministry of Labor.

According to the statistics of the Ministry of Labor, the number of disputes in 2009 was 121, 13 cases more than that of 2008 (108 cases), but the number of lost working days decreased to 627,000 from 809,000. No major disputes took place, except two strikes of the railway union. The metalworkers' union of Hyundai Motors which continued with wage strikes every year ever since its formation didn't go on strikes in 15 years and agreed on wage/collective bargaining negotiation.

Another feature in labor relations is that the number of declarations of labor-management cooperation and concession bargaining has greatly expanded.

On the Ministry of Labor's 2009 analysis on wage bargaining status at workplaces with 100 and more employees, there were 6,394 cases of declarations of labor-management cooperation (2,672) and concession bargaining (3,722), which is 2.4 times the level of the previous year. There were 2,689 cases of the declarations (2,574) and the bargaining (115) in 2008 when the global financial crisis hit the nation. In particular, concession bargaining, in which labor and management agreed to maintain employment, wage freeze or wage return, and no-strike deal, grew as much as 32 times during the same period. As a result, the averaged increase rate of agreed wage of 5,168 companies out of 6,718 workplaces with 100 and more employees, which agreed to conclude a wage bargaining, recorded the lowest 1.7% since the 1998 foreign exchange crisis.

As such, labor relations in Korea have been overcoming the confrontational and conflicting phase of the past. Although labor disputes are ongoing in some companies in 2010, most of them are foreign-nationality ones that are in the process of close-off, liquidation, production quantity transfer, factory relocation, and employment adjustment, etc. Few are suffering from serious labor conflicts out of demand for excessive wage increase or welfare services.

Indeed, labor relations in Korea has been greatly stabilized over 20 years since 1987 when the Great Struggle by Workers was waged. The labor has focused more on 'negotiation' than 'struggle'. No big strikes have been waged after the struggle to revise the labor law in December 1996. Besides that, as a foreign exchange crisis swept the nation in 1997–1998, the atmosphere changed and strikes were no longer regarded as the union's first choice to the problem solution. Not only the Federation of Korean Trade Unions (FKTU), which kept a moderate stance, but the Korean Confederation of Trade Unions

88 Current Labor Situation in Korea 2010, *supra* note 69, at 54. *See generally*, Youngmo Yoon, *Industrial Disputes and Dispute Resolution Mechanisms in South Korea* 107, in COMPARATIVE INDUSTRIAL RELATIONS: CHINA, SOUTH KOREA AND GERMANY/EUROPE (Rudolf Traub-Merz and Junhua Zhang eds. 2010).

(KCTU) which pursued for a more progressive labor movement, started to employ a combined strategy mixed with 'struggle and negotiation'.

. . . .

———

National Labour Law Profile: Republic of Korea (South Korea)[89]

Liliane Jung

. . . .

Suspension

Suspension is not legally defined, but the LSA provides that a worker may be suspended for disciplinary reasons (Arts. 30 para. 1). This, however, requires justifiable reasons, which are to be defined by collective agreements and work rules. Also, the business may be suspended for reasons attributable to the employer (Art. 45 para. 1 of the LSA). In this case, the employee in principle is paid 70 % of the average remuneration. In addition, a generally accepted legal theory understands the mutual duties under the labour contract as being suspended during industrial actions. Thus, the worker has no duty to work and the employer is released from paying wages, while the contract itself remains in force.

Termination of employment

According to the Civil Code, a labour contract may be terminated at either party's initiative for any reason with an advance notice of one month. A termination at the employer's initiative, however, is restricted by labour acts, the LSA in particular. This restriction applies to labour contracts of an unlimited period as well as to those fixed term contracts that have been unlawfully extended.

In principle, an employee may be dismissed with and without advance notice. In case of an advance notice dismissal, the notice has to be given at least 30 days beforehand or equivalent wages must be paid instead (Art. 32 para.1 of the LSA). This protection does not apply to the following kind of workers (Art. 35 of the LSA):

- workers within the first three months of their probation period,
- workers who have been employed for a fixed period not exceeding two months,
- seasonal workers who have been employed for a fixed period not exceeding six months,
- monthly paid workers who have been employed for less than six months, and
- workers being employed on a daily basis for less than three consecutive months.

Any dismissal with advance notice must be based on justifiable reasons as defined by collective agreements and work rules. The fact of joining a trade union or a legal collective action, however, must never be a justifiable reason (Art. 81 No. 1 and 5 of the TULRAA). Also, the dismissal of a woman must not be based on her gender (Art. 8 para. 1 of the Equal Employment Act). Justifiable reasons may be classified into personal reasons, behavioural reasons, and management reasons, of which the latter are further restricted in Art. 31 LSA. The managerial need should be urgent, and every effort to avoid dismissals must have been made. Additionally, the selection of workers to be dismissed

[89] Jung, *supra* note 73.

has to be fair and rational, and the enterprise trade union must be informed 60 days in advance. When recruiting within two years after dismissal for managerial reasons, the employer should re-employ the workers dismissed. In any case, the dismissal of the following workers is prohibited according to Art. 30 para. 2 of the LSA:

- workers being on maternity leave
- workers being medically treated due to an occupational injury or disease (including a period of the following 30 days).

As an exception, any worker may be dismissed without advance notice, which is specified in Art. 32 para. 1 of the LSA. It requires either considerable business troubles which have been caused by the worker or cases of natural disaster, calamity, or equivalents that make business impossible to continue.

In case of a possibly unjustified dismissal, the employee legally can file a criminal complaint with the District Labour Office or a civil complaint with the Labour Relations Commission. Other claims, which are related to the contract of employment, can only be made before the Civil Court.[90]

Strikes and Lockouts

Strikes

The workers' right to collective action is constitutionally guaranteed (Art. 33 para. 1). Some workers within the defence industry are, however, excepted – production of defence goods, electricity, and water (Art. 41 para. 2 of the TULRAA). No worker can be detained for violation of law, if he/she participates in legal industrial action. The legitimacy of industrial action requires the following conditions:

- Adjustment procedures must be completed unsuccessfully (Art. 45 para. 2 of the TULRAA). A distinction must be made between mediation and arbitration, which are both conducted by the Labour Relations Commission (see below). Labour disputes can also be settled by the industrial parties themselves on a private basis, but this has in fact not been done often.
- Any industrial action must be led by a registered trade union, of which the majority of members has voted to take industrial action (Art. 37 para. 2 and Art. 41 para. 1 of the TULRAA). The vote is to be by direct, secret and unsigned ballot.
- The action must be reported in advance to the administrative authority and the Labour Relations Commission (Art. 17 of the Enforcement Decree).
- The intended result must be the improvement of either working conditions or the workers' economic status (Art. 2 no. 4 of the TULRAA).

Violence and destruction as well as the occupation of production facilities are prohibited (Art. 42 para. 1 of the TULRAA). The maintenance and the operation of security facilities of a workplace must also not be stopped, closed or interrupted (Art. 42 para. 2 of the

90 *Id.* The Labor Relations Commission has the authority to reinstate an unjustly dismissed employee. Under section 33 of the Labor Standards Act and sections 82–86 of the Trade Union and Labor Relations Adjustment Act, "[t]he Labor Relations Commission is empowered to conduct any investigation it deems necessary and to set up an inquiry[.]" ILO, Termination of Employment Digest 278, http://www.ilo.org/public/english/dialogue/ifpdial/downloads/term/digest.pdf (last visited Oct. 2, 2010).

TULRAA). The most common form of industrial action is the strike. A distinction must be made between walk-out strikes, where workers leave the workplace, and sit-down strikes, the effect of which is the occupation of the workplace.

Lock outs

In order to protect industrial facilities, the employer may conduct a lock out but only in response to an ongoing strike (Art. 46 para. 1 of the TULRAA). The lock out needs to be reported in advance to the administrative authority and the Labour Relations Commission (Art. 46 para. 2 of the TULRAA). During industrial action, the employer is prohibited from hiring further non-striking workers or subcontracting work. He/she is, however, released from paying wages (Art. 44 of the TULRAA).

. . . .

---

b. Labor Dispute Resolution Processes

National Labour Law Profile: Republic of Korea (South Korea)[91]

Mediation and arbitration are adjustment procedures. Mediation can be requested [with the Labor Relations Commission (LRC)] by either party and must be completed . . . in general businesses within 10 days (Arts. 53 and 54 para. 1 of the TULRAA). It is conducted by either a tripartite committee or a single mediator authorized by the Labour Relations Commission. The mediation proposal needs to be accepted by both parties, for it to have the same effect as a collective agreement (Art. 61 paras. 1 and 2 of the TULRAA).

An arbitration procedure must be agreed on by both parties or may be requested by only one if the possibility is established in the previously applicable collective agreement (Art. 62 of the TULRAA). It is conducted by an arbitration committee, which is composed of three members representing the public. After arbitration has started, industrial action must not be conducted for 15 days, and the arbitration award of the committee has the same effect as a collective agreement (Arts. 63 and 70 para. 2 of the TULRAA).

. . . .

Collective Labor Dispute Settlement

Labor Relations Commission[92]

The [L]abor [R]elations [C]ommission [LRC] is an administrative agency which adopts the agreement system among employee, employer, and public interest members. According to its jurisdiction, there are three types of labor relations commissions: National Labor

[91] Jung, *supra* note 73; *see also* Current Labor Situation in Korea 2010, *supra* note 69, at 64.

[92] Current Labor Situation in Korea 2010, *supra* note 69, at 63. The Labor Relations Commission is a "quasi-judicial authority . . . [with] three categories of Labor Relations Commissions[:] . . . (1) National Labor Relations Commission . . . reviews the appeal to the ruling by a Regional Labor Relations Commission . . . (2) Regional Labor Relations Commission . . . handles labor dispute cases under its jurisdiction or cases transferred from the National Labor Relations Commission . . . [and] (3) Special Labor Relations Commission." Won-Bo Lee, *Understanding on Korea's Labor Relations*, KOILAF,

Relations Commission, regional labor relations commissions, and special labor relations commissions (seamen's labor relations commission). In addition to the plenary session in which all the members of relevant labor relations commission participate, there are sectional committees such as adjudication committee, mediation committee, discrimination redress committee, special mediation committee, arbitration committee, teachers' labor relations adjustment committee, and public officials' labor relations adjustment committee. The labor relations commission is an independent quasi-judiciary organization of which work is judging, mediating, and arbitrating interest or rights disputes between labor and management.

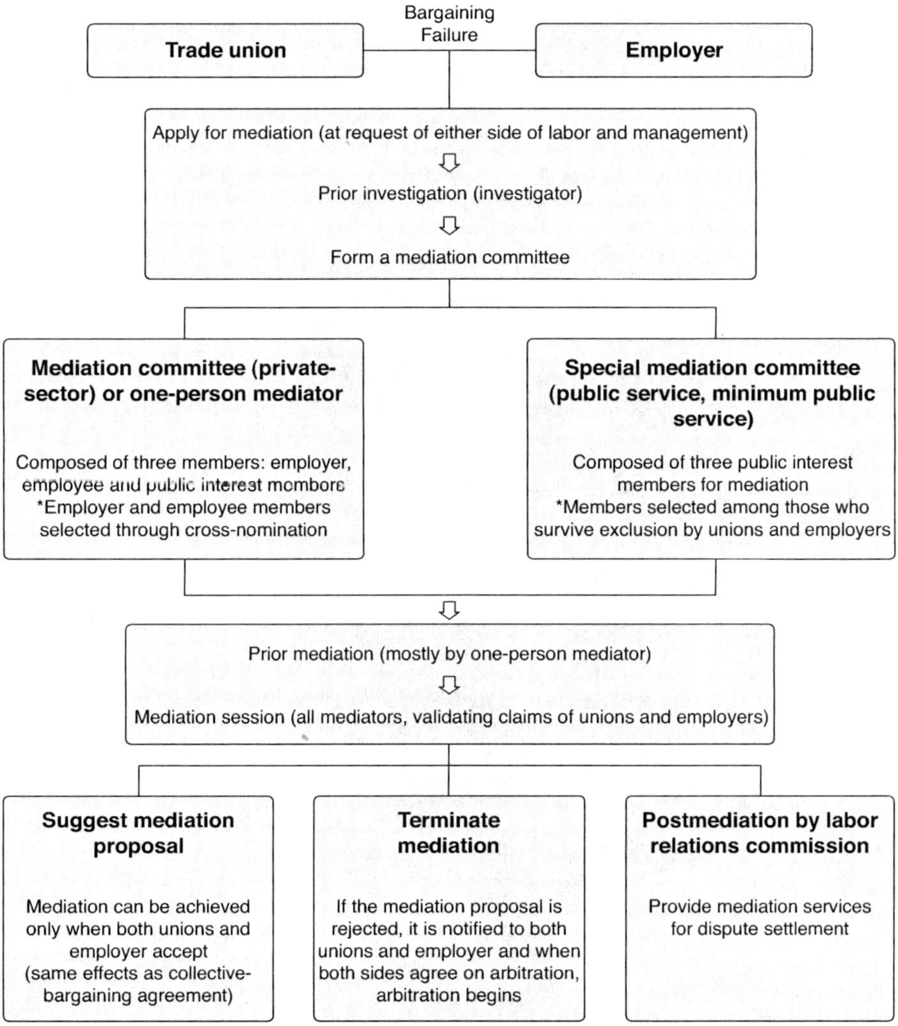

Source: "Labor management manual for foreign investors" (Ministry of Labor, KOILAF)

available at http://www.koilaf.org/KFupload/kfpublication_file/2006semi (en).pdf (last visited Sept. 29, 2010) [Formatting altered].

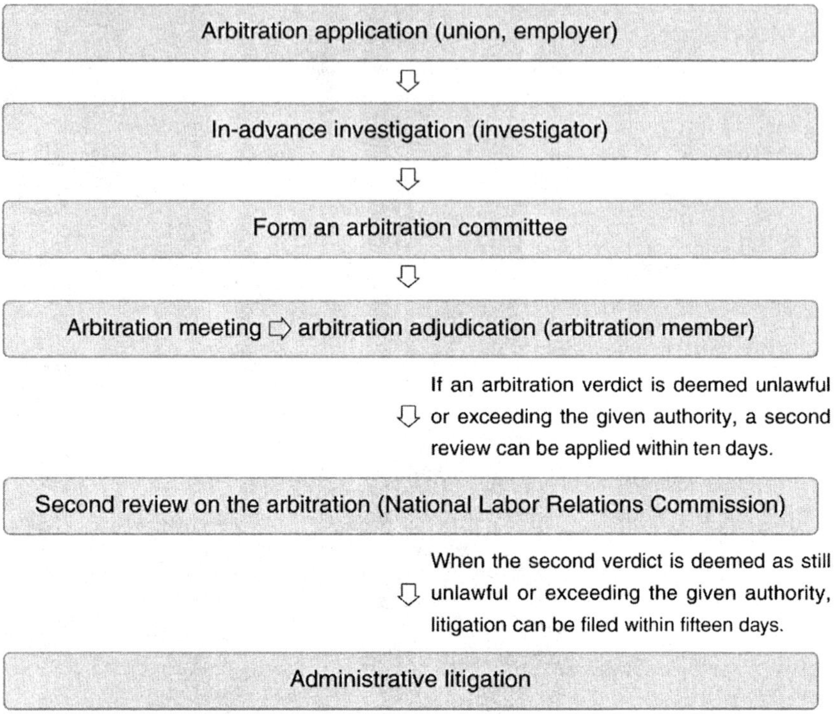

Source: "Labor management manual for foreign investors" (Ministry of Labor, KOILAF)

. . . .

Individual Labor Dispute Settlement

National Labour Law Profile: Republic of Korea (South Korea)[93]

Individual labour disputes are settled by the Civil Courts. Civil litigation in South Korea is, however, very time consuming and costly. It is thus often of interest to make a complaint with another body. In case of a possibly unjustified dismissal, the employee legally can file a criminal complaint with the District Labour Office or a civil complaint with the Labour Relations Commission (see above under *Termination of employment*). Other claims, which are related to the contract of employment, can only be made before the Civil Court.

Civil litigation is ruled by the Code of Civil Procedure, which was enacted in 1960 and extensively revised in 1990. The District Court is generally the court of the first instance, and it is usually a single judge who presides over the trial. A body of three judges is required only in exceptional cases such as where the sum in dispute exceeds

[93] Jung, *supra* note 73.

50,000,000 Won. At the end of the trial, a written judgment usually stating the reasons for the decision is made. Only in small claims actions not exceeding 20,000,000 Won, is the procedure simplified, and the written judgment does not need to state reasons.

Appellate jurisdiction is exercised by a collegiate panel of three judges within the District Court if a judgment made by a single judge is appealed. The appeal against a judgment of panel, on the other hand, is lodged with the High Court. In the second instance, the case is again investigated. The court of last resort is the Supreme Court, where only questions of law are heard.

. . . .

QUESTIONS

1. Describe the legal avenue for redressing an individual labor dispute.
2. Describe the legal avenue for redressing a collective labor dispute.
3. What is the role of the Labor Relations Commission in each of the previous cases?
4. Are work stoppages legal?
5. What is the role of the union, if any, in the previous four situations?
6. How does a Labor-Management Council operate and relate to a labor union in the Korean workplace in resolving labor disputes?

---

5. *Critique under International Labor Standards*

ITUC, Internationally Recognised Core Labour Standards in the Republic of Korea, Report for the WTO General Council Review of the Trade Policies Of Korea[94]

Executive Summary

The Republic of Korea has ratified four of the eight core ILO labour Conventions. In view of restrictions on the trade union rights of workers, discrimination, and other legal restrictions, further measures are needed to comply with the commitments the Republic of Korea accepted at Singapore, Geneva, and Doha in the WTO Ministerial Declarations over 1996–2001, and in the ILO Declaration on Fundamental Principles and Rights at Work.

Korea has ratified neither of the ILO core Conventions on trade union rights. The government's labour laws do not meet international standards or Korea's own commitments

[94] ITUC, Internationally Recognised Core Labor Standards in The Republic of Korea, Report for the WTO General Council Review of the Trade Policies of Korea, (Geneva, October 8 & 10, 2008), *available at* http://www.ituc-csi.org/IMG/pdf/Korea-_FINAL-3.pdf (last visited Sept. 29, 2010) [Formatting altered]; *see* ITUC, *Annual Survey of violations of trade union rights* (2011), http://survey.ituc-csi.org/+-Korea-44-Republic-of-+.html (last visited June 7, 2011).

to the OECD. The government continues to interfere in and, in some cases, to repress unions' activities. Many public workers are deprived of their right to organise. Police violence against strikers remains a problem, sometimes resulting in serious injuries. In practice migrant workers are not able to enjoy their fundamental trade union rights.

Korea has ratified both ILO core Conventions on discrimination and on equal remuneration. Discrimination in employment and occupation is prohibited by law. However, in practice discrimination against women and foreign workers is both frequent and serious. The measures adopted by the government to address women's disadvantaged position on the labour market have not yielded the promised results. The current employment permit system puts foreign workers in a particularly vulnerable situation, rendering them easily abused and exploited.

Korea has ratified both ILO core Conventions on child labour. Child labour is not considered to be a widespread phenomenon in Korea. Education is compulsory up to the age of 15, the minimum age to enter work. Work performed by minors younger than 18 is regulated. Official data on the prevalence of children involved in the sex industry is lacking, however.

Korea has ratified neither of the ILO Core Conventions on Forced Labour. Forced labour is prohibited by law and in practice Koreans are not subject to forced labour, but there have been reports of conditions faced by certain migrant workers that could amount to forced labour.

Internationally Recognised Core Labour Standards in the Republic of Korea

I. Freedom of Association and the Right to Collective Bargaining

The Republic of Korea has not ratified ILO Convention No. 87 on the Freedom of Association and Protection of the Right to Organise, nor Convention No. 98 on the Right to Organise and Collective Bargaining.

The right to form and join a trade union

The law provides workers with the right to organise. However there are many restrictions and limitations to that right.

The law on the Establishment and Operation of Public Officials' Trade Unions that went into effect in January 2006 gives civil servants the right to organise within administrative units predefined by the law. However, there are numerous categories of public officials who are still denied their trade union rights, including managers, human resources personnel, personnel dealing with trade unions or industrial relations, and special public servants such as military, police, fire-fighters, politically-appointed officials, and high level public officials. In its June 2007 report, the ILO Committee on Freedom of Association asked the government to ensure that all public servants who are entitled, based on international standards, to form their own associations to defend their interests, should be granted that right. Up to this date the government has failed to act.

In addition when public sector trade unions are allowed, they are not permitted to get involved in any sort of political activities. The law also prohibits public sector unionists from engaging in "acts in contravention of their duties prescribed in other laws and regulations when doing union activities". This very broadly worded provision leaves the door open for abuses.

In the private sector, the 1997 Trade Union and Relations Adjustment Act (TULRAA) allows for immediate trade union pluralism at industrial and national levels. However since 1997 implementation of this provision at the company level has been repeatedly delayed. Originally, the formation of competing unions at the workplace was to be allowed by 2002, but then the ban was extended until the end of 2006. In 2006, it was again decided to push back the implementation of this provision until 2009 [now 2011]. In its June 2007 recommendations, the ILO Committee on Freedom of Association asked the government to take rapid steps for the legalisation of trade union pluralism at the enterprise or establishment level. Local and international trade union organisations have also criticised the government's continued ban on union pluralism. Indeed in a context where pluralism at the plant level is prohibited by law, many employers have resorted to creating management-controlled unions, known as "paper unions". As those unions are impossible to democratise from within, owing to management's hostility, and since it is legally forbidden to organise alternative unions, such workers are left with few, if any, rights and cannot engage in genuine collective bargaining.

The TULRAA initially prohibited employers from remunerating union leaders from January 2002 onwards. Unionists strongly protested against this restriction, stating that this matter should be left to the discretion of negotiations between the employer and union, and succeeded in delaying implementation of this provision until 2006. Then through a tripartite agreement signed in September 2007, implementation of this provision was deferred until 2009 but the law was not changed. The ILO Committee on Freedom of Association noted in its 309th report that "the prohibition of the payment of full-time union officials by employers is a matter which should not be subject to legislative interference" and called upon the government to repeal this particular section of the TULRAA. The ILO Committee on Freedom of Association noted in its 309th report that "the prohibition of the payment of full-time union officials by employers is a matter which should not be subject to legislative interference" and called upon the government to repeal this particular section of the TULRAA.

The law bans dismissed workers from remaining members of a union, and states that nonunion members are not eligible for trade union office. However under ILO standards, such matters should be left to the discretion of the trade unions' statutes. In June 2007 the ILO Committee on Freedom of Association asked the government to repeal the provisions of the law that allow this interference. As of this date the government has not responded.

The Right to Organise and Bargain Collectively

The law provides for workers' right to collective bargaining and collective action. However there are important restrictions.

In practice, the right to organise is limited by the abusive use of Article 314 of the Korean Criminal Code on "Obstruction of Business". Employers often rely on this article to harass and seek the incarceration of union leaders. Indeed the charge of "Obstruction of Business" can lead to heavy penalties under the law including imprisonment up to five years and exorbitant fines. Examining a complaint of the Korean Federation of Construction and Industry Trade Union (KFCITU), affiliated to the Building and Wood Workers International (BWI), the ILO Committee on Freedom of Association in March 2006 expressed its concern that the KFCITU's legitimate trade union activities in the defence of construction site workers, including through collective bargaining, had been perceived as a criminal activity warranting arrest and imprisonment.

Despite the fact that the many industrial actions conclude with agreements between unions and employers, the government as well as employers are continuing to sue union members for damages as a result of their actions. Some of these trials are still in progress as in the case of 13 union leaders of a branch of the Construction Plant Workers Union from whom damages of over US $400,000 are being sought for actions they conducted in 2005. In the case of the Pohang Construction Plant Workers Union, POSCO is seeking damages of over US $1,000,000 for actions they conducted to support a strike in 2006. In the case of a strike led by a branch of the Incheon Electricians Local Union, the government is seeking damages of over US $10,000.

In the public sector, civil servants have the right to collective bargaining, but the subjects of negotiation are limited to matters concerning trade unions, members' pay and welfare, and other working conditions. Trade unions cannot address other economic and social issues.

Strikes are illegal if they are not specifically about labour conditions, such as wages, welfare, and working hours. This is contrary to ILO standards. In addition given the complicated legal procedures for organising a strike, collective actions on labour conditions often become "illegal" for breach of procedure. Unionists striking "illegally" often receive a one year prison sentence or heavy fines.

The 1997 Trade Union and Labour Relations Adjustment Act (TULRAA) and public service legislation ban strikes by people working for the central government or local governments, and by those involved in the production of military goods. According to the 1999 law on the establishment and operation of trade unions for teachers, members of this profession do not have the right to strike.

In addition there is a long list of "essential services" – including railways, utilities, public health, the Bank of Korea, and telecommunications – for which the right to strike can be heavily restricted by the imposition of mandatory mediation and arbitration procedures. In its June 2007 report, the ILO Committee on Freedom of Association asked the government to limit the restrictions on the right to strike to those services that are strictly essential. The government did not react.

At the end of 2006, there was an amendment to the Trade Union and Labor Relations Adjustment Act (TULRAA). Major revisions were made regarding limitations on collective action at essential public enterprises. The government advertised the abolition of compulsory arbitration, which had been recommended by the ILO, as a significant achievement of the revision. However, the amended bill actually expanded the scope of essential public enterprises, introduced essentially maintained services and allowed replacement workers, which in effect annulled the effect that abolishing compulsory arbitration could have by excessively limiting the right to strike. It has, through these multi-level mechanisms and institutions, potentially rendered collective action powerless.

Moreover, emergency arbitration remains in place, which can outlaw collective action in public services and large workplaces. Such emergency arbitration goes far beyond the ILO's definition of services that are truly essential, as covered in the ILO's definition, by applying multiple restrictions on the right to strike and excessively limiting workers rights to collective action. Fully allowing replacement workers is also a serious deviation from the ILO's principle that they should be allowed only as an exception during disputes in essential services and when the situation is deemed a national emergency.

In practice prosecutors are quick to issue arrest warrants as soon as workers go on strike, or sometimes when one simply is announced. Police or security agencies mount surveillance operations in order to capture strike leaders. Unions' offices and telecommunications are routinely monitored.

Unions insist police action is often unnecessarily provocative and disproportionately brutal. This was the case in 2006 when the South Korean supermarket chain E. Land had dismissed 1,000 part-time and contract workers, just before the introduction of new laws that would have helped them become full-time employees. The workers went on strike. Later the Labour Relations Commission ruled that the dismissals were unfair, but the strike was harshly repressed with women employees beaten and ejected from the company's premises in Seoul. Union leaders were arrested and charged with obstructing business.

The right to demonstrate is also seriously limited. For example, the negotiations for a free trade agreement between South Korea and the United States led to a strike in June 2007, organised by the Korean Metal Workers' Union. Public authorities demonstrated intolerance of this peaceful form of expression: 27 arrest warrants were issued against KMWU leaders and 67 of the union's members were summonsed by the police intelligence unit on charges of criminal "obstruction of business".

New laws eroding protection

According to the Government, contract and other "non-regular" workers account for approximately 35.5% of the workforce. These non-regular workers performed work similar to regular workers but receive approximately 60% of the wages and are ineligible for national health and unemployment insurance and other benefits.

In 2006, a new law was introduced which allows companies with more than 300 workers to expand the length of temporary contracts for up to two years. Trade unions argue that this law might be used as a way of evading employers' obligation to grant permanent contract to their workers. This is why they fear that it may have the effect of multiplying the number of temporary contracts, hence undermining already declining job security. In addition, in most cases unionised workers do not have their contract renewed when they expired.

In 2007, the Korean Metalworkers' Federation (KMWF), the KCTU, and the International Metalworkers' Federation (IMF) lodged a complaint with the ILO Committee on Freedom of Association. The complaint concerned anti-union practices including physical violence and imprisonment against workers unfairly employed on a subcontracting basis between 2004 and 2006 in Hyundai Motors' Corporation (HMC) Ulsan, Asan and Jeonju plants, Hynix/Magnachip, Kiryung Electronics, and KM&I. All these companies illegally used "dispatch" workers disguised as subcontractors to hide their real employment relationship.

Export processing zones

The law on Special Economic Zones (SEZs) of July 2003 contains preferential provisions in relation to foreign companies investing in the SEZs. It exempts them from many national regulations on the protection of the environment and labour standards. For example, foreign-invested enterprises located in free economic zones are exempt from otherwise mandatory monthly leave, paid holidays, or menstruation leave for women. They are also exempt from recruiting persons with disabilities for at least 2 percent of their workforce, an obligation which applies to Korean companies with more than 300 workers.

Migrant workers

Although the right to belong to a legally recognised trade union is protected under the Korean constitution (with some restrictions placed on public sector workers), the government continues to refuse to register the Migrant Trade Union (MTU), founded in April 2005, and a member of the KCTU, on the basis that it was founded by undocumented migrant workers. As such, the government does not recognise the MTU's right to engage in trade union representation or bargaining. Yet in February 2007 the Seoul High Court ruled that all migrant workers have the right to form and join unions, no matter what their residence status in Korea is. The Ministry of Labour appealed this decision to the Supreme Court and their ruling is still pending.[95]

At the present time therefore, the right to form and join trade unions of an estimated 224,000 undocumented foreign workers is not being respected. While the roughly 465,000 foreign workers with legal working status (figures from the Ministry of Migrant Workers) are allowed by law to join trade unions, their highly unequal relationship with their employers, a result of the Employment Permit System which gives overwhelming authority to employers with regards to contract renewal and dismissal, means that the exercise of that right is nearly impossible.

Conclusions

The government's labour laws do not meet international standards or Korea's own commitments to the OECD. The government continues to interfere in and in some cases to repress unions' activities. Many public workers are deprived from their right to organise. Police violence against strikers remains a problem, sometimes resulting in serious injuries. In practice migrant workers are not able to enjoy their fundamental rights, including trade union rights.

II.I. Discrimination and Equal Remuneration

The Republic of Korea ratified Convention No. 100 on Equal Remuneration in 1997 and Convention No. 111 on Discrimination (Employment and Occupation) in 1998.

By law, discrimination is prohibited on the basis of gender, religion, disability, age, social status, regional origin, national origin, ethnic origin, physical condition or appearance, marital status, pregnancy and child delivery, family status, race, skin colour, thought or political opinion, record of any crime for which the sentence has been completed, sexual orientation or medical history. The practice varies however, as documented below.

95 [Author's note.] The case was still not decided as of June, 2011; *see* Amnesty International, *South Korean government must not deport migrants' trade union leader* (Mar. 3, 2011), http://www.amnesty.org.au/news/comments/24988/ (last visited June 7, 2011)].

Discrimination against women

The Equal Employment Act penalizes companies found to discriminate against women in hiring and promotion. A company found guilty of practicing sexual discrimination could be fined up to approximately 5,300 US dollars and have its name published in the newspaper. The law also provides for a public fund to support victims in seeking legal redress.

Although the principle of equal pay for work of equal value is enshrined in the Equal Employment Act, this principle is applied at the workplace level only. Yet the Convention extends the application of this principle beyond cases where work is performed in the same establishment or business, and makes it possible to address discriminatory effects of horizontal occupational segregation based on sex. This has led the ILO Committee of Experts on the Application of Conventions and Recommendations (CEARC) to ask the government to take measures to promote and ensure the application of this principle as widely as allowed by the level at which wage policies, systems, and structures are coordinated.

Recently in order to extend the application of the principle of equal pay for work of equal value, the Government has started different activities ranging from offering consulting services to awareness-raising actions in human resource management. However as pointed out by Korean trade unions, workers' representatives are not allowed to participate in the elaboration of objective job evaluation systems on which the remuneration system relies.

In March 2006 amendments to the Equal Opportunities Act entered into force. They aimed at extending the scope of affirmative action programme to both the public and private sectors. However only workplaces with more than 500 employees are covered.

Despite these governmental initiatives, discrimination against women persists in practice. Women continue to experience serious discrimination in both pay and access to employment. Indeed, the current rate of women's labour force participation (about 50%) remains low compared to men's (74%). Likewise women remain significantly under-represented in senior and top management positions. Although the proportion of women in the occupational group of legislators, senior officials, and managers grew from 5% in 2005 to 8% in 2006, overall only 0.4% of working women in 2006 held positions in this category compared to some 4% among men.

The gender pay gap remains very wide (at about 34% for work of equal value). It is a matter of concern that requires the Government's urgent attention and action. There is also an urgent need to examine wage disparities affecting workers according to their employment status, particularly their regular or non-regular status.

Under section 12 of the Equal Employment Act, employers, senior workers, or workers shall not engage in sexual harassment at work. Employers have an obligation to conduct educational programmes on sexual harassment and to take disciplinary or other measures against sexual harassers. However, in practice sexual harassment remains a problem.

Discrimination against foreign workers

Trade unions have expressed serious concerns about the inflexible nature of the Employment Permit System (EPS), established under the Act on Foreign Workers' Employment.

Indeed, the renders foreign workers excessively dependent on their employers, hence vulnerable to exploitation and abuse. It also inhibits their access to higher-paying jobs.

Under the Employment Permit System, low-skilled foreign workers can work in certain sectors of the economy under renewable one-year contracts for a period no longer than three years. As a general rule, foreign workers may not change their employers during the three-year period. On an exceptional basis, a worker may apply for a transfer to another business or workplace if the employment permit is cancelled by the authorities because the employer has violated the provisions concerning working conditions as stipulated in the labour contract or labour laws. Following the three-year period, foreign workers must leave the country for at least six months. This period can be reduced to one month if the employer makes a request for reemployment. Employers often abuse this power to renew workers' visas through re-employment by promising re-employment only if workers will give up wages or severance pay or endure other poor working conditions.

Section 22 of the Act on Foreign Workers' Employment provides that an employer "shall not give unfair and discriminatory treatment to foreign workers on grounds of their status". Foreign workers are also covered by the labour legislation, including the Labour Standards Act, the Minimum Wage Act, and the Industrial Safety and Health Act. However, it is worth noting that domestic workers, who are predominantly women, remain outside the scope of the labour legislation and the Equal Employment Act. This raises serious doubts as to how foreign domestic workers are protected from discrimination and abuse.

A third of all migrant workers in Korea are women. According to Amnesty International, women migrant workers face discrimination in levels of pay compared to men migrant workers and they face enhanced risk of sexual harassment at the workplace compared to Korean women.

Under the current system, to be granted permission to change his/her workplace, the migrant worker suffering abuses needs to bring a complaint to establish that the employer has violated the contract or legislation. However, in practice migrants refrain from bringing complaints out of fear of retaliation by the employer.

Despite the labour inspections carried out in industries with a high concentration of foreign workers and the existence of migrants' help centers, foreign workers' rights are frequently violated. Testimonies gathered from migrant workers show that they continue to have their wages withheld and to have to work excessively long hours for lower wages than Korean workers in similar jobs. They also experience high levels of verbal and physical abuse in the workplace. Their work is often dangerous and there are many reports of serious industrial accidents where injured migrant workers have received inadequate treatment and little or no compensation.

Migrant workers face targeted arrest, detention, and deportation for trying to organise to improve their working conditions, as illustrated by the detention and expulsion of three MTU senior officials in 2007 and two in 2008. All five trade union officers were involved in campaigns to stop proposed changes in the immigration laws and other repression against migrant workers. While authorities gave their illegal residence status as reason for their arrest, it is clear from the pre-planned and targeted nature of the arrests that these were tactics to stop the officers' organising efforts.

In 2007 the Committee on the Elimination of Racial Discrimination expressed serious concerns over the persistence of widespread societal discrimination against foreigners, including migrant workers, in all areas of life, including employment. Likewise, in its 2008 observation the ILO CEARC stated that efforts are necessary to address discrimination against foreign workers and to ensure full compliance with both the national legislation and the Conventions.

Conclusions

Discrimination in employment and occupation is prohibited by law. However, in practice discrimination against women and foreign workers is both frequent and serious. Measures adopted by the government to address women's disadvantaged position on the labour market have not yielded expected results. The current employment permit system puts foreign workers in a particularly vulnerable situation, rendering them easily abused and exploited.

III. Child Labour

The Republic of Korea ratified Convention No. 138 the Minimum Age Convention in 1999, and Convention No. 182, the Worst Forms of Child Labour Convention, in 2001.

Education is compulsory from age 6 to 14. Primary school begins at age 6 and lasts 6 years. Virtually all students who enroll in primary school reach the last grade. Secondary education begins at age 12 and lasts 6 years.

Work by minors is regulated. Children under age 18 may not work more than 7 hours per day and 42 hours per week. Children are prohibited from engaging in work that is detrimental to their morality or health. Night work is also prohibited. Employers can require minors to work only a limited number of overtime hours.

Employment of children under the age 15 is prohibited without a special employment certificate from the Ministry of Labour. In practice very few certificates are issued. Children aged 16 and 17 must have written approval from parents or guardians to be able to work. However, parents or guardians may not enter into a labour contract on behalf of a minor but they may terminate a contract if it is disadvantageous to the child.

In practice child labour is not considered to be a widespread phenomenon is Korea, since the government effectively enforces the laws protecting children from exploitation at the workplace through regular inspections. However, in its Concluding Observations, in 2003 the Committee on the Rights of the Child expressed some concerns about the limited amount of data available on the prevalence of child sexual exploitation.

Conclusions

Child labour is not considered to be a widespread phenomenon in Korea. Education is compulsory up to the age of 15, the minimum age to enter work. Work performed by minors younger than 18 is regulated. Official data on the prevalence of children involved in the sex industry is lacking.

IV. Forced Labour

The Republic of Korea has not ratified Convention No. 29, the Forced Labour Convention nor Convention No. 105, the Abolition of Forced Labour Convention.

The Constitution provides that no person shall be subjected to involuntary labour, except as provided by law and through lawful procedures. The Labour Standards Act prohibits employers from forcing their employees to work against their will through the use of violence, intimidation, confinement, or by other means. Employers found to abuse workers are subject to criminal charges.

In practice, Koreans are not subject to forced labour, but the case of certain migrant workers deserves careful attention. As reported in Section II of this document, there are reports of foreign workers being beaten and having their wages or passports withheld. Such treatment can amount to a situation of forced labour in the sense of the Conventions. This is particularly the case when employers have seized official documents, including passports and work permits, and preventing migrant workers from leaving the workplace.

Many migrant workers have accumulated huge debts in order to pay high recruitment fees for jobs in Korea. Once in Korea, some of them find that the jobs are very different from those they were promised and are more dangerous or more poorly paid than they had expected. With few rights to negotiate a change of job, those workers may either accept working conditions below national standards, or give up their legal employment and go on working as undocumented migrant workers with a particularly high risk of being exploited and abused. The lack of legal status makes it extremely difficult for migrants to assert their rights or to seek redress for abuses.

The law prohibits all forms of trafficking in persons. However, there are some reports that persons were trafficked to and from the country for the purpose of sexual exploitation and domestic servitude.

Conclusions

Forced labour is prohibited by law and in practice Koreans are not subject to forced labour, but there have been reports of conditions faced by certain migrant workers that could amount to forced labour. It is essential that Korea ratify ILO Convention No. 29, the Forced Labour Convention and ILO Convention No. 105, the Abolition of Forced Labour Convention.

Final Conclusions and Recommendations

1. The government of Korea must ratify ILO Conventions No. 87 and 98 on trade union rights, as well as Conventions No. 29 and 105 on forced labour.
2. Various legal provisions have to be brought in line with Conventions No. 87 and No. 98. In particular, the government must allow all workers including those in the public sector to join and form trade unions. The government should not arbitrarily and unilaterally limit the subjects of collective bargaining.
3. The government of Korea must allow for trade union pluralism at the workplace.
4. The government should refrain from interfering in trade union activities especially with regard to the eligibility of workers to become trade union members and leaders.
5. Remuneration of union leaders should, in accordance with international labour conventions, be the outcome of negotiations between the employer and trade union. Therefore the government must repeal the section of the Trade Union and Labour Relations Adjustment Act (Article 24.2) relating to that issue.

6. Article 314 of the Criminal Code must not be abusively used to harass and seek the incarceration of trade unionists.
7. The government of Korea must put an end to brutal police actions against workers on strike.
8. The government should register the Migrants' Trade Union and let it engage in trade union representation and bargaining.
9. In the area of discrimination against women, the government of Korea must do more to address wage gaps and occupational constraints on employment for women, including greater encouragement to women to upgrade their skills and more positive action programmes, as well as a better enforcement of the laws on equal rights.
10. Migrant workers should be allowed to change business or workplace.
11. Enforcement of the legislation applicable to migrant workers has to be strengthened, with a view to eliminating and preventing discriminatory or abusive practices.
12. The government of Korea should ensure that migrant workers have access to effective complaints procedures.
13. The government should ensure that domestic workers fall within the scope of both the national labour legislation and the Equal Employment Act.
14. Policies and programmes need to be implemented so as to reduce the discrimination and abuses, including sexual abuses, faced by women migrant workers.
15. The government of Korea should collect information on the prevalence of children involved in the sex industry.
16. In line with the commitments accepted by Korea at the Singapore and Doha WTO Ministerial Conference and its obligations as a member of the ILO, the Government of Korea should provide regular reports to the WTO and the ILO on its legislative changes and implementation of all the core labour standards.
17. The WTO should draw to the attention of the authorities of Korea the commitments they undertook to observe core labour standards at the Singapore and Doha Ministerial Conferences. The WTO should request the ILO to intensify its work with the Government of Korea in these areas and provide a report to the WTO General Council on the occasion of the next trade policy review.

QUESTIONS

1. Drawing upon the above ITUC Report, list and discuss the top three labor issues in South Korea demanding attention and reform.
2. What role will unions likely play in any labor reforms that may occur? What support is there for your position?
3. How well has the South Korean government responded to the call for labor reform? *Current Labor Issues in Korea* 2010 has stated that the "year 2010 is likely to be remembered in history as a year with remarkable changes." With respect to your answer in question number one and the following article, have they come into place, and if so, how well are they working?

Current Labor Issues in Korea 2010[96]

A. *Wage for Full-time Trade Union Officials and Union Pluralism*. With revisions of the Trade Union and Labor Relations Adjustment Act, wage for full-time trade union officials shall be banned as of July 1st, 2010 and union pluralism shall be allowed from July 1st, 2011. The issues of the two systems, which were introduced along with the controversial Trade Union Act in 1997–1998, but of which implementation have been postponed for three times during the last 13 years, have finally come to the conclusion.

B. *Increasing Flexibility in Wages and Work Hours*. Flexible wage and working hours are two of the issues that the government is actively promoting. To this end, the government plans to associate wage peak system and extension of retirement age, while flexible work program is to be expanded for flexible work hours. In addition, associating changes in corporate wage system to flexible work hours is another plan of the government to promote raising retirement age. Labor Minister Lim, Tae-hee said, on his interview with media in March 2010, "Now that baby boomers have begun to retire, a long-term and comprehensive measures need to be taken to cope with structural changes in society and population" and emphasized, "It's time to discuss extension of the retirement age."

C. *Labor Relations in the Public Sector*. One of the biggest labor issues in 2010 is labor-management relations in the public sector, like government employees and teachers. Korean Railway Workers' Union of the KCTU, Korean Government Employees' Trade Union, and the Korean Teachers and Educational Workers' Union (KTU) are against the government. The railway union, which waged strikes in 2009 twice, warned at an assembly held in March 2010, "If collective bargaining doesn't go back to normal, we might go on a third strike". While the railway labor and management have yet to complete its collective bargaining which started in 2008, the union notified of the expiration of the extant collective agreement and the expiration falls in May, 2010.

D. *Betterment for Non-Regular Workers*. The government and the National Assembly enacted a bill to protect non-regular workers, the first of its kind, to dissolve discrimination and abuse against them, which has been named one of the reasons of bi-polarization in Korean society since the economic crisis at the end of the 1990s. The Non-regular Workers Protection Act passed the National Assembly on November 30, 2007 and was promulgated on December 21, 2007.

. . . .

C. CHINA

1. *Regulatory Sources, Structures, and Administration*

The evolution of Chinese law since 1949 has been phenomenal, as the development on the following issues shows. The rule of law has evolved from Mao slogans to viable and credible legal institutions and laws; although China still espouses rule "*by*" law, labor laws have gained many of the aspects of "rule of law."

[96] Current Labor Situation in Korea 2010, *supra* note 69, at 71–79 (2010) [Formatting altered].

The early socialist system of the "iron rice bowl" was transformed into labor contracts in a "socialist market economy," with workers' legal status changing from government agents to free agents and it is a status from which they can be fired.[97]

China has evolved into a recognizable system of human resource management under a profit-seeking private economy. It is fairly free from Party interference, such as was witnessed in the early Beijing Jeep venture where the Party was said to be too deeply involved in management without the necessary business expertise.[98]

The trade union (ACFTU), long associated with the Chinese Communist Party, is still aligned with the government and the Party, but is seen by some to be morphing as it seeks a meaningful identity. It is reacting to being "muscled out," if not displaced by profit-seeking employers from its early responsibility of enforcing "labor discipline."

Labor dispute resolution has evolved from early internal employer and Party-domination to outside, government arbitration.

Health and safety in the workplace continue to improve, with current law standards that require safety equipment in the workplace and provide workers' compensation.

Social security has grown from a sparse socialist system of minimal cradle-to-grave benefits to a new reformed law poised for passage in NPC, providing comprehensive coverage, funded by employers, employees, and the government. It will join the new Health Law affecting the medical benefits of workers.

China's labor reforms since the 1995 labor law include:

1. Labor Contract Law (2008)[99]
2. Employment Promotion Law (2008)
3. Labor Mediation and Arbitration Law (2008)
4. Collective Negotiation Regulations (2004)
5. Also passed and implemented in the 2000s were laws and regulations dealing with Work Safety, Occupational Disease, Work-Related Injuries, Minimum Wages and Overtime, and Social Security covering medical, maternity, work-related injuries, unemployment, and pensions (all of which are further upgraded under the new Social Security Law, etc.).

---

[97] See discussion in MARY GALLAGHER, FROM THE IRON-RICE BOWL TO INFORMALIZATION: MARKETS, STATE, AND WORKERS IN A CHANGING CHINA (Sarosh Kuruville et al. eds., 2011). Eli Friedman & Ching Kwan Lee, *Remaking the World of Chinese Labor: A Thirty-Year Retrospective*, 48 BRIT. J. INDUS. REL. 507 (2010). Hilary K. Josephs, *Measuring Progress Under China's Labor Law: Goals, Processes, Outcomes*, 30 COMP. LAB L. & POL'Y J. 373 (2009).

[98] JIM MANN, BEIJING JEEP: A CASE STUDY OF WESTERN BUSINESS IN CHINA (1997).

[99] *See* Virginia Harper Ho, *From Contracts to Compliance? An Early Look at Implementation Under China's New Labor Legislation*, 23 COLUM. J. ASIAN L. 35 (2009); Sean Cooney et al., *China's New Labor Contract Law: Responding to the Growing Complexity of Labor Relations in the PRC*, 30 U. NEW S. WALES L. J. 786 (2007). It is argued that the new employment and labor laws in China are having the effect of raising working conditions, increasing the transfer of knowledge from multinational companies to Chinese managers and workers, and increasing costs to employers in China. See discussion in Marisa Anne Pagnattaro, *Is labor really "cheap" in China? Compliance with labor and employment laws*, 10 SAN DIEGO INT'L L.J. 357–379 (2009).

Understanding Labor and Employment Law in China[100]

Ronald C. Brown

. . . .

Balancing Economic Development and Labor Reforms

The story of how labor and employment issues are dealt with on an everyday basis begins with an understanding of China and insight into its system of legal regulation. The Chinese workplace is a reflection of the diverse impacts of phenomenal economic development, tightening regulations, and an evolving safety net in the workplace. It is set in urban and rural areas; in manufacturing, construction, and heavy and light industries; and in white-collar jobs. In many sectors, there is a more stable and slowly evolving skilled workforce that has come to expect and demand better labor standards and protections. Add to this the ebb and flow of more than 150 million migrant workers into the urban areas and the absence of traditions of labor laws and law enforcement, and the image of China's workplaces come into clearer focus. It is the story of how those workplaces accommodate to China's labor and employment laws and make them work.

Relatively low wages and labor standards for workers in China are usually initially credited for its continuing economic development and its sustained annual growth in the double digits. In recent years, with the transition to a market economy and privatization, these same low labor standards have evoked international and domestic pressures; in response, China's leaders have introduced labor reforms. These reforms attempt to meet worker needs while at the same time maintaining economic development and economic competitiveness. Since the issuance of the Labor Law in 1994, there has been a steady growth in labor legislation seeking to find that balance, provide a worker safety net, promote social and political stability, and address the often disparate effects of the economic miracle.

Labor reforms, like economic reforms, have had an uneven impact on China's 800 million workers. Rural workers too often fall outside the protection of the labor laws; and better wages and working conditions are more likely available in the urban areas that have benefitted from economic development, particularly the eastern coastal regions and cities. This concentration of workplace opportunities has worked like a magnet to attract the migration of nearly 150 million rural workers to urban areas. These migrant laborers are concentrated in manufacturing and construction and are often the victims of unpaid wages and substandard working conditions.

The great diversity of China's workplaces continues to hinder the focused application and enforcement of the newly emerging labor laws. State-owned enterprises (SOEs), former SOEs, private enterprises, foreign-invested enterprises (FIEs), and large and small enterprises all present varied challenges to local governments seeking to regulate the workplace. Employers are also mindful that they risk the loss of competitiveness if they comply with labor standards while their competitors do not.

[100] Ronald C. Brown, Understanding Labor and Employment Law in China 3–12 (2010) [Footnotes omitted].

Use of Laws to Regulate the Workplace

China's new legal system was developed since the *Four Modernizations* in the late 1970s. Centuries of traditions and China's more recent socialist and civil law heritage have blended together to create its present legal system, laden with Chinese characteristics. Although legislatures and government agencies serve as sources of law, as in the West, in China other legal institutions, such as the Supreme People's Court that issues interpretations guiding the courts in their application of the laws, serve that purpose as well.

China's recent explosion of new labor laws, implemented in 2008, ranging from the Labor Contract Law (LCL), the Employment Promotion Law (EPL), and the Labor Dispute Mediation and Arbitration Law (LMA), as well as laws dealing with related topics of mergers and acquisitions and bankruptcy, must be understood in the context of China's burgeoning economy and concern for social stability. Chinese legal regulations, based on legal traditions in civil law and of course with "Chinese characteristics," may appear somewhat similar to Western laws. However, under China's political-legal system, the lawmaking organs and the enforcement mechanisms often function differently from those in the West. The National People's Congress (NPC) and its Standing Committee enact legislation, the State Council issues regulations, and the Ministries formulate rules; their local government counterparts also issue laws and regulations. The legal system operates under a "rule-by-law" approach (with legislative supremacy), and the enforcement processes are distributed differently from Western law, involving numerous layers of government and legal institutions.[101]

How Chinese laws operate is surprising to many in the West. The relationship between central and local governments and their relative authority in legislation and enforcement form a practical reality that must be dealt with. Although China is a former socialist state, it generally has a decentralized government. Central government laws (such as the 1994 Labor Law) are often merely general guidelines that thereafter depend on consistent "local implementing regulations," legislated and enforced by appropriate local authorities. For that reason, it has taken some time to provide meaningful labor protections to its workers. Labor disputes are channeled through familiar routes of alternative dispute resolution machinery, though they play out somewhat differently than in the West.

Labor laws are generally administered by the various divisions of the local labor bureaus, which are under the central ministry but, in large part, are horizontally (locally) financed and staffed. Likewise, enforcement is generally handled at the local level. In recent years there has been a growth in the number of specialized administrative agencies that, with their local labor bureau counterparts, administer and supervise specific labor law programs. One of the constant criticisms of China's labor laws is the lack of consistent enforcement by the government. However, labor disputes in China are resolved mostly by individual workers through local governmental mediation and arbitration. The number of these cases has risen dramatically every year as new laws are passed and an increased awareness of labor rights takes hold in the workforce. In the heavy manufacturing area of Guangzhou in 2008 there was a more than 200 percent increase in the number of labor disputes after the new Labor Contract Law took effect. Courts are available to enforce

[101] *See* Randall Peerenboom, CHINA'S LONG MARCH TOWARD RULE OF LAW (2002). See discussion of the extent to which rule by law may overlap with Western concepts of *due process* in Ronald C. Brown, "*Rule of Law with Chinese Characteristics*" – *What's in a Name?*, *in* Understanding Chinese Courts and Legal Process: Law with Chinese Characteristics 133–39 (1997).

or review many of these labor arbitrations. Recently, the courts have been authorized to directly determine certain wage claims without the prior requirement of undergoing the labor arbitration process.

Disparate Economic Impacts in the Workplace

China's economic development began in earnest after Deng Xiaoping began his "Four Modernizations" in 1979. Since that time many economic and legal reforms have taken place. This economic development has been uneven, causing regional and urban/rural disparities that, in turn, have brought about an influx of millions of rural workers into the cities for better work opportunities, though not necessarily better treatment or working conditions. Many of the significant labor and employment laws are applied only in the urban areas, with some additional laws applying to certain aspects of employment in the rural areas.

With the transition from the "iron rice bowl system" to labor contracts, China has moved from a socialist planned economy using SOEs to a socialist market economy.[102] Privatization, layoffs, and new management strategies emphasizing profits and competition have produced both a "wage consciousness" and feelings of unfairness among workers because of regional wage disparities, occupational wage gaps, unequal job opportunities, and sagging labor and security safety nets.

Economic growth has produced a 100 to 150 million person "floating population" (predominantly underpaid migrant workers) seeking to earn their share of the pie. It also has produced national scandals in which employers refuse to pay the wages of migrant workers, presently an underclass in China. Coal miners are dying by the thousands each year because of unsafe working conditions. Consequently, the issue of better enforcement of the labor protections provided in the labor laws is part of the labor reform agenda.

China is at a crossroads. On the one hand, it has the necessary resources to make its labor law system work much better than it does. On the other hand, labor relations have seemed to come second to the forces of economic development, and China seems unsure whether, if it makes the choice to better enforce its labor laws, it will be placed at a competitive disadvantage internationally. Employers who might otherwise follow the labor laws are in a quandary; why spend the money to follow these laws if they are not enforced?

. . . .

When adding up some of the ill side-effects of economic reforms, such as slow-rising wages, widening wage gaps, and unpaid wages of migrant workers (who make up the "floating population" of 100 to 150 million Chinese citizens) – with each affected employee seeking to find his or her share of the new economic development, one can understand why the central government has had as a high priority putting a social security safety net in place with accompanying labor law protections. This effort brought into existence the 1994 Labor Law, which broadly outlined labor standards requirements. By 2004, many of the standards had been more formally enacted into specific laws and regulations including new regulations on minimum wage and hours. Notwithstanding the progress in legislation, employees continued to demand that the laws be made to work and some collective protests have taken place demanding improved benefits.

. . . .

---

[102] For discussion of workers in SOEs see WILLIAM HURST, THE CHINESE WORKER AFTER SOCIALISM (2009).

Labor and Employment Laws and Administration[103]

Ronald C. Brown

. . . .

Ministry of Human Resources and Social Security (MOHRSS)

At the central government level under the State Council, the Ministry of Human Resources and Social Security (MOHRSS) administers labor and employment policies. In March 2008, this ministry took over the functions of the Ministry of Labor and Social Security (MOLSS) (see table below) and the Ministry of Personnel (MOP). It maintains vertical supervision at the local level through local labor bureaus, which are at the same time also greatly controlled by local governments through their funding and appointments power.

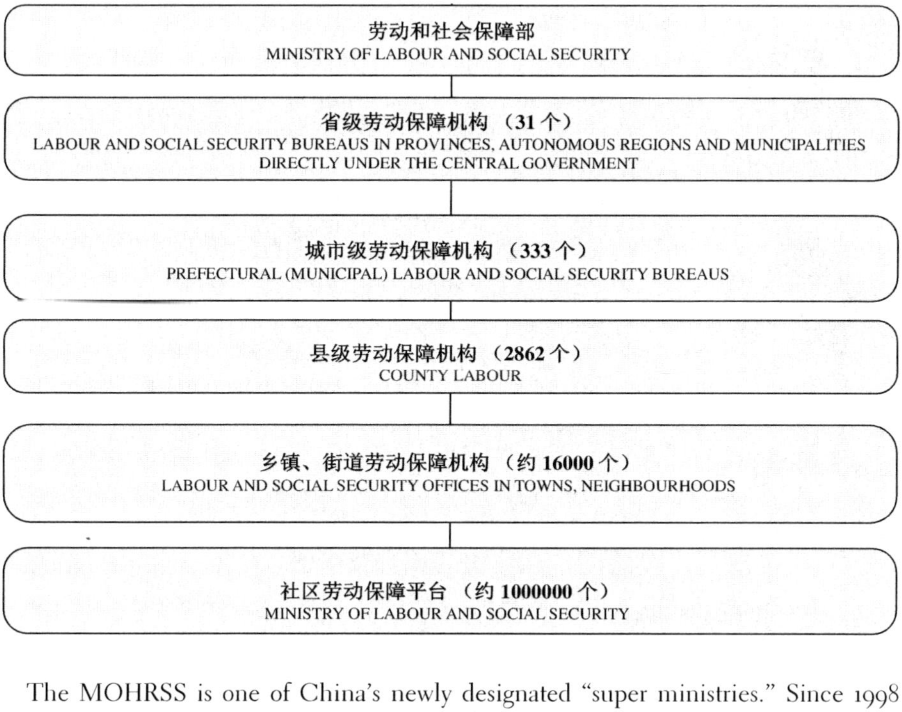

The MOHRSS is one of China's newly designated "super ministries." Since 1998 its predecessor, MOLSS, has been responsible for social security management and development of policies and legislation for urban, rural, and government workers. Before its 2008 reorganization, it was organized into the following departments: legal affairs, planning and finance, training and employment, labor and wages, pension insurance, unemployment insurance, medical insurance, work-related injury insurance, rural social insurance, social insurance fund supervision, international cooperation, and personnel and education. With the reorganization in 2008, it assumed the functions of the former

[103] Brown, *supra* note 100, at 13–19 [Footnotes omitted].

MOP, with the exception of its civil service department, which is now part of the State Public Servants Bureau.

The reorganized ministry has twenty-three departments, including several new ones (see table below).

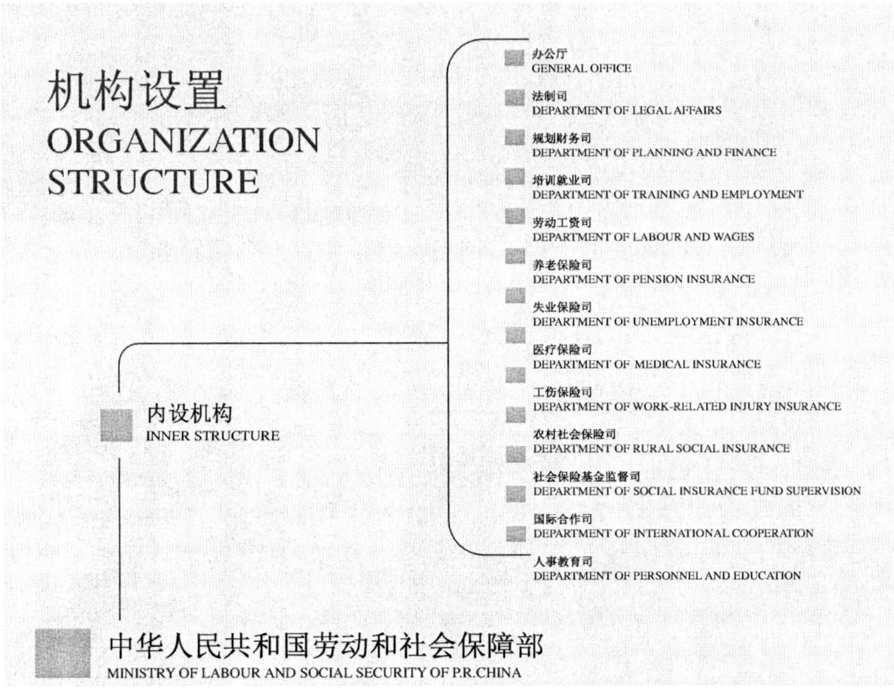

The new ministry set up 23 functional internal offices, including several new offices, for human resource market, labor inspection, rural migrant workers, labor dispute mediation and arbitration, labor relations, and wage and compensation, as shown by the table below.

MINISTRY OF HUMAN RESOURCES AND SOCIAL SECURITY (MOHRSS) 人力资源和社会保障部 **INNER STRUCTURE** 内设机构
GENERAL OFFICE 办公厅
DEPARTMENT OF POLICY & RESEARCH*** 政策研究司
DEPARTMENT OF LEGAL AFFAIRS 法规司
DEPARTMENT OF PLANNING AND FINANCE 规划财务司
DEPARTMENT OF EMPLOYMENT PROMOTION* 就业促进司

DEPARTMENT OF HUMAN RESOURCE MARKET 人力资源市场司
DEPARTMENT OF JOB PLACEMENT FOR DEMOBILIZED MILITARY OFFICERS 军官转业安置司
DEPARTMENT OF PROFESSIONAL CAPACITY-BUILDING* 职业能力建设司
DEPARTMENT OF PROFESSIONAL AND TECHNICAL PERSONNEL MANAGEMENT 专业技术人员管理司
DEPARTMENT OF PERSONNEL MANAGEMENT FOR INSTITUTIONS 事业单位人事管理司
DEPARTMENT OF SERVICE FOR MIGRANT WORKER* 农民工工作司
DEPARTMENT OF LABOR RELATIONS* 劳动关系司
DEPARTMENT OF WAGE AND BENEFITS* 工资福利司
DEPARTMENT OF PENSION INSURANCE 养老保险司
DEPARTMENT OF UNEMPLOYMENT INSURANCE 失业保险司
DEPARTMENT FO MEDICAL INSRUANCE 医疗保险司
DEPARTMENT OF WORK-RELATED INJURY INSURNACE 工伤保险司
DEPARTMENT OF RURAL SOCIAL INSRUANCE 农村社会保险司
DEPARTMENT OF SOCIAL INSURANCE FUND SUPERVISION 社会保险基金监督司
DEPARTMENT OF LABOR DISPUTE MEDIATION AND ARBITRATION MANAGEMENT* 调节仲裁管理司
DEPARTMENT OF LABOR INSPECTION* 劳动监察司
DEPARTMENT OF INTERNATIONAL COOPERATION 国际合作司
DEPARTMENT OF PERSONNEL 人事司

[*Id.* The newly established departments (or those adjusted for functions) of the original Ministry of Labor and Social Security (MOLSS) are marked by an asterisk.]

Responsibilities and Functions

The MOHRSS, through its departments and subordinate institutions (unchanged from MOLSS, see table below), is responsible for formulating and implementing policies in the following areas. It drafts laws and regulations that promote employment and labor market development and exercises supervision and inspection functions over programs and local labor agencies. In vocational training, it drafts national standards for occupational classifications and skills, training, and certification. In labor relations, it formulates the principles for labor relations adjustment, enforcement of regulations and labor contracts, dispute settlement, and labor arbitration, and it works out policies on labor standards and protections. In wage regulation, it drafts macro-level policies and measures concerning wage guidelines and regulatory policies. The ministry formulates policies and standards on social insurance and manages the funding, implementation, supervision, and inspection of government programs on old age, unemployment, medical, work-related injury, and maternity benefits. The MOHRSS also is in charge of compiling and disseminating statistical information concerning national labor and social insurance and forecasting trends. It organizes and engages in scientific research in the fields of labor and social insurance. Lastly, it is responsible for international exchanges and cooperation, including participation in international organizations such as the International Labor Organization (ILO) and technical projects.

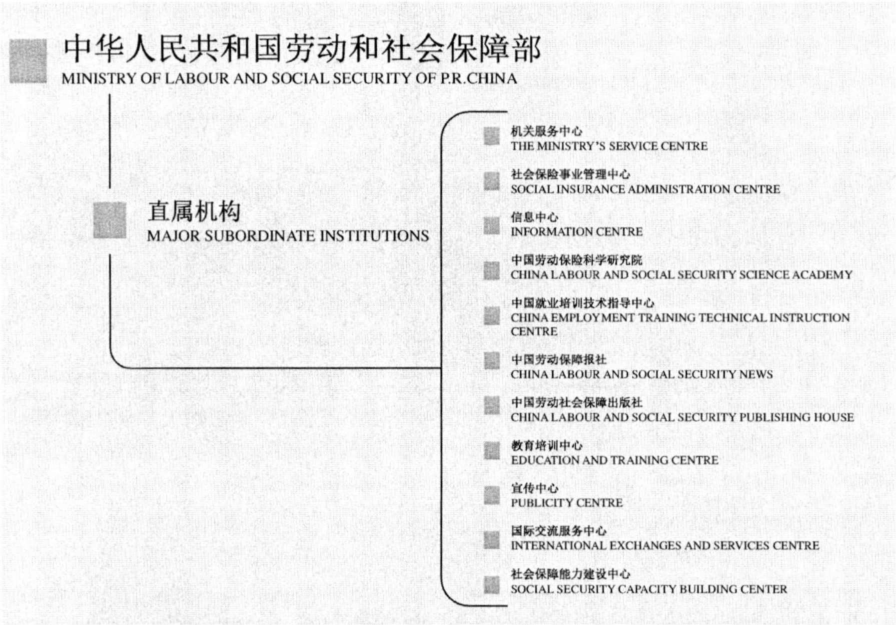

. . . .

QUESTIONS

1. Describe the sources of China's current labor law in comparison with Japan and South Korea?
2. Is China's modern legal system more civil law or common law in nature?
3. What are the similarities and differences between China's MOHRSS and the Department of Labor in the United States? Which works better? Why and how?

---

2. *Workers' Labor Rights and Benefits*

An introductory overview of employment laws and their requirements is presented next from the perspective of a labor lawyer practicing in China. This is followed by an exposition on the new labor contract law and the laws and regulations that address employment discrimination in China.

Guide to Employment Law in China[104]

Gregory Sy

I. Employment Law Legislation

1. What legislation governs employment law in China?

Employment law in China is governed by a relatively comprehensive set of laws, more recently supplemented in late 2007 to strengthen workers' rights.

Major laws include:

- Labour Law of the People's Republic of China (1994)
- Labour Contract Law of the People's Republic of China (2007)
- Labour Arbitration and Dispute Resolution Law of the People's Republic of China (2007) (effective May 1, 2008)
- Trade Union Law of the People's Republic of China (1994)
- [Employment Promotion Law of the People's Republic of China (effective January 1, 2008)]

These laws are then supplemented by a myriad of national and local laws, regulations, measures, and circulars.

. . . .

II. Labour Agreements

1. What are the different types of employment contacts?

Employment in China, like most other jurisdictions, is divided into full-time and part-time. According to the Labour Contract Law, part-time employment is defined as a labour relationship in which the employee works, on average, no more than 4 hours per day and no more than the aggregate of 24 hours per week.

[104] Gregory Sy, Grandall Legal Group, *Guide to Employment Law in China (2008), Part I*, http://www.chinasuccessstories.com/2008/04/16/chinese-labour-law/ (last visited Sept. 30, 2010); and *Part II*, http://www.chinasuccessstories.com/2008/04/22/chinese-employee-regulations/ (last visited Sept. 30, 2010). A version of this article was first published in ASIAN-MENA COUNSEL (www.inhouse community.com).

For a complete exposition of China's labor and employment laws, see Brown, *supra* note 100 (2009).

Employment relationships which exceed the hours in this definition are termed full-time employment, which is further divided into 3 types:

1. fixed term: expiry date agreed upon at outset;
2. open-ended/non-fixed term: no expiry date stipulated; or
3. project-based/completion of defined task: contract to expire on completion of predefined project or task.

2. What are the requirements of a contract?

According to the Labour Law and the Labour Contract Law, other than part-time employment, all labour contracts must be in writing and contain the following terms:

- name, address and legal representative of the employer;
- name, address and identification number of the employee;
- term of labour contract;
- job description and work site;
- working hours, rest, and vacation;
- labour remuneration;
- social insurance;
- labour conditions, working conditions, and occupational hazard prevention; and
- other matters stipulated by laws and regulations.

If the labour contract contains a probationary period only (sometimes called "a probationary period contract"), then the probation term set out therein is deemed to be the term of the labour contract and the probationary period is invalidated.

3. What are the penalties associated with not signing a written employment agreement?

If a labour contract is not concluded within the one month of commencement, the employer will be liable to the employee for double labour remuneration, of up to 1 year. After 1 year with no written labour contract, fixed-term labour contracts are deemed to be open-ended.

4. What is the maximum probationary period allowable by law?

Maximum probation periods allowed by law are as follows:

- less than 3 months: no probation period;
- 3 months to 1 year: 1 month;
- 1 year to 3 years: 2 months; and
- 3 years or more or open-ended: 6 months.

III. Wages, Benefits, and Social Security

1. What are the components of wages or salaries?

According to the Provisional Regulations for the Payment of Wages (1994), wages or salary are composed of:

- wages based on time;
- wages based on piece-work;

- bonuses;
- subsidies;
- allowances;
- overtime payments; and
- wages paid under special circumstances.

According to the Minimum Wages Provisions (2004) and based on the minimum wage standards promulgated locally, employers may not pay their employees less than the current minimum wage standard.

2. What are the standard working hours and when am I required to pay overtime?

The standard working hours in China are 8 hours per day, 5 days per week, for a maximum working period of 40 hours, with 2 rest days (typically Saturday and Sunday). Any additional requirements by the employer must be compensated according to the standard set out below here:

- Working days: 150% standard wages;
- Rest days: 200% standard wages; and
- Holidays: 300% standard wages.

3. What are the national public holidays?

National public holidays (as of 2008) are set out below:

- New Year's Day (January 1): 1 day;
- Spring Festival (lunar new year, typically January or February): 3 days;
- Women's Day (March 8): half day for women;
- Qingming Festival (April 5): 1 day;
- May Day (May 1): 1 day;
- Dragon Boat Festival (5th day of 5th lunar month): 1 day;
- Mid-autumn Festival (15th day of the 8th lunar month): 1 day; and
- National Day (October 1 – 3): 3 days.

4. What are the social security payments required by law?

Employers are obligated to provide the following benefits and social security payments to employees:

- Basic old age insurance;
- Unemployment insurance;
- Medical insurance;
- Maternity insurance; and
- Work-related injury insurance;

The employee and employer jointly contribute to the first 3 types of insurances, while the employer alone contributes to the latter 2, with rates varying based on location of employment.

IV. Non-Compete And Confidentiality

1. Can all employees be subjected to non-compete obligations?

Not all employees can nor should be bound by non-competition obligations. The Labour Contract Law limits employees who may be bound by non-compete obligations to:

- senior management;
- senior technical personnel; and
- those employees who have access to business secrets of the employer.

It is required that the employee and employer conclude a written agreement, either separately or in the labour contract, with regards to term, scope, territory, compensation during the non-compete period, and liquidated damages for employee breach.

The maximum term is 2 years.

2. What are the typical compensation requirements for non-competes?

Although it is required that compensation be paid on a monthly basis to the employee during the non-compete period, the law does not state a standard amount. In practice, it is common to pay at least 50% of the employee's wages.

3. Are liquidated damages permissible for breach of non-compete obligations?

Yes.

V. Termination and 'Layoffs'

1. Under what circumstances can an employee be terminated without notice?

An employer may terminate an employee without requirement for notice in the following situations:

- during the probation period, if the employee is determined to be unfit for the position;
- employee materially breaches employer's rules and regulations;
- employee engages in serious dereliction of duty, graft or corruption causing substantial damages to the employer's interests;
- employee has established an employment relationship with another employer and that relationship affects the completion of his tasks and he refuses to appropriately remedy the situation after employer notification;
- employee used fraud in concluding the labour contract; or
- employee is subject to criminal investigation.

2. Under what circumstances must an employee be given notice of termination?

An employer must give 30 days' prior written notice or payment in lieu thereof, if it terminates the labour contract under the following situations:

- the employee is unable to perform his original duties or re-assigned duties, after returning from medical leave or non-work-related injury;
- the employee is incompetent and remains incompetent after training or adjustment of position; or

- the occurrence of a major change of objective circumstances which were relied upon when signing the labour contract, and the employee and employer are unable to agreed on modified terms of the labour contract.

3. Under what circumstances may an employee terminate the labour contract without notice?

An employee may unilaterally terminate the employment contract without requirement for notice in the following instances:

- employer fails to provide labour protections and working conditions in accordance with the labour contract;
- employer fails to pay remuneration in full and on time;
- employer fails to pay social security payments in accordance with the law;
- employer's rules and regulations violate laws and regulations, harming the employee's rights and interests;
- employer uses fraud, coercion or the employee's unfavorable position to conclude the contract; or
- other situations set out in laws and regulations.

4. In what instances is compensation required and how much?

Severance compensation is due in a number of situations, which are summarized below:

- termination by employee under situations which result in his right to terminate the contract immediately (Item 3, discussed previously);
- termination by employer under situations which require 30 days' prior written notice (Item 2, discussed previously);
- the employee is terminated due to restructuring or difficulties in business operations;
- the labour contract is terminated after being proposed by employer and there is mutual agreement on termination;
- a fixed-term labour contract expires (except where employee refuses to renew the contract on terms equal to or better than previously concluded);
- termination of labour contract due to revocation of employer's business license; and
- termination of labour contract due to bankruptcy.

Employers must pay severance in the amount of one month's salary for each year of service, with half a month's salary for each partial year.

If the employee earns more than 3 times the average monthly wage of the locality, then the compensation will be capped at 3 times the average monthly wage, up to a maximum of 12 months.

5. Can employees be 'laid off'?

Under the following circumstances, labour contracts may be terminated due to business difficulties:

- restructuring due to the Enterprise Bankruptcy Law;
- serious difficulties in production or operations;
- a staff reduction is necessary due to changes in production, technical innovation or adjustment of management operation style; or

- other major changes in economic circumstances relied upon at the time of conclusion of the labour contract, rendering them non-performable.

For large-scale layoffs (20 or more employees, or in smaller organizations where employee layoffs are less than 20 employees but this accounts for 10% or more of the total employees), the employer must first explain the circumstances to the trade union or all employees (where there is no trade union) 30 days in advance, and may reduce the workforce only after consideration of the opinions of the trade union or employees and reporting the restructuring plan to the labour administration.

VI. Labour Arbitration and Dispute Resolution

1. How are labour disputes resolved in China?

Like most jurisdictions, mediation is the preferred method of dispute resolution, however, this is a voluntary process. The Labour Arbitration Law provides that mediated settlement agreements for salaries, medical fees for job-related injuries, severance, and penalties may be entered into court for enforcement.

Labour dispute claims, according to the Labour Law and the Labour Arbitration Law, must first be submitted to the local labour arbitration committee located in the jurisdiction of the employer. The labour arbitration committee must then render its award within 45 days after the dispute has been accepted. Arbitration decisions are final for employers in the following instances: salaries, medical fees for job-related injuries, severance, and penalties, where the disputed amount does not exceed an amount equal to 12 months' local minimum wage.

Employees and employers (with the exception of those instances set out previously) may within 15 days of the arbitration award submit the dispute to the people's court for hearing.

2. What is the statute of limitations for bringing a labour dispute claim?

The limitation period is 1 year after the employee knew or should have known that their rights have been infringed; however, if the dispute occurs under an existing labour contract, the limitation period does not start until the labour contract has expired or has been terminated.

Labor Contract Law[105]

Ronald C. Brown

A. Introduction: Context

China has issued its long-anticipated and much-discussed Employment Contract Law, effective January 1, 2008.

[105] Ronald C. Brown, *China's New Labor Contract*, 3 CHINA L. REP. 4 (2007), *available at* http://meetings.abanet.org/webupload/commupload/IC860000/newsletterpubs/ChinaLawReporterNo.8(July).pdf (last visited Sept. 30, 2010); *see also* Brown, *supra* note 100, at 36–43.

Process: Transparent and Participatory

Since its first draft was released in March, 2006, the process of its consideration, and the subsequent two drafts, was marked by transparency and wide-based participation. Not only the usual Chinese experts and officials took part, but also foreign entities from around the world, including U.S. business representatives, such as the U.S. Chamber of Commerce and the U.S. China Business Council. Also, nearly 200,000 comments came from the public, largely from workers.

Modifications of Early Drafts

Numerous provisions were introduced and vigorously debated. Some European and American businesses and associations were immediately alarmed at what they felt were the serious challenges to costs and profitability that were presented by the provisions of the early drafts. This precipitated a response by some that foreigners were intruding too deeply into China's internal affairs. It even, for the first time, caused an American union, the Steelworkers, to come out in support of the new law, in that it was intended to further workers' rights. Exchanges on the drafts continued and after the Standing Committee's consideration of the final draft, the new law was issued on June 29, 2007.

New Employment Contract Law: Many Bullets Were Ducked

The new law eliminated, re-drafted, or re-formulated many of the more controversial provisions. These modifications, for many, have accommodated the early concerns raised by the business communities. To be sure, the law imposes new and greater liabilities on employers, grants some new rights and protections for workers, places some hard-to-miss enforcement requirements on the government, grants increased self-help remedies to the labor unions and the workers, and authorizes actions against negligent government enforcers of the new labor law. It moves the prior 1994 labor contract law provisions into a posture more compatible with China's other new laws covering bankruptcy, mergers and acquisitions. While China may absorb some "hits" on its economic development and "competitive advantage" by improving labor law provisions, as always, "the proof is the pudding" – will enforcement be meaningful . . . this time? If enforcement works well and provides fairer competition, it can not only boost the rights of workers, but also "level the playing field" for the "good citizen-and-law-abiding" . . . companies operating in China.

B. Scope and Substance of Employment Contract Law: Highlights

Formation and Content: Tightening the Relationship

Many existing statutory provisions continued, but clarifications and new sanctions were added. For example, all employment contracts must be written (Art. 10); and, if not concluded and signed within 30 days, the employer must pay double wages for the period of the violation. Shortened *probationary time limits* were established, depending on the length of the contract, with maximum periods of one month for contracts between three months and one year; two months for contracts one to three years; six months for contracts three years or more or open-ended (Art. 19).

Three types of contract were prescribed – fixed term, open-ended term, and project contracts (Arts. 12–15). Workers employed for more than 10 years may be entitled to an open ended contract (Art. 14(1)); and *workers whose second consecutive term expires will be entitled to have an open-ended contract, if they so demand* (Art. 14(3)), as will workers without a written contract after one year (Art. 14). Protection of *confidential information* on trade secrets and intellectual property is authorized and a competition restriction may also be included, though limited to certain senior management and technical personnel (Art. 23). The limit on competition requires post-employment compensation, paid in monthly installments, and is limited to two years.

Liquidated damage provisions are permitted for violations by those personnel (Arts. 23–24), but for no other reason (Art. 25), except to recoup certain professional technical training costs (Art. 22). Lastly, different practices of *employer misconduct* in the formation of employment contracts are specifically highlighted and prohibited. There is a long list of "don'ts". Article 26 invalidates an employment contract secured by a contractual party's deception, coercion or taking advantage of the worker's difficulties; an employer cannot refuse to give a written contract (Art. 11). Furthermore, an employer cannot keep a worker's ID card, require a security paid by a worker (Art. 9); employers, placement or accepting unit, cannot require a fee to be paid by the worker (Art. 60); the employer cannot "disguise" overtime (Article 31); and most worker liquidated damage provisions are prohibited (Art. 25). Also prohibited are acts of violence, threats, or unlawful restriction of personal freedom to compel a worker to work (Art. 38).

Performance Provisions

There are only six provisions in this chapter, some old, some new. Article 30 reiterates the employer's obligation to *pay wages on time* and in full, with possible further damages if not (Art. 85). Interestingly, Article 30 allows the unpaid worker, "in accordance with the law", to apply to the court for an order to pay; presumably, this "labor dispute" would still need to be preceded by labor arbitration (see discussion below). Article 31 provides that an employer *may not compel overtime*, a clearer mandate than the prior law's right to negotiate same; again, if enforced, this worker's "right" could provide an obstacle to termination for exercising it under Article 39. Finally, without breaching their employment contracts, workers may withhold their services rather than performing certain dangerous operations (Art. 32).

Mergers and acquisitions, a growing phenomenon in China and under new legislation, are addressed by Articles 34 and 33, respectively, which clarify the continuing validity of incumbent workers' employment contracts, absent a proper termination or amendment of the workers' employment contracts.

Termination and Ending Employment Contracts

The 15 provisions of Chapter 4 clarify and create some new rights and obligations.

Workers may terminate their employment contracts by mutual agreement (Art. 36) or by providing 30 days notice (or 3 days notice if during probation, Art. 37). Workers also can terminate if the employer fails to provide contracted labor conditions, labor protection, full and timely compensation, social security premiums, employer rules in compliance with laws, employment contracts formed free of coercion and deception, or for a reason otherwise specified by law (Article 38).

If the employer uses violence, threats, or unlawful restriction of personal freedom in compelling a worker to work or in requiring performance of certain dangerous operations, workers may terminate their contract (without notice) (Art. 38). Perhaps this could have some relevance in the types of recent cases where the Chinese Government has "cracked down" on employers found to be using involuntary labor in some brick factories. Provisions of the employment contract law would make a covered employer liable for damages and could impose administrative and criminal penalties (Art. 88). Under this law, an *employment contract "ends"* upon its expiration, death of worker, employer bankruptcy, business closure or liquidation, or its business license is taken away (Art. 44).

The *employer may terminate workers* for the same reasons as existed under prior law (without having any obligation for severance pay); failed probation, material breach of employer's rules or regulations, serious dereliction of duty or graft causing substantial damage to the employer, and criminal liability (Art. 39 (1–3) and (6)).

The *new employment contract law adds two additional grounds* (which also do not require severance pay): (1) continuing an employment relationship with another employer (after primary employer's request to rectify), which materially affects the completion of the worker's tasks; and (2) worker uses deception, coercion, or takes advantage of the employer's difficulties to conclude or amend an employment contract (Art. 39(4)and (5)).The employer may also terminate a worker (1) unable to perform original or arrange work, following the medical treatment period for illness or a non-work-related injury or (2) incompetent, even after training or adjustment, or (3) if work is rendered unperformable by a major change in circumstances in underlying premises (Art. 40). In these cases, severance pay is due (Art. 46).

Layoffs of a certain size must be explained by an employer and are permitted only under specified circumstances. A reduction in force of at least 20 workers or if fewer than 20, then by 10 percent of the workforce is permitted if necessitated by one of the following four justifications: (1) restructuring pursuant to Bankruptcy Law; (2) serious difficulties in production and/or business operations; (3) changes in production, innovation, business method, and after amendment of employment contracts; or (4) major change in the objective economic circumstances relied upon making the contracts unperformable (Art. 41). The provision also grants *priority retention rights to workers* with relatively long fixed term or open-ended contracts or *to a worker* who is a family's sole employed member and there is an elderly person or minor needing to be cared for. Dismissed workers are provided *preferential hiring* if the employer re-hires within six months.

Provisions protecting workers from termination are expanded from three to five provisions. The original three are (1) lost or partially lost capacity to work due to occupational disease or a work-related injury attributable to the employer; (2) during medical treatment period for illness or a non-work-related injury; or (3) during pregnancy or lactation period. The *new law added two provisions*: (4) workers exposed to occupational disease hazards before pre-departure health check-up or are suspected of having contracted an occupational disease and are under medical diagnosis or observation; and (5) workers with employer for at least 15 years and are less than five years from retirement (Art. 42). Likewise, an *expired* employment contract cannot be *ended* for those workers protected by Article 42 (except for lost or diminished capacity to work, Art. 42(2)) and will be extended until the circumstances described therein have ceased.

Severance Compensation and Unlawful Termination

Article 46 stipulates the *employer must pay severance pay to the worker terminated under Articles 38, 40, or 41; and, under Article 44 where the contract ends due to a bankruptcy or closure under Article 44 (4) or (5); and, in cases of expiration of a fixed-term contract,* unless the worker refuses to renew even though the employer offered same or better conditions as contained in the current contract (Art. 44(1)). Some employers view this as a Hobson's choice, as either a new fixed or open contract must be given or severance paid.

The *computation for payment of severance was adjusted* in the employment contract law, greatly reducing the separation costs projected from earlier drafts of the law, particularly for senior management employees. Article 47 provides the original law's formula of one month's wage for each year of service, but the computation is now capped at 12 months' wages in all cases, and is limited where it exceeds three times the average wage of all employees in the municipality where the employee works (Art. 47). The main concern for employers relates to the higher-paid workers. Article 48 provides that in cases of *unlawful termination or ending* of an employment contract, if the worker does not demand reinstatement or if it is not possible, then the worker shall be paid *damages at twice the rate of severance* provided in Article 47 (Art. 87).

C. Special Provisions

Collective Contracts

Obligations and procedures under the new law follow the 1994 Labor Law, subsequent State Council regulations, and the ACFTU's 2006 *Trial Regulation on the Work of Enterprise Trade Unions* provisions calling for "consultation", "negotiation", etc. . . . Of particular interest to employers is Article 51 that states *where there is no union, the employer shall conclude a collective contract with an employee representative under the guidance of higher level unions.* A newly developed feature is the shifting emphasis from enterprise-level negotiations to industry-wide or area collective contracts in industries such as construction, mining, catering services, etc. within areas below the county level (Art. 53). Article 54 stipulates that these contracts are binding on employers and workers in the industry or in the area in the locality concerned.

Placement

Early drafts dealing with the "dispatch" worker issue were very controversial. The new law, which appears to reduce employers' wide use of "agency" workers from staffing firms, reached accommodation on the issues as follows. *Staffing firms* now must be established under the Company Law, are liable as an "employer", must have fixed term contracts of not less than two years with its workers, and must pay minimum wage compensation when there is no work assignment for the worker (Articles 57 and 58). The placement must be based on "actual" requirements of the job position and the parties may not conclude several short-term placement agreements to cover a continuous term of labor use (Art. 59).

Therefore, these temporary assignments should be limited to temporary, auxiliary or substitute openings and wages paid must be equal with the regular workers at the accepting unit (Art. 63). Additionally, the staffing firm is prohibited from "pocketing" any of the compensation paid by the accepting unit for the workers or from charging fees from the workers placed (Art. 60). Finally, these temporary workers are accorded the right to join the labor union of either the staffing firm or the accepting unit (Art. 64).

Obligations of the accepting unit also include implementing state labor standards, working conditions and labor protection; paying overtime, performance bonuses and normal wage adjustments; and providing training necessary for the job position (Art. 62). Termination is to be done by the staffing firm (Art. 65) and accepting units are prohibited from setting up their own staffing firms (Art. 67).

Part-Time Labor

Part-time workers are limited to an "average" of not more than four hours per day or 24 hours per week for the "same" employer (Art. 68); but if there is a second employer, the subsequently concluded contract cannot prejudice the performance of the first (Art. 69). Wages are usually paid on an hourly basis and must meet local minimum wage standards (Art. 72). The contract may be oral and terminable "at-will"; there is no requirement for severance pay, and there cannot be a probationary period (Articles 69–71). Some questions may remain regarding use of student "workers" not as "regular" workers, but as interns or participants in work-study programs where per MOLSS interpretation they fall outside the 1994 Labor Law, sub-minimal compensation is often paid, as in the recent *McDonald's* and *KFC* cases.

D. Administration: Monitoring Inspections

The administration and monitoring provisions add few, if any, changes. The authority of the inspectors is emphasized stating they have the authority to review employment contracts and conduct on-the-spot inspections of the work premises (Art. 75). Workers whose rights are infringed have the right to "request" government action or to apply for arbitration or sue in court, as may be permitted by law (Art. 77). Labor unions are permitted to complain about violations, file for arbitration (Art. 56), and assist workers if they arbitrate or go to court (Art. 78).

E. Legal Liability

These 15 articles set forth *remedies and damages for violations* of the aforesaid obligations. For example, failure to provide a written employment contract in the first year requires the employer to pay twice the wages for the period in violation (Art. 82); failure to pay owed compensation can render the employer liable for damages at 50–100 percent of the amount owed (Art. 85); or if an employer unlawfully terminates or ends a contract, it must pay damages to the worker at twice the rate of severance pay due (Art. 87).

Other miscellaneous provisions include employer liability for (1) "*raiding*" another worker who is still employed (Art. 91) and (2) *violation of the employment contract law by an "individual" who is* an *employer's "contractor"* (jointly and severally liable, Art. 94). Lastly, there is a provision for *sanctions against the government labor-contract-enforcers* (including the labor agency, other offices, or *"a member of its working personnel")* who act negligently or fail to perform their duties and cause harm to a worker or the employer (Art. 95). *Transition from employment contracts existing at the time of implementation* of this new law are dealt with in Article 97, with employers retaining some residual liabilities.

F. Analysis/Observations

Some themes and questions emerge.

Workers' rights have been improved in the wording of the law, including as against employer misconduct and failure to pay wages. Provisions on probationary periods, types of contracts (including placement contracts), protection of confidential information and post-employment competition were added to clarify the formation and content of employment contracts. Some new protections from termination were added for workers possibly exposed to occupational disease hazards and those close to retirement. Part-time workers remained largely at the employer's discretion, although entitled to minimum labor standards.

Employers' obligations were increased for severance pay, though for a lesser amount than proposed in earlier drafts. Employers also are *"encouraged"* to offer open-ended contacts or pay severance. The law addressed the emerging impacts caused by mergers, acquisitions, and layoffs, seeking to find some balance between employer and worker needs. *Some employer rights* were provided; for example, training costs can now be recouped by the employer allowing for damages and fixed term of service.

How has the role of the labor union been affected? On the one hand it lost its right proposed in the earlier drafts to veto employer rules, but it did gain the statutory wording that seeks to provide enhanced emphasis on its dominant role as the representative of the workers in collective negotiations, in arbitration, and in the policing and enforcing of this new law. Some will observe that there is nothing new in this rhetoric and that this law brings little change to labor relations, arguing, for example, that Wal-Mart and others took little risk when they embraced the labor union. Still, there are some interesting provisions that would challenge this somewhat cynical approach. For example, the law now grants unions, by statute in Article 53, the right to move its emphasis from enterprise-level negotiating to industry and area wide negotiation; and Article 56 does explicitly state that the union may take a labor dispute to arbitration or the court and otherwise act as an advocate in termination cases (Art. 43) and other disputes. Now, even American unions are engaging China's unions to see if they can support the further development of the unions' role as protector of workers' rights.

How this law may affect labor arbitration is another area of interest. As stated, Article 56 (even in the 1994 Labor Law) grants the right to the *union itself* to take a case to labor arbitration *and court.* This is in addition to its usual more passive role as reiterated in Article 78 that provides for union *support* when a worker brings arbitration. However, labor arbitration in China, since at least the 1994 Labor Law, has first required a "labor dispute", followed by arbitration – before access to the court is granted. Article 85 appears to confirm that approach, yet Article 30 states that in disputes over payment of *wages* the worker *"in accordance with the law"* may apply to the court for an order to pay. Whether this application to the court in Article 56 is an independent right to directly proceed to court or whether the worker, to be "in accordance with the law", must first proceed with labor arbitration is unclear . . . [however, see the 2008 law on mediation and labor, discussed subsequently].

G. Conclusion

Following the compromises produced from prior drafts, the new employment contract law, if meaningfully enforced, should make workers feel more secure and employers less displeased with their new obligations. China's labor reforms appear to have found that "harmony" that retains the competitive advantages in labor which draw Western investment and yet still allow for China's continued economic growth. Still there will be the inevitable need for clarification, regulations, and amendments to eliminate new mischief, and – above all – increased and consistent enforcement of the new law. In final observation, the Employment Contract Law should force the discussion of future labor law reforms in China to a new and higher level, carrying with it the processes of *transparency* and *wide participation* that took place in its drafting.

Employment Discrimination

Ronald C. Brown[106]

. . . .

1. Protected Status and Hiring Practices

In China, there are a number of protected classes against which employment discrimination is prohibited. There also are some statuses that are largely unprotected, such as age and height and some that lack meaningful enforcement provisions, such as disability. Maternity and child labor and sexual harassment have special protections.

In China, hiring procedures often openly discriminate on the basis of gender, social origin, and age. It is not uncommon to see or hear the following solicitation in a recruitment ad: "[S]eeking an office clerk. Female, decent height, and appearance. All five facial organs must be in the right place (*wu guan duan zheng*)." Today in China, job advertisements with those facial requirements are widely seen. Such ads, of course, are but an explicit articulation of what many employers around the world take implicit note of in the employment hiring process. In practice, other factors in considering applicants and employees in China include sex, ethnicity, social origin, health, disability, age, or migrant status, but some of which are prohibited by Chinese labor laws. The 1994 Labor Law's antidiscrimination provisions covered only employees and not *applicants*. The EPL extends this coverage to include applicants.

Of course, inequality and discrimination against different categories of employees occur in every society. China is interesting both because of the diversity of workers

[106] Brown, *supra* note 100, at 75–77 [Footnotes omitted]; *see also* Ronald C. Brown, *China's Employment Discrimination Laws During Economic Transition*, 19 COLUM. J. ASIAN L. 362 (2006).

reportedly facing obstacles to equal employment opportunities and because of the sheer size of its labor force. That size makes the number of workers within each category economically significant both because of the possibility of an enormous explosion of arbitration and litigation and the potential waste of capable and employable human resources.

Since the 1994 passage of the Labor Law, protected statuses include "ethnic groups, race, sex, or religious belief." However, Article 14 exempts from protection "people of minority ethnic groups," along with the disabled and demobilized army men where "special stipulations in laws, rules and regulations" apply. In fact, other laws protect members of ethnic minority groups and the disabled in addition to gender and religion, disability/health conditions, and migrant worker status. The Regulations on Labor Market Management also prohibit discrimination in recruitment or employment based on race, gender, religion, and ethnicity.

The 2008 EPL both expands the categories of protection (ethnicity, communicable diseases not directly transmittable, and rural residences [migrant workers]) and reiterates protections to those in a protected status. The means of enforcement of the EPL is through litigation initiated by the employee; however, as there are no monetary damages provided in the law, claimants may be more inclined to use labor arbitration as applicable. The 2008 LCL also prohibits discrimination against employees within certain categories of occupational diseases and those, in certain circumstances, with not less than fifteen continuous years of working for the employer.

. . . .

QUESTIONS

1. Are labor rights in China more commonly found in employment contracts or in statutes and regulations?
2. Assuming the labor and employment laws are comprehensive, what is their practical shortcoming? How can lack of consistent enforcement be explained?[107]
3. What are the primary areas of employment discrimination? Do the laws adequately address these issues; if so how, if not, how are they not?
4. Discuss the various types of remedies for which the employer is liable should it violate the labor laws.

---

[107] *See* Sean Cooney, *China's Labor Law, Compliance, and Flaws in Implementing Institutions*, 49 J. INDUS. REL. 673 (2007); Anita Chan, *American Chicken Feet, Chinese Tires, and the Struggle for Labor Rights*, 18 NEW LAB. F. 57 (2010); Anita Chan & Kaxton Siu, *Analyzing Exploitation: The Mechanisms Underpinning Low Wages and Excessive Overtime in Chinese Factories*, 42 CRITICAL ASIAN STUD. 167 (2010).

3. *Labor Unions and Industrial Relations*

China has and allows only one labor union, the All-China Federation of Trade Unions (ACFTU). The union is organized on a national, regional, and local level and has multifunctional roles, though pressures exist for it to assume a more employee advocacy-oriented approach. Recently, China has sought to reintroduce the Workers' Congresses to deal with some of the labor and employment issues in the companies. Collective bargaining exists in its own form as described later; and its use may be on the increase. Workers' labor disputes in 2010 have resulted in strikes in greater numbers, particularly in foreign-invested companies such as in the auto industry.[108] Lastly, there is some evidence to suggest that the ACFTU may be increasing its cooperation and exchanges with foreign trade unions. Following is the ACFTU's self-description.

All China Federation of Trade Unions[109]

The All-China Federation of Trade Unions (ACFTU) is a mass organization of the working class formed voluntarily by the Chinese workers and staff members. Founded on May 1, 1925, it now has a membership of 134 million in more than 1.713 million primary trade union organizations. There are 31 provincial trade union federations, 10 national industrial unions, and 1.324 million grassroots trade union organizations (in 2.753 million enterprises and institutions) affiliated to the ACFTU.

The membership of the ACFTU totals 169.94 million (of which 61.778 million are women, accounting for 36.4% of the total number of union members, and 40.978 million are migrant workers, accounting for 24.1% of the total); the membership rate is 73.6%.

There are 543,000 full-time trade union cadres and 4.568 million part-time cadres.

It is stipulated in the Constitution of the Chinese Trade Unions that membership in trade unions is open to all manual and mental workers in enterprises, undertakings and offices inside China whose wages constitute their principal means of livelihood and who accept the Constitution of the Chinese Trade Unions irrespective of their nationality, race, sex, occupation, religious belief or educational background.

The Chinese trade unions apply the organizational principle of combining leadership along industrial lines with that on a locality basis. Now, under the leadership of ACFTU, there are 31 federations of trade unions of provinces, autonomous region, and

[108] Anita Chan, *Strikes in China's Export Industries in Comparative Perspective*, 65 CHINA J. 27 (2011).

[109] All-China Federation of Trade Unions (ACFTU), *Organizational Structure of the ACFTU* (Sept. 30, 2007), http://www.acftu.org.cn/template/10002/file.jsp?cid=64&aid=213 (last visited Sept. 30, 2010). For a historic and critical perspective of how the ACFTU operates, see Research Report, China Labor Bulletin, *Protecting Workers' Rights or Serving the Party: The way forward for China's trade unions* (March 2009), *available at* http://www.clb.org.hk/en/files/share/File/research_reports/acftu_report.pdf (last visited Sept. 30, 2010).

municipalities directly under the Central Government and 10 national industrial unions, namely,

1. National Committee of the Chinese Educational, Scientific, Cultural, Medical and Sports Workers' Union;
2. National Committee of the Chinese Seamen and Construction Workers' Union;
3. National Committee of the Chinese Energy and Chemical Workers' Union;
4. National Committee of the Chinese Machinery, Metallurgical and Building Material Workers' Union;
5. National Committee of the Chinese Defense Industry, Postal and Telecommunications Workers' Union;
6. National Committee of the Chinese Financial, Commercial, Light Industry, Textile and Tobacco Workers' Union;
7. National Committee of the Chinese Agricultural, Forestry and Water Conservancy Workers' Union;
8. All-China Federation of Railway Workers' Unions;
9. National Committee of the Chinese Aviation Workers' Union;
10. National Committee of the Chinese Banking Workers' Union.

The supreme power organ of the Chinese trade unions is the National Congress of Trade Unions. It is convened once every five years. The 14th National Congress of the Chinese Trade Unions was held in September 2003. Composed of 267 members, the Executive Committee is the power organ when the national congress is not in session, and it elects the chairman, vice-chairmen of the Executive Committee and members of the Presidium, thus forming the Presidium. When the Executive Committee is not in session, the Presidium comprising 39 members exercises its power. The Secretariat is set up under the Presidium and consists of a first secretary and a number of members who are elected from among the members of the Presidium. The Secretariat takes care of the routine work of the ACFTU.

The Chinese trade unions take the Constitution of the People's Republic of China as the fundamental criterion for their activities, conduct their work in an independent way and in accordance with relevant laws and the Constitution of the Chinese Trade Unions, and play an important role in the political, economic and social affairs of the country.

The fundamental task of the Chinese trade unions is to carry out the various social functions of the trade unions in line with the guiding principle of reflecting and safeguarding concrete interests of the workers and staff members in a better way while safeguarding the overall interests of the people throughout the whole country, and, united with the broad masses of workers and staff members, strive for the realization of China's socialist modernization. The major social functions of the Chinese trade unions are as follows: (1) to protect the legitimate interests and democratic rights of the workers and staff members, (2) to mobilize and organize the workers and staff members to take part in the construction and reform and accomplish the tasks in the economic and social development, (3) to represent and organize the workers and staff members to take part in the administration of the State and social affairs and to participate in the democratic management of enterprises, (4) to educate the workers and staff members to constantly improve their ideological and moral qualities and raise their scientific and cultural levels.

The basic duty of the Chinese trade unions is to protect the legitimate rights and interests of the workers and staff members. In the course of developing the socialist market economy, the Chinese trade unions, in accordance with the regulations of the State's Labour law and other relevant laws, actively safeguard workers' political rights, their right to work, and their material and cultural interests; participate in coordinating labour relations and regulating social contradictions and make efforts to promote the economic development and a long-term social stability of the country.

In their international affairs, the Chinese trade unions extensively develop friendly relations with the trade union organizations of various countries on the basis of the principles of independence, equality, mutual respect and non-interference in each other's internal affairs and irrespective of the differences in ideology and their international affiliations, for world peace, development, workers' rights and interests as well as social progress together with the workers and trade unions all over the world. Now the Chinese trade unions have established relations with more than 400 national trade union centres of over 130 countries.

Organizational Structures of the ACFTU

Membership

All manual and mental workers in enterprises, institutions, and government departments within the territory of China who rely on wages or salaries as their main source of income and who accept the constitution of Chinese trade unions, irrespective of their nationality, race, sex, occupation, religious belief, or educational background, are eligible to apply for membership of Chinese trade unions.

Anyone who wishes to join the trade union can file an application, which shall be discussed and accepted by his trade union group first and then approved by the grassroots trade union committee. All members have the freedom to withdraw from their trade unions, on condition that they put in a request to the grassroots trade union committee for approval. In case a member retires or becomes unemployed, his membership shall be retained and he is free of membership dues.

Union members enjoy the following rights: the right to elect and be elected as well as the right to vote; the right to criticize and supervise trade union organizations and their work and to demand the removal or replacement of any union personnel; the right to demand that trade unions relay their criticisms and suggestions concerning problems in the state and social life to departments concerned; the right to demand that trade union give them protection when their legitimate rights and interests are infringed upon; the right to enjoy preferential treatment in terms of culture, education, sports, tourism, convalescence and recuperation as well as incentives given by trade unions; and the right to participate in discussions about trade union work and issues of interest to workers.

Organizational System

Chinese trade unions apply, as their organizational and leadership structure, the principle of combining union organizations formed along the industrial line with those formed on the locality basis. Members in the same enterprise, institution and government department may organize into one grassroots trade union; an industrial union at the national or local level can be formed in one industry or several industries of similar nature, if necessary. Except for a few industries, industrial unions mainly follow the leadership of local All China Federation of Trade Unions trade unions, and accept the leadership of industrial unions at higher levels at the same time. The national committee of an industrial union is elected for a five-year term.

Local trade union federations in various provinces, autonomous regions, municipalities directly under the Central Government, autonomous prefectures, cities and counties exercise leadership over trade union organizations and industrial unions in their localities. The congresses of local trade unions in various parts of the country are held every five years. The ACFTU is the leading organ of local trade union federations and various national industrial unions.

The supreme organ of power of Chinese trade unions is the National Congress and the ACFTU Executive Committee it elects. The national congress of Chinese trade unions is held every five years. When the congress is in recess, the Executive Committee directs the work of trade unions around the country. The plenary meeting of the Executive Committee is held at least once a year. The ACFTU Presidium is elected by the Executive Committee and exercises the power of the Executive Committee when the latter is in recess. The Presidium elects its members to the Secretariat of the ACFTU, which takes care of its routine work.

The leadership of the ACFTU is composed of one chairman, vice-chairpersons and a number of secretariat members. The first secretary of the Secretariat attends to the routine work of the ACFTU.

All types of grassroots units including enterprises, institutions and government departments should establish trade union committees, which are elected for a three or five year term. A unit with a staff of less than 25 can establish a trade union committee either independently or in collaboration with other units, or elect an organizer or trade union chairman to take charge of the routine of the trade union committee. The membership meeting of the trade union committee is held once a year. Trade union committees are set up in branches of a factory or workshops; trade union groups are formed in work teams. A full-time trade union chairman shall be appointed if an enterprise or institution has more than 200 workers.

Trade unions at all levels establish an audit committee to inspect the trade union funds and property to ensure they are properly used and managed. Trade unions at all levels set up a women workers' committee to represent and protect women workers' rights and special interests.

Source of Funding

1. Union members contribute 0.5% of their monthly salaries as membership dues;
2. Enterprises, institutions, and government departments earmark 2% of their payroll for trade union funds;
3. Contributions from enterprises and undertakings run by trade unions;
4. Other

[The organizational structure of the ACFTU is provided in the figure on the next page.]

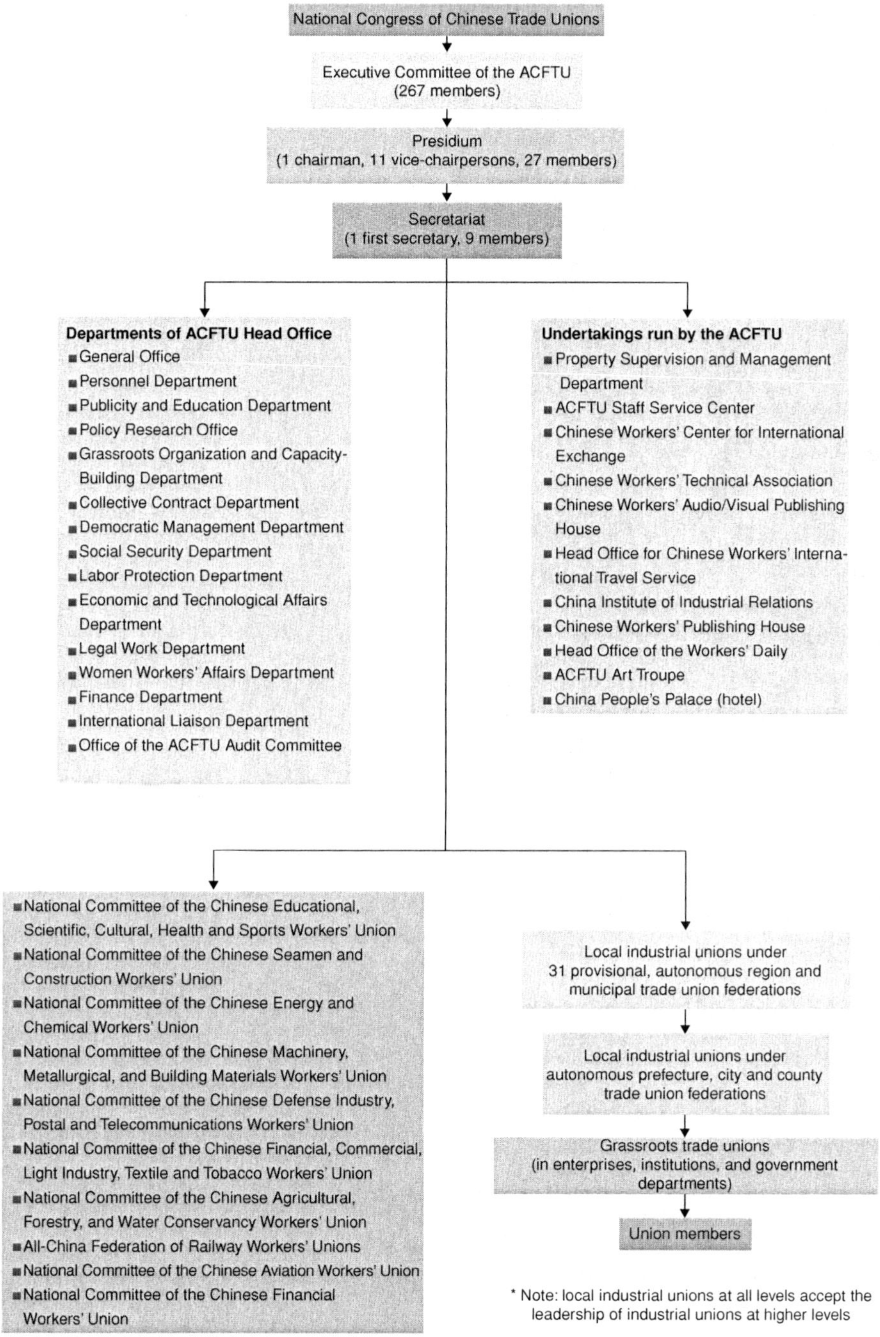
National Congress of Chinese Trade Unions
Executive Committee of the ACFTU (267 members)
Presidium (1 chairman, 11 vice-chairpersons, 27 members)
Secretariat (1 first secretary, 9 members)
Departments of ACFTU Head Office
General Office
Personnel Department
Publicity and Education Department
Policy Research Office
Grassroots Organization and Capacity-Building Department
Collective Contract Department
Democratic Management Department
Social Security Department
Labor Protection Department
Economic and Technological Affairs Department
Legal Work Department
Women Workers' Affairs Department
Finance Department
International Liaison Department
Office of the ACFTU Audit Committee
Undertakings run by the ACFTU
Property Supervision and Management Department
ACFTU Staff Service Center
Chinese Workers' Center for International Exchange
Chinese Workers' Technical Association
Chinese Workers' Audio/Visual Publishing House
Head Office for Chinese Workers' International Travel Service
China Institute of Industrial Relations
Chinese Workers' Publishing House
Head Office of the Workers' Daily
ACFTU Art Troupe
China People's Palace (hotel)
National Committee of the Chinese Educational, Scientific, Cultural, Health and Sports Workers' Union
National Committee of the Chinese Seamen and Construction Workers' Union
National Committee of the Chinese Energy and Chemical Workers' Union
National Committee of the Chinese Machinery, Metallurgical, and Building Materials Workers' Union
National Committee of the Chinese Defense Industry, Postal and Telecommunications Workers' Union
National Committee of the Chinese Financial, Commercial, Light Industry, Textile and Tobacco Workers' Union
National Committee of the Chinese Agricultural, Forestry, and Water Conservancy Workers' Union
All-China Federation of Railway Workers' Unions
National Committee of the Chinese Aviation Workers' Union
National Committee of the Chinese Financial Workers' Union
Local industrial unions under 31 provisional, autonomous region and municipal trade union federations
Local industrial unions under autonomous prefecture, city and county trade union federations
Grassroots trade unions (in enterprises, institutions, and government departments)
Union members
* Note: local industrial unions at all levels accept the leadership of industrial unions at higher levels

. . . .

COOPERATION WITH U.S. LABOR UNIONS. In recent years, the vestiges of Cold War antipathy[110] toward the ACFTU emanating from the AFL-CIO have given away to tentative explorations through exchanges and cooperation between American labor unions and the ACFTU. This is illustrated by the recent exchanges between American unions led by the Service Employees International Union (SEIU), and the cooperation agreement between China's Shanghai Municipal Trade Union Council, affiliated with the All-China Federation of Trade Unions (AFCTU) and the Los Angeles County Federation of Labor.[111] This is the first time a U.S. central labor council has established "sister-city" relations with a central labor council in China.[112] The union's case for increased cooperation between the labor unions in China and the United States is outlined next in testimony before the Congressional-Executive Commission on China.

Financial Crisis and the Changing Role of Workers in China[113]

Earl V. Brown, Jr.

. . . .

How Trade Unions Can Help:

[110] Ronald C. Brown, *East West Labor Union Cooperation; Falling Walls and Opening Doors: Communism, Cold War Era Barriers, and the Immigration Act of 1990*, 7 AMER. U. J. INT'L L. & POL'Y 1 (1991), *available at* http://www.auilr.org/pdf/7/7-1-1.pdf (last visited Sept. 30, 2010).

[111] UCLA Ctr. Lab. Research & Educ., *L.A. Labor Builds Solidarity in Shanghai*, LAB. EDUC. NEWS (2007), *available at* http://www.labor.ucla.edu/publications/newsletters/pdf/07sumfall.pdf (last visited Sept. 21, 2010). A more detailed description of the visit, from the Chinese point of view, is reported in Wang Jiao Ping, *Change to Win Delegation Visits China*, THE WORKERS' DAILY, May 22, 2007, http://www.ihlo.org/LRC/ACFTU/250907.html (last visited Sept. 21, 2010). *See also* New China News, *U.S. Trade Union Leaders: U.S. and China Trade Unions make their first move to deepen cooperations* (She Li-Na ed., May 23, 2007), *available at* http://www.clntranslations.org/file_download/13/CLNT_CtoWin_deeper_ cooperation.pdf (last visited Sept. 21, 2010) (trans. from Chinese version, available at http://www.shaanxi.cn/admin/pub_newsshow.asp?id=1056371&chid=100009 (last visited May 26, 2007)). For a report on the return visit by the Chinese, see SEIU Local 721, President's Report to the Executive Board (Feb. 18, 2009), *available at* http://localsdev.seiu.org/about/President's%20Report%202009-02.pdf (last visited Sept. 21, 2010).

[112] Renuka Rayasam, *SEIU's Andy Stern: Going Global*, US NEWS & WORLD REP., June 5, 2007, http://www.usnews.com/usnews/biztech/articles/070605/5stern.htm (last visited Sept. 21, 2010); *see also* Mei Fong & Kris Maher, *U.S. Labor Leader Aided China's Wal-Mart Coup*, WSJ, June 22, 2007, *available at* http://walmartwatch.org/blog/archives/wsj-u-s-labor-leader-aided-chinas-wal-mart-coup/ (last visited June 7, 2011); Kent Wong, *The AFL-CIO and China*, US/CHINA MEDIA BRIEF (2008), *available at* http://www.aasc.ucla.edu/uschina/ee_aflciochina.shtml (last visited Sept. 30, 2010) (urging the need for international labor union cooperation between the U.S. and China).

[113] Earl V. Brown, Jr., The Financial Crisis and the Changing Role of Workers in China, Roundtable before the Congressional-Executive Commission on China, 111 Congress, 1st Sess. (June 19, 2009), *available at* http://frwebgate.access.gpo.gov/cgi-bin/getdoc.cgi?dbname=111_house_hearings&docid=f:51190.wais (last visited Sept. 30, 2010) [Formatting altered]. The author is also the union and employee co-chair of the International Labor and Employment Committee of the American Bar Association.

A. Unions and Labor and Social Bargaining

China's workforce is not monochromatic. It includes millions of "unskilled" industrial workers; many are internal migrants of marginal legal status and limited access to schools, health care and housing. It also includes millions of high-tech workers and knowledge workers, service employees, workers in supply chains for foreign brands, and state enterprise workers and civil servants. Labor relations at US, Australian and EU companies are distinctly different from labor relations in Japanese companies, which in turn are different from labor relations in overseas Chinese and Korean companies. Many Chinese workers are under the age of 30, and have distinctive attitudes towards work and their rights at work and in society.

Each of these segments confronts different problems; in the private sector, however, too many workers do not have an accessible union to represent them. China has a web of official union institutions that parallel the state structure. The official union, ACFTU has not yet attained a wide presence in the private sector.

However, the 2008 law reforms afford this union a huge role in labor relations. Not only does the union have an important advisory and gatekeeper role in formulating labor law and regulations, it also has an invigorated mandate to collectively bargain for workers, including migrant workers. Curiously, the 2008 labor law reforms cover most workers within the boundaries of formal employment. This is in contrast to a global tendency to create exceptions to laws governing formal employment of such sweep that they undermine labor law and support the creation of a precarious and vulnerable work force without rights and collective voice. The ACFTU is now specifically charged with insuring the rights of all workers covered by the law. But the law has not created an institutional stage for this larger, encompassing role. China is also staging Hamlet without the Prince of Denmark, because it has not yet developed the necessary autonomous worker institutions at the grass roots to implement collective bargaining.

At the same time, China has experienced a significant growth of worker advocacy institutions and voices outside the union, in NGO worker centers, in GONGOs,[114] in legal aid societies, in universities and in government regulatory agencies. These articulate voices for worker rights often provide a welcome contrast to quiescence in the official union, and may spur the union to assume a more active role in worker representation and labor rights enforcement. Assuming a more active representational role in labor relations, however, will cause the official union to change profoundly. At a minimum, it will need to establish a grass roots presence; it must consult with and secure the allegiance of members; it must have a research department and it must organize employers under agreements in relevant labor markets, sometimes from the bottom up rather than from the top down.

The importance of this new role for the union in this downturn is clear. The union has invoked Article 41 of the 2008 Employee Contract Law to require prior notice to it by the employer of all lay-offs without exception. The union is further using the extensive notice and consultation provisions of Article 41 (governing mass lay-offs of 20 employees or over) to forestall and to initiate bargaining over lay-offs in this downturn.

[114] [Author's note.] GONGO is an organization created by a government and resembling an NGO, usually created for the purpose of promoting issues that the government wants to bring attention to. It is not a traditional NGO. *See government-operated nongovernmental organization (GONGO)*, BUSINESSDICTIONARY.COM, http://www.businessdictionary.com/definition/government-operated-non-governmental-organization-GONGO.html (last visited June 17, 2011).

Article 41 requires extensive consultation with the union and workers prior to any "mass lay-off", and protects certain older and ill employees from lay-off altogether. Via this Article, the union in some places is forcing employers to bargain towards a Singapore solution – reduced hours and/or furloughs instead of unilateral mass dismissals. Although this economic environment has forced many into a Hobson's choice, the law here does force the employer to bargain with the union and workers before initiating terminations. The employer cannot act unilaterally. Bargaining and labor negotiation is thus occurring prior to the creation of viable local unions and other similar industrial relations institutions. We cannot foreclose the possibility that the law will force the union into a more active representational role.

Our labor movement can assist in enhancing the capacity of interested officers and staff of the ACFTU union and other worker rights advocacy groups to begin to step into the industrial relations roles assigned unions and workers by the 2008 laws:

- We can provide expertise on structuring unions internally to equip them for the functions of organizing, bargaining, and rights advocacy;
- We can provide expertise and collaboration on occupational health and safety (OSH) technical issues, and on establishing worker capacity to enforce fundamental occupational health and safety norms via worker committees;
- We can share models on how to represent public sector employees;
- We can help enhance the capacity of activists to provide legal and other assistance to injured workers and their families, and the families of deceased workers;
- We can provide expertise on researching labor markets and employers;
- We can provide training in bargaining;
- We can provide training in organizing;
- We can provide models for broad rights advocacy;
- We have expertise in the distinct field of representing high-skilled technical workers and younger workers in service industries and working as contractors.

Labor movements in the US and elsewhere are uniquely equipped to provide such assistance as they possess the specific and time tested bargaining and organizing expertise that academics, development firms, and NGOs often lack. Mobilizing this experience during this crisis to assist internal actors advocating for worker rights in the Peoples' Republic of China will enable us to participate in addressing, in a targeted way, the universal problems of the global economy – lack of stable employment, competition based on labor law avoidance, and lack of worker voice and purchasing power – as well as assist our Chinese counterparts in addressing those very problems in China. China also needs a labor movement that is also capable of acting outside the formal employment relationship to advocate for and to represent marginalized informal sector workers. The US labor movement has made some strides in giving voice to informal and marginalized wage earners by establishing worker centers and networks of advocates and service providers that operate outside traditional craft and other formal union categories. Interaction between US and Chinese advocates for marginalized workers would be helpful to both sides. In this respect, the Solidarity Center has brought Chinese union lawyers and labor rights activists to US worker rights centers and initiated a dialogue which we hope will continue on how to provide voice to and enforce law on behalf of marginalized workers.

We should understand that EU and Japanese models of industrial relations are also relevant, and that we are not internal actors in China. Nonetheless, Chinese discourse about industrial relations has reached the stage where concrete private sector trade union expertise and skills are needed to assist in building capacity in Chinese labor institutions of all kinds – in the formal union, in worker centers, NGOs, and in legal aid institutions.

This crisis has established that economics premised on the race to the bottom – on relentlessly depressing labor costs and living standards – is not sustainable. One answer to this imbalanced global economy is an invigorated Chinese labor movement. We should seek a role in reversing the race to the bottom with the aid of invigorated labor movements in China, both for the sake of U.S. workers and Chinese workers. This necessarily entails working appropriately with counterparts in China.

Labor, Lawyers and the Rule of Law, Even in Crisis Times

The labor issue in China is also at the heart of a broad debate about human rights and the rule of law. Until 2008, many employers in China simply discounted labor law compliance. Other employers under imperatives to comply strictly with PRC law, such as foreign employers with their own legal requirements to comply with Chinese law, or those subject to consumer pressure, were constantly undermined competitively by employers who violated Chinese labor norms. This fueled a larger problem: a culture of impunity with regards to compliance with the law. While aspects of labor and employment law, such as the technicalities regarding workers' compensation and work place health and safety may seem arcane, they are critical in China, where industrial death, disease and injury remain at high levels. Unregulated labor competition means that workers are maimed and slaughtered to save on labor costs. Insuring that effective OSH and worker compensation laws and regulations are in place and enforced is central to a rule of law culture in China as elsewhere.

US union lawyers and activists can assist Chinese counterparts in union, NGO and legal aid society staffs with concrete and particular practice-based advice on infusing rule of law norms into workers' compensation structures, into regulation of work hazards in dangerous industries such as mining, and into providing for social security and protection within the framework of a private economy.

Further, US union lawyers and their colleagues can engage in a continuous dialogue on Chinese labor law compliance with US and other international lawyers who represent multinationals in China. The Solidarity Center has initiated just such a dialogue through participation in relevant ABA committees and finds that foreign lawyers representing employers in China have openly committed to advising compliance with PRC labor law and regulations. This is a major step – in which responsible employers and responsible employer counsel play an indispensable role – towards pushing back the culture of noncompliance and impunity in labor law. Foreign employers have thus often become a force for labor law compliance. Of course, there are many countervailing examples of foreign employers violating basic labor norms.

As noted above, younger and more highly skilled workers in China seem to part of the growth of regional "civil" rights movement among younger workers in East and South East Asia. This movement arises from expectations about autonomy and individual choice that are becoming widespread among all younger workers, and among more skilled workers like IT workers and airline pilots. Many elements of the 2008 labor law reforms address the needs of young and more skilled workers, and they have been used by those workers, both spontaneously and with assistance of union and legal aid staff.

Union lawyers and staff in the US movement have attained considerable expertise in representing and reaching out to such workers and can be of assistance.

There is a widely acknowledged problem in China with enforcement of judgments. In this respect, US trade union lawyers can assist Chinese counterparts on the staff of unions, legal aid societies and NGOs to enforce wage and worker compensation judgments. In enforcing judgments, workers' lawyers may find allies in the business community who also encounter this very problem.

The need to include the labor movement in the core of rule of law dialogue has become even more acute given the massive increases in international and internal migration of workers in the past decade. These migrant peasant-workers are invariable legally disenfranchised and cut off from the most basic rule of law institutions. The international labor movement and its allies realize that the rule of law cannot co-exist with huge populations of marginalized and abused migrant workers cut off from justice institutions and any means of redressing fundamental deprivations of human and worker rights.

The US and international trade union movements can play, by virtue of their institutional networks, a broad role in providing forums and assistance to Chinese worker rights advocates regarding enforcement of rights across national boundaries, against foreign employers, or in enforcing the rights of the ever increasing number of Chinese guest workers abroad. No other institution can match the capacity of the international labor movement to reach across the globe and down into societies through affiliates.

Conclusion

We should assist Chinese worker rights advocates in unions, law faculties, NGOs and legal aid societies to take up the invitation presented by 2008 labor law reforms to implement the mandate for collective bargaining. In doing so, we will be contributing in a modest way to solutions for Chinese workers and workers everywhere in this global crisis sparked by a race to the bottom that has gone too low.

Our assistance should be delivered with deference to the agency of our Chinese colleagues, and with complete awareness that only the Chinese will determine the contours of their labor relations system. Since this global crisis has exposed "Western" and Asian workers, and workers everywhere, to the dire effects of the unregulated race to the bottom, we can contribute to overcoming the crisis by technical assistance in the area of industrial relations and collective bargaining.

WORKERS' CONGRESSES

Staff and Workers Representatives Congress under Chinese Labour Law Introduction[115] .

The aim of this research paper is to present the legal context of an aspect of Chinese industrial relations that is rarely mentioned outside China, let alone understood. The

[115] *Staff and Workers Representatives Congress under Chinese Labor Law Introduction*, ILHO, http://www.ihlo.org/LRC/ACFTU/000804.html (last visited June 17, 2011). For another good introduction, see Zhu Xiaoyang & Anita Chan, *Staff and Workers' Representative Congress: An Institutionalized Channel for Expression of Employees' Interests?*, 37 CHINESE SOC. & ANTHROPOLOGY 6 (2005).

term *zhigong daibiao dahui* is generally translated as 'staff and workers representatives' congress', which we have shortened to SWRC.

The working title for this project was originally "'Workers' Councils under Chinese Labour Law'. However, this is confusing on two fronts. Firstly, the term "workers' council" is too similar in name to the institution of Works Councils that operate under law in Germany and are a feature of labour relations in some multinational corporations. Secondly it is evocative of the phenomenon of Workers' Councils that tend to emerge during profound social unrest. Such bodies are generally shop-floor based committees of workers that may or may not fall under trade union control. Their emergence is usually indicative of a revolutionary challenge to the political and economic order. In contrast, SWRCs are a top-down institution the purpose of which is to head off social upheaval, not lead or reflect it. However, as we discuss in the later stages of this paper, workers often refer to the SWRCs when they take on the State and/or employer in China.

The format of this paper is as follows. This introduction will be followed by an examination of the relevant laws and regulations that govern SWRCs and, where appropriate, provide examples of how workers have attempted to use the institution to defend wages and conditions. This format will hopefully also shed light on the relationship between 'democratic management', (see below) the official trade union (ACFTU) and the SWRCs.

The methodology has been to use exclusively Chinese-language research material in the form of academic papers, laws, and media reports and meetings with mainland labour law experts as well as interviews with workers.

Before concluding this introduction, we attempt to summarise the official discourse on how SWRCs fit into labour relations in China, firstly with regard to state-owned and collectively-owned enterprises (SOEs and COEs) and then in relation to foreign-invested and private enterprises.

In the former, they are seen as the basis and main form of so-called "democratic management" (*minzhu guanli*). Democratic management refers to the traditional and still constitutionally-recognised concept that:

> All working people in State-owned enterprises and in urban and rural economic collectives should perform their tasks with an attitude consonant with their status as masters of the country.

In theory, SWRCs are one of the vehicles through which workers can give concrete expression to their status as "masters of the country". At the same time, democratic management is not an institution through which workers decide on enterprise policy – as has historically been the case under the aforementioned "workers' councils" – but rather a channel through which workers can, in certain carefully defined and regulated circumstances, veto or reject management decisions. SWRCs give form to the expression of such rights.

In foreign-invested and private enterprises, democratic management is scaled down to trade unions having the right to sit on management boards, carry out normal trade union activities, and to merely 'discuss' issues related to workers' rights in the enterprise.

It should be noted that the increasing privatisation of state-owned enterprises (SOEs) and hazy ownership status of collectively-owned enterprises (COEs) limit the usefulness of these summaries. In a country where the issue of ownership remains at the apex of with the provisions of laws, rules and regulations, take part in democratic China's political struggles at all levels – from the courts, to the politburo to the shop floor and the street – defining and explaining the actual status of enterprise ownership would be another paper altogether.

SWRCs and the Law

Apart from the Constitution itself, there are two laws which refer to democratic management in general and SWRCs in any detail. There are also a crucial set of administrative regulations that set out a detailed procedural framework for SWRCs in publicly-owned enterprises (state and collective), their relationship with trade unions and the rights and duties of worker's representatives. The two laws are the Labour Law (1995) and Trade Union Law (2001), and the regulations are entitled Regulations on SWRCs in public-owned enterprises (hereafter Regulations). Also important is Article 20 of the Bankruptcy Law (Trial Implementation) 1988, which stipulates that the views of the staff and workers' congress must be actively listened to prior to a formal declaration of bankruptcy. For reasons of space, this paper will not examine the Company Law which addresses democratic management in both public and private companies but only makes brief reference to the actual term "democratic management" (Article 16). It should be noted that worker representation either on the company board or shareholders' committee is mentioned fairly extensively in the Company Law (1993, amended 1999) and is a topic worthy of further research by trade unions.

The Labour Law

There are two articles in the national labour law that make reference to SWRCs. Article 8 states that:

> Labourers shall, through the assembly of staff and workers or their congress, or other forms in accordance with the provisions of laws, rules and regulations, take part in democratic management or consult with the employing units on an equal footing about protection of the legitimate rights and interests of labourers.

There are two important points. The Labour Law is applicable to all types of enterprise which is why Article 8 refers to the assembly of staff and workers or their congress – an SWRC. The former is included because most private- or foreign-invested enterprises do not have SWRCs and so democratic management is meant to proceed via an assembly of all staff and workers. Except in small-scale enterprises this would obviously be an unwieldy and impractical arrangement. Indeed in private and foreign-invested enterprises, the All China Federation of Trade Unions (ACFTU) has prioritised the setting up of union branches – at least in name – and SWRCs are seen as something to tackle further down the road to regulate industrial relations in the private sector. SWRCs are thus just one of four manifestations of democratic management that focuses on the trade union role. These are:

- The establishment of a regular management-trade union consultation system to discuss issues related to management, labour, wages, and workers' welfare.
- Trade union participation in company board meetings and the union's right to question board decisions related to the bonuses and punishment, wages, welfare, labour protection, and labour insurance.

- The union's duty to reflect its members' opinions on major company issues such as production plans and division of labour, occupational safety and health, and training.
- The establishment of an SWRC system to discuss all matters relating to workers' rights in the enterprise.

The second point to note is that Article 8 makes no reference of the SWRC representing – or upholding – workers' interests. We will expand on this point in the section on SWRC regulations, but it needs to be stressed that the SWRC is not meant as an alternative to trade unions and indeed its structure rules out any potential capacity to represent class, specifically working class, interests.

This said, Article 33 presents an opportunity for a possibly more concrete role for the SWRC should an employer agree to negotiate a collective contract:

> The staff and workers of an enterprise as one party may conclude a collective contract with the enterprise on matters relating to labour remuneration, working hours, rest and vacations, occupational safety and health, and insurance and welfare. The draft collective contract shall be submitted to the congress of the staff and workers or to all the staff and workers for discussion and adoption.

It is important to note that the employer is not legally obliged to provide or begin negotiations for a contract with his or her workforce. The onus is on the workers to take the initiative. This lack of compulsion becomes a major obstacle when placed in the political context of China lacking freedom of association and the nature of the ACFTU. More positively however, there is some room to manoeuvre. At least on paper, workers can combine and demand a collective contract in the absence of the ACFTU and if the enterprise refuses, it is breaking the law.

Such an act of combination could theoretically be extended to take organisational form: a workers' committee operating under the auspices of a SWRC or even a preparatory committee to set up an SWRC. Research suggests that such a scenario has not been seen to date. This doesn't mean that it can't happen, especially in the context of so many large multinationals who deal with and sign collective contracts with their employees in other countries. Article 33 also states:

> A collective contract shall be concluded by the trade union on behalf of the staff and workers with the enterprise; in an enterprise where the trade union has not yet been set up, such contract shall be concluded by the representatives elected by the staff and workers with the enterprise.

As always, political realities can easily force such idealistic initiatives, based as they are on what appear to be legal loopholes, back into an oppressive actuality. Nevertheless SWRCs, in the context of China's national labour law at least, have the capacity to influence the process of forming a collective contract with an employer.

The Trade Union Law (TUL)

TUL goes some way to clarify the often confusing relationship between the SWRC and the trade union itself. Article 6 awards the trade union the role of organising workers and to participate in democratic decision-making, management, and supervision. The

SWRC is the principle conduit for such activity. Article 20 reaffirms the SWRC's role of deliberating on and approving a collective contract negotiated by the trade union. It is interesting to note that no mention is made of a meeting of union members to approve such a contract, which is perhaps a tacit acknowledgement of the ACFTU's organisational weakness on the shop floor, particularly in the private sector.

Articles 35 and 36 speak to the complex interface between ownership, trade union, and SWRC, which we examine more closely when we come to the SWRC regulations. After reaffirming that the "congress of the workers and staff members is the basic form of democratic management of the enterprise and the organ by which the workers and staff members exercise their right to democratic management," Article 35 states:

> The trade union committee of the State-owned enterprise is the working body of the congress of the workers and staff members and takes care of the day-to-day work of the congress, checks and supervises the implementation of the resolutions adopted by the congress.

The sentence successfully puts the running of the SWRC into the hands of the union. In theory this maintains workers' status as 'masters of the enterprise' as – again in law and theory as opposed to practice – the SWRC is made up of workers, technicians, and managers in varying proportions. By awarding the day-to-day running of the SWRC to a workers' organisation (the union) the law is passing a great deal of potential power to that organisation. No doubt law makers felt able to do this safe in the knowledge that Article 10 of the same TUL excludes independent workers' organisations at all levels and furthermore the ACFTU's own constitution entirely accepts that its activities are guided and led by the main source of power in Chinese society, the Chinese Communist Party.

Article 36 refers to COEs and brings the SWRC and the trade union even closer together:

> The trade union committee of a collectively-owned enterprise shall support and organise the participation of the workers and staff members in democratic management and democratic supervision, and defend their rights in electing, removing managerial personnel and deciding on major questions concerning operation and management.

The exact definition of a collectively owned enterprise is difficult. In urban areas COEs are generally small-scale SOEs nominally 'owned' by the workers and subject to the same political culture as SOEs. In the countryside COEs became known as township and village enterprises (TVEs) during the 1980s. Despite offering generally dreadful working conditions, they soaked up huge amounts of rural surplus labour throughout the eighties and first half of the nineties. Most of the township enterprises were operated by township and town governments, but a large number of very small units were operated by private cooperative organisations called 'rural economic unions'.

The fact is that most rural COEs (later TVEs) do not have trade unions or SWRCs. And moreover, the specific and seemingly spectacular powers that Article 36 gives to the trade union and SWRC in COEs are duplicated in the regulations on SWRCs, which apply to all publicly-owned enterprises' powers anyway.

Regulations on SWRCs in publicly-owned enterprises (*Quan min suo you zhi gongye qiye zhigong daibiao dahui tiaoli*)

These important regulations became effective in 1986. This was the same year that enterprise managers were given dramatically expanded power over hire and fire, wages and working conditions in SOEs. The long haul to smashing the 'iron rice bowl' or job security was officially embarked upon and the resurrection of SWRCs, which had been dormant for three decades, was clearly aimed at providing a check on the raw new power of SOE managers. A comparison of the industrial landscape of 1986 with that of today (2004) would reveal extraordinary changes as SWRCs along with the ACFTU have proved largely incapable of defending workers' interests against either government policies or illegal corruption.

But if the Regulations were introduced as an attempt to place a check on the authority of managers, avoid abuses, and hopefully head-off labour unrest which the CCP undoubtedly saw coming, their failure does not mean they are going to go away anymore than increased management autonomy has done. Despite their being something of a political maverick in a country whose current policies are mostly concomitant with its membership of the World Trade Organisation, the State in general, the ACFTU in particular, and the working class on occasion continue to see a future in both democratic management and SWRCs that distinguishes the 'socialist market economy' from other 'capitalist' economies.

The Regulations are divided into five chapters and 29 articles. This section will summarise and comment on the most important articles – mainly contained, for the purposes of this report, in the first three chapters.

Chapter One: General Principles

Article 3: States that the trade union looks after the day-to-day running of the SWRC. This implies that without a trade union, an SWRC cannot function and this certainly seems to be the case in practice. However, as noted above, other regulations state that in enterprises where a trade union does not exist, important decisions such as approval of collective contracts can be put to a congress of staff and workers or their representatives. As these regulations appear to be exclusively addressed to publicly-owned urban enterprises, the drafters appear to have assumed a trade union is in operation, an assumption that has since proved to be incorrect, especially after the mass lay-offs of the nineties "washed away", to use the words of former chairman of the ACFTU, so many trade union branches.

Article 4: States that an SWRC shall accept the ideological leadership of the enterprise's Party Committee. Obviously the impact of this clause, especially when workers are struggling against a 'false' bankruptcy of their SOE, depends on the situation on the ground. Generally speaking, it can be assumed that an enterprise Party Committee is going to back and implement State policy and that the ideological influence it exerts over the SWRC is going to be negative in terms of defending jobs and conditions from restructuring, privatisation and bankruptcy.

Chapter Two: Rights

Article 7 maps out five basic rights. The right to:

Consider and make suggestions on major production-related issues. Although management is responsible for drawing up and implementing company plans and proposals, it is legally obliged to consider the views of the SWRC on matters pertaining to operational policy, long term plans, annual reports, staff training, and wage allocation.

Examine and Approve. Namely enterprise rules and regulations pertaining to wages adjustments, bonus allocations, labour protection, and general bonus and punishment schemes. The SWRC has the right to veto any management decision on these matters.

Consider and decide on matters pertaining to workers' housing and general welfare. Obviously the dramatic selling off of enterprise housing in home ownership reforms as well as the replacement of enterprise welfare with pay-as-you-earn social insurance schemes have substantially reduced the capacity of this right which now mainly deals with charity and welfare relief rather than administering social insurance schemes.

The right to evaluate and monitor. The SWRC has the right to evaluate the performance of "leading cadres", a category which includes factory management right up to and including factory director. The evaluation includes suggestions on management pay levels and the promotion or dismissal of managers.

The right to elect the factory leader. While the final decision that results from a vote has to be approved by relevant local government departments, this right along with the right to dismiss a manager provides the SWRC with considerable potential power – on paper at least.

These rights must be tempered with the fact that all major decisions require the approval of "relevant" government departments. Moreover, Article Six states that the SWRCs shall follow the organising principle of democratic centralism and thus each decision must be in line with leadership policy – i.e. government policy. As the ACFTU serves as the SWRC "operating mechanism" (*gongzuo jigou*) and is in charge of day-to-day running of the SWRC, it is more or less inconceivable that it will defend or implement an SWRC decision that goes against government policy.

. . . .

Chapter Three: Staff and Worker Representatives

. . . .

According to Article 10, representatives are directly elected from different shifts and workshops within a factory. In the case of large-scale SOE with more than one factory, candidates are elected on the basis of plant sites and workshops. In effect workers are split up into groups according to the nature of their work in the factory, and/or the workshop they are employed in and/or their shift times.

Article 12 illustrates the cross-class nature of SWRCs and our earlier assertion that they do not have either the capacity or legal space to defend working class interests as separate and independent. This is not to say, as can be seen by the example cited above, that they are always neutral in the face of privatisation. Article 12 stipulates that staff and worker representatives shall be selected, via direct election from shop floor workers, technicians, managerial personnel, leading cadres (senior managers) and other divisions of staff and workers in the factory. Generally speaking, the numbers of leading administrative personnel shall not exceed more than a fifth of the overall number of representatives. Young workers and women shall be represented in proportion to their numbers at the plant.

Chapters four, five and six of the Regulations deal mainly with the administrative procedures such as times of meetings, reporting, the establishment of small groups to work on certain issues and the trade unions' responsibility to educate SWRC delegates.

Conclusion

This paper has confined itself to explaining the basic functions and procedures of SWRCs under Chinese labour law, their political context in the form of democratic management and also briefly mentioned two examples of how they have become embroiled in disputes between laid off SOE workers and SOE management and/or the State. A longer and more detailed report would certainly reveal more examples of SWRCs' role in labour disputes and allow a more thorough appraisal of whether they are a viable channel of support to Chinese workers. Our conclusion is that SWRCs are undeniably a concept from the command economy that has been practically panel-beaten into the 'socialist market economy'. The inevitable ideological dents notwithstanding, their legal status provides a forum at which workers assemble in the work place specifically to discuss work place labour rights issues. In this context, the point is not so much the inherent weaknesses in the institution itself, but the capacity for individual workers to make use of it and forge a collective critical mass that can translate into a collective voice at the very least.

In 2008, the ACFTU issued a new call for use of workers' representative congresses and promulgated draft regulations for review by the State Council.[116] The draft Regulations for the Democratic Management of Enterprises indicate that companies with at least 100 employees may be required to establish employee representative congresses – collective employee representation bodies that meet once or twice a year to discuss employee-related matters.[117] The 2008 Labor Contract Law further empowered the workers' representative congress to be consulted before an employer may implement rules or rule changes.[118] "Shanghai recently introduced a new 'Guiding Opinion' to increase the power of 'Staff and Workers' Representative Congresses' (or simply 'workers congresses') in the city.[119] 'Workers' congresses' are similar to Western European 'works councils' and, at least in principle, ensure representatives of ordinary workers a voice in enterprise decision making. Precursors

[116] Brown, *supra* note 100, at 46–47.

[117] Phil Taylor, *Employment: Unions increase the pressure*, CHINA L. & PRAC., Dec. 9, 2009, *available at* 2009 WLNR 26474605; first appeared in the International Law Office, www.internationallawoffice.com Andreas W. Lauffs et al., *ACFTU pushes forward on collective bargaining and democratic management*, INT'L L. OFF. (Sept. 8, 2010), (on file with author), *available at* http://www.internationallawoffice.com/newsletters/detail.aspx?g=a1b1d295-897e-472f-ab07-ce84663dcc8b (last visited Sept. 30, 2010).

[118] LABOR CONTRACT LAW, art. 4 (2008) (P.R.C.).

[119] Regulations of the Shanghai Municipality on the Workers Congress, *available at* http://shwomen.eastday.com/renda/node5902/node5908/node6573/u1a1729811.html. *See also* Manfred Elfstrom, *New Guidelines for Shanghai Staff and Workers Representative Congresses*, LABOR IS NOT A COMMODITY (July 23, 2008), http://laborrightsblog.typepad.com/international_labor_right/2008/07/according-to-an.html (last visited Oct. 3, 2010).

of today's congresses were created as far back as 1949 and the system was revived during the early reform era (. . .)."[120]

COLLECTIVE BARGAINING. Collective contracts have existed for many years, but they most usually were concluded without the Western notions of collective "bargaining" and their content often merely reflected statutory requirements. This has to do with the nature and role of China's only union, the ACFTU. Most collective contracts, until recently, have largely consisted of existing statutory requirements, as described later. The legal framework for meaningful negotiations may be in place, as is argued next, and all that is needed are some modifications and meaningful law enforcement. The ACFTU is aggressively promoting collective negotiations and has provided manpower and funds in pursuit of having a high percentage of unionized workplaces with collective contracts. There are indications that changes to permit increased collective bargaining and even strikes are being moved forward by government law makers.[121] Currently, there is no legal prohibition on strikes; the legal role of the union is to mediate an end to a strike.

The China Daily reports, "[T]he All-China Federation of Trade Unions (ACFTU) is working to implement a collective-bargaining system nationwide among the trade union-established enterprises in China by 2012. According to the goal set up by the union, collective contracts are to be signed in more than sixty percent of enterprises in China by the end of 2010, and more than eighty percent by 2011. At present, thirteen cities and provinces in China are developing collective bargaining, and twenty-three cities and provinces have enacted rules and regulations on collective bargaining. According to the union, a special committee consisting of about 60,000 members was put together by the ACFTU to negotiate the wage issues between enterprises and employees across the country. ACFTU also planned to invest 100 million yuan in the first batch of trial cities for collective bargaining."[122]

---

[120] *Id.* Shanghai presently has workers congresses in 7479 state-owned enterprises, of which 6088 or 81.4 percent are carrying out "democratic evaluations." *Id.*

[121] "In a somewhat unexpected move, Guangzhou businessman and national legislator, Zeng Qinghong, has made a proposal to the National People's Congress (NPC) to protect the right of Chinese workers to go on strike. Zeng pointed out that, in a market economy, the right to strike should be a basic right of workers and a natural adjunct to the right to work. Moreover, he said, it was a widely recognized civil right in many developed countries and was urgently needed in China in order to ensure social stability and the healthy development of labor relations and the legal system. Zeng, who is the general manger of the Guangzhou Automobile Group, played an important role as a mediator in the Nanhai Honda strike in Foshan last summer, and is keenly aware of the impact of strikes on the automotive industry." *Chinese legislator calls for restoration of the right to strike*, China Labor Bulletin (Mar. 11, 2011), *available at* http://www.clb.org.hk/en/node/101005 (last visited June 7, 2011).

[122] Chen Ziyan, *Collective bargaining a goal for Chinese unions*, China Daily, July 29, 2010, *available at* http://www.chinadaily.com.cn/china/2010-07/29/content_11067381.htm (last visited Sept. 30, 2010). Anita Chan, *Organizing Wal-Mart in China: Two Steps Forward, One Step Back for China's Unions*, 16 New Lab. F. 87 (2007).

ACFTU Pushes Forward on Collective Bargaining and Democratic Management[123]

Andreas W. Lauffs, Jonathan Isaacs, Bofu An

The government and the All-China Federation of Trade Unions (ACFTU) have been preparing for a further push for the implementation of collective bargaining and an increase in what they describe as "democratic management" at all companies. They are clearly still considering how to implement the policy and no practical steps have been taken. However, significant recent developments indicate what employers may expect.

At national level, the ACFTU and the National People's Congress are reportedly considering an amendment to the Labour Union Law, which would probably be passed into law by the second half of 2011. Among other things, the draft amendments are understood to stipulate more detailed procedures for forming an employee representative council. Such a move would be intended to strengthen democratic management at enterprises and encourage more collective bargaining at industry level – at present, most collective bargaining is at company level. Employee representative councils are like works councils and normally co-exist with enterprise unions.

Another amendment reportedly under discussion would require all companies to pay the union fee (equivalent to 2% of the company's payroll) to the local tax bureau, rather than directly to the company union's bank account, as is the case in most cities. This would give the government greater control over the payment and allocation of union fees, preventing companies from negotiating with the ACFTU for lower fees. In a related local development, local authorities and ACFTU officials in Beijing are planning for Beijing to follow other localities, such as Jiangsu province, in requiring companies without unions to pay a union preparation fee – which would be the same amount as the union fee – to the local tax bureau.

In Guangdong province, a third draft of the Guangdong Enterprise Democratic Management Regulations was posted on the provincial government's website for public comment on August 23, 2010. The draft sets out a detailed procedure for forming an employee representative council, as well as a description of a council's powers. It also stipulates that a company may be forced to engage in collective wage bargaining if at least one-third of the employees so request. If the company does not respond to the request within 15 days and fails to provide the required conditions or information for collective bargaining (or if it bargains in bad faith), and as a result a strike or work slowdown takes place, the employer may not terminate the striking employees. If implemented, this would be the first specific protection in legislation for striking workers since the right to strike was omitted from the 1982 Constitution. However, the draft states that if employees strike without first requesting collective bargaining or during collective bargaining, they may face legal consequences.

The Shenzhen People's Congress issued a draft of the Shenzhen Economic Zone Collective Bargaining Regulations for public comment in August 2010. Under the draft, employees may ask the employer to provide information and materials necessary for collective bargaining; except in a few narrowly defined cases, such a request may not be unjustifiably refused. The draft regulations also prohibit collective bargaining in bad faith, which includes either party (i) willfully delaying the bargaining process by focusing on minor procedural issues, or (ii) persistently sticking to its position or resisting the

[123] Lauffs et al, *supra* note 117.

other party's reasonable proposals without justification. If employers conduct collective bargaining in bad faith and fail to correct the violation as ordered by the competent labour bureau, they may be fined up to Rmb 50,000.

In a related development, a draft of the Payment of Wage Regulations is under review at the national level. It reportedly contains a provision that if an employer unjustifiably declines its employees' request for collective bargaining over wages and fails to correct such violations within the period determined by the competent authorities, it may be fined up to Rmb 200,000.

The national ACFTU, as well as the Beijing ACFTU, have publicly announced that they are considering plans to have the union chairman's salary paid directly by the ACFTU, rather than the company, in order to ensure independence from company pressure. The ACFTU has also discussed training professional collective bargaining representatives to be dispatched to companies to assist employees with collective bargaining, and has even contemplated sending in individuals from outside companies to be union chairmen.

China's Collective Contract Provisions: Can Collective Negotiations Embody Collective Bargaining?[124]

Ronald C. Brown

Introduction

. . . .

This article examines whether China's new "collective negotiations" law, in the context of Chinese conditions, can blossom into "collective bargaining," as referenced by International Labor Organization (ILO) standards and compared with U.S. approaches. Admittedly, it is hard for many to imagine that multinational corporations such as Wal-Mart, Samsung, Dell, along with increasing numbers of Chinese domestic companies, could be negotiating labor terms and benefits above statutory minimums. It is harder, perhaps, to convince the Chinese that in doing so, China can still maintain its areas of comparative advantage. However, recent developments in China's labor legislation suggest that, beyond sheer imagination, Chinese laborers now seem more enabled than ever to negotiate or bargain their working standards.

On May 1, 2004, Provisions on Collective Contract (Provisions) issued by the Ministry of Labor and Social Security (MOLSS) became effective on a national level. These Provisions build upon China's experience since the mid-1980s with individual labor contracts and with the 1994 Labor Law's mandate to create a system of collective contracts. The 2004 Provisions provide that a collective contract can be negotiated on behalf of the employees to protect their employment and workplace interests. Prior to 2004, several hundred thousand collective contracts, which covered seventy-six million workers, were

[124] Ronald C. Brown, *China's Collective Contract Provisions: Can Collective Negotiations Embody Collective Bargaining?* 16 Duke J. Comp. & Int'l L. 35 (2006) [Footnotes omitted].

already in existence under earlier regulations. As will be discussed, many of these collective contracts could be described as bare-boned reflections of labor statutory minimums. In contrast, the 2004 Provisions provide more detail and apparently seek to eliminate some of the obstacles observed under the earlier negotiated agreements and to achieve more comprehensive contracts.

The 2004 Provisions authorize employees to initiate the process through more authentic representatives to prepare proposals on a wide scope of subjects clearly beyond the usual statutory labor standards and protections. The process of negotiations is delineated, with "good faith" requirements built in to facilitate cooperative exchanges of proposals. The government's Labor Bureaus are given regulatory responsibility to supervise and intervene in the negotiations to ensure fair dealing. They also are authorized to resolve disputes arising prior to final agreement.

Lastly, there is a process of formality in "finalizing" the collective contract. The enforcement of the rights arising under this concluded contract are the same as those arising under the law regulating labor contracts, both of which utilize dispute resolution procedures within the enterprise, government-administered labor arbitration and the courts.

This article examines the 2004 Provisions on collective negotiations, sets forth some of the issues of the current Provisions, and draws comparative references to collective bargaining approaches in the United States and under the ILO's labor standards; discusses their likely viability in China; and proposes a number of labor reform "possibilities," when viewed in the context of China's existing and evolving labor law environment.

I. China's 2004 Collective Contract Provisions

A. *Legal Origins*

The new collective negotiation Provisions grew from a rather short legal history. There was interest by China's trade union, the All China Federation of Trade Unions (ACFTU), in the early 1990s and it began to experiment with collective negotiations. [This experimentation continues as of 2010[125]]. The 1992 Trade Union Law in fact first authorized unions at the enterprise level to conclude collective contracts with the employer. The 1994 Labor Law further formalized the process and provided that the ACFTU was responsible to utilize this system nationally. The Trade Union Law as amended in 2001 continued to strengthen the union's mandate in collective wage negotiations. Toward the end of 2001, the ACFTU reported it had over 510,000 such collective agreements at the enterprise level covering over 75 million workers.

Other legal documents contributing to the legal origins of collective negotiations were issued by the MOLSS in 2000 and 2001. The first, the 2000 Interim Measures of Collective Wage Consultation, rather comprehensively provides for annual wage

[125] The All-China Federation of Trade Unions announced that it planned to pilot the collective bargaining system in ten provinces as part of efforts to protect workers' rights after a string of strikes across the mainland and work-related suicides at Foxconn's Shenzhen plants. The proposal, submitted to the Standing Committee of Guangdong People's Congress last week, says negotiations will be able to cover workers' wages, overtime payments, bonuses, and general welfare. Fiona Tam, *Guangdong lawmakers mull labor reforms after recent pay protests*, SOUTH CHINA MORNING POST, at 8, Jul 28, 2010 [Formatting altered].

negotiations between the employer and union. It includes requirements of "good faith" negotiation and "fair representation." This emphasis on "wage" negotiations would seem to reflect the government's moving toward market-based determinations by the parties at local levels, yet still under a nationally-structured regulatory process.

A second legal edict was issued on November 14, 2001, by several interested government organizations – MOLSS, ACFTU, State Economic and Trade Commission (SETC), and China Enterprise Management Association, entitled, Joint Circular on Promoting Collective Consultation and Collective Contract. It reiterated the duty of employers to engage in collective negotiations and it called upon governments, unions, workers' congresses, and party members to participate in tri-party consultation to accomplish objectives. The likely significance of this Joint Circular, promulgated in the month following the newly amended Trade Union Law of 2001, is the political statement to the ACFTU, leading the collective negotiations, that the union must be mindful that there are other important interests and stakeholders in this process and the implementation of the collective agreement.

B. *2004 Provisions on Collective Contract*

The 57 new Provisions are divided into eight chapters:

One: General Rules (Arts. 1–7)
Two: Content of Collective Negotiation (Arts. 8–18)
Three: Collective Negotiation Representative (Arts. 19–31)
Four: Collective Negotiation Procedures (Arts. 32–35)
Five: Conclusion, Alteration, Recession, and Termination of Collective Contract (Arts. 36–41)
Six: Review and Examination of Collective Contracts (Arts. 42–48)
Seven: Resolution of Disputes on Collective Negotiation (Arts. 49–54)
Eight: Supplementary Articles (Arts. 55–57).

1. Coverage and Purposes

The Provisions are enacted in accordance with the Labor Law and the Trade Union Law. Article 56 of the Provisions emphasizes the union's authority by subjecting the "employing unit" (employers) to the Trade Union Law and other related laws and regulations if employer refuses to engage in collective negotiation requirements. The purposes of the Provisions are "regulating the behavior of collective negotiation," the "signing of the collective contract," and the "protecting legal rights and interests of laborers and employing units." All "enterprises and public institutions that practice commercialized management within the P.R.C." are covered by the Provisions. This broad coverage parallels the coverage of employers and employees under China's individual labor contract system.

2. Negotiating Representatives

There shall be legal negotiating representatives of equal numbers (at least three) on each side and each with one chief representative. The representative in the "employee party" shall be selected by the trade union of the unit (or, if none, then by democratic recommendations, agreed upon by one-half of the staff in that unit). The chief representative is the chair of the trade union unless an alternative is selected by the chair by written delegation (or if a union does not exist, the chief representative shall be elected from the negotiating representatives through democratic means).

Perhaps a significant change from past practice, Article 24 of the 2004 Provisions stipulates, "negotiation representatives of the employing unit and those of the staff shall not act as each other's representatives." This would appear to foreclose an employer designating a trade union official as a negotiating representative of an employer, even where that official is a managerial employee of the employer, a scenario all too familiar under earlier practices. The employer otherwise selects its own negotiating representatives.

An interesting provision, Article 23, permits both sides to select "professional personnel" (*Zhuanye Renyuan*) to act as the negotiation representative. Limitations exist, as their number may not exceed one-third of one side's representatives, and no person outside one's own unit can act as chief representative.

Certain traditional responsibilities and functions, such as participation, sharing information, etc., are fixed upon the negotiating representatives. Additionally, they are called upon to "safeguard the normal order of work and production and shall not adopt any action of threatening, buying popular support and deception."

Employee representatives' terms of service are determined by the represented party and their employment tenure is protected during that term against employer's retaliation of terminating the representative's labor contract. If the labor contract were to expire during the representative's tenure, Article 28 automatically extends the contract up to the completion of his representative obligation. Exceptions exist where the representative seriously violates employer rules, other employment-related duties, or has been investigated for criminal violations.

3. Scope of Negotiable Subjects

References to the delineated subjects for negotiation are in Article 33 of the Labor Law, and Articles 3 and 8–18 of the 2004 Provisions. Article 3 of the Provisions describes the content of the collective contract as follows:

> [W]ritten agreement signed through collective negotiation . . . concerning labor remuneration, working time, rest and holiday, labor, security and sanitation, professional training, and insurance and welfare in accordance with the stipulation of laws, regulations, and rules; the special collective contract as set forth refers to the special written agreement signed between the employing unit and employees of that unit, in accordance with laws, regulations, and rules, concerning the content of collective negotiation.

Article 8 includes the scope of negotiable subjects that can be covered in the collective contract listing some 15 categories relating to employment. Articles 9–18 then list examples under each category.

4. Labor Bureau Supervision of Collective Negotiations

General Provisions in Chapter One provide the principles and supervision for the conduct of negotiations. Article 4 says negotiation shall mainly adopt the form of consultation "conference." The negotiation conduct shall observe the following principles: act legally, respectfully, honestly, fairly, consult, cooperate and collaborate equally and in consideration of legal rights, and finally, "no drastic behavior is allowed."

Responsibility for supervising the collective negotiation process, and the "signing, reviewing and performing" of the signed collective contracts or special collective contracts shall be with the Labor Bureaus above county level. For any unresolved disputes that occur during the collective negotiations, but prior to the signing, either or both parties may submit a written application to the Labor Bureau requesting resolution. The Labor Bureau may also initiate resolution procedures on its own, as necessary. The procedures in most cases should be ended within thirty days of acceptance of the case by the Labor Bureau. The Labor Bureau at the conclusion of its process formulates an Agreement on Dispute Resolution. Thereafter, the Labor Bureau and the parties must agree and sign to be bound by the Agreement before it is effective. Some items in the Agreement where there was no unanimous resolution shall be carried on with continuous consultation.

Separate dispute resolution provisions protect the rights of individual employees, who are also negotiating representatives, against improper termination and modification of their normal work status. Such disputes are to be resolved by the local labor arbitration commission. The same forum is used to resolve any rights disputes which arise out of the performance of the concluded collective contract.

5. Collective Negotiation Procedures

Within the General Rules of convening a conference, wherein the meetings take place following prescribed rules of conduct conducive to negotiation, certain other procedures are provided in the Provisions. To initiate the process, Article 32 states a party of collective negotiation may make written request of the other party; and a written response must be given within twenty days; and this request to negotiate may not be refused without proper reason. The "preparation phrase" then calls upon parties to familiarize themselves with the laws and regulations concerning collective negotiations, collective recommendations from the employer and employees and identify topics for discussion during negotiation. After a location, time, recorder are chosen, the parties are prepared to begin.

The collective negotiation begins with each chief representative, in turn, addressing the agenda and procedures of the meeting. Thereafter, each will put forward concrete proposals and the other side will respond and discussion ensues regarding the proposals. During the negotiations, the chief representatives shall make summaries of the recommendations. Those unanimously agreed upon shall be formed into the collective contract or special collective contract and signed by the chief representatives of both parties. In case there is no agreement on issues, the negotiation may be suspended, and the parties shall negotiate the next meeting place and content.

To conclude the collective contract, the agreed upon draft is presented to the employees for discussion. Thereafter, a two-thirds quorum must be present, and the draft must be approved by a majority of the workers' congress representatives or a majority of the total employees (if a workers' congress has not been established). Thereafter, the chief representatives of each side sign the contract, which is usually of one to three years in duration and can be extended by request and agreement of the parties. The contract, though binding on the parties, may be modified by the parties, or altered or terminated by certain conditions causing an inability to perform, such as bankruptcy, force majeure, or conditions in the agreement.

The final step is to submit (register) the concluded collective contract to the Labor Bureau for review and examination. It is examined to ensure compliance with legal requirements. If there is an "objection" by the Labor Bureau, the parties will be notified and the contract will be referred back to the parties who can renegotiate or re-sign, absent those portions. There seems to be a practice of little or no referral back to the parties. In the case of no objection by the Labor Bureau, the contract is effective within 15 days of receipt of the document. The law requires the contract to be promulgated "by the negotiation representative" to all employees on the day it becomes effective.

6. Duties of Proper Conduct for Collective Negotiation

The regulatory framework of collective negotiations is set up to be monitored by a government agency, viz., the Labor Bureau and its special division with responsibility to supervise and to resolve disputes. The numbers of negotiating obligations, some mentioned earlier, for clarity can be organized under the following three categories.

a. Fair and Consultative Representation

The negotiating representatives must "participate" in the negotiations after having consulted with employees regarding negotiating topics and must accept inquires from their constituency, publicize the status of negotiations, collect opinion, and provide information concerning collective negotiations.

b. Negotiating Duty

Objective measures of negotiating include the following. The negotiating representative must be legally authorized to conduct negotiations on behalf of the represented party's interests, must "not refuse" to respond to requests to engage in collective negotiations, and must "participate." The negotiating representative must provide "information" concerning collective negotiations and determine the time and place for negotiations. The employer is prohibited from refusing the collective negotiations requirements without "proper reason," and a violation of said provision is expressly subject to the Trade Union Law, which confirms in Article 53(4) that "[R]ejecting consultation on an equal footing without justifiable reasons" is a violation. Subjective measures of the conduct of negotiating duty include "honesty," "keeping promises," "fair collaboration," and "consideration of legal rights and interests for cooperation."

The Provisions are based on and incorporate the Labor Law and the Trade Union Law that also set forth standards on negotiating conduct as well as duties of fair treatment of employees. Furthermore, Article 25(6) of the Provisions obligates the negotiating representatives to those other obligations stipulated by laws, regulations, and rules.

c. Fair Treatment of Employees

While the 2004 Provisions do not directly regulate fair treatment of employees, said Provisions incorporate the Trade Union Law on the subject, including employees' right to organize and join the union. Article 3 of the 2001 Trade Union Law provides in pertinent part the following basic guarantee:

> [Employees] who rely on wages . . . regardless of their nationality, race, sex, occupation, religious beliefs, or educational background, have the right to organize and join trade unions according to law. No organizations or individuals shall obstruct or restrict them.

Article 11 provides that:

> [T]rade union organizations at higher levels may dispatch their members to assist and guide the workers and staff members of enterprises to set up their trade unions, no units or individuals may obstruct their effort.

Article 50 instructs that if anyone violates Article 3 or 11 by obstructing employees in joining trade union organizations, or obstructing higher trade unions in assisting and guiding employees in preparation for establishing trade unions, then the violation shall be ordered to be corrected by the "administrative department for labor" (Labor Bureau), with appeals to appropriate government offices. There is also possible criminal violation if there is violence or intimidation.

Article 51 prohibits anyone from retaliating against any staff member of a trade union by modifying the employee's job. Said provision also prohibits insults, slander, or personal injury to any staff member of a trade union who performs his or her duties "according to law." Punishment for violations includes criminal prosecution or administrative sanctions by the public security (the police). Article 52 provides that if an employee or a staff member of the union has his or her labor contract cancelled because of joining the trade union, there is entitlement to reinstatement with retroactive pay or an order by the Labor Bureau to pay "two times the amount of his annual income."

Article 53 prohibits obstructing the trade union in its work to organize employees to exert "(1) democratic rights through the congress of the workers and staff members and other forms;" (2) unlawfully "dissolving or merging trade union organizations;" and "(3) preventing a trade union from participating in the investigation into and solution of an accident causing job-related injuries or death to workers or staff members or other infringements upon the legitimate rights and interests of the workers and staff members."

Employees who are negotiating representatives are protected by the 2004 Provision from retaliation. For example, an employee who is a negotiating representative cannot have his or her labor contract terminated when it expires during performance of representative obligations, rather it must be automatically extended up to the completion of his or her representative obligations. Such employee can only be terminated upon a sufficient showing by the employer of serious violation of duty or employer rules. Similarly, an employer shall not adjust or remove the employee's working position without proper reason, and the employee shall be regarded as performing normal work when participating in collective negotiations. Moreover, additional provisions of the Trade Union Law likewise provide protections for trade union funds, and proscribe improper conduct by trade union staff members against employees or the trade union.

The negotiating representative also has two affirmative obligations under Article 26 of the Provisions. The representative has a duty to "safeguard the normal order of work and production and shall not adopt any action of threatening, buying popular support and deception." The first part appears to obligate the union representative to act affirmatively to avoid or end of any employee disruption of services, while the second part seems to place an obligation of proper conduct upon both employee and employer representatives, as leaders in negotiations. The second affirmative obligation is to keep the commercial secrets of the employer acquired during the collective negotiations.

Disputes relating to "proper conduct" regarding the objective and subjective aspects of the negotiations, including disagreements or impasses on proposals, are to be resolved by the Labor Bureau. Other disputes that relate to retaliation against employee representative's rights, and under Articles 27 and 28, are to be resolved before the local labor arbitration commission.

. . . .

C. *Prior Experience with Collective Negotiations*

Recent studies in China on industrial relations aspects of collective negotiations concluded before the new 2004 Provisions have examined SOEs, private enterprises, and FIEs and point out some of the deficiencies, which the 2004 Provisions addressed, dealing with process, content, and the role of the trade union. First, with regard to *process*, the Clarke study observes the following:

> [T]he system of collective consultation is not merely a means for the state to intervene in enterprises, but nor does it provide the framework for a new industrial relations system in China. At the present stage of its development, it is essentially a development of the anachronistic system of "workers' participation in management" and a (rather ineffective) adjunct to the juridical regulation of labour relations, providing a means to remind employers and trade union officers of their legal obligations and, in principle though not in practice, a means by which industrial conflict can be defused by channeling it into juridical procedures.

The authors feel there will be no change "until the enterprise trade union develops into an organization that, in its structure and practice, disengages from management to represent the interests of its members." Another recent study concludes on a similar note:

> The system of collective contracts, theoretically designed by the superior authorities as an effective mechanism to help adjust labour relations, has undergone major revision when it comes to be applied in practice. Even though the collective contract could be concluded between the management and the union in many enterprises, the whole process of consultation is little more than administrative compliance with quotas assigned from above.

Next, with regard to *content* of the collective contracts, the Clarke study concludes the following:

> Employers remain reluctant to incorporate any substantive detail in the collective contract, so that the contract adds little or nothing to the existing legal regulation of the terms and conditions and employment. At best, the collective contract provides a means of reminding employers of their legal obligations and monitoring the implementation of labour legislation in the workplace.

In its analysis of the content of collective contracts of SOEs, the Chang study observes that there were three categories of contract clauses in the agreements: the first deals with principles and formalities, such as who are the parties, etc.; the second contains the clauses to be implemented by the parties; the third category deals with commitments of the parties and duration. The study shows the second category of implementation clauses took up an average of about 70 percent of the total number of clauses. Further examination reveals over 60 percent of these clauses were defined by the labor law (usually a duplication), 20 to 30 percent were made in reference to the law (e.g., time schedule for implementing certain required female medical examinations), and about 10 percent of the clauses, on average, dealt with subjects relating to improvement of the employees' benefits.

Interestingly, the Clarke study observes that *wage negotiations* were often conducted separately from the collective contract negotiations, with the negotiated wages reflecting the minimum wages at the enterprise. Likely, this bifurcated approach may be because wages are often revised annually, whereas a collective contract may stay in effect for two or three years.

Lastly, the controversial *role of the trade union* has drawn much attention in recent studies. The primary hindrance is continually identified as the employees not having a real advocate for their interests under the current system in China. It appears to some that "the predominant functions of the trade union at the workplace still tend to be management functions." Clarke's study concluded that the following was the principal function of the trade union:

> [To] "take economic development as its central task," encouraging workers to increase productivity, enforcing labor discipline and conducting extensive propaganda on behalf of management. 'Protecting the rights and interests of employees' is at best interpreted as monitoring managerial practice to ensure that it conforms to all the relevant laws and regulations, and implementing the social and welfare policy of the enterprise – visiting sick workers, dealing with personal problems, distributing benefits, organizing picnics and arranging celebrations.

The concept of the trade union being something other than "just a branch of management" and of representing and protecting employee interests "in opposition to those of the employer is something unfamiliar, if not entirely alien, to [the union's] traditional practice and to [its] traditional conception of [that] role." Part of the explanation is the identity of the trade union officials. A typical official at the enterprise level has been described as follows:

> Trade union officers are drawn largely from the ranks of management. A full-time trade union president is paid by the employer and normally enjoys the status (and salary) of a deputy general director of the company; the personal careers of union leaders revolve around the positions of party cadre, union leader and enterprise manager; they are usually members of the Board of Directors and/or the Supervisory Board of the company; and they (rightly) regard themselves as members of the senior management team. Whether or not there is a formal election of the trade union chair, the latter is normally appointed by management.

Clarke's study found many examples where the "real parties" in interest were obfuscated; it illustrated the often lock-step harmony of interests:

> In some enterprises senior members of management participated in the negotiations on the trade union side. In one enterprise the finance director was a member of the trade union in the consultation committee; in another a senior financial manager participated on the trade union side in an advisory capacity. At the same time, the trade union president, as a member of the Board of Directors or Supervisory Board, usually participates in the formulation of management's response to the trade union proposals for the collective contract.

Left out of the equation is whether the employees feel their interests are being properly negotiated and protected; although theoretically, and under the law, they can refuse to ratify the proposed final agreement.

In prior years, the CCP would have played a more direct and active role to ensure the employer and union worked "harmoniously," but in recent years the CCP works more indirectly, usually through the trade union. In that respect, the above study shows that "at least five of the 12 trade union presidents also held the post of party secretary or deputy party secretary." This ambiguity of *who is the employer and who is the union* (though not necessarily who is the *boss*) is further complicated by China's legacy of SOE's being units of larger integrated bureaucracies in the planned economy, the periodic use of Workers' Congresses, and the absence of unions in many enterprises across China. The traditional SOEs utilized "employers" and trade unions as agents for controlling bureaucratic entities of an economic plan. With economic reforms and new laws, legal responsibility is increasingly fixed on the "employing unit" – the employer. However, at the enterprise level, there is little meaningful influence to prevent the union and the employer from "wearing each other's hats" and in the process basically becoming the same voice.

The Worker's Congresses, set up in SOEs to provide workers' democratic management, are not used, particularly in private enterprises. However, when used in SOEs, they can be one more "player" in the complexities of relationships in the negotiations relating to the welfare of the employees and the enterprises. They were re-established in 1981 to provide for workers at the enterprise level to participate in management. The Congress is supposed to meet at least once a year and its executive body, the trade union, generally executes its functions. These functions include review and approval or disapproval of management's plans, appointments, and decisions. Its efficacy in practical terms is suspect, and, post-1979 history and rapidly changing governance structures in China seem to have overtaken its usefulness. For example, the current Corporation Law greatly diluted and reduced the power and role of Worker's Congresses to merely "exercise democratic management" and "democratic supervision." The former "legal" functions of the Workers' Congress to appraise and supervise the cadres and elect the Director of the enterprise are deleted and replaced by a corporate board of directors and supervisory committee. Whether this will be a *fatal blow* to the Workers' Congresses in SOEs remains to be seen.

Another emerging role of trade unions in collective negotiations, observed in the pre-2004 studies, is the introduction and possible institutionalization of *industrial unions*.[126] Due to the increased presence of small to medium FIEs, Privately Owned Enterprises (POEs), and Town and Village Enterprises (TVEs) in the new socialist market economy, a large number of workers coming from rural or less industrialized areas of China are being employed, and, as is well documented, their labor rights are exploited. The unionization rate in these enterprises is very low, and there is little expectation of labor law enforcement, let alone negotiation of collective contracts. It has been suggested that these largely overseas-funded enterprises do not necessarily resist collective negotiations, rather they see unions and negotiations as "irrelevant" and the government and the CCP as either reluctant or impotent to induce the enterprises to sign agreements. The ACFTU has taken notice, and as early as 1996 in a document issued jointly by then Ministry of Labor, the ACFTU, the SETC, and China Enterprise Confederation an approval was given for the use of "professional or industrial unions" of the primary trade union to negotiate collective contracts on behalf of the employees at these various enterprises.

Pursuant to this policy of using industrial unions, the ACFTU has reportedly established these types of local trade union organizations in 25 provinces since 1996. The agreements under these industrial unions cover all of the private enterprises in one district or industrial sector. The union signs the agreements with the "employers' associations" at the same levels. These "associations" are described as "established under the relevant government departments rather than genuine employers' organizations." Clarke's study, under pre-2004 Provisions, indicates that in at least one area, Chengdu (where there were some 30 agreements), there has been an increase in union membership following the agreements. An added bonus for workers in Chengdu is that the city-level ACFTU had "successfully been taking cases to the City Arbitration Committee when the employers had failed to abide by the agreement." A downside noted, was that it worked because of *government intervention* (as "employers' associations" were local government authorities supervising local private enterprises) rather than as *voluntary* regulation of collective negotiations by private employers.

There were some positive aspects observed in the pre-2004 collective negotiation process. The "existing system provides an effective method of soliciting the reactions of employees to management proposals;" however, due to the great amount of discretion a union has, the ability of employees to have an effective channel to articulate their own aspirations is more limited. In some cases involving large FIEs who wish to be

[126] In 2011, 450,000 restaurant workers in Wuhan were promised a major pay hike after marathon talks between unions and bosses. The collective contract, the largest in China so far in terms of numbers of workers covered, includes a guaranteed wage at least thirty percent above the local legal minimum. Xiao Huanhuan, *Wuhan success of the collective wage negotiations restaurant industry rose 30% minimum wage*, China News, May 3, 2011, *available at* http://www.cnkeyword.info/wuhan-success-of-the-collective-wage-negotiations-restaurant-industry-rose-30-minimum-wage/. Some concern has been expressed regarding the status of the negotiation representatives and the lack of available enforcement procedures in case there is a breach of the agreement. "The key problem is how to implement this agreement," Chang Kai, dean of the Labor Relations Institute at Renmin University, said in a CCTV interview. "Unlike formal collective contracts which entail specific legal responsibilities and procedures in case the relevant parties default, this agreement seems to have neglected that part." "In addition, the workers' representative in this collective bargaining agreement is the industry trade union federation rather than the enterprise trade union. Without a union official on site, it will be difficult for these 450,000 workers to ensure that the boss honors the agreement." *What lies behind trade union "success stories?"*, China Labor Bulletin (May 17, 2011), http://www.clb.org.hk/en/node/101052 .

"good citizens," such as Beijing Jeep Ltd., Babcock & Wilcox Company, and Shanghai Volkswagen Automotive Company Ltd., there have been comprehensive collective contracts, though not necessarily prompted by the laws. Willing unions have also evidenced their abilities "to design sophisticated negotiation strategies involving high, medium and bottom lines for their wage negotiation."

. . . .

IV. "Imagining" Change: Possibilities for Labor Reform

An objective examination of the 2004 Provisions may reveal to some the possibility that China's collective negotiations could, with additional labor reforms, take on essential characteristics of collective bargaining, as reflected in ILO standards and U.S. experience. While actual implementation is yet to be seen, one can be hopeful, within reason, that the steady evolvement in recent years' labor legislation can be matched by labor reforms in practice. Imagining what is possible, tempered by what is likely within "Chinese conditions," can move forward the possibilities of real labor reform. It is within that spirit that the following possibilities for labor reform in China are suggested.

A. *Defining the Parties and Adjusting the Role of the Union*[127]

Insisting on an "arm's length" relationship between the employer and the union in representing entrepreneurial and employee welfare interests is a beginning and adheres more closely to the ILO labor standards. Presently, the ACFTU is set up in labor relations to be all things to all people. It is possible, without systemic changes in China's political-legal system, to "de-integrate" the employer and union in their "symbiotic" relationship and still allow the union to have a dual purpose, similar perhaps to a Japanese-style, functioning to represent the employees while at the same time protecting the economic best interests of the enterprise. Arguably, it can even indirectly serve a third purpose, the economic development of the country and its social stability. Some years ago, the CCP pulled back from its direct intervention in enterprise management activities and perhaps that policy change could be a model for labor reform in collective negotiations. But clearly under international standards, it should be the business of the employer, not the union, to make the case for its own interests. Details of separating trade union representatives and management could be worked out and consideration might be given to the NLRA's 8(a)(2) unfair labor practice limiting employer domination and interference with the labor union (or in China's case, perhaps also visa-versa).

The role of the Chinese union can be slightly adjusted under existing policies. Because China primarily uses "enterprise unionism" (bargaining at the employer level), as has been mentioned, it has become enmeshed with the employer and management interests. One way to intervene in this "sweetheart" relationship is to require a regional (or "outside") union to participate or perhaps have a leading role in the local negotiations, as the "professional representative" as is provided for in the 2004 Provisions.

127 [Author's note] For proposal to reorient the ACFTU, see Ronald C. Brown, *Reform for the benefit of workers*, China Daily (July 14, 2010), *available at* http://www.chinadaily.com.cn/opinion/2010-07/14/content_10102732.htm (last visited Sept. 30, 2010).

Current Chinese law now permits the ACFTU to have national or regional unions and to provide assistance to local unions. This practice is commonplace in the United States, and it allows for more independence in the negotiation. Additionally, this "outside" union representative can bring into the negotiation examples of "real" model contracts that show numerous negotiated contractual supplements to statutory labor rights. Professional representatives of the union may also more easily propose limitations on employer rules and regulations, which under the labor contract provisions can be the basis for employee discipline and discharge. Finally, perhaps some creatively delegated responsibilities and adherence to established international standards could be devised to guard the respective interests of the parties, especially those of the employees, to provide against mixed loyalties and conflicts of interests by the negotiating parties.

An additional method of achieving increased autonomy of the union during collective negotiations is to place and enforce a stronger "duty of fair representation" on the union, so that the union will have to be accountable to represent its own constituency. Presently, a duty of fair representation by the union already exists to a limited degree, as the union bears the responsibilities to solicit input from employees' proposals, to report on the progress of discussions, and then to seek ratification by the employees of the negotiated contract. But there seems to be no effective consequence for the union's refusing or arbitrarily disregarding employee input on contract provisions or of not fully or fairly representing the employees' interests in labor rights disputes.

Moreover, at the present time, without a stronger duty of fair representation, there seems little adverse consequence to the union representatives for exchanging confidential negotiating positions with the employer, unless that will indicate "bad faith" negotiating. Placing an affirmative obligation on the union and creating a legal cause of action by which the union's action or inaction could be challenged by employees (not just through internal union processes) would encourage union responsibility to keep employees' rights and interests in mind. Internal union review presently is a mechanism in Article 55 of the Trade Union Law, which states: "[S]taff members to trade unions who, in violation of this Law, damage employees' or trade union interests, shall be ordered to make corrections or be imposed sanction by trade unions at the same levels or higher trade unions."

The weakness is the absence of a clear definition of what "damages" employees' interests; nor is there a clear consequence for these types of violations. As a reference, unions' constitutions and internal processes in the United States were determined to be inadequate by themselves to address such employee concerns. As a result, the NLRB and the courts were made guardians of the employees' treatment by the union in fair representation cases.

Another adjustment that can be made from existing law and practice is for the union to expand its current use of industrial unions. This provides protection to untold numbers of heretofore unrepresented employees in need of protection of their labor rights and the ACFTU has already had successes in its use. And, even where the union is successful, employers can still benefit by avoiding competitive disadvantages from non-covered employers, as all in the industry would be subject to the same labor provisions, though perhaps with some local market variances.

B. *Adjusting the Scope and Content of Negotiated Contracts*

First, because collective wage negotiations reportedly are often conducted independently from collective negotiations, a natural adjustment would be to combine the negotiations and put into the negotiated agreement a "re-opener" clause on wages after one year, but to keep the remainder of the collective contract in full force for its entire duration. Such a provision is common in the United States. This comprehensive agreement brings economic issues back to the negotiating table where there can be part of a larger discussion on payment of employee welfare and benefit provisions. The past practice in China of artificially removing wages and related items undercuts the emphasis of the new Provisions, which have a very broad scope for economic and non-economic topics for negotiation. But without the subject of wages, the negotiation on economic issues is diminished.

Related to the negotiation process and the statutorily expanded number of negotiation topics, the union must aim to achieve contractual labor rights above and supplementary to statutory labor rights. It would seem that is part of the CCP's interest in having the ACFTU promoting social stability, especially among society's potentially volatile employee force. By the same token, the ACFTU can better serve its role of improving employment rights and benefits and channeling the conflicts into dispute resolution processes as prescribed by the Provisions. The union of course, in its "dual purpose" role, can reasonably take into consideration the market condition of the employer in formulating realistic negotiating proposals.

Lastly and as briefly mentioned earlier, there seems to be, under the labor contract provisions of the Labor Law, an unnoticed and largely unlimited ability for employers in the form of "employer rules" to write into labor contracts innumerable grounds for legal termination. Employer rules and regulations are authorized by Articles 4 and 19 of the 1994 Labor Law, and they are apparently limited only in that they not be unlawful. Nevertheless, they are rules by which employees can be "lawfully" disciplined or terminated under their labor contracts. Article 25(2) of the Labor Law states that, where employees seriously violate the employer's labor discipline (rules and regulations), they may be terminated. There is a legal requirement that these rules be placed in a labor contract; therefore, it is interesting that studies did not find contract clauses in the content of the collective contracts that would place contractual limitations on such seemingly unlimited employer power.

An example of a case involving employer rules was where an employee's termination for quarreling with her supervisor was upheld in arbitration because it violated an employer rule that an employee should never "publicly contradict a supervisor." In the United States, while employers may impose certain rules of conduct on employees, the unions always address their concerns over these rules through other provisions in the collective bargaining agreement, such as a "good cause" limitation or a requirement of "progressive discipline."

C. *Clarifying Authority and Remedies of Labor Bureau*

Of great aid to a meaningful and consistent collective negotiations process in China is to consider clarifying and strengthening the administrative authority and remedies of Labor Bureaus to supervise the conduct of the collective negotiations. In China, the legal enforcement mechanism of labor rights and interests lies with government administrative agencies, viz., the Labor Bureaus. The Labor Bureaus supervise the collective negotiation process, whereas the labor arbitration commission and tribunals adjudicate the labor rights violations. However, the Labor Bureau has only a vaguely defined mediation role in seeking to resolve negotiation disputes, and the labor arbitration forum for labor rights is there for employees who use them. The Chinese system must use the labor arbitration commission and its tribunal as a "quasi-labor court" handling labor rights disputes arising from all sources, statutory and contractual.

In contrast, the United States uses only the NLRB for issues relating to the statutory negotiation process and related unfair labor practices but leaves collective contract rights disputes to private arbitration and the courts. Other statutory rights in the United States are typically enforced through other government administrative agencies, which are usually "housed" under the governing statutes. There are benefits to both approaches, single versus multiple forums, assuming each is equipped with meaningful and effective authority and remedies to correct and stop the labor law violations. However, in the example of China's collective negotiations provisions, an employee, and even the Labor Bureau itself, may need to search in many "houses" for sources of labor rights and interests that might be violated, and possible remedies, which may vary. For example, in collective negotiations, obligations can arise from the Labor Law, the Trade Union Law or the 2004 Provisions on collective negotiations, as well as from other miscellaneous legal directives. However, such "diffused" authority may ameliorate the efficacy of the laws, even as they now exist.

For instance, what if the employer were to engage in negotiation misconduct, such as "bad faith" bargaining? Is it a violation of a labor interest for the Labor Bureau to resolve, or a labor right for the Labor Arbitration Commission and a Labor Arbitration Tribunal to resolve? And, what is the remedy? Do any of these government labor agencies have the authority to issue a "go back to negotiation" order? And even if so, how will the agency by legal means enforce that order against a recalcitrant employer? The court will enforce a labor arbitration decision, but how will the Labor Bureau, in a timely fashion, obtain such an order and also supervise the negotiation conduct of the parties? If the negotiation misconduct also violates labor rights, how will the Labor Bureau, if at all, coordinate its supervision with the potential remedies coming from the Labor Arbitration Tribunals?

One reform that could strengthen the administrative authority of the Labor Bureau to supervise negotiation conduct is to "clarify" Article 54 of the Provisions to broadly interpret "any disputes" as including disputes about negotiation conduct. A second clarification would be to remove the requirement that the parties must consent to a "Dispute Settlement Agreement," as to negotiation conduct violations (as opposed to substantive terms of a collective contract).

An alternative to providing the Labor Bureau sufficient authority to supervise the negotiation conduct is to provide the parties direct access to the courts. This would allow the employer or the trade union (and possibly employees) to directly file a lawsuit on the "group labor dispute" in the appropriate court to determine if there were any legal violations of the requirements of negotiation conduct. Presumably, the court could fashion an appropriate remedy if a violation were found.

Appeals from the administrative organs in China again are bifurcated. For disputes arising out of the negotiations, the Provisions provide no clear guidance for review beyond the Labor Bureau level. Therefore, it is assumed that there could be a request for an administrative appeal within the MOLSS, and possible a review by the court. By contrast, for labor rights, employees go to intra-enterprise mediation or directly to the Labor Arbitration Commission that will set up Labor Arbitration Tribunals. An appeal from this decision can be made to the courts, but it will be a de novo review causing added delay and expense for the worker. Some workers also have shown interest in class-action suits (e.g., on the case of mass nonpayment of wages by an employer). In the United States, the courts generally defer to the administrative decisions of the NLRB over statutory labor disputes and also to the decisions of the private arbitrator in contract labor disputes, thus providing employees with a much quicker decision than would exist if the case were re-litigated in the courts in the normal course of appeals.

Workers in China also have sought remedies through options other than using the Labor Bureaus. Strikes and economic protests in China do occur, often when an employer has refused to pay wages or honor safety conditions, and the employees erupt in frustration. However, strikers, and particularly strike leaders, are not well protected under the law and risk legal consequences. Of course, strikes in the United States are not entirely risk-free, as employers have the legal right to permanently replace private employee strikers in order to keep their business operating.

There are other remedies that could be provided as an alternative to unregulated strikes and protests and could channel these volatile labor disputes into a regulated forum. For example, in the United States, some local government employees are provided "interest arbitration" in lieu of a strike. Indeed, strikes in state and local government are usually outlawed, and proposals have been made for using interest arbitration, partial strikes, and other mechanisms as alternatives to the strike.

Of course, national characteristics always dominate, as they should, in the formulation and implementation of legislation. In the area of collective negotiations some of the "Chinese national characteristics," or "Chinese environment," include non-confrontational negotiations, unions born as implementers of national policies (rather than as employee advocates), enterprise unionism, the legacies of a socialist planned economy (such as the role of the trade union), and law enforcement and rule of law concepts that still need further development in the minds of everyday citizens. Implementation of the above suggested "clarifications" could certainly bring the practice of collective negotiations closer to meaningful collective bargaining under international standards; and, in the process can ultimately lead to a better safeguarding of Chinese workers' labor rights.

. . . .

Recent events indicate that collective negotiations will be used much more in the future.[128] On April 15, a meeting of party worker and labor unions was convened in Guangzhou where it was determined, before the end of 2011, sixty percent of companies that have set up trade unions should establish collective wage negotiation systems. That proportion is expected to reach seventy percent by 2012 and eighty

[128] "The Standing Committee of the Fujian Province People's Representative Congress passed new regulations on collective bargaining on November 29, 2010 which will take effect on January 1, 2011. Under these regulations, if an employer refuses to collectively bargain or delays such bargaining after being requested to by the union or other employee representatives chosen by a majority of employees, then the labor bureau may fine the company up to RMB 30,000 and may also fine the legal representative or main person in charge at the company up to RMB 10,000." Baker & McKenzie, *China Employment Law Update*, LAW FIRMS (2009), http://digitalcommons.ilr.cornell.edu/lawfirms/53 .

percent by 2013. Further, it was decided all Fortune 500 companies in Guangzhou should build the system within two years. "According to Chen Weiguang, head of Guangzhou Municipal Federation of Trade Union and deputy director of the Standing Committee of Guangzhou People's Congress, more guidance will be provided to trade unions at lower levels on the work of collective wage negotiation over the next three years. First, the system will be built through the third-party negotiation mechanism; second, basic wage standard should be decided through the negotiation between the trade union of an industry or company and the industry or company; third, wage guidelines should be formulated jointly by competent labor departments of the city, federation of trade unions, and association of enterprises to provide guidance to enterprises. It was also emphasized at the meeting that for enterprises refusing to or delaying the building of the system without just cause, trade unions of the city at different levels will subject them to legal actions by labor administrative department."[129]

On August 5, 2010, Guangdong Province published the *Guideline for Collective Bargaining on Wages in Enterprises of Guangdong Province* (hereinafter the "*Guideline*"), for the Human Resources and Social Security Bureaus to regulate collective wage negotiations between the enterprises and the trade unions or employees.[130] The *Guideline* contains detailed provisions for the entire bargaining process, including the election of the employee bargaining representatives, the request for bargaining and the reply to it, the commencement and suspension of the bargaining, and the signing and reviewing of the collective wage agreements, etc. According to the *Guideline*, when one party, the management or the employees, makes a request for collective wage bargaining, the other party must give its reply within fifteen days and may not refuse bargaining absent good cause. The *Guideline* also specifies safeguard measures to protect the rights and interests of employee representatives who participate in the collective bargaining. If the employment contract of an employee representative expires during the collective bargaining, the contract shall be automatically extended to the date when the employee representative completes his/her negotiation duties. And the employer without good cause may not change the post of an employee while he/she as an employee representative participates in the bargaining process. Since that time, it is reported that Wuxi and Shanghai are moving ahead on authorizing more meaningful collective negotiations.

QUESTIONS

1. What is the role of the ACFTU?
2. Is the ACFTU effective in meeting the needs of industrial relations?

[129] *Guangzhou to Build Collective Wage Negotiation System*, GUANGZHOU INTERNATIONAL (Apr. 19, 2011), http://english.gz.gov.cn/publicfiles/business/htmlfiles/cngzyw/s4171/201104/789322.html.

[130] *Guangdong: Guideline on Collective Bargaining of Wages*, KING & WOOD (2010), http://www.kingandwood.com/article.aspx?id=Guangdong-Guideline-on-Collective-Bargaining-of-Wages&language=en (last visited June 12, 2011).

3. What are the likely consequences if strikes were explicitly authorized by law?
4. Can collective negotiations succeed under current regulations? What adjustments would you suggest, if any?
5. Is the workers' congress a good alternative to a union?
6. How should and how do workers' congresses and the ACFTU relate to each other in the workplace?
7. Explain the advantages and disadvantages in the Wuhan restaurant workers' negotiated agreement.[131] Who benefits more – the union, the workers, or the employers, and why?
8. What are the advantages and disadvantages of the ACFTU cooperating with the United States and exchanging visiting delegations and experts? How would you advise the ACFTU on these types of exchanges, and why?

---

4. *Dispute Resolution*[132]

a. Labor Disputes[133]

Labor disputes arising from statutory or contractual bases are resolved by the governmental labor mediation and arbitration process. The mediation process traditionally occurs within the enterprise and is voluntary. Arbitration is available, but claims must be filed within time limits. The Labor Mediation and Arbitration Law (LMA) became effective on May 1, 2008. It provides increased accessibility for employees and greater finality to the arbitration process. It also clarifies the relationship of arbitration awards to judicial appeal. Certain exceptions to the usual exhaustion requirement are now included where direct access to the court is permitted. The new law seems to have spurred an increased use of arbitration: "Guangdong's courts and arbitrators handled more than twice as many labor disputes this May than a year earlier, after introduction of rules giving workers more rights and making arbitration free."

. . . .

The scope of labor arbitration is large and increasing, often varying by region.[134] The number of labor arbitration cases grew from 10,326 in 1989 to about 350,000 in 2007, an increase of more than 3,000 percent and an annual rise of 10.4 percent from 2006 to 2007. In 2007, the 350,000 cases involved 650,000 workers. At the same

[131] *See* Xiao Huanhuan, *supra* note 126.

[132] *See generally* Ronald C. Brown, *Resolving Labor Disputes by Mediation, Arbitration, and Litigation*, *in* Understanding Labor and Employment Law in China, ch. 14, 168–183 (2009). [Footnotes omitted].

[133] *Id.* at 168–171.

[134] Ronald Brown, *China Labor Dispute Resolution, Rule of Law in China: Chinese Law & Business*, Found. for L., Just. & Soc. 2 (2008), *available at* http://www.fljs.org/uploads/documents/Brown%231%23.pdf (last visited Oct. 2, 2010).

time the number of arbitration cases has been increasing, the number of *collective* labor disputes has declined. It decreased from 14,000 cases in 2006 involving 350,000 workers to 13,000 cases in 2007 involving 270,000 workers, or about 41.5 percent of the total workers involved in labor disputes. Collective disputes often lead to collective actions indicative of social unrest, such as demonstrations, strikes, or even violence. In the first three quarters of 2008, China's labor dispute arbitration committees accepted 520,000 new cases, a 50 percent increase over the same period in 2007. This figure is expected to increase sharply in the fourth quarter, reflecting the rise in the number of factory closures and mass layoffs in the southeast coastal region.

There are significant regional disparities in which labor arbitration cases arise. As might be expected, where industry, investment, and economic development activity are high, there is a correspondingly high incidence of labor disputes. In 2005, Jiangsu, Guangdong, Shandong, Shanghai, Beijing, and Zhejiang each had between 15,000 and 61,200 labor arbitration cases. Regions of heavy industry (involving mostly SOEs, which are making the transition to a market economy and are undergoing restructuring, which affect significant numbers of workers) also have a relatively large number of labor disputes. These include Liaoning, Hubei, Fujian, Chongqing, and Sichuan, which typically have between 8,000 and 10,000 cases per year, compared with fewer than 2,000 cases per year in many of the provinces.

The characteristics of labor arbitration cases vary widely. Topics of labor disputes include (in order of the number of cases) wages, termination, insurance, and work injury. In 2006, 64 percent of Shanghai's 24,000 labor arbitration cases involved the failure to pay wages or social insurance. The type of ownership is also an identifiable characteristic, with most labor disputes being with either an SOE or a foreign-invested enterprise (FIE). An interesting side note is that, although more large-scale mass protests occur with SOEs, more work stoppages and strikes occur in the FIEs.[135] Moreover, in Guangdong most of the labor disputes have occurred in Japanese-, Taiwanese-, Hong Kong-, and Korean invested enterprises, where workers' rights are reported to be more often violated.[136] Lastly, although the worker is the complainant in nearly 95 percent of the cases, the employer may bring a claim as well. Over the years, employers have filed as the moving party in 4 to 13 percent of the arbitration cases, usually on topics dealing with deliberate damage to employer property or other labor contract violations.

[135] Mayoung Nham, Note, *The Right to Strike or the Freedom to Strike: Can Either Interpretation Improve Working Conditions In China?*, 39 Geo. Wash. Int'l L. Rev. 919, 930 (2007). Currently in China, there is no law banning worker strikes; in 2009 there were between 60–80,000 mass disputes, many of which involved labor disputes. *See also* Anita Chan, *Labor unrest and role of unions*, China Daily, June 18, 2010, http://www.chinadaily.com.cn/opinion/2010-06/18/content_9987347.htm (last visited Feb. 20, 2011); Fang Lee Cooke, *The dynamics of employment relations in China: An evaluation of the rising level of labor disputes*, 50 J. Indus. Rel. 111 (2008).

[136] In 2010, there were numbers of strikes, especially those involving foreign investors. For example, see Kevin Soh, *Strikes end at two Chinese automotive suppliers*, Reuters, *available at* http://www.reuters.com/article/idUSTRE66L0A220100722 (last visited Oct. 2, 2010); Phelim Kine, *China's Summer Of Labor Unrest*, Forbes.com, http://www.forbes.com/2010/07/23/china-labor-migrant-worker-strikes-markets-economy-wages-union-human-rights-watch.html (last visited Sept. 30, 2010).

In China, labor disputes involve violations of contractual and statutory labor rights. Generally speaking, resolving a labor dispute between an employee and an employer through labor arbitration is mandatory, if initiated by either party, and in most cases is a prerequisite for a court to have jurisdiction. The LMA, Article 2, defines a "labor dispute" as one arising from formation of an employment relationship. The LCL provides further definition, stating that "an employment relationship with an employee is established on the day it starts using the employee." Thus, "applicants," not yet having formed an employment relationship, would seem to fall outside this definition, whereas "retired employees" may have residual rights to use arbitration over pensions and other benefit entitlements. The LMA, Article 2, continues, stipulating the following as labor disputes: (1) disputes arising from the confirmation of a labor relationship; (2) disputes arising from the conclusion, performance, amendment, termination, or ending of a labor contract; (3) disputes arising from dismissal or from a formal or de facto resignation; (4) disputes arising from working hours, rest and leave, social insurance, benefits, training, or labor protection; (5) disputes arising from labor compensation, medical bills for a work-related injury, severance pay, or damages; and (6) other labor disputes specified in laws or statutes.

. . . .

---

b. Labor Dispute Resolution Processes[137]

. . . .

Mediation

The 1994 Labor Law, Section 80, states that enterprises may establish internal mediation committees to assist in resolving labor disputes. The 2008 LMA broadens this to also include local mediation organizations. Within each enterprise, guidance for the mediation procedures comes from its own rules. If filed, the process must be reconciled within the legal time requirement of filing for arbitration, within one year. The mediation process is voluntary, and usually the employee has no explicit right to an individual representative. If no mediation settlement agreement is reached within fifteen days of submission, then either party may file for arbitration. If a mediation agreement is reached, it is legally binding. If either party fails to fulfill the mediation agreement, the other party may apply for arbitration. However, a mediation agreement on certain subjects, including agreements on payment of overdue labor remuneration, medical

[137] Brown, *supra* note 100, at 171–183; *see also* Vicki Waye & Ping Xiong, *The Relationship between Mediation and Judicial Proceedings in China*, 6 ASIAN J. COMP. L. 1 (2011). On November 30, 2011, China's MHRSS issued a Decree, effective January 1, 2012, requiring the creation of a labor dispute mediation committee in large and medium size enterprises. *Regulations on Enterprise Labor Dispute Negotiation and Mediation, Decree No. 17. See China Briefing, China to Further Regulate Labor Mediation, available at* http://www.china-briefing.com/news/2011/12/07/china-to-further-regulate-labor-dispute-mediation.html.

bills for a work-related injury, severance pay, or damages, is directly enforceable by the courts.

Under the LMA, there is a tripartite mediation committee, with one representative each appointed from the employer, the workers, and the trade union. However, many enterprises do not have a union, and those who do typically provide no meaningful training in mediation and are said to lack the ability or credibility to mediate labor disputes. In fact, this process can be, and often is, bypassed, and the claiming party may directly proceed to arbitration. As early as 1997, the number of cases being taken directly to arbitration was the same as the number being processed from enterprise mediation. The number of enterprise-mediated settlements continues to decline even as the number of arbitration cases rises. However, even with dramatically declining numbers of cases using enterprise mediation, the percentage of cases settled remains high.

Arbitration

Labor arbitration has proven quite successful in resolving cases; the resolution rate is higher than 92 percent, including conciliation/mediation and arbitration awards, which in 2006 were 34 and 46 percent of the total settlements, respectively. Of a total of 310,780 cases filed and settled in the arbitration process, 104,435 cases were mediated, whereas 141,465 cases were settled by arbitration. The other 20 percent were dispensed with by withdrawals, rejections, and the like. Workers prevailed in 146,028 cases, employers in 39,251, and there were split decisions in 125,501 cases. Since 1999, the annual number of arbitration awards has exceeded the number settled by conciliation/mediation. Statistics show workers win nearly four cases for every one by the employer, and win partial victories in a majority of the split decisions.

The LMA has 34 articles in Chapter 3 that outline the arbitration requirements and process. They increase accessibility to employees by extending the filing deadline from sixty days to one year and eliminating any fees. The law affirms the use of the previously established, government-based Labor Arbitration Commission (LAC). Pursuant to the Organization Rules of the Labor Dispute Arbitration Commission, the LAC is staffed by representatives from the labor administrative authorities (labor bureau), the labor union, and a government-appointed representative with management authority. It is in charge of the following functions: (1) retaining and dismissing full- and part-time labor dispute arbitrators, (2) accepting and hearing labor arbitration cases, (3) discussing major or difficult labor arbitration cases, and (4) overseeing labor arbitration activities. The total number of commission members must be an odd number.

Arbitrators who serve on the LAC's Labor Arbitration Tribunals must meet certain qualifications under the LMA. In addition to being "just and upright," they must have: (1) once served as a judge; (2) been engaged in legal research or education with a mid-level or higher title; or (3) possess legal knowledge and been professionally engaged in human resource management, labor union work, or other such work for at least five years; or (4) practiced as a lawyer for at least three years.

Earlier qualification standards for arbitrators do not appear to have been explicitly displaced by the LMA. A 2008 Notice by the Beijing Labor Dispute Arbitration Commission on referring part-time labor arbitrators provides a good example on how the two sets of standards may be currently applied. The qualifications for the nominees are (1) labor arbitrators who have been licensed since 2004; (2) labor union public lawyers; (3) previous experience as a judge; (4) been engaged in law research or a professor with a mid-level or higher professional title; (5) a bar license and more than two years of experience in labor union work; (6) legal knowledge and more than five years of experience with labor union legal aid or legal counseling; or (7) a law degree and labor union work experience for more than five years.

Labor arbitrators must undergo training and take a qualification exam; there is a permit system for labor arbitrators as well. Anyone with the background and experience described in the previous paragraph has the right to apply to be a labor arbitrator. For example, the Beijing Labor Dispute Arbitration Commission issued a notice on referring part-time labor arbitrators on September 1, 2008. The notice asked all local levels of the labor union, the city's various industry departments, workers' committee, employee University, and legal service centers to nominate part-time labor arbitrators to the city-level labor union for approval. Each permit is effective for three years. However, LAC members, once nominated by the government, automatically receive this permit.

The LAC will convene Labor Arbitration Tribunals as needed, composed of one, two, or three arbitrators, or if the case is a collective arbitration (involving more than thirty claimants), an odd number of more than three arbitrators is selected. Most arbitration cases are handled by one arbitrator under simplified procedures. Arbitrators may be full- or part-time, with the former usually drawn from the administrative staff of the Labor Bureau. Training of arbitrators is often provided, but few had legal education before the LMA. At the end of 2007, it was reported that there were 7,424 full-time and 12,906 part-time arbitrators nationally. In addition to conducting the arbitration, arbitrators are also called on to attempt mediation before rendering the arbitration award.

In 2006, more than one-third of the decided cases filed in arbitration were mediated. Arbitrator fees vary according to local standards. Under the old system, the party who lost the labor arbitration paid for the arbitration fees. Now, under the LMA, labor arbitration is free for the parties, and local governments pay the fees. Several provinces have issued special local regulations on labor arbitration fees (e.g., Hunan, Fujian, and Guangdong). Under those local rules, the local ministry of finance at the same level as the labor arbitration authority reimbursed the labor arbitration fees from May 1, 2008, to December 31, 2008; the labor arbitration fees became part of the government-spending budget in 2009. In most cases, this amount is relatively modest. For example, the standard in Taizhou, a small city in Jiangsu Province, which is relatively wealthy, depends on the labor arbitrator's qualification: at the senior level, 120 yuan per case; at the junior level, 100 yuan per case; at the associate level, 80 yuan per case; and at the assistant level, 50 yuan per case. In Guangxi province, which is relatively poor, labor arbitrators receive a flat subsidy of 30 yuan per case, and there is a ceiling of 60 yuan per month for each arbitrator.

Because the majority of the full-time labor arbitrators are actually public servants working for the Labor Bureau, they typically do not receive additional compensation for arbitration, but this can vary by locale. Part-time arbitrators usually receive only a nominal reimbursement or subsidy. This is quite different from commercial arbitration in China, in which the Chinese arbitrator can get paid a very high hourly rate and/or a percentage of the total amount under dispute.

Arbitration Process

Arbitration is mandatory if requested by either party and has three phases: filing, the hearing, and the award. The applicant for arbitration must file with the LAC within one year of the alleged violation, and there is no prior requirement to use mediation. As described earlier, since the LMA became effective on May 1, 2008, labor arbitration is free of charge.

MOLSS published its latest working rules on labor and personnel disputes arbitration on January 1, 2009. These rules supersede all previous procedural rules, and although there are few major changes, they provide more details and instructions. Article 4 provides that the Labor Dispute Arbitration Commission will give priority to disputes involving more than ten workers or to collective contracts. Article 8 allows shareholders, mother companies, or supervisory departments to be joined as co-defendants when the employer in dispute has its business license revoked, is shut down or dismissed, and is unable to be responsible for the liability. Article 20 provides that when parties cannot collect evidence by themselves because of objective reasons, the Labor Dispute Arbitration Commission can collect evidence based on the PRC Civil Procedure Law. Article 26 provides that the case records of the LAC are open to the parties or their representatives for review and copying, except for those cases involving national or military secrets.

The filing deadline of one year may be tolled in certain circumstances, such as when an applicant is currently seeking a remedy from a relevant government authority, or there has been an intervention of *force majeure*, or if the labor dispute involves overdue remuneration during the ongoing employment relationship. The applicant must provide pertinent information in the arbitration application, including the nature of the claim, supporting evidence, and witnesses. The LAC must accept or reject the application (with a stated reason) within five days from its receipt, or else the applicant may proceed directly to court, as is also the case if the application is rejected. The respondent is notified within five days after acceptance of the application and has ten days to respond.

The LAC first designates a Labor Arbitration Tribunal (LAT) and notifies the applicant of its composition within the five-day period from receipt of the application. The one to three arbitrators are bound by ethical standards and must recuse themselves or be challenged by the parties for violating any listed areas of impropriety, such as being related to a party, having a material interest in the case, etc. The LAT will attempt mediation before issuing its award, and if a resulting written mediation agreement is signed by the arbitrator(s) and the parties, it is enforceable in the courts.

The arbitration hearing process allows for the parties to cross-examine, argue, and make final comments, and a record is maintained. Evidence accepted as genuine by the LAT is used as "the basis for determining the facts," and the burden of production, if not proof, is on each party, except where the evidence is in the possession or under the control of the employer and the employee is unable to submit it, in which case the employer must produce it by a deadline, and failure to do so will be held against the employer's burden of proof. Although there is some guidance available on determining the "burden of proof" in court cases, it is not expressly binding on arbitrators in the arbitration process.[138] The arbitration award must be rendered within forty-five to sixty days from

[138] According to general principles of Chinese law, if an employee makes a claim for overtime pay, he or she assumes the burden of proof. But it is almost always difficult, in practice, for an employee to provide such evidence. As a result, Article 9 of [the Supreme People's Court's] Labor Disputes Interpretation III provides that, where an employee makes a claim for overtime pay, he shall assume the burden of proof as to the fact he has done overtime work; but where the employee has evidence that the employer possesses but has failed to provide evidence proving there was overtime work, the

the date of acceptance by the LAC of the application for arbitration. When the LAT is composed of more than one arbitrator, the written award is based on majority opinion, or if none can be reached, it will be in accord with the opinion of the chief arbitrator, along with dissent(s) also placed in the record. The award is final and legally effective on the date it is rendered in two areas of labor disputes: (1) labor remuneration, medical bills for work-related injuries, severance pay, or damages, in any amount not exceeding the equivalent of twelve months of the local minimum wage and (2) working hours, rest, leave, social insurance, etc., arising from the implementation of state standards.

An employee dissatisfied with an award in those two areas may appeal to the court within fifteen days, whereas an employer within thirty days may seek to vacate the order in intermediate court only on errors in law, jurisdiction, or statutory procedure; fabricated or concealed evidence; or if the arbitrator demanded a bribe or committed graft. All other non-Article 47 appeals may be brought to court by either party within fifteen days from the date of the receipt of the written ruling. In 2008, in the first reported case under the LCL, a district court in the Chaoyang District of Beijing upheld an arbitration ruling that awarded an employee an open-ended labor contract based on her circumstances, including her prior employment with the employer, and notwithstanding her leave of absence.

Arbitration awards tend to be brief, without elaborate analysis, as contrasted with, for example, longer American arbitration decisions. Access to Chinese awards is limited, with only the appealing parties granted access to the award. In 2009, new Procedure Rules provided that the case records of Labor Arbitration Commission are open to the parties or their representatives for review and copying.

There are mixed views about whether the new law will resolve the growing number of labor disputes. Most see it as a further improvement; whereas advocacy groups argue the LACs are ill-equipped to deal with the surging workload.

Litigation

The number of labor dispute cases appealed to the courts from labor arbitration decisions has grown dramatically from 28,285 in 1995 to 114,997 in 2004 and to 122,480 in 2005 (involving about 2.37 billion yuan).[139] In 2005, about 94 percent of appeals were initiated

employer shall bear the adverse consequences (an admittedly vague clause, most likely meaning the court will adopt the employee's claims and hold that he or she did indeed work overtime). John V. Grobowski et al., *Interpretation on Several Issues Concerning the Application of Laws in the Trial of Labor Disputes (III)*, FAEGRE & BENSON (Dec. 1, 2010), http://www.faegre.com/12422; *see also* Jiang Junlu & Li Jing, *Responding to Change*, 8 ASIAN-COUNSEL 35 (2010), *available at* http://www.inhousecommunity.com/controlPanel/download.php?id=770.

[139] It is reported that in 2009, labor dispute arbitration organizations nationwide handled 875,000 cases. Some 684,000 cases were accepted for arbitration, a decrease of 1.3 percent compared to the previous year. The cases involved 1.017 million workers, a decrease of 16.3 percent compared to the previous year. *China's Human Resources*, GOV.CN, http://www.gov.cn/english/official/2010-09/10/content_1700448_16.htm (last visited June 13, 2011). Interestingly, it was reported that in 2008, the courts handled about 295,000 labor dispute cases, an increase of 95 percent from 2007; whereas the 2009 figure was up to about 318,000 cases. *See China's labor dispute resolution system*, CHINA LABOR BULLETIN (Nov. 26, 2009), *available at* http://www.china-labour.org.hk/en/node/100618; *see also Chinese courts complete 317,000 labor dispute cases in 2009*, XINHUA, Sept. 13, 2010, http://www.china.org.cn/china/2010-09/13/content_20917787.htm.

by workers, and they prevailed in more than half of them; in some courts, such as in Ningbo in Zhejiang and Zhongshan in Guangdong, as many as 90 percent of the appeals were settled in favor of the worker. The LMA seeks to add more finality to arbitration decisions in stipulated areas, as discussed in this section.

In 2005, 121,516 court cases were settled (resolved) – 62,608 by court judgment, 27,944 by mediation, – and 20,998 were withdrawn, with 7,115 rejected. Interestingly, the court successfully mediated nearly one-third of the settled cases.

Chinese law ordinarily distinguishes between "labor contracts" and "contracts for work," with the latter treated as a civil contract case able to be taken directly to court. In contrast, the former is treated as a labor case in which resolution of the labor dispute through labor arbitration is required before court access is granted. The LCL and a 2006 SPC Interpretation (preceding the LMA) authorize direct lawsuits in court on certain limited topics, such as back wages owed for which the amount is not in dispute. A recent court case in Shanghai, basing its holding on the Civil Procedure Law (CPL) Article 191, ordered a wage payment of RMB 200,000 to an employee whose employer had agreed the money was due, and the date for payment was past.

There may be some question as to how best to reconcile this narrow exception with Article 44 of the LMA, which requires first going to arbitration and requesting authorization for "advance execution," as discussed in this section. However, a limited number of non-performed mediation agreements (settlements) may be taken directly to court for enforcement, and the LMA authorizes other non-conflicting related laws to continue in force. Some of these related laws, such as the Women's Rights and Interests Law (Women's Law) and the Employment Promotion Law specifically grant the right to "institute a legal action in a People's Court." Whether that precludes first exhausting this "labor dispute" in labor arbitration is doubtful, though debatable, in view of current court cases.

Uncontested arbitration awards, except those falling under Article 47, or those qualifying for *advance execution* under Article 44, will be final after the fifteen-day appeal period. Under new provisions of the LMA, the usual right of appeal and full review, largely de novo, of the arbitration award by the court can be avoided either by a successful application for advance execution or an arbitration award in two stipulated areas under Article 47.

An advance execution can be made in qualifying cases involving recovery of "labor remuneration, medical bills for a work-related injury, severance pay, or damages." The employee applies to the LAT for an award for advance execution and transfer of the case to the court for execution. Two conditions are required: (1) the rights and obligations are clear and (2) the failure to grant will "materially affect the livelihood of the applicant." Article 47 provides for "final and legally effective" arbitration awards on the date they were rendered in two areas: (1) labor remuneration, medical bills for a work-related injury, severance pay, or damages "not exceeding the equivalent of twelve months of the local minimum wage rate" and (2) disputes over working hours, rest, leave, social insurance, etc. arising from the implementation of government labor standards.

If an employee is dissatisfied with the arbitration award under Article 47, he or she may make an appeal to the Intermediate People's Court within fifteen days. An appeal by an employer to vacate the award is limited to six circumstances: (1) error in the application of laws; (2) the LAC lacked jurisdiction; (3) a statutory procedure was violated; (4) evidence on which award was based was fabricated; (5) the other party concealed evidence sufficient to affect the fairness of the award; and (6) the arbitrator demanded or accepted a bribe, committed graft, or rendered an award that perverted the law. If the award is vacated, it will be final unless either party, within fifteen days, takes the labor dispute to the People's Court.

There are certain requirements for and barriers to court review of labor disputes. As discussed earlier, an appellant first must have a "labor dispute" arising from an employment relationship and, second, must have first exhausted the labor arbitration procedures, except where this requirement has been excluded. A mediation agreement reached in court, like a mediation agreement reached in arbitration, is binding, except on the legality of the agreement.

Arbitrated labor dispute cases, taken by the courts, unless otherwise directed by laws or Supreme People's Court (SPC) guidance, will be enforced in accordance with the law. The Civil Procedure Law includes rules on evidence, review standards, appeals, etc., and, according to the SPC's 2001 Labor Dispute Interpretation, the employer has a burden to produce evidence within its control, and in cases of termination, reduction of compensation, or recalculation of an employee's length of service, it has the burden of proof.[140]

. . . .

QUESTIONS

1. If employees most often prevail, at least partially, in remedying labor disputes in arbitration, what are the still-existing shortcomings of the current system?
2. In what forum(s) may mediation be applied?
3. May an employer (e.g., an MNC) substitute an "in-house" grievance system for the statutory arbitration process? Why or why not?
4. In view of the new mediation-arbitration procedures, how would you explain the recent leveling off of the number of arbitrations and the increase in the number of labor cases taken to court?

---

5. *Critique under International Labor Standards*

In addition to the previous overview description of China's labor and employment laws, there are some sources following that "critique" those laws, emphasizing the purported "shortcomings" of the laws as measured against international standards.

[140] *See discussion in* Grobowski et al., *supra* note 138; *see also* Jiang Junlu & Li Jing, *supra* note 138.

Together, the overview and critique raise issues of how law works in practice and what issues need to be further addressed.[141]

Internationally Recognised Core Labour Standards in the People's Republic of China, Report for the WTO General Council Review of the Trade Policies of the People's Republic of China[142]

Executive Summary

The People's Republic of China has ratified four of the eight core ILO labour Conventions. In view of severe restrictions on trade union rights and the prevalence of child labour and forced labour as well as discrimination, determined measures are needed to comply with the commitments WTO members accepted at Singapore, Geneva and Doha in the WTO Ministerial Declarations over 1996–2001, and in the ILO Declaration on Fundamental Principles and Rights at Work.

China has not ratified either of the core ILO Conventions on freedom of association and collective bargaining. Workers do not have the right to organise in trade unions of their choice. Legal trade unions have to be affiliated to the ACFTU and accept its control. Although there have been some efforts to establish collective wage consultation systems, the right to collective bargaining is restricted as is the right to strike, both in law and in practice. The lack of proper representation is reflected in the number of protests and labour disputes that have been rising over the years. Under extensive state secrets legislation it is a crime to publish unofficially sanctioned data, even on national strike figures or unemployment numbers, resulting in a lack of official public data on labour related issues.

China has ratified the core ILO Conventions on equal remuneration and discrimination. Discrimination is prohibited by law but in practice, while there is an absence of gender segregated data, clearly it is prevalent. Women, ethnic minorities and persons who live with HIV/AIDS and Hepatitis B frequently suffer from discrimination in remuneration and in access to employment, education and public services. Institutionalised discrimination against migrant workers from rural areas remains a serious problem, despite recent legislation.

141 For a detailed analysis from the perspective of the U.S. State Department, see Bureau of Democracy Human Rights and Labor, *2010 Human Rights Report: China (includes Tibet Hong Kong, and Macau)*, U.S. Department of State (Apr. 8, 2011), *available at* http://www.state.gov/documents/organization/160451.pdf. *See also* discussion in Qiu Yang, *ILO Fundamental Conventions and Chinese Labor Law: From a Comparative Perspective*, *available at* http://www.pennealr.com/media/articles/vol2/CLPR_v2i1ps10pe35.pdf (last visited Sept. 30, 2010).

142 ITUC, Internationally Recognized Core Labor Standards in The People's Republic of China, Report for the WTO General Council Review of the Trade Policies of the People's Republic of China, (Geneva, May 10 & 12, 2010), *available at* http://www.ituc-csi.org/IMG/pdf/Chinal_Final-2.pdf (last visited Sept. 30, 2010); *see* ITUC, China – 2011, *available at* http://survey.ituc-csi.org/+-China-+.html (last visited June, 13, 2011).

China has ratified the core ILO Convention on the worst forms of child labour and the ILO Convention on minimum age. Child labour, although prohibited under the age of 16, is a serious problem in China. Children are sometimes employed under forced conditions or performing the worst forms of child labour. Law enforcement officers often fail to apply the law effectively. Work-study programmes, run under school auspices, frequently result in forced child labour.

China has not ratified the core ILO Conventions on forced labour. Forced labour is prohibited in China but does occur in commercial enterprises. There is forced prison labour in the form of "re-education through labour camps," including prison labour by children. Progress in prosecuting traffickers and in protecting and assisting victims of trafficking, which affects women, men, and children, has been limited so far.

. . . .

I. Freedom of Association and the Right to Collective Bargaining

The People's Republic of China has not ratified ILO Convention No. 87 on Freedom of Association and Protection of the Right to OrganiseOrganize or ILO Convention No. 98 on the Right to Organise and Collective Bargaining.

Freedom of Association

Workers are not free to form or join trade unions of their choice. Only the All China Federation of Trade Unions (ACFTU) is recognised in law. The ACFTU therefore exercises a trade union monopoly. As Art.11 of the Trade Union Law states:, "the establishment of any trade union organisation, whether local, national or industrial, shall be submitted to the trade union organisation at the next higher level for approval." Trade union organisations at the higher level "shall exercise leadership" over those at lower level. Organisers of independent trade unions which resist ACFTU assimilation are generally arrested, detained, or imprisoned. On the other hand organising trade unions with "Chinese characteristics" is strongly encouraged by ACFTU officials. "Chinese characteristics" comprise, according to the official press agency Xinhua, "the principle of the leadership of the Communist Party of China over the unions", as well as "*protecting workers' rights and interests in line with laws and in a scientific manner. Pursuit of harmonious labour relations is another requirement of building trade unions with Chinese characteristics.*"

The ACFTU is part of the government and party bureaucracy, and has the task of assisting the government in ensuring social stability during economic changes in the Chinese industry and protecting workers in the privatised economy while working to organise the workers before they organise themselves independently. Relatively recent reforms within the ACFTU include a push for direct trade union elections at the enterprise level, and the opening of the union to migrant workers. This has resulted in official statistics stating that around 66 million migrant workers now belong to the ACFTU. However despite these reforms, the level of autonomy of most unions at enterprise level remains low, with the majority of officials appointed directly or indirectly by the Party. The number of workers organised by the ACFTU in multinational enterprises over recent years has increased rapidly. ACFTU branches have been established in firms such as Walmart, Carrefour, McDonalds, Motorola, Kentucky Fried Chicken, Samsung and Nestlé despite the initial well publicised opposition of management.

Collective Bargaining

There is no comprehensive national law on collective bargaining procedures but rather a plethora of regulations which govern "collective contracts". The Labour Law effective from 1995 adopted collective consultation as a key medium for settling disputes between employers and workers, even in enterprises with no established trade union. However, the Labour Law only dictates that enterprises "may" engage in consultations, leaving this as an option up to the management of each enterprise. Several further regulations including the revised Trade Union Law have provided guidance on the negotiation process and content of collective contracts. The *Minimum Wage Regulations*, *Regulations on Collective Contracts*, and *Provisional Regulations on Wage Payments* are non-binding administrative regulations.

In practice, however, genuine collective bargaining remains limited, as the ACFTU engages in negotiations and represents workers in negotiations with management and government without workers having a real say and input in these negotiations. At the same time the ACFTU remains either nonexistent or ineffective in much of the private sector and workers, because of the impossibility to organise independently, are unable to establish adequate collective contracts. According to official reports, wage demands are at the core of the collective contract system, but trade unions in small and medium enterprises rarely undertake negotiations with management.

According to ACFTU statistics for 2008, a total of 1.9 million enterprises have signed 1.1 million collective contracts, covering 150 million workers. As of September 2008, 60.2 per cent of workers were covered by collective contracts. However, many collective contracts reflect the minimum legal requirements and do not cover enough areas to be of much use to workers. There is little data available on the number of sectoral collective contracts.

In July 2009, the ACFTU formulated its *Guiding Opinion Regarding Actively Launching Industrial Wage Collective Consultation Work*, which stipulates that industry-wide union representatives will represent workers in collective consultations with employers' organisations at the same level with the aim of signing industry-wide collective contracts covering the issues of wage setting, labour quotas, and the minimum wage.

Over recent years, there have been several high profile experiments in collective bargaining and a number of apparently successful pilot projects including bargaining efforts in Zhejiang Province and Shenzhen. Since late 2007, in Luoyang the local government has executed a programme of establishing a collective wage consultation system in the city's enterprises. The Luoyang's pilot programme has been followed by the Henan Provincial Federation of Trade Unions, which decided to extend it throughout the province. The ACFTU's branch in Luoyang has completed a study which found that workers' wages in enterprises that implemented the Luoyang programme increased an average 10 to 20 per cent depending on the industrial sector, however that many entrepreneurs are not cooperating and prefer to stick to verbal agreements on wages with their employees. Others accompanied the implementation of the collective wage consultation system with creative accounting, such as counting in the insurance contribution, in order to keep the wages on the levels before the implementation. The Luoyang programme revealed that trade unions' effectiveness of negotiating is limited by lack of access to company's sheets on operations and profitability, contrary to the 1998 ACFTU's *Guiding Opinion on Trade Unions' Participation in Collective Wage*

Consultations. Trade union leaders are reported to be dependent on their employers who often threaten and sack militant unionists for their activities. In addition to this, the law does not prescribe penalties for Luoyang's enterprises that fail to comply with the collective wage consultation program.

Other examples of province specific approaches with a view to developing collective contracts are the Hebei Province's *Regulations on Enterprise Collective Consultations between labour and management* and the 2007 Shanghai *Collective Contract Rules*. The latter provides procedures and legal requirements governing collective contracts, dispute settlement and collective bargaining covering issues of wages, health and safety, social insurance and benefits, training, labour discipline, production quotas, working time and days-off.

China ratified the ILO Convention on Tripartite Consultation in 1990 but the Convention has only started to be implemented recently. The Convention envisages that tripartite mechanism should perform three basic functions: exchanging information, consultation, and negotiation. As of September 2008, over 12,000 tripartite consultation organisations have been established, however, in China they are used only for exchange of information.

Labour Contract Law

The Labour Contract Law entered into force on January 1, 2008 after public and internal consultation. The Labour Contract Law "mandated contracts for all employees without exception, stabilized employment through the use of non-fixed-term contracts for workers who were on their third contract and for those who had worked at a single enterprise more than ten years, strengthened penalties for non-compliance with existing labour regulations, and opened more space for collective bargaining and consultation by the ACFTU."

A survey by the National People's Congress found that less than 20 per cent of small- and medium-sized private companies had signed contracts with their workers before the law's entry into force. The law provides specific penalties for companies failing to observe labour laws and regulations concerning contracts and related issues, such as providing written contracts and abiding by the terms of the contracts. However, the Labour Contract Law does not provide support for increased worker participation in negotiating contracts or conditions of work apart from through the official trade union and does not contain any sanctions for enterprises that refuse to implement a collective wage consultation system.

The law was preceded by a public comment period where employers, including the US and EU Chambers of Commerce in China, expressed their fierce opposition and labour defended the new law. The employers massively laid off long standing workers prior to the law's ratification. The telecommunications firm Huawei, for example, intended to require 7,000 workers with seniority to resign before January 1, 2008, and then renegotiate a new labour contract, until such action was prevented by an intervention from the ACFTU.

Since entry into force of the law in January 2008, companies have reacted in a variety of ways including use of more covert ways to reduce employee numbers such as increased use of subcontracted work; demotions of more senior workers, and so forth. Some have sought to argue that a number of export processing firms have closed due to a tougher operating environment due to the Labour Contract Law (when in reality, it is mostly due to the global financial crisis). In response to the crisis, the Guangdong government issued an Opinion stipulating that law enforcers should exercise caution in prosecuting white-collar criminals and ordering them not to arrest factory owners and managers accused of crimes such as corruption. By contrast, with regard to workers the Opinion stressed that "prosecutors should crackdown on any crimes that harm the legitimate interests of enterprises or jeopardize production."

Many multinational corporations, such as Coca-Cola and Swire Beverages, outsource labour contracts to labour supply companies with a view to avoiding labour disputes and reducing costs. Yet if dispatched workers work full time in the premises of an enterprise, as frequently is the case, the companies act in violation of the Article 66 of the Labour Contract Law, which stipulates that supply workers should only fill temporary or supporting positions.

According to an independent survey of foreign-owned businesses, the total cost increase directly related to the Labour Contract Law was between two to three per cent. However, local governments are under severe pressure from local businesses to relax enforcement of the Labour Contract Law. Up to this moment, the enforcement has not been strict: in Huangpi, for example, in over a thousand small enterprises, especially kilns and mines, employing over 100,000 workers, only some 5,000 workers were in companies that had signed labour contracts.

Dispute resolution and the right to strike

The right to strike was removed from the Constitution in 1982. The revised Trade Union Law (Art 27) is not clear on strikes but says: "In case of a work stoppage or a go slow in an enterprise, the trade union shall represent staff and workers in consultation with the enterprise, institution, or relevant party, and shall reflect the opinions and demands of staff and workers as well as raise solutions. The enterprise or institution shall strive for a settlement with the reasonable demands made by the staff and workers." The Trade Union Law also stipulates, "when a work-stoppage or go slow occurs in an enterprise or institution, the trade union shall assist the enterprise or institution in its work so as to enable the normal production process to be resumed as quickly as possible". While strikes have a tenuous legal existence, in practice the number of strikes continues to grow. In general, however, strikes are often repressed with police force and are not supported or endorsed in any way by the official trade union.

The only allowed action comes in the form of "health and safety work stoppages," which are foreseen in the Work Safety Law of 2003. Workers who encounter a situation at work that directly endangers their personal safety have the right to refuse orders, which violate health and safety rules, to stop work, and to leave the workplace. Similar provisions are contained in the Labour Law, notwithstanding, the Trade Union Law stipulates that in the case of unsafe conditions the union has the right to propose solutions but it does not extend to allow industrial action. Many accidents occur every year in China due to a widespread disregard for basic health and safety standards. As in previous years mining remains a dangerous occupation with several reported instances where miners died while working in unsafe environments after they were forced to continue work. Government statistics for 2009 show that the number of coal mine accidents decreased by 338, and the deaths decreased from 3,215 in 2008 to 2,631 in 2009. Most of the accidents and deaths occur in small and private mines, which run with minimum safety regulations and obsolete equipment. However, many large state-owned mines outsource their operations to the private sector with direct consequences for the safety of workers.

In 2008, the Labour Dispute Mediation and Arbitration Law entered into force. The new law abolished arbitration fees for both employees and employers and accelerated the resolution of internal disputes by encouraging management to set up labour mediation committees to solve internal disputes. The extensive dispute resolution system consists of three stages: mediation, arbitration and the courts. Tripartite labour dispute arbitration committees are chaired by the local labour bureaus.

According to the Chinese Ministry of Human Resources, the number of labour dispute cases accepted by labour dispute arbitration committees more than doubled from 314,000 in 2005 to 690,000 in 2008. Civil courts accepted 280,000 labour dispute cases in 2008, almost 93 per cent more than in the previous year. In the first half of 2009, the accepted cases rose another 30 per cent and in the most industrialised areas, Guangdong, Jiangsu, and Zhejiang, labour disputes increased respectively by 41 percent, 50 per cent, and 159 per cent.

There are signs that authorities, at least in Shenzhen, become more tolerant to events of work stoppages and other similar industrial action. The Shenzhen Municipal People's Congress published the *Draft Regulation on the Growth and Development of Harmonious Labour Relations in the Shenzhen Special Economic Zone* in June 2008. The Regulation does not legalise strikes but it no longer obliges trade unions to assist the quick resumption of production when they decide to take action. However, it regulates that in case of a strike, employers and workers are obliged to take no more action for 30 days in order to provide time for the dispute to be resolved by mediation or arbitration.

The number of strikes both spontaneous and planned, but always without the official recognition of the union, is increasing; figures suggest that each day around 1,000 workers are involved in industrial action in Guangdong Province alone. The long-standing oppression of workers' rights has resulted to an unprecedented radicalisation of incidents that jeopardises the Chinese "harmonious society". For example, in July 2009, a senior enterprise manager was beaten to death in Tonghua and in August in Lingang steel mill, a vice-director was held captive for 90 hours. Local governments and employers often turn to violent repression of protests with large-scale deployment of armed riot police as well as ordinary public security forces. In some instances, companies hired security forces to beat and threaten workers protesting or taking other forms of industrial action, often with deadly results.

In the majority of disputes at the enterprise level, the ACFTU appears to be unwilling or unable to genuinely support workers and overall, direct assistance to them remains limited. The ACFTU does not play a role in the majority of labour disputes and collective actions involving migrant workers in manufacturing zones where private businesses are located. Nonetheless, since at least 2008 the ACFTU has been leading a high profile campaign aimed at obtaining wages in arrears for migrant workers, as well as more recently wage increases for migrant workers.

The main reasons for the increasing number of labour dispute cases include substantial long term wages arrears, frozen wages, collective agreement breaches, unresolved issues and readjustment in private companies on the pretext of the global economic crisis including wage and social benefits decreases and suspended overtime payments. As in the state-owned enterprises (SOE), such readjustment in private companies is generally not negotiated with the employees. Furthermore many foreign small scale entrepreneurs typically sell off their assets quickly, including machinery, shut down the factories and depart from China leaving workers' wages in arrears. In response to this practice the Supreme People's Court issued a *Guiding Opinion* in 2009 which stipulates that the issue of wages in arrears should be dealt with urgency with a view to preventing the employers from fleeing the country and workers from protesting. It also dictates that the courts should discourage lay-offs and in case they are inevitable that the workers be compensated as the law prescribes, even in installments. Most importantly, the courts should put the survival of the enterprises first, by allowing the use of sealed assets for business purposes and by prohibiting the sell-off of assets necessary for the operation of the enterprise, such as machinery and factory equipment.

Labour disputes are also on the rise due to the restructuring of SOEs. Although in 2009 there were not many lay-offs in such companies, restructuring opens up windows of opportunity for corrupt officials who, according to an article in the magazine of the official Xinhua News Agency, "declared bankruptcy without proper authorisation, and sold off assets directly linked to enterprise survival, disregarded the fate of the employees, and national interests, and in some cases, sold off national assets at below market price."

. . . .

Export Processing Zones

There are no specific labour laws or exemptions from labour laws relating to collective contract signed in the Export Processing Zones although a number of significant labour law clauses can be circumvented by employers who obtain exemptions from local authorities on issues such as working hours or overtime, although it should be noted that such exemptions are not unique to the zones.

Conclusions

Workers do not have the right to organise in trade unions of their choice. Legal trade unions have to be affiliated to the ACFTU and accept its control. Although there have been some efforts to establish collective wage consultation systems, the right to collective bargaining is restricted as is the right to strike, both in law and in practice. The lack of proper representation is reflected in the number of protests and labour disputes that have been rising over the years.

II. Discrimination and Equal Remuneration

The People's Republic of China ratified ILO Convention No. 100 on Equal Remuneration in 1990 and ILO Convention No. 111 on Discrimination (Employment and Occupation) in 2006.

Gender Discrimination

Gender equality has been an official government policy objective since 1949. The Constitution states that "women enjoy equal rights with men in all spheres of life." The law stipulates equal remuneration for work of equal value. The Law on the Protection of Women's Rights and Interests was designed to assist in curbing gender-based discrimination, and with an amendment in 2005 sexual harassment was declared a crime. The recent Employment Promotion Law prohibits discrimination based, among other grounds, on gender and age. It stipulates that "other than for types of work or posts that are not suitable for women as prescribed by the State, no employer shall refuse to employ women or raise recruitment standards for women on the grounds of gender. When an employer recruits female employees, the labour contract shall not stipulate any requirement such as one restricting female employees from marrying or bearing children". However, women continue to experience discrimination, unequal remuneration, sexual harassment, unfair dismissals, demotion and wage discrepancies.

The financial crisis has reportedly hit women harder than men, as statistics from Huangzhou province show; female unemployment increased by 40 to 60 per cent during 2008 and 2009, while men's unemployment increased by 35 per cent. In reforming the SOEs, women have been the first workers to be laid off or dismissed. Indeed, throughout the past decade women have suffered disproportionately from layoffs and it is estimated that in some areas up to 70 to 80 per cent of the laid off workers are women, especially in the northeast of China. In many instances, women workers are not technically laid off but are asked to take prolonged "rest" from work or are forced into early retirement. Regulations governing the reforms of SOEs allow for women to be forced to "retire" at 40 or to take enforced two-year maternity leave without pay. Lower retirement ages for women mean reduced pensions, which are based on the number of years worked. The official retirement age continues to set two ages for men and women – 60 years for men and 55 for women.

In terms of re-employment, women workers find it harder than men to find new jobs. Some figures show that about 75 per cent of laid-off women are still unemployed after one year, compared with 50 per cent of men still unemployed after one year.

Effective job segregation means women generally find employment in the unskilled, labour-intensive, and lower-paid textile and manufacturing industries. For professionals and white-collar workers, there is a distinct preference towards male graduates while young non-married women are preferred for assembly line posts, thus increasing gender segregation of work. Moreover, even women with advanced degrees reported discrimination in the hiring process, citing the employers' concerns with regard to the costs of maternity leave and other special benefits. Job advertisements often specified height and age requirements for women, which is now declared illegal by the Employment Promotion Law which imposes more detailed requirements for recruitment advertisements placed by employers. "The employer must not stipulate any discriminatory requirements, which often include: males only, people who are registered residents of a specific city only, etc." Information on the application and effectiveness of this law is very limited.

Many employers prefer to hire men to avoid the expense of maternity leave and child care. For many women, becoming pregnant entails the end of their working life at a particular factory. Laws regarding non-termination of work contracts for pregnant and nursing mothers are often not enforced and women are dismissed.

Chinese law provides for equal pay for equal work. However, discrimination in remuneration exists; women earn 65 per cent of men's compensation and in rural areas this percentage is reported to be even lower. Women accounted for 60 per cent of those below the poverty line in the country. According to older statistics, average incomes of female executives and senior professionals were only 58 per cent and 68 per cent, respectively, of their male colleagues' salaries. Furthermore, it is difficult for women to litigate a sex discrimination suit because of the vague legal provisions. Agencies tasked with protecting women's rights tended to focus on maternity leave related lay-offs and benefits and discarded cases of gender discrimination, violence, and sexual harassment. Women are also underrepresented in certain highly skilled and highly paid positions. For every 5 male senior officials and managers, only one woman occupies a position of the same level. However, in terms of professional and technical work, women occupy slightly more positions than men.

While illiteracy rates are officially lower than 2 per cent, 2008 official government statistics show that women comprised more than 70 per cent of all illiterate persons.

In the private sector, many of the migrants employed at the lower end of the wage scale in small and medium enterprises in the south and eastern parts of China are young women between the ages of 16 and 25. Some statistics show that the migrant labour male-to-female ratio nationwide is 2:1 while in the Pearl River delta the ratio is reversed. Typically, young female migrants earn less than their male counterparts.

Although the law clearly forbids sexual harassment, including at the workplace, the law's application is under question. Many labour offices tasked with receiving and processing complaints are not used to dealing with such cases and many complaints go uninvestigated. In one much-reported case, a 28 year-old office worker was dismissed in 2008 after complaining about sexual harassment by her boss. The vice-chair of the union and member of the union's women's committee proposed the victim's dismissal due to alleged absenteeism. The victim undertook a successful lawsuit. Some months before that, another court was the first to decide in favour of a sexual harassment victim using the 2005 amendment of the Law on the Protection of Women's Rights and Interests.

Internal Migrant Workers

....

Workers from the countryside are discriminated against in several ways. First, there are extensive restrictions on freedom of movement brought about by the "*hukou*" system, a form of household registration whereby each family member is registered according to his or her family residence. Once classified it is hard to change status. The majority of rural residents, despite living in urban areas, therefore keep their rural status, which is passed onto their children. As an integral part of the *hukou* system, rural migrants are disqualified from freely seeking and obtaining better-paid opportunities in the cities unless they can obtain temporary residency and work permits. On the other hand, the Employment Promotion Law expressly stipulates that migrant workers in the cities enjoy equivalent employment rights to those of urban labourers, and that no discriminatory restrictions are to be set. The law also prescribed that workers that have been in the city for more than 6 months are entitled to unemployment benefits and services from the local government. In practice, however, most migrants receive little or no local government support.

Many of the millions of migrants living in urban areas are illegal. This poses grave problems, as residing illegally in an urban area makes one illegible to receive education, access to medical care, housing and other public services. Even legally employed rural migrants living in cities do not enjoy the same access rights to health, medication, and education opportunities as urban residents. For example, the UNDP China Human

Development Report of 2007/08 showed that 74.8 per cent of migrants are not covered by any insurance.

While recent reforms have loosened the *hukou* system for the well educated and rich, the reforms have not addressed the core problem facing most rural migrants, which is the link between their *hukou* status and public services. One serious issue is the lack of affordable and accessible provision of educational opportunities for the children of migrants, which in turn continues to impact on the growing number of child labourers. Migrants' first jobs in the cities are most often obtained through labour recruiters who travel to villages and rural towns looking for groups of people to work on projects. In many cases, the potential migrants have no idea what type of work they will undertake and if they will be paid what they are promised. In practice, promises often fail to materialise, leading many migrants to work illegally in the cities with no contracts or benefits. This makes them very vulnerable to arbitrary dismissal, illegal working conditions, and wage arrears or simply non-payment of wages. The ILO's 2007 Global Report on Discrimination noted that migrant workers cannot obtain an urban *hukou* to give them better access to housing, health care, and education. It said that some progress has been made in redressing these inequalities by ensuring a minimum wage for migrant workers, the enforcement of a labour contract, and access to employment services and job training.

The financial crisis caused a sharp drop in foreign demand, and many export-oriented enterprises and labour-intensive industries massively laid off workers. Migrant workers who had been laid off found it particularly difficult to stay in the cities, because, in addition to the lack of social protection, they had no other safety net to fall on. The crisis provoked a tide of returning migrants putting more pressure on the rural economy. Before the Spring of 2009, an estimated 70 million migrant workers returned home, roughly the 50 per cent of the migrant worker workforce. A reported 4 million of migrants, 5.8 per cent, who went back to the countryside in 2009 were owed wages in arrears, in many cases by entrepreneurs who shut down their operations and fled.

The urban-rural wage gap is high, officially standing at 3.36:1 in 2009. The average wealth gap has now reached 11,100 yuan, 1360 more than it was in 2007. The majority of rural migrants are employed in low paid, labour intensive industries, such as mining, earning far less than urban residents. In 2009, a People's Daily survey showed that rural migrant workers earned 1,417 yuan per month, a wage rise of 5.7 per cent comparatively to the year before. The wages of locals are one third more to double this amount, depending on the sector and the city of employment. For most migrants, the minimum wage set in particular areas is in practice the maximum and recent inflation has seriously cut away the value of recent wage increases.

According to official figures, the total wage in arrears across China from 2005 to July 2007 was 66 billion yuan The problem is most severe in the construction industry, which accounts for over 70 per cent of the total amount owed. The vast majority of those employed in the construction industry are migrant workers. In the construction industry, part of the problem comes from poor employment practices, such as illegal recruitment and lack of formal contracts, and a lack of clear accountability in legislation.

Ethnic Minorities

Government policy provides members of recognised ethnic minorities with preferential treatment in birth planning, university admission, access to loans, and employment.

Nevertheless, in practice minorities are often discriminated against in terms of access to equal education opportunities and employment. Discrimination is the source of deep resentment in some areas, such as in the Xinjiang Uyghur Autonomous Region (XUAR), the Inner Mongolia Autonomous Region and the Tibetan Autonomous Region and areas. It is widely reported that despite extensive, large scale development projects in the XUAR, many ethnic Uyghurs failed to benefit from newly created construction jobs and instead Han migrant workers were brought in to work, particularly on road construction and oil and gas pipelines.

....

In the Tibetan Autonomous Region (TAR) and surrounding Tibetan autonomous prefectures and counties, there are frequent claims of discriminatory employment practices and economic opportunities which favour the Han Chinese and disadvantage Tibetan nationals. Unemployment in some areas among Tibetan youth has been put at around 70 to 80 per cent, while the disparity in Chinese language skills required for well-paid jobs perpetuates the already skewed system of preferential recruitment against ethnic Tibetans.

Persons with Disabilities

Chinese law prohibits discrimination against persons with disabilities. Nonetheless, unemployment of disabled persons is a problem. Although the Employment Promotion Law expanded the legal protection of disabled persons, it seems that the implementation of the law is lax. In respect to the employment situation, out of 83 million persons with disabilities, only 21.7 million are employed and another 10 million receive social protection benefits. Official data demonstrate that almost 25 per cent of disabled persons live in extreme poverty and that children with disabilities have far higher illiteracy rates when compared to the national average. Moreover, universities can legally exclude persons with disabilities otherwise qualified to follow their programmes. The government operated 3,731 vocational education and training schools in 2008, providing training and job-placement services for 774,000 disabled persons.

Persons Living with HIV/AIDS and Hepatitis B

Despite provisions in the Employment Promotion Law, discrimination against persons with HIV/AIDS and hepatitis B remains a problem. China is estimated to have 93 million hepatitis B carriers and discrimination against this group in access to opportunities of employment and education has been significant. In May 2007, the Ministry of Labour and the Ministry of Health enacted a regulation prohibiting tests for hepatitis B during recruitment and prescribing that companies pay 1,000 yuan for demanding the tests. The application of this law is lax according to a survey published in *China Daily* in February 2009 stating that 84 per cent of companies require such a test from their candidates.

Conclusions

Discrimination is prohibited by law however in practice it is prevalent. Women, ethnic minorities, migrant workers and persons who live with HIV/AIDS and Hepatitis B suffer from discrimination either in remuneration, or in access to employment, education and public services. In particular the institutionalised discrimination against migrant workers from rural areas remains a serious problem, despite recent legislation.

III. Child Labour

The People's Republic of China ratified ILO Convention No. 138, the Minimum Age Convention in 1999, and ILO Convention No. 182, the Worst Forms of Child Labour Convention in 2002.

Child labour is prohibited by law and restrictions are in force for those aged between 16 and 18, legally named "juveniles". The law foresees fines and revocation of licenses of companies that fail to apply the law. However, child labour is widespread.

Only under special circumstances can children legally be employed, such as in sports, arts or through occupational training and educational labour, but only if their personal health and safety is not affected. On April 1, 2009 the government established a reward system to encourage reporting of child labour cases. Nonetheless, China does not publish any data on child labour or on tried lawsuits and other investigations. The penalties prescribed by the law are not stringent; measures against offenders are limited to fines and forced return of the children to their parents. Criminal law provisions apply only to cases of child trafficking, employing minors in strenuous or hazardous work, excessive forced child labour and offering a child for prostitution or pornography; furthermore, the CEACR has reported that in some cases the penalties foreseen by the criminal code for certain labour crimes are not dissuasive enough.

Competence for dealing with child labour resides with labour bureaux at all levels of local government. Labour bureaux can act alone or in conjunction with public security, officers of industry and commerce bureaus and trade unions. The inspection can be regular, irregular and extraordinary based on media or public reports. However, lack of proper enforcement of regulations, lack of sufficient resources, and corruption continue to block efforts at improving the situation. The problem persists, even in cases where the law has officially been applied, because of officers' mistakes, negligence and extensive corruption. For example, despite the massive media coverage surrounding the discovery of hundreds of slaves found working in Shanxi brick kilns in 2007 many of those freed have not been returned home. The case resulted in a few high profile prosecutions but most local officials and others involved in the case remain in their positions.

There is substantial employment of children under the age of sixteen in China. Studies have revealed that child labour is a result of the poor conditions of the rural education system. Education is supposed to be free and compulsory for nine years, however, inadequate resources are provided for education, which has resulted in a range of fees being demanded from parents. Despite government initiatives to subsidise school fees for poor families, parents send their children to work because their children's education is costly. Work-study programmes, which are regulated by the Ministry of Education, allow schools in poor areas to set up income generating schemes in agriculture and manufacturing, employing children to earn money for their school fees as well as learn skills. Although some schemes are limited to seasonal agricultural work, improving school facilities or making small handicrafts, many of these programmes have resulted in abuses such that child labour is forced and used in dangerous and labour-intensive industries such as agriculture, construction and factories working long hours under harsh conditions.

The work-study programmes are inadequately regulated as they fall under the responsibility of the Ministry of Education and not the Ministry of Labour and Social Security, with few public rules on working hours, job descriptions, or age limitations. According to Human Rights Watch (HRW), more than 400,000 middle and junior high schools are running work-study schemes. One example, cited by HRW in June 2007, is the case of 500 children from a middle school in Sichuan working 14 hour shifts in a factory during summer. They slept in overcrowded dormitories, got insufficient food, suffered work-induced health problems and were fined for production mistakes.

. . . .

Apprenticeships are also used to employ children in factories. These can be extended apprenticeships whereby children are employed for several months working long hours. Children particularly from rural areas and migrants' children may be sent as apprentices to craftsmen and small enterprises. The law does not prohibit the employment of underage apprentices and this enables certain employers to conceal their use of child labour. The CEACR has asked that China bring its law in line with Convention No. 138 and set the age of 14 as the minimum age limit for apprentices to work. It is reported that apprentices only receive board and lodging and in the best cases, some pocket money. One example uncovered in June 2007 concerned the Longzhen Connector Component Factory in Dongguan where some 300 students, most of them under 16 from Sichuan Province, were working 14 hours a day on 8 month apprenticeships. Another example was Yonghong Electronics in Shenzhen where a 2006 report indicated that the company recruited 14 and 15 year old children as apprentices to work for low pay and long hours in the electronics factory, beyond the summer period. Interviews among the student workers showed that the workers were not free to leave the factory. They were sent by their schools and told to work until enough payments were received for their school fees. They were not allowed to return before payments were made and were kept beyond school holidays.

Conclusions

Child labour, although prohibited under the age of 16, is a serious problem in China. Children are sometimes employed under forced conditions or performing the worst form of child labour. Law enforcement officers often fail to apply the law effectively. Work-study programmes, run under school auspices, frequently result in child labour and forced child labour.

IV. Forced Labour

The People's Republic of China has not ratified ILO Convention No. 29, the Forced Labour Convention, nor ILO Convention No. 105, the Abolition of Forced Labour Convention.

Chinese law prohibits forced and compulsory labour, including by children. However, the ILO's CEACR has deemed the punishment for forced labour offenses not stringent enough: penalties range from an administrative fine to a maximum of three years' imprisonment.

In practice, forced labour is a serious problem. Many employers withhold employees' payments until the contract's expiration, in order to avoid early departures of their workers. Workers not having the choice of leaving their work are vulnerable to forced labour and other abuses of their rights.

In May 2007, several hundred children and mentally ill people were rescued from scores of brick kilns in Shanxi province, resulting in one of the biggest scandals in recent years. Despite the alleged strengthening of monitoring and oversight, in February 2008, in Huangpi a brick kiln owner was found guilty of forcing 20 mentally retarded people into work. The incident was revealed by media after the kiln caught journalists' attention when a worker was killed by his co-workers. The "employer" paid the slaves the equivalent of a week's pay for the labour of a whole year. In May 2009 another brick kiln, in Anhui Province, was found guilty for forcing 32 retarded persons into work.

Forced labour systematically occurs in China's penal institutions, with regard to prisoners sentenced by the criminal justice system to "reform through labour" and those undergoing the administrative punishment of "re-education through labour" which bypasses the criminal justice system altogether. Detainees in "re-education through labour" facilities are required to work, often for very long hours with little or no remuneration. Sometimes the prisoners are contracted out to non-prison enterprises. There is no efficient control over prison labour products to bar them from being exported and in recent investigations the Chinese authorities controlled all information provided. Such labour camp based enterprises are a key economic player in some regions, such as Xinjiang where many such penal institutions are based. In 2006, the ITUC pointed out that children between 13 and 16 years can be sent to "custody and re-education" programmes by the local public security bureaux without recourse to the criminal justice system. Children working in re-education through labour camps have little safeguard against overwork and poor conditions. Generally, when placed in re-education through labour camps, there is little avenue for appeals except to the public security bureau itself. Moreover, forced labour is also used in detoxification and rehabilitation centres for drug addicts.

Trafficking in human beings is prohibited by law but remains a serious problem. The scope of the definition of trafficking does not cover debt bondage, forms of coercion other than abduction or offences against males. The fight against trafficking is largely perceived as anti-prostitution measures. The Trafficking Report of the US Department of Labor states that "there were numerous confirmed reports of involuntary servitude of children, migrant workers, and abductees in China."

. . . .

Conclusions

Forced labour is prohibited in China but does occur in commercial enterprises. There is forced prison labour in the form of "re-education through labour camps,", including prison labour by children. Progress in prosecuting traffickers and in protecting and assisting victims of trafficking, which affects women, men, and children, has been limited so far.

Recommendations

1. The Chinese government should ratify ILO Conventions No. 87, on Freedom of Association and Protection of the Right to Organise, and No. 98, on the Right to

Organise and Collective Bargaining. The government should allow the formation of independent unions.

2. Chinese law should provide for the right to collectively bargain and the government should design policies to actively promote collective bargaining as the primary step for labour disputes settlement and labour relations management. The Labour Contract Law should provide support for increased worker participation in negotiating contracts apart from through the official trade union and should contain sanctions on enterprises that refuse to implement a collective wage consultation system.
3. The government should lift limitations and impediments on independent labour rights groups, law firms, human rights organisations and workers' individual efforts to pursue their cases through the courts of justice. Those currently imprisoned for the peaceful exercise of these activities should be released.
4. The right to strike needs to be recognised and workers enabled to exercise it freely.
5. The Chinese authorities must thoroughly investigate and effectively prosecute and punish those who commit violence and other crimes against protesting workers.
6. Women's representation in skilled positions should be increased through more effective government equality programmes and wage equality must be promoted.
7. Law enforcers should investigate cases of sexual harassment effectively and take measures against offenders in a timely fashion.
8. China needs to amend its housing registration system, "*hukou*," in order to allow rural migrants to register and enjoy the local governments' social benefits and look for better employment opportunities. The government needs to apply the Employment Promotion Law's provisions on the issue with a view to improving the livelihoods of migrant workers who live in cities.
9. China has to end discrimination in employment against Chinese citizens of Uyghur, Tibetan or other origin in employment opportunities, access to public services, education opportunities and access to decision making.
10. State authorities have to take additional measures in order to provide equal opportunities of employment and education to disabled persons and children.
11. The government should take measures against companies which ask for HIV/AIDS and Hepatitis B tests before hiring, and which discriminate in any way against such persons.
12. The state should start gathering statistical data on child labour and publicise lawsuits and prosecutions against offenders.
13. The law prohibiting child labour should become stricter and provide dissuasive penalties for offenders. It should establish the age of 14 as the minimum age limit for apprentices to work.
14. The government needs to increase expenditure on education in order to make it free and accessible to all, especially poor families. It should urgently stop the practice of work-study programmes, which has been abused in some cases amounting to child slavery.
15. The government should ratify ILO Conventions No. 29, on Forced Labour, and No. 105, the Abolition of Forced Labour Convention.
16. The law prohibiting forced labour should become stricter and enact dissuasive penalties for offenders. Wage withholding and other measures resulting in debt bondage should be explicitly outlawed and punished.

17. China should abolish the administrative punishment of "re-education through labour". Penal work undertaken through "reform through labour" for prisoners and drug addicts, including the "custody and re-education" for children detainees, should also be ended.
18. The Chinese law on trafficking in human beings needs to be amended in order to cover debt bondage, non-violent forms of coercion and offenses against males in the definition of trafficking. China should become more efficient in prosecuting and punishing traffickers, as well as assisting and protecting the victims of trafficking through public shelters, legal and psychological assistance. It should closely cooperate with foreign governments on issues of trafficking and facilitate NGOs in protecting victims. It should stop deporting migrants, refugees and victims of trafficking to North Korea.
19. The Chinese government should reinforce labour bureaux, inspectorates and other authorities with financial and human resources, including training, in order to achieve better, quicker, and more efficient law enforcement. Labour inspectors should be enabled to recognise cases of violations of the laws regarding child labour, safety, and health regulations, forced labour, and equality, and thoroughly investigate them. Courts of justice should be efficient and quick in prosecuting and punishing offenders.
20. In line with the conclusions of the Singapore and Doha WTO Ministerial Conferences and China's obligations as a member of the ILO, the government of China should provide regular reports to the WTO and the ILO on its legislative changes and implementation of all the core labour standard.
21. The WTO should draw to the attention of the authorities of China to the commitments they undertook to observe core labour standards at the Doha Ministerial Conference. The WTO should request the ILO to intensify its work with the government of China in these areas and provide a report to the WTO General Council on the occasion of the next trade policy review.

QUESTIONS

1. Comparing laws with practices, list the top three areas of labor law in China needing reform. Explain what types of reforms might be most effective, and explain why.
2. How is it to be explained that China has ratified more ILO Conventions on core labor rights than has the United States?
3. Does the Labor Mediation and Arbitration Law encourage more arbitrations or more court litigation of labor disputes, or both? Do statistical data support this position?[143] Explain.

---

6. *Taiwan and Hong Kong: Brief Survey and Critiques*

Taiwan and Hong Kong, being Chinese communities, are a necessary component for understanding China and East Asia and the comparative and competitive advantages

[143] *See* Brown, *supra* note 100 at 180, discussing litigation.

of doing business in East Asia. However, for purposes of this book and the utility of providing contextual materials for comparative study, only a brief description of labor laws is referenced in this section. This is intended to keep the primary comparative emphasis on China, Japan, and South Korea.[144]

---

a. Taiwan

Revised Labor Law Encourages Union Membership[145]

Philip Liu

The Legislative Yuan passed a revision of Taiwan`s Labor Union Law on June 1, [2010] setting in place a complete legal framework for the protection of worker rights on the island.

[144] For a more complete overview of Taiwan's labor and employment laws, see Council of Labor Affairs, Overview, http://www.cla.gov.tw/cgi-bin/siteMaker/SM_theme?page=48eaf454 (last visited Sept. 30, 2010). For discussion on the economic significance of Taiwan and Hong Kong with China, see Kevin Honglin Zhang, *Why does so much FDI from Hong Kong and Taiwan go to Mainland China?*, 16 CHINA ECON. REV. 293 (2005), *available at* http://www.aiecon.org/advanced/suggestedreadings/PDF/sug365.pdf (last visited Sept. 30, 2010) and see WILLEM VAN KEMENADE, CHINA, HONG KONG, TAIWAN, INC.: THE DYNAMICS OF A NEW EMPIRE (1998).

[145] Philip Liu, *Revised Labor Law Encourages Union Membership*, CENS.COM (June 10, 2010), http://www.cens.com/cens/html/en/news/news_inner_32591.html (last visited Sept. 30, 2010). See also, a report in the Pacific Bridge, Inc. – Asian HR eNewsletter. "In June 2010, the Taiwanese government passed the Labor Unions Act. This new law will work in conjunction with the Group Contract Law (2008) and Law for Settlement of Labor-Management Disputes (2009); it will further regulate employee rights at both local and foreign companies in the country. The Labor Unions Act is expected to become effective sometime in early 2011. Under the new law, full-time workers are required to join unions where available. Dispatched workers are not included under the regulations. Companies that are deemed to have treated workers unfairly (i.e., job transfer, dismissal, salary reduction, etc.) for joining a labor union can now be fined up to NT$300,000 (about USD$9330). Banning employees from taking time off from work to handle union activities may also result in a fine of up to NT$100,000 (about USD$3110). The Labor Unions Act also for the first time allows foreign laborers working in Taiwan to join trade unions and even to be elected as union leaders. Legislators expect the new law to increase union membership among Taiwan's workforce significantly. The 2009 estimates by Hewitt Associates show that there were more than 4500 unions in Taiwan with around 3 million members. The country's total labor force is estimated to be around 11 million." Pacific Bridge, Inc., *LABOR UNIONS ACT PASSED IN TAIWAN*, ASIAN HR ENEWSLETTER (July 15, 2010), http://www.pacificbridge.com/asianews.asp?id=465. "According to the government's Council of Labor Affairs (CLA), the main objective for amending the law was 'to solve the current problems for the development of the labor unions, such as limitation of exercising workers' right to organize, inflexibility of the labor union framework, insufficient protection of workers' right to organize, defective financial management mechanism of the labor unions and so on . . . The simultaneous implementation of the three labor laws will provide a comprehensive shield of three labor rights' of the right to negotiate, to organize, and to strike, said Wang Ju-hsuan, CLA minister." Susan R. Heylman, *Taiwan Labor Union Law Expands Workers' Right to Organize, available at* http://www.shrmindia.org/taiwan-labor-union-law-expands-workers%E2%80%99-right-organize.

The law complements the Group Contract Law and the Law for the Settlement of Labor-Management Disputes, which were passed in 2008 and 2009, respectively, and guarantees local laborers the right of negotiation, dispute, and solidarity.

[T]he three labor laws will be implemented simultaneously . . . on May 1, 2011 . . . , after eight subsidiary laws are enacted and arbitration mechanism for labor-management disputes is set up.

The Labor Union Law stipulates that local laborers "should" join labor unions. This is of the nature of an instruction, a compromise between two opposing proposals: free participation and mandatory participation. Employers who block the formation and operation of labor unions will be subject to continuous heavy penalties.

. . . .

. . . although union membership will not be mandatory, the government will put in place stipulations that encourage membership. The Group Contract Law, for instance, will prohibit non-union members from benefiting from the fruits of labor-union negotiations.

The revised Labor Union Law imposes an NT$300,000 fine on employers who give employees unfavorable treatment – job transfers, pay cuts, or dismissal, for instance – for joining labor unions. Union leaders will be entitled to take leave for handling union affairs.[146]

The law divides labor unions into three categories: enterprise unions, trade unions, and vocational unions. [The Government states] . . . trade unions can represent a company's laborers in negotiations with its management, so long as half of the company's workers are its members. Foreign laborers will be allowed to serve as union leaders. Teachers will also be allowed to organize trade unions, but not unions of their specific schools. They will also not be allowed to strike. The new laws are expected to boost the ratio of union membership among local laborers, which now stands at only 3%.

Below is a chart showing the chronology of Taiwan's labor and welfare legislation (as of 2008).[147]

[146] In accordance with Article 6 of the Labor Union Law, labor unions can be categorized into craft union and industrial union. The term "industrial union" shall mean the union organized by workers of different crafts in various divisions of one and the same industry, whereas the term "craft union" shall mean the union jointly organized by workers of one and the same craft. Based on Article 47, 48, 49, and 50 of the Law, unions can organize federation of labor unions when all the legal terms are met. Statistics of labor union in Taiwan as of the end of 2007 are listed: (1) Number of basic industrial unions: 995, with 580,315 members. (2) Number of basic craft unions: 3376, with 2,453,347 members. (3) Number of general federation: 75, with 3783 group members. (4) Number of federation of labor unions: 141, with 1122 group members. (5) Number of labor unions: 4574, with 3,026,508 members, and 35.8 percent organization rate. Chih-Poung Liou, *The Roles of Labor Unions and Employee Representatives in Taiwan*, *available at* http://www.jil.go.jp/english/events_and_information/documents/clls06_08taiwan.pdf (last visited June 13, 2011).

[147] National Policy Foundation, Establishment of the Pension System in Taiwan (March 13, 2009), http://www.npf.org.tw/post/3/5577 (last visited Sept. 30, 2010).

Social Welfare Legislation and Policies in Taiwan

Year	Social welfare legislation	Social welfare programs, measures
Before 1949	Factories Act, Factory Inspection Act, Minimum Wage Act, Labor contract Act, Workers' Benefits Rules, and Labor Disputes Handling Act	1947 Department of Social Affairs, Taiwan Provincial, set up
1950		Servicemen Insurance and Labor Insurance launched
1952		Veterans Affairs Commission, Executive Yuan, R.O.C. set up
1953	Army, Navy, and Air Force Servicemen Insurance Rules	
1958	Labor Insurance Rules, and Civil Servants Insurance Act	
1963		Assistance of children service program from the Children's Fund of the United Nations
1964		Social policy of Present Stage for the Principle of the People's Livelihood
1965		Social Welfare Fund set up
1966		Strengthening Social Welfare Measures of Provinces and Cities (Phase I)
1967	Social Assistance Investigation of Taiwan Province Law	
1968	Labor Insurance Rules (amended)	Community Development Eight-year Plan for Taiwan Province, and the Outlines for Community Development Program
1969		Outlines for present social construction program
1970		Four-year community development plan for Taipei City, Ten-year community development plan for Taiwan Province
1971		Strengthening Social Welfare Measures of Provinces and Cities (Phase II)
1972		Plan for Family Well-off, Plan to Re-construct the Poor and Disabled
1973	Children's Welfare Act, and Labor Insurance Rules (amended)	Plan for Health and Wealth
1974	Occupational Safety and Health Act, and Civil Servants Insurance Act (amended)	Strengthening Social Welfare Measures of Provinces and Cities (Phase III)

Year	Social welfare legislation	Social welfare programs, measures
1975	National Housing Rules, and Factories Act (amended)	Asylum Plan for the Impoverished Mentally Ill, and Program for Improving Present Social Welfare Services and Assistance
1978		Strengthening Social Welfare Measures of Provinces and Cities (Phase IV)
1979	Labor Insurance Rules (amended)	Measures for Reforming Current Social Work, and Plan to Initiate Social Workers System in Taiwan Province
1980	Old Age Welfare Act, Handicapped Welfare Act, Social Assistance Act, and Private School Staff Insurance Rules	
1981	Implementation Byelaws for Old Age Welfare Act, Implementation Bylaws for Social Assistance Act, and Insurance Rules for Dependents of Public Servants	Community Development Plan in the first five-year period in Taiwan Province
1982	Compulsory School Rules, Implementation Byelaws for Child Welfare Act	
1983	Vocational Training Act	Program to Strengthen Infrastructure of Grassroots Level, and Program to Increase Farmers' Income
1984	Labor Standards Act	
1985		Health Insurance for Retired Civil Servants and Their Spouses, Health Insurance for Private School Staff and Their Spouses, and Farmers' Health Insurance
1987	Implementation Byelaws for Civil Servants Insurance Act	
1988	Juvenile Welfare Act, and Labor Insurance Rules (amended)	Outlines for Present Labor Policy, and Plans for the Elderly in Taiwan Province – Welfare Measures for Caring for Senior Citizens
1989	Farmers' Health Insurance Rules	Implantation Project of Cooperatives to Supply Daily Necessities for Civil Servants
1990	Handicapped Welfare Act (amended), Employment Service Act, Implementation Byelaws for Farmers' Health Insurance Rules, and Labor Standards Act (amended)	Six-Year National Development Plan

(*continued*)

Year	Social welfare legislation	Social welfare programs, measures
1991	Occupational Safety and Health Act (amended), Disabled People Health Insurance Scheme, Helping Nursery in Taiwan Province Scheme, and Implementation Byelaws for Handicapped Welfare Act	Six-Year National Development Plan – National Health Insurance, Outlines for Work of Community Development, Implantation Program for Emergency Life Aid of Unfortunate Women in Cities and Counties of Taiwan Province, and Management Rules for Funeral Facilities of Taiwan Province
1992	Employment and Welfare Act, Points to Help Abandoned Baby in Taiwan Province, and Implementation Points of Community Activities for Classroom of Mother	Work Program for Present Community Development in Taiwan Province, Work Program for Children, Juvenile and the Old Health Care in Cities and Counties in Taiwan Province, and Program for Society Peace in Taiwan Province
1993	Children's Welfare Act (amended), and Old Age Welfare Act (amended)	
1994	National Health Insurance Act	Outlines and Implementation Program for Social Welfare Policy
1995	Byelaws for the National Health Insurance Act, Handicapped Welfare Act (amended) Child and Youth Sexual Trade Prevention Rules, and Labor Insurance Rules (amended)	
1996		Women's Welfare Aids in Cities and Counties of Taiwan Province
1997	Sex Crime Prevention Act, Social Worker Act, Physically and Mentally Handicapped People Protection Act, Social Assistance Act (amended) – first reading, and Old Age Welfare Act (amended)	
1998	Domestic Violence Prevention Act	
2000		Provision of Assistance for Women and Households in Difficulties
2001	Voluntary Service Act	
2002	Gender Equality in Employment Act	
2003	Children and Youth Welfare Act	
2007	Employment Insurance Act (amended), National Pension Act, and Disabled People Protection Act (formerly Handicapped Welfare Act)	
2008	Labor Insurance Rules (amended) – pension insurance system	

Labor Arbitration in Taiwan[148]

New arbitration rules seen easing labor disputes

The Council of Labor Affairs has formulated new arbitration regulations to facilitate the settlement of labor-management disputes, council officials said Oct. 19, [2010].

The new rules, pending Cabinet approval, will greatly expand the scope of issues for which parties to a dispute can file for arbitration, the council said.

According to the CLA, the new regulations increase the range of issues that can be handled via arbitration to include "labor rights items," such as worker contracts, payment of outstanding salaries, overtime pay, severance packages and collective agreements.

The current regulations state that a dispute between management and labor must first be handled according to the mediation process, with arbitration or the appeal process only to be used to resolve cases in which mediation has failed to achieve a result.

However, applications for arbitration can only be filed for disputes that involve "adjustments to labor conditions," such as requests for salary increases or protests against pay cuts. Also, only groups are allowed to file for arbitration.

In addition, applications for arbitration in labor-management disputes have to be submitted by unions or by 10 or more workers in order to be accepted. The new regulations will allow for a single employee or member of management to request arbitration.

Nevertheless, the rules state that both parties in a dispute must agree to arbitration for it to move forward; otherwise the dispute must be resolved via the legal process.

The new regulations will also allow for the selection of neutral third-party arbitrators to settle labor-management disputes. This stipulation is expected to save at least two weeks in the process of resolving such disputes as the two parties will no longer be required to wait for an arbitration committee to handle their case.

The council explained that the new regulations are drafted in accordance with the amended Settlement of Labor Disputes Act that recently passed third reading in the Legislative Yuan. (SB).

. . . .

A critique of the current status of Taiwan's labor laws follows.

2009 Country Reports on Human Rights Practices: Taiwan[149]

. . . .

Section 7 Worker Rights

[148] *New arbitration rules seen easing labor disputes*, TAIWAN TODAY, Oct. 20, 2010, http://www.taiwantoday.tw/ct.asp?xItem=123837&ctNode=445; *see also*, The Settlement of Labor-Management Disputes Act (May 1, 2011), *available at* http://laws.cla.gov.tw/eng/EngContent.asp?msgid=200 .

[149] Taiwan Bureau of Democracy, Human Rights, and Labor, American Institute in Taiwan, 2009 Country Reports on Human Rights Practices (Mar. 11, 2010), http://www.ait.org.tw/en/officialtext-ot1007.html (last visited Sept. 30, 2010) [Formatting altered]; *see* ITUC, Taiwan – 2011, http://survey.ituc-csi.org/+-Taiwan-+.html (last visited June 13, 2011).

a. The Right of Association

The right to unionize is protected by law but is highly regulated under the Labor Union Law (LUL). Some public employees have limited rights to form unions. Teachers and civil servants were allowed to form professional associations to negotiate with the authorities but were not allowed to strike. These restrictions led to a long-running dispute between the authorities and groups representing teachers and civil servants. Foreign workers are not allowed to form their own unions or to assume union leadership positions in existing unions.

A number of laws and regulations limit the right of association. While labor unions may draw up their own rules and constitutions, they must submit them to county and city authorities as well as to the CLA for review. Labor unions may be rejected or dissolved if they do not meet CLA certification requirements or if their activities disturb public order.

As of June approximately 29 percent of the 10.9 million-person labor force belonged to one of the 4,721 registered labor unions. Many of them were also members of one of eight island-wide labor federations.

The right to strike is provided by law, and workers exercised this right in practice. However, legal constraints make it difficult to strike, undermining the usefulness of collective bargaining. Workers may strike over issues of compensation and working schedules, but not living or working conditions. Teachers and defense industry employees are not afforded the right to strike. The law requires mediation of labor disputes when the authorities deem them to be sufficiently serious or to involve unfair practices. The law prohibits labor and management from disturbing the "working order" while mediation or arbitration is in progress. Critics contended the law has a chilling effect on the right to strike because it does not clearly state what conduct is prohibited. The law mandates stiff penalties for violations of no-strike and no-retaliation clauses.

b. The Right to Organize and Bargain Collectively

The law gives workers the right to organize, bargain, and act collectively, although some positions are not afforded this right. As of September, there were 49 collective bargaining agreements in force; however, they covered only a small proportion of the labor force, mainly in large companies; 95 percent of industrial labor unions had no collective agreements. No special labor laws or labor law exemptions apply to the export processing zones in Kaohsiung and Taichung.

The LUL prohibits discrimination, dismissal, or other unfair treatment of workers because of union-related activities. Labor unions charged that during employee cutbacks, labor union leaders were sometimes laid off first or dismissed without reasonable cause. According to the Taiwan Confederation of Trade Unions and the Taiwan Labor Front, there is no specific penalty for the improper dismissal of a labor union leader.

c. Prohibition of Forced or Compulsory Labor

The law prohibits forced or compulsory labor. However, there were reports that such practices occurred. There was evidence of trafficking in persons into forced labor in such sectors as household caregivers, farming, fishing, manufacturing, and construction (see section 7.e.). The anti-trafficking law criminalizes forced labor, and public awareness campaigns included worker education pamphlets, foreign worker hotlines, and Ministry of Education programs on trafficking as part of the broader human rights curriculum.

d. Prohibition of Child Labor and Minimum Age for Employment

The Labor Standards Law (LSL) stipulates age 15, when compulsory education ends, as the minimum age for employment. County and city labor bureaus effectively enforced minimum-age laws.

e. Acceptable Conditions of Work

The LSL provides standards for working conditions and health and safety precautions. As of May, the LSL covered an estimated 6.5 million of the 7.9 million salaried workers. Those not covered included health-care workers, gardeners, bodyguards, teachers, doctors, accountants, lawyers, civil servants, and domestic workers.

Foreign household caregivers and domestic workers were covered instead by the Employment Services Act, which does not guarantee a minimum wage or overtime pay, set limits on the workday or workweek, or provide for minimum breaks or vacation time. At the end of June, 172,000 of the 341,000 foreign household caregivers and domestic workers had applied for coverage under the Employment Services Act. There were no plans to increase the minimum monthly wage of NT$17,280 (approximately $532) or the minimum hourly wage of NT$104 ($3.20) which were established in 2007. While sufficient in less expensive areas, the minimum wage did not provide a decent standard of living for a single-income family in urban areas such as Taipei. Labor rights activists alleged any benefit to foreign workers from previous increases to the monthly minimum wage failed to cover the increase in the maximum NT$5,000 ($154) monthly deduction the CLA allowed employers to collect. The average manufacturing wage was more than double the legal minimum wage, and the average wage for service industry employees was even higher. Nevertheless, the real monthly average wage in the first half of the year at NT$42,909 ($1,321) was the lowest in the 13 years. Many workers either lost their jobs or took unpaid leave in the first half of the year. To assist jobless workers, the authorities revised the Employment Insurance Act in May to extend unemployment relief payments from six months to nine months. Legal working hours were 336 hours per eight-week period (for an average of 42 hours per workweek). A five-day workweek has been mandated for the public sector, and according to a CLA survey, more than half of private sector enterprises also had a five-day workweek.

The law provides standards for working conditions and health and safety precautions and gives workers the right to remove themselves from dangerous work situations without jeopardy to continued employment. There was widespread criticism that the CLA did not effectively enforce workplace laws and regulations. In the first half of the year, CLA's 318 inspectors conducted 80,354 inspections, an increase of 38 percent from the same period in 2008. Those 318 inspectors were responsible for inspecting approximately 300,000 enterprises covered by the Occupational Safety and Health Law. Labor NGOs and academics argued that the labor inspection rate was far too low to serve as an effective deterrent against labor violations and unsafe working conditions. Regulations require intensified inspection and oversight of foreign labor brokerage companies. NGOs reported that labor brokers and employers regularly collected high fees or loan payments from foreign workers, frequently using debt as a tool for involuntary servitude, and that foreign workers were unwilling to report employer abuses for fear the employer would terminate the contract and forcibly deport them, leaving them unable to pay back debt accrued to brokers or others.

An employer may only deduct labor insurance fees, health insurance premiums, income taxes, and meal and lodging fees from the wages of a foreign worker. Violators face fines of NT$60,000 to 300,000 (approximately $1,850 to 9,240) and lose hiring privileges. Critics, however, complained that these practices continued and that the CLA did not effectively enforce statutes and regulations intended to protect foreign laborers from unscrupulous brokers and employers.

In 2008 the CLA opened a Foreign Worker Direct-Hire Service Center. The center allowed local employers to rehire their foreign employees, especially caregivers, without a broker. NGOs, however, argued that restrictions on eligibility to use the service prevented widespread implementation and advocated lifting restrictions on transfers between employers. This year the CLA expanded the program to permit rehiring of foreign workers engaged in manufacturing, fishery, construction, and other industries. In April the LY ratified the two UN Human Rights Covenants, including the UN Covenant on Economic, Social, and Cultural Rights, without reservation and passed an implementing law that mandates that the laws meet obligations outlined in the covenants. Civic groups and labor rights advocates lauded these actions but noted room for improvement. NGOs and academics urged the CLA to provide basic labor protections such as minimum wage, overtime, and a mandatory day off for household caregivers and domestic workers.

The NIA is responsible for all immigration-related policies and procedures for foreign workers, foreign spouses, immigrant services, and repatriation of illegal immigrants.

Foreign workers, not victims of trafficking or employer abuse, deemed to have worked illegally faced heavy fines, mandatory repatriation, and a permanent ban on reentering Taiwan.

———

ITUC 2007 Annual Survey of Violations of Trade Union Rights[150]

Trade Union Rights in Law

Many restrictions: Prior to 1971, when it was displaced from the ILO by the People's Republic of China, Taiwan had ratified ILO Convention no. 98 on the right to organise

[150] ITUC, 2007 Annual Survey of violations of trade union rights, http://survey07.ituc-csi.org/getcountry.php?IDCountry=TWN&IDLang=EN (last visited June 13, 2011). This critique was updated in 2011, as follows in the *Annual Survey of violations of trade union rights* 2011 – *ITUC*, Taiwan, *available at*, http://survey.ituc-csi.org/Taiwan.html#. "Taiwan and China signed a free-trade agreement on 29 June [2011].... Changes to labour laws have strengthened the protection of trade union rights. Most recently, the Labour Union Law was amended on 1 June 2010 and brought a number of significant improvements. Teachers are now allowed to join unions and migrant workers now also have the right to take part in unions' director and supervisor elections. A number of workers, including fire-fighters and medical personnel are still denied the right to organise, and civil servants may only form associations.... In 2009, the Settlement of Labor-Management Dispute Act was also

and collectively bargain. Despite this early international commitment, while the right to organise is generally protected by law there are also significant restrictions on this right. Defence industry workers, fire fighters, teachers, civil servants, doctors and Medicare personnel, defence industry workers, and domestic employees are still not permitted to form trade unions. Army personnel and police are also not permitted to form or join trade unions.

The Civil Servants' Association Law allows civil servants the right to organise professional associations. These do not in any way equate to trade unions. Teachers had hoped that they would be given the right to join and form unions, but the necessary amendments to the Labour Union Law, proposed by unions and their allies in the Legislative Yuan in January, were not considered. Under the Teachers' Law, teachers may form associations, but cannot form trade unions or take strike action.

Migrant workers can join trade unions, but only Taiwanese citizens may hold leadership positions.

The Labour Union Law states that labour union leaders must be elected regularly by secret ballot.

Government interference permitted: The legislation authorises the government to interfere directly in the internal affairs of trade unions. Trade unions must submit their articles of association and rules to the authorities at three levels of government (city, county, and national) for review prior to official registration. The authorities can also dissolve unions if they do not meet certification requirements or if their activities constitute a "disturbance of public order".

Restrictions on the right to strike: There are many restrictions on the right to strike, and government officials are given broad authority under the law to take decisions which curtail or prevent strikes. As a result, it is difficult to hold a legal strike, and workers complain that this effectively undermines their ability to develop leverage to collectively bargain. Strikes are only permitted concerning issues of wages/compensation, or working schedules. Government authorities can impose mediation or arbitration procedures for disputes that they consider sufficiently serious, or which involve "anti-competitive practices", or which they deem to involve 'unfair practices'. During such procedures, the law prohibits workers from interfering with the "working order". Severe sanctions are applied for failure to comply with the law, workers are not allowed to strike and employers are not allowed to take retaliatory action.

Collective bargaining limited: Collective bargaining is recognised by law but is not mandatory.

Limits to coverage of salaried workers under Labour Standards Law: The Labour Standards Law, which governs the rights and obligations of both workers and employers, and provides oversight for working conditions, does not apply to numerous sectors of the labour market, including civil servants, teachers, doctors, nursery employees and gardeners, domestic workers, lawyers, and bodyguards/security personnel. An estimated 15 to 20 per cent of the salaried workforce is outside the purview of this law, further

amended to better secure the right to strike. Limited collective bargaining: Barely 5% of the work force is covered by the 49 collective agreements in force, the majority in large companies. The content of these conventions rarely exceed the minimum stipulated by law.

Trade union members are first in line when it comes to dismissals: Even if the 1929 law on trade unions prohibits anti-trade union discrimination, it does not provide for penalties in case of the wrongful dismissal of leaders or members of trade unions. Many trade unionists are amongst the first to be dismissed during a restructuring or are dismissed for minor reasons. . . ." *Id.*

undercutting a minimum floor of standards upon which collective bargaining can be based.

Export Processing Zones (EPZs): Companies operating in the export processing zones are subject to the same labour laws as the rest of the country, with the exception of some high-tech industries.

Trade union rights in practice

Labour unions, as distinct from the many "craft" unions registered, are small and disorganised and represent just over three per cent of the workforce.

Collective bargaining limited: Very few workers are covered by collective agreements. Collective bargaining generally only takes place in large companies, which account for a mere five per cent of companies in the country. By 2006, only 22 per cent of existing industrial labour unions had been able to successfully negotiate a collective agreement for their members.

Employers loath to work with unions: Many employers were frequently unwilling to bargain agreements or otherwise discuss labour issues with unions, and many enterprises readily locked out or fired workers for union activities. There are no legal penalties for discrimination against union leaders.

Systematic abuses of the rights of migrant workers: Legal migrant workers pursuing justice in the civil courts for violation of contracts, damages for injury on the job, or non-payment of wages are frequently deported before their day in court arrives. The Council of Labour Affairs (CLA) regularly denies migrant workers an extension of their employment permit while their cases are pending in court, thereby depriving them of the right to remain in Taiwan. Migrant workers employed in homes as domestic workers continued to be denied coverage under the labour law, and therefore faced significant obstacles in seeking legal redress in instances when their rights are abused.

In November, the CLA introduced a new set of labour regulations governing the work of migrant workers. Employers of migrant workers are required to reach an agreement with their worker on key conditions of work such as hours of work and overtime, living quarters and meals, and holidays/time off. Contract terminations of migrant workers must be signed by a city or county government official in order to end inappropriate use of deportation as a threat against workers to keep them in line.

Violations in 2006

Background: The year was marked by political controversy and conflicts arising from charges of alleged corruption by President Chen Shui-bian's wife, son-in-law, and top aides. Votes in June and September in the Parliament to recall the President failed, but as protests mounted on the streets, the result was political deadlock for the remainder of the year.

False promotions to sideline union leaders at Bank of Overseas Chinese (BOOC): When Polaris Financial Group, one of the top securities firms in Taiwan, took over the BOOC, the bank's union [affiliate of the National Federation of Bank Employees Union (NFBEU)] stood in the way of the new owners' intention to restructure the bank to strengthen its appeal to potential buyers among international banking corporations.

On 13 March, without any prior notice the management notified union president Lee Ying-chung that he had been promoted to the position of deputy director-general of the BOOC Human Resources Department. According to the labour law, representatives of management human resources divisions are not allowed to be members of the union. The NFBEU reported that the intent of management was to change the union leadership to ensure that a more pliable, management-friendly union representative be appointed. Lee Ying-chung promptly refused the promotion and filed a complaint to office of the local labour authority requesting immediate revocation of management's appointment letter. Nevertheless, BOOC management pushed the union to immediately hold an election to replace President Lee and turn over the leadership of the union. To pressure the union, the BOOC temporarily cut off the union's internet access and threatened to deny access of the union leaders to the union's office on BOOC property.

After the Polaris Financial Group assumed control, the BOOC refused to negotiate with the union concerning changes in the conditions of employment or to provide guarantees of job security for employees in the case of a foreign take-over of the bank. The NFBEU further reported that management sought to intimidate union leaders to stay away from union meetings, and threatened to withdraw advertising from media publications that actively covered the expanding labour dispute. The union threatened to call a strike on 29 December to underline the demand for a collective agreement to protect the jobs of the BOOC employees, but the strike did not materialise. Nevertheless, as the year ended, the BOOC terminated Chen Hui-chih, the acting president of the union, and another leading union activist for their activities to rally support for employees' demand for an agreement. The union called the lay-offs illegal and planned to appeal.

Lawsuit in retaliation at collective action by migrant workers: In February 2006, Hua Pan Manpower Consultant and Management filed a civil lawsuit against 14 Thai workers for damages caused during massive riots in August 2005 and demanded they pay the company NT $19.67 million. The riots followed months of inaction by Kaohsiung authorities over complaints of abuse by the Kaohsiung Rapid Transit Company (KRTC). Hua Pan supplied KRTC with Thai workers, who complained of many abuses, including beatings, forced overtime, and massive illegal deductions from their salaries. The lawsuit was filed despite a finding by the CLA's Foreign Labour Department that the unrest resulted from poor management of workers by Hua Pan, for which the company was fined $NT 1.5 million. A Cabinet-level CLA official was publicly quoted calling Hua Pan's lawsuit "unacceptable and unjustifiable." With the support of labour unions and NGOs, five of the 14 Thai workers countersued Hua Pan, claiming they had been held as slaves. Public pressure on Hua Pan later compelled the company to reduce the compensation demanded to a nominal amount, but the workers were not prepared to settle the dispute.

The reason for the Kaohsiung authorities' inaction became clear when a major scandal emerged in the contracting arrangements for the Thai workers. KRTC records showed one third of each worker's salary was being diverted into the pockets of other unknown persons. Over 22 Kaohsiung city and provincial officials, KRTC senior managers, and Chen Che-nan, a former top aide to President Chen Shui-bian, were indicted and tried on charges of corruption and breach of trust connected to arrangements made by Hua Pan. Meanwhile, Yen Shih-hua, the General Manager of Huapan, and his wife were tried for taking kickbacks from manpower agents in Thailand, as well as extorting money from the workers themselves.

. . . .

QUESTIONS

1. How well does the new labor legislation in Taiwan address the deficiencies outlined above?
2. Describe the similarities between the labor and employment laws of China and Taiwan.

b. Hong Kong

A brief description of Hong Kong's labor and employment laws is provided next, followed by a "critique" of the current status of Hong Kong's labor laws under international standards.[151]

Highlights Concerning Hong Kong and Chinese Employment Law[152]

. . . .

Although the Hong Kong Special Administrative Region ("Hong Kong") is part of the People's Republic of China ("PRC" or "China"), Hong Kong and China have fundamentally different legal systems with very different approaches to employment law. The Hong Kong legal system is based on the English legal system, although with many "Hong Kong characteristics." Hong Kong's flexible employment law regime is generally considered to be one of Hong Kong's selling points when foreign companies establish subsidiaries or offices in Asia. PRC law is a continental legal system, and employment law is based on the 1995 Labor Law and a 2007 Labor Contract Law, together with other associated legislation. PRC labor legislation favors the employee and the (government-backed) trade union, and is much less flexible than its Hong Kong counterpart. Some of the provisions in the new Labor Contract Law reflect an attempt by the government to stop some of the abuses that occurred because of legislative and enforcement inadequacies. Hong Kong employment law is generally familiar to Americans, and favors a free market approach, although it imposes certain statutory requirements on employers generally not seen in U.S. employment law. The primary source of Hong Kong employment law is the Employment Ordinance, although other Hong Kong legislation, as well as the common law, is also relevant.

. . . .

[151] A brief introduction to Hong Kong employment law, from an employment law practitioner's perspective follows, and is available at, Winston & Strawn LLP, *Hong Kong and Chinese Employment Law Update*, BRIEFING, January 2009, *available at* http://www.winston.com/siteFiles/publications/Hong_Kong_and_Chinese_Employment_Law_Update.pdf (last visited Oct. 2, 2010).

[152] *Id.*

Labor Regulation[153]

The Labor Department has four primary areas of work, namely, Employment Services, Labor Relations, Safety and Health at Work, and Employee Rights and Benefits. The objectives of these areas are given here:

Labor Relations: The aim is to foster harmonious labor relations through promotion of good employment practices and resolution of labor disputes.

Employment Services: The aim is to improve the utilization of human resources by providing a range of employment services to meet challenges and needs in the labor market.

Safety and Health at Work: The aim is to ensure that risks to people's safety and health at work are properly managed by legislation, education, and promotion.

Employee Rights and Benefits: The aim is to improve and safeguard employees' rights and benefits in an equitable manner.

Employment Ordinance, Chapter 57[154]

The Employment Ordinance is the main piece of legislation governing conditions of employment in Hong Kong. Since its enactment in 1968, the benefits provided for under the Ordinance have been substantially improved. It now covers a comprehensive range of employment protection and benefits for employees including the following:

- Wage Protection
- Rest Days
- Holidays with Pay
- Paid Annual Leave
- Sickness Allowance
- Maternity Protection
- Severance Payment
- Long Service Payment
- Employment Protection
- Termination of Employment Contract
- Protection Against Antiunion Discrimination

. . . .

Employment Law in Hong Kong[155]

The primary piece of legislation, the Employment Ordinance (the "EO"), prescribes certain basic rights and protection for all employees. The EO applies to every employee engaged under a contract of employment in Hong Kong with only a few minor exceptions,

[153] *Program Areas*, Labor Department of The Government of the Hong Kong Special Administrative Region, http://www.labour.gov.hk/eng/home/index.htm (last updated Aug. 25, 2009).

[154] Employment Ordinance Chapter 57, *available at* http://www.labour.gov.hk/eng/legislat/content2.htm. (last visited Dec. 6, 2011).

[155] Mayer Brown LLP, Guide to Employment Law in Hong Kong (2009), *available at* http://www.mayerbrown.com/publications/article.asp?id=4515&nid=6 (last visited Sept. 30, 2010).

for example, in relation to family members employed in family businesses and merchant seamen. The EO applies equally to locals and foreign nationals working in Hong Kong. Provided that the contractual terms of service are no less favourable than the basic protection afforded by the EO, the contract of employment will govern the relationship between employer and employee. To the extent that any contractual terms are less favourable, the EO will prevail.

There are a number of labour organisations/trade unions in Hong Kong but no closed shops. These are principally established on a trade-by-trade basis, although some of the larger corporations with substantial numbers of employees have labour unions particular to that corporation. Membership of trade unions in Hong Kong on a percentage basis is relatively low compared to its European or American counterparts. However, with the down turn in the economy, collective bargaining and union organised activities are gathering momentum. The EO contains protection against anti-union discrimination.

. . . .

Summary of Minimum Statutory Entitlements

Wages

[A Minimum Wage ordinance was passed by the city's Legislative Council on July 17, 2010, effective May 1, 2011.][156]

. . . .

Hours

Except in relation to the employment of young persons employed in industrial undertakings where special regulations apply, there are no statutory provisions which prescribe maximum working hours. The EO does however, provide that in addition to paid statutory (public) holidays, an employee is entitled to not less than one rest day in every period of seven days.

Benefits

Vacation

Employees are entitled a minimum of between seven days and fourteen days annual leave for each period of twelve months' employment, calculated on the basis of length of service.

For additional highlights of recent legal developments, see also Fiona Loughrey & Shun Fong Kung, *Keeping one eye open*, 8 ASIAN-COUNSEL 47 (2010), *available at* http://www.inhousecommunity.com/controlPanel/download.php?id=770.

[156] A Minimum Wage ordinance was passed by the city's Legislative Council on July 17, 2010, effective May 1, 2011. According to the ordinance, wages payable to an employee in respect of any wage period, when averaged over the total number of hours worked during that time, should be no less than the statutory minimum wage rate of 28 HK dollars (3.6 U.S. dollars). *See Minimum wage enforced in Hong Kong*, XINHUA, May 1, 2011, http://news.xinhuanet.com/english2010/business/2011-05/01/c_13854256.htm; *see also* Laney Zhang, *Hong Kong: Minimum Wage Law Takes Effect*, LIBRARY OF CONGRESS (May 17, 2011), http://www.loc.gov/lawweb/servlet/lloc_news?disp3_l205402674_text.

Bonuses
Many employers in Hong Kong pay an automatic annual bonus of one month's salary at Chinese New Year, although the trend is to replace this with a performance related bonus.

Pensions
The Mandatory Provident Fund Schemes Ordinance requires that every employer in Hong Kong contribute an amount equal to at least 5% of an employee's salary (up to a maximum of HK$20,000 per month) to a retirement scheme that is registered as an MPF scheme. Every employee will also be required to contribute at least 5% of his or her salary (again up to a maximum of HK$20,000 per month) to the scheme. There are certain exceptions to this general rule. Certain employers provide additional benefits through occupational retirement schemes. These are regulated by the occupational Retirement Schemes Ordinance.

Workmen's Compensation
Employers are required to maintain insurance coverage pursuant to the Employees Compensation Ordinance in respect of work-related injuries but otherwise, there is no statutory requirement to provide medical benefits.

Social Security

Hong Kong has a non-contributory social security system to provide a basic social safety net. No deductions are made from salary in respect of social security contributions.

Other Conditions

Maternity leave
Subject to the qualifying requirements, female employees are entitled to paid maternity leave of ten weeks or as provided by the terms of the employer, whichever is more favourable. Maternity leave pay is paid at the rate of 4/5ths of the employee's average wage over the preceding 12 month period.

Sickness leave
Employees are entitled to paid sick leave at the rate of 4/5ths of the employee's average wage over the preceding 12 month period. Entitlement to sickness leave may be accumulated at the rate of two paid sickness days for each completed month of employment during the first twelve months of employment and at the rate of four paid sickness days for each month thereafter, up to a maximum of 120 paid sickness days. The entitlement to sickness pay only applies, however, to periods of absence due to sickness of not less than four consecutive days.

Severance pay
An employee who has been employed for not less than 24 months is entitled to severance pay if he is dismissed by reason of redundancy or if the employee is laid off (i.e., where

the remuneration of an employee depends on his being provided with a particular kind of work and he is no longer provided with a sufficient amount of such work). The amount of severance pay is two-thirds of one month's pay for each year of employment or two-thirds of HK$22,500, whichever is less, subject to a maximum payment not exceeding HK$390,000. The amount of any contractual gratuity based on length of service is deductible from the amount of severance pay entitlement. In addition, that part of a retirement scheme payment which is due to the employer's contributions may be deducted from the amount of the severance pay.

. . . .

Long service pay

Certain employees who have been employed under a continuous contract for not less than five years are entitled to long service pay on dismissal. The amount of long service pay is calculated by reference to the same formula as for severance pay.

Annual Leave

Statutory Entitlement

Under the EO, employees are entitled to a minimum of 7 to 14 days statutory annual leave for each period of 12 months' employment, calculated on the basis of length of service. . . .

. . . .

Contractual Entitlement

An employee's contractual entitlement (i.e., entitlement in excess of the statutory entitlement) to annual leave varies depending on the nature of the employer and the employee's position. The EO, however, only regulates statutory annual leave and therefore the comments made in this section relate solely to an employee's statutory annual leave entitlement.

Time of Taking Leave

Employers are entitled to determine when annual leave is to be taken and must give 14 days' notice in writing to the employee of the time that they have selected. Annual leave must, however, be granted within 12 months of the end of the leave year, although in practice, most employers allow annual leave to be taken as it accrues.

. . . .

Maternity Leave

Eligibility

A female employee who is employed under a continuous contract of employment (i.e., she has been employed for four or more weeks and has worked at least 18 hours in each week) immediately before the expected date of her commencement of maternity leave, is entitled to take maternity leave in accordance with the EO (or as provided by the terms agreed with the employer, whichever is more favourable).

. . . .

Prohibition Against Termination

After a pregnant employee has served notice of pregnancy on her employer, her contract of employment cannot be terminated by the employer (other than for reasons permitting summary dismissal) from that date until the end of her maternity leave or the date of cessation of pregnancy (otherwise than by reason of birth).

. . . .

Sickness Benefits

Eligibility

An employee who has been employed under a continuous contract for a period of at least one month immediately preceding a sickness day is entitled to paid sickness allowance in accordance with the EO. There is no entitlement to take sick leave for reasons other than the employee's own poor health or injury. So, for example, a female employee cannot claim sickness allowance in respect of a day where she has been absent from work to care for her sick child.

. . . .

Prohibition Against Termination

There is a specific prohibition against the termination of employees whilst entitled to statutory sickness allowance.

. . . .

Form of Contract

There is no requirement in Hong Kong for a contract of employment to be in writing. However, upon written request before commencement of employment, the employer is required to give written particulars of certain conditions of employment. Where the contract of employment is in writing, the employer must provide a copy of it to the employee immediately after it is signed. The basic conditions which are required to be stated are the wages and wage period, the amount of end-of-year payment or the proportional entitlement and the length of notice required to terminate the employment.

Termination

Termination by Notice

The services of an employee on probation may be terminated by the employer or the employee without notice during the first month and by not less than seven days' notice thereafter.

In all other cases, the employee is entitled to:

- Not less than one month's notice of termination where the contract is deemed to be for one month renewable from month to month under the EO (i.e., where the employee has worked for 18 hours or more each week for a period of four weeks) and does not otherwise provide for the length of notice required to terminate the contract or
- Seven days or the agreed period, whichever is the longer, where the contract is for one month renewable from month to month and the length of notice of termination is provided for in the contract or
- In every other case (e.g., a fixed term contract), the agreed period, but not less than seven days in the case of a continuous contract. The length of notice for the termination of employment contract mentioned above does not include annual leave and maternity leave.

Termination by Payment in Lieu of Notice

An employment contract may also be terminated without notice by either party agreeing to pay to the other a sum equal to the amount of wages which would have accrued to the employee during the requisite period of notice.

. . . .

Employees' Entitlements on Termination

Accrued Wages and Unused Annual Leave

All outstanding wages and payments in respect of accrued but unused annual leave (only statutory leave, unless contract specifies otherwise) up to the time of termination are payable.

End of Year Payments

Where the employees are contractually entitled to an annual bonus, they will be entitled to a proportional payment thereof in respect of the year in which they are dismissed, unless the bonus is payable solely at the discretion of the company or they have not been employed for a continuous period of three months or more in the payment period. If an end of year payment is not specified in the employment contract, a sum equal to the monthly average wage of the employee will be awarded.

Severance Payments

An employee who has been employed under a continuous contract for not less than 24 months is entitled to severance payment if dismissed by reason of redundancy or if the employee is laid off (that is, where the remuneration of an employee depends on their being provided with a particular kind of work and they are no longer provided with a sufficient amount of such work).

"Dismissal" includes:

- Termination by an employer with or without notice or payment in lieu other than by summary dismissal
- The expiry of a fixed term contract which is not renewed with comparable terms and

- Constructive dismissal where an employee is entitled to terminate their contract without notice by reason of the employer's conduct. Redundancy occurs where the employer has ceased, or intends to cease, to carry on the business for the purpose of which the employee was employed, or in the place where the employee was so employed or where the requirements of that business for employees to carry out a particular kind of work or to carry out such work in the place where the employee was so employed have ceased or diminished or are expected to cease or diminish.

....

Long Service Payments

An employee with at least five years of service (other than an employee who retires) will be entitled to a long service payment if they are dismissed and his employer is not liable to pay them a severance payment. "Dismissal" has the same meaning as that under the provisions relating to severance payments described above. The amount of the long service payment is calculated according to the same formulae used to calculate severance payments. The calculation is also subject to the same restrictions on maximum payments.

As with severance pay, long service payments may be reduced by the total amount of any contractual gratuities based on length of service and the employer contribution element of any retirement scheme benefits paid to the employee in respect of any or all of the years of service for which severance pay is due.

Employment Protection Under the EO

Requirement for valid reason

The EO enables any employee who has been employed under a continuous contract for a period of not less than 24 months and who is dismissed or whose contract is varied without his or her consent to make a claim for "unreasonable dismissal" to the Labour Tribunal. Once such a claim is made, the employer is required to produce a valid reason for the dismissal or variation. Valid reasons include:

- The conduct of the employee
- The capability or qualifications of the employee for performing the work of the kind which he was employed by the employer to do and
- Redundancy of the employee or other genuine operational Requirements

Remedies

Even if an employee files a claim with the Labour Tribunal and their claim is upheld, the remedies available to the employee are unlikely to be significant unless the employer has terminated the employee in contravention of certain sections in the EO prohibiting the termination of employees on the grounds of pregnancy, while they are on a paid sickness day, or for participation in trade union activities (for which there are greater remedies). Assuming that termination of an employee is not for a prohibited ground, the Labour Tribunal can only make an order for reinstatement of conditions and/or re-engagement if the parties, including the employer, agree. Otherwise, the Tribunal may only make an award of terminal payments.

Terminal payments are, in effect, unpaid statutory and contractual entitlements which the employer should already have paid upon termination of the employee's contract. Although the Labour Tribunal may also award pro-rata entitlements where the employee has not attained the qualifying length of service, this is really only relevant to severance and long service pay. Severance and long service pay awarded by the Labour Tribunal can be set off by the amount of any contractual gratuity based on length of service or the employer's contribution element of any retirement scheme payment paid to the employee upon termination of employment.

Discrimination Laws

Generally

Discrimination on the grounds of sex, pregnancy, marital status (Sex Discrimination Ordinance "SDO"), disability (Disability Discrimination Ordinance "DDO"), family status (Family Status 20 Guide to Employment Laws in Hong Kong Discrimination Ordinance), race (Race Discrimination Ordinance "RDO") and trade union membership (EO) is currently prohibited by legislation in Hong Kong. Specifically, there is no protection against discrimination on the basis of age or sexual orientation nor is there any equal pay legislation. Each of the anti-discrimination Ordinances prohibits "direct" and "indirect" discrimination.

. . . .

It is unlawful for an employer to discriminate against an employee on a prohibited ground:

- In the way they afford that person access to opportunities for promotion, transfer, or training, or to any other benefits, services, or facilities or
- By refusing or deliberately omitting to afford that person access to them by the terms of employment they afford that person or
- By dismissing that person, or subjecting them to any other detriment.

There are very few exemptions in the four Ordinances that apply to private sector employment. All four Ordinances also prohibit victimisation – which is discrimination against a person on the ground that the person has made allegations of unlawful discrimination or harassment, has given evidence, or has taken steps to enforce one of the four Ordinances.

Finally, each Ordinance provides that an employer will normally be held vicariously liable for an unlawful act of an employee in the course of employment regardless of whether the act was done with the employer's consent or knowledge. However, an employer can avoid vicarious liability by demonstrating that it took such steps as were "reasonably practicable" to prevent the employee from committing the unlawful act. This is intended to encourage employers to institute and enforce equal opportunity policies.

Disability Discrimination

"Disability" is defined broadly in the DDO to include:

- Total or partial loss of bodily or mental functions
- Total or partial loss of a part of the body

- The presence in the body of organisms causing disease or illness
- The presence in the body of organisms capable of causing disease or illness
- The malfunction or malformation or disfigurement of a part of the person's body
- A disorder or malfunction that results in the person learning differently from a person without the disorder or malfunction
- A disorder or illness or disease that affects a person's thought processes, perception of reality, emotions, or judgment or that results in disturbed behaviour

The DDO covers a current disability, previous disability, future disability, and imputed disability.

. . . .

Race Discrimination

The RDO prohibits less favourable treatment of employees on grounds of race. The legislation is modelled on concepts contained in the existing anti-discrimination legislation. A Code of Practice on Employment under the Race Discrimination Ordinance has been issued by the Equal Opportunities Commission to provide practical guidance in preventing race discrimination in the employment field. The term 'race' means 'race, colour, descent, or national or ethnic origin of the person'. The following considerations (among others) are excluded from 'race' for the purposes of the ordinance:

- Whether the person is an indigenous inhabitant of the New Territories
- Whether or not a person is a Hong Kong permanent resident;
- Whether or not a person has the right of abode or the right to land in Hong Kong
- Whether or not a person is subject to any restriction or condition of stay imposed under the Immigration Ordinance (Cap. 115)
- Whether or not a person has been given the permission to land or remain in Hong Kong under the Immigration Ordinance (Cap. 115)
- The length of residence in Hong Kong of a person or
- The nationality, citizenship or resident status of a person under the law of any country or place concerning nationality, citizenship, resident status or naturalisation of or in that country or place
- Genuine occupational qualifications operate as a (limited) exemption to race discrimination in the field of employment. Under the RDO, genuine occupational qualifications apply only in five specified circumstances. The job involves participation in a dramatic performance or other entertainment in a capacity for which a person of a particular racial group is required for reason of authenticity.
- The job involves participation as an artist's or photographic model in the production of a work of art, visual images or sequence of visual images for which a person of a particular racial group is required for reason of authenticity.
- The job involves working in a place where food or drink is provided to and consumed by the public in a particular setting for which, in that job, a person of that racial group is required for reasons of authenticity.
- The holder of the job provides persons of a particular racial group with personal services promoting their welfare, and those services can most effectively be provided by a person of that racial group.

or

- The job involves providing persons of a particular racial group with personal services of such nature or in such circumstances as to require familiarity with the language, culture and customs of and sensitivity to the needs of that racial group, and those services can most effectively be provided by a person of that racial group.

Racial Harassment

Racial harassment in the workplace is specifically prohibited under the RDO. It occurs where the harasser:

- Engages in unwelcome conduct on the grounds of the race of the victim where a reasonable person would have anticipated that such person would be offended, humiliated or intimidated, or
- Engages in conduct that renders hostile or intimidating the environment in which the victim works or carries out related activities.

Calling employees derogatory names based on their ethnic group is likely to amount to harassment. Also, inappropriate racial jokes or pictures making fun of a particular ethnic group in the workplace may amount to unlawful harassment.

Sex Discrimination Specifically

The SDO prohibits the less favourable treatment of employees on the grounds of sex, marital status, and pregnancy. Genuine occupational qualifications operate as a (limited) exemption to sex discrimination (but not pregnancy, marital status, or family status discrimination) in the field of employment. Under the SDO, genuine occupational qualifications include:

- Where the essential nature of the job requires a person of a given sex for reasons of physiology or reasons of authenticity in dramatic performances
- Where the job needs to be held by a person of a given sex to preserve decency or privacy
- Where the job is likely to involve people doing the work or living in a private home and objection may reasonably be taken to a person of a given sex because of the degree of physical or social contact with that person in the private home or
- Where the holder of the job provides individuals with personal services promoting their welfare or education, or similar personal services, and such services can be best provided by a person of a given sex.

Separate exemptions exist under the SDO for affirmative action programmes and the withholding of housing, education, and similar benefits to a married employee on the basis that his or her spouse receives the same benefit.

Sexual Harassment

Sexual harassment in the workplace is specifically prohibited by the SDO. There are two types of behaviour that can amount to sexual harassment.

The first and more obvious form of sexual harassment arises from the conduct of a manager or employee (the harasser) towards another employee or applicant (the victim). Sexual harassment occurs where:

- The harasser makes a sexual advance or request for sexual favours, or engages in other conduct of a sexual nature towards the victim in circumstances where the victim does not welcome such conduct, and
- The harasser should reasonably have anticipated that the victim would be offended, humiliated or intimidated.

The second form of sexual harassment occurs where one or more co-employees engage in conduct of a sexual nature which creates a sexually hostile or intimidating work environment. This provision may transform seemingly trivial sexual conduct or conversations, and conduct or conversations which are not specifically addressed to a single employee, into cases of sexual harassment. Where a sexual harassment claim is made by an employee against one or more other employees, the only defence open to an employer is to demonstrate that it took all steps which were reasonably practicable to prevent the sexual harassment occurring.

Remedies

Proceedings under the anti-discrimination Ordinances in Hong Kong are commenced either by lodging a complaint with the Equal Opportunities Commission (EOC) and/or in the District Court. Prior conciliation by the EOC is not a pre-requisite to lodging proceedings in the District Court.

. . . .

Data Privacy Legislation

Generally

The collection, use and handling of personal data of employees in Hong Kong is governed by the Personal Data (Privacy) Ordinance (PDPO). With certain exemptions, the requirements of the PDPO are principally contained in six data protection principles set out in Schedule 1 of the Ordinance. Section 4 of the PDPO states that "a data user shall not do an act or engage in a practice that contravenes a data protection principle unless the act or practice as the case may be, is required or permitted under this Ordinance."

. . . .

The Mandatory Provident Fund

Obligation to Contribute

Under the Mandatory Provident Fund Schemes Ordinance ("the MPF Ordinance"), every employer in Hong Kong must contribute an amount equal to at least 5% of an employee's salary (up to a maximum salary of HK$20,000 per month) to a retirement scheme that is registered as an MPF scheme. Every employee will also be required to contribute at least 5% of their salary (up to a maximum salary of HK$20,000 per month) to the scheme. There are certain exceptions to this general rule.

Employee Compensation

The Employees' Compensation Ordinance (ECO) obliges every employer to obtain a policy of insurance for a specified minimum amount in respect of its liability to compensate employees for "injury by accident" or "death" arising "out of and in the course of employment."

....

The ECO also preserves common law remedies against employers whose negligence, breach of statutory duty (such as the Occupational Safety and Health Ordinance), or other wrongful act or omission has caused injury to the employee although the amount of damages awarded to an employee who has brought a common law action will be reduced by the amount of any compensation payable under the ECO.

....

Hong Kong: Trade Unions[157]

Hong Kong has a labour force of 3.1 million, distributed as follows: 17.5 percent in manufacturing, 8.1 in construction, 28.9 in distribution and catering (including 236,000 in hotels and restaurants), 11.4 in transport and communication, 11.6 in banking, insurance, real estate and business services and 21.5 in public services, health and education.

There are three trade union confederations: the HK Federation of Trade Unions (FTU), which claims 257,000 members in 135 unions, the HK Confederation of Trade Unions (HKCTU), 140,000 members claimed in 42 unions, and the HK Trades Union Council (HKTUC), has an estimated 30,000 members in 69 unions.

The FTU has no international affiliation but is controlled by the CPC and follows the policies of the Chinese government. The HKCTU is part of the democratic opposition and its leadership is active in the Democratic Party and in Frontier (see above). The HKTUC is controlled by the Kuomintang and is aligned with the government of the Republic of China (Taiwan). Both HKCTU and HKTUC are ICFTU affiliates.

In addition, there are unions not affiliated to any of the confederations (mostly in the civil service), which are pro-Beijing or independent.

The conditions under which the three confederations operate are by no means comparable. The FTU membership, for example, must be seen against the background of massive financial support the FTU has received from China which has enabled it to build up a network of business enterprises and services which no other union organisation can match. This includes the second-largest vocational training system in Hong Kong and assets including over 40 branch offices. After 1989, the FTU bought nine offices for HKD10–20 million each and expanded its head office. It provides benefits to its members which include support for mortgages, discounts in supermarkets and on

157 *Hong Kong: Trade Unions*, GLOBAL LABOR INSTITUTE (Sept. 5, 2007), http://www.globallabour.info/en/2007/09/hong_kong_trade_unions.html.

travel through its own travel agency, and free lifetime VISA cards issued by the Bank of China. It nets HKD36 million in business revenue per year from a printing press, a construction company, and the South China Travel Agency, which sells package tours to China.

The HKCTU has a total annual revenue of HKD3 million in a normal year (HKD6.5m. in 1997 which included funds raised to purchase its new office). It raises its revenue mainly from membership dues and from street collections. For example, it set up a stand at the Kun Tong subway station on December 13 to demonstrate for Labour Rights Week (an event instituted by the ICFTU), at which it gave away 3,000 copies of a 45-page brochure explaining the Employment Ordinance and at the same time collected HKD14,000 in four hours in voluntary contributions from passers-by (which paid for the brochures and generated a substantial surplus). In 1997 the HKCTU applied for a HKD400,000 project to the ICFTU, which was supposed to pay for two organisers and their activity. This application was substantially cut back to HKD110,000 to be shared by the HKCTU and the HKTUC.

The fragmentation of the FTU membership in 135 unions should also be noted. This reflects a policy of maintaining small affiliates which are easier to control (those who are familiar with the CGTP in Portugal or the CTM in Mexico, for example, will recognise the pattern). HKCTU policy is the opposite: unifying its affiliates into larger units.

Relations between the FTU and the HKCTU are tense. The FTU attacks the HKCTU as an "arm of a foreign power" (because of its international affiliation) and as "too radical" (radical methods, like strikes, demonstrations, etc. and unrealistic demands, like implementation of ILO conventions). It also attacked the HKCTU for lodging a complaint with the ILO against the HKSAR government in October 1997, which it called "attempting to internationalise internal affairs." The FTU, however, was itself criticised in the media (two TV channels) for failing to support the labour legislation which was adopted by the Legco and subsequently suspended by the Provisional Legislature.

The HKCTU Trade Union Rights Week demonstration on December 13 also featured an exhibit of twelve panels telling the story of HKCTU-led struggles for trade union rights, including those against the dismissals of union activists at the Welcome supermarket (1993), at HK Telecom (1993), at the bus company (for campaigning against noise hazards), and the Cathay Pacific 17-day strike in 1993 against increased flying time. One panel shows the decline of real wages (from 1.5 to 23 percent, depending on the sector) as a result of suppression of workers' rights. (Photographs of panels available).

Contrary to some predictions, the post-handover situation has not led to a weakening of the HKCTU, which actually increased its membership since July by about 7-8 percent. FTU membership has also increased in about the same proportion, whereas HKTUC membership is ageing and in decline.

An assessment of the trade union situation in Hong Kong would have to conclude that the HKCTU is the representative organisation of free and democratic trade unionism whereas the FTU is a wholly controlled subsidiary of the Communist Party of China although, like all unions in Hong Kong, it is based on voluntary membership (the same can be said of the Beijing-controlled Macau Federation of Trade Unions). The decline of the HKTUC is likely to be terminal.

. . . .

Alternative Dispute Resolution[158]

. . . .

The Labour Relations Division of the Labour Department of The Government of the Hong Kong Special Administrative Region is responsible for the maintenance of harmonious labour relations in the non-government sector. They provide "voluntary conciliation service to employers and employees to help settle their disputes and claims."

"Conciliation service is accessible to both employers and employees. In case of a labour dispute, either party involved may contact [one of 10 branch offices] to make enquiries in person. The staff of the branch office will interview the enquirer to understand the problem involved and explain the provisions of the Employment Ordinance. If the party concerned requires conciliation, a meeting for the purpose would be arranged, and the other party would be requested in writing to turn up at the conciliation meeting at the scheduled time.

At the conciliation meeting, the conciliation officer would assist both parties in exploring the crux of the problem concerned, and in analysing the situation. He would also draw their attention to the relevant requirements under the Employment Ordinance, thus facilitating them to reach a mutually acceptable settlement. If necessary, a settlement agreement would also be signed by the parties. If the settlement involves compensation by cash payment, the conciliation officer would make arrangements for effecting payment.

If either party fails to attend the conciliation meeting, or no settlement is reached between both parties at the meeting, the conciliation officer will arrange another conciliation meeting, or at the request of the party concerned, refer him, depending on the claim amount, to lodge a claim with the Minor Employment Claims Adjudication Board or the Labour Tribunal where the dispute will be adjudicated by the Adjudication Officer of the Minor Employment Claims Adjudication Board or the Presiding Officer of the Labour Tribunal."[159]

. . . .

Labour Tribunal[160]

What work does the Labour Tribunal carry out?

The Labour Tribunal offers a quick, informal, and inexpensive way of settling monetary disputes between employees and employers. There is no upper limit on the amount of claim.

The Tribunal hears claims arising from the failure of a person to comply with the provisions of the Employment Ordinance (Cap. 57) or the Apprenticeship Ordinance

[158] Conciliation Service of the Labor Relations Division, *available at* http://www.labour.gov.hk/eng/public/wcp/ConciliationServiceLRD.pdf (last visited Dec. 6, 2011).

[159] Conciliation Service of the Labor Relations Division, *available at* http://www.labour.gov.hk/eng/public/wcp/ConciliationServiceLRD.pdf (last visited June 1, 2011). The Hong Kong Federation of Trade Unions provides labor services at their Labor Services Centre, which "[p]rovides free consultation on Labor Law and assistance in settling disputes between employers and employees." *Labor Service*, Hong Kong Federation of Trade Unions, http://www.ftu.org.hk/eng/index.html (last visited June 1, 2011).

[160] *Court Services & Facilities*, Judiciary of The Government of the Hong Kong Special Administrative Region, http://www.judiciary.gov.hk/en/crt_services/pphlt/html/labour.htm (last updated May 24, 2011).

(Cap. 47). It also deals with cases involving breaches of a term of a contract of employment, whether for performance in Hong Kong or under a contract to which the Contracts for Employment Outside Hong Kong Ordinance (Cap. 78) applies, and claims arising from the breach of a term of a contract of apprenticeship.

In order to maintain the impartial role of the Judiciary, our staff will not provide any legal advice or offer any comment on the conduct or merits of specific court cases and proceedings.

What types of claim does the Tribunal hear?

The most popular items of claim lodged by employees include:

- wages due for work done
- wages in lieu of notice of termination of a contract of employment by an employer without giving the required notice
- pay for statutory holidays, annual leave, or rest days
- severance pay, long service payment or terminal payments
- end of year payment, double pay or annual bonus
- commission
- unpaid wages of up to 2 months against the principal contractor and superior sub-contractors in the building and construction industry

Common items of claim lodged by employers include:

- wages in lieu of notice on resignation or termination of contract of employment

The Tribunal only hears cases where the amount of claim exceeds $8,000 for at least one of the claimants in a claim or where the number of claimants in the claim exceeds 10. Claims lodged by not more than 10 claimants for a sum of money not exceeding $8,000 per claimant are dealt with by the Minor Employment Claims Adjudication Board, located at 10/F, Cheung Sha Wan Government Offices, 303 Cheung Sha Wan Road, Kowloon (Tel: 2927 8000).

The Limitation Ordinance (Cap. 347) stipulates that actions founded on simple contract or on tort and certain other actions shall not be brought after the expiration of 6 years from the date on which the cause of action accrued

. . . .

Can both claimant and defendant appeal?

Yes, but an appeal can be lodged only on the grounds that the award or order is erroneous in point of law or outside the jurisdiction of the Tribunal.

Either party may apply to the Court of First Instance of the High Court for leave, i.e. permission, to appeal within 7 days after the date on which the written award or order was served on him, or within such extended time as may be allowed by the Registrar of the High Court on good cause. Parties applying for leave to appeal will need to complete Form 14 – "Application for Leave to Appeal on Point of Law". The form is available at the Tribunal registry and the Clerk of Court's Office of the High Court. The form has to be filed with payment of a prescribed fee at the Clerk of Court's Office of the High Court, located at G/F., High Court Building, 38 Queensway, Hong Kong.

A refusal by the Court of First Instance to grant leave to appeal is final. If leave is granted, the Court of First Instance will hear and determine the appeal.

Can a decision of the Court of First Instance be appealed?

Yes. Both claimant and defendant may apply to the Court of Appeal for leave to appeal within 7 days after the date of the decision of the Court of First Instance. The Court of Appeal may grant leave to appeal if it considers that a question of law of general public importance is involved.

Procedures for Settling Monetary Disputes between Employees and Employers

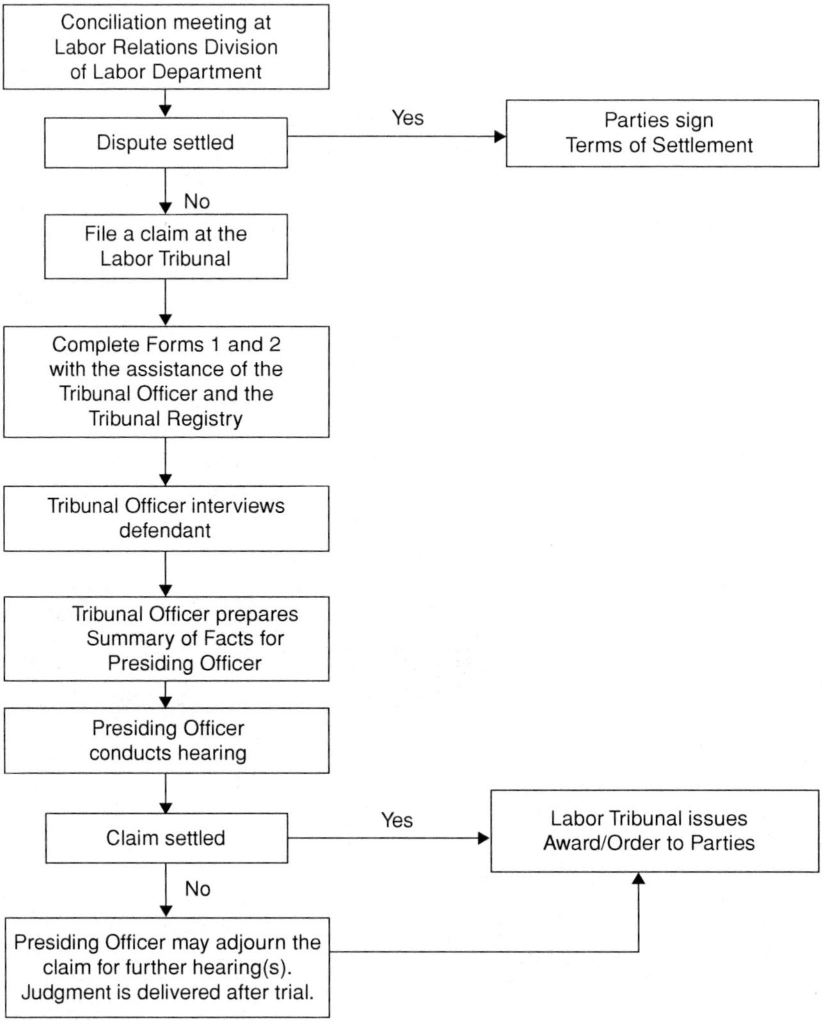

. . . .

2009 Human Rights Report: Hong Kong[161]

. . . .

Section 7 Worker Rights

a. The Right of Association

The law provides for the right of association and the right of workers to establish and join organizations of their own choosing. Trade unions must register under the Trade Unions Ordinance and must have a minimum membership of seven persons for registration. At the end of 2008, there were 796 registered trade unions, consisting of 752 employee unions, 19 employers' associations, and 25 mixed organizations of employees and employers. During the first half of the year, 13 new unions were registered and three unions were deregistered upon request.

Government statistics indicated that, as of the end of 2008, there were 708,953 salaried employees and wage earners claiming affiliation with a union, totaling 21.5 percent of the workforce.

The 1997 Employment and Labor Relations (Miscellaneous Amendments) Ordinance bans the use of union funds for political purposes, requires the CE's approval before unions can contribute funds to any trade union outside of the SAR, and restricts the appointment of persons from outside the enterprise or sector to union executive committees.

Work stoppages and strikes are legal. There are some restrictions on this right for civil servants. Although there is no legislative prohibition of strikes, in practice most workers had to sign employment contracts that typically stated that walking off the job is a breach of contract, which could lead to summary dismissal. In addition, there is no legal entitlement to reinstatement in the case of unfair dismissal. Four strikes, collectively involving 655 workers, were held during the first half of the year.

b. The Right to Organize and Bargain Collectively

The law provides for the right to organize, and this right was implemented in practice; however, it does not guarantee the right to collective bargaining. The 1997 Employment and Labor Relations (Miscellaneous Amendments) Ordinance does not provide a legal framework for trade unions to engage employers in collective bargaining. In all but a few trades, unions were not powerful enough to force management to engage in collective bargaining. A motion supported by union activists in the LegCo that called on the government to promote collective bargaining and legislate on the right to collective bargaining failed due to opposition by the government and business representatives.

The government did not engage in collective bargaining with civil servants' unions. According to an International Trade Union Congress report, only 1 percent of the workforce was covered by collective agreements, and these were not legally binding.

The Workplace Consultation Promotion Unit in the Labor Department facilitated communication, consultation, and voluntary negotiation between employers and

[161] Consulate General of the U.S. Hong Kong & Macau, U.S. Department of State, 2009 Human Rights Report: China (Hong Kong), Mar. 11, 2010, http://hongkong.usconsulate.gov/ushk_hr_2010031101.html (last visited Sept. 30, 2010); *see* ITUC, Hong Kong SAR (China) – 2011, http://survey.ituc-csi.org/+-Hong-Kong-SAR-China-+.html (last visited June 13, 2011).

employees. Tripartite committees for each of the nine sectors of the economy included representatives from some trade unions, employers, and the Labor Department.

There is no provision guaranteeing reinstatement of workers dismissed because of their trade union membership.

There are no export processing zones in the SAR.

c. Prohibition of Forced or Compulsory Labor

The law prohibits forced or compulsory labor, and there were no reports that such practices occurred.

d. Prohibition of Child Labor and Minimum Age for Employment

The Employment of Children Regulations prohibits employment of children under the age of 15 in any industrial establishment. The regulations limit work hours in the manufacturing sector for persons 15 to 17 years of age to eight hours per day and 48 hours per week between 7 A.M. and 7 P.M. They also prohibit overtime in industrial establishments with employment in dangerous trades for persons less than 18 years of age.

Children 13 and 14 years of age may work in certain nonindustrial establishments, subject to conditions aimed at ensuring a minimum of nine years of education and protection of their safety, health, and welfare. The Labor Department conducted regular workplace inspections to enforce compliance with the regulations. During the first half of the year, the Labor Department conducted 78,441 inspections. Three employers were convicted of offenses involving employment of children 13 to 14 years of age without written parental consent and valid school attendance certificates. Fines were between HK$1,000 and HK$4,000 (approximately $130 to $515).

e. Acceptable Conditions of Work

There is no statutory minimum wage except for domestic workers of foreign origin. Aside from a small number of trades where a uniform wage structure exists, wage levels customarily are fixed by individual agreement between employer and employee and are determined by supply and demand. Some employers provided workers with various kinds of allowances, medical treatment, and subsidized transport. Two-income households were the norm. There are no regulations concerning working hours, paid weekly rest, rest breaks, or compulsory overtime. Workweeks of up to 60 hours and more were not uncommon.

While the government provides assistance to many low-wage earners through the Comprehensive Social Security Assistance scheme and housing assistance programs, workers and labor unions contended wages in many low-level positions were insufficient to guarantee workers a decent standard of living.

On July 8, the government's Minimum Wage Bill had its first reading in the LegCo. The bill would create a minimum wage (but not set its rate) and establish a Minimum

Wage Commission which would advise the CE on the rate to be set. On February 7, the government appointed a Provisional Minimum Wage Commission made up of academics, employers, and organized labor representatives, and government economic and labor officials. At year's end both the bill and the wage rate remained under discussion.

Unionists alleged workers increasingly were tricked by employers into signing contracts that changed their terms of employment to "self-employed," and thus they were not entitled to employer-provided benefits such as paid leave, sick leave, medical insurance, workers' compensation, or Mandatory Provident Fund payments.

The Occupational Safety and Health Branch of the Labor Department is responsible for safety and health promotion, enforcement of safety management legislation, and policy formulation and implementation. The Factories and Industrial Undertakings Ordinance, the Occupational Safety and Health Ordinance, the Boilers and Pressure Vessels Ordinance, and their 35 sets of subsidiary regulations regulate safety and health conditions. During the first half of the year, the Labor Department's Occupational Safety and Health Branch conducted 59,475 workplace inspections. There were 842 convicted summonses, resulting in fines totaling HK$6.06 million (approximately $780,000). In addition to prosecuting offenses under the safety legislation, the Labor Department also issued improvement notices requiring employers to remedy contraventions of safety laws within a specified period and suspension notices directing removal of imminent risks to life and limb in workplaces. During the first half of the year, 709 improvement notices and 41 suspension notices were served.

Although worker safety and health continued to improve, serious problems remained, particularly in the construction industry. In the first quarter of the year, the Labor Department reported 8,512 occupational injuries, including 2,842 classified as industrial accidents. In the same period, there were two fatal industrial accidents. Employers are required under the Employee's Compensation Ordinance to report any injuries sustained by their employees in work-related accidents. There is no specific legal provision allowing workers to remove themselves from dangerous work situations without jeopardy to continued employment.

The media reported on the danger of working on bamboo scaffolding. It cited a Labor Department study showing "falling from height" as the primary source of fatalities in the construction industry, with 8,000 workers injured and 149 killed between 1998-2007.

There are no laws restricting work during typhoon or rainstorm warning signals save a Labor Department recommendation that employers have only essential staff come to work during certain categories of typhoon or rainstorm warnings.

The minimum wage for foreign domestic workers was HK$3,580 per month (approximately $460). The standard workweek was 48 hours, but many domestic workers worked much longer hours. The standard contract law requires employers to provide foreign domestic workers with housing, worker's compensation insurance, travel allowances, and food or a food allowance in addition to the minimum wage, which together provided a decent standard of living. Foreign domestic workers can be deported if dismissed. After leaving one employer, workers have two weeks to secure new employment before they must leave the SAR. Activists contended this restriction left workers vulnerable to a range of abuses from employers. Workers who pursue complaints through legal channels may be granted leave to remain; however, they are not able to work, leaving them either to live from savings or to depend on charitable assistance.

Domestic workers were required to live with their employers (who do not always provide separate accommodation for the worker), which made it difficult to enforce maximum working hours per day or overtime.

The government contended that the "two-week rule" was necessary to maintain effective immigration control and prevent migrant workers from overstaying and taking up unauthorized work. Regarding maximum hours and rest periods, the government stated that the Employment Ordinance rules on these issues cover local and migrant workers. However, in its explanation of why live-in domestic helpers (both local and foreign) would not be covered by the anticipated statutory minimum wage, the government explained that "the distinctive working pattern – round-the-clock presence, provision of service-on-demand, and the multifarious domestic duties expected of live-in domestic workers – makes it impossible to ascertain the actual hours worked so as to determine the wages to be paid."

During the first six months of the year, seven employers were convicted for labor law maltreatment violations under the Employment Ordinance relating to the employment of foreign domestic workers. During the first seven months of the year, 86 foreign domestic workers filed criminal suits, 43 of which were against employers, for maltreatment including rape (five), indecent assault (four), and injury and serious assault (34).

. . . .

QUESTIONS

1. What are the similarities and differences between Taiwan and Hong Kong in their regulation of labor?
2. Describe how labor laws in Taiwan and Hong Kong affect ongoing businesses.
3. Explain the significance, if any, of Taiwan and Hong Kong labor and employment laws for those businesses investing in China or in East Asia. What are the comparative and competitive advantages?
4. Hong Kong has a reputation for being "laissez-faire" in its approach to legal regulation; is this reflected in its labor and employment legislation? If so, how, if not, why and how?
5. What is the ADR approach used in Hong Kong for resolving labor disputes? What is the difference in approach in resolving monetary versus nonmonetary employment disputes?
6. Compare the Hong Kong approach to ADR to that in Taiwan; is one preferable? If so why; if not, why not? Is one more business-friendly?

V

Advising on Comparative and Competitive Advantages in East Asian HRM Practices

Those wishing to understand the competitive and comparative advantages of investing and operating in East Asia might usefully reflect on the various legal systems and labor law regimes existing in Japan, South Korea, and China before going forward. Which legal environment is better for the type of operations to be undertaken? Generally, there is no clear-cut answer without applying the laws to specific details of the business activities. Low-skilled jobs might involve frequent turnovers of personnel, which involve unemployment and severance pay laws that might negate the savings from low-cost labor; high-skilled jobs involving intellectual property of the employer require understanding the legal obligations of restrictive covenants and nondisclosure provisions. In all countries, the issue of a possible relationship with a union and the resulting collective negotiations and contractual restrictions are germane to doing business. And, of course, the likely enforcement of the existing labor laws is of great importance to many employers.

To evaluate competitive and comparative advantages, a working definition may be helpful. *Comparative advantage* is believed by some economists to be a key determinant of international production and trade patterns, whereas noneconomists typically think otherwise. In business, much greater emphasis is placed on the role of *competitive advantage* as a predictor of the economic fortunes not just of firms, but of nations as a whole. What exactly is competitive advantage? And how, if at all, does it relate to and interact with comparative advantage? It has been said, "[O]ne possible answer is that it is something to do with more competitive markets: lower barriers to entry or simply a larger number of firms may give an industry an advantage in competing with foreign rivals. A different answer is that competitive advantage is just a synonym for absolute advantage: some natural or policy-induced superiority (such as lower taxes or greater labor-market flexibility) that reduces costs for all home sectors."[1]

---

1 J. Peter Neary, *Competitive versus Comparative Advantage* (Sch. of Econ, Univ. Coll. Dublin, Working Paper No. WP02/19, 2002), *available at* http://www.ucd.ie/economics/research/papers/2002/WP02.19

Human rights interests in China have described China's competitive advantage to be largely in labor, as reported next.

> China's economic "miracle" has long hinged on five elements: cheap labor, market reforms, disregard for intellectual property rights, loose environmental standards, and cheap capital from state-controlled banks. Together, they've offered global investors a unique combination of nineteenth-century business practices and twenty–first-century infrastructure that have allowed China to attract almost $900 billion in direct foreign investment since 1979, mostly in the labor-intensive manufacturing sector.
>
> But China's economic ground realities are changing. Ecological devastation is forcing better environmental standards. Beijing is under pressure from the West to enforce intellectual property rights. And the public listing of major state-owned banks is reducing the banks' ability to make political loans to China's gargantuan state-owned companies. That's left China's cheap and disempowered labor force as the country's only unchanged manufacturing "competitive advantage."[2]

To aid in exploring the variant outcomes arising from different East Asian legal environments, a number of vignettes are presented from which the legal advisor or the reader can apply the laws and practices of Japan, South Korea, and China and determine, based on considerations of labor and employment laws, how the venues differ. This is followed by questions calling for comparative analysis.

A. VIGNETTES

Compare outcomes in Japan, South Korea, and China. Are there comparative and/or competitive advantages in dealing in or with each?

---

1. *Hiring and Discrimination*

On December 2, 2011, the Employer, a private corporation, unilaterally issued new "Work Rules" that are used to discipline employees who violate them. On March 19,

.pdf (last visited Oct. 2, 2010). It is also noted, "[I]ndustry-level determinants jointly create a microeconomic business environment that impacts companies' productivity. They are a central force linking a nation's comparative advantage with firms' competitive advantages in wealth creation. While country-level and industry-level advantages together provide a context for improving country competitiveness, firm-level and individual-level determinants are direct 'hands' in creating and improving this competitiveness. These 'hands' can be stronger or weaker, depending on both country-level and industry-level conditions." Oded Shenkar & Yadong Luo, International Business 148 (2002).

[2] Jehangir S. Pocha, *The Last 'Competitive Advantage': Letter From China*, Yale Global Online, June 12, 2007, http://yaleglobal.yale.edu/content/last-competitive-advantage-letter-china (last visited Sept. 30, 2010).

2012, part-time employee Ivana Lee was discharged for violation of the rules. The Rule stated that "older workers who reach 55 must retire." Ms. Lee became 55 on March 15, 2012, and refused to retire and was fired under the Rule. Is the Rule effective? Is there any statutory relief? She also claims the real reason for her termination was that she refused her supervisor's sexual advances at work. Please advise her on any rights and processes to which she may be entitled.[3]

QUESTIONS

1. Is a part-time worker an "employee" for purposes of application of pertinent labor laws?
2. Does Ms. Lee have or need a written labor contract? What is the consequence if she does not?
3. Is there a law prohibiting discrimination based on age? Is the retirement age a legitimate exception to the prohibition?
4. Are there legal limits on the issuance of such "work rules"? Are they valid without the review and advice of the union or employee-based representative?
5. Are sexual advances prohibited by law? Are there employer obligations to have internal procedures? What type of remedy is available for violations? Do they include punitive damages?
6. Are there potential violations in contract and/or statute? Does that difference affect the appropriate forum for redress?
7. How do answers to these questions translate in terms of labor costs for the employer? Are the labor costs significant?

Irregular Workers

Irregular workers are employed throughout the world, often as an economic cushion against the changing economic needs of the company.[4] Typically, they are paid less than regular, full-time, permanent workers and receive fewer benefits. In 2007, South Korea passed a law mandating conversion of these part-timers to full-time, permanent employees after two years of employment.[5] In 2009, during a global economic downturn, many Korean employers were faced with the issue of whether

[3] See discussion in Fang Lee Cooke, *Women's Participation in Employment in Asia: A Comparative Analysis of China, India, Japan, and South Korea*, 21 INT'L J. HUM. RESOURCE MGMT. 2249 (2010).

[4] *See* Katherine V. W. Stone, *Legal Protections for Atypical Employees: Employment Law for Workers Without Workplaces and Employees with Employers*, 27 BERKELEY J. EMP. & LAB. L. 251 (2006). *See also* European Foundation for the Improvement of Living and Working Conditions, *Part-Time Work in Europe* (2005), http://www.eurofound.europa.eu/ewco/reports/ES0403TR01/ES0403TR01.pdf.

[5] For discussion of why employers in Korea often use irregular workers, see Lee Hyun-sang, *Why do irregular workers need protection?*, JOONGANG ILBO, June 26, 2007, http://joongangdaily.joins.com/article/view.asp?aid=2877209.

to convert their workers or dismiss them.[6] In Japan, irregular workers constitute about a third of the workforce and total about fifteen million workers with nearly half being women.[7]

QUESTIONS

1. Are irregular employees eligible for statutory protection of labor rights in Japan, South Korea, and China?
2. Can irregular employees be dismissed more easily? What are the governing provisions in each country?
3. Is the South Korean law that converts part-time workers to full-time status after two years a good model for other countries? If so, why; if not, why not? How can the competing interests be best balanced?

---

2. *Labor Contracts: Individual and Collective*

The private employer has been requested by a union to engage in collective bargaining. The employer is willing, but an issue has come up whether it must bargain over health and safety issues, specifically over a provision that "the employer must not unlawfully discriminate against applicants or employees who have Hepatitis B." Please advise the employer as to the duty to bargain, scope of subjects, and any other relevant information.

QUESTIONS

1. Is there a legal duty to bargain with the union; if so, how is it satisfied, who are the permissible bargaining representatives, and what institution, if any, oversees the process?
2. What is the legal scope of subjects that must be bargained about and how is that determined?
3. Is economic coercion authorized, such as picketing and strikes? Is the use of armbands a form of economic coercion; if not, what is it?

6 *See* Lee Eun-joo, *Why do we keep hearing about those irregular workers?*, JOONGANG ILBO, July 11, 2009, http://joongangdaily.joins.com/article/view.asp?aid=2907268 (discussion of employers forced between retention or dismissal of part-time employees converting to full-time status).

7 See discussion in Paul Wiseman & Naoko Nishiwaki, *Japan offers a lifetime job if hired right out of school*, USA TODAY, Mar. 6, 2009, http://www.usatoday.com/money/world/2009-03-05-japan-lifetime-employment_N.htm. *See also Give "irregular" workers a fair shake*, THE JAPAN TIMES, Feb. 28, 2004, http://search.japantimes.co.jp/cgi-bin/ed20040228a1.html.

4. Must a non-unionized employer provide a written individual labor contract to an employee in Japan, South Korea, and China? What is the legal consequence, if any, for failure to do so?

---

3. *Working Conditions and Benefits*

For the past three years Mr. I. M. Pai worked as a manager in a fast food chain operation with thirteen people reporting to him. Although he still had many "hands-on duties," much like the other employees he worked very long hours and one day he realized he made more money per hour as an employee than he did as a "manager." He consulted local counsel who advised him he may well be an "employee" under the law and not a "manager." He is considering filing for overtime wages for the time he served as manager. Please advise him as to his rights and possible remedies.

QUESTIONS

1. Is Mr. Pai an "employee" covered by a wage and hour law for which he is entitled to overtime pay, or does he fall under an exception/exemption for certain types of managers?
2. What is the remedy for a violation and the practical implications for the employer?
3. Is there a way the employer might restructure the position to exempt Mr. Pai from overtime eligibility?

---

4. *Employer Discipline, Termination, and Alternative Dispute Resolution*

Yoko Kim suffered an injury at work while working on her machine. She filed a claim for Worker's Compensation, but to her surprise she was terminated because she had not taken her break as required by the employer and the injury occurred during that time. The employer felt she was negligent and would not have suffered the injury if she had taken the break and rested at her designated time, which was before the injury. You determine she is a regular full-time employee and has the standard labor contract and there is no union or union contract. Advise her as to specific rights she may have, any limitations on termination, and which processes she may use to possibly secure a remedy.

QUESTIONS

1. Does the Worker's Compensation law prohibit discrimination because of the injury?
2. May Ms. Kim be terminated for violation of this employer rule? Even if so, is she still eligible to apply for Worker's Compensation benefits?
3. Is there a choice of forum to proceed under either the administrative processes of the Worker's Compensation law or to proceed on an arbitration or judicial forum? What is the interrelationship, if any, of these forums?
4. If there are any violations of law, what remedies are available to Ms. Kim?
5. Is Ms. Kim entitled to unemployment compensation?

Dismissing Employees

When a company in Japan considers the dismissal of an employee, what type of grounds, if any, must be provided? Generally, the employee must fall under at least one of the reasons for dismissal set forth in the company's work rules. Lawyers in Japan suggest the following difficulties in dismissing an employee in Japan.

Assessing the Consequences[8]

For this reason, companies in Japan often have a provision in their work rules that stipulates that poor job performance is a possible ground for dismissal. However, a company cannot always dismiss an employee just because the employee's performance is poor and one of the grounds for dismissal under the work rules is satisfied, because, as Article 16 of Japan's *Labor Contract Act* (the Act) states, 'a dismissal shall, if it lacks objectively reasonable grounds and is not considered to be appropriate in general societal terms, be treated as an abuse of right and be invalid.'

As Article 16 of the Act stipulates, poor performance is generally considered to be one of the "objectively reasonable grounds" upon which an employee can be dismissed. Yet in practice, the performance of the employee in question must be remarkably poor so that it is acceptable as an objectively reasonable ground. Generally speaking, it can also be said that the Japanese courts tend to consider that dismissals are appropriate in general societal terms only where: (a) the grounds upon which the employee was dismissed were grave; (b) there were no other ways to avoid the dismissal; and (c) there were little or no reasons to tolerate the employee. A tendency to give tough judgments against companies can be observed in respect of employees who are in continuous employment under a system of long-term employment. On the other hand, courts have shown more leniencies toward

[8] Hironobu Tsukamoto & Toshiaki Kobayashi, *Assessing the Consequences*, 8 ASIAN-COUNSEL 40 (2010), *available at* http://www.inhousecommunity.com/controlPanel/download.php?id=770. *See also* UTU, *University Teachers Union Information* (2008), *available at* http://nugw.org/utu/downloads/UTUInformation.pdf.

the dismissal of employees who were recruited mid-career for their high level of skills but whose actual performance after the commencement of their employment turned out to be below expectation.[9]

QUESTIONS

1. Would the same outcomes as decided in Japan's court decisions be more or less likely under Japan's Labor Tribunal?
2. How would this case be dealt with under South Korean labor laws?
3. How would this case be dealt with under Chinese labor laws?
4. How would this case be dealt with under U.S. labor laws?
5. Will the ADR analysis change if there is an allegation of gender discrimination?
6. What difference will there be if the discharged employee was an American or Japanese citizen working in Japan? Consider the extraterritorial application of the U.S. Civil Rights law; what is the relevancy, if any, whether the employer is controlled by Japanese or American interests?
7. What are the differences in approach and likely outcomes if the labor dispute over the dismissal were decided in Japan's Labor Tribunal, South Korea's civil court, or China's Labor Arbitration Commission?

Strikes

Strikes by workers, whether legal or not, do occur in East Asian countries as well as throughout the world. In the summer of 2010, a number of strikes occurred in China at the Honda auto plants and the Foxconn electronics assembly company. Both were foreign-invested firms and employee complaints were raised about wages and working conditions.[10] News accounts reported as follows.

> Reports suggested disputes were beginning to spread from China's coastal manufacturing zones after 900 workers in the interior city of Xian halted at a complex operated by Japan's sewing machine maker Brother demanding better pay and conditions. The news came as Honda announced it would resume production in Guangdong on Friday morning after settling two strikes by offering wage increases rumored to be 24 [percent] only to be hit by a third strike at a factory that makes locks for its cars. 'All it takes now is a single spark and news will spread all over

[9] For further analyses of leading Japanese court cases, see discussion in Hironobu Tsukamoto & Toshiaki Kobayashi, *supra*, note 8. The authors, Hironobu Tsukamoto and Toshiaki Kobayashi, are practicing lawyers in Japan.

[10] Jeffrey Hayes, *Foxconn Suicides and Honda and Toyota Strikes*, FACTS AND DETAILS, http://factsanddetails.com/china.php?itemid=1657&catid=9&subcatid=60 (last visited June 13, 2011).

China, which could lead to similar industrial action in other factories,' said Paul Tang, chief economist at Bank of East Asia in Hong Kong. The latest round of strikes follows the huge 70 [percent] pay rise offered to workers by iPod-maker Foxconn last week, which has been hit by a spate of worker suicides this year. However, analysts said the growing power of workers also reflected an underlying tightening of the Chinese labor market which has led to a growing shortage of migrant labor in China's manufacturing heartlands.[11]

QUESTIONS

1. Are such strikes legal in China, in South Korea, and in Japan?
2. How significant, if at all, was the fact the strikes were at foreign-invested companies in China?
3. How legally significant is it whether the purpose of a strike is for economic improvement at the workplace versus political change? Does that differ from experience in Europe?
4. What is the role of the labor union in strike activities, if any, in each East Asian country?
5. In each East Asian country, how, if at all, does this type of strike activity relate to collective bargaining?

Mechanisms for Resolving Individual Labor Disputes in East Asia[12]

Ronald C. Brown

A. Introduction

Resolving *individual labor rights* disputes in East Asia and the United States in recent years has taken on new significance and prominence for both domestic and multinational corporations.[13] New laws and approaches that have been put into place in Japan, China, and the United States deal with individual rights under either individual and/or collective contract or statutory labor disputes. In 2004, Japan passed the judicial labor tribunal system and in 2008 China implemented a new Mediation and Arbitration Law, each with heralded success. In 2009, the U.S. Supreme Court completed its approval of the use of private arbitration under individual and collective contracts to resolve both contractual and statutory labor disputes.

There are common themes and comparative contrasts in the uses of mediation and arbitration in the approaches of each country. They may use governmental and/or private structures to house dispute settlement processes of individual and/or collective labor

[11] *China's factories hit by wave of strikes*, BBC, June 28, 2010, http://www.bbc.co.uk/news/10434079.

[12] Ronald C. Brown, *Comparative ADR for Individual Labor Disputes in Japan, China, and the U.S.: Lessons from Asia?* 86 St. Johns L. Rev. (2012).

[13] Labor *rights* are to be distinguished from labor *interests*, not discussed in this chapter.

disputes, and mediation falls both inside and outside the arbitration process. There are some interesting differences with the U.S. providing the legal authority to privatize much of the labor and employment law dispute resolution processes, whereas China and Japan keep the processes largely under government regulation and institutions

. . . .

The processes of resolving labor rights disputes in the U.S., China, and Japan, while appearing to use diverse approaches, actually have common themes, as well as their comparative contrasts. Understanding their functionalities may present an opportunity for countries to choose the best practices from among these processes. This may also afford the many multinational companies (MNC) and others doing business in these countries the vantage point of evaluating the different methods of alternative dispute resolution (ADR) processes and keeping the benefits of in-house mediation processes and their time- and cost-saving mediation settlements (even while using external neutrals).

The variables in these ADR procedures include the degree of governmental regulation, if any, and whether to house the institutional processes within the government, in the private sector, or in some combination of the two. ADR procedures vary on defining "labor disputes" for channeling into specific ADR processes; they may include individual and/or collective disputes, which can arise from either or both of contractual (individual or collective bargaining contracts) and/or statutory labor rights.

The usual mechanisms of mediation, arbitration, and litigation are employed by all, though in different ways and with different legal effect. While arbitration decisions may or may not be legally binding in different settings and in different countries, mediated settlements almost always are legally enforceable regardless of when or where they occurred – inside the company or in the mediation process preceding an arbitration, or in the arbitration process itself, or in judicial proceedings before, during, or after any litigation.

Existing mediation and arbitration institutional procedures each has its own time and cost considerations. It will be proposed that perhaps consideration of the models of ADR used in labor disputes in Japan, China, and the U.S. may provide some guide in possible redesigning of current ADR systems.

. . . .

---

5. *Global Human Resource Management*

In doing business globally, a global company like Honda, a Japanese auto company, has international labor law and human resource management issues. In doing business, it is necessarily involved in many aspects of business, ranging from mergers and acquisitions (M&As), to managing and operating production, sales, and marketing, to staffing issues, such as hiring, setting wages and conditions, as well as disciplining and terminating employees. These issues often involve local and legal questions and understanding of cross-cultural customs and expectations. From these legal requirements come negotiations to resolve the issues. In its cross-border business dealings, these companies may have need of advice on the following issues that occur outside and inside China.

QUESTIONS

1. In the United States or Europe, what might the lawyer expect of its Japanese client regarding its home-country perception of "how to do business" in the United States or Europe? What are the industrial relations concepts that may also come with the client, such as employee loyalty, unions, and gender issues? Discuss the issues under U.S. or European law that might be generated by these cultural expectations.
2. Answer the same question as above when the U.S. or European employer locates in China, Japan, or South Korea.

B. GROWING ISSUES AND AREAS FOR FURTHER INQUIRY

1. What are the legal factors to consider in knowing if and when the laws of a foreign country, such as the United States, apply in Japan, South Korea, and China?
2. Discuss the labor law-related *comparative* advantages of locating a business in Japan or South Korea or China.
3. Are the *competitive* advantages the same or different as discussed under the previous question? What are the variables?
4. What are the differences in functions, if any, of the Workers' Congress in China and the Labor Management Councils in South Korea?
5. What are the differences in functions, if any, of the Labor Arbitration Tribunal in China and the Labor Tribunal in Japan?
6. Are written employment agreements required in China, Japan, and South Korea?
7. Why might an East Asian government place more emphasis on providing procedures resolving individual versus collective labor disputes or strikes?
8. Are strikes permitted or tolerated in Japan, South Korea, and China and what are their limits?
9. What are the employers' legal liabilities, if any, for violation of labor laws by its subcontractors in Japan, South Korea, or China?
10. What legal limitations, if any, exist in each country on hiring "contingent" employees, such as part-time or foreign workers?
11. What are the requirements in China, Japan, and South Korea for payment of severance pay?

FUTURE ECONOMIC GROWTH PREDICTED IN EAST ASIA. Future economic growth is predicted in East Asia, making it an attractive venue for business investment. Businesses require managers and workers to achieve success; thus labor and employment and HRM issues will remain a significant component of that success. Lawyers, HRM managers, employees, and those connected to or interested in this growth will want to understand the cultural and legal practices and requirements present in each country: Japan, China, or South Korea. Compliance and navigation with labor and employment laws increasingly are key factors in keeping on course.

> According to the report released today [by the United Nations], East Asia remains the fastest-growing region in the world. Economic activity expanded by 8.8 percent in 2010 as the region recovered rapidly from the global crisis. China and the highly export-oriented economies of Singapore and Taiwan Province of China achieved the fastest growth rates in the region. . . . The outlook for East Asia is favorable, although growth is expected to moderate owing to weakening global conditions and fading government stimulus. Regional growth is forecast to average 7.2 percent in 2011 and 7.4 percent in 2012. Given the subdued outlook in developed economies, countries with large and buoyant domestic markets, such as China . . . are in a better position to maintain the growth momentum than the economies more heavily dependent on exports, says *WESP* [World Economic Situation and Prospects Report]. GDP growth in China is forecast to decelerate from 10.1 percent in 2010 to 8.9 percent in 2011 and 9.0 percent in 2012. *WESP* says labor market conditions in East Asia generally improved in 2010. Strong growth boosted employment across the region, especially in the manufacturing, construction, and service sectors. In most economies, unemployment is back to or below pre-crisis levels. Average real wages increased, with China seeing significant minimum-wage hikes in several provinces. In the outlook, unemployment and underemployment rates are expected to decline slowly and real wages are forecast to increase further.[14]

[14] *World Economic Situation and Prospects* is produced at the beginning of each year by the UN Department of Economic and Social Affairs (UN DESA), the United Nations Conference for Trade and Development (UNCTAD) and the five United Nations regional commissions. UN Department of Public Information, *Asia's developing economies sustain robust growth, leading global recovery* (Jan. 18, 2001), *available at* http://www.un.org/en/development/desa/policy/wesp/wesp_current/2011wesp_pr_asiadeveloping_en.pdf.

Index